The Priestly Vision of Genesis 1

THE PRIESTLY VISION OF GENESIS 1

Cover image: Rising moon over mountains ©iStockphoto.com/Daniel Bobrowsky
Cover design: Ivy Palmer Skrade

Library of Congress Cataloging-in-Publication Data
Smith, Mark S., 1955-
  The priestly vision of Genesis 1/by Mark S. Smith.
    p. cm.
  Includes bibliographical references and indexes.
  ISBN 978-0-8006-6373-5 (pbk.: alk. paper)
1. Bible. O.T. Genesis I—Criticism, interpretation, etc. 2. Creationism. 3. Creation—Mythology. 4. Priesthood. I. Title.
  BV1235.52.S65 2009
  222'.11066—dc22

                                                                    2009017570
The paper used in this publication meets the minimum requirements of American National Standard for Information Sciences—Permanence of Paper for Printed Library Materials, ANSI Z329.48-1984.

Manufactured in the U.S.A.

14 13 12 11 10 1 2 3 4 5 6 7 8 9 10

The Priestly Vision
of Genesis 1

Mark S. Smith

*For Donald and Kay Titus,
With great appreciation
for your interest,*

Mark

Fortress Press
Minneapolis

For my folks,
Barbara Pindar Smith
and Donald Eugene Smith,
and
to my sisters and brothers,
Gregory,
Cecily,
Andrea,
Veronica,
Teresa,
Valerie,
Jeffrey,
and
Stephanie
—gifts of a lifetime

Contents

PART TWO

Literary Issues concerning Genesis 1
and its Position in the Hebrew Bible

Preface

This book examines the priestly vision of the creation account in Genesis 1:1—2:3 (which I will call Genesis 1 from now on). Its vision of God, humanity, and the world has inspired readers for centuries, and as a result, it has been regarded as one of the all-time classics of biblical literature. In recent decades, scholars have arrived at a number of insights about Genesis 1 worth sharing with a wider readership. One central purpose in writing this book is to bring what biblical scholars have learned about Genesis 1 to people interested in the Bible and in ancient Israel.

The scholarly approaches taken to Genesis 1 have long acknowledged its priestly background. It has become evident to scholars that Genesis 1 drew on the language and imagery of the priestly tradition, known from priestly books of the Bible—especially Leviticus and Ezekiel. While Genesis 1 also shows features known from other creation accounts in the Bible and in the ancient Near East, it typically depicts creation after the image and likeness of the Bible's priestly texts. Viewing Genesis 1 in the context of other priestly texts therefore helps us to get at its worldview. It is this priestly dimension of Genesis 1 that this book focuses on. In addition to the priestly texts in the Bible, the ritual texts discovered at the ancient site of Ugarit (located on the coast of modern day Syria) can also help us to appreciate the priestly sensibility of Genesis 1. As the largest group of nonbiblical ritual texts predating the literature of nearby ancient Israel, the Ugaritic ritual texts offer an important context for understanding the priestly tradition of the Bible and for interpreting a number of specific priestly details in Genesis 1.

In drawing on this older tradition, Genesis 1 was participating in a larger discussion that was going on among Israelites during the sixth century BCE about the origins of the universe and about the nature of God and reality. While Genesis 1 weighs in on this discussion in a major way, we may also hear other voices engaged in this conversation. This discussion included two major prophetic works of the sixth century BCE. One such work was the book of Ezekiel. This figure was a priest exiled to Babylon in 597 BCE who had a prophetic career there spanning from the year 593 down to 571. The other was Isaiah 40–55, an anonymous addition made to the book of Isaiah (which scholars often call "Second Isaiah"). Deuteronomy as well as Job perhaps belonged to this discussion. Like Ezekiel, Genesis 1 offered a priestly response and vision. All of these biblical works offered reflections on the world in light of the terrible experience of Jerusalem's destruction and the exile of its leadership in 586 BCE, vividly captured by Psalm 74 and the book of Lamentations. This experience of Israelite suffering occurred not only at home but also abroad, as mournfully recounted by Psalm 137 ("by the rivers of Babylon, there we sat and wept. . ."). All these reflections by these great writers took place in the sixth century and reflect this time of dramatic and traumatic change for Israel.

Genesis 1's vision of God and the world that this deity created spoke to Israel's dire conditions in the sixth century. The world may change, at times with great violence. It may seem to have become a "void and vacuum" (Genesis 1:2) or a world without divine blessing (Genesis 1:22, 28; 2:3). Whatever the world was coming to in the sixth century, the God who had created this world remained the God of Israel. The account of creation in Genesis 1 was designed to teach Israel not simply about the distant past. Creation also served to instruct Israel about the world that God had brought into being in order to benefit humanity and especially Israel throughout time. God's creation in Genesis 1 offered to Israel a vision of life and blessing, of order and holiness, in the midst of a world marred by violence and disaster, servitude and death.

For centuries readers of the Bible have been drawn to ponder this story. In their contemplation of the seven days of creation, they join the author of Genesis 1 in considering the nature of God. My aim in this book is to trace the path taken by the writer of Genesis 1 to arrive at its priestly vision, here presented for a broader audience just as it was intended when it became the beginning of the Bible.

Acknowledgments

This book has a lengthy history going back to 1995. As a result, I have a lengthy list of institutions and individuals to thank. Chapter 1 began from two lectures. The first, "The Politics of Creation in the Bible," was delivered on February 21, 1995 at Saint Vincent's College in Latrobe, Pennsylvania. I am particularly indebted to Professor Elliott C. Maloney, OSB, of Saint Vincent's College, for the kind invitation to lecture there. The second address, "Psalm 8 and the Politics of Creation," was given at the annual meeting of the Society of Biblical Literature in November 1995 in Philadelphia.

Chapter 2 began as a presentation given at the Society of Biblical Literature in 2002 and appeared in 2008 in the Shalom Paul Festschrift. For decades, Professor Paul has been a sharp commentator on biblical and ancient Near Eastern parallels. I am grateful for his generous support and friendship since my student days at the Hebrew University in 1983-1984. Baruch Schwartz and Jeffrey Tigay also provided very helpful comments on this chapter, as acknowledged in the endnotes. I would also like to acknowledge the original inspiration for a major part of this chapter (concerning the light of the first day), namely the 1998 book by James Kugel entitled *Traditions in the Bible*.

Chapter 4 was presented before the Columbia University Bible Seminar in January 2002, and before the Old Testament Colloquium in March 2002. My thanks go to the members of these groups for their many suggestions, especially David Carr, Alan Cooper, David Marcus, and Bob Wilson. David Carr also offered helpful comments on an earlier draft of this chapter. As readers will see, my discussion here is particularly indebted to the works of the scholars involved in the discussion of scribal activity in ancient Israel, in particular David Carr but also Seth Sanders and Karel van der Toorn.

An earlier form of chapter 5 was delivered at the Society of Biblical Literature in 2006, at the "Bible, Myth, and Myth Theory" consultation, thanks to the kind invitation of Dexter Callender and Neal Walls. It appeared subsequently in a volume honoring Professor Bernd Janowski. For this book, I have revised this essay specifically with Genesis 1 in mind.

I was able to rethink and rewrite these chapters thanks to the semester that I spent at New York University Madrid in the spring term of 2008. I am thankful both to my home department and to the university for facilitating this arrangement, which gave me time to concentrate on this project. My thanks would be incomplete without also mentioning the many helpful comments that I received at this time from Aaron Tugendhaft, a doctoral candidate at NYU. It has been a pleasure to work with him. Two of my departmental colleagues, Dan Fleming and Elliot Wolfson, also gave me many useful suggestions and bibliography for which I am grateful.

The course that I gave at NYU Madrid was an introduction to the Hebrew Bible, which provided me with a lovely setting to work on Genesis 1 and on the biblical texts used in this study to help understand Genesis 1. I am grateful for the hospitality and help that I received at NYU Madrid, especially from its director Anjouli Janzon, her staff—particularly Justin Byrne—and the students in the course: Jacob Gross, Kristin Gualano, and Andrea Sper. During my semester in Madrid I had the opportunity to discuss this project with colleagues at the Complutense University, in particular Julio Trebolle Barrera and Andrés Piquer Otero. During this term I was also a visiting scholar-researcher at the Centro de Ciencias Humanas y Sociales (Instituto de Lenguas y Culturas del Mediterráneo y de Oriente Próximo), which is part of the Consejo Superior de Investigaciones Científicas (CSIC) in Madrid. I am deeply indebted to my sponsor there, Ignacio Márquez Rowe. I am appreciative of the many members of the CSIC for their hospitality, and in particular to Barbara Böck and Javier Castano. The CSIC also invited me to give a presentation, which helped me to rethink some aspects of chapter 2. I am grateful to the hosts for my talk, Mariano Gómez and Javier del Barco. Toward the end of my time in Madrid, Tryggve Mettinger most kindly read the manuscript and offered many helpful suggestions, for which I am very grateful. Professor Mettinger read the manuscript a second time in November 2008, and offered several more comments. I have happily incorporated these.

On August 3, 2008, chapters 1 and 2 were the subjects of discussion at the "Divinity in Ancient Israel" seminar, held at the meeting of the Catholic Biblical Association at Fordham University. I owe a debt to John McLaughlin for inviting me to present this material at his seminar and to its various members, in particular Steven McKenzie for his fine response, and to others for their remarks: Corrine Carvalho, Stephen Cook, Shawn Flynn, Gordon Hamilton, Heather Macumber, Sara Mandell, Pamela Miles, and Bill Morrow. At the Colloquium for Biblical Research held at Dartmouth College August 13-16, 2008, I was afforded the opportunity to discuss this work with Bill Brown, Sidnie White Crawford, and Leong Seow, who gave me some very helpful feedback. I also wish to thank Susan Ackerman for hosting this meeting. In the summer of 2008, Ronald S. Hendel generously offered access to his unpublished commentary on Genesis 1, to appear as *Genesis 1–11: A Commentary* (Anchor Bible series, volume 1A; Yale University Press). This fine commentary covers much of the same territory as chapters 2 and 3 of my book. I have included citations from Hendel's work (labeled as personal communications) on points where my discussion has particularly benefited from his insights.

In the fall of 2008, I had the opportunity to discuss the book with Jerome Marcus and Martti Nissinen. I thank them for their responses. Toward the end of the work on this book, Bruce Zuckerman most generously offered to go over the entire manuscript (apart from the appendix). I am immensely grateful for his meticulous editing and for a number of valuable suggestions about the book's content. I have also made some final changes in light of a presentation that I made on Genesis 1 on February 26, 2009, for a series that the University of Nebraska sponsored for the bicentennial of Charles Darwin's birth. I am grateful to Sidnie White Crawford and Dan Crawford for this invitation and for the opportunity to refine my thinking on a number of points. My conversations with them were a pleasure. While the book was in press, Peter Machinist offered a number of helpful comments, for which I thank him.

I wish to thank my wife, Liz Bloch-Smith, and our daughter, Shulamit, especially for our time together in Madrid. As usual, Shula has suggested a number of titles for this book; these include: "Wurr da priestz at?? (answer: Genesis 1)," "Pokemon in the priestly text," "The Destruction of Myth in Genesis One: The Beginning of an Epic Story"; and "Shula goes to town, a story of family and maaaaaaagic." (Perhaps I should have used one of these.) Shula also served as a first member of the focus group that examined this manuscript. In this capacity, she gave me several helpful suggestions for improving this work.

I also thank my in-laws, Sonia and Ted Bloch. For Sonia's eightieth birthday, the whole family went to the Galapagos Islands. Many of these islands had beautiful, lush vegetation and all sorts of animals that attracted the attention of Charles Darwin; we also swam in the sea and saw an underwater seascape that Darwin never experienced. For me, these moments echoed the origins of the creation of animals on days 5 and 6, as Genesis 1 expresses it. We also spent time on some islands with very little vegetation and animal life. There, too, we stood and glimpsed something of the world's primordial quality as though it had risen from the primeval waters; day 2 of Genesis readily came to mind. Wonder is something, I think, that Genesis 1 conveys, and my time in the Galapagos brought this home to me in a way that no other experience ever has. For this, I thank Sonia and Ted. I also thank Ted for reading much of this book and for his feedback.

I also wish to thank Sheila Anderson of Fortress Press for her superb help.

I end these acknowledgements with the pleasure of dedicating this work to my folks, Donald Eugene Smith and Barbara Pindar Smith, and to my eight siblings. Their affection and encouragement have carried me throughout my academic life. As one of my parents' greatest gifts to me, my six sisters, and two brothers have been long and deep sources of care and support.

Abbreviations for Reference Works, Translations, and Text Versions

Abbreviations for journals and series follow the *SBL Handbook of Style* (ed. Patrick H. Alexander et al.; Peabody, Mass.: Hendrickson, 1949). The following abbreviations are used frequently in the text and notes.

11QPs^{a}	Psalms Scroll from Cave Eleven at Qumran
AHw	Wolfram von Soden, *Akkadisches Handwörterbuch*. Wiesbaden: Harrassowitz, 1965–1981.
ANEP	*The Ancient Near East in Pictures Relating to the Old Testament*. Edited by James B. Pritchard. Princeton: Princeton University, 1954.
ANET	*Ancient Near Eastern Texts Relating to the Old Testament*. Edited by James B. Pritchard. Third edition with supplement. Princeton: Princeton University, 1969.
BDB	Francis Brown, S. R. Driver, and C. A. Briggs, *Hebrew and English Lexicon of the Old Testament*. Oxford: At the Clarendon, 1907.
BHS	Biblia Hebraica Stuttgartensia
b.T.	Babylonian Talmud
CAD	*The Assyrian Dictionary of the Oriental Institute of the University of Chicago*. Chicago: The Oriental Institute; Glückstadt: J. J. Augustin, 1956–.
COS	*The Context of Scripture*. Edited by Willliam W. Hallo

	and K. Lawson Younger. Three volumes. Leiden/Boston/Köln: Brill, 1997, 2000, 2002.
DCH	*The Dictionary of Classical Hebrew.* Edited by David J. A. Clines, John Elwolde Executive Editor. Sheffield: Sheffield Academic, 1993—.
DNWSI	J. Hoftijzer and K. Jongeling. *Dictionary of the North-West Semitic Inscriptions.* Two Volumes. Leiden/New York/Köln: E. J. Brill, 1995.
DUL	Gregorio del Olmo Lete and Joachin Sanmartín, *A Dictionary of the Ugaritic Language in the Alphabetic Tradition. Part One [('a/i/u – k]; Part Two [l – z].* Translated by Wilfred G. E. Watson. Handbuch für Orientalistik, volume 67. Leiden/Boston: Brill, 2003. With continuous pagination.
D-stem	Factitive or transitivizing conjugation or stem ("binyan") in Semitic languages ("piel" in Hebrew)
GKC	*Gesenius' Hebrew Grammar.* Edited by Emil Kautzsch. Second edition revised by A. E. Cowley. Oxford: Clarendon, 1910.
G-stem	Basic conjugation or stem ("binyan") in Semitic languages ("qal" in Hebrew)
HALOT	Ludwig Koehler and Walter Baumgartner, *The Hebrew and Aramaic Lexicon of the Old Testament.* Subsequently revised by Walter Baumgartner and Johann Jakob Stamm, with assistance from Benedikt Hartmann, Ze'ev Ben- Hayyim, Eduard Yechezkel Kutscher, and Philippe Reymond. Translated and edited under the supervision of M. E. J. Richardson. Leiden/New York/Köln: E. J. Brill, 1996. Five volumes, with continuous pagination.
KB	E. Schvader, ed. *Klein in schriftliche Bibliothek.* 6 Vols. Berlin, 1889–1915.
KTU	M. Dietrich, O. Loretz and J. Sanmartín. *The Cunieform Alphabetic Texts: from Ugarit, Ras Ibn Hani and Other Places.* Second enlarged edition. Münster: Ugarit-Verlag, 1997.

LXX	The Septuagint Greek translation of the Hebrew Bible
MT	Masoretic Text (text of the Bible in Jewish tradition)
NAB	New American Bible translation of the Bible
NJPS	New Jewish Publication Society translation of the Hebrew Bible
NRSV	New Revised Standard Version translation of the Bible
N-stem	Passive or middle-passive conjugation or stem ("binyan") in Semitic languages ("niphal" in Hebrew).
SBLWAW	Society of Biblical Literature Writings from the Ancient World.
*	An asterisk is put before a word in Hebrew without the grammatical elements that may be on it as it is actually attested in a passage. These grammatical elements include prepositions that in Hebrew can be attached at the beginning of a word or suffixes marking pronouns such as "my" in English that can be attached to the end of a noun in Hebrew. Example: *bere'shit*, the first word in the Bible consists of *be-*, "in," plus **re'shit*, "beginning (of)."

Introduction

1. The Purpose and Parameters of This Book

The Genesis creation story does much more than just commence the Bible. It is at once the sacred story of God's wondrous creation and an important cultural icon that has inspired readers for centuries. The Bible's first story continues to fascinate readers, laypeople and scholars alike. The sweep of this narrative and its imagery do more than keep the readers' rapt attention. It leads them to consider and contemplate the profound realities of creation as they unfold in the story. The beautiful and highly literate structure of its narrative, with its deep symbolism and masterfully sparse rhetoric, offers its readers more than just an inspiring vision of creation. It also gives them a first grand look at the nature of the one God who through just a few spoken words brings about creation.

This opening account runs from Genesis 1:1—2:3, which, for the sake of simplicity, I will call Genesis 1 from now on. How Genesis 1 expresses its priestly vision is what I want to explore in this book. Building on the work of many scholars, this book studies the first creation story from a number of perspectives in five chapters and an appendix. The titles of the first four chapters capture four basic aspects of this study. First of all, Genesis 1 is one of many biblical passages that discuss creation. Different creation texts reflect differing concerns and worldviews. Comparing and contrasting these passages with Genesis 1 will help us see its particular emphasis.

Second, the nature of the specific perspective of Genesis 1 is priestly, which refers to the priesthood responsible for the Jerusalem temple and its sanctity, its sacrificial regimen, and calendar. The priestly perspective of Genesis 1 is deeply informed by the religious ritual of the Jerusalem

Temple.[1] This priesthood wrote and passed down texts reflecting their concern for order and holiness. This includes Genesis 1. An examination of priestly expressions and concepts in this account will open up the world of priestly literature more broadly in the Bible and illuminate the priestly vision of Genesis 1 in particular.

Third, Genesis 1 uses expressions that compare closely with prior traditions and texts. Its choice of words and phrases sometimes shows the author's response to these literary forerunners. By looking closely at these terms, we will see how Genesis 1 offers a sort of implicit, narrative "commentary" on other sources.

Fourth and finally, the placement of Genesis 1 at the very beginning of the Bible stakes a claim, asserting the primary status of its account over and above other biblical versions of creation. Thanks to this placement, it inevitably looms over other creation accounts and allusions to creation found thereafter in the Bible. I will describe how its priestly vision took its place within the larger context of Genesis. As a result, we will come to understand better how, in the minds of many readers, Genesis 1 has come to be the creation account *par excellence* in the Bible.

2. The Plan of This Book

The chapters of this work look closely in turn at each of these points. I would like to explain how. Chapter 1 opens the work with a broad discussion of creation in the Hebrew Bible. It pays special attention to many creation texts of the Bible, thereby showing that ancient Israel never really knew a single version. In fact, we can identify different ideas about creation in the Bible. In its various models of creation, the process of creation might be characterized as a product of divine conflict, divine wisdom, and divine presence. Genesis 1 drew on all these different models. By looking at them in some detail in chapter 1, we can get a better sense of the traditional material and ideas that the composer of Genesis 1 knew and used. Indeed, these essential, traditional themes represented the basic templates on which the author relied in composing Genesis 1. In illustrating these commonalities, chapter 1 serves as a prelude to the next two chapters.

Part 1, consisting of chapters 2 and 3, focuses on the specific priestly vision of Genesis 1. This approach has engaged biblical scholars for over a century. Scholarly study of the first five books of the Bible, (the Pentateuch, or in Jewish tradition, the Torah), has devoted intense energy to what has come to be known as the Documentary Hypothesis or the Four Source Theory. This theory holds that the Pentateuch is constituted from four separate written sources brought together over the course of several centuries, beginning during the monarchy and essentially completed in the Persian period. In this analysis, Genesis 1 came to be assigned to the priestly source (often called "P" for short). While other aspects of the Documentary Hypothesis have eroded in the past quarter century, the view of a priestly source, or at least priestly material, has stood the test of time. In chapters 2 and 3, I am not terribly concerned with the specific arguments over source theory or over the question of whether the priestly material in the Pentateuch really constitutes a single source or tradition. (These issues are addressed in the appendix.) Instead, these chapters are devoted to exploring the priestly vision of reality in Genesis 1.

Scholars have long recognized the priestly character of Genesis 1. But what is specifically meant by this? What is the priestly vision of God, humanity, and the world, and how do the various actions in Genesis 1 express this vision? For the priestly composer, what is conveyed by divine speech and light on day one and by divine blessing and Sabbath on day seven? To answer these questions, we will look into priestly texts especially in the Pentateuch/Torah and Ezekiel in order to understand the priestly worldview that informed Genesis 1. These parts of the Bible, as well as other texts from that time, show Genesis 1 participating in a dialogue over these questions about reality in the face of the crises of the sixth century BCE. Genesis 1 offers its response to these questions in the form of a priestly vision of reality. This vision was designed to inspire a sense of hope grounded in an order, specifically labeled as "good." In turn, this good order provided a sense of the ultimate connection between the transcendent Creator and the immanent creation.

Chapter 2 addresses a number of questions about creation raised by the description of the first day in Genesis 1:1-5. Several are commonly asked questions. The answers to them can help us to understand the outlook of the priestly composer. In addition, this chapter looks closely at the words and phrases of this passage, with particular attention paid to the association of divine speech with "light" on the first day. The light on the first day of creation has fascinated commentators since antiquity. Unlike most modern commentators, many ancient writers argued that the light of the first day was not "created" as such, but represented the very light of God. I will take up this argument and show why this view has merit. The implications of this reading for understanding Genesis 1 are immense and point to its powerful, perhaps even mystical, vision of reality.

Chapter 3 explores major priestly features evident in the rest of the first week. Most of these are well known, such as the allusion to the Sabbath on the seventh day. Others have attracted less attention. The nuances of all these priestly features are worth probing. This chapter will help us to see Genesis 1 within the larger context of priestly thinking. In its vision of reality, the universe is presented in terms of a cosmic temple. God is not only its builder, but also its priest who offers blessing to the world.

The next two chapters, which form part 2 of this work, turn to broader issues involving the interpretation of Genesis 1 and its placement at the head of the Bible. Chapter 4 studies the significance of Genesis 1's position at the very head of the Bible. To grasp the matter of the placement of Genesis 1, we will look at how the priestly tradition came to write out its rituals and stories. I will describe the emergence of priestly literature and then broadly situate the priestly placement of Genesis 1 within the context of this tradition of priestly literature. The purpose of Genesis 1 as the Bible's initial chapter will also be considered by comparing it with what has sometimes been called the "second creation story," namely Genesis 2:4b–24. (For the sake of convenience, I will sometimes refer to this second creation account as Genesis 2.) We will look at the points of contact between these two creation narratives as well as their literary design as a larger, single narrative. The first creation story of Genesis 1:1—2:3 was not meant to stand as a separate narrative, but to serve as a preface or prologue to the second creation story of Genesis 2:4b and following. The first creation story was designed to be read with the second creation story as a single whole. The final achievement of creation in the first account is the emergence of humanity, the very act of creation that begins the second creation story. We might say that the first leaves off where the second begins. In this way, the two stories were meant to dovetail with one another and be taken as a larger whole.

Working with this view, I further suggest in chapter 4 that specific expressions in Genesis 1 serve to balance, modify, and comment on some of the views expressed in the second creation account in Genesis 2. In this respect, one may view Genesis 1 as an implicit form of "commentary" on Genesis 2. To be sure, this is not commentary in the usual sense of this word, namely an explicit exposition or explication of a biblical text. Instead, Genesis 1 offers an implicit sort of commentary conveyed through its narrative form.

In this interpretation of Genesis 1–2, Genesis 1 serves a dual role as both prologue to and implicit commentary on Genesis 2. It offers a cosmic vision of God, humanity, and the world to balance and complement the earthly perspective of Genesis 2. Separately, the two accounts would stand ostensibly in opposition: the first favors a heavenly or cosmic perspective, while the second emphasizes a more concrete perspective, one that is literally more "down to earth." Placed together in their present order, they offer a fuller perspective, with priority of order given first to the creations of the heavens and then with greater focus on the earth. The net effect of having the first account before the second is not simply to offer balance, but also to orchestrate a narrative movement from God the Creator at the very beginning to the world of humanity on earth.

In chapter 5 I will take a look at an issue that has been central to the scholarly study of Genesis 1 for decades. Readers since the Enlightenment have asked whether Genesis 1 is a myth or not. This issue became particularly critical in light of texts that came to light from archaeological excavations in Mesopotamia (modern Iraq). These narratives raised questions about how we are to understand Genesis 1 in a broader, ancient Near Eastern context. The Mesopotamian creation stories that we will discuss in chapter 1 show important resemblances with Genesis 1. These similarities lead to questions about just how unique Genesis 1 really is, and therefore whether it represents a unique, divine revelation about creation. It would seem clear that Genesis 1, in the broader cultural milieu, is not the beginning of creation narratives. Rather, it is another variation on long standing ancient traditions. In light of this, one may well raise the question whether Genesis 1 itself might be better regarded as a myth like Mesopotamian creation stories.

Chapter 5 compares Genesis 1 with extrabiblical stories commonly regarded as myths and addresses the question whether or not it is to be considered a myth compared to them. As we will see, the answer is yes and no. Although Genesis 1 in its content conforms to most definitions of myth, its position makes a further statement about it. As part of the larger construction of the Pentateuch, Genesis 1 has the effect of making other creation accounts and allusions in books such as Psalms, Job, or Proverbs recede from view. Due to its placement at the very beginning of the Bible, Genesis 1 becomes—at least in biblical terms—*the* account that begins it all. It is not regarded as only one of a number of creation stories, but as the creation story that looms over all others. By placing the story of Genesis 1 as the very beginning of the Bible, its author makes a claim to its authority and a claim about the nature of reality; in this respect, it is unlike what scholars have otherwise regarded as myths. Standing at the head of the longer narrative of the Bible, Genesis 1, despite its older mythic material, is not simply a myth.

The appendix at the end of this book offers a discussion of modern scholarly approaches to the Bible in general and to Genesis 1 in particular. Readers interested in knowing about these scholarly approaches may wish to consult this appendix. This can be a bit daunting for people unfamiliar with biblical studies, since it often involves terms and ideas used by biblical scholars. Still, I would encourage those of you who may be interested to wade into the appendix, as it provides an opportunity for you to think about how and why you read and study the Bible.

Before I conclude these comments, I want to briefly mention two other matters. First, this study does not work through each day of creation. While many biblical and ancient Near Eastern parallels are noted,[2] this book is hardly a comprehensive study of all aspects of Genesis 1, especially where the priestly imprint is less marked. Second, this study draws heavily on the work of other scholars. To my mind, biblical scholarship has a great deal to offer to interested readers. It is my hope that this effort to understand Genesis 1, drawing as it does on the best, modern scholarship available, will interest a wider readership.

3. The Format of This Book

This is the general plan of the book. Before we move to chapter 1, it may be helpful to offer comments about this book's format, which is designed for readers with an interest in the Bible and in ancient Israel, but who are not specialists in the field of biblical studies.

Spelling of Hebrew Words

To make for a less taxing reading, I generally spell out the names of biblical books instead of using abbreviations. I also use simplified spellings of Hebrew words in English (called transliterations by scholars); they usually appear in parentheses following their English equivalent. In my transliterations of Hebrew words, I do not indicate the lengths of vowels, as is the common practice for scholarly publications. I have also simplified the spellings for a number of Hebrew consonants. The spelling "sh" is used for the letter *shin* and "h" for both of the Hebrew letters, *he* and *het* (sometimes spelled *chet*). I also employ "s" not only for the letters *samekh* and *sin*, but also for the letter *sade*. Hebrew readers will be able to tell which letter is transliterated by consulting a Hebrew Bible. Occasionally I put an asterisk before a Hebrew word to indicate the "consonantal root," or the base form of the word. In other words, I show the word without the prepositional prefixes or pronoun suffixes often affixed to Hebrew words. An very important example for this study is *bere'shit,* the first word in the Bible, which consists of the preposition *be,* "in," plus *re'shit,* "beginning (of)."

Endnotes

The main text is aimed for a broader readership; it is not necessary to consult the notes in order to understand this book. I have placed these notes at the end of the book so that they won't distract readers who are not interested in scholarly technicalities. On the other hand, readers who do wish to know the underlying basis for claims made in the main text will find documentation and scholarly references in these notes. The notes aim for a representative citation of scholarly literature; they are hardly exhaustive. I would mention in passing that there is some occasional duplication of material; this is to avoid interruption in reading through the book.

Translations Used

Readers may find it helpful to know the main translations used for this book. For translations of passages from the Bible, I often use my own translations, which tend toward the more literal in order to bring out the flavor of the original Hebrew. I also cite the important translations of the New Revised Standard Version (NRSV)[3] and the New Jewish Publication Society version (NJPS).[4] I also sometimes use the New American Bible (NAB). Where the verse numbers differ in the Hebrew text and the English translation of the NRSV or NAB, I follow the convention of using the Hebrew numbering with the NRSV numbering added in parenthesis, preceded by the word "English" or "E." Occasionally I note the versification of the traditional Hebrew text (Masoretic Text) by adding MT.

For Mesopotamian texts, I have used the fine translation by Yale professor Benjamin Foster.[5] I often cite as well the accessible and handy translation of Mesopotamian literary texts produced by Stephanie Dalley of Oxford University.[6] For Ugaritic literature, I have mainly cited the collection edited by the late Simon B. Parker (formerly professor at Boston University).[7] This edition has the advantage of having the English translation on facing pages with the Ugaritic text spelled out in English letters. This translation allows readers with some basic knowledge of Hebrew to gain some sense of the Ugaritic words involved. Interested readers are encouraged also to consult the translations of Dennis Pardee, professor at the University of Chicago and today the world's leading scholar of Ugaritic studies.[8] For the Ugaritic rituals cited in this study, Pardee has also provided a handy edition,[9] and curious readers may wish to look further into his massive two-volume edition of these texts.[10]

At this point, we are ready to address different models of creation in the Bible. Sketching out these models will help us see the general contours of creation traditions in ancient Israel and provide a framework for exploring the specific character of Genesis 1 that we will examine in chapters 2 and 3. Now we may start with chapter 1 and its survey of the models of creation in the Bible.

Prelude

Creation in the Bible

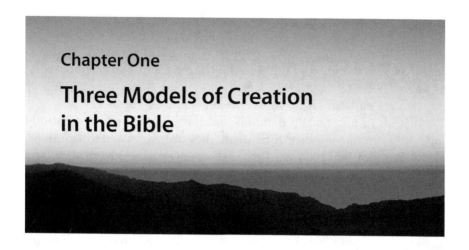

Chapter One

Three Models of Creation in the Bible

To understand the priestly vision of Genesis 1, a look at the Bible's creation traditions is a good starting point. In ancient Israel, people told the creation story in different ways, as we see in various biblical books.[1] There are allusions to the creation story in the prophets (for example, Jer. 10:12; Amos 4:13, 9:6; Zech. 12:1), and it is recounted in various wisdom books (Prov. 8:22-31; Job 26:7-13, 38:1-11; Ben Sira 1:3-4, 24:3-9). The creation story was also a topic in Israel's worship (Pss. 74:12-17, 89:11-13, 90:2, and 148). These passages show us that in ancient Israel many different creation accounts existed, not just one single creation story.[2] In fact, these passages indicate that there were various ways of telling the creation story.

In the Bible, creation refers to the divine production of the physical world, mostly involving divine making or manufacturing. The common terminology for creation involves words for manufacturing, such as "to make" (*'sh*), "to form, fashion" (*°ysr*) and "to create" (*°br'*).[3] Most creation passages use one or more of these verbs. When a passage describes creation using one of these verbs we have a creation *text*. If a passage also involves a narrative, then we have a creation *account*. Other biblical verses mention creation only in passing; these we may call creation *allusions*.

Creation passages in the Bible differ in important ways. The Bible's ways of telling the story of creation may be grouped into a number of categories or models. We may identify three major models of creation: God created the universe by divine *power*, with divine *wisdom*, or with some form of the divine *presence*. Divine power, wisdom, and presence also characterize the connection between God and the world outside of

11

creation contexts.[4] In emphasizing these three models, I am not claiming that the Bible does not have other models of creation.[5] For example, creation by divine procreation enjoyed a long and venerable tradition in the ancient world,[6] and it lies in the deep background of Genesis 1,[7] as we will see later in chapter 3. Still, in general, these three models of creation are particularly useful for understanding Genesis 1.

It is also important to mention that these models are not entirely separate from one another. First of all, they are all related to kingship.[8] Power, wisdom, and presence (especially in the palace) are all attributes associated with kings. In addition, the king is responsible for building temples. In accordance with these ideas, various creation accounts present God as a warrior-king, as a wise ruler, or as the great monarchic presence in his palace or builder of his sanctuary space. All of these were old ideas in the ancient world well before the historical emergence of Israel around 1200 BCE.[9] Finally, we should note that more than one model is sometimes operative in a creation text. All three models inform a number of biblical passages, such as Genesis 1, Psalm 104, and Second Isaiah (Is. 40–55, a sixth-century addition made to the book of Isaiah).[10] In some cases, it may be that an older royal model was adopted and modified under other influences. Perhaps some of the wisdom texts should be viewed in these royal terms. Similarly, Genesis 1 might be seen as a priestly text that has drawn extensively on royal ideas and reshaped them with priestly concerns.[11]

The three models of creation that we will examine in this chapter will help us to identify and organize the various features in creation texts. By grouping the ways of telling or alluding to the creation story according to these models, we will able to appreciate the contours of specific creation accounts, and in particular the version of creation in Genesis 1.[12] I would like to begin by offering a summary of the three models. Then we will discuss each model in more detail.

The First Model of Creation: Divine Power

The first model that we will explore entails creation issuing from God's powerful victory over cosmic enemies,[13] for example in Psalms 74:12-17 and 89:11-13.[14] In this model, the universe is the stage on which God engages in battle against a cosmic enemy understood to be either the waters personified or a monster dwelling in the waters. In the aftermath of his victory, the divine warrior-king reconfigures the elements, such as the waters, from the divine conflict into creation. This model sometimes uses verbs of making, but they are not necessarily the dominant way of expressing creation in this model. For example, Psalm 74:12-17 uses only one such verb. Instead, this passage focuses on God's power (see also Psalms 65:7-8 and 68:35).

In the first model of creation, the deity is viewed primarily as a warrior-king, and power is the primary idea in this divine reality.[15] This king has a palace (also regarded as his temple), from which he marches to battle and to which he gloriously returns after the divine victory.[16] The proper human response is to honor the divine king as a servant would, by paying him homage. In religious terms, this translates into sacrificial cult and praise of the warrior-king at the temple. In this model, God punishes enemies with acts of powerful violence.[17]

In ancient Israel, this first model sometimes involved the figure of the human king. In various Bible passages, the human king functioned as mediator between the divine king and his subjects. As God's intermediary, the human king drew his own power from the power of the divine king.[18] In some cases of the first model, it is through the human king that divine power is made manifest in the world. For example, in Psalm 89:10-11 (MT 11-12), creation occurs in a context concerned with the king's power and his divine support. In this psalm, the king derives his power from God's own power, as expressed by God in verse 25 (MT 26): "I will set his hand on Sea and his right hand on River(s)."[19]

The Second Model of Creation: Divine Wisdom

The second model involves creation accomplished by divine wisdom, for example, in Psalm 104 and Job 38:1-11 (especially vv. 5-6; compare Job 28:25-27).[20] This model often presents creation as the work of the divine craftsman,[21] who works variously as builder, engineer, and architect (see Job 28:25 and 38:4-6), and occasionally as a metal worker (see Job 37:18).[22] Isaiah 40:12-14 describes God as the wise craftsman of creation in contrast to the human craftsmen who make idols in 40:18-20. In Proverbs 8:22-31,[23] the wisdom of divine creation is embodied by Wisdom personified as a female figure who was with God at the beginning of the divine acts of creation (see also Wis. 6:22).[24] In this model, wisdom is the primary idea, in contrast to power in the first model.

In the second model, the human response to God as creator builds on the first model's idea of human reverence to God: "the fear of the LORD is the beginning of knowledge" (Prov. 1:7); and "the beginning of wisdom is reverence for God" (Ps. 111:10; compare Eccles. 12:13).

Biblical texts in this second model call men (and often not women) to acknowledge the wisdom of the universe as created by God, to learn wisdom and understand it, and accordingly, to live a life of wisdom. If in the first model the king is the mediator of divine power, it is wisdom itself built into the world's fabric that mediates between God and people. In order to become wise, one is to learn God's wisdom in the world, or in the terms presented by Proverbs 1–9, to approach Wisdom herself and to learn from her. As a result, people gain divine wisdom, which helps them to withstand challenges over time. Sinners instead perish from their lack of wisdom, and not necessarily through the instrument of divine punishment. Instead, because of their foolishness, they set themselves on their way to the underworld (see Ps. 49). The biblical scholar Adele Berlin remarks of Psalm 104:35: "sinners undermine God's favor to the world: they may cause God to hide his face."[25] It is hoped that they disappear from the earth (Ps. 104:35).

Instances of this model may draw on the first model of divine conflict, for example, in Psalm 104:6-7: the waters of creation "fled at your rebuke,[26] rushed away at the sound of your thunder." On the whole, however, the second model emphasizes how creation is an expression of divine wisdom. The wisdom vision of Psalm 104, which is the focus of the second section of this chapter, corresponds to Genesis 1 in a number of ways.

The Third Model of Creation: Divine Presence

The third model offers a view of the universe as the place of God's presence, and this idea is expressed by various terms that connect God to the world. Like the first model, the third involves the notion of the divine palace-temple, but its emphasis is not so much on divine power, with the warrior-king marching from his palace. Instead, it focuses on the idea of temple, imbued with aspects of divine presence, such as holiness. In some cases, we see the ideas of divine power and holiness together, for example in the heavenly divine home referenced in Psalm 150:1: "Praise God in his sanctuary (holy place), praise God in the firmament, his stronghold!" The firmament is not only the divine fortress; it is also God's holy place, the divine sanctuary (as we see also in Isaiah 40:22, 57:15; see also Ezekiel 1). From the heavenly temple-palace, God makes the divine presence manifest in a variety of ways.

Parallel to the heavenly palace or temple is God's temple-palace on earth. It, too, is regarded as a sacred space established by God in the wake of divine victory. The praises of Exodus 15 include a reference to the sacred space that God provided for the people (v. 17) following the divine triumph over the Egyptians:

> You brought them and planted[27] them
>   on the mountain of your inheritance,
> The place for your dwelling that you made, O Lord,
> The sanctuary, O Lord, that your hands established.

The divine temple, whether in heaven or on earth, is God's sanctuary that mediates divine presence in different ways. It is this sense of temple that informs the third model.

In the third model of creation, the universe bears some characteristic of God associated with the temple[28] or the divine presence[29] in it. The Psalms in particular convey God's connection to the world in contexts describing creation.[30] Following its initial reference to creation, Psalm 8 discusses the divine *name* in the universe.[31] Psalm 33:6 states that God made the world by the divine *word*.[32] Psalm 148 depicts various parts of creation joining in praise of God because God created them (v. 5); the divine *name* and *splendor* are over all heaven and earth (v. 13).[33] God's *light* is prominent in the account of creation in Psalm 104:2, and it is also notable in Temple contexts. For example, Psalm 36, which describes an experience of God in the temple, declares in verse 10: "In your light we see light."[34] Divine light is a well-attested element of temple experience linking human worshippers to their deity.[35] For example, Psalm 27:1 calls God "my light," and verses 4-7 describe the speaker's desire to be in God's temple.[36]

Divine name,[37] word,[38] holiness,[39] and light[40] are all features[41] relating to the divine presence associated with the temple,[42] in contrast to the stress put on power in the first model and wisdom in the second model.[43] In addition, there is devotion centered on divine teaching (see Pss. 1, 19, and 119), a verbal manifestation of the divine *word* (see Ps. 33:6).[44]

The human response in this third model builds on the first. It certainly includes giving proper service to God. In addition, people are to acknowledge God's presence in the world through praise (see Ps. 33, especially vv. 1-2). The divine name is a source of trust for the upright (Ps. 33:21). The wicked honor neither God nor the divine presence in the world. In a sense, it is the self-inflicted punishment of the wicked to remain outside of the upright community, which recognizes God and the divine presence in the world. The wicked stand outside this worldview (for example, in Ps. 8). As a result, they perish, as expressed in Psalm 1:6: "The LORD knows the way of the upright, but the way of the wicked perishes." In this case, they perish not because God violently punishes them as in the first model, but because they do not ground their lives in God's presence mediated by divine teaching, so they do not prosper like the upright (see vv. 2-3). As a result, they simply fall away like chaff (see v. 4) and will not stand in the assembly of the upright (v. 5). In short, they place themselves outside of life with God, and so they pass away. In the third section of this chapter, we will explore this third model, especially in Psalm 8 as it compares with Genesis 1. For now, I would emphasize that this model assumes the idea of the created universe as comparable to the Temple; within this Temple the divine presence is at work. Outside of this Temple are threats of cosmic waters (see Jonah 3:3-9), which correspond to the potential threats of violence to humanity and the traumas of human experience.

In this discussion I may give the impression that the Bible delineates these three models clearly and keeps them separate. On the contrary, they were used with a great deal of flexibility, and they can overlap. So we should be careful not to distinguish them too strongly. Different biblical authors combined motifs from different models as they suited their purposes. For example, Psalm 104, a passage that emphasizes the wisdom of God's creation (v. 24),[45] also mentions the divine light (v. 2) and the divine presence or "face" (v. 29).[46] Biblical texts that clearly belong to the second or third models skillfully play off the first model.

Genesis 1 alludes to and works off the first model, as we will see in chapter 2. In addition, it uses the language of divine making, as found in the second model.[47] In our discussion of Genesis 1, we will also see signs of divinity which comprise the third model: divine *word* and *light* are important beginning with the first day; and divine *holiness* along with divine blessing marks the seventh day. Genesis 1 draws on all three models, with divine speech and light as well as other features informing its vision of creation.

To understand the use of older creation traditions in Genesis 1, we may draw on an observation made by Ronald S. Hendel about biblical worldviews and their social settings. Hendel comments as follows: "The cosmology corresponding to a particular social context should be defined not as an ideal pattern as such, but as the consequence of an interpretation of a preexisting cultural tradition."[48] In the case of Genesis 1, its worldview emerged from the priesthood and its interpretation of preexisting cultural traditions. The ideal order that Genesis 1 expresses did not develop in isolation. Instead, its vision of creation came about as a response to earlier traditions, including older Israelite traditions about creation. The three models examined in this chapter will help us to see how the priestly account of Genesis 1 responded to nonpriestly traditions. We will be able to identify nonpriestly features of creation in Genesis 1, which in turn will help to highlight its priestly features that we will explore in the following chapters.

At this point, we may address the three models in greater depth; for each model one biblical passage will serve as an illustration. We may begin with the first model of creation.

1. Creation as Divine Might

In the Bible, the most common model of creation involves divine might and conflict that issues in creation. In this model, elements involved in the battle figure also in creation. Psalm 74:12-17 offers a good example. In its appeal to God to provide help against enemies, this passage describes creation in the wake of the divine battle against the cosmic enemies:[49]

> 12 Yet God my[50] King is from of old,
>   Working salvation in the midst of the earth.
> 13 You—you scattered[51] Sea by your might;
>   You smashed the heads of the Tanninim on the waters.
> 14 You—you crushed the heads of Leviathan,
>   You made him into food for the work of sea-beasts (?).[52]
> 15 You—you split open springs and brooks;
>   You—you dried up mighty rivers.
> 16 Yours is the day, yours also the night;
>   You—you established[53] the luminary of the sun.[54]
> 17 You—you fixed all the boundaries of earth;
>   Summer and winter,[55] you—you fashioned.

The passage is marked by invocations of God in the second person, each one with a display of divine power. The divine victory here depicts God smashing the primordial enemies, Sea, Tanninim, and Leviathan, which in verse 14 serves as food for animals. In this case, one of the primordial enemies is transfigured to serve in God's creation. Creation in this context hardly uses verbs of making, and it does so only at the very end, in verse 17. Instead, the focus falls on God's power. Psalm 74:12-17 makes the divine conflict over the cosmic enemies of the waters the basis for the establishment of the sun, moon, and stars as well as the boundaries of the earth. Genesis 1 largely follows the format of creation found in Psalm 74:12-17. These shared features indicate that the overall format was a basic one known in ancient Israel. We will return to this passage in chapter 2, but for now it is important for illustrating the idea of divine conflict in ancient Israel.

For examples of the first model, we could marshal additional passages, such as Psalm 89:11-13. This model also underlies the presentations of the divine conquest of the cosmic waters in Job 26:7-13 (especially v. 10) and Job 38:1-11 (especially v. 8), as well as Psalm 104 (especially vv. 6-9).[56] Other passages alluding to creation likewise mention the divine subjugation of the waters (Jeremiah 31:35; Job 9:8). It is for this reason that some creation passages specifically mention God's might or strength at creation, for example, Psalm 65:6-7 (MT 7-8), Job 26:12, Isaiah 66:1-2 and Jeremiah 27:5 (compare Amos 5:8 and 9:6). These as well as other passages would suggest that cosmic might and conflict issuing in creation was perhaps the best-known model of creation in ancient Israel.

The idea of ancient divine conflict was a very old one in the ancient Near East. The text perhaps cited most often as an example of creation emerging from conflict between divine wills is the Babylonian classic known from its first two words, *Enuma Elish* ("When on high"), or as it is called in some translations, the *Epic of Creation.* In this story, after various generations of deities have come into existence, a divine conflict ensues between the older gods and the newer generations of high deities. In the course of the story, we meet the older goddess, Tiamat. Her name identifies her as the cosmic waters; it is related to the word "deep" (*tehom*) in Genesis 1:2. Tiamat conspires to destroy the newer gods in revenge for their slaughter of her mate, Apsu. To address this challenge, the younger gods meet as a divine council and choose the warrior storm god Marduk as their divine champion. After they accept his terms for agreeing to fight Tiamat, he meets her in battle. He suffers an initial setback, but then he slays her with his weapons of weather. He cuts her carcass into two parts that form the top and bottom of the perceivable universe. At this point, creation emerges explicitly out of the defeated enemy. Marduk then creates the constellations of the stars, identified as the abodes of deities. In turn, humanity is created in part with the blood of Tiamat's right-hand man, Qingu. The center of the newly created world is Esagila, the palace of Marduk and his temple on earth, which the text locates by name in Babylon. *Enuma Elish* then closes with fifty names given to Marduk as an expression of praise.

This epic poem has been read against the political events of the late second millennium BCE Babylon and the later Assyrian and Babylonian empires of the first millennium BCE. The late second millennium witnessed a rise in the worship of Marduk, and in the first millennium his power symbolized the power of Babylon. In their own versions of *Enuma Elish,* Assyrian kings would sometimes substitute the name of their patron-god Assur, for the name of Marduk. One Assyrian king, Esarhaddon, had an inventive political strategy to integrate Babylon more fully into the neo-Assyrian empire.[57] He combined construction projects with symbols and imagery associated with Marduk in order to demonstrate what a good friend Esarhaddon was to Babylon. Later in his reign Esarhaddon went further, trying to use Marduk as a symbol of unity between Babylon and Assur. It is clear from this history that Marduk and *Enuma Elish,* which celebrates the god's cosmic achievements, in turn celebrated the rulers who patronized this epic.

The universe that the epic depicts is not altogether unlike the human world that celebrated it. On the heavenly level, deities face off in battle like the human royalty who patronized the epic. In the wake of this divine conflict, creation emerges. The worldview of the epic corresponds to the human world. Marduk, like the human rulers who revered him, faces cosmic enemies who threaten him with their primordial powers. The enemies of the divine king and his human counterpart can be threatening in the world that he created. Both divine and human kings reign from Babylon; the temple of the god in Babylon is the cosmic center on both divine and human levels. The heavenly world corresponds to the earthly world. The relationship might be expressed in the following diagram:

| heavenly level | god | divine enemies |
| earthly level | king | human enemies |

On these two levels, the god and the king mirror one another in status and power, and both face hostile enemies who threaten the kingdom.

When we move from Mesopotamia toward the Mediterranean coast, closer to the world of the Bible, we see a number of texts that refer to the cosmic conflict between the storm-god and his enemies. The conflict story served to reinforce human kingship in a variety of texts hailing from the city of Mari (lying on the great bend of the Euphrates River) all the way to Egypt. A letter sent by a prophet named Nur-Sin of Aleppo to King Zimri-Lim of Mari quotes to him the following words of the storm-god Adad: "I brought you back to the throne of your father, and I handed you the weapons with which I battled Sea."[58] In other words, the king had received the very power of his god. We also see this idea of divine power of the king in some of the Amarna letters written to the Egyptian king by his vassals living in various cities up and down the Mediterranean coast in the fourteen century. In some of these letters, local vassals of the pharaoh compare him with "Baal in the heavens" (El Amarna letters 108:9; 147:14; 149:7; 159:7; 207:16).[59] Here again there is an association of the king with the power of the god.[60] The Baal Cycle, the longest religious text from the ancient city of Ugarit (located on the coast of modern day Syria), does not explicitly make this link between Baal and the Ugaritic king. At the same time, the royal line, whose patron god was Baal, sponsored the Baal Cycle, because this text embodied the royal ideals of divine support for the Ugaritic royal line. Baal's enemies such as Sea and Death as well as the better known Leviathan mirrored the Ugaritic king's enemies.

The imagery in some of these cases (for example, the letter to King Zimri-lim) does not simply express a correspondence between the divine and human kings. Rather, it goes further in making the king sound like his patron storm god.[61] The language was not a mere figure of speech, but a statement of the king's power and how it was linked to the power of his patron god.[62] In the first model, power is what fundamentally connects the divine and the human.[63] The king's power flowed from the god. The human king and his power were thought to come from the power of God, the divine king.

The political use made of the conflict between storm god and cosmic enemies passed into Israelite tradition. The biblical God is not only generally similar to Baal as a storm god, but God inherited the names of Baal's cosmic enemies, with names such as Leviathan, Sea, Death, and Tanninim (see Ps. 74:13-14; Job 3:8, 26:12-13, 41:1; Is. 25:8, 27:1). Baal's home on Mount Saphon is identified with Zion in Psalm 48:3. God's titles, "Rider in the heavens" and "Rider of the Steppe" (for example, Ps. 68.4) are also echoes of Baal's own title, "Rider of the Clouds."[64]

As we see in *Enuma Elish* and in Ugaritic, biblical passages draw a parallel between God, the divine king, and the Davidic ruler, the human king. This correspondence of the divine and human kings may be seen in Psalm 89. Its description of the victorious power of God in verses 5-18 matches its praise of the divine favor that God bestows upon the Davidic monarch in verses 19-37. Creation belongs to this divine scheme in verses 5-18, as expressed in verses 10-13. The parallelism between God and the king changes, however, in verse 26, and a different sort of notion appears: God extends his power to the monarch in language that recalls Baal in Ugaritic: "I will set his hand on Sea and his right hand on Rivers."[65] Here God invests the king with power capable of mastery over the cosmic enemies, Sea and River, which are elsewhere titles of God's cosmic enemy (just like Sea in Ps. 74).[66] Psalm 89:26 expresses a correspondence between heavenly and earthly levels, which may be put in the following way:

heavenly level	God, the divine king	divine enemies
earthly level	the Davidic human king	national enemies

The image of the Davidic monarch receiving martial power from God also informs the simile used for the house of David in Zechariah 12:8: "On that day the Lord will put a shield about the inhabitants of Jerusalem so that the feeblest among them on that day shall be like David, and the house of David shall be like God, like the angel of the Lord at their head."[67]

The mirroring of divine enemies and earthly enemies appears in other texts of the Hebrew Bible. This sort of divine imagery worked its way into various biblical images not only for the enemies of the king, but also for people's personal enemies. We see various echoes of cosmic imagery known from the Ugaritic texts appearing in biblical passages aimed against wicked human beings. Habakkuk 2:5 and Proverbs 1:12 compare the wicked with the underworld (Sheol) personified with its insatiable mouth. These descriptions echo Death's appetite as in the Ugaritic story of the god Baal, and in the story of the destructive gods known as the "Goodly Gods."[68] Both Death and the Goodly Gods are said to have "a lip to Earth, a lip to Heaven," and they swallow the animals of creation.[69] Similarly in Psalms, the Underworld is said to have a mouth that threatens the speaker, and the cosmic Deep can likewise "swallow" the speaker (Ps. 69:16). Human enemies, too, "would have swallowed us alive," if not for God's saving help (Ps. 124:3). Like these foes, human foes in Psalm 73:9 set their mouth against heaven. Isaiah 9:19 draws on the image of enemies, devouring on their left and their right. (This particularly echoes the description of the "Goodly Gods.")[70] These passages suggest that this was stock language for cosmic enemies applicable to various sorts of earthly foes, whether king or commoner. Just as the cosmic enemies parallel earthly kingdoms opposed to the Judean king, this language of cosmic enemies is used to describe enemies or wicked persons who threaten individuals. This imagery was used for a long time, both for kings and for people more generally.

After the monarchy fell in 586, the royal view of creation did not disappear. In biblical texts dating to the postexilic period (from 538 on), the idea of divine conflict was not only a matter set in the primordial past. It also became a way to talk about the future, definitive moment of God's salvation of Israel. Among the texts after the exile, Isaiah 27:1 may be the most poignant expression of this theme: "In that day the Lord with his hard and great and strong sword will punish Leviathan the fleeing serpent, and he will slay the dragon that is in the sea." We hear a more consoling voice along these lines in Isaiah 25:6-8 (RSV):

> On this mountain the LORD of hosts will make for all peoples a feast of fat things, a feast of wine on the lees, of fat things full of marrow, of wine on the lees well refined. And he will destroy on this mountain the covering that is cast over all peoples, the veil that is spread over all nations. He will swallow up death forever, and the Lord GOD will wipe away tears from all faces, and the reproach of his people he will take away from all the earth, for the LORD has spoken.[71]

The later apocalyptic visions of Daniel 7 and Revelation 13 describe beasts rising from the Sea. They are political empires that God the divine warrior will ultimately sweep away (Dan. 7:23-27 and Rev. 19:17-21).

The book of Revelation contains a dramatic example of this old tradition in 21:1-4 (NRSV). This passage echoes the sequence of events known all the way back in the Late Bronze Age story of the Baal Cycle, with Baal's defeat of Sea, the building of his palace and his conquest of Death (as marked by my italics):

> Then I saw a new heaven and a new earth; for the first heaven and the first earth had passed away, and *the sea was no more.* And I saw *the holy city, the new Jerusalem,* coming down out of heaven from God, prepared as a bride adorned for her husband; and I heard a loud voice from the throne saying, "Behold, the home of God is among mortals. He will dwell with them as their God; they will be his peoples, and God himself will be with them; he will wipe every tear from their eyes. *Death will be no more,* mourning and crying and pain will be no more, for the first things have passed away."

In this passage the cosmic Sea is destroyed, then the heavenly city (the divine palace-city) appears, and finally Death is overcome.

The political link between these beasts and world empires was not a late invention. It echoed the old mirroring of divine and human kings and the cosmic and human enemies. Throughout Israel's monarchy and even over the centuries of domination by several political empires, the model of divine power endured. Divine power not only expressed the political fortunes of Israel's monarchy; it also expressed hope through Israel's times of trouble and powerlessness.

2. Creation as Divine Wisdom

Ancient Israelites conceived of creation as being infused with divine wisdom.[72] Psalm 104:24 views God's creation in terms of wisdom: "How many are Your creations, O LORD; all of them You made with wisdom." Proverbs 3:19-20 similarly proclaims: "The LORD established earth by wisdom, He established Heaven by understanding."[73] Here Proverbs 3:19-20 adds understanding to wisdom as the means God used to make the world. Psalm 136:5 attributes understanding to the divine creation of the heavens. Proverbs 8:22-31 presents the figure of female Wisdom personified as present with God throughout creation. With personified Wisdom, this passage, in a sense, "anthropomorphizes" the traditional idea of divine wisdom present in creation. According to Job 11:6, it is God who could tell "the secrets of wisdom" (see also Job 12:13),[74] and according to Job 38:16, God put wisdom into the hidden parts of the world. Wisdom is commonly associated with God as creator in the book of Job, for example, in Job 28:20-28 specifically, but see also Job 39:17, 26. Wisdom, in the divine speeches of Job 38–40, is not only a matter of an architect's wise order, but it also presents creation's wondrous beauty made by the divine artist.[75]

Of all these texts, it is Psalm 104 that most fully elaborates a picture of creation based on divine wisdom.[76] In several respects, it also offers a valuable comparison with Genesis 1. To facilitate our appreciation of the similarities with Genesis 1, I provide a translation of Psalm 104, with my own section headings marked in bold letters[77]:

Opening Invocation of the Creator of the Heavens

1   Bless the LORD, O my soul![78]
     O LORD, my God, you are so great!
     In splendor and majesty you are clothed,
2   Wrapped in light like a robe.
     Spreading the heavens like a tent-curtain,
3   Putting beams in the waters for his upper chambers;
     He is the one who sets the clouds as his chariot,
     The one who moves on the wings of the wind;[79]
4   Making winds into his messengers,
     Fiery flames, his servants.[80]

Praise of the World's Creator

5   He established the earth on its foundations,
     So that it would never shake.
6   As for the ocean (*tehom*), you covered it like clothing,
     Above the mountains the waters stood.
7   At your roar they fled,
     At the sound of your thunder they hurried.[81]
8   They went up the mountains, went down the valleys,[82]
     To the site that[83] you had established for them.
9   You set a boundary they would not cross,
     And never again cover the earth.

Praise of the Creator of Waters on Earth

10   You are the one who makes springs gush in torrents,
     Between the mountains they flow.
11   They give drink for every beast of the field,
     Wild asses quench their thirst.
12   Beside them the birds of the sky dwell,
     Among the foliage they sing.
13   Watering the mountains from his upper chambers,
     By the fruit of your work the earth is sated.

Praise of the Creator of Food

14   Growing grass for the beasts,
     Herbage for humanity's labor:
     To yield food from the ground,
15   And wine that[84] gladdens the human heart;
     To make the face shine[85] with oil,
     and food that sustains the heart.
16   The trees of the LORD have their fill,
     The cedars of Lebanon that he planted,
17   Where birds nest,
     The stork has its home in the junipers.
18   High mountains are for wild goats,
     Cliffs are a refuge for badgers.

Praise of the Creator of Seasons and Days

19   He made the moon to [mark] seasons,
     The sun knows when to set.

20   You make it dark, and it is night,
       Then every beast of the forest roams.
21   The lions roar for prey,
       Seeking their food from God.
22   The sun rises, they retire,
       And they lie down in their lairs.
23   Humanity goes out to its work,
       To its labor, until evening.

Praise of the Creator of the Seas

24   How many are your creations, O LORD!
       All of them you made with wisdom,
       The earth is fully your property.[86]
25   There[87] is the sea, great and vast,
       There with creatures beyond number,
       Living things, small along with great.
26   There ships go about, Leviathan as well,
       Whom[88] you formed to play with.

Creatures' Dependence on the Creator

27   All of them hope in you,
       To give them food in due season.
28   You give to them—they gather,
       You open your hand—they are sated with good.
29   You hide your face—they are terrified,
       You take away their spirit—they expire,
       And they return to their dust.
30   You send forth your spirit—they are created (°*br'*),
       And you renew the face of the earth.[89]
31   May the glory of the LORD be forever,
       May the LORD rejoice in his creations,
32   The one who looks to the earth and it trembles,
       Touches the mountains and they smoke.
33   Let me sing of the LORD throughout my life,
       I will rejoice in my God while I live.
34   May my discourse[90] be pleasing to him,
       I—I will rejoice in the LORD.
35   May sinners vanish from the earth,
       And the wicked be no more.
       Bless the LORD, O my soul!
       Hallelujah

The overall sense of creation is a dynamic interaction of its parts, especially the waters flowing from the beginning of the psalm. It also shows various relationships between these parts of creation. They are designed with wisdom (v. 24) so that they help one another.[91]

We may also note that in its treatment of the waters in verses 6-9, Psalm 104 draws on the model of creation of divine conflict. The storm god rides on his chariot in verse 3,[92] and the waters of the psalm "flee" at the sound of the divine "rebuke" (v. 7). As in the first model, these waters are left over from the implied conflict and are transformed into beneficial components of nature. Similarly, Leviathan, another maritime cosmic enemy,[93] appears in this psalm. At the same time, the psalm moves away from the model of conflict. The waters are not accorded any status as opponents, and Leviathan here is no more than God's pet. While Psalm 104 draws on elements of the first model of the warrior god's battle against the cosmic waters, its presentation is informed by the considerably different concept of divine wisdom. In keeping with the second model of creation, creation is imbued with wisdom (v. 24). Moreover, the wicked are not punished by divine violence, as in the first model; instead, the author of the psalm wishes that they would vanish from the earth (v. 35).

Readers may recognize some similarities between this psalm and Genesis 1. Many elements of creation and their overall order as known from Psalm 104 also appear in their essence in Genesis 1. Scholars have generally noted the following similarities:[94]

> Psalm 104:2-4; Genesis 1:6-8: God as Creator presented with respect to the cosmic waters.
>
> Psalm 104:5-9; Genesis 1:9-10: God establishes the earth with respect to the waters and establishes bounds for them.
>
> Psalm 104:10-13; Genesis 1:6-10: With the cosmic waters under control, they provide sources for springs.
>
> Psalm 104:14-18, Genesis 1:11-12: Vegetation is produced and feeds living creatures.
>
> Psalm 104:19-23, Genesis 1:14-18: The moon and sun are created to marks times and seasons.
>
> Psalm 104:24-26, Genesis 1:20-22: In the remnant of watery chaos live the sea creatures.
>
> Psalm 104:27-30, Genesis 1:24-30: Humanity's place in creation is shown.

The similarities and the fairly similar order in these two passages are impressive. They share in common a general schema, reflected in different degrees in a variety of biblical texts (see also Ps. 89:10-13; cf. Job 38–39): description of God as creator of the universe; sea and the sea monsters overcome; fixing of the earth on its foundations; release of springs; creation of day and night; creation of the sun as well as the seasons; and human creation. The authors of Genesis 1 and Psalm 104 incorporated the traditional outline into their presentations. Genesis 1 structures the outline into its scheme of seven days, as we will see in chapter 3.

With its dynamic vision of creation, Psalm 104 offers a constructive and appealing presentation of humanity, nature and God. The parts of creation in this psalm serve and help one another in many respects. Unlike the ordered picture of Genesis 1, with boundaries set for various realms and animals, the effects of these realms and their animals in Psalm 104 interconnect with one another, to their mutual benefit. Unlike the picture of humanity in Genesis 1, humanity in Psalm 104 is not the ruler of creation; humanity is woven into the pattern of creation with other beings.[95] In its presentation of humanity, Genesis 1 stands closer to Psalm 8, to which we now turn.

3. Creation as Divine Presence

The model of creation as divine presence works off the model of creation as divine conflict. This model expresses its sense of divine presence in creation by using any number of terms, such as divine name and holiness. A good example is Psalm 8. In several ways, this psalm resembles the priestly vision of Genesis 1.[96] Both evoke the image of the word or speech in the universe, which is metaphorically or analogously God's temple.[97] In this section, I would like to look at Psalm 8 in some detail, with the purpose of using it to understand some aspects of the priestly vision of Genesis 1 that we will see in chapters 2 and 3. As we will discover, the visions of reality in these two biblical passages also differ in some respects.

Let us begin with a translation of Psalm 8, which I have laid out according to its poetic structure (following the prose label, or what scholars call the "superscription"). I have also highlighted some key words with italics and marked my headings in bold:[98]

Prose Label (Superscription)

Musical Personnel:

S (MT 1)   For the director

Musical Information

On the *gittit* (?)

Type of Composition:

Song

Putative Authorship:

Of David.

Poem

A: The Divine Name throughout the Earth

1 (MT 2)   O Lord, our God,
How (*mah*) mighty is your Name (*shem*) in all the Earth!

B: Heavenly Creation

Let me acknowledge [= sing of][99] your splendor over the heavens (*shamayim*):

2 (MT 3)   From the mouth of babes and suckers,
You established a strong place[100] because of your foes,
To put an end (*lehashbit*) to the enemy and avenger.

3 (MT 4)   When I behold your heavens (*shameka*),
The works of Your fingers,
Moon and stars that you established[101, 102]

C: The Question of Humanity in the Universe

4 (MT 5)   What (*mah*) is the human being that you remember her,
The human that you are mindful of him?

5 (MT 6)   You made her little less than divinities,[103]
And with glory and majesty you crowned him.

B': Earthly Creation

6 (MT 7)   You made him rule (*tamshilehu*)
The works of your hands,
All you set beneath her feet:

7 (MT 8)   Sheep[104] and cattle, all of them,
              Also, beasts of the field.
8 (MT 9)   Bird of heaven (*shamayim*) and fish of the sea,
              The path-crosser of the seas.

A': The Divine Name throughout the Earth

9 (MT 10)   O Lord, our God
        How (*mah*) mighty is your name (*shem*) in all the Earth!

This hymn of praise opens and closes with a communal invocation of "Lord, our God" followed by a proclamation of the divine name's power throughout the world (vv. 1 and 9). This proclamation at the psalm's beginning and end frames the rest of the poem and gives it a universal horizon. The first major section of the poem (vv. 1-4)[105] opens with a first person proclamation of the divine honor (v. 1), which continues the cosmic horizon of the introduction. The divine victory at creation that neutralized the enemies of old prepared a place for humanity (v. 2). Here we may sense the old model of creation as conflict,[106] but the psalm does not dwell on the matter.[107]

Instead, the psalmist is moved to contemplate the creation of the universe, which issued in the astral bodies (v. 3). This reflection leads to the speaker's question, which does not praise God either for that creation or for the divine power as the source of this creation.[108] Rather, it leads to the speaker's question about the nature of humans.[109] The next part (vv. 5-8) answers the question with a reflection on humanity and the world. The psalmist presents humanity as the ruler of creation exalted nearly to the level of the minor divinities of the divine council (v. 5) and above the creatures known from human experience (vv. 7-8). From this vision of the universe, the psalmist is led to finish with one final expression of "hymnal elation."[110] The hymn is directed to God, and the basis for its praise is humanity itself.[111] For this presentation of humanity as a reason for divine praise, Psalm 8 is perhaps unique in the Bible.

Consistent with this theme, the literary structure of Psalm 8 places humanity at the center in its arrangement, as reflected in the following scheme[112]:

A verse 1 = verse 9: envelope of praise;
     B verses 2-3: heavenly creation ("the works of your fingers");
          C verse 4-5: humanity as the crown of earthly creation;
     B´ verses 6-8: earthly creation ("the works of your hands");
A´ verse 9 = verse 1: envelope of praise.

The structure here has what is called a "chiasm" or envelope structure (which I have labeled above as A and A′ and B and B′). This structure is reinforced through a three-fold repetition of the particle "how, what" (*mah*). This word is used twice at the beginning in verse 1 and at the end in verse 9, and also once in the middle of the psalm in verse 4.[113] In addition, we see the consonants "sh" (*shin*) and "m" (*mem*) standing in prominent positions: the word "name" (°*shem*) in both verses 1 and 9; "heavens" (°*shamayim*) in verses 1 and 8; and, "your heavens" (*shameka*), the second word in verse 3, and "you made him rule" (*tamshilehu*), the first word in verse 6. This alliteration using the sounds "sh" and "m" links creation with the name (°*shem*) of the Creator.

The divine splendor and divine name are within the heavens, as in all creation (vv. 1 and 9). Creation bears the signature of the Creator, and more, because "splendor" and "name" are also cultic expressions of the divine. These two terms suggest a model of the heavens and earth as the site of God's manifestation to humanity. In other words, the heavens are metaphorically like a temple or sanctuary containing divine splendor, and the earth analogously is the part of this sanctuary where the speaker senses the name of God.[114] To this picture of the divine name, we may compare the glorious manifestation of the divine name in Psalm 29:2 (made manifest in v. 9), the personification of the divine name as a warrior in Isaiah 30:33, or the idea that God's sanctuary is where God establishes the divine name, for example in Deuteronomy 12:5, 11, and 14:23-24.[115]

To the idea of the divine name in the universe, we might also compare the notion of the divine "glory" (*kabod*) filling the earth.[116] We see this idea in the famous exclamation of the seraphim in Isaiah 6:3: "Holy, holy, holy is the Lord of hosts; the whole earth is full of his glory."[117] It also occurs in the priestly divine speech of Numbers 14:20-21.[118] Here God describes himself in the third person: "the glory of the LORD fills all the earth." These passages show a temple or priestly sensibility. For Genesis 1, creation embodies the priestly vision of holiness and proper ordering, with humanity as the highpoint of creation and Sabbath rest evoked as its concluding moment.[119] Where the first model of creation stresses divine might, and the second model emphasizes divine wisdom, Psalm 8 offers a picture of the divine name made manifest in creation. Somewhat similarly, Genesis 1 proclaims divine holiness, embodied specifically in its picture of divine rest and Sabbath.

Psalm 8 and Genesis 1 are similar in other important ways.[120] For example, humanity is featured as the literary highpoint of both accounts.

For the prose account of Genesis 1, this highpoint is the sixth day of creation, while for Psalm 8 the reference to humanity is the poem's middle-point. Both passages make humanity the highpoint of creation. They also draw on similar imagery to describe humanity. They evoke the royal notion of the king as *'elohim,* a Hebrew word that may mean, "divine," "divinities," or "God," depending on the context. In the royal worldview, the king could be exalted as a minor divinity (*'elohim*) because of his relationship to God, as seen, for example, in Psalm 45:6 (MT 7) in its address to the monarch, "Your throne, O divine one, is forever and ever" (compare the king being called "my son" by God in Psalm 2:7). Psalm 8:6 draws on this royal idea for its understanding of humanity. At the same time, the verse qualifies the status of humanity by positioning it only slightly lower than *'elohim,* sometimes understood as "God" (for example, in the Greek versions of Aquila, Symmachus, and Theodotion as well as the Latin Vulgate of Jerome), but elsewhere as "angels" (for example, in the Greek Septuagint). A similar movement away from the royal worldview is made in Genesis 1, which applies the notion of the king as created in the image of God (*'elohim*), an idea that we will see in chapter 3.

The similarities between Psalm 8 and Genesis 1 extend also to the notion of human rule in the world. God has placed the world at the feet of humanity in Psalm 8:6 in a manner recalling the verb "to rule" (*°rdh*) in Genesis 1:28.[121] In Psalm 8:5-6, royal terms again are applied to humanity,[122] "majesty" (*hadar*) like that of God (Psalms 29:4, 90:16, 104:1, 111:3 and 145:5) and perhaps also like the king's (see Psalm 21:5; cf. Psalm 45:3-4).[123] In Job 40:10, God taunts Job by asking: "Can you dress in glory and majesty?" These are God's characteristics, and humanity is graced with these divine qualities in Psalm 8:6. Finally, there is some similarity in the presentation of the animals and their realms in Psalm 8:7-8 and Genesis 1.[124] In sum, Psalm 8 and Genesis 1 draw on ideas and motifs from the first model, that is, that creation emerges from conflict waged by the divine warrior king over the cosmic enemies. At the same time, these passages recast the worldview of divine conflict. Psalm 8 focuses on the divine name filling the world, while Genesis 1 presents the sacred plan of space and time, as we will see in chapter 3.[125]

The two passages also display some significant differences. While Psalm 8 resembles Genesis 1 in evoking a picture of the universe as a divine sanctuary, it does not include the specifically priestly emphases found in Genesis 1, in particular its themes of sanctification and divine rest. Genesis 1 presents the created world with the holiness of the Sabbath on the seventh day. This sense of the universe as a divine sanctuary is also conveyed, as we will explore in chapter 3, by its picture of God acting as a divine priest who utters blessing upon creatures, including humanity (Genesis 1:22, 28). The verb, "to cease, end" (*shbt*) in the two texts may mark a subtle difference within their overall similarity: in Genesis 1 this verb, which refers to the divine rest, may play off the older notion of this root that we see in Psalm 8, that God put an end to the divine enemies.[126]

Conclusion

Let me close this discussion with some general comments on the three models. As we consider these models, it is important to reflect on their limitations as well as their insights. They are all deeply indebted to Israel's patriarchal society, primarily reflecting the experiences and perspectives of men: in the first model, the monarchy; in the second, the sages; and in the third, the priesthood. Moreover, these were primarily men of elite status. It is evident that they offer limited intellectual horizons within Israel's overall experience. They do not offer reflections from the experiences of women or from the generally less privileged of Israel's society. At the same time, they offer the best (or at least some of the best) of what Israelite elites in their times had to say about the nature of God, humanity and the world. We may further appreciate the dire conditions in which many of them wrote their works. Several of Israel's writers, especially those of the sixth century, sought to speak with hope at Israel's critical moments and through its terrible crises. All three models convey a quality that speaks to the human condition. The language of divine power, wisdom, and presence address the situation of human beings enmeshed in the realities of power, engaged in the search for understanding, and attuned to a sense of the divine in the world.

All three models have conceptual advantages and disadvantages. At first glance, the first model of divine conflict today would seem to be the least satisfying of the three. It works on a premise of divine power and violence, and it casts God in the leading role in this drama of violence. Because such biblical portraits of God may be used to justify violence,[127] this model seems least helpful for creating a world without violence. Divine conflicts such as Job's can feel like the violent clashes initiated by a sort of a divine, misguided Don Quixote in the name of order and justice.[128] At the same time, the first model has the distinct theological advantage of exploring the chaos of the world and human experience. Violence and chaos are real parts of our world. The first model permits an examination of the unruly character of our reality. While we may be—and arguably should be—uncomfortable with the idea of a God who takes up violence to punish or test, such a way of looking at the world reminds us that God both cares about the world and cares enough that God is prepared to act. When we feel our discomfort at this side of God, we may also be forgetting the terrible violence of the ancient world in which Israel lived—and in which many people around the world live today. To my mind, the first model acknowledges not only God's power; it also calls us to resist human power and human structures in which our lives are intractably embedded. Moreover, I am often struck by the comfort that the first model gives to people who themselves have little or no recourse in this world. While I recoil at the idea of the violent God, many people who take comfort in it are consoled not so much by the picture of divine violence, but by the sense of divine attention and care that it conveys to them for the possibility of overcoming terrible human power in the world. I may recoil perhaps in part because I can afford to; as a fairly privileged upper middle-class American, I suffer little from the world's violence and thus far—thank God—it has not intruded much into my existence. But this is hardly the case for the vast number of people who look to the Bible for how it may speak to their lives.

In this context, it may be helpful to mention Hannah's prayer in 1 Samuel 2:1-10 and the Hymn of Mary in Luke 1:46-55 (known as the Magnificat). Many people find great consolation in these poems. These two poems also include images of God not simply in control of human history, but also exercising divine power: "The Lord kills" (1 Samuel 2:6); and "He has shown strength with his arm" (Luke 1:51). Hannah's prayer belongs in the worldview of the first model, especially with its mention of divine power (vv. 4 and 10) and the human king (v. 10). Despite the violence of these poems, people take great comfort in them, as do I. To my mind, they point to an important consideration about the first model, that it might be read less as a model to be emulated and more as a model of creation offering hope. It tells us that the world does not have to be the way that it is. It tells us that there is a power in this universe that hears the cries of the oppressed, the lonely, and the abandoned against the powers of this world and their destructive effects, and that somehow God acts. From this perspective, this first model can seem closer to the problems of our world than the second or third models.

The second model is quite appealing for today's world. It gets away from violence that many people find repugnant. We saw, for example, how Psalm 104 departs from the violence of the first model. In addition, the wisdom model conveyed in this psalm offers an ecological vision that is particularly attractive.[129] Its balance of humanity with other species may resonate in a culture increasingly sensitive to human dominance of other species.[130] In the next chapter of this book, we will also see joy, play, and wonder in the second model; these themes, too, are appealing today. All of these aspects of the second model I find very compelling. People engaged by the physical universe and its secrets may also find inspiration in the second model. The science of the Bible in passages such as Job 38–41 may look more like myth than science (so may the Big Bang theory two millennia from now), but it offers a biblical basis for human beings to exercise their intelligence in the search to understand the world. The second model's contribution, then, is not only the particular pictures of the universe that it yielded in the Bible. It is additionally the recognition of our God-given intelligence and the importance of using it as fully as possible to understand the world. It calls for thinking about the world.

At the same time, we need to be attentive to the potential abuses of the second model. Its biblical versions often assume a wise balance and order in the world that might serve too easily to justify things in the world as they are. Sometimes it can seem just too optimistic about reality. The model can also be misused to justify a hierarchical social order that might claim its blessings point to its divine approval. A wise order may also leave little room for exploring evil and suffering in our world. However, the search for wisdom can go beyond the Bible's particular pictures of the universe's wise order. The very search for wisdom sanctioned by the second model calls for exploring its weaknesses and its inability to explain certain problems of human existence, such as the problem of evil in the world. The wisdom search modeled in biblical wisdom texts provides a check on the limitations of traditional understandings of reality in those texts. The search for wisdom embodied by the second model also challenges us not to accept any one picture produced by this search, but to pursue this search with the same energy and insight that the biblical authors mustered.

The Bible itself recognizes the problems with the wisdom model. This issue comes out in Job and Ecclesiastes (*Qohelet*). These books go beyond the simple vision of a wise and good order imprinted on the universe. Their search for wisdom acknowledges the issue of God's power and the problem of human finitude: if God's creation is wise, then why do people suffer without understanding (Job), or why must people struggle with their mortality and never fully understand (Ecclesiastes)? Creation in Job shows the darkness of creation, and not only its light (see Job 3). Ecclesiastes 3:21 asks whether people really know in the end that the human life-force (*ruah*) rises upward to God. These two biblical books acknowledge humanity's finite capacity to understand creation. In the end, this wisdom search may seem like a failure to disclose true knowledge. The limitations of the human condition seem to keep humanity in the dark with respect to God's wisdom (see Job 28; Eccl. 3:11). This is hardly a consolation, much less any answer, and we might identify with "The Secret Sits," a two-line poem by Robert Frost: "We dance round in a ring and suppose, But the Secret sits in the middle and knows." People may feel tempted to dismiss the premise of the wisdom search that God is powerful, good, and wise.

Despite humanity's limitations, these biblical books affirm the search to keep pressing toward the Creator's ways in creation. We learn from Job and Ecclesiastes not only their views of creation, but also the central importance of the search for wisdom, a God-given capacity that we need to exercise as we try to understand the world around us. For Ecclesiastes, it is a capacity arguably built into people by God. Ecclesiastes (3:11) says that God has put eternity into the human heart and people cannot reach to the end of the matter.[131] The eternity put into the human heart perhaps gives it an intuition into the Eternal One who made us so. And despite Ecclesiastes' initial sense that the human condition is ultimately little different from animals' (3:18-21), the search affirms the basic goodness of God's blessings; these include the ability to enjoy what God has given (2:24-26; 3:12-13; 11:7-10), and especially in the form of human companionship (4:9-12). It also affirms that the human life force (*ruah*) does return to God in the end (12:7), the very matter questioned earlier in the book (3:21).

Job's search for wisdom leads to the fundamental insight that the wisdom search does go somewhere. At the end of Job, it is the experience of God that ends up as a response to the sorts of traditional theories about God (42:2-6). Experience is a sort of answer for Job who says to God at the end: "I had indeed spoken but without my having understood, Of things too wonderful for me, without my having known. . . I had heard of you by the hearing of the ear, but now with my eyes I see you." And despite Job's difficulties, God affirms his search for understanding in the end (42:6-16). For all the limitations of human understanding, people can come to understand something of the reality of the world. Even when the world may seem like "void and vacuum" (Genesis 1:2), it still offers the prospect of some God-given knowledge and good.[132]

The third model of divine presence may be the most difficult of the three models for people today. Having a sense of God strikes many people as a difficult proposition; having a sense of divine presence in the world is even a harder proposition. The idea of divine presence barely resonates in our culture. We stand at such a massive distance from the ancient traditions of the Jerusalem temple that supported this sense of divine presence in the world. As the decades pass, our culture seems increasingly removed from the Christian and Jewish religious traditions that drew upon the experience of temple. Divine presence seems little more than an outmoded relic of our religious past. Even for people of faith, a sense of divine presence may seem increasingly difficult to grasp, as our religious communities suffer from fragmentation and strife. The third model of divine presence can feel like an impossible challenge in today's world.

At the same time, the third model appeals to our basic intuition that our lives are not simply physical power struggles or intellectual and emotional pursuits. People often sense that there is more to their lives, and the third model takes account of this fact. It suggests that faith is central to the human person. People recognize that they act on faith all the time. In our human interactions, we act on faith every day. We continue to hope for things, often with little empirical basis. For example, people deeply believe in love. So while faith in God and a sense of divine presence offer great challenges, the third model offers people an invitation to discover within themselves the light and life-force that links them to God and to one another.

Potentially the third model offers great comfort. For my conclusion of this discussion of the third model, I have saved one final example, the beautiful Psalm 23. This psalm talks about the pilgrimage with God, who walks with people to the Temple as their shepherd (in vv. 1-4) and who serves as divine host there (in vv. 5-6). This vision culminates in verse 6 with the idea of life in the Temple "all the days of my life." This famous psalm presents life in the divine presence on the way to the temple and in the temple as a model for life and not simply for a particular occasion of pilgrimage.[133] For Christians, such a model for life is embodied in the figure of Jesus, who according to the Gospel of John (1:14) lived in the world (more literally, "pitched a tent") as the living tabernacle of God's word and glory. The model of the temple and tabernacle is not only an ancient one; it continues today. Jewish and Catholic traditions use temple language and imagery in their Sabbath services, offering moments of sanctuary.

The third model, as much as it is a challenge of faith, speaks to the human desire and urge to overcome the limitations of this world and to sense the wider connections of life within it. It further acknowledges that somehow the great giver of the life force of our universe is near, that the universe is not simply an empty and impersonal "void" (Gen. 1:2), but a reality where the transcendent can become immanent and personal. As a consequence, the third model adds motivation and inspiration to the search for understanding the world's challenges, and it is a call to act on them. It summons our best selves to respond to the worst in ourselves and our world.

All three models offer distinct theological advantages, and together they suggest a powerful way for thinking about reality. The first model recognizes the real problems of power in the world. The second calls for a life of the heart and mind to examine and understand these realities. The third connects this life to a sense of the divine that can guide and give hope in responding to the world's challenges. If we can set aside the limitations of these models and focus on their insights, we may gain a view of the world's goodness, grace, and wondrous potential for the divine, even as we acknowledge the world's unruliness, its chaotic quality, and the potential for terrible human evil. The three models, and the visions that they express, contribute toward our understanding Genesis 1. Over the next two chapters, we will see how Genesis 1 transforms the language and imagery of these models into its own priestly vision of reality.

Part One

Creation and the Priestly Vision of Reality

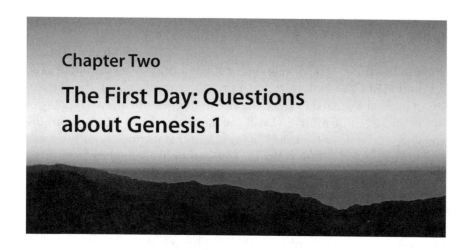

Chapter Two

The First Day: Questions about Genesis 1

In chapter 1, we saw that Genesis 1 is one of a number of creation passages in the Bible. We also saw that these other passages have some of the themes and ideas that we find in Genesis 1. So what makes Genesis 1 special? To answer this question, this chapter begins with the very first day of creation. We will see how it draws on all three models of creation, and how it put its own priestly imprint on its version of creation. To get at the priestly vision of creation in Genesis 1, I will address a number of questions commonly asked about the first day. Along the way, we will also look at some important details, in particular the divine speech and "light" in verse 3, and also the act of separation of light and darkness in verse 4.

Before we turn to these matters, we need to set the historical context for Genesis 1. Many biblical scholars date Genesis 1 to the sixth century BCE.[1] For years, I have questioned whether this is true; indeed, I have been skeptical as to whether we have enough evidence to pin down the time of the writing of Genesis 1. Still, over the course of working on Genesis 1 in this study, I have come to the tentative conclusion that a sixth century date remains the best theory, especially since this is the century when many of the biblical chapters that relate to Genesis 1 were written. One such passage is Psalm 74, which can be chronologically fixed to this time, since it refers to the destruction of Jerusalem in 586 BCE. Other biblical texts that we will meet over the course of this chapter may come from the sixth century as well. (Here I am thinking of Ezekiel 1–3 as well as Isaiah 45 and 51.) Other considerations likewise work in favor of a sixth century date for Genesis 1.[2] Unfortunately, it is hard to be more specific than this. We do not know whether the composition was before the destruction of Jerusalem in 586 BCE,[3] or during the Exile in Babylon (ca. 586-538 BCE),[4] or in the following decades.[5]

Thanks to the many parallels that Genesis 1 shows with priestly literature in the Bible, scholars agree that it has a priestly background.[6] The attribution of Genesis 1:1—2:3 to a priestly writer has been the consensus of biblical scholarship since the rise of the Documentary Hypothesis in the nineteenth century.[7] (I will say more about this later.) From the language and style of Genesis 1, it is evident that its priestly author was a highly literate and cultured figure. This author likely held a place within a leading institution that enjoyed considerable advantages and status under the monarchy and later during the Persian empire. This priestly author drew on traditional creation material known in ancient Israel (as we saw in the preceding chapter) and was clearly familiar with priestly terms and ideas (as described in this chapter and the next).

As a literate writer and reader, this author may have been familiar with some of the wider currents of thought about the universe known during the sixth century BCE, as reflected in works as diverse as the Mesopotamian creation account of *Enuma Elish*, the Egyptian Memphite Creation text, and the Phoenician cosmogony of Philo of Byblos.[8] Scholars have noted that the seventh and sixth centuries BCE witnessed great literary production and crosscultural influence across the eastern Mediterranean and the Middle East. During this great international epoch, these sorts of works may have directly or at least indirectly influenced Genesis 1. According to the Egyptologist Donald Redford, the Memphite Creation text (commonly known as the Memphite Theology) is among those creation narratives that would not have had any impact "on the outside world" until the time of the 24th to the 26th dynasties,[9] which he dates roughly to the years 725-525 BCE. This timeframe would fit with the idea of a broad circulation for this text (perhaps via the sea-trading Phoenicians),[10] extending to the sixth-century context of Genesis 1. This sense of our author's working knowledge of international literature is speculative. Still, it appears plausible when we take into account the prophet Ezekiel, another priestly figure of this period. The book of Ezekiel is exceedingly literate, reflecting knowledge of priestly tradition as well as various facets of Phoenician and Egyptian culture.[11] A similar case for seeing Second Isaiah both as a priest[12] and as a literate figure aware of wider international currents of thought[13] has been made as well.

Whatever the precise reach and range of his knowledge, the author of Genesis 1 was evidently a sophisticated priest.[14] As a member of an important group in ancient Israel,[15] this author belonged to a privileged class within the larger society. We may suppose that this figure would have been a man and not a woman, since the priesthood was an occupation only held by males in ancient Israel in this period. The writer of Genesis 1 was also someone who shared the fate of Israel's society living in an oppressed "colonial" situation,[16] perhaps under the Babylonian or Persian empire. In sum, the author of Genesis 1 wrote as an elite figure in a colonized society dominated by a foreign power.

Broadly speaking, Genesis 1 spoke to the same imperial world of Jeremiah,[17] Ezekiel[18] and Second Isaiah,[19] works all rooted in the sixth century. These great biblical works all contain important creation texts[20] that probe the nature of God's power and the reality of God for Israel in a time dominated by foreign powers. All of these writings try to understand God's relationship with Israel in the context of God's presence in the world.[21] Job, too, has sometimes been thought to belong to this period;[22] it also contains very important creation passages[23] that explore the nature of God and the ways of God in the world.[24] To my mind, these major biblical works[25] were engaged in a conversation over the nature of God and the world during this period of Israel's deepest crises.[26]

It is generally in this context that we may locate the priestly vision of Genesis 1. Over the course of this chapter, we will see priestly ideas; at the end of this chapter, I will raise the question of the intended audience for this creation account. At this point, let's begin with an important question about the beginning in verse 1.

1. Does Genesis 1:1 Begin in "the" Beginning?

Most readers assume that the answer to the question of whether Genesis 1:1 is the absolute first moment in all of history is yes. They read the first verse of Genesis 1 as describing the beginning of reality. For this view, they may be influenced by the translation of Genesis 1:1 in the King James Version (KJV) and the New International Version (NIV): "In the beginning, God created the heaven and the earth." In this translation, God seems to begin creation in verse 1, and so it seems logical that there was nothing before God began creating. "The heaven and the earth" here is what is called a *merismus*. In other words, the biblical phrase stands for everything encompassed by "the heaven and the earth."[27] So it seems that everything is created beginning in Genesis 1. The idea that everything was created by God in Genesis 1 may be reinforced for Christian readers by the common English translation of the opening words in John's Gospel (1:1), which echoes the first verse of Genesis 1: "In the beginning was the Word."

In fact, the story with Genesis 1:1 is more complicated when we become engaged with the actual Hebrew text. First of all, there is no "the" before "beginning" in the Hebrew phrase at the beginning of the verse. The omission of "the" before "beginning" in verse 1 is likely not an error, since it is well attested in the oldest Genesis texts and traditions. The early Greek translation of the Bible known as the Septuagint leaves out the definite article, and the Greek wording of John 1:1 also does not have the article. These sources seem to recognize the lack of "the" in the Hebrew, as they knew it. Well before the King James Version in 1611,[28] scholars noted that it was incorrect to translate the opening words of Genesis 1:1 "in the beginning." The famous rabbinic commentators, Rashi (1040-1105) and ibn Ezra (1092-1167), observed the critical facts about *bere'shit*. Rashi noted that the form of the word *bere'shit* means "in beginning of," as it does elsewhere in the Bible (Jeremiah 26:1; Proverbs 8:22).[29] As ibn Ezra emphasized,[30] the word in Hebrew has no definite article ("the") with the noun.[31] We will further note the contributions of these medieval figures shortly.

As these two scholars saw, the first three words of Genesis, *bere'shit bara' 'elohim*, are not a simple phrase, and the sense grammatically speaking is not "In the beginning, God created."[32] These words really mean something like "when at first God created," or "in the beginning[33] of when God created," or less literally, "when God began to create."[34] Several modern Bible translations follow this approach to Genesis 1:1. The *New Revised Standard Version* (NRSV) and the *New American Bible* (NAB) both translate: "In the beginning when God created the heavens and the earth."[35] The *New Jewish Publication Society* (NJPS) translation is similar: "When God began to create heaven and earth." These Bible translations basically have it right.[36] To be exact, the opening of Genesis 1:1 consists of a preposition ("in," *be-*), plus a noun ("beginning," *re'shit*) standing in an "of" (construct or possessive) relationship to what follows. In this case,[37] what follows is a relative clause, "(that) God created" (*bara' 'elohim*). This relative clause is "unmarked" (that is to say, it omits the relative pronoun, "that" or "which").[38] In this structure, the relative clause, "(that) God created," defines or "restricts" the preceding noun. It is the relative clause that makes "in beginning" definite in the NRSV and NAB translations, which allows for their translation "the beginning," instead of an indefinite rendering, "a beginning." At the same time, this translation may make it seem that the verse is talking about the beginning. So it is better to avoid using "the beginning" in a translation. It is for this reason that I have instead adopted the translation: "When at first

God created" (this is fairly similar to the NJPS translation: "When God began to create").

This understanding of verse 1 affects the translation of verses 2 and 3. Scholars generally agree that verse 1 is not a complete sentence by itself; instead, it is a part of a sentence connected to what follows. So, from the standpoint of grammar, verse 1 is a subordinate clause that depends on what follows. Verse 2 may be the main clause for verse 1,[39] but many scholars see verse 2 as a parenthetical statement describing the conditions that prevailed at the time God first began to create. For these scholars, [40] verse 2 is not the main sentence that verse 1 depends on. Instead, they understand verse 3 as the main clause of a long sentence that begins with the dependent (subordinate) clause of verse 1 and continues with a parenthetical statement in verse 2. In other words, Genesis 1:1-3 is one long sentence as in the following translation: "(1) When at first God created the heavens and the earth (2)—the earth was void and vacuum, and darkness was over deep, and a wind of God was moving over the face of the water—(3) (then) God said, 'Let light be,'[41] and light was."[42]

Most modern translations, such as NRSV, NAB, and NJPS, follow this understanding. The reasons in favor of this interpretation of Genesis 1:1-3 have been nicely expressed by the biblical scholar Jack M. Sasson, professor at Vanderbilt University:

> Although there are competent philologists who still defend the traditional translation, I personally think that this exegesis is really beyond dispute: first, because it is supported by grammar and syntax; second, because other creation narratives similarly open with temporal or circumstantial clauses; and third because the first of God's creative injunctions does not come until v. 3.[43]

Despite the length of such a sentence, Genesis 1:1-3 falls entirely in line with the openings of creation accounts from Mesopotamia. For example, Enuma Elish, which we discussed above, begins in this manner. Such introductions start with a clause beginning "when," and often follow with a description of the conditions lacking for life, followed by a "then" statement describing an important, initial act of creation.[44] Significantly, this is also essentially the structure of Genesis 2:4 (in the second half of the verse) through Genesis 2:7: verse 4, second half, is the when clause, verses 5-6 are the parenthetical clause describing the conditions prevailing at the time, and verse 7 describes the divine act.[45]

The implication of this interpretation is that Genesis 1:1 does not talk about "*the* beginning" in an absolute sense. Instead, it simply refers to the remote time when God began to create. We will study the meaning of the word "in beginning of" (*bere'shit*) shortly, but we should be careful that we not allow the traditional interpretation of the meaning of Genesis 1:1 to dictate about how we think about it. This verse presents the situation of the world when God first started creating—a point that was well recognized by ancient writers. The great Jewish philosopher Philo of Alexandria (roughly, a contemporary of Jesus) put the point this way: "'in (the) beginning he made' is equivalent to 'he first made the heaven first.'"[46] Modern commentators have followed this approach as well. According to the giant of German biblical scholarship of the nineteenth century, Julius Wellhausen, *re'shit* does not denote "the commencement of a process which goes forward in time, but the first. . . part of a thing."[47] The account talks about "the beginning," namely the beginning of God's creating the world, not the absolute beginning of everything. In the words of the great scholar Wilfred G. Lambert, Genesis is "about the processes by which the universe we know reached its present form, with no attempt to delve into the question of ultimate origin."[48] This is the general understanding of biblical scholars today. As we will observe below, the idea of creation from nothing arose in the Greco-Roman period and is alien to the Hebrew Bible. With this question about "the beginning" addressed, we may turn to the specific words of verse 1.

"When at first"

Now that we have discussed the grammatical syntax of *bere'shit*, "when at first" (or literally "in beginning of"), we can turn to its meaning. The same noun is used in other creation references. In Proverbs 8:22-23, the figure of Wisdom personified says:

> The Lord established me at the beginning (*re'shit*) of his way,[49]
> The earliest of his works from of old.
> In the distant past I was fashioned,
> At the beginning (*ro'sh*), at the early ages of earth.[50]

The words for "beginning," as well as "from of old" and "distant past," refer to primordial antiquity.[51] Job 40:19 calls the bovine beast Behemoth "the first (*re'shit*) of God's works." Both of these passages have creation contexts reminiscent of Genesis 1. In Job 15:17, God asks Job: "Were you the first (*ri'shon*) human born?" In Isaiah 48:16, the similar noun, "head" (*ro'sh*), refers to this time as "the beginning."[52] This verse also refers to "the beginning" as "the time of its coming to be."[53] As in Genesis 1:1, *re'shit* and *ro'sh* in these passages do not point to the absolute beginning of time, but the beginning of the time when things were first created.[54]

In Isaiah 46:9-10, the word refers to the beginning of time as known to humans:

> Recall beginning things (*ri'shonot*) from eternity;
> I am God, and there is no one like me,
> foretelling the end from the beginning (*mere'shit*).

These verses are talking about primordial time, at the beginning of creation. In this connection, we may note that other passages in Second Isaiah (Isaiah 40–55) refer to God as "first" (*ri'shon*), as well as "last."[55] This view of God is combined in Isaiah 41:4 with the divine rhetorical question: "Who has accomplished and done this? The One who has announced the generations from the beginning (*mero'sh*)." Isaiah 48:16 presents a similar idea. Following the declaration that God is the first and the last in verse 12, verse 16 claims: "from the beginning (*mero'sh*) I have not spoken in secret; from the time of its being I was there." As in these passages, the word *bere'shit* in Genesis 1:1 locates the story in the most ancient of times.

We may note that Genesis 1 and Second Isaiah (Isaiah 40–55) are sixth century BCE works that probe the primordial character of God. Their statements about God in the beginning of creation provide a way for them to ground their claim for the unique character of Israel's God. In the case of Second Isaiah, the claim is sometimes aimed against other gods (Isaiah 44:6; compare 44:6-8 with 48:5-6). While Genesis 1 offers no such overt polemic,[56] its attention, too, is directed to the God of Israel as the one and only deity of creation. Both Second Isaiah and Genesis 1 show a common set of concerns, and they both use the term *beginning* to discuss them. Both of these biblical texts were part of a larger discussion over the nature of God and creation, which was to help their audiences come to grips with the challenges of their sixth century situation.

Another priestly text from around this period offers some insight into *bere'shit* in Genesis 1:1. Ezekiel 45:18 uses *bari'shon* for the first month of a priestly offering: "Thus said the Lord: 'In the beginning (month) on the first (day) of the month, you shall take a bull of the herd without blemish, and you shall cleanse the sanctuary.'" What makes this verse particularly relevant for our discussion of *bere'shit* is that *ri'shon* occurs in close proximity to *'ehad*, which contextually designates "(day) one"[57] that is "the first day" of the month. This combination of "in the beginning" (*bari'shon*) with "(day) one" (*'ehad*) is reminiscent of "in beginning of" (*bere'shit*) in Genesis 1:1 and "day one" (*yom 'ehad*) in Genesis 1:5. Ezekiel 45:18, in using *bari'shon* and *'ehad* together in reckoning a date for sacrifices, points to the priestly flavor of events beginning on day one in Genesis 1:1 and 5. Taking these various comparisons together, it would seem that Genesis 1:1 and its use of *bere'shit* conjures up both cosmic and priestly associations.

"God created"

Following *bere'shit*, the next word in Genesis 1:1 is "(he) created" (*bara'*). The sound of the two words together resonates rather nicely; both words have three consonants in common in Hebrew. The verb marks the act to follow as a specifically divine one, since this particular verb[58] is used to denote only acts of God.[59] In this respect, this verb differs from other, more common verbs utilized to denote "to make" in creation texts. Second Isaiah tends to use the verb, "to create" (**br'*), rather than more common verbs of making in portraying divine acts, which is hardly surprising in view of its emphasis on God's unique capacities.[60] Genesis 1 seems no less concerned with God's uniqueness. We may also note the distribution of the verb **br'* within Genesis 1. It occurs at the very beginning in 1:1, and it closes the account in 2:3 and 4. In between, this verb applies to the creation of sea creatures and humanity on days 5 and 6 of creation (1:21 and 27). In contrast, a more generic verb, "to make" (**'sh*),[61] occurs on days 2 and 4 and in combination with the verb, "to create" (**br'*) on day 6 (see also 2:3). The verb, "to create" (**br'*), in Genesis 1 frames the account, and in this way it stresses God's unique role as the Creator.

The term for "God" (*'elohim*) in Genesis 1:1 and throughout this account is not the divine name as such.[62] Within the context of Genesis 1, we might say that it might further signify the one and only God, since this word can mean "gods." But with the singular verb following, clearly this context implicitly asserts that what other texts commonly view as plurality is, as far as Genesis is concerned, a divine singularity. There may be an implicit expression of monotheism here, that this is the one and only God acting in all of the creation that is about to unfold.

"The Heavens and the Earth"

Verse 1 continues by naming what is to be created, "the heavens and the earth." This order, as opposed to "earth and heaven" as in Genesis 2:4,[63] is quite traditional in biblical creation texts. We see it in many creation passages, for example, in Jeremiah 32:17 (see also 10:11, 23:24; 31:37, and 33:25), Amos 9:6, and Psalm 136:5-6; see also Isaiah 45:8, 48:13 and 65:17. It also appears in hymnic usage more broadly, as in Deuteronomy 32:1, Isaiah 1:2 and 66:1 (likewise a creation context), Jeremiah 51:48, and Psalms 69:34 (MT 35) and 135:6.[64] Creation accounts from Mesopotamia also have this order.[65] For the author of Genesis 1, the order may further signal a sense of priority, reflecting the heavenly or cosmic perspective of the account, as opposed to the more earthly perspective of Genesis 2:4b, which instead begins with "earth and heavens." We will return to the significance of this difference in chapter 4.

"Heaven-and-Earth" appears as a pair of old primordial deities in Ugaritic literature,[66] which matches the order in Genesis 1:1. (Like the order, "earth and heaven" in Genesis 2:4b, we also see the divine pair, "Earth-and-Heaven," in two Ugaritic god-lists.[67]) The divine pair of "Heaven" and "Earth" also occurs in Ugaritic ritual contexts.[68] This type of divine pairing reflects an older tradition of recounting the origins of the universe by a series of procreating generations of old paired divinities.[69] "Deep" and "water"[70] in verse 2 constitute another pair of this sort. This is not to suggest that the author of Genesis 1 thought that these were deities, or that he even was aware of traditions of this nature (although this is possible), only that with these pairings, Genesis 1 stands in a long line of creation traditions going back to the Bronze Age.

Finally, we should note that the word "earth" is used two different ways in verses 1 and 2. In verse 1 it refers to what is to be created: "in the beginning of (when) God created the heavens and the earth." In verse 2 it serves to characterize the situation of the universe[71] before creation takes place: "the earth (ha'ares) was void and vacuum (tohu wabohu)." So in the first two verses of Genesis, earth functions in a double manner that we will explore in the following section.

2. Did God Make Creation from Nothing in Genesis 1:1-2?

Before we proceed to a detailed discussion of the words in verse 2, it is important to explore the common idea that God created the universe out of nothing (creatio ex nihilo).[72] With regard to this question, ancient Israel seems to have known two views. On the one hand, some texts suggest that all creation was made by God. In Isaiah 45:6-7, God declares:

> "I am Yahweh, and there is none else,
> fashioning light and creating darkness,
> making well-being and creating strife;
> I am Yahweh who makes all these."[73]

This passage presents both darkness and light as coming from God's creative activity. Psalm 148:4-5 also understands the cosmic water as created. The second century BCE Jewish work known as the Book of Jubilees goes even further. Jubilees 2:2-3 counts the "seven great works on the first day"[74] as heavens, earth, waters, the ministering spirits, the void, darkness, and light.[75] This passage includes not only light and darkness, but also the cosmic waters. The late second century BCE work of 2 Maccabees 7:28 includes anything that is perceptible: "I beg you my child, to look at the heaven and the earth and see everything that is in them, and recognize that God did not make them out of things that existed."[76] This passage is thought to be the oldest text that explicitly reflects the idea of the universe as created from nothing (*creatio ex nihilo*).[77]

As we have already noted, many people today may also think of the universe in Genesis 1 as created from nothing. This idea may seem right if they are familiar with the King James Version's translation: "In the beginning, God created the heaven and the earth." However, as we have seen, this translation is not correct. Even so, there might seem to be room for the idea of creation made from nothing. It might appear to readers that this idea of creation from nothing is expressed or symbolized in Genesis 1:2 by the mention of "void and vacuum" (*tohu wabohu*). These two nouns, connected by a conjunction and forming a fixed, compound phrase, would seem to describe precisely the kind of nothingness that facilitates the concept of *creatio ex nihilo*. The phrase is thus translated as "a formless void" by NRSV and as "unformed and void" by NJPS. While these translations are fairly true to the basic meanings of these words, readers might think that these are symbols for complete nothingness.[78] They are not.

"Nothingness" is not the picture of the situation at the beginning. Unformed as the world is, *tohu wabohu* is far from being nothingness or connoting nothingness. Indeed, the context that immediately follows in verse 2 characterizes them as "waters" that form a "deep," which would seem to suggest a universe filled with a great watery mass rather than nothingness. I will use "void and vacuum" to translate *tohu wabohu*, not to suggest a general emptiness, but a lack of form and structure, and more specifically a lack of those realities that make the world beneficial for life.[79] Thus Genesis 1 depicts God turning *tohu wabohu* into something more useful. Likewise, other biblical creation stories and allusions also attest to "earth," "deep," and "water," as being in existence prior to creation. To take only a few examples, water appears in the creation account in Psalm 74:13, while heavens, water, and deep occur in Psalm 104:2-3 and 6 (see also sea and deep in Job 38:8 and 16). Similarly, the creation account beginning in Genesis 2:4b, with its earthly perspective, presupposes that the earth is there, but that it lacks for plants and herbs (verse 5). Ancient Near Eastern accounts also work with the idea that creation involved preexisting, tangible realities of various sorts, in particular the primordial water. Genesis 1 does not relate the "beginning of everything except God."[80] Instead, this account opens with what we might call a "preworld,"[81] before creation begins. (Later passages, such as Wisdom of Solomon 11:17, assume the idea of creation out of "unformed matter.")[82] So how are we to understand the process of creation in Genesis 1?

Genesis 1:2 presents reality as not yet formed in the manner that it was known to humanity. The universe was essentially "unformed" (the term used by the NJPS translation to render the word, *tohu*). In a sense, "heaven and earth" existed before creation, as expressed in the creation allusion in Amos 9:5-6: "It is my Lord of hosts. . . who built his chambers in heaven, and (as for) his vault on earth he established it" (in this vein, see also Job 9:8-9). In this passage, the universe[83] was already there when God created: heaven is where God made his "chambers," and the same goes with his "vault on earth." The picture in this verse is that heavens and earth were there when God acted to create. However, prior to creation, the heavens and earth were not yet in the form that humans are familiar with; they are transformed over the course of God's six days of creation.[84] Genesis 1:1-3 expresses the state of the "preworld" in terms of the deep, darkness and the waters as well as the "void and vacuum" (*tohu wabohu*). These are expressions of the lack of formation, but not of nothingness.

Let's consider this more closely. Creation is a process in which a deity makes the world, as it came to be experienced by human beings. Genesis 1 envisions creation not simply as God making; it is as much as a process of "separation" and differentiation (in Hebrew, *lehabdil*) of elements from one another (verses 4, 6, 7, 14, and 18), as we will see in chapter 3. It involves a transformation from an unformed, watery mass into the world that sustains human existence with water.[85] In its allusion to creation, Psalm 33:6-7 nicely expresses this transformation:

> By the word of the Lord the heavens were made,
> By the breath of his mouth, all their retinue;
> He gathers the waters of the sea like a mound,
> Sets the deeps in vaults.

As in Genesis 1, the waters were there when God began creating. In short, creation accounts, whether in the Bible or in Mesopotamian literature, presuppose the prior existence of a tangible universe in some manner. For all these creation accounts, creation is not a transition from utter nothingness to something. Instead, it involves a divine transformation of preexistent water and other elements deficient for life as humanity knows it. In the words of Isaiah 45:18, God the Creator "created it not as a void (*tohu*), but he formed it for dwelling." The undifferentiated mass represented by the unruly waters in Genesis 1 eventuates in a world beneficial to human life, with plentitude provided by God. Different biblical creation accounts convey how this transformation of the primordial situation took place.

To describe the author's understanding of the conditions of reality prior to creation, Genesis 1:2 makes three statements: "the earth (*ha'ares*) was void and vacuum (*tohu wabohu*), and darkness (*hoshek*) was over the face of deep (*tehom*), and the wind (*ruah*) of God was moving over the face of the water (*hammayim*)." Then the first divine act follows with divine speech that leads to the light of the first day (verse 3). The components preceding the description of creation, as mentioned in verse 2, are literally "the earth" (*ha'ares*), "(watery) deep" (*tehom*), "darkness" (*hoshek*), "a wind" (*ruah*), and "the waters" (*hammayim*). (We might leave *ruah* out of this list, since this is a feature attributed specifically to God.) To understand verse 2 better, we might note the correspondences between the three statements. To show what I have in mind, we may lay out the translation of verses 1-3, with the middle verse 2 arranged in poetically corresponding lines[86]:

> (1) When at first God created the heavens and the earth—
> (2) the **earth** was[87] ***void and vacuum***,
> and **darkness** was over the face of ***deep***,
> and **the wind of God** was sweeping over the face of ***the waters***—
> (3) (then) God said, "Let light be," and light was.

I have put in bold the subjects of the three clauses that correspond to one another in verse 2, and I have put the predicate nouns that correspond in bold italics. This arrangement shows the correspondence between the subjects, namely earth, darkness, and wind (or life-breath; *ruah*)[88] of God. This layout also shows the correspondence of the objects, void and vacuum, deep, and water. I have also aimed for alliteration within lines with my translation: void and vacuum, darkness and deep, wind and water.[89]

Now that we have addressed the overall structure of verse 2, we may turn to its particular words, beginning with the subjects and then the objects of the three clauses.

Earth, Darkness, and a Wind of God
The use of "earth" in verse 2, after its earlier use in verse 1, is striking since the same word first designates part of what existed before God began

creating in this account. In verse 2, the word designates the nature of the raw material divinely employed just as creation starts. Thus the word "earth" is used for the situation both before creation begins and after it starts.[90]

In verse 2, the picture of precreation is enlarged by the introduction of a second subject, "darkness," which is the polar opposite of what is to appear with the divine words in verse 3: "God said, 'let light be,' and light was." As we have noted, "earth" appears in older traditions of creation often paired with "heaven." However, in its second occurrence in Genesis 1, "earth" is immediately associated with "darkness." Darkness is also a condition of reality prior to creation in Mesopotamian creation accounts.[91] A later Greek source containing Phoenician creation traditions presents darkness with primordial wind: "The beginning of everything he posits as a dark and windy air, or a blast of dark air, and turbid dark chaos."[92]

The third subject, *ruah 'elohim*, which I have translated "the wind of God," presents formidable challenges for interpreters.[93] This phrase is different from the subjects in the preceding two lines. We no longer have the static mention of the rather unclear "earth" of the first line or the second line's characterization of the situation as "darkness." Instead, the focus shifts to naming a force operating within this situation. The hard question is the meaning of the two words in the phrase, *ruah 'elohim*, as both words have been interpreted in a variety of ways. The word *'elohim* is literally "God" or "gods" since it is a plural form, but it has also been translated as a sort of superlative such as "mighty" or simply as "divine." As we will see shortly, the *ruah* elsewhere is God's, and so *'elohim* in Genesis 1:2 probably should be understood in a similar fashion, as a specific designation of the creating deity, rather than a more generalized qualification, such as "mighty." This view is reflected in many translations; both NJPS and NRSV translate, "a wind from God." At a minimum, if "a mighty wind" or the like were the correct translation, it is a force powered by God.

The word *ruah* is perhaps more challenging to interpret, given its range of meaning in other creation contexts in the Bible.[94] On the one hand, it specifically marks divine force or wind. On the other hand, the word may have a nuance more in the sense of spirit.[95] In Job 26:12-13 we see the first meaning of the divine *ruah* serving as one of the divine instruments of creation:

> By his strength (*koah*), he stilled the sea,
> By his skill (*tebunah*), he smashed Rahab,
> By his force (*ruah*), heaven was calmed,
> His hand (*yad*) pierced the Twisty Serpent.

The four nouns that I have put in italics are all qualities of God. The first two nouns, "strength" and "skill," conjure up a picture of a skilled or trained warrior. The fourth, literally "hand," commonly refers to "power," which would be in keeping with the first two nouns. The third noun in the group, *ruah*, may be read along similar lines, as God's force, one that is analogous to human strength. It is like the *ruah* of Samson (Judg. 14:6, 19; 15:14). The Samson story also uses the word, "strength" (*koah*) to characterize his acts of *ruah* at several points (Judg. 16:5, 9, 15, 17, 19).[96] The narrative makes it clear that this *ruah* comes from God (16:20). Samson, the human warrior, gets the *ruah* that instills *koah* from Yahweh, the divine warrior. In short, the stories about Samson describe him with "strength" (*koah*) and "force" (*ruah*), much as Job 26:13 describes God's strength.

The word *ruah* is also an important term in creation passages with the sense of "wind." We already saw "wind" in the Phoenician creation account. This presentation has resonances in the Bible, for example in Psalm 104:3: God "setting the clouds as his chariot, moving on the wings of the wind."[97] This *ruah* carries Yahweh's wind-chariot. For this idea, scholars compare the storm chariot of the Mesopotamian god Marduk in the so-called "Epic of Creation."[98] In the same text, Marduk summons winds to fight Tiamat. The winds of the god Baal are also an integral part of his meteorological entourage.[99] Psalm 104:4 describes God as one who "makes winds his messengers." In Psalm 104:3-4, it is clear that the word *ruah* means, "wind," and that it is divine.[100] Many scholars support this sense of *ruah* also in Genesis 1:2.[101]

Two biblical passages that seem to be linked to Genesis 1:2 also favor this approach. The first text is Genesis 8:1. In this priestly passage, God generates "a wind (*ruah*) over the earth," a phrasing that is reminiscent of Genesis 1:2.[102] Since both of these texts are priestly, they would seem to reflect a priestly idea of *ruah* in creation. Second, commentators have noted that Daniel 7:2 deliberately echoes Genesis 1:2: "In my vision at night, I saw the four winds of heaven stirring up the great sea" (NJPS).[103] In drawing on Genesis 1:2, the later author of Daniel 7:2 indicates that contextually he understands *ruah* as "wind" in the creation story.

At the same time, the idea of God's *ruah* as divine breath in creation is also known in Psalm 33:6-7:

> By the word (*debar*) of the Lord the heavens were made,
> By the breath (*ruah*) of his mouth, all their retinue.[104]

The image specifically indicates that *ruah* is something that emanates from God's mouth. So there is some basis for translating the word as "breath." Support for this approach can also be seen in Psalm 104. I just noted above the evidence for *ruah* as "wind" in Psalm 104:3-4, but this is not the end of the story in this psalm. The end of Psalm 104 implies that *ruah* has the full range of nuances as "spirit," "breath," and "life-force." Verses 29-30 match human *ruah* with divine *ruah*:

> (When) you hide your **face**, they are terrified,
> (When) you take away their *ruah*, they expire,[105]
> And to their dust they return;
> (When) you send your *ruah*, they are created,
> And you renew the **face** of the earth.

This passage depicts God infusing creatures with divine breath or force of life.[106] The first instance of *ruah* in these verses is for the human life force or breath (see also Is. 42:5; Ps. 146:4; Eccles. 3:21, 11:5, 12:7),[107] while the second would be the divine source of this human *ruah*.[108] For Psalm 104:29-30, an important scholarly team working on ancient pictorial art has offered an interesting comparison to this passage. Othmar Keel and Christoph Uehlinger have compared a depiction on a rectangular plaque from Taanach, portraying a striding deity with outstretched arms, which they take to be a gesture of supporting the heavens. One side of the plaque shows the god's mouth with a scorching breath and on the other side his "reinvigorating breath of life (see Ps. 104:29f.)."[109] As this remark suggests, Keel and Uehlinger see in the plaque the divine "breath" (*ruah*) of the sort that we have in Psalm 104.[110] In sum, Psalm 104 uses *ruah* in both senses, and perhaps the same semantic range applies to *ruah* in Genesis 1:2.

These biblical passages show how understanding the nuances of *ruah* in specific cases depend on their contexts. So we must return to the context of Genesis 1:2. Context is an important, if not the most important, indicator of the word's sense in this verse. In context, the divine *ruah* is described as "moving[111] [*merahepet*] over the face of the water." The verb denotes a physical activity of flight over the water. (The same root is used in Hebrew and Ugaritic for birds soaring or gliding.)[112] The picture is perhaps like the wind-chariot of Psalm 104:3 riding on *ruah*. This physical sense of the verb works with *ruah* understood as "wind." At the same time, this is no ordinary wind, since it is specifically associated with God. God is able to speak in the next verse, so some anthropomorphic sense of the word, as expressed by the translation, "breath," arguably fits the context.[113] In sum, the translation "wind" conveys the natural side of the action, while "breath" captures the divine anthropomorphism here.

As this exploration suggests, *ruah* in Genesis 1:2 may involve both meanings of wind and breath. The biblical scholar Agustinus Gianto has emphasized that the word conveys a double meaning.[114] It is the divine breath, and it sweeps as a wind over the water.[115] It would be best to adopt a translation that conveys these two sides of *ruah*, but I am unable to find an English word that captures both meanings. Closest in English to the broader semantic range of the Hebrew term would be the compound, "life-breath," but since this seems a bit awkward, I find it difficult to adopt it. It is simply a problem to find an ideal translation for *ruah*. We should be aware that the limitation in translation may reflect the limitations of English. Moreover, the problem of translation may reflect a more basic difficulty. Nuance in language may be an indicator of conceptual thinking; and as this case indicates, there is often a significant difference between ancient Israelite thought and modern thought in English. We must recognize that, generally, there is much more of a separation of the natural from the supernatural or between the physical and anthropomorphic in English religious thinking and language than would be the case in biblical Hebrew. We may not have a suitable term, simply because our language, as a tool of our way of thinking, constructs divinity differently than biblical Hebrew. In the end, I have settled on "wind" for three reasons: it enjoys a wide range of evidence within the Bible; it is accurate for the physical side of the description in verse 2; and it is appealing for the alliteration that it adds to the line with the word, "water." At the same time, it is important to bear in mind the double aspect of Hebrew *ruah*.

One might assume that *ruah* plays no further role in Genesis 1 (in contrast to Psalm 104, for example, where it returns at the end of the psalm), since it is not mentioned again. However, I suspect that since *ruah* is associated with God's speech (as in Psalm 33:6-7, noted above), it is better viewed as implicitly empowering the speech of God throughout Genesis 1. Seen in this light, the universe in Genesis 1 is completely infused with this *ruah*. This, at least, was the view of Psalm 104:27-30, which we cited in part above. In this more expansive quotation, we can see how strongly it echoes Genesis 1 on this point:

> All of them hope in you,
> To give them food in due season.
> You give to them—they gather,
> You open your hand—they are sated with good.
> You hide your face—they are terrified,
> You take away their spirit (*ruah*)—they expire,

And they return to their dust.
You send forth your spirit (*ruah*)—they are created (°*br*'),
And you renew the face of the earth.[116]

The last two lines of this passage strongly recall Genesis 1:2, not only with the words *ruah* and "to create" (°*br*'), but also with the two expressions, "face of the" and "earth." If the comparison of *ruah* in Psalm 104 with Genesis 1 on this point is right,[117] then Genesis 1 may be no less animated by the idea of God's *ruah* in the world.[118] At the same time, this *ruah* in Genesis 1 is channeled into expressions of divine speech, as we will see later.

Void and Vacuum, Deep, and Water

The alliterative phrase "void and vacuum" (*tohu wabohu*)[119] has a parallel in Jeremiah 4:23: "I looked on the earth, and see—it was waste and void (*tohu wabohu*); and to the heavens, and they had no light" (NRSV).[120] This passage describes the reversal of creation, with the prophet witnessing the terrifying prospect of God turning the earth back into *tohu wabohu*. In view of this phrasing, Jeremiah 4:23 may be a deliberate echo of Genesis 1:2.[121] The two nouns *tohu* and *bohu* also stand in parallelism in Isaiah 34:11, which may also allude to Genesis 1:2. Here the two nouns appear in a description of God taking the measurements and the weight of Edom, which will become a wasteland: "He shall stretch out over it a line of *tohu* and weights of *bohu*."

Both nouns basically connote "emptiness,"[122] or in the case of Genesis 1:2, reality as an empty space. The word *bohu* is not entirely clear, as we have relatively little evidence for this noun.[123] In contrast, *tohu* appears several times in the Bible. It occurs the most in Second Isaiah (Isaiah 40-55), for example, in God's view of the nations (40:17) and their rulers (40:23), their false gods (41:29, compare verse 24, where they are "nothing," *'ayin*), their makers of idols (44:9); and their wasted effort (49:4). It applies similarly to worthless things in 1 Samuel 12:21, to bad speech in Isaiah 59:4 and to false speech in Isaiah 29:21.

In other passages, *tohu* applies to desolate places or spaces,[124] which fits the cosmic situation of the universe in Genesis 1:2 as lacking form and structure as well as the content of creation as produced by God in the rest of the chapter. The universe is not empty in a literal sense since it is clear that it is filled with water; it is empty of all that is about to be created in Genesis 1. Elsewhere the word describes the condition of the destroyed city in Isaiah 24:10 and Edom destroyed in Isaiah 34:11. In Deuteronomy 32:10, the word is in parallelism with wilderness or steppe (*midbar*).[125] In this connection, we may mention the same usage of the related Ugaritic word, *thw*, in the story of the god Baal. There the word refers to where lions live, specifically the wilderness.[126] Baal's enemy, the god Death, describes his voracious appetite in these terms: "My appetite is like a lion's in the wilderness (*thw*)."[127] In this passage, the word is parallel to "sea," another term denoting a vast expanse. In Death's speech, the word conveys the idea of a desert or wilderness.

We also have the Hebrew word *tohu* used for place or space in two creation contexts. Following a string of creation titles for God, Isaiah 45:18 presents God as claiming that the earth was not created as *tohu*, but that it was formed for human dwelling. In other words, *tohu* is a wasteland, a place that is not habitable. Creation in this context involves turning *tohu* into a habitable world. The next verse also uses *tohu* in a way that echoes creation. Isaiah 45:19 states that "I did not speak in secret (or a secret place), in a place of a land of darkness; I did not say to the seed of Jacob: 'in *tohu* seek me.'" The "land of darkness" and *tohu* are places unfit for God's creations, and they are suggestive of conditions before creation. Job 26:7 offers a distinctive use of *tohu*. It is parallel with *beli-mah*, literally "without-what." NJPS translates *tohu* here as "chaos" and *beli-mah* as "emptiness"—quite literally a terra incognita.

Before proceeding to address *tohu* in its connection with *bohu*, we should take note of the dates of the texts that we have been considering. Isaiah 45:18-19 belongs to the sixth-century BCE work of Second Isaiah, and as we noted at the outset of this chapter, Job may also date to this century. The use of *tohu* in these particular contexts then may have been meant to make a more contemporary, hopeful comment—namely that God has destined Israel to live in a place that will be transformed from the *tohu* that seemed ready to engulf it in the sixth century.[128]

Now let us turn to the question of how best to translate *tohu wabohu* in Genesis 1:2. In an insightful comment, Jack M. Sasson calls this expression, "a farrago, wherein two usually alliterative words combine to give a meaning other than their constituent parts."[129] Sasson nicely recognizes the alliterative quality of the phrase, which derives in part from their both having the same last two consonants as well as the same Hebrew noun form.[130] With his translation "hodgepodge," Sasson nicely captures the pair's sonant quality. At the same time, the first term may have carried the connotations of desolate space or wilderness, and its combination with *bohu* in Genesis 1:2 may not have eclipsed this meaning. One might conclude that *tohu wabohu* means "wilderness and desolation," in other words "a vast wilderness." To convey the meaning of two words in the expression as well as its character as an alliterative farrago, I suggest translating the phrase "void and vacuum."[131] I do not mean to suggest that the universe has nothing in it. On the contrary: it is indeed filled with waters. However, "void and vacuum," as I am using this translation, is to convey that these waters are empty of all that makes up the creation to be generated by God in Genesis 1. In fact, the universe is full of waters, but a "void and vacuum" with respect to life.

The phrase, *tohu wabohu*, is almost immediately echoed by the similar sounding word, *tehom*, "deep," the second object in Genesis 1:2. With *tohu wabohu* suggesting a vast universe empty of life, *tehom* suggests a world filled with water. Like heaven and earth, "deep" as the great cosmic waters is attested in cosmological traditions in the Bible. For example, Genesis 49:25 lists blessings of various divine figures, including "the blessings of Heaven above, blessings of Deep crouching below."[132] "Deep" in this passage is feminine, and here she is paired with Heaven. This verse echoes the old cosmological pair of "Heaven" and "Deep" known outside of the Bible. This pair is attested as divinities of cosmic origins in earlier West Semitic tradition (as known from the Ugaritic texts),[133] where the word, "Deep" (*thm*) is paired with "Heaven."[134] The third of our three objects in Genesis 1:2, "water," is also a term for the cosmic water; we may compare the expression, "mighty waters," in Psalm 93:3.[135]

We may close this discussion of the subjects and objects of verse 2 with a brief consideration of the relationships between them, as expressed by the verbs. The first line uses the verb, "was," to state the characterization that "the earth was void and vacuum." The second line provides a more precise relationship and a more descriptive characterization in stating that "darkness" was "over the surface of deep." In this case, there is no verb, but a prepositional phrase evoking the surface of the water of the deep.[136] Third and finally, the divine wind or life-breath is "moving over the surface" (literally "face"[137]) of the water. With this description completed, we are poised to address a critical issue in the interpretation of Genesis 1:2.

3. Does Genesis 1 Explain the Origins of Good and Evil?

At this point, it may be helpful to address a popular misconception about the waters of creation in Genesis 1. In his important book, *Creation and the Persistence of Evil*,[138] Jon D. Levenson explored many of the themes that we are examining. Levenson's book uses the term, "evil," to characterize the symbolism of the water.[139] Through his title, Levenson is suggesting that the waters defeated by God in some biblical passages (other than Genesis 1) are deemed to be evil, or represent a symbol of evil.[140] When it comes to some passages, Levenson is quite right. When it comes to Genesis 1, Levenson suggests that the story is about the "control" of evil.[141] Edward L. Greenstein goes further, in seeing the "great sea monsters" (*tanninim*) of Genesis 1:21 as evil things made by God.[142]

This approach certainly works with passages other than Genesis 1. In the sixth century BCE situation of Genesis 1, the waters would have evoked the terrible, traumatic, and violent events of that century for Israel. In some passages, the waters embody the terrifying threats to human existence. Traditionally the cosmic waters include the waters of the underworld that threaten to drown and kill human beings (Jonah 3:3-9). Waters can be destructive for human life, and in their greatest natural manifestations as raging oceans, they are unruly. They are not controllable by human beings, even as they are restrained by God (Job 7:12, 38:8-11; Psalm 104:9; Proverbs 8:29). Life in sixth century Israel did indeed seem to be precariously set adrift amid invasive and destructive world empires and could easily have been viewed as akin to the primordial times when the cosmic waters and its threatening cosmic beasts in it could hold sway. Psalm 74 compares the terrible situation of the sixth century with the waters with its threatening cosmic beasts. The sea monsters specifically mentioned in Genesis 1:21 are also known as cosmic enemies in this psalm (in verse 74:13).[143] Psalm 74 seems to equate cosmic waters and cosmic enemies to imperial manifestations of evil in the world. As a result, the world could seem like the "void and vacuum" (*tohu wabohu*) of Genesis 1:2. The waters never go away; they "persist" (to echo the title of Levenson's book). So the waters of Genesis 1:2 might also seem to be equated with evil, or to serve as a symbol for evil.

This is not so. Genesis 1 depicts a different view of the primordial waters. In Genesis 1:2, the waters are simply there. There is no hint in the text that they are evil.[144] As Levenson notes, it offers no resistance to God.[145] In Ronald Hendel's formulation, Genesis 1:2 presents the waters in "the image of the calm, passive, and purely material ocean."[146] The waters do not have any will to act. Similarly, the sea monsters (*tanninim*) are said in Genesis 1:21 to be "good" in God's eyes.[147] In Genesis 1, the waters are channeled into useful purposes within creation (see also Psalm 104:10-11 and 25-26). The waters within the world become a positive part of creation, serving as home to the sea creatures (see verses 20-23; compare Psalms 104:10-11 and 25-26).

So what is the meaning of the description of the waters in Genesis 1:2? They indeed do do more than "persist" in Levenson's terms; they offer benefit within the scheme of creation. It is within God's power to hold the waters at bay and to use them to generate and support life. They are a "natural symbol," to use a phrase coined by the anthropologist, Mary

Douglas, [148] for potential benefit to human life and not only for its potential as a force of destruction. The waters in Genesis 1 are not "evil," but express both a lack of order on the margins of creation and a part of the divine order within that creation. The waters evoke both the potential threat of destruction from the periphery and its positive life-giving capacity within creation.

The waters before creation begins may evoke the possibility of terrible and terrifying threats to human life as found in other biblical passages, yet in Genesis 1 they manifest God's beneficial plan for the world.[149] The presentation of the waters in Genesis 1 may in fact be a calculated response to a well-known view, found in other passages, that the waters embody what is threatening about the world. As we have seen, the waters sometimes offer resistance to God (Psalm 74). This darker side of God's creation is evident in yet other passages (for example, Isaiah 45:6-7).[150] Perhaps as a response to these concepts, Genesis 1 offers a positive, hopeful vision of God's capacity for well-being in the midst of an uncertain and dangerous world. The role of the waters in Genesis points to God's power to generate a world that supports prosperity and blessing. Genesis 1 presents a world that often flies in the face of human experience, with a deity that is all-powerful producing a world that is very good (cf. verse 31).[151] This picture of the world cannot be rationally reconciled with human experience, since the existence of evil in a world created by an apparently all-powerful God cannot be reconciled with a depiction of a universal beneficence created by a good God.[152] The picture of the world in Genesis 1—even as it contradicts human experience—is offered by the priestly writer as a faithful response to his perception of God's goodness; it is presented as something that has to be taken on faith. As the verses of Genesis 1 repeatedly remind its readers, creation comes from God's speech; it is the product of divine words. This "very good" world is a world of profound hope. Presenting the waters as positively as it does, Genesis 1 radically transforms them into a symbol of God's power that lies beyond any possible resistance to the divine vision of good.

Seen from this perspective, Genesis 1's presentation of the waters seems to bring up a problem. As we have seen, the account never says that the preexisting elements, such as the waters, are bad or evil or wicked, but it does tell us that all creation is divinely deemed to be "very good" to God (verse 31; see also 4, 10, 18). This presentation does not really address evil.[153] Because evil goes unmentioned in Genesis 1, one might entertain the possibility that the word "good" (*tob*) in Genesis 1 might not mean moral good, as most commentators understand it.[154] Instead, we might consider the idea that it simply refers to benefit or well-being balancing *tohu wabohu*. Taking this approach toward the word for "good" would remove any sense of moral imbalance between good and evil. However, limiting goodness to so narrow a nuance without seeing it in context as having any moral or even holy dimension seems rather dubious, as a consideration of the evidence for the semantic range of *tob* will demonstrate.[155] Let's look briefly at the evidence for the meanings of *tob*.

To begin with, Genesis 1 certainly does entail the creation of benefit and well-being and not just goodness in an abstract or moral sense.[156] In a similar fashion, the creation account of Psalm 104:28 also uses *tob* to connote benefit. So one might see the semantic range of *tob* in Genesis 1 to encompass the "peace, well-being, weal" (*shalom*) invoked in Isaiah 45:7. In this creation passage, the God of creation makes both "weal" (*shalom*) and "woe" (*ra'*).[157] Outside of creation texts, the word *tob* may mean well-being or prosperity, as opposed to doom or destruction (cf. Proverbs 11:10). In this connection, we may also note "goodness and kindness (*hesed*)" in Psalm 23:6; these are the blessings or benefits derived from the speaker's relationship with God. So there is plenty of support for taking *tob* in Genesis 1 with the nuance of benefit. Note that in such contexts, it bears no particular moral connotation.

In contrast, the priestly plan of Genesis 1 suggests that "good" here is not simply limited to so narrow a characterization of benefit. As we will see in the next chapter, Genesis 1 lays the foundation for priestly holiness. Indeed, *tob* in this narrative establishes the norms for holiness and good or moral behavior. Elsewhere the word, "good" (*tob*) functions in a moral sense as a term for righteous or upright people. "Good" persons are contrasted with wicked or bad people (Proverbs 2:20-22, 12:2, 13:22, 14:14, and 15:3).[158] Similarly, "good" applies to deeds (Psalms 14:1, 3 = 53:1, 3). In an obvious example, Amos 5:14-15 commands: "seek good and not evil" and "hate evil and love good." Some creation allusions also show a concern for moral good (see Psalm 33:4-7).

So we may conclude that both meanings apply in Genesis 1; creation is good in both meanings as benefit and moral good. Within the priestly worldview, both aspects of "good" fall under the rubric of holiness.[159] God is good in all these respects, and when God creates, creation is likewise good. So it appears that Genesis 1 provides a picture for the origins of creation and its goodness, but it does not explain the origins of wickedness or evil in a moral sense.[160] It makes no concrete effort to explain evil or to justify the existence of evil, nor does it offer an explanation for the unruly cosmic waters[161] at the outset of creation in verse 2; they are a "given," existing at the time when God begins to create.

This manner of presentation of good without evil perhaps calls for some broader comment. At this point, it bears noting that the depictions of the world one encounters in traditional stories such as those found in the Bible are not exactly explanations in the modern sense.[162] They differ in that they do not depend on what people today regard as modern scientific criteria or rational reasoning. To illustrate this, we may draw on some observations made by the literary critic Jonathan Culler about the difference between scientific explanation and explanation in stories. We use stories, he says, as

> the main way we make sense of things, whether in thinking of our lives as a progression leading somewhere or in telling ourselves what is happening in the world. Scientific explanation makes sense of things by placing them under laws—whenever a and b obtains, c will occur—but life is not like that. It follows not a scientific logic of cause and effect but the logic of story, where to understand is to conceive of how one thing leads to another, how something might have come about.[163]

Culler also compares stories in literature with the stories that historians tell: "We make sense of events through possible stories; philosophers of history. . . have even argued that the historical explanation follows not the logic of scientific causality, but the logic of story."

The distinction that Culler draws between the logic of scientific reasoning and the logic of stories is helpful for thinking about biblical creation and in particular about the situation of reality, as it was understood to be before creation began in Genesis 1:3. Genesis 1 does tell readers about how things came about. At the same time, it does not offer an explanation in any manner approaching a rational or scientific sense. It tells the story, and to set it up, it tells readers what was there at the outset of things in verse 2. It shows no effort to get at the story "behind" the preexisting water or to provide any philosophical insight as to either the source of evil in the world or its justification for being in the world. For whatever reasons, Genesis 1 displays little or no interest in these concerns—these are largely postbiblical and especially modern issues. As we have seen, its composer had drawn on a traditional idea of the cosmic waters. Elsewhere the waters are inimical to God (Psalm 74:13) or "flee" from God (Psalm 104:7), but in Genesis 1 they are simply there at the time of God's beginning to create. Evil is not the concern; good is decidedly the sense emphasized in Genesis 1. Perhaps in omitting evil from creation and so stressing the good, Genesis 1 responds to other biblical works that do emphasize the evil of human experience or creation (such as Job 3). Genesis 1 does not deny evil (certainly not in any explicit way), but it simply ignores it and instead elevates a vision of good, perhaps in response to Israel's experience of trauma and evil during the sixth century BCE. We might say that Genesis 1 offers a decidedly hopeful vision, perhaps even a wildly optimistic one. In any case, it is clearly a world of good. The good creation begins in verse 3, with its expression of divine speech and light. These related features of speech and light are the subjects of the following two sections.

4. What is the Significance of Divine Speech in Genesis 1:3?

One feature fundamental to creation in Genesis 1 is divine speech. Divine speaking begins each act of creation on each of the six days (verses 3, 6, 9, 20, 24, and 29). It is used additionally to begin the creation of humanity (verse 26). Divine speech is not only a matter of God speaking. It involves divine naming in the first three days of creation (verses 5, 8, 10)[164] and divine blessings in the last three days (verses 22, 28, and 2:3). Overall, verbs for divine speech occur thirteen times; this is more than the eleven times verbs are used for narrating divine manufacture (Genesis 1:1, 7, 16, 21, 25, 27 [three times]; 2:2 [twice]; 2:3). This is the only creation story in the Bible that narrates God speaking, calling, and blessing as acts of creation.[165] Divine speech appears to constitute the basis for creation just as much as divine manufacture. More importantly, the two are tied together in this account. To signal this connection between divine speech and creation, the verb *qara'*, "he called," in verse 5 echoes the sound of the word, *bara'*, "he created" in verse 1. Thus the acts of divine speech are made to sound like divine pronouncements initiating creation.[166]

The idea of creation by divine speech was hardly novel, as divine speech occurs in both Egyptian and Mesopotamian creation accounts.[167] We have already noted Psalm 33:6-7 in this regard, which expresses creation by divine word in succinct fashion:

> By the word[168] of the Lord the heavens were made,
> By the breath of his mouth,[169] all their host;
> He gathers the water of the sea like a mound,
> Sets the deeps in vaults.

"Word" here appears in rather human (or anthropomorphic) terms, as suggested by its parallelism with the phrase, "the breath of his mouth."[170] The creative word here perhaps is the closest biblical analogy to the divine speech of Genesis 1:3.[171]

Psalm 19 presents the speech of creation in more detail with a variety of nouns and verbs. The psalm[172] is translated with my headings added in bold and italics for purposes of clarification (and without the prose label):

Part I: Hymn to Creation

The Speech of the Heavens

1   The heavens declare the glory of God,
     The firmament proclaims his handiwork.
2   Day by day pours forth speech,
     Night by night states a statement.
3   Beyond speech, beyond words,
     Their sound cannot be heard.
4   In all the earth their sound[173] goes forth,
     To the end of the world, their words.

Praise of the Sun

     For the sun, he set in them a tent.
5   And he proceeds like a groom from his wedding canopy,
     Exulting like a warrior in running the race.
6   His departure lies at one end of the sky,
     And his circuit at the other end,
     And there is no hiding from his heat.

Part II: Hymn to Teaching

Hymn to Divine Teaching

7   The teaching of Yahweh is perfect, renewing a person;
     The decree of Yahweh is firm, making the simple wise.
8   The precepts of Yahweh are just, giving joy to the heart.
     The command of Yahweh is pure, giving light to the eyes.
9   The fear of Yahweh is pure, standing forever,
     The judgments of Yahweh are true, altogether righteous—
10   More desirable than gold, or much fine gold,
     And sweeter than honey or honeycomb.

Prayer against Transgression

11   Moreover, your servant is enlightened by them;
     There is much reward in obeying them.
12   Who can discern errors?
     Clear me of hidden faults,
13   Moreover, hold back your servant from the wicked,
     So that they do not rule me.

> Then I will be blameless,
> And cleared of grave transgression.
> 14   May the words of my mouth be pleasing,
> The utterance of my heart, before you,
> O Yahweh, my rock and my redeemer.

The labels for the two main sections of the poem are in bold. These show the divine speech of the heavens corresponding to divine teaching on earth. Speech is central to divine revelation in the heavens and on earth. In Psalm 19, divine speech and teaching are present realities, while Genesis 1 situates the divine acts of speaking in a past narrative about creation. Genesis 1 does not simply describe teaching like Psalm 19. As we will see, divine speech provides the basis and blueprint of divine teaching in Genesis 1. Speech in Psalm 19 permeates creation. The notion of nature speaking in praise of God is hardly exceptional (Psalms 50:6 and 148:7-10),[174] and it suggests an ancient "nature theology," suggesting that all living creatures, not just humanity, praise God. This natural word, which tells of God in praise, is paralleled in Psalm 19 by the divine word given to humanity. In short, divine word and the created world are linked in Psalm 19. For Genesis 1, word and world are also linked, yet they are separate, with acts of the divine speech serving as the basis of creation. Moreover, speech in Genesis 1 involves divine blessings culminating in the blessing of the Sabbath day.

With the particular prominence that Genesis 1 gives to divine speaking, it has been long thought that "the word" is "the principle of creation" in this account (as we find in the beginning of the Gospel of John).[175] I would put the point in a slightly different way, since "word" does not occur in Genesis 1. Rather, it is divine speech that is foundational to the divine acts of creation. In the words of Richard J. Clifford, "divine speech. . . [is] the animating principle of creation activity."[176] We might ask, then, what the significance divine speech in this account might have held for the priestly writer. This question about God speaking in Genesis 1 is poignant, when we recall that priestly narrative material tends to make God less human-like (anthropomorphic) than other narrative traditions in Genesis (for example, God walking and conversing with humanity in Genesis 3:8-13, or smelling the offering in Genesis 8:21). The acts of divine speaking, calling, and blessing are foundational for Genesis 1. Why is such prominence given to divine speech in a priestly text such as Genesis 1?

We know that for the priestly tradition, divine speech expresses divine authority and revelation. The priestly tradition believed that priestly instruction came from God. This tradition held that God's speech, often quoted in the form of priestly teaching or instruction (*torah*), formed the basis of revelation and instruction. For the priestly tradition, the divine speech in Genesis 1 authorized priestly instruction.[177] The association of divine speech and priestly revelation also affected the representation of God in Genesis 1. This is perhaps clearest with the blessings that God gives on the last three days of creation; we will explore this particular feature in the next chapter. The divine pronouncements in Genesis 1 were modeled not only on the priestly role of blessing, but also of teaching. In ancient Israel, instruction (*torah*, and the related verb, "to teach," **yrh*) was associated especially with priests, as suggested by many biblical passages: Deuteronomy 33:10; Jeremiah 18:18, Ezekiel 7:26, Hosea 4:6, Micah 3:11, Zephaniah 3:4, Haggai 2:11, and Malachi 2:6-9 (compare Jer. 2:8, 5:31, and Lam. 2:9).[178] The parallel texts of Isaiah 2:3 and Micah 4:2 note the instruction received at the temple, quite likely also from priests. In using verbs of speech, Genesis 1 presents God's primary role of speaking the world into existence (so to speak); this perhaps echoes the priestly role of teaching aloud to the Israelites at the Temple.[179] Here we must pause and highlight a very crucial point about the idea of God in Genesis 1: God is presented as the ultimate priest. As we will see later in reference to God's blessings, Genesis 1 understands the universe in terms of a divine temple, with God serving in the role of its priest.

We may look at divine speech in Genesis 1 from another angle. To understand its massive importance in this narrative, we may consider what Genesis 1 *omits* from its creation story. Perhaps the most dramatic omission is the overt assertion of divine power.[180] Divine power is displaced by the divine wind and speech on day one. In chapter 1, we already saw how in the first model of creation, divine conflict, sets the stage for creation. A number of biblical passages develop the idea of a divine conflict between the Lord and cosmic forces before creation.[181] For example, consider Isaiah 51:9-10a, a passage usually dated by scholars to the sixth century BCE:

> Awake, awake, put on strength,
> O arm of the LORD;
> Awake, as in days of old,
> The generations of long ago.
> Was it not you who cut Rahab in pieces,

> Who pierced the dragon?
> Was it not you who dried up the Sea,
> The water of the great deep?[182]

An example closer to Genesis 1 is Psalm 74:12-17, a passage that we also made note of in chapter 1. It decries the destruction of Jerusalem in the sixth century BCE. In its appeal to God to provide help against enemies, this passage discusses creation in ways that relate to Genesis 1. It places creation in the wake of the divine battle against the cosmic enemies:

> 12 Yet God my king is from of old,
>   Working salvation in the midst of the earth.
> 13 You—you scattered Sea by your might;
>   You smashed the heads of the Tanninim on the water.
> 14 You—you crushed the heads of Leviathan,
>   You made him into food for the work of sea beasts (?).
> 15 You—you split open springs and brooks;
>   You—you dried up mighty rivers.
> 16 Yours is the day, yours also the night;
>   You—you established the luminary of the sun.
> 17 You—you fixed all the boundaries of earth;
>   Summer and winter, you—you fashioned.

For Psalm 74:12-17 the divine power exercised in the primordial conflict continues in God's establishment of the sun as well as the boundaries of the earth.

Genesis 1 largely follows the format of creation found in Psalm 74:12-17. After the introductory statement in vs. 12, the passage continues in verses 13-14 with the preexistent waters that are presented as the cosmic enemy of God. Genesis 1 also opens with a description of the same cosmic water, but it pointedly omits the conflict. Psalm 74:15 mentions the creation of water and land, which occurs on the second and third days of creation in Genesis 1. Psalm 74:16 mentions day and night, which came into being on day one in Genesis 1. Psalm 74:16 mentions the sun, created on day four in Genesis 1. Psalm 74:14 mentions the cosmic enemy "Sea," which in Genesis 1:9-10 is simply depicted as the waters gathered together. In this connection, Jonas C. Greenfield commented: "The biblical writer sought in Genesis to lessen the primordial nature of Yam, by making it not a participant in creation."[183] As we noted above, Psalm 74:13 also mentions God's enemies as watery foes, called the *tanninim* ("dragons" in NRSV, "monsters" in NJPS). These are mentioned also in Genesis 1:21 as the "sea monsters" (in both NRSV and NJPS).[184] However, unlike Psalm

74:12-17, Genesis 1 omits God fighting these sea monsters; they are simply part of creation.

Genesis 1 contains other elements that appear with divine conflict in other creation accounts, but it omits conflict. At the same time, it seems to set up the expectation for the divine battle in its opening reference to the watery depths in verse 2, especially with the term, "deep" (tehom). Many scholars compare this term with the related name of the Akkadian female figure, Tiamat; she faces off against the warrior-god Marduk in Enuma Elish. They further accept that here Genesis 1 is working off the sort of picture presented in Enuma Elish.[185] It is not necessary to see a particular Mesopotamian background at work behind Genesis 1 in order to compare tehom with Tiamat. This word for the ocean occurs in the Ugaritic texts not only in god-lists,[186] but also in mythological contexts.[187] Evidence from the sites of Mari and Aleppo[188] shows that tehom in a battle context is an old West Semitic idea and not just a Mesopotamian one.[189] It also appears to be a royal idea. The West Semitic background is suggested also by the appearance of the word in Psalm 104:6. John Day has suggested further that tehom in Genesis 1:2 was in fact borrowed from Psalm 104:6, since Genesis 1 and Psalm 104 show so many similarities.[190] The old idea of cosmic conflict can be seen also with the figures of Sea and Leviathan in Psalm 74:12-17 or in Isaiah 27:1.[191]

What would be the point of this omission of divine conflict in Genesis 1? The aim would appear to be to substitute divine speech for divine conflict and thus read conflict out of creation. In this way, God can be viewed as a power beyond conflict, indeed the unchallenged and unchallengeable power beyond any powers. Creation does not occur in the aftermath of divine powers in opposition. It is not the result of two wills in opposition, but it evinces a God unopposed, bringing about creation simply by expressing good words. This omission of conflict, just at the moment in the narrative when it might be expected, is so marked that its absence indicates a paradigm shift away from the traditional presentation of creation as the product of divine conflict. With respect to divine conflict, Genesis 1 stands at one end of the spectrum opposite from Psalm 74 at the other end, with Psalm 104 (as well as the Job speeches of Job 38–41) lying in-between. While probably well aware of the first model of divine conflict, Genesis 1 decisively turns in a different direction.

If Genesis 1 omits conflict, then how does the creation work? Creation, as it unfolds over the course of the first six days, is described not as destruction manifest in the strife of battle, but rather through construction issuing in a sort of divine temple. As we noted in chapter 1, creation and temple-building in biblical texts are analogous to one another (they represent a "homology," to cite Jon Levenson's expression).[192] What this means is that in some descriptions, creation and temple-building are sometimes understood in terms of one another. The temple in Psalm 78:69 is represented with images of creation: "He built his sanctuary like the heavens, like the earth that he established forever." [193] The creation story in Genesis 1 works in the opposite direction: the universe is envisioned in terms of a temple. The world is cast in this manner as God's temple also in Isaiah 66:1, a text perhaps dating to the late sixth century BCE:

> Thus said Yahweh:
> The heavens are my throne
> And the earth is my footstool.

In this verse, the universe is imagined in terms of divine furniture within the divine palace. The world created by God in Genesis 1 is like the divine temple.[194] In short, in Genesis 1, the good, structured creation is built like a temple. In this metaphorical temple, the human person imitates holiness and rest, the order and holiness of the Deity in whose image humanity is made. This vision leaves conflict out of the process of creation.

Just as Genesis 1 omits divine conflict as understood in the first model of creation, it also omits a feature from the second. While Genesis 1 uses the verbs of divine manufacture known from the second model, it leaves out the affective dimension of the second model, its joy and rejoicing as well as its sense of play.[195] When God sees creation in Genesis 1, he sees that it is good, but in Job 38:7 when the morning stars saw God's creation, "they sang and shouted for joy." In Proverbs 8:30-31, the female figure of Wisdom was God's "delight day by day," "always playing (°shq) before" God (verse 30). She was "playing in the inhabited world" and "delighting (°shq) in humanity" (verse 31). Psalm 104 is very much concerned with the wise arrangement of creation's parts so that they serve and aid one another, and this wise creation inspires joy and play. God made wine to "make the human heart rejoice" (°smh) in verse 14. God made Leviathan in verse 26 in order to play (°shq) with him. God joins in the play with his pet Leviathan (see also Job 41:29); by contrast, the great sea monsters (tanninim) of Genesis 1:21 are simply dwelling in the sea. In Psalm 104:31, the speaker requests: "May the Lord rejoice (°smh) in his creations!" And the psalmist adds the declaration in verse 34: "I will rejoice (°smh) in the Lord." The rejoicing, the joy, and the play are inspired by God's wise creation. If creation in the first model inspires awe at divine power, creation in the second model is an ode to joy. Genesis 1 steps back from the expression of divine power in favor of divine speech, and it also invests no energy in associating wisdom or joy with God's creation.[196] Instead, Genesis 1 conjures up a creation worthy of admiration and wonder inspired by its divine grandeur, as captured in its massive literary architecture; all of these are the result of divine speech, suggestive of the role of priestly speech in teaching and blessing.

This vision of the universe in Genesis 1 would serve Israel in exile (586-538 BCE) and beyond.[197] If we think about Genesis 1 in terms of the sixth century situation when it appears to have been written, the theme of royal power of the first model perhaps made less sense for Israel. At this time, Israel's monarchy was deposed, and the idea of conflict as a way of thinking about God may not have seemed particularly suitable. God now was the God beyond any conflict or any other power. Similarly, the theme of wisdom informing the second model of creation, with its joy and play, may have seemed less fitting in the context of the terrible loss suffered at this time. Order, whether expressed in royal or wisdom terms, seemed entirely violated and decimated by the traumatic events of this time. With the monarchy no longer viewed as a viable protector of Israel in a world dominated by foreign empires, the priesthood offered strong leadership within the Israelite community. Genesis 1 in a sense mirrors this change: the royal model has been altered in favor of a priestly model; the politics of creation have changed. There is still a king in this world, but it is the King of Kings, the One Will that rules heavens and earth alike, with no serious competition, and this king in Heaven is, as importantly, the Holy One. There is no mirror, no royal agent on earth whose human foes match the cosmic foes of the divine king. Instead, it is the Holy King who rules all, enthroned over the universe that is the divine temple. Humanity is to serve in it as God's appointed agent on earth (as we will discuss in the next section). This God only needs to speak, and the divine speech makes the world hospitable to humanity. With this background in mind, we turn to the first act of creation.

5. Was the Light on Day One in Genesis 1:3 Created?

At first glance, this question hardly seems worth asking.[198] The answer would seem to be obvious; of course, light was created. After all, this is the first act of creation on the first day in Genesis 1:3: "And God said, 'let light be,' and light was." However, as we are about to see, the issue is more subtle. It involves looking at how this light was understood among ancient and modern commentators as well as in other ancient texts.[199] Our exploration of these authorities will help us to uncover the deep and important meaning that the light held for ancient Israel. As a result, we will also see what it meant in Genesis 1:3 and what was at stake for its author.

Most modern scholars and readers generally assume that the light in this verse is "created,"[200] like the other parts of creation that unfold over the days that follow. Some ancient commentators likewise viewed the light as created. As we noted earlier in this chapter, Jubilees 2:2-3 counts light as one of the "seven great works on the first day,"[201] along with heavens, the earth, waters, the ministering spirits, the void, and darkness.[202] In understanding the waters as well as darkness and light as created, Jubilees follows the view expressed in Isaiah 45:6-7. In this passage, God declares: "I am Yahweh, and there is none else, fashioning light and creating darkness, making peace and creating evil; I am Yahweh who makes all these." This passage places light as well as darkness within the acts of creation. Jubilees 2:2-3 extends this view by including the waters and the void among the works of divine creation and not presenting them as existing before creation begins. All in all, Jubilees holds a stronger view of the created character of the primordial elements of creation than either Isaiah 45:6-7 or Genesis 1.

Perhaps we should read the evidence of Genesis 1:3 as these sources do. Seeing the light as created would seem, as many have concluded, the obvious implication of Genesis 1. The light might be understood as created, since it belongs to the order of creation of six days, as emphasized at the outset in Genesis 1:1. Unlike the primordial elements named in verse 2, light is the subject of divine action taken in the process of creation, specifically in the form of divine speech. In other words, perhaps it was not necessary for Genesis 1 to mention that God "made" light, especially since verses 4-5 are clear in understanding light and darkness to be the outcome of creation on the first day. Moreover, Genesis 2:1-2 and 2:4 presuppose that the divine effort on days one through six constitutes the work of creation. So the light of the first day might seem to be no less a tangible creation than the works of days two through six.[203]

But there is a very clear problem with this assumption, even when Isaiah 45:6-7 is taken into account: Isaiah 45:6-7 represents darkness as being created, the opposite of the way darkness is presented in Genesis 1. This should give us pause, for if Second Isaiah holds a different view of darkness, this author may as well have had a different view of light. In fact, several scholars argue that the author of Isaiah 45:6-7 knew the text of Genesis 1:3 and went out of his way to differ from it on this very point. For Moshe Weinfeld and Benjamin Sommer, Isaiah 45:6-7 constitutes a polemic against Genesis 1:1-3, while for Michael Fishbane, it represents an interpretation of it.[204] Both Isaiah 45:6-7 and Genesis 1:2 were weighing in on the understanding of primordial creation, and they took different views of the darkness and the light. Why might they do that?

The two texts offered different visions of creation perhaps to convey different points about the Creator to their audiences. Second Isaiah was promoting a view of God's absolute control over reality as a way to console an Israel that had suffered terrible events; this effort at comfort is the note sounded at the very opening of Second Isaiah (Isaiah 40:1-2). In attributing the creation of all things to God, Isaiah 45:6-7 is telling Israel that God has control over things and therefore God really is powerful enough to control the course of human history, including the situation of Israel in exile. By comparison, the creation account of Genesis 1 offers a different message of hope about the Creator for Israel at the time of its writing. It highlights the light within the darkness, anticipating what is to come for Israel. It points to a divine light that is to be perceived and received by Israel, no matter how terrible its circumstances. This divine light emerging out of the darkness also expresses that God is at once knowable and unknowable to human beings. We have in the divine light of Genesis 1 a powerful statement of God's presence: God has indeed given some element of the divine self to the world.

In contrast to Isaiah 45:6-7 and the book of Jubilees, other ancient commentators support the reading of the divine light in Genesis 1:3 as primordial and not created.[205] For example, 4 Ezra, a work preserved in several languages and perhaps going back to an Aramaic or Hebrew original (dated ca. 100 CE), [206] offers an important witness to this idea. In 4 Ezra 6:40, the figure of Ezra is presented as saying to God: "Then you commanded that a ray of *light* be brought forth from your treasuries, so that your works might then appear."[207] Another example comes from 2 Enoch,[208] which survives only in Slavonic and whose date is widely debated. In its longer version, it shows God speaking in the first-person (25:3): "And I was in the midst of the great *light*. And *light* out of *light* is carried thus. And the great age came out, and it revealed all creation which I had thought up to create."[209] Other passages from this period also show this view, though less explicitly.[210]

The idea of the divine light of Genesis 1 is sometimes connected with the divine word in the Greco-Roman period, for example in the work of the Jewish philosopher Philo of Alexandria.[211] The divine light resonates also in the portrayal of Jesus as the divine word in the New Testament Gospel of John (1:4-5):

> What has come into being in him was life, and the *light* was the light
> of all people. The *light* shines in the *darkness,* and the *darkness* did
> not overcome it.[212]

Here Jesus is the light to the world that follows from his capacity as
word, as announced in the very opening words of John's Gospel (1:1): "in
the beginning was the word (*logos*)."[213] For John, Jesus was this word.
These words evoke the opening of Genesis 1, and John's description of
the light calls to mind the light of the first day in Genesis 1. Like Philo,
John views the light of Genesis 1:3 not as created; it is God's own light.
What is also interesting about these descriptions of the divine light is
its relationship to the word (*logos*), which in Greek philosophy denoted
"reason, law exhibited in the world-process," or more specifically for
Stoic philosophy, "the divine order."[214] The *logos* was very important in
Greek philosophy of this period, and it is not surprising to see it featured
in both Philo and John. What is notable is how both their accounts connect word with the light: the light is the perceptible image of the word
spoken by God. For John, the light comes from the word, understood
as the figure of Jesus. The preexistent light comes into the created, perceptible realm through the word. As we will see later, the connection
between divine word and God's light is a fundamental part of the picture
also for the priestly tradition of Genesis 1.

The image of divine light from the Prologue of John is echoed in the
Nicene Creed in its reference to God the Father and God the Son: "light
of light, true God of true God, begotten not made, one in being with the
Father, through whom all things were made." In this creedal statement,
Christian tradition preserved the notion that this light was not created. For
Jewish tradition, this idea of the light was a standard reading.[215] The great
medieval Jewish work, the Zohar, offers an extensive mystical commentary on the five books of the Torah.[216] The opening comments on Genesis
1 state: "At the head of potency of the King, He engraved engravings in
luster on high."[217] The luster or light is God's own light. The commentary
becomes more explicit in its statement on verse 3: "And there was light—
light that already was."[218] Already at the very beginning of God's creative
activity, the Zohar intimates God's own light, following Genesis Rabbah
1:15.[219] This tradition of understanding the light raises a challenge to the
modern scholarly consensus that the light of Genesis 1:3 was made.

Several reasons for seeing the light as God's own reveal themselves
when we look more closely at the biblical context of the light of creation.
To begin with, Genesis 1 never actually states that God "created" the
light. It simply says: "God said, 'Let light be (*yehi*),' and light was." No

verb of making appears before the creation of the firmament in verse 7. If the writer wished to express the point that the light was made, he might have been more explicit about this. In fact, the author did exactly that in Genesis 1:7 and 16.[220] In these verses, the expression, "let (there) be" (*yehi*) is followed by the narrative account of these acts of creation, "and God made" (*wayya'as 'elohim*).[221] Scholars have noted that the priestly author of Genesis 1 chooses his wording very carefully and deliberately. In his commentary on Genesis, Gerhard von Rad expressed this sense of the chapter: "[Genesis 1] is Priestly doctrine—indeed, it contains the essence of Priestly knowledge in a most concentrated form. . . . Nothing is here by chance."[222] William Brown comments similarly: "No other text is so densely structured in the Hebrew Bible; every word seems to bear the mark of extensive reflection."[223] It might be expected that Genesis 1:3 says what it means, and that the light was not created but more precisely was "spoken."

This approach would answer a question that the light in verse 3 poses for many modern readers: how can there be light on the first day, in verses 3-5, when sources of light, namely the sun and the moon (called "two great lights"), are not created until the fourth day, in verses 14-19? However, the question is answered when the light of day one is recognized to be God's own light, which "the great lights" of verses 14-19 were thought to reflect.[224] The divine light of Genesis 1:3 would explain how there could be light before the creation of the sun and the moon, and it would also explain where the light originally came from.

So one might conclude that God did not make the light. At the same time, we need to be careful. My conclusion so far is based only on what is missing from Genesis 1:3. Further corroborating evidence is needed.[225] At this point we may turn to the wider context of Genesis 1. Following Benno Jacob, Martin Buber, and Franz Rosenzweig,[226] scholars have noted the specific verbal parallels between Genesis 1 (actually Genesis 1:31—2:3) and Exodus 39–40. On this basis, they have posited a literary relationship between these two passages.[227] For the sake of convenience the parallels are laid out here,[228] with the similar wordings put in italics:

> Exodus 39:43 "and when Moses *saw* all the work, and *behold*, they had *made* it—just as the Lord commanded, so they had *made*— Moses *blessed* them."

> Genesis 1:31a: "and God *saw* all that he had *made*, and *behold* it was very good."

> Genesis 2:3: "and God *blessed* the seventh day and sanctified it because on it he ceased from all its work that God had created for *making*."

Exodus 40:33b: "and Moses *finished* the *work.*"

Genesis 2:2a: "and God *finished* on the seventh day his *work.*"

Exodus 39:32a: "and all the work of the tabernacle of the tent of meeting was *finished.*"

Genesis 2:1 "and the heaven and the earth and all their host were *finished.*"

These verbal connections tie the Tabernacle account in Exodus 39–40 to creation in Genesis 1:31—2:3. In addition to the specific links in the wording of the two passages, they also show a general conceptual resemblance. Both describe the construction of a sacred space, the creation of God in Genesis 1 and the creation of the Tabernacle for God's glory in Exodus 39–40. In this comparison, the divine light (*'or*) in Genesis 1:3 corresponds to Exodus 40's divine "glory" (or perhaps better, "effulgence" or "gravitas," in Hebrew, *kabod*). The glory of Exodus 39–40 is not created; rather, it is God's own.[229] This, too, seems to be the case for the light of Genesis 1:3. This comparison is further instructive for the sense of the light in Genesis 1. In Exodus 40:34, the glory of God goes into the tabernacle, while the light of God comes into creation.

A number of other biblical passages also suggest that the light of Genesis 1:3 is not created. The most relevant passage for interpreting the light of Genesis 1:3 is the opening of Psalm 104.[230] This psalm is particularly important for discussing Genesis 1; as we saw in chapter 1,[231] these two texts follow the same overall format in describing creation. The opening of creation in Genesis 1:3 corresponds to Psalm 104:1-2:

In glory and majesty you are clothed (*labesh*),
Wrapped in light (*'or*) like a robe,
Spreading heaven like a tent-cloth.

This passage presents God dressed in glory and majesty, a picture that is hardly exceptional (for example, Psalm 93:1; note the sarcastic use of this motif attributed to God in Job 40:10). Psalm 104:1-2 elaborates this glorious picture of God by characterizing "light" as divine clothing. The psalm ends this initial presentation of divine creation by using the image of a tent being stretched out. This image is found in other references to creation.[232] The image of the tent is a way to express creation of the heavens; it corresponds to the picture of the firmament in Genesis 1, understood as a thin shell shaped or hammered from metal.[233] The vast majority of scholars accept the comparison of the light in Genesis 1:3 and Psalm 104:1-2.[234]

Another text suggests this view of the light in Genesis 1:3. Isaiah 60:19 describes the reversal of the order of creation:

> No longer shall the sun serve as your light (*'or*) by day,
> Nor for brightness shall the moon provide light (*°'wr*) for you;
> The LORD will serve you as an eternal light (*'or*),
> Your God, as your glory.

In this passage, God is promised as Israel's light in the future. As noted by the Israeli scholar Yair Zakovitch, the picture of the future end (*Endzeit*) here in Isaiah 60:19 reverses the order of the beginning-time (*Urzeit*); it promises the divine light of Genesis 1:3 and not the light of the sun and moon in Genesis 1:14.[235] Both passages reflect the notion of the light at the beginning of creation as God's own light. This passage dates to the early post-exilic period and is not so far removed in time from Genesis 1.

Zechariah 14:6-7 shows a similar theme,[236] and it deserves particular mention in view of its wording. NRSV renders the passage (with my italics added): "On that day there shall not be either cold or frost. And there shall be *continuous day* (it is known to the LORD), not *day* and not *night,* for at *evening* time there shall be *light.*" In suggesting a reversion to the primordial light, this passage echoes Isaiah 60:19, and it also echoes Genesis 1 quite strongly (as suggested by the terms put in italics). Zechariah 14:7 uses the expression, *yom 'ehad* (translated as "continuous day" by NRSV), the same expression employed for the end of "day one" in Genesis 1:5. It also uses the same words that we find in Genesis 1:5 for day and night as well as evening. With these terms in common, it would appear that Genesis 1:5, with the light of its first day, is echoed deliberately in Zechariah 14:7.[237] Zechariah 14:6-7 promises the light of God "on that day," like the beginning in Genesis 1. In both cases, it seems to be characterized by a divine light. This would fit with the presentation of divine light also in the priestly book of Ezekiel, not only in the heavenly vision of chapter 1,[238] but also later in the vision of the return of the divine presence to Jerusalem in chapter 43.[239] As the depiction of divine light in Ezekiel 1–3 would suggest, God's light was perhaps thought to be located in the heavenly palace above the firmament.

For the notion of the light of creation, we should briefly take note of some texts outside the Bible. As we observed in the introduction, ancient Near Eastern comparisons have long been a staple of scholarly discussion of Genesis 1. In Mesopotamian literature, light belongs to heaven, while earth was dark. A Sumerian text from Nippur expresses the picture of primordial reality in this manner: "An, (being) Bel, made heaven resplend[ent], earth was in darkness, the lower world was [invi]sible."[240] As we saw, *Enuma Elish* has often been compared with Genesis 1.[241] In his commentary on Genesis, the great Assyriologist of the post-World

War II era, Ephraim Speiser, listed what he took to be the correspondences between Genesis 1 and *Enuma Elish*. These include what he called "Light created" in Genesis 1 and "Light emanating from the gods" in the Babylonian narrative.[242] For purposes of comparison with Genesis 1, it is to be underscored that in *Enuma Elish*, this light is prior to creation. In fact, it is the god's own light. It appears in *Enuma Elish's* presentation of the god Marduk in tablet I, lines 101-104:[243]

> 101 The son UTU (the Sun), the son UTU (the Sun),
> 102 The son, the sun, the sunlight of the gods!
> 103 He wore (on his body) (*lbš*) the auras of ten gods,
>   had (them) around his head too,
> 104 Fifty fears are heaped upon him.[244]

In these lines, Marduk appears in theophanic light. It is called "the sun" and "sunlight" as well as "aura."[245]

This presentation of Marduk compares with biblical passages of God's appearance. We may note in particular the use of the same verb, "to clothe" (**lbsh*), both in *Enuma Elish* I, line 103 and in Psalm 104:2.[246] It is to be observed that this light of Marduk appears in the story before his creation of the world. It is only after his victory over Tiamat that he creates the universe, which includes heavenly abodes of the other deities associated with astral bodies (compare the divine stars of Job 38:7, which we will discuss in the next chapter).[247] The descriptions of Marduk represent the god's divine light before and at creation. This fits with the presentation of the divine, preexistent light not only in Psalm 104, but also in Genesis 1:3, as I am proposing.[248]

As suggested by several biblical texts discussed in this section, the light at the beginning of creation was known in ancient Israel to be an inherent divine light that preceded creation. This, in turn, suggests the possibility of this view for the light in Genesis 1:3. Despite possible objections,[249] the overall weight of the evidence favors this view. The light was a primordial, divine brilliance made perceptible in the created world. The composer of Genesis 1 allowed a number of primordial elements prior to the creation to fit into creation (for example, darkness, watery deeps, and water in verse 2). The light of verse 3 seems also to be one of these uncreated components. The question is: why is Genesis 1:3 not more explicit in saying so? At the end of this chapter, we will return to the issue of why the composer of Genesis 1 did not describe the light in more explicit terms.

Before turning to the next question about Genesis 1, we need to consider the light in the larger context of this story. In their study of light in the context of social experiences and material culture,[250] Mikkel Bille and Tim Flohr Sørensen suggest that "light may be used as a tool for exercising social intimacy and inclusion, of shaping moral spaces and hospitality, and orchestrating movement, while working as a metaphor as well as a material agent in these social negotiations."[251] This quote nicely captures the power of the light in Genesis 1:3. The divine light marks something of the divine presence in the world; it informs the moral vision of the world in Genesis 1; and it helps to draw people toward this vision. To use a term drawn from the study of Bille and Flohr, Genesis 1 is a textual "lightscape," designed to affect those who "enter" it. In their terms, "lightscapes" have a purpose: "*lightscapes* are socially constructed to shed light *for* the world."[252] They may offer a sense of divine presence in the world that attracts people. In the case of Genesis 1, this divine "lightscape" expresses a deep sense of God's presence in the world, and at the same time it also points to the ultimate unknowability of God. We may see God's light, but it is also so dazzling that we cannot see God face to face. Instead, for Genesis 1, we see God's light in and through all that God has created. We may see this point more clearly for light in Genesis 1, as we examine the divine acts of sight, separation, and speech on the first day.

6. Why are Divine Sight, Separation, and Speech in Genesis 1:4-5 Important?

The emergence of the light is followed by the divine perception that the light was good. The first half of verse 4 reads "and God saw the light that it (was) good."[253] The divine perception in Genesis 1:4 is no incidental detail, as it is echoed in the creation allusion in Job 28:27: "then he saw it and declared it; he established it and searched it out" (see also verse 24). This verse recognizes the fine proportions of creation mentioned in verse 25. In Job 28, God takes stock of the divine act involved in the divine measurements of the creation under construction. By contrast, Genesis 1:4 uses the motif of divine perception at creation to express its goodness. Creation is not simply a fine construction, nor is it imbued primarily with wisdom or strength, as we saw in chapter 1. It is "good," a divine perception repeated over the course of the six days.

According to verse 4, God separated the light from the darkness. The verb, "to divide" (*lehabdil*) is a hallmark priestly term. In fact, of all creation accounts in the Bible, it is only Genesis 1 that uses this verb, and it does so several times, in verses 4, 6, 7, 14, 18.[254] (I will discuss this verb in more detail in the next chapter, as it applies to the six days of creation in Genesis 1.) Amos 4:13 uses a poetic image in its description of darkness in contradistinction to light, saying that God "makes darkness into dawn."[255] Genesis 1 perhaps understands the revelation of the original divine light on the model of early dawn, when the light emerges from the darkness. Perhaps light was present with the already existing darkness, and in separating these two preexisting entities in verse 4, the divine light emerged from the darkness in the universe so as to be perceptible to the creatures created on days four through six.

In verse 5, God names[256] the separated light and darkness day and night. In contrast, Psalm 74:16 directly associates day and night of day one with the sun of day four: "Yours is the day, yours also the night; you established the luminaries and the sun." Jeremiah 33:25 expresses the creation of day and night in different terms: "I surely established my covenant with day and night, the statutes of heaven and earth." This passage offers a rather evocative sense of day and night, personified as God's covenant-vassals given the responsibility for regulating time. Isaiah 43:12-13 refers to this primordial time by reference to the first day: "And I am God. Ever since day was, I am he." The beginning of the primordial day goes back to God.

The first day ends in verse 5 with the statement that "there was evening and then was morning, day one." It is clear from this verse, and from the other summaries for the days that follow, that a day in this biblical account covers an evening and morning.[257] It is a period consisting of twenty-fours. When day is contrasted with night in Genesis 1:14-19, it covers half a day. This is implicit from the creation of the sun and moon in these verses, which are to regulate day and night. "Day" in Genesis 1 is not an expression or metaphor for a longer unit of time.[258] More specifically, a "day" is not meant to be equivalent to one geological age, an idea sometimes used to reconcile views of the earth's age based on astronomical, geological, biological, and other scientific evidence.

The biblical parallels to "day one" in Genesis 1:5 also point to "day one" as a period of twenty-four hours. Other biblical passages use "day one" (*yom 'ehad*) for marking calendar time: Ezra 3:6 ("from the first day of the seventh month they began to make burnt offerings"); 10:16 ("the first day of the tenth month"); 10:17 ("the first day of the first month"); Nehemiah 8:2 ("the first day of the seventh month"); and Haggai 1:1 ("in the second year of King Darius, on the first day of the sixth month").[259] *Yom 'ehad* in these passages clearly refers to one day.[260] We may also note the expression for "day one" elsewhere in priestly literature, where it omits the word "day." We see this use of *'ehad* for "(day) one" in Genesis

8:5, 13, Exodus 40:2, 17; Leviticus 23:24; Numbers 1:1, 18, 29:1, 33:38; and Ezekiel 26:1, 29:17, 31:1, 32:1, and 45:18.[261]

It has largely gone unnoticed that the expression "day one" also appears in one of the Ugaritic ritual texts.[262] As we will see, the comparison offers some help in understanding Genesis 1. The ritual has four sections. The first names the king as the officiant who is to offer sacrifices in a temple. The other sections present shorter sets of instructions. The fourth and final section, which is the one germane to our discussion, is very brief: "And (an offering of) a turtle dove for QLH (on) day one (ym 'aḥd)." Dennis Pardee comments on this usage:

> This formula is attested only here, and its precise signification is unclear. The interpretation of "day one" (of a longer sequence) appears to be belied by the word 'id at the beginning of the text, which already indicates that this rite is part of a longer series; in such a context "day one" could only mean "this is the end of cultic activity on day one; proceed to the following cultic act as appropriately designated chronologically." Interpreted as "one day," the essential function is the same, but the day in question is not defined as the first.[263]

As these comments suggest, there are some differences in how "day one" is used here and in Genesis 1:5.[264] Despite some considerable dissimilarities, the comparison is helpful, as it suggests that the usage of "day one" does not mark Genesis 1:1-5 as the beginning of time in any sort of absolute way. It suggests that the events on "day one" in Genesis 1:5 express what God did first when beginning to create the universe. It is important to mention as well that this Ugaritic parallel comes from the sacrificial, ritual world of the priesthood.[265] Loren Fisher points to the ritual sensibility in both the Ugaritic parallel and Genesis 1:5,[266] suggesting something of the priestly world that the expression "day one" seems to reflect in Genesis 1:5. This sense also fits with the several priestly texts of the Bible that attest to "one" ('eḥad) for reckoning the first day in a month.

This parallel and others within the Bible are suggestive of the ritual world of Genesis 1. In its concepts, it is a narrative infused with a temple and ritual sensibility. This ritual sensibility perhaps contributed also to Genesis 1's literary style, with its repetition over the course of the seven days.[267] (We will return to this observation in chapter 4.) We may conclude this chapter with a consideration of the audience of Genesis 1, based on what we have seen with the first day.

7. Who is the Audience for the Divine Speech and Light in Genesis 1?

I would like to close this chapter by addressing an issue of special significance: the nature of the audience of Genesis 1. To get at this issue, I would like to return to the question of whether or not the light was created. As we saw above, the answer is not made explicit from the presentation in Genesis 1:1-5. Despite the other biblical passages cited and the arguments presented, the case in favor of the light as preexistent in Genesis 1 is suggestive but not certain. The phrasing seems deliberately calculated to leave the interpretation open. Considering how careful the priestly writer is in choosing his language, this ambiguous presentation of the light in Genesis 1:3 is itself worthy of close consideration. In fact, I would look at the style of presentation as a piece of evidence. In other words, I would like to explore what I take to be its deliberately muted presentation of the light in this extremely important context. We need to account for the manner of this presentation of light, which differs considerably from the other biblical passages (such as Psalm 104:1-2) that we discussed in an earlier section. The fact that Genesis 1:3 does not explicitly present the light as not created is not simply a problem. It is also important information for us to explore.

To put the issue succinctly: what is Genesis 1:3 doing with the light and why is it presenting the light in this manner? The verse does not present a divine theophany that moves about the created world—as in Ezekiel 1–3—so what does it intend to present? Before proceeding further, let me mention a fact about priestly texts that is relevant to the presentation of the light. Some priestly material appears not to have been originally intended for laypeople in general (for example, Leviticus 1–16), but it nonetheless eventually became more broadly accessible. Other priestly teaching was always designed for a popular audience (for example, Leviticus 17–26). If the ultimate goal of the final compilation of the Pentateuch was to extend priestly views beyond the priesthood,[268] then Genesis 1 offered priestly teaching for a wider audience so that they could better understand the priestly perspective on creation.

Within this situation, let us first consider this audience of laypeople. What should the light mean for them, from the perspective of a priestly writer? Genesis 1 was designed to teach the divine blueprint of creation in order to help people follow priestly teaching. As we will explore in chapter 3, Genesis 1 expresses a vision of divine time and space that its audience was encouraged to emulate, the Sabbath evoked in day seven being the most conspicuous in this regard. The image of the light plays a role in this teaching purpose. Genesis 1 perhaps operates with the idea found in Psalm 119:130: "the unfolding of your words gives light" (NRSV).[269] In other words, divine speech enables light. This divine light issues in divine salvation, as in Isaiah 9:2 (MT 1): "The people going in darkness have seen a great light."[270] This relationship of divine light and speech is also echoed in Isaiah 51:4, "for teaching shall go forth from me, my way for the light of the nations."[271] In this passage, divine teaching provides a conduit for divine enlightenment.

Genesis 1 also presents the idea of divine word providing light in creation. The priestly composer builds light into the very fabric of creation immediately following the divine speech, "let light be." Divine speech is basic in authorizing the manifestation of this light,[272] and in Genesis 1:3, this light emanates from God's utterance. In its compact formulation of six words, this verse expresses the deep relationship of divine teaching and light, which was recognized by Philo of Alexandria and in John's Gospel, as we discussed earlier. By walking in the ways of priestly teaching, Israelites are invited to enter into the light of God first heralded by the divine speech of Genesis 1:3. This verse would seem to offer a priestly precursor to the view expressed in the Babylonian Talmud (Megillot 16b) that "Light is Torah."[273] Genesis 1 is concerned with instruction, or we might say, with both moral and cultic illumination. Light issues from the divine words in Genesis 1:3, authorizing the priestly teaching to be followed by the Israelite community. For a popular audience, light was to be understood as a means to reflect the divine words.

Still we may ask: why isn't the text more explicit about the precise nature of the light? The answer to this question may have to do with a possible, second audience of Genesis 1, namely the members of the priesthood that supported the composition of Genesis 1. For them, there may have been a more covert yet highly meaningful dimension to the narrative. Indeed, the idea of divine light as expressed in Genesis 1 may have been an integral aspect of traditional priestly lore,[274] a subject of discussion, speculation, and perhaps even a concept with mystical aspects.

As we noted, Ezekiel 43 suggests a priestly tradition that promotes the concept of an inherent divine light. More broadly, and especially in the first three chapters of this prophetic book, this prophet may be representative of priestly thinking on the nature of God's light. Contemplation of this sort in priestly circles is not restricted to Ezekiel. It appears also in the book of Zechariah. In chapter 3, the prophet has a vision of Joshua the high priest in the heavenly council. The priest is promised in verse 7 that if he walks in God's ways and keeps his charge, then God declares:

"I will permit you walking among these attendants."[275] These attendants, as shown elsewhere in Zechariah,[276] constitute the heavenly council of God.[277] This is the divine court that Zechariah 3 mentions. Thus the high priest is being promised access to the heavenly court, and was thought to enjoy the experience of mystical ascending to heaven.[278] Zechariah 3 and Ezekiel provide different glimpses into priestly mystical thinking. In its muted presentation, Genesis 1:3 may represent an implicit nod to such a mystical, priestly view of the primordial light. As we see in Zechariah 3, the priesthood laid claim to mystical experience, and the light of Genesis 1:3 was likely seen as an element in this sort of experience. That this is a feature of the Temple landscape is evident from Zechariah 4:2 and 10, which connect the Temple's light with God (see also 1 Kings 7:49; cf. the Tabernacle's lampstand in Exodus 25:31-32, 27:20, 31:8 and 39:37).[279] Given information about light in sanctuary spaces in other priestly passages in the Bible, the priestly sense of the Temple light is palpable in Genesis 1:3.

To get at a clearer sense of this priestly understanding, I want to turn to further passages in the priestly book of Ezekiel that bear on divine light. These may reflect the prophet's reaction against the idea of divine light that he condemns in Ezekiel 8:16. According to Ezekiel 8, the prophet was brought by God into the inner court of the Jerusalem Temple. There the prophet is shown about twenty-five men. Because of the Temple's location, most commentators assume that these men are priests. They are said to be facing east "and bowing low to the sun in the east." Though there is no mention of sacrifice, they may be offering some form of devotion[280] that focused on the sun as a symbol. Perhaps this was a form of priestly piety toward Yahweh mediated through the sun that Ezekiel is condemning.[281] In its criticism, Ezekiel 8:16 may constitute a polemic by one priestly voice, Ezekiel himself, aimed against veneration by other priests who practice a form of devotion to Yahweh as the divine light symbolized by the sun.[282] Perhaps then in their depictions of the divine light, Ezekiel 1 and 43 reconfigure the picture of Yahweh's divine light in reaction to this priestly practice. In these two chapters of Ezekiel, the sun itself drops out of the picture. The texts focus on God without reference to the sun, yet the light remains important in the cosmic portrait of God. Divine light then was part of priestly thinking. As a matter of priestly speculation, it can hardly be expected to be conspicuous in the Bible, and it may be for this reason that the presentation of the light in Genesis 1:3 is as muted as it is. It is precisely the sort of esoteric material that would be rare for a work used as instruction for laypeople.[283]

Looking back over this discussion, the difficulty of interpreting the light may mirror differences due to its different audiences. For most ancient Israelites, Genesis 1 was intended for their moral illumination through priestly teaching. The light following in the wake of divine speech constitutes the primordial foundation of priestly teaching. For the Israelite priesthood, the light may have been additionally an object of contemplation. In Genesis 1, we may have evidence for priestly devotion to the divine light and speech. This picture is important for the early history of Judaism and Christianity. In recent decades, mystical thinking, long recognized as an important aspect of medieval Judaism, has been traced back to earlier texts, such as the Songs of the Sabbath Sacrifice in the Dead Sea Scrolls.[284] Like so many features of later Judaism and Christianity, it is possible that mysticism may have forerunners in biblical texts and beyond in the ancient Near East.[285] Within this context, the divine light may have been an esoteric element in biblical tradition, just as it was acknowledged in later Judaism.[286]

Some of the issues raised in this final section bear on features found later in the first week of creation. It is to these features that we now turn.

Chapter Three

The First Week: The Priestly Vision of Time and Space, Humanity and Divinity

I n this chapter, we will look at a number of priestly terms and concepts that appear in days two through seven in Genesis 1. We will not proceed verse by verse. Instead, we will examine the prominent priestly features in creation as they appear through the week.[1] As we will see, the week is informed by a priestly vision that links creation to the Creator. This vision begins with the order of time and space.

1. Priestly Time and Space

Genesis 1 is as deliberately ordered as the creation it describes. This is no surprise. Literary texts don't give us information like a recipe or a phonebook. They make their impact through their structure and form as well as their imagery and metaphors. Crucial to Genesis 1 is its most prominent organizational feature—the seven days. This now seems so integral to the modern view of biblical creation that we tend not to recognize its dramatic importance, namely that this was a completely priestly innovation.[2] No other creation account in the Bible, or more broadly speaking, in the ancient Near East, uses this structure. In contrast, the seven-day structure for other sorts of biblical narratives is well known.[3]

Seven-day units are common in biblical literature. For the scale of numbers up to ten,[4] seven was the number used to mark completion or fullness.[5] Seven days is the length of the journey in Genesis 31:23.[6] It applies also to the time of the Samson's wedding feast in Judges 14:12-15 and to the period of Job's lamentation in Job 2:13. It is the number of times the psalmist praises God in Psalm 119:164 and the number of persons to whom the generous soul is to make donations in Ecclesiastes 11:2.

Seven days was traditional for other religious periods in both Ugaritic and biblical literature. It was on the seventh day of Danil's rite in the temple that Baal interceded for him and El blessed him (KTU 1.17 I 15-16),[7] just as it was on the seventh day that God called to Moses on the cloud-covered mountain (Exodus 24:16).[8] In what the biblical scholar Michael David Coogan cleverly calls a "final parade example," the fall of Jericho occurred on the seventh day after seven priests with seven trumpets marched seven times around the city (Joshua 6:15-16).[9] Seven is also the well-known number of years of prosperity and scarcity in the Joseph story in Genesis 41:26-31;[10] the best silver is refined seven times according to Psalm 12:6 (MT 7); and seven is the number of abominations harbored in the mind of the deceitful enemy in Proverbs 26:25.

Clearly the use of seven was a widespread cultural convention. It also made its way into priestly material. We may note the seven-day counting of time, for example in the priestly calendar in Leviticus 23:3, 7-8, and 36.[11] The priestly calendar in Numbers 29 marks seven days of offerings (verses 17, 20, 23, 26, 29, and 32).[12] Its use of numbers for days two through seven of the ritual matches the numbers used for the second through the seventh days of creation in Genesis 1.[13] One may suspect that the seven-day marking of time of festivals that we see in the priestly calendars informed the development of the Sabbath in priestly tradition.

To illustrate how this may have happened, we may look at one Ugaritic ritual that says that the seventh day marks the end of obligations within the cultic realm. The seventh day in this case is not the last day in a week, but the end of a sequence of days in a seven-day ritual: "On the seventh day (of the festival of the full moon), when the sun rises, the day will be free (of cultic obligations); when the sun sets, the king will be [free (of cultic obligations)]."[14] Dennis Pardee comments: "The seventh day would have begun at sundown on the day before the sun-rise mentioned here; the point of the two commands seems to be that, though no specific activity is required, the king must remain in his holy state throughout the daylight hours."[15] The point pertinent for our discussion of Genesis 1 is that "no specific activity is required." The day itself is free of the normal ritual obligations involving cultic acts. The "free" day in this liturgy is the seventh and final day of the festival; it is free of obligations unlike the preceding six days. Likewise, Genesis 2:2 marks the seventh day as the last in the series of days, and it too is to be free from obligations, but in a different way. This verse evokes the notion of the Sabbath day as "free" from nonsacral obligations.

Genesis 2:2 may be read in light of the Ugaritic ritual text, with the seventh day marked apart from the preceding six days. For all their differences, both point to the idea of the seventh day as distinctive from the other days involved. Both convey a shift to inactivity from the duties to be conducted in the initial six days, life's basic tasks (represented in human "rule" over the animals and human reproduction) in the case of Genesis 1 and ritual acts in the case of the Ugaritic ritual. The underlying analogy is hardly a distant one: the first involves life's tasks or secular work while the second involves cultic service. So the Ugaritic ritual perhaps hints at how the idea of the Sabbath as free from obligations might have developed out of the seven-day units that we see in the larger ritual calendars in Leviticus 23 and Numbers 29. We will return to the meaning of the Sabbath in Genesis 1 later in this chapter. For now we may note that seven-day units are unknown for creation accounts apart from Genesis 1, and this structure seems to be part of its particular priestly imprint.[16]

Overall the structure of seven days in Genesis 1 conveys the impression of ordered creative activity and thus an ordered creation:[17]

Day 1: light	Day 4: bodies of light
Day 2: heavens and water	Day 5: creatures of heavens and water
Day 3: land and vegetation	Day 6: land creatures, vegetation, and humanity
Day 7: God resting from work (*shabat*)	

Creation proceeds in an orderly fashion, with each day largely following the same pattern: divine speech proposing creation of some part of the universe; the creation (or "letting there be") of what is proposed in the divine speech; the divine separation of elements of creation; the divine naming of these components; God seeing that it is good; the mention of evening and morning, numbered as successive days of the week.[18] The result of this repetition is a correspondence among all the days. If this pattern sounds like the recitation of rituals over the course of six days with a culminating seventh day, this should occasion no surprise. After all, we are being presented a world created to the rhythm of ritual repetition, a vivid reality for a priestly writer.

Genesis 1 is also intentionally structured so that there is a balance between two sets of corresponding days. As the chart above shows, days one through three balance days four through six,[19] a structure that is reinforced by two acts of creation occurring respectively on days three and six. In addition, the days balance divine speech, with divine naming on days one through three, and divine blessing on days five through seven;[20] on this score, day four is a middle point in the week.[21] Finally, we should mention in this context the observation of William P. Brown that the motif of seven informs the repetition of certain key-words in Genesis 1: "God," "good," and "earth."[22] The seven-fold repetition of these three words expresses the basic message of Genesis 1, that God's creation of the earth is indeed a seven-fold good.

The order of Genesis 1 is not entirely balanced in every respect. There is marked variation in this account, both on the overall level of the text and also in the details of various days. The reasons for these variations are not always clear, and they may be read in different ways. Different modern approaches (which we address in this book's Appendix) look at Genesis 1 from different angles. Literary interpretation in the spirit of New Criticism might see interesting and pleasing effects in the account's variation, while an interpretation informed by a deconstructionist perspective might take these differences as signs of ideological and cultural discord.[23] New Criticism might see textual beauty where deconstructionism might see textual warfare. Gender readings might assert that what is seen in Genesis 1 is a priestly instrument of male, heterosexual power within the Israelite community. A postcolonial reading might put more emphasis on the text as a colonized intellectual's effort at maintaining his culture's identity in the face of foreign domination; in short, an expression of literary resistance. In a sense, all of these dimensions are present within Genesis 1. To my mind, the writer of Genesis 1 composed his vision in a paradoxical and polarized situation, as a figure at the top of a society that was in ruins. The author of Genesis 1 sought to create order out of this "void and vacuum" (verse 2), in order to maintain his community in the face of a terribly threatening world that could destroy the Temple and could kill royalty and priests or take them into exile. The picture of the orderly structure of creation represented by Genesis 1 offered a contrast to the present situation of Israel. It offered an expression of hope, imbued by a priestly sensibility on several fronts.

Let us consider, then, how this was done. First and foremost, Genesis 1 uses a hallmark priestly term for expressing the division of space and time, namely the verb, "to divide" (*lehabdil*). Of all of the Bible's creation accounts, Genesis 1 is the only one to use this verb. Granted some ancient Near Eastern accounts refer to the division of heaven and earth.[24]

The separation of heaven and earth in Mesopotamian accounts reflects the larger notion that they constitute a cosmological pair that helps give birth to the world. As noted in both chapters 1 and 2, the pair "Heaven and Earth" is also known in Ugaritic and biblical poetic tradition (see Gen. 27:28, 39; compare Gen. 49:25). So this background seems to lie behind the presentation of heaven and earth in Genesis 1.[25] At the same time, this biblical account differs from ancient Near Eastern accounts by using the idea of separation more extensively.

In verses 4, 6, 7, 14, and 18,[26] Genesis 1 employs this verb "to separate" for its blueprint of priestly space and time.[27] The verb is used for the separation of light from darkness in verse 4—a spatial separation. In a sense, this might also be considered a temporal act, as it takes place as the first act of creation at the beginning of creation. Time, as known to human beings, begins with this act.[28] It marks the beginning of the chain of time: evening and morning, day one (verse 5). The second act of separation follows in day two (vv. 6-7). Waters above are separated from waters below by a *raqia'*, what is traditionally called a "firmament," also rendered "dome" (NRSV) or "expanse" (NJPS).[29] A corresponding second act on the third day does not use the phrase, "to separate." This involves the gathering of the waters under heaven into a single space, so that dry land may appear (vv. 9-10) and therefore functions, as it were, as both a culmination and consolidation of the three-day process of separation. This division (*lehabdil*) of the universe into heavens, earth, and seas (see 1:4, 6; cf. verses 9-10),[30] corresponds to the assignment of the animals to these spheres.

In view of its prominence in Genesis 1, it is also important to see how this term, "to separate" (*lehabdil*) serves a central function in other priestly works of the Bible. The structure of creation and its separation into realms in Genesis 1 foreshadows the priestly requirement regarding animals permissible and forbidden for eating in Leviticus 11.[31] The division of animals in these realms in Genesis 1[32] is matched in Leviticus 11, which lists the animals permissible and forbidden (what is today called *kashrut* or "keeping kosher" in Jewish tradition).[33] The relationship between the contents of Leviticus 11 and Genesis 1 is further important to note, since Leviticus 11 uses several of the same headings for various animals as are found in Genesis 1.[34] Leviticus 11 mentions "the animals that are on the land" (Leviticus 11:2); those "that are in the waters" (11:9, 10); "the winged" (11:13); "all winged swarming" (11:20, 23); and "all that swarm on the earth" (11:41). Genesis 1 uses several of the same terms: "swarms of living creatures (1:20) and "all the living creatures that move that swarm in the waters" (1:21); "the winged" (1:20) and "the winged bird" (1:21); "living creatures, animals, creepers" (1:24). Leviticus 11:47 ends its listing of the animals in these categories with this summary: "These are the instructions of animals, birds, all living creatures that move in the water, and all creatures that swarm on earth, in order to distinguish (*lehabdil*) between clean and unclean, between living things that may be eaten and living things that may not be eaten." Leviticus 20:25 also uses this verb to distinguish clean and unclean beasts and birds. The same verb occurs in Leviticus 10:10 as a general prescription to distinguish between the holy and the nonsacral, and between clean and unclean.[35]

We also see the same verb employed in Ezekiel 22:26, in a passage that has a priestly context (see Ezekiel 1:3 for Ezekiel's priestly background). This passage from Ezekiel condemns priests who cannot make the proper distinction between the holy and the profane. In this way, the priestly tradition systematized their terms for animals by classifying them according to their natural realms and then further by adding their binary pair of priestly terms, "pure" and "impure," in order "to distinguish" between the animals within each of these domains of the world. In this manner, the practice of temple *kashrut* is detailed in Leviticus 11. In a somewhat similar fashion, the priestly author of Genesis 1 deployed this priestly schema for the division of the animals over days five and six of creation. One might therefore say that Leviticus 11 represents the concrete prescriptions that underlie the narrative description of creation in Genesis 1. The acts of separation on days one and two serve to balance the creation of animals on days five and six and to present the notion of separation of realms in order to facilitate the separation of animals within these realms. For the priestly tradition, the language and structure in Leviticus 11 were designed to uphold the dietary prescriptions for animals, as maintained by priests in the Temple.[36] Correspondingly, Genesis 1 provides a proper sense of separation of realms and animals in creation.[37]

The implications for the picture of God are of singular importance. What is foundational in priestly thinking is represented as primordial in the divine plan of creation. God not only creates; God is also the one who inaugurates separation into proper realms, and these realms are maintained in terms that echo the priestly regimen of the Temple. In this respect, God is presented not simply as the first builder. Genesis 1 further intimates that the universe is like a temple (or more specifically, like the Temple), with God presented as its priest of priests.[38] At various points,[39] I have mentioned the idea of numerous scholars that creation in Genesis 1 is analogous to the creation of the Tabernacle in Exodus 39–40. In particular, there are strong verbal links between the two passages that suggest this relationship. Within this worldview, creation in Genesis 1 is, in a sense, taking place in God's divine sanctuary. Within this sanctuary, God generates the proper division of realms and animals, as the priests correspondingly do in the Temple. This Temple operates on days that are holy days, as symbolized by the Sabbath, and on days that do not specifically constitute sacred time, as represented by the first six days of creation. As we saw in the preceding chapter, the light of God is to be always present in the world, much like the lamp stand and lamps of the Temple (Zech. 4:2; 1 Kgs. 7:49; cf. the Tabernacle's lamp in Ex. 25:31-32, 27:20, 31:8, and 39:37).[40] This way of envisioning God in the image and likeness of the Temple priesthood will be explored further below when we get to the discussion of the seventh day.

In the end, the priestly account generates a vision of unity within reality that also links what is separated. The priestly time, marked for day seven and separated from the other days, is matched on the other days by the marking of priestly space in terms of animals and their realms. As scholars have long noted, the priestly binary construction of the world in terms of holy versus unholy, clean versus unclean, and pure versus impure[41] are portrayed as a series of distinctions within an overall unity. The unity, as it is narrated, unfolds in a series of divisions cast in terms of opposition, whose overarching unity points back to the One God who made it all.

2. Priestly Time: The Lights of Day Four

In the preceding section, we explored the priestly separation of space on days one and two. We also mentioned the idea that the separation of light and darkness marks the beginning of time as experienced by humanity in the form of days. This notion of separation of time becomes explicit on day four. Within the scheme in Genesis 1, the fourth day of creation in verses 14-19 offers a particularly priestly view of time. Verse 14 sets out the purpose of the lights on day four: "God said, 'let lights be in the firmament of the sky, to separate day from night, and they will become signs for the appointed times [literally, "signs and appointed times"] and for the days and years.'"

Genesis 1:14 expresses a traditional idea about creation that the lights mark the days and years,[42] which is elaborated in verse 16: "And God made the two great lights, the great light as ruler of day and the small light as ruler of night, and the stars."[43] The verb "to separate" applies here to time as well as space in Genesis 1. In other words, creation in Genesis 1 is about the creation of both spatial and temporal reality as generally known to the Israelites.

The sun and moon were matters of considerable interest in Israel as well as the rest of the ancient Near East. The characterizations of the sun and the moon found in Genesis 1:16 are traditional. In the Ugaritic story of Kirta, the sun is called "Great Sun" and the "Great Light." [44] The sun is also called "Great Light" in one of the Ugaritic ritual texts and "Divine Light" in the Ugaritic stories about Baal.[45] These titles have been compared with the designations for the sun and moon in Genesis 1:16.[46] Just as the sun and moon are subservient[47] to God in Genesis 1 and in biblical tradition more generally, so both the sun and the moon in Ugaritic literature are subservient to the chief god, El. The sun, in particular, acts on El's orders. The sun and moon are also his divine children, as are other astral figures (such as Dawn and Dusk). One Ugaritic text provides an excerpt of a creation account of deities (or, "theogony"); it describes El's fathering of the Dawn and Dusk, evidently the last of his astral children to be born.[48] Following their birth, an offering is ordered for Lady Sun and to the other stars. Other divinities associated with stars likewise belong to El's astral family, such as Athtart and Athtar, who are the morning and evening stars respectively.[49]

The tradition of the stars as divine figures was known also in ancient Israel. For example, Isaiah 14 displays this sort of knowledge. It draws on an old tradition about the fall of one of these old astral divinities as a parable for the fall of Babylon. Verse 12 addresses the king of Babylon as the divine figure, "Helal, son of Dawn," and verse 13 alludes to "the stars of El." Here these divine, astral figures are under El's power. They also survive in other biblical passages and in Israelite proper names. A remarkable treatment of the stars comes from Job 38. In this chapter, God relates many of the wondrous things that the figure of Job has no experience of. Job has challenged God, and God responds in Job 38:1-11:

1   Then Yahweh replied to Job out of the storm and said:
2   Who is this who darkens counsel
     With words lacking knowledge?
3   Gird up your loins like a strong man;
     I will question you, you will inform me.
4   Where were you when I laid the earth's foundations?
     Tell if you have understanding (of such matters).

5   Who fixed its measurements—do you know?
    Or, who measured it with a line?
6   On what were its bases sunk,
    Or, who set its cornerstone,
7   When the morning stars sang together
    And all the divine children (*bene 'elohim*) shouted for joy?
8   And who closed the sea behind doors,
    When it gushed forth from the womb,
9   When I clothed it with clouds,
    Covered it with dense cloud,
10 When I decreed breakers for it,
    And set up bars and doors,
11 And I said: 'Up to this point you may come, but no farther;
    Here your surging waves are stopped'?

The speech goes on to discuss God's power over the day and dawn (verses 12-15), and then God asks Job if he has ever experienced the cosmic sources of the sea or surveyed the expanses of the world (verses 16-18). Overall the speech points out to Job that his understanding of the universe is limited, hinting that his knowledge of God is at least as limited and that his questioning of God may be out of place in the many chapters before Job 38.

The divine speech in chapter 38 provides an overview of creation, as it was known in ancient Israel. In some respects, it complements the information provided in the accounts of creation that we have seen in earlier chapters with Psalms 74 and 104. While creation accounts commonly provide some details lacking in the others, all three of these texts know the idea of the unruly (perhaps even hostile) nature of the cosmic waters that God subdued at creation. Like Psalm 104, Job 38 mentions God as the divine builder of the world, with its foundations toward the beginning of creation (Psalm 74 does not mention this feature). Job 38 mentions in verse 7 a significant detail missing from the other creation stories. This verse 7 tells us that at creation "the morning stars sang together." This line stands in poetic parallelism with the second half of the verse, "and all the divine children (*bene 'elohim*) shouted for joy." These "divine children" (often translated as "divine beings") are known in the Bible in a variety of passages (for example, Ps. 29:1). By the time of Genesis 1, they may have been thought of as little more than servants of God, perhaps like angels (as in Job 1:6 and 2:1; see also Zech. 14:5). In Job 38:7, "the morning stars" and "all the divine beings" stand in parallelism, and they provide two corresponding ways of referring to the same divine group. In other words, Job 38:7 recognizes that at the time of creation, the morning stars are minor divinities, perhaps enjoying no more power than angels, who recognize the sovereignty of their divine overlord, Yahweh. In Genesis 1:16, the deified aspect of these stars is given no emphasis, and their part in creation is only mentioned in passing. Perhaps closer to the sense of Genesis 1:16 is Psalm 147:4: "He reckoned the number of the stars; to each he gave its name." As in Genesis 1, this creation allusion simply exalts God without much sense of the stars as powers in their own right.

It has sometimes been thought that the lack of reference to the sun and the moon by name in Genesis 1:14-19 is significant. Some scholars argue that this omission represented an implicit attack directed against worship of the "sun, moon, and the stars." [50] In some biblical passages, such polemical attacks are known, for example, in 2 Kings 23:5. The picture is not uniform, however. The divine assembly that serves God is sometimes referred to as "the host of heaven" in a neutral manner. While it is condemned in Zephaniah 1:5, it is assumed in 1 Kings 22:19 to be an acceptable way to refer to the heavenly council. It is true that Genesis 1 does not personify these lights, as we see in Job 38:7. These texts treat the sun and moon differently, but neither passage seems to involve polemic. In this regard, we may also note the characterization in Jeremiah 33:25: "I surely established my covenant with day and night, the statutes of heaven and earth." At least on a metaphorical level,[51] this text represents the sun and moon as entities that can enter into a covenantal relationship with God. They are not considered deities as such, nor are they condemned. The same may be involved in Genesis 1. In any case, it is clear that the passage does not assign the sun, moon, and stars the status of even minor deities. Whatever their precise status, they are brought into the order of divine creation, and unlike the light of day one, the lights of day four are explicitly made by God (verse 18). Thus Genesis offers not so much a monotheistic polemic as a vision of monotheistic harmony in the universe.

The sun and the moon in Genesis 1 seem more like elements in creation, as we see in some ancient Near Eastern texts. The opening of Sumerian and Akkadian versions of the astrological series, "When Anu (and) Enlil," shows this idea:

Sumerian

When Anu, Enlil, and Enki, [the great gods],
In their infallible wisdom,

Had, in the plans for heaven and earth,
      Laid down the crescent-shaped vessel of the Moon,
Had established it as a sign for heaven and earth,
The stars came out, to be visible in heaven.

Akkadian

When Anu, Enlil, and Ea, the great gods, in their wisdom,
Had laid down the plans for heaven and earth,
Had confided to the hands of the great gods to bring forth
      The day, to start the month for humankind to see,
They beheld the Sun in the portal of his rising,
The stars came out faithfully in heaven [52]

This Mesopotamian representation of the sun and moon as components of creation should serve as a caution before assuming that Genesis 1:14-19 constitutes a polemic against worship of the sun and moon as divinities. If the Mesopotamian text could present the sun and moon more as things than as deities, it is also possible that this is the case for Genesis 1. The comparison does not prove the point, but it is suggestive of this possibility.

Instead of presenting a polemic against other deities, Genesis 1:14-19 may reflect an astronomical sensibility that would be hardly exceptional for biblical creation accounts. In this connection, we may note this feature in two other creation accounts that we discussed in chapter 1. Psalms 8:4 and 74:16 both use the verb, "set in place" (hiphil, or causative form of the verb, *kwn). The first passage uses it for the moon and the stars, while the second applies it to the sun. In Akkadian astronomical texts, the same verb is used of stars in the sense "to be stationary" and "to make stationary," for example "(the planet) Venus becomes stationary in the morning."[53] In this connection, we may note that reliance on astronomical knowledge for predicting the future is criticized in Isaiah 47:13: "The scanners of heaven, the star-gazers, who announce month by month whatever will come upon you" (NJPS). In Isaiah 44:25, the Lord annuls the "signs" or omens of diviners.[54] Jeremiah 10:2 advises that Israelites should "not be dismayed by signs in heaven" (compare Joel 2:30 [MT 3:3]).[55]

Genesis 1:14 may utilize astronomical terminology as well, but with its own religious purpose in mind. The idea of the sun, moon, and stars as "signs" ('otot)[56] in Genesis 1:14[57] may be a common one drawn from astronomical usage, as suggested by the Sumerian quote above about the moon as "a sign for heaven and earth." The importance of omens and signs located in heaven and on earth is emphasized in a remarkable Babylonian diviner's manual that explains: "The signs on earth, just as those in the sky, give us signals. Sky and earth both produce portents, (and) though appearing separately, they are not, (because) sky and earth are interrelated."[58] Genesis 1:14-19 may be playing off such an astronomical sensibility, as Baruch Halpern has suggested.[59] In any case, this priestly account offers a specifically priestly qualification about the astronomical role of the sun and moon as "signs." The lights in Genesis 1:14 serve a specifically religious function, in marking the "appointed times" (*mo'adim*), in other words, the festivals as known from the priestly calendars in Leviticus 23 and Numbers 28–29.[60] The same word for festivals occurs at the head of the calendar in Leviticus 23:4. This usage also fits in with the Sabbath in Leviticus 23, since it treats the calendars along the lines of the priestly Sabbath (see the discussion of the Sabbath below).[61] In Genesis 1, the signs of the astral bodies are not for divination (as in the words of Isaiah 47:13 just cited above), but for religious devotion.

By the time of Genesis 1 in the sixth century BCE, the sun and the moon may not have played much of a role in Israel's worship,[62] although they did remain well embedded in the traditional lore of creation. In Genesis 1, these bodies made on day four appear to be designed to correspond to the light of day one. The text is not explicit on the point, but it seems that the lights of day four are to reflect the light of day one.[63] The text is explicit in placing the sun and moon within the larger design of divine creation, signaling first the time of the day and the year, as we see in Psalm 104:19: "He made the moon for the appointed times." The appointed times are the "seasons" of the year (so NJPS). In Genesis 1:14, they are to also serve the priestly purpose of marking the "times" of the festivals. The priestly account makes no distinction between the roles of the sun and moon for marking natural time (sunrise and sunset) and cultic time (the ritual calendars). All functions of time are part of the same unified, organized creation.

3. Priestly Person: Humanity on Day Six

Another priestly trait in the first creation story involves the making of the human person.[64] God proposes in verse 26: "let us make (the) human in our image (*selem*), corresponding to our likeness (*demut*)."[65] The narrative description of this divine creation in verse 27 takes the form of a three-line poetic unit with different words between the lines corresponding to one another (what scholars call "biblical parallelism").[66] The poetic form of the verse demarcates the human person from other parts of creation:

> And God created (*bara'*) the human in his image (*selem*),
> In the image (*selem*) of God he created (*bara'*) him,
> Male and female he created (*bara'*) them.

Perhaps most strikingly, this verse uses the verb, "he created" (*bara'*) three times. This three-fold use occurs in no other verse of the Bible, and as we saw in chapter 2, the verb itself is reserved for the deity, marking human creation as a divine act. Second, the two-fold use of "image" (*selem*) and its omission of "likeness" (*demut*) in the poetic unit of verse 27 are conspicuous compared with the preceding verse 26. Perhaps the word "image" is stressed here for a reason (we will explore the background of these terms below). Third and finally, scholars have regularly noted that the presentation of the human person here stands in marked contrast with the sort of description for divine creation of the human person, for example in Genesis 2:7: "the Lord God shaped the human with dust from the earth and he blew into his nostrils breath of life." This way of understanding human creation is common both in the Bible and in the ancient world more broadly.[67] Genesis 1:26-27 stands out for the different approach that it takes to the human person. We will return to the contrast between the two accounts of human creation in chapter 4, but for now we may say that the "image" and "likeness" together mark the human person as more directly linked to God than any other part of creation.

For many years, scholars compared the image and likeness in Genesis 1:26-28 with ancient Near Eastern texts that understand the king as the image of his patron-god.[68] As we will see shortly, resonances of this royal sensibility can be found in the context of Genesis 1:26 and 28, with the command to "rule" (**rdh*). We may see in this passage an echo of an older royal notion reused in the priestly context of Genesis 1. The human person is the royal regent or representative of the god on earth. This royal background is expressed in a particularly poignant way in an Aramaic-Akkadian bilingual inscription, as scholars have noted since it was first published.[69] The inscription is written on a statue of a king and the Aramaic portion refers to the statue of the king as his "likeness" (*dmwt'*, in lines 1, 15)[70] and his "image" (*slm*, in line 12; cf. *slmh* in line 16). According to the inscription, this king is the servant of his overlord, the Assyrian emperor. W. Randall Garr comments on the rhetorical functions of the terms "likeness" and "image" in the inscription:

"'Likeness' is petitionary and directed at the deity; it is cultic and votive. 'Image' is majestic, absolute and commemorative; it is directed at the people. Thus, these two Aramaic terms encode two traditional roles of the Mesopotamian ruler—that of devoted worshipper and that of sovereign monarch."[71] The statue, this image and likeness, in this case represents the image of the vassal of an overlord. We may read the terms in Genesis 1:26-28 in a similar manner. As the image and likeness of the god, the human person is to be the devoted worshipper of the god who also serves God the sovereign as servant and agent on earth. This second notion leads into the verbs in verse 28: the human person is to master and rule the earth.[72]

While the older, royal sense of the passage is present in Genesis 1, we also need to be mindful that our author is priestly. So we may ask about the sensibility that the terms of divine image and likeness might have held for a priestly composer.[73] To put the description of the human person as God's "likeness" in its priestly context, Ezekiel, another priestly work, offers us some help. (As Ezekiel 1:3 tells us, the prophet came from a priestly family, and it is clear from many aspects of the book that it reflects a specifically priestly viewpoint.) The language for the creation of the human person in Genesis 1:26-27 echoes the priestly description of God in Ezekiel 1:26.[74] This verse describes the appearance of the divine in the following way: it was "an image like the appearance of a human" (*demut kemar'eh 'adam*).[75]

In its context, this description of God in Ezekiel 1:26-28 represents an effort to qualify and arguably reduce the anthropomorphic presentation of Yahweh in the heavenly divine council, a feature that we see in Ugaritic and biblical texts especially Isaiah 6. Indeed, Ezekiel 1 builds on the very same sort of prophetic call narrative represented by Isaiah 6. Isaiah 6 is a particularly good parallel, since it includes a vision of the heavenly beings with a straightforward reference to the prophet's seeing God in human-form: "I saw the Lord seated on a high and lofty throne" (verse 1). Both Isaiah 6:1 and Ezekiel 1:27 use the verb "I saw" (*r'h*) to describe the prophets' experience of seeing God. Ezekiel 1:26-28 provides a comparable representation of God, but it does so in a far more elaborate, yet far less straightforward manner. The anthropomorphism is made explicit, as it describes God's "likeness" (*demut*) as "like the appearance of a human" (verse 26).[76] Yet even at this initial mention of God's appearance, the anthropomorphism is highly qualified, "it was *like* the appearance of a human." Verses 27 and 28 go on to elaborate the character of this appearance: the appearance of the divine loins was "*like* the appearance of amber, *like* the appearance of fire, . . and above the loins was fire and light." [77] Compared with other representations of God, Ezekiel's is more baroque and less direct.

The language of the divine "likeness" (*demut*) is one component within the elaborate description of God in Ezekiel 1. It is also the one that bears on the description of the human person in Genesis 1:26-27 (see also 5:1). Ezekiel 1:26-27 sees God in human terms, while Genesis 1:26-27 describes humanity in divine terms. Ezekiel 1:26-28 conveys the prophet's vision of the divine with the language of "likeness" of the human person ("an image like the appearance of a human"). In turn, Genesis 1:26-28 presents a vision of the human person in the likeness of the divine. Ezekiel 1:26 casts Yahweh in human terms, and its various uses of "like" and "appearance" seem to acknowledge the problem inherent in reducing God to mere human terms. Using the same language of likeness, Genesis 1:26-28 moves in the opposite direction, in magnifying the human person in divine terms. As a result, Genesis 1 provides a vision of the human person that leads back to the Creator. The creation of the human person is a sign on earth of the reality of God the Creator. Humanity is not only the representation of God on earth; the human person is the living representation pointing to a living and real God, perhaps unlike the lifeless images of other deities made by human hands. [78]

Genesis 1:28 describes what is entailed by the creation of the human person. As we have seen, humanity is to "subdue" (*kbsh*) the earth and to "rule" (*rdh*) over the animals. [79] Some scholars see in these two verbs language modeled on the figure of the king as the divine representative on earth. [80] To a considerable degree, this is correct, especially in regard to the verb, "to rule" (*rdh*). However, there is perhaps more to the story, since the other verb, "to subdue" (*kbsh*) does not seem to be particularly royal in character. Instead, this verb elsewhere has a priestly use that may help us understand the further nuance that the term may have held for a priestly author in Genesis 1:28. The verb occurs in the priestly context of Joshua 18:1. [81] This biblical chapter begins by relating how "the land was under the control" (*kbsh*) of the Israelites. [82] The chapter goes on to list the portions or land "inheritances" (*nahalah*) that the Israelite tribes are to receive from God (see also Numbers 32:22 and 29). In this context, [83] the verb evokes God's power to allot the land to the Israelites. Similarly, the verb in Genesis 1 suggests the divine allotment of the world to humanity. While we may hear the royal background of monarchic power in the verb, "to rule" (*rdh*) in Genesis 1:28, the verb, "to subdue" (*kbsh*) conveys a priestly sense of the divine allotment of the world to humanity. Like the language of likeness in Genesis 1:26, the verbal usage here is a priestly one. Joshua 18 attributes the victory to God, and the verb conveys the control of the land that results from this divine achievement (see also Numbers 32:22). In this context, this is not so much a human conquest, much less a royal one. Rather, it points to God, and further to God's allotment of the land as a divine gift to Israel. In Genesis 1, the verb denotes God's gift to humanity. Perhaps through the comparison with other priestly passages, we may sense that the verb conveys the notion of humanity not only constituted in the image of God, but also empowered by being made in the divine image. God, the Power over the world, extends this capacity to humanity in the divine blessing in Genesis 1:28.

Within its priestly context, the creation of the human person in Genesis 1:26-28 contains a further dimension. God blesses the human person in verse 28, suggesting that the image further involves male and female[84] in the procreation of humanity.[85] It has been debated whether for a priestly author of Genesis 1, the creation of human male and female might express a norm against sexual relations between humans and animals (Leviticus 18:23, 20:15) or same-sex sexual relations (see Leviticus 18:22; 20:13).[86] In any case, this role of humans in Genesis 1:26-28 echoes, or we might say, "images," God's role as creator.[87] As we have seen, we have older royal language and imagery in this description, recast in priestly terms. The description of the human person in Genesis 1:26-28 reflects this shift. We will return to the creation of the human person in the next chapter. For now, we may note the priestly imprint on the description of the human person in this account. This priestly sensibility about God is more evident with the blessing and the Sabbath of the seventh day.

4. Priestly God: Divine Blessing and Sanctification on Day Seven

Day seven contains the important priestly features of divine blessing and echo of the Sabbath (Gen. 2:3): "And God blessed the seventh day and sanctified it, because on it God ceased (*shabat*) from all his work that he had done." The major difficulty for interpreters of this verse is the verb *shabat*, followed by the phrase "from all his work." Does the verb mean, "to desist" or "to cease" from work, or does it mean "to rest," as it has been traditionally understood? Or, should we see contextually some or all of the nuances in the semantic range of the term? We will consider the various nuances of *shabat* shortly, but before we do so, we need to focus on divine blessing in this verse.

Blessing is a traditional role for the deity,[88] a divine gift made to human beings.[89] For example, God blesses creatures with fertility in Genesis 1:22[90] and humanity with fertility in 1:28. God also blesses the seventh day in 2:3, again with humanity's wellbeing in mind.

Blessing is a particularly priestly expression in Genesis 1.[91] To illustrate this point, let us consider some cases of priestly blessing in the Bible. Mediating the blessing of God to the people was considered a traditional function of priests, according to "the priestly blessing" in Numbers 6:22-26 (NRSV):[92]

> The Lord spoke to Moses, saying: "Speak to Aaron and his sons,
>   saying,
> 'Thus you shall bless the Israelites: You shall say to them:
> "May the Lord bless you and keep you;
>   May the Lord make his face to shine upon you,
>   And be gracious to you;
>   May the Lord lift up his countenance upon you,
>   And give you peace.""

The mediation of blessing was an old priestly role in Israel. 1 Samuel 2 describes the annual pilgrimage made to Shiloh by Elkanah and his family. According to verse 20, the priest Eli would bless the family every year (NRSV): "Then Eli would bless Elkanah and his wife, and say, 'May the Lord repay you with children by this woman for the gift that she made to the Lord'; and then they would return to their home." Similarly, Genesis 14:19 indicates that the priest Melchizedek blesses Abraham at Salem (understood as Jerusalem, as in Psalm 76:2). The poetic blessing in verse 19 first blesses Abram and then in verse 20 turns to the deity directly (compare the cultic blessing in Psalm 115:12-15):

> He blessed him and said:
> "Blessed be Abram by (l-) God Most High (El Elyon),
> maker of heaven and earth;
> and blessed be God Most High
> who has delivered your enemies into your hand."

In turn, Abram offers a tithe to the priest (verse 20b). In this passage, Melchizedek represents the classic model of a priest blessing a person at a shrine. The second part of the blessing, in particular, marks the priest as mediating God's blessing to Abram.

The tradition of the priestly blessing is known from later texts. The book of Ben Sira (also known as Sirach or Ecclesiasticus) presents blessing to the people as one of the roles exercised by Aaron as priest (45:15; cf. 45:26). Ben Sira also describes the high priest, Simon,[93] offering blessing to the people after completing sacrifice in the Jerusalem temple (50:20-21; NRSV):

> Then Simon came down and raised his hands
> over the whole congregation of Israelites,
> to pronounce the blessing of the Lord with his lips,
> and to glory in his name;
> And they bowed down in worship a second time,
> to receive the blessing from the Most High.

Here Simon pronounces God's blessing on the people. In this manner, the high priest mediates the divine blessing by pronouncing it in the people's presence. From these texts,[94] it is evident that blessing was recalled as a priestly function in shrines and the Jerusalem temple from early Israel through the Hellenistic period.

Priestly blessing informs the divine blessing on the seventh day in Genesis 2:3. This idea fits with the notion of the world as analogous to the divine Tabernacle of Exodus 39–40 and with the Jerusalem Temple, a theme noted in chapter 2. In Genesis 1, God's blessing combines both the divine role of giving blessing and the human priestly role of offering blessing to the creatures in verse 22 and to the human persons in verse 28. God not only provides the force of the blessing; God also articulates it by pronouncing it as priests do. In this respect, God is in the image and likeness of the priest. Blessing is clearly an important role for the author of Genesis 1; it appears not once but three times in this account, yet appears in no other creation narrative.

Genesis 2:3 stresses the idea of divine blessing, by presenting God as blessing the Sabbath.[95] Blessing time or a measure of time is not a common biblical notion.[96] As we have seen, blessing generally is pronounced over persons. By implication, the blessing of the Sabbath day suggests that the blessing is for those who keep the Sabbath as commanded. The Sabbath day in Genesis 2:3 is not only blessed, it is also sanctified. Sanctification flows from this God, who commands Israel: "You shall be holy because I, the Lord your God, am holy" (Lev. 19:2). The idea of imitation of God underlies the Genesis 1 narrative about God. We may also note that the Sabbath in passages thought to date to the eighth century (for example, 2 Kgs. 4:23; Is. 1:13; Hos. 2:11; Amos 8:5) is associated with sacral celebrations involving the moon.[97] These would have been carried out at holy places, including the Temple. From these texts as well as priestly calendars that locate the Sabbath with annual feasts (Lev. 23:3; Num. 28:9), it seems that the Sabbath was part of a monthly public regimen and not only a family or domestic practice. When we look at the evoking of the Sabbath in Genesis 1, we should bear in mind its connection with public ritual and the Temple.

Sanctification of the day by God is to be imitated by the observance of the day by the Israelites, as commended in Leviticus 23:3: "For six days work may be done, but on the seventh day there is to be a Sabbath of complete rest as a sacred time; no work shall you do—it is a Sabbath to Yahweh in all your dwellings." Desisting from work is a paramount expression of rest in imitation of God.[98] Echoing Genesis 2:2-3, the Ten Commandments in Exodus 20:8-11 explicitly commands that the Sabbath rest of God is to be imitated by Israel.[99] In this passage, "rest" is explicitly tied to the Sabbath.[100] Exodus 16:29-30 likewise connects the Sabbath with the phrase, *wayyishbetu ha'am*, "and the peoples rested" ("remained inactive," in NJPS).[101]

At the same time, it is important to note that in the phrase, "'shabbated' from all his work" in Genesis 2:2, "rest" is not the literal meaning of the verb. Rather, it means, "to cease."[102] Outside of contexts dealing with the Sabbath, the word shows this sense. For example, Jeremiah 31:36 promises: "If these laws should ever be annulled by me, declares Yahweh, only then would the offspring of Israel *cease* (*shbt*)." This word is also used for ceasing from work in a late seventh-century BCE Hebrew inscription from Mesad Hashayyahu: "And your servant harvested and measured (*wykl*) and stored, according to the schedule, before stopping (*shbt*)."[103] From this passage, it is evident that "to cease" or "to stop" is the basic sense of the word in relation to work.

The meaning of Sabbath rest is developed further in Exodus 31. This chapter describes the Sabbath as the sign of the covenant (see verse 17). In its allusion to the establishment of the Sabbath in creation, Exodus 31:17 intimates the purpose of this sign of the relationship between God and the people, "for in six days the Lord made heaven and earth, and on the seventh he ceased (*shbt*) from work and was refreshed (*wayyinnapash*)." This passage adds the notion that desisting from work permits the restoration of the *nepesh*,[104] one's "life" or "self" (sometimes translated "soul").[105] Similarly, Exodus 20:11 uses another word for rest (*nwh*) in connection with the Sabbath, in reflecting on the commandment to keep the Sabbath in verse 8: "He rested (*wayyanah*) on the seventh day."[106] Here "rest" is associated with the Sabbath and its requirement to cease from labor.

The priestly notion in Exodus 31:17 that the Sabbath is the day to refresh or restore oneself may build on earlier nuances of the word, such as the king's rest from enemies following victory. As we noted in chapter 1, the meaning "to cease" occurs also for the root *shbt* in Psalm 8:3,[107] where it applies to defeated enemies in the sense "to cause to cease," in other words, "to put an end to" such foes. In this psalm, the word signals divine victory. It is this victory that leads to divine enthronement and rest, the ideal condition for a king.[108] In Genesis 1, the God who speaks and creates without conflict against cosmic enemies enjoys divine rest at the end of creation.[109] In ceasing from work, God is viewed as an enthroned king, enjoying rest following victory.

This motif of divine rest in Genesis 1 offers an interesting comparison when considered in the context of Mesopotamia literature. In *Enuma Elish* and *Atrahasis*, the creation of humanity allows the gods to rest from their work.[110] These Mesopotamian texts understand that divine rest comes at the expense of human rest. Yet unlike the Mesopotamian perspective, for Genesis 1 rest is designed not only for the deity, but also for humanity as an imitation of the deity. The human person is made for work, but not on the seventh day. On that day, humanity is to participate in the divine rest. Genesis 1 also locates this rest or desisting from work within a religious life. It is in this spirit that various prophetic works of the sixth century BCE decry violation of the Sabbath.[111] It also lies at the center of the priestly vision of Genesis 1.[112] To mark the special character of the Sabbath, Genesis 2:3 says that God blessed and sanctified it and that God desisted from work on it. In other words, this rest is an expression of the sacred. This is a very special feature of this creation story. Indeed, the combination of blessing, sanctification, and rest appears in no other creation account; it is central to the priestly vision of Genesis 1.

Before we turn to summarizing the overall priestly vision of Genesis 1, there is one detail about the Sabbath that we need to consider, because it has troubled commentators for a long time. The difficulty involves Genesis 2:2. The first part of the verse says that God completed the work on the seventh day, which would seem to imply that God was still working on the seventh day when he finished. As we have seen, the priestly tradition sees work being only on days one through six and not on the seventh. There are a number of ways to resolve the problem.[113] One way has been to read "sixth" day in Genesis 2:2 instead of "seventh." The verse in the versions of the Greek Septuagint, Samaritan Hebrew and Peshitta Syriac texts in fact reads "sixth" day instead of "seventh."[114] In contrast, cases of seven-day sequences in Ugaritic literary texts have the activity in question ending sometime on the seventh day,[115] and so they would seem to favor the reading of the Hebrew Masoretic text.[116] So what is going on?

It seems that the formulation that God ceased from work on the seventh day, as expressed in both Genesis 2:2 and Exodus 31:17, was not meant to suggest that God was still working on the seventh day. At the same time the formulation was not explicit on this point. Other passages, as we see in Exodus 31:15-17 (paralleled in Exodus 35:2), could have provided the needed clarification, but the formulation wasn't sufficiently clear enough on this point for the tradition behind the reading of Genesis 2:2 in the Greek, Samaritan, and Syriac Peshitta versions. These texts strive to remove any ambiguity. In general, the difference may reflect an ancient discussion that may have been going on already in the biblical period itself over the formulation. On the one hand, we see one formulation that was rather general and seemingly too open-ended, and on the other hand, there was another tradition of formulation that was more precise and clear on the point. As this discussion seems to suggest, perhaps we are witnessing how the understanding of work and the Sabbath itself involved interpretation and clarification among scribes and priests in ancient Israel.

As we reach the end of our priestly story, we may return to the remarkable correlation between the end of Genesis 1 and the end of Exodus 39–40, which we noted in chapter 2. Exodus 39–40 describes the completion of the building of the Tabernacle that is to house the glory of Yahweh. I mentioned this series of correspondences in the preceding chapter,[117] but it bears revisiting at this point, in order to illustrate the final effect of the priestly vision of Genesis 1:

> Exodus 39:43: "and when Moses *saw* all the work, and *behold,* they had *made* it—just as the Lord commanded, so they had *made*—Moses *blessed* them."
>
> Genesis 1:31a: "and God *saw* all that he had *made,* and *behold* it was very good."
>
> Genesis 2:3: "and God *blessed* the seventh day and sanctified it because on it he ceased from all its work that God had created for *making.*"
>
> Exodus 40:33b: "and Moses *finished* the *work.*"
>
> Genesis 2:2a: "and God *finished* on the seventh day his *work.*"
>
> Exodus 39:32a: "and all the work of the tabernacle of the tent of meeting was *finished.*"
>
> Genesis 2:1: "and the heaven and the earth and all their host were *finished.*"

These correlations suggest that the priestly author of Genesis 1 thought of God's creation as similar to the Tabernacle, that both are structures sanctioned by God for the divine presence. In this similarity of phrases, as we have previously noted, we glimpse the most fundamental aspect of priestly thinking in this entire account, namely that the world is like a temple. But we need to consider the implications of this comparison further if we are to understand the intentions of the priestly writer of Genesis 1. In his view, the world, like the Temple, is the very site of divine goodness given by God; it is informed by the light of God like a theophany in a temple, and it is imbued with divine word and revelation in the forms of divine speech and blessing, like the teaching taught by priests and like the blessings that they give in the Temple. Taken together, the correspondences between the end of Genesis 1 and the end of Exodus 39–40 offer a profound vision of reality. In arriving at the end of Genesis 1 and seeing its correspondences with Exodus 39–40, readers come to understand that as they have watched the unfolding of creation at its very beginning, all the while they have been contemplating the very temple of the world,[118] made by God with divine word and light, blessing and rest.

5. The Priestly Vision of Genesis 1

With the priestly elements of Genesis 1 now addressed in some detail, it is time to summarize its vision.[119] This account builds into the construction of the world a priestly vision of time and space that could speak to Israel in the sixth century BCE. God in Genesis 1 is known primarily by divine deeds. This God is God beyond all powers who only speaks and makes it so, and no other powers in the universe can contravene what God has spoken into reality. God does not fight the "Deep" (*tehom*) as in Psalm 74. Instead, the waters in Genesis 1:2 simply become part of God's good order. In Genesis 1:21, the *tanninim* are also part of God's good creation; they are not the enemies that they are in Psalm 74 and in older divine battle stories. In the midst of the "void and vacuum" (*tohu wabohu*), Israel's God is poised to respond.

With the first three divine words in Genesis 1:3, the divine light suffuses the universe. The divine acts of creation respond to the void of reality, or as it may seem to ancient Israelites, the reality of the void represented by world empires that dominated it. Thanks to divine goodness and blessing crowned by the seventh day, Israel is to live in the world not as combatants in its conflicts, but as pilgrims brought to God's Temple. The universe, wherever people are, provides place and time for observing Sabbath and festivals. Further, the divine order hints at the role of dietary law (*kashrut*), and the divine word hints at divine teaching (*torah*). These help to express and perhaps even generate the blessings spoken by God the Divine Priest. Like the high priest who turns to the people in the Temple and blesses them, God pronounces the divine blessing over all creatures that have God's life force in them. God's blessing at the primordial beginning of the world will continue for all time.

The divine capacity to act is expressed not as power, for this God is God beyond all powers. God but speaks and it is so. Speech continues as a very important verb involved in the process of creation. It marks the very first moment of creation with God's own light, which infuses the world for all time. In every day of creation, God speaks in a way that builds with various verbs of making. All six days of creation open with God speaking. On day one, God only has to speak and there is light. On day two, God speaks and makes. On day three, God again speaks and the waters below heaven are gathered into one area. Moreover, on all of the first three days, God gives names to the parts of creation. On day four, God again speaks and makes. On day five, God's speech is followed instead by the verb exclusive to God, "to create" (**br'*). Here God blesses animals. On day six, God speaks, God makes, God creates, and God blesses humanity. On day seven, God blesses the Sabbath. Divine speech, in its various modes, is a particular hallmark of Genesis 1. Divine speech infuses creation. It is first in creation, before any making.

With the divine speech in Genesis 1:3, God's light comes into the universe. No darkness of the past or the present can alter this reality. In the midst of a dangerous and unruly world, the divine acts of creation create space and time for Israel to experience divine goodness and blessing crowned by the seventh day, a day of holiness. Like the Temple, the world as created by God supports the proper order of priestly space and time. The universe is the site for the observance of Sabbath and festivals. The holiness is not entirely separate from the other days. Like the Temple priesthood that maintains sacrifice and festivals, God creates a time ordered for the celebration of festivals and a space for the *kashrut* of the Temple. With this order of time and space, the creation is like a cosmic temple overseen by God for the good of humanity.

Within this order, the human person is in the image and likeness of God. Humanity is empowered by God to act like God with respect to (pro)creation and dominion in the world. Humanity also receives the gift of the Sabbath to rest from work, emulating God's own cessation from work. As we have seen, rest is a particularly divine gift, the very mark of divine existence. In imitating the divine creator of this order, the human person practicing this routine of rest fulfills the calling of being made in the image of the divine. This process of imaging does not end with rest and Sabbath. The temporal and spatial parameters constitute the order ordained and blessed by God, like the priesthood that teaches and blesses. Particularly echoing the priestly role of blessing, the divine blessings uttered to humanity and the Sabbath offer the prospect of human prosperity and human imitation of God. Even the blessing of fertility to animals ultimately serves to aid human prosperity. Like the high priest who turns to the people in the Temple and blesses them, God pronounces the divine blessing over all creatures that have God's life force in them. God blesses the world at the primordial beginning for all time, and it is a gift to Israel to have received God's blessing. Likewise, God's teaching, whether in Genesis 1 or elsewhere in priestly texts, serves to instruct people through time. Those serving in the Temple of God stand poised to offer praise and devotion in the life ordained by God and to welcome the divine teaching and blessings of life uttered by its divine high priest. This divine blessing and teaching is set within a structure represented by the process of separation over the course of the week. This sense of separation, too, is a specific priestly contribution to the presentation of creation in Genesis 1.

According to the account, this order goes all the way back to the beginning, to the very origins of the universe as it was ever known to human beings. Here a glimpse of God and the very beginning of God's own ways are unveiled before the audience that would seek to walk in them for their blessing. The God of divine speech and divine light infuses creation with life and structure. This God is power beyond any power in the universe[120] and a craftsman beyond any natural craftsmanship. In this story, God makes (*ʿsh) just as humans do, and yet God creates (*br') unlike humans. This Creator God is at once like and unlike humans. Moreover, God as Creator in Genesis 1 is knowable to some extent, but not entirely. The complex character of God's presence to humans is captured in this creation narrative. God is mediated through what God gives of the divine self in the world, namely the divine light of day one, which is refracted to humanity through the lights of the sun and the moon made on day four. This divine light in its fullness is not perceptible directly by humans. Similarly, divine speech is not spoken directly to humanity, with the single exception of the blessing in 1:28 and 29. It is particularly in blessing that humanity is directly addressed by God.

God's paradoxical presence through creation is nonetheless a rich one benefiting humanity. God is the power beyond any powers, the sage maker of the vast universe, the model and maker of human holiness, and the source of blessing and wellbeing. The world that God created is full of blessing for the world. And despite any situation in the world, whether in the sixth century BCE or at any other time, this order of reality is so because it was the order spoken and created by God at the very beginning of the world.[121] In short, the description of the world's creation in Genesis 1 is God's priestly prescription for the world.

This priestly vision of creation in Genesis 1 was not simply descriptive of the ancient past. It was also an ongoing prescription for Israel. The primordial situation of Genesis 1:2, of "void and vacuum" (*tohu wabohu*), of "waters" (*mayim*) and "Deep" (*tehom*), expressed the situation for the world not only at the beginning of creation; it also captured many dramatic and difficult moments in Israel's history. Even when the world may seem like void and vacuum, it still offered the prospect of some God-given good.[122] The world seemed like void and vacuum to Jeremiah in the sixth century BCE when he looked out at the world and its great empires threatening Israel. He says, in 4:23: "I looked at the world, and it was *tohu wabohu;* and at the heavens, and they had no light." For Jeremiah, the threatening circumstances imagined in the ancient past put a name on the world of his time. Israel was inundated, as it were, by the cosmic "waters" of the great empires that engulfed it.[123]

In the midst of these threatening waters, the life-force (*ruah*) of Israel's God remained poised to respond, according to Genesis 1:2. So the unknown author of Psalm 104 could similarly hope. This sentiment is expressed in particular in verses 27-30, with its description of God's creatures:

27   All of them hope in you,
     To give them food in due season.
28   You give to them—they gather,
     You open your hand—they are sated with good.
29   You hide your face—they are terrified,
     You take away their spirit—they expire,
     And they return to their dust.
30   You send forth your spirit (*ruah*)—they are created (°*br'*),
     And you renew the face of the earth.

Despite any critical situation in the world, whether in the sixth century BCE or at any other dangerous time, creation in Genesis 1 is the way it is because it was the order spoken and created by God at the beginning of the world. The divine wind or life-force (*ruah*), divine speech and light are for the world for all time. Genesis 1 is not simply an expression of hope in the midst of a threatening, potentially evil and destructive situation; the world, we are told, is good through and through. God stands in this cosmic Temple of the universe as its priest, pronouncing blessing on animals and humanity. Genesis 1 is not simply a description of the past, but a prescription of what good is to be hoped for. For Israel's priesthood, this was the hope for Israel through time.

The prescriptive role of Genesis 1 is clear from other passages that connect to this creation story. Genesis 1 is located within a web of biblical memories that provide a foundational point of reference for Israel's life.[124] Genesis 1 belongs to the priesthood's memory of the beginning. For the priestly worldview, it functioned not only as a community reminder of the Sabbath, but also as a link to the Ten Commandments. The priestly version of the Ten Commandments commands each Israelite to "remember the Sabbath and keep it holy" (Exodus 20:11) and explicitly links this command to the priestly view of creation: "for in six days the Lord made heaven and sea and all that is in them, and he rested on the seventh day; therefore He blessed the day of the Sabbath and sanctified it." Similarly, Exodus 31:17 marks observance of the Sabbath as a sign of the covenant between God and Israel. Genesis 1 was understood as a text between these texts or underlying and informing them; it was an "intertext" that perhaps required no explicit citation. At this primordial, rather "magical" moment, God spoke and it was, and all priestly tradition looked back to this text for inspiration.

Genesis 1 enjoyed a particularly paradoxical place in priestly thinking. The composition of this text flowed from a priestly tradition attested throughout the priestly writings of the Pentateuch and beyond (as we will see in the next chapter). At the same time, Genesis 1 served as the foundational memory for these writings and their vision of the world. It was not simply the first text of ancient priestly memory. Genesis 1 is more than an important piece of priestly memory or a cornerstone in the construction of its past memory. When it is viewed in the contexts of Exodus 20:11 and 31:17, it is evident that Genesis 1 is the text that authorizes the commemoration of priestly thought in Israel and gives to it a primacy of place. The evocation of the primordial past in Genesis 1 authorizes the text's priestly vision as the primordial reality. This single priestly construction describes and prescribes one reality consisting of one good and blessed order created by the one God acting alone.

In the end, this vision of the world can be taken in several ways. It may inspire those who treasure the element of priestly vision in their own traditions. It may also challenge readers to follow God's ways, as understood by Israel's priesthood and developed in later religious traditions. Yet Genesis 1 may also offend, with its apparent effort to assert the priesthood's traditional status and power in ancient Israel. Readers who react negatively to priestly prerogative stand within good biblical tradition, as an offensive attitude toward the priesthood was already active in biblical times.[125] At the same time, Genesis 1 also offers a vision of hope in the world of the sixth century BCE, when Israel's existence was under such terrible threat. I think that all of these perspectives have some basis, and perhaps the complexity of such a text and its context calls for a comparably complex response on the part of its readers. The challenge for readers today is how to appreciate this priestly vision without accepting its problematic aspects.

In closing this discussion, we may ask, as did many authors of biblical books, how the world made by God relates to us. What position and status do we hold as creatures in this creation? If Genesis 1 is any guide for our thoughts, it reminds us that we are obligated to do more than ponder only the terrible things of this world as real and as tangible as they are to us—and they are. Genesis 1's vision is wildly optimistic, a vision of good that can be hard to accept in the face of real experience. Nonetheless, for Jews, Christians, and Muslims alike, this vision of goodness remains the bedrock and beginning of our traditions. At the same time, we need to be mindful of how our traditions began. While we may think of the Bible itself as the beginning of our modern traditions, we have seen in this work that it is not.

The process of revelation of Genesis 1 involved an engagement with other models of creation known in ancient Israel, a point generally recognized quite insightfully by Joseph Cardinal Ratzinger (now Pope Benedict XVI).[126] As we have seen, these models are not only Israelite, but go back to the rest of the ancient Near East, again as Ratzinger in general terms has recognized.[127] The resulting revelation of Genesis 1 comes in the form of its own carefully worded vision that sees God, humanity, and the world in a way that no other text does. In the end, the revelation of Genesis 1 yields a unique picture, yet it is one that is also "incarnational" in the sense that it is produced out of prior traditions, both priestly and nonpriestly ones. These ultimately include nonbiblical traditions to which ancient Israel was heir; in this sense, one might regard ancient Near Eastern traditions as containing some measure of "pre-revelation." While the path of revelation begins with Abraham (to paraphrase Ratzinger),[128] this path of revelation is indebted to nonbiblical or pre-Abrahamic traditions, and it is in this sense that I would refer to these as "pre-revelation." In short, Genesis 1 is an utterly unique creation account, even as various aspects of its language and ideas are indebted to earlier traditions.

One dimension of Genesis 1's revelatory force lies in its combination of the descriptive and prescriptive. As we have seen, Genesis 1 not only offers a description of the world at the beginning, but also intimates a prescription for humanity. This sense of the prescriptive is evoked specifically in the Sabbath (Genesis 2:2) and the festivals (1:14) and more broadly in the proper sense of separation of time and space, perhaps embodied as well in the priestly dietary practice (kashrut). This combination of description and prescription in Genesis 1 is central to understanding this account. It offers both a description of the world and humanity and a prescription for humanity's place in this world. In other words, Genesis 1 combines an understanding of reality with an understanding of proper action on the part of humans. This combination of the prescriptive and descriptive is, in philosophical terms, a combination of the ontological and the ethical, what reality is and how humanity is to act. In this combination, Genesis 1 offers a sort of systematic vision of reality in narrative form. This linkage of the prescriptive and descriptive, of ontology and human behavior, may be the first of its kind in ancient Israel.[129] We see no other creation text in the Bible making this sort of linkage of what I am calling here the descriptive and prescriptive. At the same time, I am not claiming either that this vision is complete, or that it even addresses most aspects of reality or human action.

At the same time, Genesis 1 sets the stage for addressing further matters, which is what the rest of the Bible attends to. Indeed, as we will see in the next chapter, whatever priestly hand wrote Genesis 1, the head of the priestly work[130] already envisioned Genesis 1 as setting the course for the descriptive and prescriptive. This function for the account was enhanced further when it came to serve as the head not only to the priestly work of the Pentateuch, but also as the head of the Bible as a whole. Genesis 1 is about the beginning, and its place at the head of the Bible is a crucial matter for fully understanding Genesis 1. Part 2 of this study is devoted to addressing the significance of the position of Genesis 1 at the head of the Bible.

Part Two

Literary Issues Concerning Genesis 1 and its Position in the Hebrew Bible

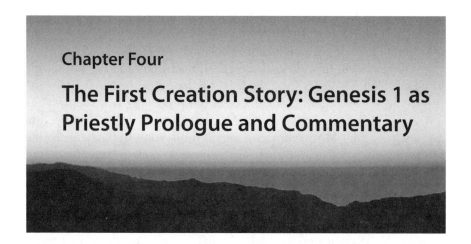

Chapter Four

The First Creation Story: Genesis 1 as Priestly Prologue and Commentary

Up this point, we have studied priestly terms and ideas in Genesis 1. What we have not discussed yet is how the priestly writer went about composing Genesis 1. This will be the concern of the present chapter. In looking at Genesis 1 from the perspective of its composition, we may appreciate its priestly vision even more. To begin the inquiry of this chapter, we may ask what the priestly author knew of other traditional narratives, and how this writer worked with and in reaction to them. As one case of priestly narrative, how did Genesis 1 fit into this larger genre?

In his book *Reading the Fractures of Genesis*,[1] David M. Carr notes that the priestly source was combined with the so-called Yahwist (known as "J") source in the editorial compilation (or redaction) of the Pentateuch, that is, the first five books of the Bible. Carr views this edition (or redaction) as priestly, as do many other critics. He also suggests, following the well-known theory of biblical criticism called the Documentary Hypothesis, that the Yahwist source was also independently known to the priestly source (known as "P").[2] Carr then raises important questions for understanding the priestly material: How was J known to P? Was the form of J in written form, oral form, or both? How and who was transmitting J as it became accessible to P? Finally, what is P doing at least in Genesis 1, considering that this text is being composed in light of his knowledge of J? Since these questions involve the activity of scribes who wrote texts in ancient Israel, they necessarily lead to other questions. What was the context of the scribal operation that produced Genesis 1? How did it operate? With these questions in mind, we shift our attention from looking at various details in Genesis 1 to exploring the process of how it was composed by its author. Compared with identifying and discussing priestly themes and vocabulary in Genesis 1, the question of its composition is more challenging terrain.

We may begin to address these questions by considering the setting in which Genesis 1 was produced. It was based on our analysis of the priestly terms and ideas that we saw in the preceding two chapters. As a result of this analysis, we concluded that Genesis 1 was produced in a priestly setting. Most scholars imagine the setting to have involved a scribe or scribes who worked in priestly circles in ancient Israelite society. From the Bible, we can see instances where the same person performed the two roles of priest and scribe. The figure of Ezra comes to mind; he was both priest and scribe (see, for example, 7:11; Neh. 8:2, 4, 9). Over the course of the Israelite and Judean monarchies (1000–586 BCE) and later in the Persian period (540–322 BCE), the priestly scribal tradition collected various texts, some of which may have had an extant oral tradition alongside the written form. In the first section of this chapter, we will look briefly at scribal practices generally as they are attested in ancient Israel. The second section addresses priestly scribal practice in particular. The third and final section turns to the scribal production of Genesis 1, and especially examines how this account may serve as the priestly prologue[3] to what follows in Genesis and as a sort of implicit priestly "commentary" on the so-called "second" creation account of Genesis 2:4 through the end of Genesis 3.

1. The Scribal Background of Biblical Texts

Understanding how biblical texts were written involves recognizing a variety of operations undertaken by scribes. These include two complementary foci: writing and interpretation, on the one hand, and reading and memorization on the other. In their work, scribes performed all these input and output operations.[4] Oral tradition embedded in Israel's collective memory alongside older written texts served as sources for scribal work. These foundational traditions were further accompanied by interpretations to these traditional texts that scribes may themselves have added. Scribes knew older texts from their circles and sometimes from other traditions, and they would draw on these textual materials to shape their own writings. They would not infrequently add their "takes" on various traditions as they had inherited them and knew them. We have already seen how Genesis 1 uses a number of priestly terms and ideas, and that has led us to conclude, as the previous chapters have made clear, that the composer of Genesis 1 was familiar with the priestly tradition.

Within the confines of a single chapter, it is impossible to do justice to all of these scribal operations; that would be a book in itself. Thankfully, two recent studies have addressed these questions in depth, and interested readers are advised to consult these.[5] The first is yet another book by the prolific scholar, David M. Carr, entitled *Writing on the Tablet of the Heart: Origins of Scripture and Literature*.[6] Carr emphasizes the role that memorization took in scribal training in ancient Near Eastern cultures, including Israel. He provides textual evidence of how scribes learned texts by heart in large measure through copying them. In a sense, scribes became the living repositories of memorized texts, and writing out the texts helped them to achieve this capacity.[7] According to Carr, written texts were aids for the memorized texts learned by scribes, and to some degree, written literary texts were the by-product more than the end-product of scribal memorization.[8]

The second book is Karel van der Toorn's *Scribal Culture and the Making of the Hebrew Bible*.[9] Van der Toorn summarizes the ancient Near Eastern and biblical evidence for scribal activity, and he offers detailed studies of the books of Deuteronomy and Jeremiah as scribal productions. The scribal additions to these two biblical works and in other ancient Near Eastern literary texts are very nicely drawn out by van der Toorn. He shows how these additions do not just add more content to the works, but also add interpretations of the works to which they are added. Furthermore, van der Toorn brilliantly sketches out a cultural history of the idea of divine revelation in Mesopotamian and Israelite scribal circles.[10] The discussion that follows in this chapter draws and builds on these two studies.

As a part of scribal learning, many, or perhaps all, texts were memorized at various levels of detail. Not a great deal is known about the scribal practice of memorization in ancient Israel, but some glimpses are available. One example involves a letter that comes from the site of Lachish in Judah (designated "Lachish Letter 3" by scholars). I provide a translation of part of the letter here with the line numbers in parentheses:[11]

> (4) Now open (5) please the eyes of (i.e., explain for) your servant about the letter that (6) my lord sent to your servant yesterday, for the heart (7) of your servant has been sick ever since you sent (it) to[12] (8) your servant.
>
> My lord said: "You don't know how (9) to read a letter."[13]
>
> As the Lord lives, no one has tried (10) to read me a letter.
>
> Moreover, (11) as for any letter that comes to me, if I have read it, (12) [the]n I can recite[14] it, (down) to any pa[rt[15]].

Lines 9-10 of this letter stress the recipient's claim that he has the ability to read documents sent to him. Lines 11-12 go on to illustrate the practice of reading together with verbal recitation. It is important to note at this point that this passage in the letter assumes a kind of middle ground in regard to memorization. Otherwise, the claim to recitation would simply be an assertion of being able to read, and the letter has already made that point. My emphasizing this point about the letter's implicit acknowledgement of memorization as a piece of the scribal practice might seem to put too much weight on a point made only in passing. After all, this passage from Lachish Letter 3 generally stresses the administrator's ability to read, not to recite from heart. Yet what is only a passing reference may betray what was generally taken for granted in scribal practice: memorization is assumed to be a part of the process of learning texts. The letter may be all the more revealing for what it assumed.

Other Lachish letters also mention the scribal aspect of the administrator's job. On Lachish Letter 4 (lines 3-4), Dennis Pardee comments: "The most likely interpretation is that the author of Lachish 4 was required to keep a running record of his official activities on a papyrus scroll with a column (*dlt*, Jer. 36:23) devoted to each set of orders."[16] Lachish Letter 5 (lines 3-7) adds a mention of the circulation of texts. These letters taken together suggest the scribal practice of reading, writing, memorizing and transmitting at a regional administrative site. All of these tasks presuppose that a competent administrator is able not only to read texts, but also to recite them by heart.

Biblical evidence suggests that this competence in reading and memorizing is a professional one extending beyond administrative functions or the genre of letters. We also see reading and memorization in the wisdom literature of the Bible. Proverbs 22:17-20 constructs an "anatomy" of scribal memorization and recitation (with parts of the body put in italics in the translation):

> Turn your *ear* and listen to the sages' words,
> And set your *heart* to my knowledge.
> For it is good that you guard them in your *belly*,
> They be together fixed on your *lips*,
> That your trust may be in[17] the Lord;
> I have informed[18] you today, indeed, you!
> Indeed,[19] I have written for you thirty[20] in counsel and knowledge.

The ear is the entry-point for texts that reach the heart.[21] There in the belly or innards they are stored; in other words, they are memorized.[22] In fixed verbal form they are recited on the lips. Knowledge embodied in sayings are in effect memorized internally and recited externally; the two processes complement one another. This piece of wisdom literature, as well as wisdom literature more broadly, represents important evidence for scribal memorization among sages.

The professional scribal praxis informed a range of texts beyond royal administration or wisdom circles. Earlier premonarchic culture had been primarily, but not exclusively oral. The verb "to recite" (*thny* referred to memorized oral recitation, sometimes without reference to written texts (Jdg. 5:11, 11:40).[23] Oral tradition was widespread in early Israel, and it was augmented by the new prestigious technology of writing developing especially from the eighth century BCE onwards.[24] By the time of the sixth century, we see in Lachish Letter 3 reading and writing as components in the process of memorization and recitation. From the eighth century (Isaiah) through the sixth century (Jeremiah and Ezekiel), prophetic accounts suggest a range of scribal activities that combine reading, memorization, writing and interpretation.[25] Some sixth century prophecy (Isaiah 40–55, Second Isaiah) shows an orientation around reading, interpretation, and writing (with arguably little or no component of oral composition).[26] Liturgical texts combining memory and writing can be discerned in the reuse of texts over time. For example, the early Psalm 29:1-2 was reused in the later Psalm 96, and then in 1 Chronicles 16.[27] The longer narrative texts of Genesis through Deuteronomy and Joshua through 2 Kings (the latter often called "the Deuteronomistic History") involved the compilation and redaction of older written sources;[28] they may have also included works known orally. In short, various combinations of reading, writing, interpretation, and memorization are represented in the Bible.

2. The Priestly, Scribal Context of Genesis 1

This brief survey provides some background for understanding the priestly scribal milieu of Genesis 1. To imagine the priestly context, we may think in terms of a priestly tradition at work for hundreds of years, beginning as early as the eighth century BCE (if not earlier) and lasting well into the Roman period when the Jerusalem Temple was destroyed in 70 CE. This priesthood maintained the routine of sacrifices and the cultic calendar at the Jerusalem Temple, and it was responsible for producing texts that helped to serve these priestly functions. In their situation, priestly writers worked with texts accessible to them through several written traditions as well as various oral channels. A wide variety of works would have been available to the priestly scribal tradition, as well as the esoteric knowledge transmitted within priestly lines (as we noted at the end of chapter 2). The book of Ezekiel is a particularly rich source in this regard. As we noted earlier, Ezekiel was a priest by background, and he drew on a very wide range of sources, including the mythology of Israel's Phoenician neighbors (see Ezekiel 28). Various written and oral sources were coming to be read and examined by priestly traditions, which is evident in Jerusalem from the late seventh century (Jeremiah), into the sixth century (Ezekiel) and beyond (late additions to Ezekiel 40–48).

Over the late seventh and sixth centuries BCE, texts and traditions were read by scribes with greater scrutiny and perhaps with more technical sophistication. In this context, issues of interpretation were raised explicitly at this time. The Bible contains explicit reflections on interpretation focusing on a number of topics.[29] One involves prophecy given in the name of Yahweh that, in the view of the biblical writers and editors, is to be regarded as false. With slightly different variations, Deuteronomy 18:20 as well as Jeremiah 14:14 and 29:23 refer to prophecy given in the name of Yahweh as that "which I did not command." The evaluation of false and true prophecy was already a long-standing issue in the period of the monarchy. With this expression, "which I did not command," these passages are refuting the claim that the prophecies in question were commanded by God. In other words, they question some commandments given through prophets that had been accepted by others as true prophecy. In short, the phrase "which I did not command" questions the commandment as it was understood at the time.

Another set of passages applies the same sort of condemnation to child sacrifice.[30] Jeremiah 7:31, 19:5, and 32:35 denounce the practice as one "which I [God] did not command" (or "never commanded," NJPS) and "which did not ascend to my heart" (that is, "never entered my mind"). In its representation of the divine role in the law of child sacrifice, Ezekiel 20:25-26 goes further than either Jeremiah 7:31, 19:5, or 32:35 by telling its audience that Israel's God "gave them statutes that were not good and rules by which they would not live."[31] These biblical expressions about God's view of child sacrifice seem to be addressing what their authors evidently thought was the wrong understanding of the law of the sacrifice of the firstborn, as expressed, for example, in Exodus 22:28.[32] More specifically, the aim of Ezekiel apparently was to dispute and disavow an interpretation of Exodus 22:28 (or the like) that would apply the law of the sacrifice of the firstborn to humans.

In the case of these condemnations of child sacrifice, the authors are arguing not only about the authority of an older text, but also about its interpretation, which had become part of their tradition surrounding authoritative texts. These later authors cannot just change the older text presumably due partially to the broadly recognized weight of tradition that has legitimized them—at least in some eyes. Instead, they refute its divine character—not so much of the text itself, but of the way that it had been understood and interpreted. What people thought was commanded, it is now claimed, represents an incorrect understanding or interpretation of the commands. The strategy of characterizing these practices as one "which I did not command them," was also applied to the worship of other gods in Deuteronomy 17:3.[33] These references to laws "which I did not command" might seem at first to be a direct denial of the laws involved rather than an argument for a more careful and nuanced interpretation of them. Still, at this time, perhaps the distinction between text and its interpretation was not yet fully articulated.[34] Using this phrase, "which I did not command," seems to be one means by which these authors express their disagreement with a known, inherited interpretation of these laws that for some has genuine authority but whose authority they wish to question.[35]

This expression of law that God says that God did not command dates to the late seventh and sixth centuries BCE.[36] This was the period when a concern was developing over how older texts may and arguably should be read. These passages in Deuteronomy, Jeremiah, and Ezekiel are among the earliest texts[37] that explicitly raise the problem of interpretation of biblical laws, and all of them may be traced to various priestly backgrounds in this period. We should perhaps further connect this development with the scribal production of prophecy and law in ancient Judah in the seventh and sixth centuries; in other words, interpretation in these texts developed in combination with their production. It may be that this scribal context engendered a sense of textual interpretation in a manner not as critically apparent as in earlier periods. This juncture in Israel's textual culture also marks the growing importance of writing in general and also for Israel's sacred traditions emerging in *written* Scriptures.[38]

In this context, we may imagine scribal training organized within priestly family lines. This is so during the postexilic period (for example, the families of scribes named in 1 Chronicles 2:55), and it was probably the case earlier as well.[39] Within priestly traditions, there are signs of different priestly lines engaged in scribal transmission: Levites, or "the sons of Levi," responsible for transmitting books such as Psalms and perhaps

Deuteronomy (see also the Levites in Nehemiah 8:8[40] and Ezra 9:5); Aaronids, or "the sons of Aaron," authors of priestly laws in Exodus, Leviticus, and Numbers as well as priestly narrative in Genesis and elsewhere; and "Zadokites," or "the sons of Zadok," the lineage of Ezekiel and probably responsible for producing the so-called Holiness Code of Leviticus 17–26 as well as the holiness redaction of the Pentateuch.[41] It is the latter two priestly families that drafted ritual prescriptions or instructions for the maintenance of sacrificial practice. Priestly scribes drafted texts for rituals, as we see for sacrifices delineated in Leviticus 1–7.[42] They also wrote out ritual instructions for the calendar of offerings, for example in Leviticus 23 and Numbers 28–29. They also drafted priestly instructions for other matters (see Leviticus 8–9), including the instructions for the Tabernacle and its furnishings (Exodus 25–31). Such priestly endeavors, of course, had significant impact on the crafting of the creation narrative of Genesis 1, as seen from the priestly perspective. In chapters 2 and 3, we paid considerable attention to parallels between the creation of the world in Genesis 1 and the building of the Tabernacle in Exodus 39–40. In these chapters, we also noted a number of parallels between Genesis 1 and ritual and priestly ideas in other biblical books. There is every likelihood that the industry of priestly scribes played a decisive role in the development of these conceptual linkages.

Informed by the style of ritual material,[43] the priestly tradition also developed narratives that reflected their ritualistic concerns. Through these narratives, matters of ritual prescription were grounded in a literary context. It seems that some narratives were added with ritual prescriptions that treat the same theme. For example, the narrative of the building of the tabernacle in Exodus 35–40 mostly follows the ritual instructions of Exodus 25–31. Similarly, the story of Nadab and Abihu in Leviticus 10 seems to be set out as an illustration for Leviticus 9. In addition, when the ritual texts were given a narrative context, they were elaborated with quotations of divine speech as well as other literary features.[44]

In the context of this scribal activity, the priestly tradition of Israel developed its versions of the major events of the foundational narrative in the Pentateuch. It is difficult to know exactly how this priestly narrative developed. This has been a matter of considerable discussion, as reflected in Carr's work, *Reading the Fractures of Genesis*,[45] and Erhard Blum's study, *Studien zur Komposition des Pentateuch*.[46] These two scholars differ over the nature the priestly narrative material. Carr favors the idea of a preexisting, separate priestly document, while Blum sees the priestly material not as a full-blown independent composition, but a series of preliminary drafts or sketches incorporated and refined in the eventual priestly redaction. (Because there may not be a full-scale separate priestly source paralleling the J source,[47] I am inclined to Blum's view on this point, but this is a difficult question, and scholars are understandably divided over the issue.) It is possible that such drafts might have been composed for the purposes of priestly instruction,[48] a role of priests that we noted in chapter 2. At some point (or at various points), they were incorporated into the larger narrative as we have it in the Pentateuch.[49] Sometimes these versions were spliced in with other nonpriestly material, for example, in the flood narrative of Genesis 6–9 with its alternation of priestly "P" material and the so-called "Yahwist" source. In contrast, the priestly account of the covenant in Genesis 17 stands in parallel with the nonpriestly text of Genesis 15. In other cases, the priestly tradition tailored its version to the narrative contexts in still other ways. In the case of Genesis 1, it would appear to have been written to serve as a prologue to Genesis 2 and following, as several scholars have noted.[50]

To offer a little further background to this picture of the priestly, scribal tradition so deeply entrenched in the Pentateuch, we may briefly note and compare priestly scribal practices as known from a series of Ugaritic ritual texts. Of course, there are some significant differences between Ugaritic ritual texts and priestly Pentateuchal narrative. For example, according to Dennis Pardee, these Ugaritic priestly texts focusing on sacrificial rituals were produced in a relatively short compass of time: "It appears likely the sacrificial texts reflect precise situations and that the vast majority of them date, therefore, to the last years of the kingdom of Ugarit (i.e., to the years 1200-1185 in round figures)."[51] So the time frame for this corpus is quite short when compared with the Israelite priestly tradition. Pardee further notes that these Ugaritic texts do not constitute a "library."[52] He comments:

> The sacrificial texts are virtually all prescriptive, laying out a series of acts to be performed over a period of time that may extend from one day to two months. They appear, therefore, to reflect the impact on daily practice of an oral priestly tradition: someone dictated (or some talented priest wrote out himself) the cultic procedures to be followed during the upcoming period.[53]

In other words, the Ugaritic sacrificial texts largely "reflect daily religious practice"[54] in a far more specific fashion than do comparable priestly texts in the Bible. The Ugaritic sacrificial texts also lack a priestly calendar of sacrifices of the sort that we see in Leviticus 23 or Numbers 28–29. As ritual prescriptions for the most part, the Ugaritic material also lacks narrative elaborations (contrast the biblical descriptions of the figures of God, Moses, and Aaron) or divine speeches that we see in biblical ritual texts.[55]

Despite these significant differences, we can note some features of the Ugaritic texts that can be helpful for understanding priestly material in the Bible. We may also take note of Ugaritic administrative texts that deal with similar subject matter. The style of these administrative texts resembles the sacrificial lists, and so these lists may be regarded as a form of priestly administration.[56] Such a "list style" of administrative proceedings also underlies a number of texts that we have in priestly sections of the Pentateuch, for example, the census lists of Numbers 1 and 26 (compare also the list style employed in Joshua 12:9-24).

Taken together, these Ugaritic sacrificial and administrative texts offer some help for understanding the development of the priestly instructional literature preserved in the Bible. The Israelite priestly tradition may have started out largely as oral tradition about ritual prescriptions for sacrifices and other matters. In Israel, this tradition began to be committed to writing initially during the monarchy. It developed and expanded into cultic calendars and prescriptions for other areas of priestly life, as well as literary representations of these priestly matters. The written priestly traditions that we now find in the Bible perhaps began much as what we see in the Ugaritic ritual texts, but over the course of centuries this material substantially developed in ancient Israel. This is true most notably in the prescriptive rituals of Leviticus 1–7, which show considerable elaboration beyond what we see in the Ugaritic ritual texts.[57] The result was an entire "priestly instructional literature," which has its own editorial additions,"[58] and other editorial touches.[59]

By way of contrast, Ugaritic also helps to put into context the biblical narratives about priestly matters, as well as priestly narratives of major events in Israel's national or foundational story in the Pentateuch. On the one hand, Ugaritic narrative literature offers important parallels to Israel's older poetic tradition, for example, in Judges 5,[60] and the style of stories in the so-called the "Yahwist" and "Elohist" sources.[61] On the other hand, the style of priestly narrative literature[62] represents a departure from what we see in the Ugaritic narrative literature. This includes the creation story of Genesis 1.[63] We see the priestly worldview of its ritual within this narrative, which is particularly evident from a comparison of Exodus 35–40, which generally follows the ritual prescriptions for the

Tabernacle in Exodus 25–31.[64] In short, Genesis 1 is a priestly narrative of the divine construction of the universe informed by priestly ritualistic concerns.

The priestly narrative style seems to come by way of priestly ritual style and background. This ritual sensibility seems to have informed Genesis 1's style. Thus, the seven days of the festivals may have given rise to the idea of the structure of seven days in Genesis 1.[65] The account's literary architecture combines repetition from day to day, and at the same time it varies this expression between days. This style seems to echo the repetition of rituals, with their counting of days and their repetitions of various actions. Even with their variations within repetition, the formulations of the days and their counting, not to mention their blessing, casts God in the role of the priest of his cosmic temple, namely the universe. This ritual, priestly background may be the inspiration for the repetitive and precise style of formulation in Genesis 1. This narrative is thus better seen as having emerged out of the tradition of priestly ritual literature[66] and not from traditional folkloristic literature. This does not mean that the priestly tradition ignored such traditional storytelling, whether in poetry or prose. Indeed, a good case has been made for Genesis 1 as showing the rhythm of biblical poetry, such as we see in traditional biblical hymns.[67] At the same time, the composer of Genesis 1 arguably drew as well on the rhythm of ritual.

In a broader context, Genesis 1 serves as a new prologue to the Pentateuch more broadly.[68] This sort of scribal creation is evident elsewhere in the biblical corpus. For example, scholars have long noted that Deuteronomy 1:1—4:43 constitutes a new prologue, added before 4:44, which is clearly designed to provide verse 44 ("This is the teaching that Moses set before the Israelites") and all that follows with a new context.[69] Indeed, perhaps this verse was the very model for Deuteronomy 1:1: "These are the words that Moses spoke to all Israel." Scholars commonly regard Judges 1:1—2:5 as a new introduction inserted into the older narrative that ran from the end of Joshua to the old beginning of Judges at 2:6.[70] The new introductory material helps to set up the picture of Israel's idolatry (see especially 2:1-5), which was central to the later edition of the book of Judges. Scholars have noted this sort of scribal production of a new prologue in ancient Near Eastern works outside the Bible as well. A famous case is the opening of Gilgamesh in its Middle Babylonian and Standard Babylonian versions, which add a perspective on wisdom, death, and immortality absent from the Old Babylonian introduction to the text.[71] Genesis 1 thus fits in with these cases where new prologues have been added to the beginning of preexisting narratives.

At the same time, Genesis 1 was designed to be more than a new initial piece. It provides both a new prologue and a new concept to the older narrative. Critics have long noted the dense and deliberate character of this text, which reflects its role as an introduction. In his commentary on Genesis, Gerhard von Rad expressed his sense of the chapter: "Gen. ch. I. . . is Priestly doctrine—indeed, it contains the essence of Priestly knowledge in a most concentrated form. . . . Nothing is here by chance."[72] William Brown comments similarly: "No other text is so densely structured in the Hebrew Bible; every word seems to bear the mark of extensive reflection."[73] In its compactness, Genesis 1 as a textual composition responds to a variety of religious and cultural matters, and part of its response likely was to older texts, as we saw in chapter 1.

In this respect, Genesis 1 includes what we might regard as an early sort of implicit "commentary" on the material that immediately follows. Scholars normally reserve this term for ancient texts such as the so-called Qumran *peshers* and volumes found in medieval Jewish and Christian tradition as well as modern commentary series. Such commentaries offer explicit exposition on a biblical text, often by way of a word-to-word or verse-by-verse commentary. We generally think of commentary as being later than the Hebrew Bible. At the same time, we may note that commentary in a preliminary form appears in technical literature already in the Late Bronze Age.[74] Dream omen literature at Ugarit provides details of dreams, followed by interpretation introduced by the term "word." This "word" has been compared with the use of the term "interpretation" (*pesher*) or "its interpretation" (*pishro*) in the Dead Sea Scrolls. Such *pesher* texts introduce a comment on a prior text, usually a scriptural work of the prophets and Psalms.[75] Between the time of the Ugaritic texts and the Dead Sea Scrolls, priestly literature as we see in the Bible developed an implicit or rudimentary form of narrative commentary,[76] which indicates that the priestly authors were keenly sensitive in interpreting prior literature that priestly tradition had inherited.

Commentary, as we see in the context of biblical texts such as Genesis 1, belongs to the larger activity of scribal transmission that involved reading, writing, memorizing, and reciting. If I may be permitted to use the word commentary not only as a particular genre but also for denoting conscious wordings mindful of other texts, then the word commentary may be applied to Genesis 1. This chapter shows the use of specific words and themes in response to another text that its author knew and "commented on," namely Genesis 2:4b and following. In a broad sense, this "commentary" involves formulations that comment specifically on the text with which the writer was dialoguing. Using the term "commentary" for this method of composition has the particular virtue of capturing the specific priestly use of verbal resonances between Genesis 1:1—2:3 and Genesis 2:4b and following.

3. Genesis 1 as Implicit Commentary in Narrative Form

The specific frame of reference for the narrow commentary of Genesis 1:1—2:4a is Genesis 2:4b and following, as we discussed above. Many commentators have remarked upon the relationship of these two creation accounts in the wake of classic source-critical divisions between these two texts. The models of editorial activity used by scholars as different as Gerhard von Rad, Brevard Childs, Richard Elliott Friedman, Erhard Blum, and David Carr would see verbal relationships operative in Genesis 1:1—2:3 relative to Genesis 2:4b and following. For example, Carr believes that the P account was placed "before the non-P account it was designed to replace."[77] I would put the point a little differently. To my mind, the effect was not so much to replace but rather more to redirect and refocus the audience's attention by giving the initial account pride of place. In doing so, Genesis 1 offers room for further clarifying commentary in a manner that we will now discuss.

We may begin by considering how the two narratives were tied together. It has often been argued that the two creation accounts were connected by means of an editorial link between the story in Genesis 1:1—2:4a and the story in 2:4b and following.[78] In this respect, the two halves of Genesis 2:4, that is verse 4a and verse 4b, serve as a kind of editorial hinge. This requires a little explanation. Genesis 2:4a contains a genealogical heading ("generations," *toledot*), as we also see in Genesis 5:1; 6:9; 10:1; 11:10, 27; 25:12, 19; 36:19, and 37:2.[79] This would suggest that 2:4a is designed to serve as the first of these other genealogical headings,[80] and that it is itself the first of these. In other words, Genesis 2:4a now stands as the head text of the generations of creation. To establish a frame for the whole story of Genesis 1:1—2:4a, verse 2:4a adopts the order of "heaven and earth" found in 1:1. To connect 1:1—2:4a with the story of verse 2:4b and following, verse 2:4a refers to creation as the "generations (*toledot*) of heaven and earth." In this respect, verse 2:4a indicates that what came before serves as prologue to what comes after. As a result, Genesis 1:1—2:3 conveys the meaning of the order of creation of "heaven and earth" in 2:4b and serves as its prologue. The implied commentary is that the generations of later genealogies are integrally related to the generations of heaven and earth in 1:1—2:4a.[81] Since *toledot* is a priestly term, the choice of this particular word shows a priestly hand at work in Genesis 2:4a. This priestly compiler and editor added Genesis 2:4a to link the two creation stories of Genesis 1–2, and in turn both narratives are linked to the rest of Genesis in characterizing it as "generations," a term woven into the fabric of the rest of the book.

The role of commentary is not confined to the editorial addition of Genesis 2:4a.[82] The text of 1:1—2:3 also functions as commentary.[83] The verbal affinities between the so-called "two creation accounts" noted by a number of scholars[84] point to commentary being made by Genesis 1:1—2:3 on Genesis 2:4b and following. Following the lead of earlier commentators, a number of observations can be made in regard to possible implicit "commentary" found in the first account in reference to the second. Proceeding roughly in order of the verses, we may note the following.

"Heavens and Earth" in 1:1 as Comment on "Earth and Heaven" in 2:4b

We have already touched on the reversal of creation in 1:1 and 2:4a ("heavens and earth") in contrast to verse 4b ("earth and heavens"). As many commentators have long recognized, there is a particular verbal affinity between Genesis 1:1 and 2:4b. Ephraim Speiser in noting the connection states: "the difference is by no means accidental."[85] Claus Westermann thinks that, "since v 4b clearly refers to Gen 1 and is similar to the introduction, 1:1, it can be understood as a prefix which makes it easier to join Gen 2–3 to Gen 1."[86] Westermann then cites a statement of Werner Schmidt: "It forms a transition from the priestly to the Yahwistic story of creation."[87] In his discussion of the change in viewpoint from God the Creator in Genesis 1 to humanity in 2:4b and following, Nahum Sarna similarly observes: "This shift in perspective and emphasis is signaled by the inversion of the regular sequence 'heaven and earth' in the opening sentence."[88] David Carr comments on Schmidt's view:

> Certainly one verse seems to have been formed in light of the other. Nevertheless, Schmidt's hypothesis would not explain why such a transition does not more closely match the text with which it links. Whereas Gen. 1:1 talks of the "creation" of "heavens and earth," Gen. 2:4b speaks of the "making" of "earth and heaven." If 2:4b had been designed to resume 1:1 in a single narrative line, it probably would have been closer in terminology and order. As it is, Gen. 2:4b appears to have been the model for 1:1, and 1:1 in turn was originally meant to stand separately from the verse on which it was

modeled [namely 2:4b], as a distinctly different beginning to a P primeval history.[89]

Carr's view rightly notes that the differences between the wordings of the two openings is intentional and meant to draw contrast as much as it is to form a transition. He is particularly correct in seeing the modeling of Genesis 1:1 on 2:4b. In this modeling, one can see an implicit sort of "commentary."

What most critics recognize is how the two openings function to connect the two passages. The priestly author knew the order "earth and heavens," a phrase also known elsewhere.[90] This order corresponds to the earthly perspective of Genesis 2:4b-24. The priestly author of Genesis 1 switched the order of these words, giving a different emphasis to mark the whole of the passage. The purpose of this commentary, as we noted above, was to redirect the readers' overall view of Genesis 1–2 first toward heaven and then to earth. Instead of starting with earth as in Genesis 2:4b with its terrestrial and anthropomorphic presentation, Genesis 1:1 informs its audience that the initial moment of creation is located in the "heavens"; it is cosmic in its orientation. If this view of the differences in word-order is correct, then Genesis 1:1 represents a deliberate comment on 2:4b.

Sometimes commentators view the outcome of this literary activity that produced a literary whole as an original literary whole. In assuming that Genesis 1–2 was originally a literary whole, some commentators interpret 2:4 also as a whole and do not see 2:4a as the end of the first account (or a sentence linking the two accounts) and 2:4b as the beginning of the second account. In his support of this view, Nahum Sarna appeals to the arguments that, if the verse is taken as a whole, the verse contains a nice chiasm of "the heavens and the earth" (2:4a) and "earth and heavens" (2:4b).[91] Sarna assumes that chiasm constitutes evidence for unitary authorship rather than sophisticated literary editorial handling.[92] However, taking the two halves of the verse as a literary whole overlooks differences between the formulations. If the same author wrote both halves of 2:4, why does 2:4a have definite articles ("the") on "the heavens and the earth," while 2:4b lacks them in the formulation, "earth and heavens"? What Sarna believes constituted a single composition of Genesis 1–2 was a matter of editorial commentary.[93] In other words, we have in Genesis 1–2 what Luis Alonso Schökel has called "secondary unity": "A later writer could take already completed pieces and bring them together skillfully to form a new and complex unity."[94]

"In beginning of" (*bere'shit*) in 1:1 and
"on the day of" (*beyom*) in 2:4b

The implicit commentary does not end with the phrases "the heavens and the earth" in 1:1 and 2:4a versus "earth and heavens" in 2:4b. Other features in Genesis 1:1-3 seem to play off of Genesis 2:4b-6. One involves the form of the sentence. Genesis 1 begins with a word that corresponds in structure to the opening of 2:4b. The composer of Genesis 1:1 chose "in beginning of" (*bere'shit*) matching "on the day of" (*beyom*) in 2:4b. So here we see modeling.[95] At the same time, the actual word in 1:1 is not "day," but "beginning," and this raises the question of what the priestly author was aiming for in selecting this wording instead. We see the specific word *bere'shit* in 1:1 in other creation accounts that have a primordial and cosmic perspective. For example, it appears in Proverbs 8:22:[96] "The Lord created me at (or as) the beginning (*re'shit*) of his way."[97] So what's going on? It would seem that the priestly writer of Genesis 1 picked up *beyom* from 2:4b and used it as a unit of time for the structure of the seven days, which was traditional in priestly thinking and in older West Semitic texts.[98] In addition, in order to provide a more profoundly grand perspective, he selected the word *re'shit* for Genesis 1:1 because of its primordial and cosmic connotation, as seen in other cosmically oriented biblical texts.

"To Create" (**br'*) in Genesis 1:1 and "to Make" (**'sh*) in 2:4b

Another feature that may be an example of "implicit commentary" involves the use of the verb "to create" (**br'*) in 1:1, compared with "to make" (**'sh*) in 2:4b. The first verb is used for activity exercised only by the deity (e.g., Num. 16:30; Ps. 51:12; Is. 42:15, 43:1, 45:18),[99] as opposed to the second verb, which may be used of either divinities or humans. We do have the verb, "to make," in Genesis 1. However, for acts of creation it is limited to days 2, 4, and 6 (see also 2:2 and 2:3). In contrast, the verb, "to create," is more extensive, used once for the creation of sea creatures on day 5 (1:21) and three times for humanity on day 6 (1:27). It also frames the story (1:1 and 2:3-4). The important use of the verb, "to create," makes a commentary about the cosmic profile of the deity. In other words, this creation is a particular activity of the deity unlike what humans do when they make things. In a sense, the initial verb of creation, "to create" (**br'*), announces at the outset in Genesis 1:1 the divine role throughout, even as the chapter employs additional terms. In also using both "to create" and "to make," Genesis 1 also generates an impression of continuity with Genesis 2:4b-24. In sum, Genesis 1 gives its own priestly imprint on creation by using "to create"; yet by using "to make," it suggests that it is fundamentally related to the second creation account.

"Earth" and "face" in 1:2 and 2:5-6

We may suspect another instance of modeling behind the imagery of cosmic water in 1:2 compared with watered desert portrayed in 2:5-6.[100] The difference directs the attention of the audience to a cosmic perspective in Genesis 1. The phrasing of Genesis 1:2 perhaps echoes the phrasing of 2:5-6:

Genesis 1:2

and *the earth* was void and vacuum,
and darkness was over *the surface* (*face*) of the deep.
(*weha'ares* haytah tohu wabohu
wehoshek 'al-*peney* tehom.*)

Genesis 2:5-6

before any plant of the field was on *the earth* (*ha'ares*),
and before any grass of the field had sprouted,
for the Lord God had not sent rain on *the earth* (*ha'ares*),
and there was no human to till the ground;
and a stream would rise from *the earth*,
and would water the whole *surface* (*face*) of the ground.
(*we'ed ya'aleh min-ha'ares*
wehishqah 'et-kol-*peney*-ha'adamah.*)

I have put the terms shared by the two verses in italics (underlined in Hebrew). We may note that both accounts use the word, "earth," to characterize the situation at the beginning of creation, and both use the expression "surface of." Perhaps the use of "earth" in Genesis 2:5-6 informed its use in Genesis 1:2. The same might apply to "surface."[101]

As we discussed in chapter 2, Claus Westermann and David Tsumura, to name a few, have attempted to relate *tohu* to its use for desert imagery, as found in Deuteronomy 32:10, Job 6:18, and 12:24 (= Psalm 107:40).[102] Was Genesis 1:2 designed to conjure up the image of the desert implicit in 2:5 but on the cosmic plane? The use of *peney* (literally, "face of") in both sentences may signal deliberate echoing here. In any case, the comparison of the two verses highlights the cosmic perspective of 1:2 with its cosmic water above and below as opposed to the terrestrial water of 2:6, which simply come from below to the earth.[103] Perhaps then the mention of water in the two passages suggests that here 1:2 offers a comment on 2:6.[104]

The Creation of Humanity in 1:26-28 and in 2:7

The creation of the human person in the two accounts has generated a great deal of discussion.[105] The picture of God blowing the breath of life into the human person in Genesis 2:7 makes God sound like a human being giving mouth-to-mouth resuscitation. This highly tangible picture of the deity making humans out of the dirt of the earth, as we find in 2:7, appears also in texts from Mesopotamia, Egypt, and Israel.[106] In contrast, the priestly text of Genesis 1 does not represent God in such human terms (anthropomorphism).[107] The priestly text of Genesis 1 shies away from such a concrete depiction of God's creation of humanity.

Both creation accounts convey the idea that the human is connected to God in a fundamental manner. In Genesis 2:7, the breath of God connects the human person to God,[108] but it is clear that human is not God, as the dirt that forms the substance of human creation comes from the ground. To echo the Hebrew words of 2:7, the "human" (*'adam*) comes from the "humus" (or "ground," *'adamah*). In Genesis 1:26-27, the human is connected to God by virtue of being in the divine image and the likeness. At the same time, this image and likeness is not to be identified as God's own self. Phyllis Trible makes this point in connection with Genesis 1:27: "The identity of vocabulary, *God* and 'the image of *God*,' establishes a similarity in meaning at the same time that the word *the-image-of* stresses the difference between Creator and created."[109] Where the dirt from the ground distinguishes the human from God in Genesis 2, it is through the idea of the image that humanity is differentiated from God in Genesis 1. God's breath is the divine means for enlivening the human person in Genesis 2; it is the image and likeness of God after which humanity is patterned in Genesis 1. So in both presentations, the human person is fundamentally related to God, but the human person is not divine as such. The question that we need to consider is this: Why did the author of Genesis 1:26-27 use a different way to express both the connection and distinction between divinity and humanity in Genesis 2?

We can answer this question by looking more closely at the idea of the image and likeness. In chapter 3, we mentioned that the Aramaic portion of an Aramaic-Akkadian bilingual inscription found on a statue discovered at Tell Fekheriyeh uses both *dmwt'* (lines 1, 15) and *slm* (line 12; cf. *slmh* in line 16) for the king's image. Genesis 1:26-27 may have derived its language of image and likeness notion from a similar notion of statuary by employing terminology that both bears an official's image and serves to represent the official's presence in a given place; the discourse may also include cultic sensibilities that can be associated with religious statuary as well.[110] To judge how these terms are employed, human dominion in the form of rule and service in a particular location is how the human person is seen as being in the image and likeness of God. This idea of rule is also suggested by God's own words in verse 26 that precede the divine act of creating humanity: "Let us make the human in our image, according to our likeness, so that they may rule." The specific command that follows, "to be fruitful and multiply," is suggestive of a further, priestly sense of the image and likeness, namely that the human person is also a creator in a manner somewhat analogous to the divine creator.

Because its picture of the human emphasizes the image and likeness of God, Genesis 1:26-27 would seem to offer a deliberately different formulation that may serve as an implicit commentary on 2:7.[111] The priestly language of "image and likeness" in 1:26-27 was apparently designed to overshadow the overt anthropomorphism of God of Genesis 2:7 where God is portrayed as fashioning humanity out of dirt and blowing life-giving breath into it.[112] Perhaps the priestly author thought this image could be potentially misleading, especially if taken literally. With this different image, 1:26-27 offers an implicit clarification of 2:7 that tones down the perceived difficulty of its strong anthropomorphic representation of God without entirely discarding the point of its presentation[113] that humanity is integrally related to God, but not the same as God. As Wellhausen observed,[114] Genesis 1:27 sounds like a response to the presentation of humanity in Genesis 2–3.

We may add one final comparison between the two creation accounts that bears on the commentary in Genesis 2 employed to qualify Genesis 1:26-28. According to the account in Genesis 2:15, the Lord God settled the human in the garden of Eden "to work it" (le'obdah) and "to guard it" (leshomrah). This passage assumes that work is the primary purpose of human life. Such a concept hearkens back to the Mesopotamian creation account of *Atrahasis*,[115] which describes how humanity was created in order to work thereby relieving the gods of the burden of doing so. In contrast, the establishment of the Sabbath day in Genesis 2:2-3 portrays a God who rests from all his work like the gods in *Atrahasis;* yet it does more, for this description is also a prescription in the priestly worldview. Leviticus 23:3 reflects this understanding: "For six days work may be done, but on the seventh day there is to be a sabbath of complete rest as a sacred time; no work shall you do—it is a sabbath to Yahweh in all your dwellings." The Sabbath of the first creation account may in context reflect a response to Genesis 2:15, that the human person is commanded to "work" the garden and "guard" it. It is to be noted that there are no verbs for the human working. The human person might be made for work according to Genesis 1, but at best only implicitly and surely not on the seventh day. On that day, humanity participates in the very rest that is divine. Without this qualification, work might be implicitly seen as mandated in the garden of Eden seven days a week.

With these specific connections between the two creation accounts noted, let us step back and consider the larger picture. On the whole, the narrative in Genesis 2 is set on earth; the earthly level is the focus of the story. As readers imagine the narrative, creation is terrestrial; the action takes place in the garden. In contrast, the priestly writer offers a cosmic perspective, in beginning with the heavens and the primordial light, paralleled by the sun and the moon. As a whole, it builds a majestic literary architecture of cosmic wonder over the course of seven days. The ordered literary presentation of the creation recapitulates and creates a majestic and well-planned world in the imagination of its audience. As commentary, the priestly writer redirects the audience away from the earthly perspective of the Genesis 2 story and points it towards a majestic presentation of God as Creator of the entire cosmic universe beyond the ground-level view of the older account.

In this chapter, it is clear that we have moved quite a distance from the idea of commentary in a traditional sense. However, if it does nothing else, this discussion illustrates the sorts of literary transformations that the priestly author of Genesis 1 was effecting in understanding reality compared with Genesis 2 and other passages. Thomas Aquinas, the great medieval Christian philosopher, observed that the order of human discovery about reality in historical time is not the same as the order in reality (or nature).[116] In its composition and its placement in the Bible, Genesis 1 captures this paradox. For although Genesis 1 came at a later point in the order of historical composition (compared with many other creation accounts), it was given pride of first place in the Pentateuch, in what its compilers regarded as more properly reflecting the order of reality. This placement—and all that it represented hermeneutically—thus serves as one of the Bible's greatest acts of commentary.

Prior to Genesis 1, multiple creation accounts circulated both in Israel and elsewhere; we discussed Psalms 74 and 104 in chapter 1. Likewise in Mesopotamia there were multiple creation narratives. The positioning of Genesis 1 arguably represents a claim that it is to be seen as *the* creation story, not simply one more among many. It is not only first relative to the second creation story. It is first in the whole Bible, and so it stands on a level different from other accounts within the biblical corpus. Placement constitutes purpose, and the purpose in this case was to distinguish Genesis 1 from the various creation accounts—indeed, from any and all other accounts and narratives within what became the biblical corpus of sacred traditions. Up to this point, various creation accounts held relatively similar status, with the sense that they offer different but equally revered perspectives on divine creation. But the placement of Genesis 1 was designed to place it above all other accounts. Genesis 1 in its position stakes a claim to be *the* narrative on the topic of creation, in fact *the* standard account. In reacting to older versions of creation, Genesis 1 was, in a sense, about asserting a master-version of creation victorious over other versions.

The Bible ultimately became the home of different versions of creation as well as many other matters. It was the site where different views vied to influence religious thought in the turmoil of postexilic Israel. This textual struggle, as we might call it, in turn affected the representation of the Deity as remembered in later tradition. The Deity shifted in nature from the monarchic warrior king at war with dangerous cosmic rivals into the priestly Holy One who has no match and no rivals at all.[117] The battle of the warrior god over the divine foes functioned to proclaim royal power in monarchic Israel. In its version of creation, Genesis 1 served as a means of asserting priestly cultural and religious traditions compared with the royal model of divine conquest.[118] Genesis 1 drew on this older royal model yet subsumed it within its own priestly viewpoint. In textual terms, the priestly tradition[119] "defeated" the other versions of creation. In its final effect, it was intended as the first and only compared with all that follows, especially Genesis 2. Genesis 1 thus emerges in several respects as the one set above and before other texts; and so it has remained the standard up into our own time. It is "the" creation story that readers first think of from the Bible.

With this chapter, we have arrived at the end of our study of the priestly vision of Genesis 1. We have explored creation accounts and their various motifs in chapter 1, and we have considered the priestly vision of Genesis 1 in chapters 2 and 3. With chapter 4 here, we have come to understand how the priestly tradition produced this vision and how it gained its placement at the head of the Bible. This issue needs to be considered in light of one final question. Because it is in large part a modern problem, I have saved this question for chapter 5 in this study. The issue is this: despite the status of Genesis 1 as the first and best-known creation accounts of the Bible and despite the high esteem in which the Bible is held, many people today consider Genesis 1 a "myth."

For many people today, it seems little more than a quaint and outmoded "fairy tale" from the distant past, comparable to the mythical stories of Greece or Mesopotamia. Given the use of the comparative approach in this study, it is worth asking how Genesis 1 measures up to ancient myths. The meaning of the term "myth" and its scholarly application to ancient Near Eastern narratives and Genesis 1 are complex matters, and they deserve our careful consideration, as we will see in chapter 5.

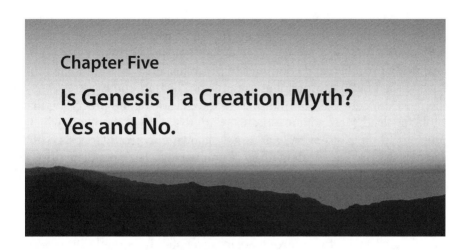

Chapter Five

Is Genesis 1 a Creation Myth? Yes and No.

1. Myth and its Modern Definers

Is Genesis 1 a myth? The answer to this question depends on what you think about myth and what you think about Genesis 1. If you view the Bible as sacred and authoritative for your religious practice, then the obvious answer would seem to be no, of course not. If you are a secular reader of the Bible, this is a question that you may take more seriously. Indeed, from the secular standpoint, the obvious may well be, yes, it is. Before either the religious or secular reader can answer this question, she or he must engage a more basic question: what do you think a myth is? In common American usage, a myth is first of all a story that refers to gods and goddesses in different societies. While a myth is also typically viewed as an important and compelling story, it also carries the connotation of an account that may not be true. The expression, "that's just a myth," conveys to people today the idea that a myth is a tale, maybe even a good tale, but also one that is of questionable authenticity.

For many readers of the Bible, the idea of biblical stories as myths became a critical issue because of the discovery of tablets with stories from ancient Mesopotamia. For centuries, the Bible was considered the word of God, but the stories found in much earlier texts emerging from excavations in Mesopotamia challenged the primacy and authenticity of such biblical narratives of the Bible. When the Bible was studied in the context of ancient Near Eastern literature during the nineteenth and twentieth centuries, it no longer seemed so easy to affirm its divine origins. Scholarly study of the Bible led to a reevaluation of the relationship of biblical literature to literature outside of and preceding the Bible. Ancient Near Eastern literature was obviously not to be considered divine revelation in Jewish or Christian traditions, yet if extrabiblical literature showed stories or traditions that appear also in the Bible, then perhaps the Bible was not so sacred either. Because of this, modern biblical study provoked and continues to provoke a crisis in traditional biblically-based faith. A prominent example to illustrate the issue: Perhaps the most dramatic case of traditions found outside of and preceding the Bible involved Mesopotamian tablets with the story of the flood, which previous to their discovery, was largely known only from Genesis 6–9.[1] The flood story was evident from a number of Mesopotamian stories (for example, Atrahasis and Gilgamesh, tablet XII), some of which were datable to many centuries before the writing of Genesis.[2] Sometimes the texts in the Bible and their Mesopotamian parallels appeared to be so close that they seemed to be part of a shared worldview and common tradition (although to be sure, scholars also noted important differences between the Bible and these Mesopotamian stories).

Such recent discoveries have affected our modern understanding of Genesis 1 in particular. As we saw in chapter 2, Genesis 1 has often been compared with ancient Near Eastern texts, in particular with *Enuma Elish* (sometimes called "The Creation Story" or "Epic of Creation"). This narrative poem exalts the central figure, the god Marduk, who creates the universe in the wake of his victory over Tiamat, the cosmic Sea personified. While scholars generally seem to have little trouble viewing *Enuma Elish* as a myth, many seem far more reluctant to characterize Genesis 1 as a myth. Yet, on the face of it, the biblical chapter resembles *Enuma Elish* in many respects, and it satisfies the common definition of myth as a story centered on divine figures or with any number of divine figures featuring prominently.[3] So for many readers of these texts, Genesis 1 could certainly seem to be a myth—perhaps even a myth written somewhat after the model of the tradition reflected in *Enuma Elish*.

Yet many readers, professional and nonprofessional alike, have rejected the significance of the similarities, in part motivated by their religious attitudes toward the Bible. They champion the Bible's inerrancy and view extra-Israelite literature as pagan and untrue. Some scholars reject the comparisons on the more formal grounds that Genesis 1 did not present the sorts of divine world and beings encountered in so many ancient Near Eastern myths.[4] Another way that some authors have tried to get around this problem has been to distinguish stories involving multiple deities in ancient Near Eastern literature from stories involving only one deity. In this approach, the Bible is monotheistic and not polytheistic, and therefore its texts are not mythical.[5] That way, religiously minded scholars could regard the ancient Near Eastern texts as myths, but Genesis 1 would not be a myth, and so its divine revelation about creation could be maintained. As it turns out on further reflection, the logic behind this distinction does not seem particularly strong: why should the form of divinity serve as the criterion for the genre of myth? In fact, many scholars see little logic in using theism as a criterion for genre, and so they do not draw this distinction. If we use the simple definition of myth as a story about the gods or divinity, then Genesis 1 is a myth.

Still the matter is not this simple. The difficulty goes back to ancient Greece where the word "myth" originated. The English word "myth" is derived from the Greek term, *mythos*. If you look the word up in a dictionary of classical Greek,[6] you will find the meanings, "word, speech," as in public speech, conversation, a saying or a command. It can also refer to a thing one thinks about or an unspoken word. It also applies to a tale, a narrative, or a story, and it was used initially without any distinction between true or false stories. Over time the word came to refer to a fiction, fable, or children's story. The Harvard scholar of classics, Gregory Nagy, attributes the lack of modern consensus about myth in part to the semantic shift of the word in antiquity to meaning something untrue, as opposed to "true things" (*alētheia*).[7] Over time, the Greek word developed the connotation of being something of questionable legitimacy.

The word "myth" has also had a complicated modern history. Recent studies, such as Andrew Van Hendy's *The Modern Construction of Myth*,[8] have shown how the word has had a long career often reflecting modern attempts to define and understand religion and science and their proper relationship to one another. The modern history of defining myth reads more like the story of trying to come to grips with a broader experience and understanding of the world. Aspects of this include the emergence of science within Europe, the discovery of other cultures outside of Europe, and the resulting efforts at finding a place for religion in light of these modern developments. Von Hendry correlates the rise of myth as a term in the second half of the eighteenth century to "epidemic defections from institutional Christianity and remarkable intellectual turmoil about the nature both of religion and of belief."[9] The rubric of "religion" is a way to speak about the phenomena associated with religious practices across cultures,[10] and "myth" has served as a useful term that has been applied to a wide range of the sacred stories from various cultures, including some biblical narratives. Myths could function to refer to religious stories both within Christianity and outside of it. In the end, "myth" is an extremely problematic term because it developed to handle modern western concerns about religion and science in relation to each other and in relation to non-Western cultures. Von Hendry put the point this way in referring to myth in the modern context as "a concept whose two-and-a-half centuries under construction constitutes one of the significant attempts at what the German philosopher of culture Hans Blumenberg calls the legitimation of modernity."[11] The history of the definitions for the word myth in modern usage does not resolve the problem of our understanding myth; indeed, this history reflects the modern problem itself. For this reason alone, we should be skeptical about discovering some relatively neutral definition of myth beyond the basic (and arguably banal) definition of myth as a type of religious story.

Hendry's book also shows another problem with defining myth: its definitions often reflect the concerns of the fields of the scholars offering the definitions. It is not uncommon for scholars to define myth in the image and likeness of their own disciplines.[12] It is unsurprising that theologians, depth psychologists, anthropologists, Marxists, or literary critics tend to see the concerns of their own fields in myths. At the same time, the different perceptions of myths by different disciplines are hardly without basis. As various approaches have suggested, myths do refer to political phenomena (for example, in *Enuma Elish* and the Ugaritic story known as the Baal Cycle). Other myths do mention social groups (for example, priestesses, at the end of Atrahasis). Religious institutions are referenced (*Enuma Elish*'s description of the temple Esagila and its mention of "Babylon, home of the great gods,/We shall make it the centre of religion").[13] Myths do evoke natural phenomena (e.g., the weather in the Baal Cycle and the Tigris and Euphrates in *Enuma Elish*).[14] Myths also commemorate the past (e.g., the characterization of Nintu's necklace in Atrahasis).[15] Myths draw widely on what scribes knew of their world, and they included all the various aspects of life and reality that different modern fields have seen in them. Out of the experience of the ancients came their literature, and out of their religious experience came their religious literature. From our modern perspective, it is valuable to see these different aspects of myth. Modern fields of academic study have made important contributions toward understanding these different dimensions of myth.[16]

At the same time, with all these particular modern fields weighing in with their own definition or approach to myth, we do not arrive at a basic definition or idea of myth. Robert A. Segal explains the reason for this situation:

"Each discipline harbors multiple theories of myth. Strictly, theories of myths are theories of some much larger domain, with a myth a mere subset. For example, anthropological theories of myth are theories of myth *applied* to the case of myth. Psychological theories of myth are theories of the mind. Sociological theories of myth are theories of society. There are no theories of myth itself, for there is no discipline of myth in itself. Myth is not like literature, in which field it has or had traditionally been claimed, but it must be studied as *literature* rather than as history, sociology, or something else nonliterary. There is no study of myth as myth."[17]

From this perspective, the problem with defining myth is not simply an etymological problem involving Greek *mythos*; it is also a modern problem involving the way knowledge is organized in modern societies. Underscoring the point that this is an especially modern problem is suggested by the explosion of interest in myth in the twentieth century.[18] We may ask what drove this interest and correspondingly what impact it has had on how modern thinkers have understood the nature of myth. I would note further problems about the modern exploration of myth. Modern theorizing about myth has largely revolved around classical mythology, and its efforts to address ancient Near Eastern myths have not been based on first-hand knowledge of them. As a result, the treatment of ancient Near Eastern material by modern theorists of myth has been rather superficial.[19]

Because of these ancient and modern problems with the study of myth, scholars have struggled to produce a proper definition. For example, the classicist Fritz Graf responds to the question of the nomenclature of "myth," "legend," or "epic poems" in this critical manner: "The question is irrelevant at best, misleading at worst: it is a matter of our categories, and there is no scholarly consensus as to what these categories mean."[20] His fellow classicist, Gregory Nagy, asks in the title of one of his essays, "Can Myth Be Saved?"[21] The issue has been addressed also by scholars of ancient Mesopotamia, including Thorkild Jacobsen[22] and Stephanie Dalley.[23] In biblical scholarship, Michael Fishbane declines to define myth in terms of a specific genre. Instead, he sees myths as accounts of deeds and personalities of the gods and heroes or their actions.[24] According to this approach, myth is as much a matter of content as it is the formal features of a genre. The classicist Geoffrey S. Kirk suggests that "myth as a broad category within which special forms and functions will require different kinds of explanation. The analysis that is to be applied to a myth must be both flexible and multiform."[25] In other words, a simple definition of myth is not so simple to pin down or to figure out.

Using a simple definition of myth could also paper over problems. It sometimes lets some dubious assumptions creep into the discussion. One assumption commonly made is that myths are traditional stories[26] designed to explain origins and are therefore set in the past. The great scholar of comparative religion of the twentieth century, Mircea Eliade, put quite a good deal of emphasis on the purpose of myth to evoke or to reestablish "the creative era."[27] In an address delivered in 1980, the anthropologist Edmund Leach defined a myth as "a sacred tale about past events that justify social action in the present."[28] Or, compare Alan Dundes' definition of myth, as a "sacred narrative of how the world or mankind came to be in their present form."[29] Now it is true that many stories that are often called myths are set in the past, for example the Mesopotamian flood narratives. Yet in view of some cases, it may be asked how much a past setting constitutes a myth. For example, it is hardly clear that the Ugaritic Baal Cycle was understood to be set in a time of primordial origins. This raises the question as to whether other narratives in the more recent past or present and perhaps even in the future may be regarded equally mythic in character.[30] Biblical and extrabiblical apocalyptic narratives, for example, in Daniel 7–12 and in the New Testament book of Revelation ostensibly predict future events, yet they arguably qualify as myth, especially given their mythic imagery.

A second problem with a simple definition of myth as traditional stories involves the word, "traditional." For many scholars of the field, "traditional" evokes an oral context of storytelling and transmission. Granted, it is true that many myths may have originated in an oral context. However, this is not always the case. Some myths probably did not originate in an oral context as such. The Mesopotamian story of Erra and Ishum might be an example of a myth that did not derive out of a traditional oral context; instead, it may have been generated within the context of writing scribes. One might say something of the same thing about Virgil's efforts to refigure Homeric myth in his Aeneid, or, for that matter, the still later effort to fuse classical and Christian myth in John Milton's *Paradise Lost*.

There is another problem with the idea of "traditional," oral myths. For ancient myths that may have had oral origins, they survive only in written forms, and we have no direct access to their oral forms. Among its many accomplishments, Susan Niditch's 1996 book, *Oral World and Written Word*,[31] has shown that some written works may very well imitate oral story-telling style. One implication of this fine insight is that we really do not have access to oral literature of the ancient Near East. We probably cannot get at traditional oral literature behind the written record. On this point, we may note Kirk's observation: "The vital fact is that myths in Greek literature exist for the most part only in brief allusions. . . . The myths were so well known that formal exposition was unnecessary, and in the high classical period, at least, it was felt to be provincial. This changed in the Hellenistic world after the conquests of the Alexander the Great."[32] In the case of Mesopotamian myths, we often have good reason to believe that this material may stand at quite a distance from a strictly oral environment.

2. Ancient Signs of What Myths Are

Our most productive strategy may be to conclude that we should not fix upon a definition of myth and then apply it in order to decide whether Genesis 1 is myth or not, because there is no scholarly consensus as to how to define myth.[33] It seems that we need another strategy to address the question of whether Genesis 1 is a myth. I would like to try an inductive approach. It might be more productive to take a look at some of the features involved in the texts generally regarded as myths and then to observe how they compare with material in the Bible, including Genesis 1. "Theories of myth may be as old as myth themselves,"[34] Robert A. Segal suggests, and so we may attempt to intuit from texts generally accepted as ancient Near Eastern myths what they seem to be and do and to see how this sort of information may help to address the question of myth and Genesis 1. It will become clear in the discussion that follows that I am drawing on observations made by different scholars working on various ancient Near Eastern texts. I am going to try to synthesize a number of their observations and to use them to help us understand the question of myth and how well this label applies to Genesis 1.

To begin, we need to decide which texts are going to be considered for our discussion. In other words, which ancient Near Eastern texts should we use as examples of myth? Among scholars, there seem to be a consensus that Akkadian myths include the stories of *Enuma Elish, Atrahasis*, the *Descent of Ishtar, Anzu*, and *Erra and Ishum*. We may also add their Sumerian counterparts and antecedents, as well as other Sumerian works such as *Enki* and the *World Order*. The vast majority of scholars who use the term myth would also include several Hittite narratives, such as *Telepinu*. They would also include some Ugaritic texts, such the Baal Cycle (KTU 1.1-1.6) as well as the Rituals and Myths of the Goodly Gods (KTU 1.23), or at least the narrative of lines 30-76, as well as the main part of *Nikkal wa-Ib* (KTU 1.24). These have been called myths in modern collections. James B. Pritchard's *Ancient Near Eastern Texts* (commonly abbreviated as *ANET*) puts them under the rubric of "myths, epics, and legends," and these texts are listed under "canonical texts with a divine focus" in *The Context of Scripture* (abbreviated in this volume as *COS*). It also may be noted that the vast majority are narrative poems, a point underscored by the title of the collection, *Ugaritic Narrative Poetry*,[35] which contains the Ugaritic texts just mentioned. To stay on the safe side, this discussion will generally stick to these texts, which seem to fit most people's sense of myth as stories about gods or goddesses.[36]

The problem we are discussing may be seen more clearly for the ancient Near East if we pose the question in this way: how are the texts that modern scholars label as myths represented? In other words, how did the ancient scribes of these texts present them? What did they say these texts were about? To begin, several of these texts explicitly name deities as their subject matter by adding explicit labels to these texts. Attached to the only known written forms of these texts, these labels represent the earliest known interpretations of the poems. The label for the Ugaritic Baal Cycle is "about (literally, "to") Baal," or perhaps more technically speaking, "belonging to (the series of tablets called) Baal" (*lb'l*, in KTU 1.6 I 1). This designation is not a genre marker for myth as such, since Ugaritic shows the same sort of markers for the stories of Kirta and Aqhat, "about Kirta" (*lkrt*, in KTU 1.14 I 1, 1.16 I 1) and "[about][37] Aqhat (*[l]'aqht*, in KTU 1.19 I 1).[38] This sort of labeling indicates that an individual figure is in some sense the focus of the narrative. For the Baal Cycle, the label is important for showing that its ancient scribes regarded the text as being about the god. The final words of *Enuma Elish* likewise represent the text as "the Song of Marduk, Who defeated Tiamat and took the kingship."[39] This quote suggests that the authors of *Enuma Elish* regarded the god Marduk as this narrative's central topic. Likewise, the end of *Atrahasis* tells its audience that it is to extol the greatness of the god Enlil.[40] So in this respect, the ancient labeling of these texts fits the modern notion that myths are about gods or goddesses.

Beyond this matter of individual divinities, the texts show a sense of what kind of text that they are. Several are narratives, but many are not simply narratives. More specifically, many of these narratives are identified as songs. This idea is explicitly stated in texts, either in their opening or at their end. For this discussion, I will briefly note a handful of cases.[41] The end of *Enuma Elish,* as I noted above, refers to the text as "the Song of Marduk."[42] A second example comes from *Atrahasis,* named after its hero by modern scholars (his name literally means "exceedingly wise"). This text combines creation and flood traditions in a single composition. As the scholars Wilfred G. Lambert and

Alan Millard note in their edition of *Atrahasis*, this narrative is called "this song" (*an-ni-a-am za-ma-[ra]*), specifically the song sung by the goddess, Nintu.[43] Lambert and Millard comment further: "Thus a deity who confesses to participating in the bringing of the flood at Enlil's command claims to have sung this 'song,' which is equivalent to authorship. The Mother Goddess is a possible candidate."[44] In this case, the text is not simply about deities or their deeds; it is also a narrative song sung by one deity in praise of another.[45] Like *Enuma Elish*, *Atrahasis* is labeled this way with the explicit purpose of praising the deity, and also like *Enuma Elish*, its performance is called for in the future as an act of praise.[46]

We have more cases from Akkadian literature. These include the Standard Babylonian version of *Anzu*, also named for its main divine protagonist. This text opens as song and as praise: "I sing of the superb son of the king of populated lands, Beloved of Mami, the powerful god, Ellil's son; I praise superb Ninurta, beloved of Mami, the powerful god, Ellil's son."[47] Again we see the idea of the text as a song to the god. Another instance is the text called *Erra* (in its Standard Babylonian version), again named for its main divine character. It closes with the description of "this song" (twice) and it opens: "[I sing of the son of] the king of the populated lands, creator of the world."[48] The end of the text says that it was revealed by the god in a dream to the scribe, as Karel van der Toorn has recently emphasized.[49] Here *Erra*, like *Enuma Elish* and *Atrahasis*, are represented as songs to the gods by deities. In this sense, the texts are regarded as having divine authorship not unlike Genesis 1.

We should note that the idea of myths as songs appears quite widely in ancient Near Eastern literature. Several Hurrian myths are called "songs," such as "the Song of Ullikumi."[50] Closer to ancient Israel, the opening of the Ugaritic text often called *Nikkal wa-Ib* (KTU 1.24), opens as a song: "let me [si]ng of Nikkal wa-Ib."[51] The text then turns to a narrative of the marriage of Nikkal to Yarikh. The last line of the text at line 39 closes with a hymnic note: O Nikkal wa-Ib, of whom I sing, May Yarikh shine, May Yarikh shine on you!" The text follows with an epilogue (lines 40-50), the first line of which is regularly reconstructed: "[Let me sing of the Kotharat. . . .]." The model for this line may be a wedding-song (compare Ps. 45:1-2).[52]

Some of the Mesopotamian examples are songs by deities about deities that their human audience is to imitate. The great Sumerian scholar Thorkild Jacobsen commented: "the strictly literary Sumerian works can be defined as praise. The praise can be for something extant and enjoyed, a temple, a deity, or a human king. It can take narrative form as myth or epic, or descriptive form as hymn."[53] The myths that I have just mentioned are, as Jacobsen characterizes them, praise presented largely in narrative form. Some biblical texts might also serve as comparable cases of praise largely in the form of narrative,[54] for example, Exodus 15 and even the laments of Psalms 74 and 89, which include narrative praise.

For this discussion, it is important to emphasize that the oral representation of these texts as songs seems to be a scribal idea, perhaps aimed to encourage oral recitation of the written text. In other words, oral singing in these texts is not simply a reflection of their older, traditional origins as oral texts, as presupposed in many discussions of ancient Near Eastern myth.[55] (Of course, they may have drawn on notions of oral performance and perhaps hearkened back nostalgically to a time when oral presentation—versus recitation based on a written text—was the norm.)[56] Instead, divine orality in these texts is a scribal representation, and it highlights the authority of the scribal production. The presentation of these myths as songs is, in short, a claim to divine performance and revelation of these texts. At the same time, it is very important to observe that many myths do not make any claims about their being songs. The Hittite narrative known as *Telepinu* is very different in this regard. It incorporates an apparent ritual of appeasement. So this myth may be regarded not so much as a narrative song but as narrative focused on appeasement.

So how is all this relevant to our understanding of myths? These cases allow us to recognize that myths are not merely narratives about gods or goddesses; more to the point, they evoke a world invoked by other means often to serve some further end. Myths narrate a world that may be sung about in songs by human devotees of the deity. Alternately, myths may describe ritual appeasement of an angry god or goddess. Myths in their narrative form evoke deities and their world through songs, incantations, or other genres inclined to ritual. This does not mean that myths were always used in rituals (though in some cases, they seem to have been); what it means is that different sorts of myths and rituals are often concerned with the same divine world as it intersects with human society. These sorts of relationships between myths and rituals are evident in some of the cases that we will consider in the next section.

3. Myths in Relation to Various Genres

How myths are to be understood in their ancient contexts depends further on whether they are connected with other sorts of textual material. Some myths appear to be self-standing, while others are combined with other genres. An example of an apparent self-standing myth would be the Ugaritic Baal Cycle. As far as one can tell from its extant material, apart from its colophon and scribal instruction, it stands alone and does not seem to be intended to fulfill any function beyond narrative. Other texts show myth in conjunction with ritual.[57] A fine example of the latter is an Ugaritic text known as "The Rituals and Myths of the Goodly Gods" (KTU 1.23). This is a single text containing a series of rituals in lines 1-29, followed by a narrative involving gods and goddesses in lines 30-76.[58]

There are other cases of texts that combine narrative about deities with ritual. In the Sumerian text *Enki and the World Order,* the narrative shifts to ritual at lines 140-154 and then reverts to narrative.[59] The narrative of Hittite *Telepinu* includes a ritual designed to appease the god's anger.[60] The Akkadian work often called the *Descent of Ishtar,* a composition of about 140 lines (compare the Sumerian *Descent of Inanna* at some 410 lines), "seems to end with ritual instructions for the *taklimtu,* an annual ritual for the month of Dumuzi, which featured the bathing, anointing, and lying-in-state of a statue of Dumuzi in Nineveh."[61] Several Egyptian narratives are prefaced by information that they constitute spells.[62]

Ritual is hardly the only sort of text combined with myth. There is a narrative that is combined with a medicinal recipe, in the prescription of the hangover in one Ugaritic text (KTU 1.114.29-31).[63] This prescription is prefaced by and separated with a scribal line from the narrative, which describes the drunkenness of the patriarchal god, El. There may be "prophecy" in myth. In her comment on a passage in *Erra and Ishum,* Stephanie Dalley notes: "This line indicates that there is an important element of pseudo-prophecy in the epic."[64] In other words, this myth contains a representation of prophecy. Myth can also be combined with other narrative material. Myths contained within an epic would include tablet XI in Gilgamesh, with its incorporation of the flood myth, or the *Descent of Ishtar* opening in Gilgamesh tablet VII.[65]

From these cases, it is clear that narrative myth may be wedded to other forms, including ritual, epic or even medicinal prescription. To what ends? Jonathan Z. Smith offers an interesting comment that addresses this question: "Myth, as narrative, I would suggest, is the analogue to the limited number of objects manipulated by the diviner. Myth as application represents the complex interaction between diviner, client, and situation."[66] In other words, what myth is and how it is meant to function depends in part on its context. It is true that some examples involve ritual, and so one might agree with Smith that the world of divination is analogous to the world of narrative. As we have seen, ritual invokes a world that myth evokes. In some cases such as "The Rituals and Myth of the Goodly Gods" (KTU 1.23), a single text that combines myths and rituals both invokes and evokes the divine world. Yet ritual is only one arena with its "limited number of objects" (to echo Smith's quote). There may be other arenas of human activity with their "number of objects" that correspond to myth. The sense of myth and the role it can play is potentially as wide as human experience and imagination.

From the combination of myths with other genres of writing, we see that scribal production is important for understanding myths and what they are. From the examples we have noted, we can see how complicated mythic narrative may be. In addition, mythic narrative may also borrow from or be modeled on older myths. For example, *Enuma Elish* was a particularly strong "textual magnet" drawing on the older story of *Anzu*.[67] (At a minimum, they at least share a common stock of material).[68] The creation of humanity in *Enuma Elish* tablet VI may have drawn on the story of *Atrahasis*.[69] Also, the figure of Marduk in battle in *Enuma Elish* appears to have been modeled on the battles of the god Ninurta in Lugal-e,[70] while the portrait of Marduk in the same text may also owe something to the West Semitic conflict myth (as represented in the Ugaritic Baal Cycle), as Thorkild Jacobsen suggested decades ago.[71]

Other Mesopotamian myths show dependence on yet other myths. Benjamin R. Foster suggests that the ending of *Erra* is modeled on the ending of *Enuma Elish*.[72] The relationship may run deeper, with *Erra* perhaps forming a sort of commentary on the world of *Enuma Elish*.[73] In short, texts may represent narrative agglomerations drawing on other cultural material as well as diverse textual traditions and texts. In this connection, one may note J. Z. Smith's comment that "There is something funny, there is something crazy about myth. For it shares with the comic and the insane the quality of obsessiveness. Nothing, in principle, is allowed to elude its grasp. The myth, like the diviner's objects, is a code capable in theory of universal application if it would only be properly understood."[74] Indeed, sometimes agglomeration with various sorts of material even involved translation and migration, whether from Sumerian into Akkadian, or West Semitic into Hurrian-Hittite (Elkunirsa)[75] and Egyptian (for example, the Legend of Astarte and the Tribute of the Sea),[76] or Akkadian into Hebrew (Genesis 6–8). This textual flexibility may represent one hallmark of ancient Near Eastern myth.[77]

4. Divine Space in Myth

Up to this point, the discussion has focused on what might be called the external or formal side of myths. Yet it is equally important to note what is inside of myths, for example, what they evoke in their literary presentation of the spatial world. As I mentioned earlier, the discussion of myth has often focused on time, in particular time past. Among scholars, there has been a similar discussion of sacred space in myths; holy mountains, for example, have been prominent in this discussion. Space in myth more generally provides a stage for expressing human perceptions about reality.

Two cases illustrate this point. In *Enuma Elish*, one effect is for the audience to contemplate the grandeur of the universe, particularly as a spatial manifestation of Marduk's power as its creator. The narrative not only presents the universe in general, but also in its details, simultaneously religious and political, astronomical and divine. The audience of *Enuma Elish* is meant to see in this world its immediate reality as their place of habitation and at the same time to understand its divine origin and dimensions. It is especially in its divine aspect that the universe of *Enuma Elish* is deserving of human wonder and praise. It is in this aspect that the world as presented in Genesis 1 is structured to evoke a similar response. It, too, constructs a divine architecture of grandeur deserving of praise. In this respect, Genesis 1 may be characterized as mythic.

A second example comes from the Ugaritic narrative known as the Baal Cycle. This story presents various gods and goddesses moving through human habitations, well known in Ugaritic culture, such as Crete and Egypt. In this case, deities do not walk in some remote non-human "mythic places" of a distant past, nor do they exist in some distant prehuman past. Rather, these deities stride through very real places known to the ancients who transmitted these traditions. It is notable that humans barely appear in the Baal Cycle, and so in a literary sense they cede their space to gods and goddesses. While rituals would invoke divine presence into human experience, narrative evokes divine presence in the world. In such a narrative, humans are drawn (or, in a sense, "redrawn") into their own worlds, which include deities. The world in this account is transformed from a mundane world into a theophanic space. This literature allows the human audience to listen in on the deities as they imagine them to be in a world that now combines the divine and the human. Myth in such a case is not simply about the narrative as such or about its sequence. It provides a literary stage that gives to deities a space to reveal who they really are, or more precisely, who they are imagined to be.

Through the Baal Cycle, humans visualize and contemplate not only who the gods are in general, but also who they are in relation to one another. This includes the intimacy among various deities or groups of deities, and their mysterious bonds with the world of human experience. In the narrative sequence of events, the text sometimes even pauses for a moment and allows its audience to overhear a private, divine conversation. Thanks to the conventions of the literary narrative, humans can then join the deities literarily as they listen in on the words that one deity directs to another, sometimes conveyed with a certain intimacy and sense of affection. For example, the god Baal sends a message to his sister Anat inviting her to come to his mountain to learn the secret word of the universe (KTU 1.3 III-IV).[78] As they learn of this tête-à-tête, mere humans learn what Anat learns, as they listen in on this intimate communication. In one sense, this sounds more like Genesis 2–3 than Genesis 1 as the Baal Cycle provides a stage for divinity on the earthly level.[79] Just as the deities walk through the world in the Baal Cycle, so, too, God walks through the garden in Genesis 3. To be sure, the Garden of Eden is no normal space for humans, but the representation of the deity on the earthly level in Genesis 3 is not so distant from what we see in the Baal Cycle. By contrast, Genesis 1 directs human attention upward from the terrestrial level to consider the divine dimensions of a wider universe. In short, myths can be narratives of revelation. They allow their human audience an opportunity to step into a deeper reality, one underlying its more mundane existence.

Deities themselves captured basic dimensions of reality for the ancients, and the relationships among the deities make certain connections between these aspects of reality. To use an analogy, we may put the point in terms of grammar. Deities are in a sense the grammatical forms or morphology of reality; their relationships are its sentence structure or syntax; and its realities of power, of life and death, of nature and society, stand in coordinate and subordinate clauses. What does this "syntax" express as a whole? Myths can explore reality; they narrate it, but they do not really "explain" it in the modern sense. They present "causes" (aetia, the base for the first part of the word aetiology or etiology in English), but these are hardly causes or explanations in the modern sense.[80] Instead, they constitute claims that certain divinely involved events are connected with conditions in the world known to humans.[81] What myths seem to do is to evoke the basic realities that humans face and to present a narration that links these realities to the world of the gods and goddesses.[82]

Myths are narratives that span across these realities of deities, humanity, and their worlds but without explaining them, in any modern sense. They narrate, even tolerate, the apparent contradictions that seem inherent in human existence, such as violence or trouble in the world, as we see in *Enuma Elish*, the Baal Cycle or the Bible (Genesis 1–3), or mortality as it is addressed in *Atrahasis* and in the Bible (for example, in Genesis 6:1-4). Myths may relate the divine source of human threat or celebrate the divine origin of human blessing. And without explaining how, these narratives may claim that the sources of blessings and threat ultimately derive from deities who may or may not care about the welfare of mere mortals. Myths refrain from explaining why things are the way they are, but they do at least tell to some extent how things came to be this way. Different scholars discuss the explanatory (or etiological) function of myth, and surely there are plenty of textual references suggesting the connection between the there and then in the myth and the here and now of its human audience. Yet, as we have noted, a myth's portrayal of the world is not explanatory in any modern sense;[83] rather, it indicates that the problems of humanity are bound up with the divine world. In sum, myths narrate realities by presenting deities and their actions in or affecting the world, and they do so by building relations between these deities with plots that cover and cross over the inexplicable difficulties of human experience. Myths also indicate that in various ways deities are related to and have an impact on humanity in the midst of its numerous hardships. In terms of this discussion, Genesis 1 surely shows these hallmarks of ancient Near Eastern myths.

Let us look at the question of Genesis 1 as a myth also in terms of the presentation of deities in earthly settings. In contrast to the Baal Cycle or the Goodly Gods, biblical narrative does not *typically* present deities operating in a human-like manner in the world, or more specifically, on the earthly plane. To be sure, there are biblical snapshots of divine activity: God walking in the garden in Genesis 3; or, the "sons of gods" in Genesis 6:1-4. To explain this overall difference in the Bible, one might be tempted to adopt any variety of generalizations to explain the relative rarity of such presentations of gods or God. One might think that avoiding anthropomorphism is key, but this hardly helps us with various prophetic or apocalyptic images of the divine. Or, one might be tempted to say that the focus of Israel's narrative in Genesis through Kings is the story of Israel, and God is mediated through this story.

Yet even in apocalyptic texts, there is plenty of material reminiscent of ancient Near Eastern myths, yet even here the divine does not inhabit the earth in quite the same immanent manner. There is divine presence in liturgy (Psalm 29) and in prophetic passages (1 Kings 22 or Isaiah 6), but descriptions of God in human or "mythic" terms do not form the backbone of biblical narratives. Whatever the presentation of God in other biblical texts, Genesis 1 does not present God in this way, and in fact, one might argue that it looks decidedly unlike myths in this regard. So in consideration of these points, is it fair to label Genesis 1 as a myth?

5. Is Genesis 1 a "Creation Myth"?

As we have seen, modern discussions of myth and the Bible have often generated definitions of myth that could be applied to ancient Near Eastern texts, but not to the Bible. Many commentators in the last quarter century have largely given up this older practice of holding up the uniqueness of the Bible as nonmyth over and against ancient Near Eastern myths.[84] Even in rejecting this approach, one may still wonder why ancient Israel did not preserve longer mythic narratives of the sort seen elsewhere. This may be not a particular function of religious belief as much as a matter of scribal tradition and its particular interests. Behind the scribal tradition that shaped the Bible, Israel did transmit a collection of myths, or at least a constellation of mythic motifs and basic plotlines. The evidence represented by biblical apocalyptic in Daniel 7–12 and later in the book of Revelation, with their rich mythic imagery and plots, would seem to support the view that Israel indeed did have a fund of myths from which it could draw. Perhaps a better question for us to pose is why Israel's elites in the period generated so many narratives that look less mythic, such as longer biblical narrative collections that ultimately coalesced into the accounts that we now find in Genesis through 2 Kings. One should be cautious even here of assuming too little presence of myth in biblical narratives. As has been noted, the Bible is full of the sorts of images associated with myth, even if it does not contain longer mythic narratives apart from apocalyptic and arguably parts of the primeval history that we find in Genesis 1–11.[85] With a little imagination, one might well be able to string together a series of biblical stories that nearly matches the Ugaritic Baal Cycle scene for scene.

When one asks about what myths are and do as literary texts and then consider biblical narratives in a similar fashion, then it should be all too evident that some myths and biblical narratives have quite a bit in common. In general, both offer a narrative about a main deity. They also reference natural, social and religious phenomena. Both show scribal use of older narrative material that include commemoration, incorporation or use of older traditions or prior mythic versions[86] as well as translation and arguably textual commentary (for example, Genesis 1:1—2:3 as commentary on Genesis 2:4bf., as in chapter 3). Like many ancient Near Eastern texts, Genesis combines myth with materials that are far less mythic looking. Bernard Batto has argued that *Atrahasis* served as the model for Genesis 1–9; both stories link creation and flood.[87] The agglomeration of Genesis 1 hardly ends with Genesis 1–9 or even the end of Exodus, in chapters 39–40, as noted by many commentators. The trajectory is arguably Sinai as a whole,[88] with the theme of the Sabbath. Calling Genesis 1–11 "primeval history," as it often is called, has a certain merit, in that these chapters are inextricably linked to Israel's so-called history (or better, its "historiographical narrative") in Genesis through Deuteronomy, and perhaps through the books of Kings.

In chapter 4, we noted genealogies in Genesis (2:4, 5:1, 6:9; 10:1; 11:10, 27; 25:12, 19; 36:19, and 37:2).[89] These locate the primordial events of Genesis 1–3 in some sort of quasihistorical time, perhaps analogous to the Sumerian King List's referencing of the flood tradition in connection with human royal figures.[90] Genesis 2:4a labels the contents of Genesis 1 as a genealogy of heaven and earth.[91] While this labeling may recall the idea of theogonic myths involving generations of old cosmic pairs, including older deities,[92] in the context of Genesis 1 it no longer appears to be functioning in this manner. Instead, it serves to express the author's own interpretation of his material as connected to the historiographical material that follows throughout the book of Genesis and beyond. Genesis 1 perhaps looks less like a myth because it stands in the context of a long historical work in Genesis through Kings.[93]

For all their considerable differences, the parallel between the Sumerian King List and Genesis 1–11 is useful for understanding Genesis 1 in its larger context and for a consideration of the related question as to whether it is a myth. The parallel has been noted, mostly for potential traces of shared traditions.[94] For the purposes of this discussion, it is useful to look briefly at the Sumerian King list for a comparison with Genesis 1 in relation to its context in Genesis 1–11. Like Genesis 1, the King List begins with the heavens ("when kingship was lowered from heaven"). It also relates sequences of time down through the flood and into historical time. Like Genesis 1–11, it details preflood and postflood figures. Compared with the reigns of its postflood figures, the Sumerian King List provides much higher dates for the preflood figures. Both Genesis 1–11 and the Sumerian King List incorporate various sorts of traditional information. Both are also recognized as now being composite works. (The preflood material in the Sumerian King List appears in many but not all of the twenty-five known exemplars of this text.)[95] What is the upshot of this comparison for the question of Genesis 1 as a myth? No one calls the Sumerian King List a myth, yet within its historiographical framework it contains references to "mythic events." Similarly, scholars do not use the label of myth for all of Genesis (much less for Genesis—Deuteronomy or Genesis—Kings), and so Genesis 1 as one component in a much larger context should not be considered a myth. For all their differences, both the Sumerian King List and Genesis 1–11 allude to mythic events, but this does not make either one of them a myth. One might characterize them as mythic in the sense that both contain elements we would associate with myth; still, it would be stretching the point from a literary perspective to call them myths.

As this comparison suggests, the position of Genesis 1 affects the question of whether or not it is to be viewed as a myth. As we noted toward the end of chapter 4, Genesis 1 stands before any other text. It is given a position above other texts in the Bible, including other creation accounts (such as Psalm 74:12-17 or Psalm 104). To the question raised by this chapter, as to whether Genesis 1 in its context is a myth, the answer is negative when its position in the Bible is considered. As the foundational account at the head of Genesis to Deuteronomy and beyond, Genesis 1 is not a myth, nor did its editors design it to be read or to be understood as the kind of narrative that we would call a myth. From a biblical standpoint, it is not simply linked to historical time; it represents the beginning of time.[96]

So as we reach the end of our exploration of myth, what is the bottom line? Is Genesis 1 a myth or not? The answer is, of course, yes and no. From the perspective of its content, it is certainly very mythic. At the same time, the issue is complicated by its position (and perhaps also by its overall lack of anthropomorphism). It is not a self-standing narrative. Its place as the head of Genesis as well as its label as "generations of Heaven and Earth" (in 2:4a) shows an effort to link it to historical time. Its textual location also represents an effort or claim to make it first and primary relative to all other biblical accounts. In effect, this placement expresses a priestly claim for its account of creation in Genesis 1 as *the* account of creation, much as readers of the Bible usually think of it today. In this manner, we might say that the priestly authors or editors of Genesis 1 fundamentally altered the nature of the myth in their presentation of Genesis 1. The priestly tradition in effect effaced the resemblance between the mythic looking content of Genesis 1 and what scholars have generally regarded as ancient Near Eastern myths. In short, the priestly tradition has made Genesis 1 into the beginning of Israel's national story. Structurally, Genesis 1 has thus ended up no longer looking like ancient Near Eastern myths despite the fact that it has so much mythic content.

For many religious readers of the Bible, it is impossible to think of Genesis 1 as a myth in the first place, in part because of the modern sense of myth as something that is not true. Yet for other readers, the content of Genesis 1 reminds them of other creation stories from around the world. For these readers, Genesis 1 still looks very much a myth, and not surprisingly some scholars and laypeople alike have described it as a myth. These readers are not uncomfortable with the idea of Genesis 1 as one myth among many or as only one of the Bible's ways of looking at creation. We might say that religious readers who view the Bible as God's inerrant word and as Genesis 1 as historically true follow the view that the priestly tradition itself intended. For the priestly tradition as for religious readers of the Bible, Genesis 1 begins as *the* creation account. In contrast, other readers less concerned with biblical inerrancy may prefer to read Genesis 1 (or perhaps Genesis 1–3 or, indeed, Genesis 1–11), in isolation from its overall position within Genesis—Deuteronomy or Genesis—Kings. In a sense, these two different modern approaches to Genesis echo the ancient situation of Genesis 1 with its mythic looking content versus the priestly claim for Genesis 1 implied by its position.

To my mind, neither view has the Bible or the biblical view of creation quite right, especially if we consider creation within the Bible's overall scope.[97] On the one hand, Genesis 1 is the creation story for the priestly tradition, and it stands at the head of the whole Bible. On the other hand, the biblical tradition did not eliminate other creation accounts, for example, the ones we saw in Psalms 74 and 104. Instead, the Bible retained both the priestly claim to the primacy of Genesis 1 and the witnesses to alternative views in other texts. As the "canonical approach" would remind us,[98] a canonical perspective then is not the same as the priestly view. Instead, the Bible preserves a more complex situation, namely a literarily dominant text in Genesis 1 that stands in dialogue with other texts that are less prominent in terms of their placement. A religiously minded person might say that the biblical truth of creation constitutes the range or sum of the truths in all of the various accounts in the Bible.

To put the point in terms of the Bible's own presentation of creation, it might be more accurate to say that the truth of creation in Genesis 1 is echoed in other biblical accounts of creation, and that their presentations of creation expand on what Genesis 1 conveys. In this perspective, Psalm 74's emphasis on God's power in creation would complement the concept of creation that Genesis 1 initially lays out for its readers. Psalm 104 offers yet another dynamic take on creation and its elements, and an inspiring sense of God's own breath of life infusing the world. This variation on the theme of creation adds a dimension missing from Genesis 1. Psalm 104's ecologically integrated vision of creation qualifies the human-centered picture presented by Genesis 1.[99] Creation is not only good, as Genesis 1 reminds its readers; it is also built with divine wisdom, as Psalm 104:24 tells its audience. Thus for the Bible as a whole, the other creation accounts magnify and harmonize with the sense of creation and its Creator found initially in Genesis 1.[100]

Other creation passages also qualify any sense of absolute truth that might be attached to Genesis 1 as the single most important biblical witness to the meaning of creation. The other biblical passages of creation remind readers that the biblical witness to creation is not to be boiled down to the single, basic truth of Genesis 1. (Nor would it be easy to do this without impoverishing our reading of the Bible.) Other passages potentially serve as foils to Genesis 1. If Genesis 1 holds up a "good" picture of creation, other passages suggest something of its "downside," as it applies to humanity. As we saw in chapter 1, the good creation of Genesis 1 does not explain human suffering or evil in the world. Other passages remind us of the dark side of God's creation (Is. 45:7; see also Job 3).[101] Finally, yet other creation accounts in the Bible remind readers that Genesis 1 is not to be taken as the single account of creation in any historical or scientific sense. To the degree that people take Genesis 1 in this way, they fail to understand the full biblical witness to creation and the biblical attitude toward creation. While Genesis 1 is certainly designed to overshadow all other creation accounts, it was never the biblical purpose—even of its priestly editors—for it to be idealized or idolized to their exclusion. As the priestly editors of Genesis 1 might be the first to point out, every one of the sacred accounts in the Bible is "good" in God's sight.

Indeed, the situation of the different creation accounts in the Bible is more complex precisely because they belong to the Bible. The Bible is not simply a combination of parts or a variety of works that includes creation texts. In this respect, it differed in the long term from creation accounts not only in Mesopotamia and Egypt, but also through most of ancient Israel's history. Creation texts of Mesopotamia and Egypt basically remained separate works offering a range of ideas about creation, a veritable kaleidoscope in their perspectives on creation. While Israel's creation texts also began as separate works, in time its kaleidoscope of creation was fused into a single work that we now know as the Bible. One of the things that ultimately makes Genesis 1 different as a creation text is that it belongs to this larger work. In this larger literary context, creation accounts and allusions are no longer separate texts, but passages meant to be read in conjunction with one another. This complex of textual activity, as we see it in later biblical texts and the Dead Sea Scrolls, might be further described as "scripturalizing." By this, I mean that texts regarded as holy or inspired were coming to be read and interpreted together; that words or complexes of terms shared by different religious texts not only could be read in tandem but should be read together across the boundaries of their original contexts, beyond the limits of any individual passage or document. It is this process of scriptural reading linking passages across their former textual boundaries that eventually distinguishes works that belong to the Bible from other such works of the ancient Near East or, for that matter, all of literature.[102] In its placement as the Bible's opening, Genesis 1 enjoys a singular place in a singular work where its voice is to be heard not only in the beginning, but also through to the end.

In the end, the question of Genesis 1 as myth depends on what we mean by the word myth and what we think myths are really about. This issue of the Bible or Genesis 1 as myth is as much a concern of our own time as it is about the Bible and its ancient authors. The resolution of this question may ultimately depend on what credence readers are prepared to give to either the Bible or to ancient Near Eastern literature in their descriptions of reality. Regardless of how readers regard Genesis 1, whether as myth or religious truth, as story or foundation of faith, it will remain a cultural and literary monument that will endure as long as the Bible endures.

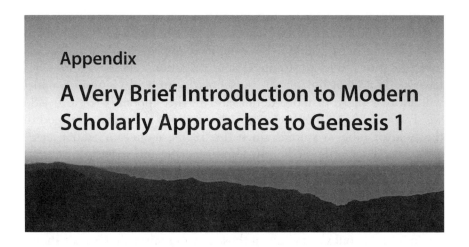

Appendix

A Very Brief Introduction to Modern Scholarly Approaches to Genesis 1

This appendix is designed to give interested readers a sense of the modern scholarly approaches taken to Genesis 1. By any account, the major areas of scholarly discussion involving Genesis 1 include textual criticism (the study of ancient manuscripts), source criticism (the study of prior sources that a biblical book may incorporate or draw on), form criticism (the study of genres), the comparative approach (comparison with other ancient Near Eastern and biblical passages), redaction criticism (the study of various editions of a biblical book or chapter as well as further editorial additions), and literary analysis (the study of a biblical text's various literary features).

Historical study of the backgrounds of biblical books has also enjoyed a prominent place in biblical studies. It has particularly benefited from advances in archaeological research,[1] which have included discoveries of inscriptions and pictorial representations (iconography),[2] both in ancient Israel and in other lands of the ancient Near East. The intensive study of Hebrew as well as other languages of the ancient world has also added considerably to our knowledge of the language and idiom of biblical works. Thanks to these areas of research, the historical and cultural understanding of ancient Israel has dramatically increased over the past few decades.

Throughout the modern era, biblical theology has also been involved in biblical studies for Christian scholars of the Bible. Biblical theology takes stock of the Bible's theological witness to God, humanity, and the world in the light of Christian experience and research on the Bible.[3] Related to the fields of theology and literary study are approaches that focus on the interpretation of biblical books during the biblical period and afterward. These include "canon criticism" (sometimes called "the canonical approach"),[4] innerbiblical interpretation,[5] and postbiblical interpretation.[6] These approaches have made a great impact on the scholarly study of Genesis 1, and I will address these in more detail later in this appendix. Before I do so,[7] I would like to mention scholarly methods that have emerged in the field of biblical studies since the 1970s, namely narrative criticism, social scientific criticism, feminist criticism, structuralist criticism, deconstructive criticism, and ideological criticism. These more recent approaches have been covered in, for example, *To Each Its Own Meaning* by Steven L. McKenzie and Stephen R. Haynes, and *Judges and Method* edited by Gale A. Yee.[8] These volumes do a good job in bringing out what many of these newer approaches are all about. (Yee's additionally applies these approaches to the book of Judges.) It is also worth consulting the introductory chapter of *The Religions of Ancient Israel* by Ziony Zevit, professor at the University of Judaism in Los Angeles.[9] Zevit has tried to mediate between various older and newer paradigms of interpretation. These books discuss many of the more recent entries into the biblical field.[10] We may also note *Reading the Old Testament* by Oxford professor John Barton and *The Bible after Babel* by Yale professor John J. Collins.[11] These cover traditional areas of biblical study quite well, and they also address some of the newer approaches. Barton also offers a defense of "historical criticism," a label often used for the older approaches. For biblical scholarship between 1450 and 1889, we have *What Have They Done to the Bible?* by John Sandys-Wunsch.[12]

In addition, we may note the Web sites for significant biblical bibliography, including matters of method. M. Daniel Carroll Rodas, Hélène Dallaire, and Richard S. Hess, "Annotated Old Testament Bibliography—2009," at http://www.denverseminary.edu/article/annotated-old-testament-bibliography-2009/, includes both traditional areas (theology; history, archaeology, ancient Near Eastern texts in translation; lexica, dictionaries and lexica; concordances and grammars) and more recent approaches (sociological and anthropological studies; feminist, minority and third world studies; literary approaches). While mostly providing bibliography for biblical books, there is some bibliography for traditional approaches and for some more recent literary matters at Bibliografia Basilare dell'a.t. = Old Testament Basic Bibliography, at http://www.biblico.it/doc-vari/ska_bibl.html.[13]

1. Recent Approaches in Biblical Studies

Many of the newer approaches expand the horizons of older research on the historical background of biblical books and authors. This includes scholarship on the Bible informed by the social sciences, such as anthropology and sociology.[14] Biblical scholars working in this intellectual paradigm reconstruct the society of ancient Israel and locate biblical books within their societal and cultural contexts. This is not simply a more sophisticated version of older historical criticism, which asked about the historical setting of biblical books. This approach goes further and asks also about the assumptions and horizons of biblical books based on their social background. Within the context of historical and cultural study, we may also note the increased attention paid to the study of scribal practices.[15] The study of scribal practices adds a further layer of refinement to the study of the social setting that produced biblical texts. It not only shows the technical techniques of scribal practice; it also connects the scribal setting of texts with various social segments in ancient Israel.

The approach known as New Historicism has made a considerable impact in biblical studies.[16] This approach goes even further than the historical approaches we've mentioned so far by looking at literature not as a reflection or product of social realities, but as an expression (or as a series of expressions) of political realities. In this approach, literature plays an important role in maintaining and asserting cultural power, which can be discovered by tracing "connections among texts, discourses, power, and the constitution of subjectivity."[17] As this quote suggests, this sort of study looks at texts in connection to their different ways of representing the world (discourses), and to their various ways of relating to power and the myriad of combinations of ways they imagine the nature of human identity (whether as a basic inner core, or a set of traits determined by one's origins and social attributes, or as an identity shaped by a person's own acts or the various positions or roles occupied in life). Literature in this view involves analyzing texts for their potential roles of "subversion and containment," how they may offer a radical critique of the religious and political ideologies of their day, and to what degree they contain subversive energies.[18] These themes can also be seen in postcolonial criticism,[19] which has become an important approach in the study of the Bible, especially for periods of foreign domination.

In connection with New Historicism and postcolonial theory, we may also mention the study of collective memory,[20] insofar as it also addresses the role of power relations. Collective memory takes up this concern in studying how cultures generate and maintain the representations of their past. Differing versions of the past involve struggles in the present. In other words, what is present often affects the understanding of the past; versions of the past may exercise power over the present. Collective memory commonly shows cultural and societal shifts over time, especially with changes in the institutions and other sites in society that produce and transmit representations of the past. The changing representation of the past reflects later changes in the institutions that guard and transmit it. Collective memory permits a more sophisticated examination of biblical texts not only as vessels of historical memory within ancient Israel, but also as potential instruments of power within that society.[21]

Other newer biblical scholarship looks at the ancient context of the Bible through perspectives of gender. It draws on a variety of theories, including psychoanalysis pioneered by Sigmund Freud and Carl Jung,[22] feminism and feminist hermeneutics,[23] as well as queer theory.[24] At its most basic, psychoanalysis has led to a literary criticism alert to psychoanalytic themes and relations in literature,[25] while feminist theory in Jonathan Culler's characterization is less a particular sort of theory as it is "a social and intellectual movement and a space of debate" that especially "undertakes a theoretical critique of the heterosexual matrix that organizes social identities and culture in terms of the opposition between man and woman."[26] In this task, feminist studies are joined by queer theory.

In these approaches, ideas about gender and sexuality in biblical passages come to the fore, and the gender assumptions of the biblical writers and their audiences are addressed explicitly. These approaches have helped the field see the Bible as the product of a deeply patriarchal society and as an instrument used to assert its patriarchy. Feminist scholars and queer theorists often question the Bible's depictions of women and men and further explore the impact of gender roles in the Bible's representations of God.[27] Aided by archaeology, feminist biblical criticism has sought to learn about the lives of women in ancient Israel without the distorting lenses of the Bible.[28] Thanks to this approach, it became possible to undertake a fresh study of history "from below" rather than work only from the Bible, largely dominated by voices asserting their authority "from above," both in ancient Israel and in modern culture.[29]

In this scholarly effort, feminist criticism has been joined by the very rich literature that looks at the Bible from the perspectives of race and class,[30] as well as ethnicity.[31] Some of this research combines these perspectives under the rubrics of ideological criticism and postcolonial theory.[32] Ideological criticism focuses on issues of power between writers and their audiences in their larger social contexts, and postcolonial theory addresses power relations between the cultures to which authors belong and the ruling cultures to which they may be responding. In this connection, we may also note ecological hermeneutics or "ecocriticism," which seeks a proper critical relationship between ecology and biblical interpretation.[33] In general, all of this research offers more sophisticated and sensitive tools for understanding the cultural situation of ancient Israel and the books of the Bible. It shows a wider concern about the production of power and the role of biblical literature in the production and exercise of power relations, both within ancient Israel and in later western culture. By asking broader questions about gender and race, and about political power and conditions, we get a fuller picture of ancient Israel than what was produced by older historical study of the Bible. These newer approaches to ancient Israel have enhanced historical understanding.

These newer perspectives on gender, race and class have also affected literary study of the Bible. As a result, literary interpretation in biblical studies has vastly expanded its horizons, compared with older sorts of literary analysis.[34] Some recent entries in the literary study of the Bible involve narratology and reader response criticism. Narratology, as its name implies, involves theory of narrative aimed at understanding its components as well as the ways that it achieves its affects.[35] It asks not simply about narrative time past and present with their possible permutations, or about narrative pace and perspective. It inquires into the nature and perspectives of the narrative voice represented and of the characters as well as the representation of their limitations and influence in the construction of the narrative. A story may be channeled or "focalized" through one of the characters and her or his point of view, and not through the represented narrative voice.

In some respects, this work is not entirely removed from the concerns of New Criticism, the literary criticism of the 1940s and 1950s that focused on texts as literary wholes. However, narratology was influenced by French structuralism of the 1960s and early 1970s,[36] trying to discern the various sorts of linguistic and social codes embedded in texts. Moreover, narratology may also bring to the interpretive task a whole range of concerns about social identities represented in the text (whether promoted, denigrated, or obscured), including gender and sexuality, race, and class.

Reader response theory does not make the text the single focus of its interpretive attention. Rather, it centers on the interplay between texts and their readers. For this approach, the meaning of the text is not "behind the text" as in historical readings, nor does it lie "in the text" as in the older literary criticism, such as New Criticism. Instead, it is "in front of the text," lying in the reader's experience of the text. How do readers take in texts? How does this process happen? How is it influenced by the differing horizons that readers and their texts have?

Other literary studies deploy what have been called deconstruction-ist and postmodern readings.[37] On one level, these readings combine perspectives "behind," "in," and "in front of" the text. They ask about the reader as a human subject, as a recipient and agent of cultural attitudes and categories.[38] On one level, they respond to the agenda of French structuralism and its method of exploring and uncovering binary oppo-sitions generated in texts. Deconstructionist readings offer critiques of hierarchical oppositions that have traditionally structured western thought, such as inside/outside, mind/body, literal/metaphorical, and nature/culture.[39] These binary oppositions are seen not as "natural" in any sense, but as social constructions often bearing political force. Deconstructionism, as its name suggests, further seeks to dismantle these oppositions. Deconstruction is, to use Barbara Johnson's phrase, a "teasing out of warring forces of signification within a text."[40]

Unlike older literary theory such as New Criticism, deconstruction-ism does not assume that biblical books represent literary wholes, and unlike structuralism, the codes uncovered are not simply uncovered and appreciated for what they tell us about texts. Instead, texts and the ways in which they express themselves are often seen to be at war with them-selves. In this approach, coherence or structure of meaning is not pre-supposed; such concerns may in fact be a hindrance to interpretation. In this mode of reading, the possibility of determinate meaning is treated as an illusion to be avoided. In addition to sharing these interpretive perspectives with deconstructionism, many postmodern readings aim at getting away from the distinction drawn between allegedly high and low culture, between "refined" literature and artifacts of popular culture. Readings play between so-called high and low culture and engage with a multitude of other facets of culture that would have seemed alien to most literary study even thirty years ago.

Many interpreters combine these approaches in a variety of ways. This situation is conveyed by the online journal, *The Bible and Critical Theory*. On its Web site, the journal states its scope as follows:

> Biblical studies is in an interesting state of flux. The various meth-
> ods of critical theory have been used by biblical critics for some

time now. The methods include poststructuralism, feminism, psychoanalysis, ideological criticism, the social sciences, Marxism, ecocriticism, postcolonialism, reader response criticism, narratology, new historicism, and utopian studies. These methods have raised questions about the Bible concerning race and ethnicity, indigeneity, gender and sexual difference, class and ideology, hegemony and subversion, the nature of history, texts and readers, and so on.[41]

This quote conveys something of the rich theoretical environment in which biblical scholarship is working today.

While many of these approaches help us better understand the ancient cultural context of biblical texts, the quote also suggests that a good deal of the biblical field has lost interest in the historical background of the Bible. For such scholars, historical reading seems to have run its course, and they prefer to move onto to something newer and intellectually fresher. The field also seems to be exhausted by the sheer volume of secondary literature, much of which has been devoted to historical interpretation. We can sometimes lose sight of the deep value that historical reading provides to our culture in combating fundamentalism[42] and in showing what interpretation of the Bible entails. In short, anyone wanting to understand the Bible cannot afford to ignore the past. The diversity of approaches signals a healthy matrix for interpretation, but the risk is an atomization of biblical scholarship into a myriad of approaches, sometimes deteriorating into hostility between approaches and their proponents. Scholars in different intellectual camps regularly lament their low status relative to others. Our annual meeting of the Society of Biblical Literature can seem like long rows of scholarly boutiques in a large mall, where groups and sections sometimes act as if their intellectual wares are better and more beautiful than the ones on display next door.[43] As an intellectual matter, this aspect of our situation is indefensible.

Roland Barthes (1915–1980), a major icon of French structuralism and literary criticism, commented on the state of traditional literary criticism in evocative, biblical terms in what is quite a compelling passage. What he says here can seem like the situation of traditional biblical criticism and biblical literature in the face of newer methods:

> The old values are no longer transmitted, no longer circulate, no longer impress; literature is desacralized, institutions are impotent to defend and impose it as the implicit model of the human. It is not, if you will, that literature is destroyed; rather *it is no longer protected*: so this is the moment to go there. Literary semiology is, as it

were, that journey that lands us in a country free by default; angels and dragons are no longer there to defend it. Our gaze can fall, not without perversity, upon certain old and lovely things, whose signified is abstract, out of date. It is a moment at once decadent and prophetic, a moment of gentle apocalypse, a historical moment of the greatest possible pleasure.[44]

This is hardly the time for diehard historical critics to despair, as I sometimes hear them lament (though that time may come). To my mind, the current situation in biblical studies offers a wonderful opportunity as well as a daunting challenge: how can biblical interpretation effectively combine data, approaches and theories?

To be sure, biblical scholars need to have a basic grounding in the primary evidence. This includes Hebrew language and knowledge of the Bible and the cultural realities to which it refers, preferably complemented by training in the extra-biblical languages and literatures, history and culture that have certainly helped us to better understand Biblical Hebrew and the Bible. So we need to have a solid grasp of the basic, traditional methods. In these basics, I am a pretty traditional biblical critic. In making this statement, I make no claim about the objectivity of these methods or their lack of ideology. What I do claim is that despite their own theological and historical ideologies (not to mention some of their own curious histories),[45] traditional methods of biblical criticism that I will outline in the following paragraphs provide a way of coming to know basic information about the Bible and ancient Israel without which interpretation is deficient. I am not saying that valuable or fresh interpretations cannot be proposed by someone deficient in either basic language skills or in the literature, culture and history of the Bible. After all, many fine observations occur in classrooms thanks to students who have never studied the Bible before. Still, basic knowledge is required to get at biblical texts and literature more deeply and to gain basic professional competence to teach people. Otherwise, it would be like having a professor of French literature who didn't know French—impossible, *incroyable!*

At the same time, I would say that the traditional foundations of biblical scholarship, while necessary, are not sufficient. I do not find the older approaches to be adequate conditions for well-rounded biblical interpretation. Instead, it is intellectually preferable to build on and to improve the old with the new—and to continue exploring further. Most of the newer methods of biblical interpretation can build on the foundations of older approaches, and the older methods can be improved by recourse to newer ones. For example, traditional philology has been immensely advanced by modern linguistic study, such as discourse analysis. To take another example, traditional historical study has been vastly improved by some of the newer interests and methods in the study of historiography, cultural history, and collective memory. An interdisciplinary approach, in which scholars work with the many older approaches along with several newer ones, will help expand our intellectual horizons. Scholars can reasonably disagree over the right balance of methods and approaches, and these may vary according to the evidence or issue under investigation. This does not mean that scholars should make arbitrary choices, but it also doesn't mean that the scholars' choices aren't going to reflect their own intellectual and affective horizons.[46] In some cases, as I will consider after the following survey of the main traditional approaches to Genesis 1, it is advisable that scholars draw on their own horizons, where their horizons somehow meet those of the texts under investigation, as long as this is done with self-critical reflection.

2. Traditional Approaches and Genesis 1

At this point, I would like to turn to the traditional areas of study as they relate to the study of Genesis 1. Afterwards I will return in some final reflections to the question of the horizons of biblical interpreters.

Text Criticism

Text criticism examines the words in different manuscripts of biblical books produced in different languages.[47] Major Hebrew manuscripts of the Bible come from Jewish tradition handed down over the centuries. This text is often called the Masoretic Text (abbreviated as MT, this is the traditional Hebrew text of the Bible). The other important source for biblical manuscripts in Hebrew comes from the Dead Sea Scrolls as well as the Samaritan Pentateuch.[48] The most important Greek translation is called the Septuagint (abbreviated as LXX, this Jewish translation was eventually adopted by Christians).[49] Translations in other languages, such as Aramaic, Syriac, and Latin, are also important witnesses to the text of the Bible. In various parts of this study, I have occasionally referred not only to the MT and LXX, but also to other Greek versions of Aquila, Symmachus, and Theodotion as well as the Latin Vulgate of Jerome.

Text criticism emerged as an important topic for Genesis 1 beginning in the 1990s. Works from this period view textual manuscripts as important information for the ancient interpretation of Genesis 1. In other words, the differences between the Hebrew and Greek show an interpretive dimension. The most dramatic study in this regard was a 1993 book by William P. Brown, professor of Bible at Columbia Theological Seminary in Decatur, Georgia.[50] Brown seeks to reverse the usual text-critical thinking that largely assumes that differences between the Septuagint (LXX) and Masoretic Text (MT) are due to LXX changes that harmonize differences in the text as represented in the MT.[51] For Brown, the Hebrew text that the Septuagint used predated the Masoretic text, and this older Hebrew text was different in some ways from the later Masoretic text. In other words, the differences between the LXX and the MT did not simply involve changes made secondarily by the LXX. Instead, the Masoretic textual tradition made some alterations to the older Hebrew version that it had inherited. In turn, Brown also sees LXX textual differences influenced by creation traditions current in its time. As examples in the LXX, he notes the positive treatment of the waters, specifically as moving and contributing to the formation of land in Genesis 1:9, as in Hellenistic creation-stories (also called "cosmogonies"), as opposed to ancient Near Eastern creation accounts.[52]

Representing a different text-critical analysis of Genesis 1 is a 1998 work by Ronald S. Hendel, professor of Hebrew Bible at Berkeley.[53] In general, it is Hendel's view that the LXX translator used a Hebrew text dependent on an older form of the MT (or, "proto-MT"), which was marked especially by harmonizations. He argues that MT retains the priestly tendency for what he claims is deliberate variation, while LXX aims for greater consistency. For Hendel, the perceived style of the priestly author of the text represents one of the major criteria in adjudicating differences between MT and LXX.[54]

In 2008, Jennifer M. Dines published a study of the Septuagint's understanding of divine power in Genesis 1 compared with the Masoretic text.[55] By comparison with the Masoretic text of Genesis 1, the Septuagint reduces the language for ruler and dominion for the luminaries in 1:16 and 18 and for the human person in 1:26 and 28. According to Dines, the language for power in these verses in the MT is "overridden" in the Septuagint translation. In turn, for the Septuagint the "beginning" (*archē*) of verse 1 carries the connotation of primacy and rule. It further connects with verse 26, which also uses this Greek root. Dines suggests: "the 'rule' of the luminaries in the LXX is infused more than in the MT with the idea of 'initiating' as well as of 'ordering,' and conversely, the very beginning of the process of creation may carry a clearer overtone of authority." She concludes that humans, who are to maintain order (*archein*, 1:26, 28; cf. 1:18) by the exercise of force and ownership (*katakurieuein*, 1:28), are not mere servants. Neither are they stewards or overseers (Genesis 2:15), nor do they merely "help" God. According to the Septuagint of Genesis 1:1—2:3, God does not share power; he hands it over to his creatures.

The work of these scholars is not simply the older style of text criticism, which was largely concerned either with sorting through the textual versions and weeding out scribal errors or with understanding the techniques of translation of the Bible in the various languages. This traditional sort of textual criticism is often called "lower criticism," because it provides the foundation for further analysis of the text by the other areas of biblical studies, which were correspondingly called "higher criticism." By comparison, areas of "higher criticism" were considered to be more interpretive in their approach than the "lower criticism" of text criticism. In the hands of Brown and Hendel, text criticism has been viewed as having been affected by matters of "higher criticism," such as priestly style. With Dines' essay as with Brown's, we see a concern for understanding translations as interpretations. In other words, in the study of Genesis 1 "higher criticism" has invaded "lower criticism." What this newer text-criticism also contributes to the understanding of Genesis 1 is a sense of the larger role of cultural and literary influences on the textual versions of the text.

Source Criticism

Source criticism has long been a major approach to Genesis 1. In the view of source criticism, the Pentateuch was understood as woven together in a series of stages from four sources or written documents (called the Documentary Hypothesis): the Yahwist (labeled as "J" from the German word for the source, "Yahwist" = Ger. "Jahwist"); the Elohist ("E"); the Priestly source ("P"); and Deuteronomist ("D").[56] In addition, Leviticus 17–26 was considered to derive from priestly work, with some different vocabulary and ideas, and was called the Holiness Code. In the classic model of source criticism, the Yahwist and Elohist sources were compiled together by an editor or redactor (often called "RJE").[57] A later priestly editor then took this work and compiled it together with the priestly source. The resulting work, with some Deuteronomistic additions, was Genesis-Exodus-Leviticus-Numbers. Deuteronomy was subsequently added as the last book.

While great controversy continues to swirl around the so-called Yahwist ("J")[58] and Elohist sources,[59] most scholars of the Pentateuch have accepted the Priestly source, or at least priestly material. In Europe and North America, critics reached a consensus about Genesis 1:1—2:3 belonging to the priestly source (P) or material, as opposed to the

Yahwist material, found in Genesis 2:4b and following.[60] (Verse 2:4a has been viewed as a secondary addition; I will discuss this under redaction criticism below.) In Israel, this basic division of sources has prevailed despite the misgivings expressed decades ago by Umberto Cassuto, who was professor at the Hebrew University in Jerusalem.[61] In general, study of priestly material has survived some of the more polarized debates in source criticism, for example, over the dates and nature of the Yahwist (J) and Elohist (E) sources. It is to be noted that source criticism has been particularly successful in heightening our sense of the worldviews informing different passages. In the case of Genesis 1, it builds into the very fabric of creation the priestly understanding of the Sabbath (Hebrew *shabbat*) and the festivals.

Building on the older consensus about Genesis 1 as P, the question of what P is not only in Genesis 1, but also more broadly in the Pentateuch, exploded in the 1990s. The most notable development involved the identification of a separate Holiness (H or HP) redaction of the Pentateuch, based on similarities between some passages historically attributed to P and the Holiness Code of Leviticus 17–26. Two professors, initially Israel Knohl of the Hebrew University and then Jacob Milgrom, professor emeritus at Berkeley, published their findings that numerous passages long assigned to P should be assigned to the Holiness redaction, based on their use of specific phrasings and vocabulary found in the Holiness Code (Leviticus 17–26).[62] Knohl also reversed the relative chronology of the Holiness Code and the P source. The Holiness Code had been regarded by scholars as older than P, but Knohl, followed by Milgrom, argued that the Holiness Code is later than P, as is the Holiness redaction of the Pentateuch. It is important to bear in mind that H and P are both priestly in nature according to these authors. Without entering into the specifics of this controversy as it applies to Genesis 1,[63] I use the term priestly in reference to this account. For our purposes, what is important to see from this discussion of H and P is that the overall priestly material and its redaction dates to different times, reflecting a complex priestly tradition.

This sense of priestly material as reflecting a tradition rather than a single written document has developed in Pentateuchal studies. Scholarship a generation ago often treated P either as a separate source or a series of additions, which included a basic, single P composition.[64] More recently, some critics have raised questions about this understanding, preferring instead to think about P as a tradition of material and composition. The uniform consensus a generation ago that P was a single composition has shifted more recently to that of a single social segment or tradition. Such a view is compatible with several observations made in older P research (for example, by the notable twentieth-century German biblical scholar, Martin Noth). This research regarded priestly expansions as signs of an ongoing priestly tradition. This approach has also allowed for a more dynamic view of the relationships between the various sorts of P material[65]: various narratives, with their different sorts of relationships with non-P material[66]; priestly laws, or what Chaim Cohen has nicely dubbed "priestly instructional literature that has its own editorial additions"[67]; and other editorial touches.[68]

A related concern in the discussion of priestly material involves its date, especially for scholars working primarily with a single or major priestly P source. Many Israeli scholars, going back to Yehezkel Kaufmann,[69] regard P as preexilic. In contrast, most European and a number of major American[70] scholars regard it as postexilic.[71] For two decades, vocal support for a preexilic date has been grounded in linguistic evidence. At this point, we turn to this arena of research.

Grammatical Study

This work is often associated with the name of the important Israeli scholar of Hebrew language, Avi Hurvitz. Stimulated by his brilliant teacher Eduard Y. Kutscher at the Hebrew University,[72] Hurvitz developed a typological approach to Biblical Hebrew that closely compared variant expressions and vocabulary in various biblical books. He has noted many cases of replacement of words and grammatical forms in one book (for example, in Chronicles), compared with an earlier usage in a passage belonging to an earlier book (for example, in Kings). According to Hurvitz, it is possible on the basis of these contrasts to distinguish preexilic Hebrew from postexilic Hebrew, or what he labeled "Standard Biblical Hebrew" (often abbreviated as SBH) and "Late Biblical Hebrew" (LBH).[73]

Hurvitz's research was important for Genesis 1, when he extended his approach to distinguishing P and Ezekiel. He demonstrated that in cases where synonyms can be identified in these two works, P was consistently prior to Ezekiel. On this basis, Hurvitz concluded that P dates before Ezekiel and is therefore part of standard Biblical Hebrew rather than Late Biblical Hebrew.[74] Among students of Hebrew language, Hurvitz's typology has gained a great deal of support.[75]

In recent years, Hurvitz's approach has been the subject of considerable debate. Some of the disagreements come from scholars studying the linguistic evidence,[76] but other criticisms arose from scholars who work on the literary and editorial history of texts and do not really address matters of language.[77] Yet questions about Hurvitz's approach have been raised. It presupposed that results deriving from a rather limited number of passages in P and Ezekiel were representative for both of these texts generally and not only for the sections of these books where the linguistic contrast could be observed. Hurvitz's critics have also complained that his linguistic approach does consider the literary history of a text. For example, the problem of the date of Ezekiel did not enter into Hurvitz's discussion in a substantial way. He assumed that the book in general could be dated to the early sixth century, a view that has been challenged in other quarters of biblical scholarship. For many scholars deploying a redactional and literary approach, the text of Ezekiel in large measure does not date to the first third of the sixth century. In this case, the priority of P before Ezekiel would not necessarily make P preexilic; both could be postexilic. The issues and evidence are quite involved and very technical. Interested readers will find more information in the endnotes, but as this review of the debate suggests, the disagreement stems in large measure from subdisciplines that are at times not addressing one another's arguments and what they regard as proper method and evidence.

To my mind, the priestly material of Genesis 1 would be suitable linguistically and culturally in the late preexilic period, or in the exilic period, or even in the decades following in the sixth century. Genesis 1 may have followed traditional prose writing coming out of the monarchic period, in keeping with Hurvitz's findings.[78] At the same time, the composition of the present text may date to a later time during the sixth century, as other critics would argue. In view of the passages in the Bible that most closely compare with Genesis 1, several often dated to the sixth century stand out (for example, Isaiah 45:7 as well as Ezekiel 1 and 43), as the preceding chapters illustrate. With these sorts of texts in mind, one might be inclined to date Genesis 1 to this century. (In this context we may also view Genesis 1 as an effort at preserving Israelite cultural identity over and against the possible domination of Mesopotamian political and cultural influences.)[79] In general, this book works with the sixth century as the general context for Genesis 1. Whether or not a sixth-century date for Genesis 1 is correct, the debates of source criticism and linguistic analysis point to a priestly tradition rather than one priestly source. This view is consistent with some of the findings of redaction criticism.

Redaction Criticism and the Canonical Approach

Redaction criticism of Genesis 1 examines biblical books for signs of editorial additions and changes. From these signs, scholars have made the case for different levels or layers. In some biblical books, this editorial activity is rather strong, and it has been possible to reconstruct rather complex editorial or redactional histories. For other biblical books, it has been more difficult to arrive at consensus. Genesis 1 has received some attention from this approach. Canon criticism, or the canonical approach, considers the editorial history of biblical books as part of its efforts to better understand how biblical books as whole works came together. In this way, the final form that biblical books take and the way that they work in their final shaping can be appreciated better. Canon criticism pursues this agenda in order to appreciate the theological dimension of the text by reading it in terms of its wider context of the Bible. More specifically, it inquires into the theological witness represented by the final form of the books.

Redaction has long been a topic of research of Genesis 1.[80] Scholars have posited earlier versions of Genesis 1 lying behind its present form. Hermann Gunkel generally regarded Genesis 1 as thoroughly redacted from an older pre-P text.[81] Martin Noth commented: "The creation of the P narrative in Gen. 1:1—2:4a has behind it a literary prehistory and that P has here incorporated into his presentation previously formed narrative material without smooshing out all the irregularities that arose thereby."[82] Noth suggests more specifically: "The narrative elements dealing with the creative *act* of God, with their articulation of the whole into individual works of creation, seem to be previously formed material which P absorbed, not altogether smoothly and harmoniously, into his presentation oriented toward the creative *word* of God and the six-day scheme."[83] The double acts of creation on days 3 and 6 have also been viewed as alterations/additions to an earlier version that would have had only a single generative act per day.[84] Other scholars have discussed further redactional or editorial changes to Genesis 1.[85] Even Umberto Cassuto, who largely rejected source-critical and redactional approaches, argued that some phrasings in Genesis 1 reflected an older epic version as opposed to a more recent composition. Cassuto suggested, for example, that the first term in the formulation of "beast of the earth" (*hayto 'eres*) in Genesis 1:24 reflected older poetic usage (for example, in Psalms 50:10 and 104:11, 20), compared with the corresponding expression in Genesis 1:25, 30, *hayyat ha'ares* (see Jeremiah 28:14; Hosea 4:3; cf. 13:8).[86]

This variation within Genesis 1 perhaps suggests a complex history lying behind this text. In the first three chapters of this book, we have seen royal themes at various points: the three models of creation generally having a royal background; temple-building as a royal role; divine pronouncements—not blessings—that arguably sound like royal pronouncements; and royal language of the image and likeness of verses 26–28, as well as the verbs "to dominate" in verse 28 and "to rule" in verse 26 and 28. We have also noted some unevenness in the chapter, such as different schemas about the animals,[87] and variant phrasings (such as the one noted by Cassuto). We may also observe that there are substantial portions of Genesis 1 without any particular priestly features. Based on these observations, it would not be difficult to entertain a theory that there was an older royal version of creation that the priestly author of Genesis 1 drew on and recast with priestly ideas and vocabulary.[88] I could also entertain the idea that this royal version was a poetic one,[89] perhaps a creation psalm with some resemblances to Psalms 8 and 104.[90] Whatever might have been the older version, it was cast in a liturgical prose, structured by the seven-days schema and marked by a number of other priestly features. If the text was the result of considerable compositional and editorial activity, then it may be regarded as a literary work with what Luis Alonso Schökel calls a "secondary unity."[91]

Even in suggesting this possibility, I hasten to urge caution. Reconstructions of this sort are highly hypothetical, and so it may be questioned whether there was a self-standing composition prior to the priestly text of Genesis 1 as we essentially have it.[92] It is quite possible that a priestly author with experience of the old Judean royal cult could have drawn on such royal themes and reworked them in drafting his priestly composition. Rather than reworking a particular psalm, the priestly author may have drawn on various prior sources. Psalm 104 has been suggested, for example.[93] A priest working in the Jerusalem temple (or at least in its traditions) could have been fully aware of royal themes such as what we see in Genesis 1. The Jerusalem temple was after all a royal institution,[94] and a literate priest could well have produced a vision of reality that at some points uses royal themes and at other points adapts such themes to priestly notions.

The chapters of my book here do not venture reconstruction of the text's prehistory. Instead, I work with the notion of a basic priestly composition. I imagine that this priestly author drew not only on the traditional creation material known in ancient Israel (as outlined in chapter 1) and not only with traditional priestly terms and ideas (as described in chapters 2 and 3), but also draws on some of the wider currents of thoughts about the cosmos reflected in works such as the Memphite Creation and Philo of Byblos (as I mentioned in chapter 2). Such a scenario seems to gain in plausibility when it is remembered that Ezekiel, another priestly work, seems to draw broadly on Phoenician tradition (for example, Ezekiel 28). Of course, without more evidence, such claims are little more than suspicions on my part.

While I have generally prescinded from a full redactional analysis of Genesis 1, this book has paid attention to an important redactional observation often made about the relationship of Genesis 1 to other contexts. Most commentators tend to take Genesis 1:1—2:3 as later than 2:4b and following, with 2:4a added as an editorial priestly addition designed to bridge the priestly creation account between the two passages. In this reading, 2:4a serves as the first of several priestly headings marking genealogies listing generations (*toledot* in Hebrew) in Genesis (5:1; 6:9; 10:1; 11:10, 27; 25:12, 19; 36:19, and 37:2).[95] As a result of this reading, commentators have recognized that the redactional link in Genesis 2:4a makes the first creation story serve as the prologue or preface to the second. We explored this issue in some depth in chapter 4.

On this point, redaction criticism dovetails somewhat with the "canonical approach," advocated by Brevard S. Childs, for many years professor of Old Testament at Yale Divinity School. In the redaction of Genesis 1–2, they are not, as commonly supposed, simply "two creation stories."[96] Childs notes that in their present canonical shaping (what he elsewhere calls "the final form of the text"), the Yahwist story has been subordinated to the priestly account.[97] In his approach, Childs builds on redactional features of the text, but he would not restrict his analysis to identifying such features. Instead, he regards the text in its "shape" as an object of historical study in its own right. The "canonical approach" draws on historical study, redaction criticism, and literary analysis of texts, but standing above these resources for study of the Bible's final form is the theological concern of the "canonical approach," and for the text's continuing capacity to speak to people. For our purposes in studying Genesis 1, Childs' reading of Genesis 1–2 together marked an important step in seeing the final production of these chapters as parts ultimately standing as a single text.

Childs' canonical approach invites broader inquiry into the meaning of creation in Genesis 1 in terms of the whole Bible.[98] For a Christian canonical approach, this means thinking about Genesis 1 in terms of both the Old and New Testaments. The meaning of Genesis 1 would depend on understanding it in terms of the major ideas of both testaments. This might be pursued by tracing intertextual relationships or themes from Genesis 1 through the two testaments.[99] Clearly the canonical approach is a matter of Christian theorizing. Some thinking along these lines can be seen in a short book on creation by Cardinal Joseph Ratzinger (now Pope Benedict XVI), published in English in 1990.[100] The drama of creation cannot be separated by the larger biblical drama of creation, fall, incarnation, resurrection, and eschaton. From one perspective, this sort of operation generates interpretation of Genesis 1 by juxtaposing it with other biblical texts that were composed without any knowledge of Genesis 1 (or vice-versa). In other words, this sort of broad canonical approach finds the fuller meaning of Genesis 1 by assuming or claiming that its meaning is not restricted to the meanings of the text as understood by its historical author and audience. In this sort of reading, secondary readings generated by seeing Genesis 1 in terms of the Christian Bible as a whole become the primary sense of the text for Christians.

At the same time, this instinct to see Genesis 1 in its broader biblical context has roots in the Bible itself, as shown by a redactional insight going back to Benno Jacob and the pair of great twentieth-century Jewish intellectuals, Martin Buber and Franz Rosenzweig.[101] They observed that the account of the building of the Tabernacle in Exodus 39–40 echoes the creation of the world in Genesis 1:31—2:3. The basic parallels are highlighted in italics:[102]

> Exodus 39:43: "and when Moses *saw* all the *work,* and *behold,* they had *made* it—just as the Lord commanded, so they had *made*— Moses *blessed* them."
>
> Genesis 1:31a: "and God *saw* all that he had *made,* and there, it was very good."
>
> Genesis 2:3: "and God *blessed* the seventh day and sanctified it because on it he ceased from all its *work* that God had created for *making.*"
>
> Exodus 40:33b: "and Moses *finished* the *work.*"
>
> Genesis 2:2a: "and God *finished* on the seventh day his *work.*"
>
> Exodus 39:32a: "and all the work of the tabernacle of the tent of meeting was *finished.*"
>
> Genesis 2:1 "and the heavens and the earth and all their host were *finished.*"

The verbal links involved with these verses tie the Tabernacle account in Exodus 39–40 to creation in Genesis 1:31—2:3.

For redaction criticism, this linkage was generated by P or by a later priestly redactor (sometimes called R[P]) linking P to prior material of JE or redacted JE (RJE).[103] This insight worked nicely with the further observation that creation and temple building in the Bible and Ancient Near East were often cast in terms of one another, a sort of literary analogy that the Harvard biblical scholar Jon D. Levenson has called a "homology."[104] The temple in biblical passages such as Psalm 78:69 is represented with images of the heavens: "He built his sanctuary like the heavens, like the earth that he established forever." Temple-construction is described sometimes in cosmic terms in Mesopotamian texts, such as Gudea Cylinder A, xxv, line 2: "the house's stretching out/ along (sub-structure) walltops,/was like the heights of heaven/awe-inspiring."[105] For many, divergent commentators such as Joseph Blenkinsopp, William P. Brown, Michael Fishbane, Loren Fisher, Bernd Janowski, Peter J. Kearney, Jon D. Levenson, Hannah Liss, S. Dean McBride, Raymond C. van Leeuwen and Moshe Weinfeld,[106] Genesis 1 renders cosmic creation in terms of temple building, a point that the chapters in this study explore.

This relationship indicates that broader readings across major parts of the Bible are already an intended dimension of religious texts during the biblical period, and it anticipates further readings across what became biblical books. Historical critics, and in particular redaction critics, may recognize such relationships when they stand at the primary historical level of the text, and may not go beyond such primary historical contexts. They may trace efforts where biblical editors made intertextual connections within what became Scripture, even where these were not made by their original authors. This is a crucial point that requires some comment. Making these sorts of connections was arguably tied to their becoming recognized as religious or sacred writings within ancient Israel. One sign of this recognition involves their becoming objects of interpretation from the eighth or seventh century on. Prior to the eighth century, sacred literature shows less explicit, deliberate acts of interpretation, and this I believe is one of the most important shifts in the ancient history of what scriptural texts are. A concomitant factor in this shift involves the intense scribal agglomeration of works that came to be considered scriptural from the seventh century onward.

For explicit reflections on interpretation, we have some points of reference within our biblical traditions. To be clear, I do not simply

mean obvious instances of reinterpretation. Instead, I mean explicit representations of interpretation and reflections on interpretation. For a
narrative description of interpretation, we have the classic postexilic text
of Nehemiah 8:8 describing the Levites reading and arguably interpreting the reading of Torah. This verse uses different terms of reading and
interpretation.[107] Interpretation of this sort seeks to divine in the traditional text understandings applicable to the context of the interpreters
and their audience. This complex of textual activity, as we see it in later
biblical texts and the Dead Sea Scrolls, might be further described as
"scripturalizing." By this, I mean that texts regarded as holy or inspired
were coming to be read and interpreted together; that words or complexes of terms shared by different religious texts not only could be read
in tandem but should be read together across the boundaries of their
original contexts, beyond the limits of any individual passage or document. (I try to avoid using the word, "book," for writings in this period,
since this word is anachronistic.) In general, the writing and collecting
of religious texts in turn reinforced collecting their interpretations and
cross-referencing the texts. Redaction critics might view this activity as
part of postexilic Israel's "Schriftgelehrte intertextuality," but for canonical critics this does not express sufficiently the larger move represented
by this textual work.[108] Childs would put this activity under the rubric of
the "canonical process," but the word "canonical" assumes the existence
of a canon, something of an anachronism for postexilic Israel and the
Dead Sea Scrolls. Prior to the emergence of the notion of canon (after
the Dead Sea Scrolls), we may speak instead of a developing collection
of sacred writings that may cross-reference to one another.

The narrative representation of Nehemiah 8:8 is not the beginning
of the interpretational activity represented by the verse. In chapter 4, we
noted earlier texts that explicitly comment on scriptural texts as revealed
(or not) by God and as properly understood (or not) by humans. As we
saw, explicit reflections on interpretation concentrate in two arenas,[109]
prophecy given in the name of Yahweh that the passages regard as false
(Deuteronomy 18:20; Jeremiah 14:14 and 29:23; cf. Ezekiel 20:25-26)
and the worship of other gods (Deuteronomy 17:3). These biblical
works, with their expressions about what the deity says that he did not
command, date to the seventh and sixth centuries. This period was the
context when a concern developed for the interpretation of older texts
that may (and arguably should) be read as allowing the practices. We
may connect this development with the scribal production of prophecy and law in ancient Judah in the seventh and sixth centuries; in this

context, interpretation developed in tandem with the scribal production of texts. It may be that scribal production brought together written texts of older and newer formulations over the same practices, which in turn engendered textual interpretation in a manner not as critically apparent in earlier periods. It may be at this juncture in Israel's textual culture that shows the beginning of its emerging scriptures and scripturalizing processes of reading across texts.

The interpretation of holy writings continued to expand and shift in the context of Second Temple Literature. The texts provide many new opportunities to address religious issues; we might say that scriptural texts become pretexts for raising such questions and resolving them in a manner consonant with the religious worldviews of those who transmitted the texts. The use of scriptural texts provided warrant for different focuses and for further interpretation; they also provided tradents with a sense of continuity with the biblical past, that foundational, mythical time. Precisely because such religious texts were considered to be scriptural in this period, they became not simply sites of textual interpretation in a detailed or in some narrow sense. In the Second Temple period, scriptural texts also became the canvases for dramatic, large-scale retellings that reflected the lives of the Second Temple composers and their audiences and the traditions in which they understood themselves. This trajectory at "reading scripturally" increased in the postexilic period and anticipates later intertextual readings made in Jewish and Christian sources. Redaction criticism and the canonical approach may contribute to an understanding of this series of changes within ancient Israel. As long as the canonical approach recognizes that it is essentially a labor of Christian theology, and as long as it does not attempt to level out the various levels of reading biblical texts and their meanings in their historical development, and as long as redactional criticism does not attempt to make historical readings stand for a full biblical theology of both Old and New Testaments, the two disciplines may work well in some conjunction. To my mind, the two enterprises may be pursued separately. At the same time, it seems to me that in the long run, the two pursued in tandem produce more powerful results for Christian readings of the two testaments.

Before closing this discussion of the canonical approach and redactional criticism as it applies to Genesis 1, we may briefly note changes in the area of redaction criticism over the past two decades. The most notable development has been the wedding of source and redaction criticism. This is evident not only in the most helpful and detailed discussion of redaction in a book by David M. Carr, professor at Union Theological Seminary in New York City,[110] but also in an influential study by Tübingen professor, Erhard Blum.[111] These two biblical scholars differ over the specifics of the nature of P: Carr favors the idea of a preexisting, separate P document, while Blum sees the P material not as a full-blown independent composition, but a series of preliminary drafts or sketches incorporated and refined in the eventual priestly redaction. (Because there does not seem to be a full-scale separate priestly source paralleling the J source,[112] I am inclined toward Blum's view on this point.) In any case, Carr's work carries forward this agenda by wedding studies of source and redaction in a wide range of texts from the ancient Near East (for example, in the work on Gilgamesh by University of Pennsylvania professor, Jeffrey Tigay).[113] We see various insights of redaction bearing on another areas such as ancient Near Eastern comparisons, to which we now turn.

Comparative Study

Perhaps the single greatest contribution to the study of Genesis 1 in the twentieth century came from comparative study with ancient Near Eastern creation texts. Scholars have long compared biblical texts with other works of the ancient world, from Egypt in the west to Mesopotamia in the east. Many texts from the ancient world show ideas and literary motifs very similar to what we see in the Bible, and they help us to understand better the sense of the concepts or worldviews expressed by different biblical authors. Moreover, the Bible sometimes shows a direct awareness of ideas from other cultures.

As the Bible was emerging in ancient Israel, it was confronting the worldviews of its own times. At some point in ancient Israel's existence, some of its worldviews were judged to be antithetical to Israel's way of life. For example, the worship of other deities may have been tolerated in early Israel, but the growing criticism of other deities from the ninth century on eventually made the sole worship of Yahweh into the normative practice for Israel.[114] Yet not all worldviews of Israel's neighbors were rejected outright. Rather, the biblical record shows that some aspects of other ancient Near Eastern worldviews were sometimes embraced or other times modified. This question of how the Bible compares with the worldviews of other cultures has been an important question of comparisons of Genesis 1 with other ancient Near Eastern creation accounts.

In the case of Genesis 1, *Enuma Elish* came to be the most cited of Mesopotamian creation narratives in biblical studies. Its publication along with several other works such as Alexander Heidel's 1942 work,

The Babylonian Genesis, illustrated the long tradition and variety among Mesopotamian cosmogonies. Umberto Cassuto's 1944 Hebrew commentary on Genesis 1:1—6:8 noted not only some of these Mesopotamian works, but also several biblical passages that help to situate Genesis 1 within the larger traditions of creation. Studies have continued to situate Genesis 1 in a longer and broader tradition of Israelite creation accounts.[115]

Enuma Elish became further prominent in discussions of Genesis 1, thanks to the 1950 translation by the University of Pennsylvania Assyriologist Ephraim A. Speiser in the widely used *Ancient Near Eastern Texts Relating to the Old Testament* (commonly abbreviated as *ANET*), followed fifteen years later by his 1964 Genesis commentary.[116] Together these two works made comparison of *Enuma Elish* and Genesis 1 a staple in biblical scholarship. In 1984, Richard J. Clifford, Professor of Old Testament and now Dean of Boston College's School of Theology and Ministry, would note how *Enuma Elish* had come to be thought of as the standard (and implicitly representative) for Near Eastern cosmogonies.[117] And many Bible scholars in turn treated Genesis 1 as the standard of Israelite thought.[118] It is true that many students of the Bible tend to think of Genesis 1 as the standard account of creation. In fact, many, if not most readers regard it as the only biblical account of creation. They are not aware of the several other biblical creation pieces, whether it is the powerful picture of God in Psalm 74:12-17, the hymnic Psalms 104 and 148, the evocative description of Wisdom personified with God in Proverbs 8:22-31, the condemnation of Jeremiah 10:12-16 = 51:15-19, or the recollections of creation in Job 26:7-13 and 38:1-11. Some of these biblical texts offer excerpts of what was known of the creation in ancient Israel. Many other passages, such as Jeremiah 27:5 and 31:35, Amos 4:13, 5:8 and 9:6, Zechariah 12:1, Psalm 89:11-13, and Job 9:8-9, contain allusions to creation. (Jeremiah 4:23-26 shows an interesting reversal of creation.)

These biblical texts show the range of themes that tended to be common to Israelite creation accounts. They also point to the fact that like Mesopotamian creation accounts, these could be molded to the specific concerns and worldview of their composers and audiences. Indeed, on the Mesopotamian side, there are numerous and varied descriptions of creation.[119] The Ugaritic texts likewise contain an excerpt of a creation tradition.[120] This text is important because it shows that the earlier tradition of creation stories is not only Mesopotamian (or East Semitic), but also Canaanite (or more accurately, West Semitic). In addition, the

Ugaritic texts provide a number of allusions to old creation ideas. The West Semitic context represented by the Ugaritic texts is also suggested by later Phoenician cosmogonies that contain some of the elements mentioned in Genesis 1.[121] The force of the scholarly studies of Ugaritic and Phoenician traditions is to suggest shared West Semitic creation traditions in later periods. Some commentators detect the combination of a West Semitic background with Egyptian influence in Genesis 1,[122] while other scholars have read the text simply against an Egyptian background.[123] Broader comparisons with Egyptian texts have also been probed without claims for direct influence.[124] Greek parallels have also been discussed.[125]

The comparison between *Enuma Elish* and Genesis 1 continues to predominate in the comparative discussion.[126] The tendency to take Genesis 1 as the standard for the Bible has led in turn to sweeping generalizations being made between ancient Israelite thought and "their more mythopoeic neighbors" (to cite Vanderbilt professor, Jack M. Sasson).[127] Both Genesis 1 and *Enuma Elish* are sophisticated products of religious thought and experience. They are not so much the standards for their respective cultures as they are representations of the apex of literary and religious expression about creation for the scribes that produced them. At the time of their writing, most Israelites and Babylonians probably did not know these versions of creation. Sasson comments: "That *Enuma Elish* was kept away from nonpriestly hands and that it was recited only in the inner recesses of Mesopotamian temples are also reasons why the text was not likely available to Israel's own priests."[128]

This is not to say that comparative studies have no role to play. On the contrary, it continues to produces insight into Genesis 1, and here I have in mind a particularly seminal article by Baruch Halpern of Pennsylvania State University, entitled "The Assyrian Astronomy of Genesis 1 and the Birth of Milesian Philosophy."[129] Similarly, many scholars have argued that the author of Genesis 1 knew *Enuma Elish*.[130] Kenton Sparks at Eastern Baptist University near Philadelphia has produced the most detailed, comparative reading of Genesis 1, specifically as a response to *Enuma Elish* and the worldview that it represents.[131] Sparks argues that the priestly writer actually used the myth.[132] While the approach can be speculative at a number of points, it draws our attention to the density of cultural information in Genesis 1 that can only be sensed through a comparative approach. Halpern and Sparks have explored the Mesopotamian side of available evidence rather thoroughly, and so my explorations of Genesis 1 focus more on evidence closer to Israel, especially from the site of ancient Ugarit, as well as the evidence from within Israel itself. Genesis 1 may well represent a reaction to Mesopotamian culture on a number of levels; at the same time for its response, it is drawing on the literary and religious traditions closer at hand. We may say that my study looks more at the context inside of Israel than at the context outside of it. Comparative evidence cited in this study is used more to contextualize Israel's creation traditions in order to understand better the "insider context" of Genesis 1.[133]

On this point, Cassuto's contributions are worth recalling. His efforts at reconstructing an ancient Israelite creation epic[134] had the merit of indicating the vast range of biblical references to primordial creation that look quite different than Genesis 1. This passage was not the original "standard" in ancient Israel. As we have already noted, other texts, such as Psalms 74:12-17, 89:11-13, Job 26:7-13, and 38:1-11, refer to a divine conflict at the beginning of creation. This basic idea of creation probably comes closer to what Israelites knew about such primordial events. Genesis 1 built on and supplanted other Israelite versions of creation that understood the primordial universe as a field of battle between two divine wills.[135] It envisions instead a single royal-priestly power beyond all powers, enthroned over the world understood as a holy place similar to a sanctuary; this understanding of Genesis 1 is explored in the preceding chapters. The royal politics of creation expressed in texts such as *Enuma Elish* and Psalm 74 were replaced partially in Genesis 1 with a priestly order imbued with the proper religious life of the Sabbath, festivals (*mo'adim*) and perhaps even dietary norms. I elaborate on this shift in chapters 1 and 2. *Enuma Elish* also plays a major role in my understanding of the light of the first day, which is explored in chapter 2. It also provides an important example of myth discussed in chapter 5.

Form Criticism and Literary Study

Form criticism and literary study of the Bible have been old areas of research in biblical studies. Form criticism has been prominent since the beginning of the twentieth century,[136] while literary criticism gained particular force in biblical studies from the 1970s on.[137] Form criticism pays attention to the genres of writing (for example, a recipe, an obituary, or a sonnet) and the expectations of each one (for example, a list of ingredients to be used in a recipe, as well as instructions for cooking). It looks at how a given piece of writing manifests the chief characteristics of a genre as well as possible optional elements. In addition, form criticism classically has been concerned for the original setting in which a genre was used (such as recipes, clearly to be used for cooking in a kitchen).

Form criticism benefited tremendously from the comparative approach, as it provided a wider range of texts used to identify biblical genres.

When it came to creation texts, form criticism noted that creation texts are narratives (in either poetry or prose) that delineate ancient events of creation.[138] Two major subgenres of creation texts are *theogonies,* which describe the creation of gods and goddesses, often as a series of generations of deities, and *cosmogonies,* which narrate the creation of the world, including humanity.[139] Many scholars have been reluctant to view Genesis 1 in terms of theogonies and cosmogonies especially of the ancient Near East, as these works are regularly classified as myths. As we noted in chapter 5, many scholars are reluctant to see Genesis 1 as a myth. Genesis 1 in its overall content arguably fits with cosmogonies, although its cosmic pairing of Heaven and Earth in verse 1 (and perhaps also the cosmic elements in verse 2) as well as its label as "the generations of Heaven and Earth" echo older theogonies.[140] Genesis 1 also manifests one of the openings found in cosmogonies, namely a temporal marker (such as "when"), plus the conditions prevailing at this time, followed by narration of creation.[141] Among form critics, there is little consensus about how to label Genesis 1.[142]

Literary study looks at biblical books the way that English professors study classic pieces of literature, like Shakespeare's plays. This approach is often not terribly concerned with the historical background of the Bible. For the literary approach, that would be like reducing the meaning of Shakespeare's plays to what we know about their historical background. Rather than reading behind the text for its editorial history or historical context, literary study devotes its attention to what is going on in the text itself. It means focusing on the text's language and imagery, and the dynamics of plot and character. Older literary reading of a text looks at the world created in it or by it, not to the historical or cultural world of the author. Under the rubric of literary criticism, we may group both literary criticism prevalent in English departments and comparative literature,[143] as well as "rhetorical criticism,"[144] an approach that emerged within the field of biblical studies under the influence of broader literary study and as a reaction to the limitations of form criticism.[145]

When it comes to Genesis 1, literary study is an old matter.[146] In more recent years, the question of the literary style and structure of Genesis 1 has reached something of a consensus.[147] The style has long been characterized as "architectonic"[148] or "lapidary,"[149] due to the series of repetitions within the first six days.[150] With their many (though hardly rigid) repetitions, the six days are highly parallel to one another in their wordings. Clearly the structure of seven days stood out as the basic over-all structural feature of Genesis 1. As we noted in chapter 3, this insight was bolstered by comparisons to units of seven days used as a structuring device in a number of Ugaritic passages.[151]

Older critics such as Cassuto also noted many particular occurrences of repeating terms. He pointed out in particular the importance of the number seven not just for the number of days but also words and motifs appearing seven times or in multiples of seven. Objections have occasionally been raised that the text contains a number of irregularities that do not conform to this larger patterning or that this patterning reflects modern sensibilities about symmetry.[152] At the same time, such minor deviations hardly detract from the effect of the many, shared expressions within each of the six days or from the evident parallelism between days 1–3 and days 4–6. In short, the literary patterning of Genesis 1 expresses the sense of order championed by its priestly writer. This sense of the text as a piece of priestly literature is central to understanding it, and it has influenced the heart of this book. Moreover, often since Cassuto, critics have repeated the observation that days 1–3 and 4–6 parallel one another in content.[153] Cassuto's approach was extended by Nahum Sarna, who was professor at Brandeis University for many years. Sarna regarded days 1–3 as the resource for the utilizers in days 4–6. (Sarna also contrasted the vegetation of day 3 as the lowest form of organic life with humanity of day 6 as the highest form of organic life.) This overall sense of the text's priestly architecture informs this study.

3. A Few Reflections

In retrospect, what is perhaps most interesting in the study of Genesis 1 is the way that the different areas of research have not simply influenced one other; they have also affected some of their ground rules. For Ron Hendel, literary perceptions about P form the basis for text-critical decisions; for William Brown, information about cosmogonies in the ancient Near East versus the Hellenistic world affects his text-critical perceptions. Brown also makes literary and redactional theory play a significant role in his text criticism. It is also to be noted how Second Temple literature too has informed biblical text criticism. Hendel incorporates the texts of Jubilees and Pseudo-Philo's *Liber Antiquitatum Biblicarum* into the text-critical apparatus. For Israel Knohl and Jacob Milgrom, redactional theory about H informs their source-criticism. David Carr, too, connects considerations of sources, redaction, and literary style. Dissatisfaction with the limits of traditional source criticism has led to more complex models of textual composition that pay particular attention to editorial history as well as scribal transmission.[154]

Related to this way of looking at scribal production are several valuable investigations into oral transmission of texts and its role in the production of written texts, for example by Susan A. Niditch (Amherst College) and Raymond F. Person, Jr. (Ohio Northern University).[155] The related role of literacy in textual production has been stressed in the otherwise widely varying treatments by Michael D. Coogan (Stonehill College), James L. Crenshaw (professor emeritus of Duke Divinity School) and Menachem Haran (professor emeritus of the Hebrew University).[156] The comparative agenda also points up issues of social location in which the text was composed. In other words, when it comes to Genesis 1, we should not be speaking simply of it as a priestly text or its priestly tradition, but we should see Genesis 1 as a priestly scribal production belonging to a priestly scribal tradition. The comparative agenda also helps us to understand better the literary motifs and structures in the Bible, for example, the structure of the seven days in Genesis 1. Similarly, the cultural sensibilities of temple building for the priestly presentation of cosmic order have come to the fore, thanks in part to the comparative approach. Here literary considerations are tied into source critical study.

As the chapters of this book illustrate, the more traditional areas of modern biblical study have strongly informed it. Some of the newer approaches mentioned at the outset of this short survey have also made an impact on this study, especially when they build on the older methods. The fruits of source criticism, the comparative approach, literary criticism, feminist criticism, canon criticism, and innerbiblical and post-biblical interpretation have left a particular imprint on my thinking. In addition, postcolonial theory, and in particular reflections by commentators from sub-Saharan Africa,[157] have led me to see ancient Israel's circumstances in light of their experience and reflections. In his conclusion to his brief survey of literary theory, Jonathan Culler makes a helpful statement about theory, in all its variety:

> Theory, then, offers not a set of solutions but the prospect of further thought. It calls for commitment to the work of reading, of challenging presuppositions, of questioning the assumptions on which you proceed. I began by saying that theory was endless—an unbounded corpus of challenging and fascinating writings—but not just more writings: it is also an ongoing project of thinking which does not end when a very short introduction ends.[158]

My book represents my effort to draw on and synthesize various approaches in order to think about the priestly vision of creation. I have drawn on various approaches to help me analyze and reflect on the meaning of Genesis 1. I must say that I don't find each approach equally valuable for this particular project. This is not to say that it would be impossible to combine more of the approaches presently available in biblical research, and in fact, it is my hope that biblical scholarship will figure out ways to synthesize these various branches of study into a more powerful and fruitful tool for understanding the Bible.

In ending this survey, I feel it's necessary to reflect on one important methodological difficulty faced by all biblical interpreters, namely ourselves and specifically ourselves as interpreters. In a sense, all of the approaches, traditional ones as well as more recent entries, make efforts at understanding the interpreter's role in interpretation. Within biblical studies, this problem has often been posed as a contrast between historical and theological approaches, as reflected in a statement made by one of my teachers, the great American biblical scholar Frank Moore Cross, professor emeritus of Harvard University. Cross says: "Our task must be a historical, not a theological, enterprise."[159] For a work that asks first what Genesis 1 conveyed for its author(s) and audience in ancient Israel, the basic task starts with studying their context and worldview. The research needs to begin with Israel's religious and cultural context, and it needs to build on this foundation.

At the same time, it seems to me that while we have been quite adept at deciphering and describing what the ancients said, by comparison we have been less adroit at understanding and sensing what they felt about the world around them. Perhaps out of a concern to avoid superimposing modern theological perspectives on ancient texts, many historically-oriented scholars tend to avoid religious matters and questions of meaning. This is a reasonable concern. It also involves a very grave difficulty for interpreters, especially for ones like myself who come not only from a strong religious background but also from a particularly privileged situation in the academic world. There is a real danger of subconsciously identifying with the situation of Genesis 1 and of unconsciously championing the sort of values that it expresses. At the same time, the historical task is not simply a description of the worldviews in ancient Israel and the ancient Near East and setting them in their proper historical and cultural context. It is also the cultural historian's task to ask about what these expressions meant to the ancients and even to ask how they might have felt and thought about divinity, humanity, and the world. In other words, what did their words mean to them and evoke for them? This study makes efforts in this direction.

In the spirit of the ancients' tendency to read the past through their own present conditions, I have drawn occasionally on later theological concepts and make some modern applications along the way. My comments of this sort work rather directly from what the ancient authors were expressing in their texts. I try to learn what the Bible says about the struggles that its authors were trying to address and the ways they tried to address them. To do so, I sometimes use ideas from later theology. I draw on theology because its ways of addressing the nature of reality help to unpack what is going on in many biblical texts. The authors of many biblical books were no less concerned with the nature of reality than later theology or philosophy; sometimes in biblical texts we may glimpse their own sorts of theological or philosophical inquiry into the nature of reality. In this sense, an effort is made on my part to relate my study of Genesis 1 to the task of biblical theology.

I am aware of the potential danger in using theology for this study because it may suit or support my own theological perspective. I could fall into the trap that Cross identifies. Indeed, it has become clear to me over the past two decades that my interest in the priestly and liturgical aspects of biblical texts, including Genesis 1, has been inspired by my religious background as a believing Roman Catholic. Readers may want to know where I am coming from; so I think it's only fair to mention this. I have written about my religious background and affiliation elsewhere, so readers interested in such matters may look at that discussion.[160] As a sacramental Catholic, I tend to think of my own religious horizons as dovetailing with the liturgical texts of the Bible, such as priestly material and Psalms. I leave it to readers to decide whether my use of theology or my religious affiliation has adversely affected my reading of Genesis 1.

Scholars should be concerned about how their religious backgrounds or the modern categories that we use affect are our interpretation. More historically-minded biblical scholars may try to "get out of the way" of the past and let the past "speak for itself." (I have heard these sorts of expressions used by historical critics.) However, it is something of an illusion for scholars to think that they can both serve as interpreters of the past and get "out of its way." This sort of position arguably involves an ideology of authority, and it sometimes serves an excuse for a scholarship that cannot face its own theoretical underpinnings. Yet more is involved. Scholars who are interested in dealing with the theoretical aspects of our enterprise have much more to be concerned with than either our religious backgrounds or the modern categories that we use in considering our situations as interpreters. The difficulty goes beyond identifying our social, ethnic, economic, and political backgrounds and affiliations and their impacts on our work on the Bible. These all play roles in affecting our work, sometimes to the detriment of our handling of biblical passages and at other times to our benefit, depending on how well our horizons and intellects meet the horizons and intellects informing the texts that we study. Certainly over the past thirty years, biblical scholars have reflected more deliberately and consciously on who we are and how that makes an impact on our work. However, the problem runs deeper.

This is the fundamental problem, as I see it. We hardly perceive how much and how rapidly our present context is changing and affecting us all the time.[161] As scholars of the past, we are aware of how the past changed, or at least we work with ideas of how we think the past changed. We have a sense of historical and cultural developments and how these influenced various texts and traditions. After all, this is what we study. However, we are not nearly as good at being students of ourselves. We are not nearly as aware of the massive changes in our lives and in our world. We may take in changes along the way in our lives (changes in family situations and employment, deaths and births, major illnesses and losses experienced). Similarly, we take note of major events in our world (for me, Vatican II and the civil rights movement, the assassinations of John and Robert F. Kennedy and Martin Luther King Jr., the Vietnam War, the feminist movement and the shift in attitudes toward sexuality, the impact of Ronald Reagan, 9–11, the Iraq and Afghanistan wars, and the ecological movement). Yet we may experience but barely acknowledge the vast majority of changes in our lives and the changes that they make in us; and whatever impact they make on us as interpreters we barely take conscious note of. Like the past that we study, our present moment is shifting all the time. Like the past, the present—and we ourselves within it—are moving targets, which is difficult for us to fathom. We interpreters are not fixed points in the present; we are moving all the time just as much as the past moves, yet we do not see most changes in our circumstances and our intellects. In a real sense, we as much as the past are mysteries to be fathomed for our own interpretation.

Robert Frost has a two-line poem that captures many things, and it applies to interpreters of the past: "We dance round in a ring and suppose, But the Secret sits in the middle and knows." For interpreters, we work for decades; we dance round in a ring. However, it is not simply the past that is the Secret that is so hard to fathom; it is also the secret of ourselves. Scholars may have high competence in the evidence of the past, and our methods especially in the past thirty years are designed to help us to come to grips with the nature of interpreters. Still, we are not very well equipped for fathoming the complexity of our own shifting conditions and their impact on our thinking and for coordinating this self-knowledge with our knowledge of the past. As a result, it lies mostly beyond us to grasp and to coordinate our understanding of the shifting contexts of both past and present; we are unable to comprehend the shifting realities of both past and present, to consider the two of them together, and to include such a consideration in our interpretation.

Our work reflects the changing reality of who we have been, as well as what our fields have been and are becoming, as much as it reflects the texts and traditions that we seek to illuminate. What we have to say will (and should) fade in the future, not only because scholarship will improve with new data emerging and methods improving, but also because what we think and have to say bears the imprints of our own shifting contexts and experiences, often in ways that we will never know. Readers understand this in general terms, as this is true of people's work and lives. Whatever we do for a living, we are all interpreters of what we do; we analyze all the time. Yet in our work, we rarely ask about the impact of life events or world events on our intellects. In this respect, we often operate on autopilot. After all, it makes life easier and leaves time for other things that we find more needed, more meaningful, or more pleasurable. For all the riches of our knowledge, even the best scholars among us are only human; if we academics cannot fathom our own place in our work, then at least we could express some humility about the limits of our interpretations.[162]

Recommended Reading for Genesis 1

William P. Brown

The Ethos of Cosmos: The Genesis of Moral Imagination (Grand Rapids, Mich./ Cambridge, U.K.: Eerdmans, 1999).

> This study includes a theologically sensitive reading of Genesis 1.

Richard J. Clifford, SJ

Creation Accounts in the Ancient Near East and in the Bible (Catholic Biblical Quarterly Monograph Series, volume 26; Washington, D.C.: The Catholic Biblical Association of America, 1994).

> A fine presentation of creation accounts from around the ancient Near East. This is a scholarly work, and a fairly accessible one as well.

Edwin Firmage

"Genesis 1 and the Priestly Agenda," *Journal for the Study of the Old Testament* 82 (1999) 97–114.

> A good, scholarly description of the priestly character of Genesis 1.

Michael Fishbane

Biblical Myth and Rabbinic Mythmaking (Oxford: Oxford University, 2003).

> An important scholarly study of myth in the Bible from a thematic perspective.

W. Randall Garr

In His Own Image and Likeness: Humanity, Divinity, and Monotheism (Culture and History of the Ancient Near East, volume 15; Leiden/Boston: Brill, 2003).

A detailed analysis that combines grammatical insights with cultural information in interpreting the creation of the human person in Genesis 1:26-27.

Markham J. Geller and Mineke Schipper, editors

Imagining Creation (with an Introduction by Mary Douglas; IJS Studies in
Judaica, volume 5; Leiden: Brill, 2007).

This book discusses a wide selection of creation stories from different cultures, regions, and periods, from the Ancient Near East and India, Bible
and Koran, to modern Africa and Europe.

Edward L. Greenstein

"Presenting Genesis 1: Constructively and Deconstructively," *Prooftexts* 21/2
(2001) 1–22.

A combination of historical-criticism and post-modern approaches to the
chapter.

Baruch Halpern

"The Assyrian Astronomy of Genesis 1 and the Birth of Milesian Philosophy,"
Eretz Israel 27 (2003) 74°–83°. This essay has been republished in Halpern's
book, *From Gods to God: The Dynamics of Iron Age Cosmologies* (edited by
Matthew J. Adams; Forschungen zum Alten Testament, volume 63; Tübingen:
Mohr Siebeck, 2009) 427–442.

A speculative, yet brilliant study that sees Mesopotamian astronomical
ideas informing the description of creation in Genesis 1.

Ronald S. Hendel

"Genesis 1–11 and its Mesopotamian Problem," in *Cultural Borrowings and
Ethnic Appropriations in Antiquity: Oriens et Occidens* (edited by Erich S.
Gruen; Studien zu antiken Kulturkontakten und ihrem Nachleben, volume 8;
Stuttgart: Franz Steiner Verlag, 2005) 23–36.

A sophisticated consideration of various aspects of Genesis 1–11 as a form
of literary resistance to Mesopotamian culture and religion.

Ronald S. Hendel

"Prophets, Priests, and the Efficacy of Ritual," in *Pomegranates and Golden
Bells: Studies in Biblical, Jewish, and Near Eastern Ritual, Law and Literature
in Honor of Jacob Milgrom* (edited by David P. Wright, David N. Freedman,
and Avi Hurvitz; Winona Lake, Ind.: Eisenbrauns, 1995) 185–198.

This article makes a number of apt observations about the priestly worldview from a sociological and anthropological perspective.

Ronald S. Hendel

Genesis 1–11: A Commentary (Anchor Bible series, volume 1A; Yale University Press, in preparation).

This volume provides a fine, concise and insightful verse by verse commentary.

Bernd Janowski

"Tempel und Schöpfung. Schöpfungstheologische Aspekte der priesterschriftlichen Heiligtumskonzeption," *Jahrbuch für Biblische Theologie* 5 (1990) 37–69.

This article is recommended for its thoughtful, wide-ranging consideration of the themes of Genesis 1.

Jon D. Levenson

Creation and the Persistence of Evil; The Jewish Drama of Divine Omnipotence (San Francisco: Harper & Row, 1988).

A highly acclaimed and accessible study that describes Genesis 1 within the context of the larger biblical tradition.

S. Dean McBride

"Divine Protocol: Genesis 1:1—2:3 as Prologue to the Pentateuch," in *God Who Creates: Essays in Honor of W. Sibley Towner* (edited by William P. Brown and S. Dean McBride Jr.; Grand Rapids, Mich./Cambridge, U.K.: Eerdmans, 2000) 3–41.

This article discusses Genesis 1 in its broader context within the Pentateuch.

Frank Polak

"Poetic Style and Parallelism in the Creation Account (Gen. 1:1—2:3)," in *Creation in Jewish and Christian Tradition* (edited by H. Reventlow and Y. Hoffman; Journal for the Study of the Old Testament Supplementary Series, volume 319; Sheffield: Sheffield Academic Press, 2002) 2–31.

A brilliant study of the poetic sensibility informing the composition of Genesis 1.

Kenton Sparks

"*Enūma Elish* and Priestly Mimesis: Elite Emulation in Nascent Judaism," *Journal of Biblical Literature* 126 (2007) 625–48.

A sophisticated comparison of Genesis 1 with the Mesopotamian classic text, *Enuma Elish*.

Moshe Weinfeld

"Sabbath, Temple and the Enthronement of the Lord—The Problem of the *Sitz im Leben* of Genesis 1:1—2:3," in *Mélanges bibliques et orientaux en l'honneur de M. Henri Cazelles* (edited by André Caquot and Mathias Delcor; Alter Orient und Altes Testament, volume 212; Kevelaer: Butzon & Bercker; Neukirchen-Vluyn: Neukirchener Verlag, 1981) 501–12.

> A thematic examination of Genesis 1 in light of other ancient Near Eastern texts.

E. J. van Wolde

"The Text as Eloquent Guide: Rhetorical, Linguistic, and Literary Features in Genesis 1," in *Literary Structure and Rhetorical Strategies in the Hebrew Bible* (edited by L. J. de Regt, J. de Waard and J. Fokkelman; Assen: van Gorcum; Winona Lake, Ind.: Eisenbrauns, 1996) 134–51.

> A fine literary analysis of Genesis 1.

Notes

Introduction

1. This is true whether or not the text was written in Jerusalem. As we will discuss in ch. 2, we do not know where exactly Genesis 1 was written. If it was produced in Jerusalem by a priest at the time when the Temple was functioning, then its priestly author would have the priestly prerogative to make sacrificial offerings. At the same time, making offerings may not have been his primary function. As I discuss in ch. 4, I imagine the author to be a priestly scribe; whether he was a priestly administrator of some sort, it is impossible to know at this point.

2. For example, see Richard J. Clifford, *Creation Accounts in the Ancient Near East and in the Bible*, CBQMS 26; and Othmar Keel and Silvia Schroer, *Schöpfung: Biblische Theologien im Kontext altorientalischer Religioneis* (Gottingen: Vandenhoeck & Ruprecht; Freiburg, Schweiz: Universitätsverlag, 2002) 173–88.

3. A particularly handy edition of the NRSV is found in *The HarperCollins Study Bible Fully Revised and Updated: New Revised Standard Version* (general ed., Harold W. Attridge; New York: HarperSan Francisco, 2006). Its notes are rather substantial and often contain the present standard scholarship; as a result its notes are also sometimes cited. Hereafter cited as *HCSB*.

4. *TANAKH The Holy Scriptures: The New JPS Translation According to the Traditional Hebrew Text* (Philadelphia/New York/Jerusalem: The Jewish Publication Society, 1988).

5. Foster, *Muses*.

6. Stephanie Dalley, *Myths from Mesopotamia: Creation, the Flood, Gilgamesh and Others* (Oxford/New York: Oxford University, 1991).

7. *UNP*. The standard text edition is KTU, 2nd ed.. A revision of this volume is planned. The field also benefits from the important work of Gregorio del Olmo Lete and Joachin Sanmartín. *DUL,* a revised edition is in the works.

8. These appear in *The Context of Scripture* (ed. William W. Hallo and K. Lawson Younger; vol. 1; Leiden/Boston/Köln: Brill, 1997) 241–83, 333–58. There is also the English trans. of Nick Wyatt, *Religious Texts from Ugarit: The Words of Ilimilku and His Colleagues* (Sheffield: Sheffield Academic Press, 1998).

9. Dennis Pardee, *Ritual and Cult at Ugarit* (ed. Theodore J. Lewis; SBLWAW 10),

10. Dennis Pardee, *Les textes rituels* (two volumes; Ras Shamra—Ougarit XII; Paris: Éditions Recherches sur les Civilisations, 2000).

Chapter 1: Three Models of Creation

1. See the fine surveys of Paul Beauchamp, *Création et separation: Étude exégétique du chapitre premier de la Genèse*, LD 346–73; and Clifford, *Creation Accounts* (Intro., n. 2), 137–97.

2. See the emphasis on this point by Pope Benedict XVI (Cardinal Joseph Ratzinger), *'In the Beginning...': A Catholic Understanding of the Story of Creation and the Fall* (trans. Boniface Ramsey, O.P.; Huntington, Ind.: Our Sunday Visitor Publishing Division, 1990), 24.

3. In alluding to creation, Isaiah 45:18 uses all three of these verbs, and it adds another one, "to establish" (that comes from the root, $°kwn$). The model of procreation underlies the verbs in Psalm 90:2 (compare the related image for human creation by God in Deut. 32:18; cf. the model of weaving for the divine making of the human person in the womb in Ps. 139:15). In extrabiblical texts, human reproduction is a common model in the creation of the universe, including the generation of deities. See Clifford, *Creation Accounts*, 45, 86–90 106, 111. For the verbs of creation generally, see also Dennis J. McCarthy, "Creation Motifs in Ancient Hebrew Poetry," *CBQ* 29 (1967), 393–406. For the verb $°qny$, "to establish," as a verb of creation, see also Clifford, *Creation Accounts*, 118. On the root $°br'$, see p. 224.

4. These are all ways of expressing the fundamental connection of the divine to the world; through these, humanity can be linked to the divine. These expressions for this sense of linkage are what I would call "biblical ontologies," which convey the basic sense of the very being of creatures connected to (or "participating in") the reality of God. For example, as we will see shortly, the power of the human king draws on, or "participates in," the power of the divine warrior-king. This idea of ontology goes back to the medieval metaphysical idea of the "Great Chain of Being," which understood finite beings as "participating in" the Being, which is God. Their being in this sense derives from the Being of God. For examples in the ancient Near Eastern context, see my book, *God in Translation: Deities in Cross-Cultural Discourse in the Biblical World* (FAT series I, volume 57; Tübingen: Mohr Siebeck, 2008) 14, 48, 69, 298–99; and see further below. The Bible shows various pictures of reality that are analogous in some ways to later philosophical descriptions.

5. My three models are quite close to Keel and Schroer, *Schöpfung* (Intro, n. 2) 100–135. Their four models are creation as procreation and birth (see the following note); manufacture; conflict; and as spell, command, and word of command ("Machtwort" in the German original, *Schöpfung. Biblische Theologien im Kontext altorientalischer Religionen* [Göttingen: Vandenhoeck & Ruprecht; Freiburg Schweiz: Universitätsverlag, 2002] 100-35). Compared with Keel and Schroer, I put more emphasis on various forms of divine presence and wisdom and less on procreation and birth; the latter is relatively less common in biblical material. The listing of Keel and Schroer is richly informed by ancient Near Eastern textual and iconographic parallels, and it is highly recommended to interested readers.

6. For Genesis 1, I am thinking primarily of the cosmological pairs such as heaven and earth. This pairing occurs also in the Ugaritic texts (see ch. 2) and in biblical poetry (see Gen. 27:28 and 39; compare Gen. 49:25). Pairs such as heaven and earth go back to the idea of creation of pairs of cosmic components imagined as successive generations of parents giving birth. See Frank Moore Cross, "The 'Olden Gods' in Ancient Near Eastern Creation Myths and in Israel," in Frank Moore Cross, *From Epic to Canon: History and Literature in Ancient Israel* (Baltimore/London: The Johns Hopkins University Press, 1998) 72–83; and Othmar Keel, *The Symbolism of the Biblical World: Ancient Near Eastern Iconography and the Book of Psalms* (translated by Timothy J. Hallett; New York: Crossroad, 1985) 30–31, 36. Keel emphasizes the two-part nature of the world as consisting of heaven and earth. Keel also characterizes earth in Gen. 1:2, 24 as a "mother earth figure." See Keel, *Goddesses and Trees, New Moon and Yahweh: Ancient Near Eastern Art and the Hebrew Bible* (Sheffield: Sheffield Academic Press, 1998) 52. See also Meier Malul, "Woman-Earth Homology in Biblical *Weltanschauung*," *UF* 32, 339–63. Outside of Genesis 1, procreation and birth inform divine creation; note, for example, creation language is used of both El and Asherah, which in turn may have influenced language for Wisdom personified in Proverbs as $°'shr$ in 3:13–18 (see below, note 88). We may also note other contexts of God as mother or father in the Hebrew Bible more generally; see Tikva Frymer-Kensky, *In the Wake of the Goddesses: Women, Culture, and the Biblical Transformation of Pagan Myth* (New York: Free Press, 1992) especially 162–67; Mayer

I. Gruber, *The Motherhood of God and Other Essays* (South Florida Studies in the History of Judaism, volume 57; Atlanta: Scholars Press, 1992); and Sarah Dille, *Mixing Metaphors: God as Mother and Father in Deutero-Isaiah* (London: T & T Clark, 2004). I wish to thank Pamela Miles for suggesting that I emphasize this model of creation more. See further in ch. 3 below.

7. The comments of Tikva Frymer-Kensky on Genesis 1 suggest a distance between this chapter and other biblical passages that draw on the model of creation as divine birth. See Frymer-Kensky, *In the Wake*, 93.

8. For this general point, I have been aided by remarks made to me by William Morrow. It has been suggested that the creation story of Gen. 2:4–24 is informed by the creation of royal gardens by kings in the ancient Near East often as part of their royal palace complexes. See Lawrence E. Stager, "Jerusalem and the Garden of Eden," *ErIsr* 26, 183°-94°. Note also Manfred Görg, "Mensch und Tempel im 'Zweiten Schöpfungstext,'" in *Textarbeit: Studien zu Texten und ihrer Rezeption aus dem Alten Testament und der Umwelt Israels*, AOAT 294, 191–215; and Terje Stordalen, *Echoes of Eden: Genesis 2–3 and Symbolism of the Eden Garden in Biblical Hebrew Literature*, CBET 25, 94–104.

9. For these two reasons, I have not been particularly concerned about being able to pinpoint the relative development of these three models within Israel. In addition, many of the texts in questions are notoriously difficult to date.

10. For example, Isaiah 40:26–28 combines might and wisdom. Compare also God as Holy One, King and Creator in Isaiah 43:15. The differences among these three models can be expressed in some biblical passages. For example, Zechariah 4:6 contrasts divine power and might with divine spirit.

11. Over the course of this study, a number of royal themes are noted, as well as the specific priestly features of Genesis 1. In the appendix (p. 175), I will make further comments about the possible significance of the combination of royal and priestly terms in Genesis 1.

12. The organization of various creation accounts and their motifs into these three models in this chapter is a heuristic exercise; it is not intended to be a statement about how Israelites grouped these various accounts or their motifs. Indeed, they were used with considerable flexibility, and one of my goals in organizing the material in this manner is to help us see the variation better. I would add that some expressions of creation do not readily conform to any of these three categories; moreover, some passages using a particular motif of creation can differ considerably from other texts with the same motif (for example, *ruah*, "breath, life-force, wind," which is discussed below).

13. The linkage of cosmic battle and creation has been undermined in recent discussions of divine conflict, for example in David Toshio Tsumura, *Creation and Destruction: A Reappraisal of the Chaoskampf Theory in the Old Testament* (Winona Lake, Ind.: Eisenbrauns, 2005). However, the linkage is clear in Psalm 74, and the effort to dismiss this case is unconvincing. To be sure, the assumption that images of cosmic waters point to divine conflict has been overstated; in this, Tsumura is correct. See further the discussion in ch. 2.

14. For the worldview of Psalm 89, see Paul Mosca, "Ugarit and Daniel 7: A Missing Link," *Bib* 67, 496–517. For a more recent study of Psalm 89 and its royal worldview, see Robert Couffignal, *Les psaumes royaux de la Bible: Étude littéraire*, CahRB 54, esp. 94–112. For a general study of the royal worldview, see Tryggve N. D. Mettinger, *King and Messiah* (Lund: C.W.K. Gleerup, 1976). As we will see in the discussion below, the same model of divine power is attested strongly in Psalm 74:12–17.

These psalms show that by the time of their composition, Yahweh was considered a divine creator. It has been debated how early this divine role was attributed to Yahweh. It might be argued that the establishment of Yahweh as a national god would imply that major divine roles such as creation would have been attributed to this divinity prior to the eighth century. By this time, Yahweh and El were identified in Judean royal cult, the apparent source of the expressions in Psalms 74 and 89. Amos 4:13 and 9:6 might be thought to provide the eighth century evidence. However, the date of these passages is highly disputed. See the discussion of Jörg Jeremias, *The Book of Amos*, OTL, 76–79. Shalom M. Paul has defended their attribution to Amos; see Paul, *Amos: A Commentary on the Book of Amos* (edited by Frank Moore Cross; Hermeneia; Minneapolis: Fortress Press, 1991)

6, 152–53. With the use of *'elohim* for God in Genesis 1, it might be tempting to trace the role of divine creator in this text back to the figure of El.

A premonarchic dating for Yahweh as creator might be defended accepting the argument that Yahweh was originally a title (or part of a title) for the old god, El, who was likely a creator god. For discussion, see Mark S. Smith, *The Origins of Biblical Monotheism: Israel's Polytheistic Background and the Ugaritic Texts* (Oxford/New York: Oxford University Press, 2001) 139–48. To my mind, the available evidence does not favor this view. Deuteronomy 32:8–9 and Psalm 82 manifest vestiges of the differentiation between Elyon (probably El) and Yahweh. For these texts, see the recent discussion of Smith, *God in Translation*, 131–43, 195–212. Furthermore, Exod. 6:2–3 has been read as an acknowledgment that El (Shadday) and Yahweh were identified secondarily. The available evidence also suggests that Yahweh was originally a warrior god (like Baal) rather than a creator god (like El). If Yahweh was not originally a title of El, then the identification of the two figures in Judah, if not in Israel more broadly, would have taken place by the eighth century if not earlier. It is to be noted that the so-called "old poetry" (to be dated anywhere from the twelfth to the eighth centuries) regularly represents Yahweh as a divine warrior, but there is little sign of Yahweh as a creator in these texts. In contrast, El language associated with creation (or at least with blessings of creation) is to be observed in Gen. 49:25–26.

15. The idea of this model is emblemized in the formulation of Psalm 62:12: "might belongs to God." See below on this idea of power as one of a number of "biblical ontologies," terms that connect the reality of God with the world.

16. The classic formulation of this worldview is by Frank Moore Cross, *Canaanite Myth and Hebrew Epic: Essays in the History of the Religion of Israel* (Cambridge, Mass./London: Harvard University, 1973) 91–111. For the deity's march back from battle, see in addition to royal psalms (see the following note) Psalm 68. For divine enthronement following divine victory and recognized in the temple, see Psalm 29. For the reading of the iconography of the Jerusalem Temple as representing divine victory and enthronement, see Elizabeth M. Bloch-Smith, "'Who is the King of Glory': Solomon's Temple as Symbol" in *Scripture and Other Artifacts: Essays on the Bible and Archaeology in Honor of Philip J. King* (edited by Michael Coogan, Cheryl Exum, and Lawrence Stager; Louisville, Ky.: Westminster John Knox Press, 1994) 18–31; and "Solomon's Temple: The Politics of Ritual Space," in *Sacred Place-Sacred Time: Archaeology and the Religion of Israel* (edited by Barry Gitlin; Winona Lake, Ind.: Eisenbrauns, 2001) 83–94. In these essays, Bloch-Smith discusses Psalm 29 and other relevant texts. The divine temple could be expressed equally as the heavenly abode of the God (see Psalm 68:29–30).

17. Psalm 89, with its creation references in verses 10–12 (MT 11–13), requests divine help for the Judean king against his enemies. For another dramatic example of divine punishment, which opens with a call to the earth to listen, see Isaiah 34; note its use of "void" (*tohu*) in verse 11 (see ch. 2 for a discussion of this term used in Gen. 1:2).

18. As noted above, this notion of divine and human power linked together is one sort of "biblical ontology." In the royal worldview, the power of the human king "participates in" the power of the divine king. In this model, power is the term governing reality (instead of being); we might say that in this model, power is a basic "biblical ontology." I have discussed this idea in my book, *God in Translation*, 14; and specifically as it applies to the king, see 14 and 69–70. This notion of "biblical ontology" is also discussed further in sec. 3 below.

19. See the insightful study of Mosca, "Ugarit and Daniel 7," 496–517, here 509, 512. As Mosca and others have noted, this verse reflects the idea of the cosmic enemies of Sea and River(s) as in the Ugaritic texts, for example, KTU 1.2 IV, 1.3 III 38–42 and 1.5 I 1–3 (presented in Mark S. Smith, "The Baal Cycle," in *UNP*, 103–4, 111, 141).

20. Scholars often compare the Egyptian god Re in his role as creator by wisdom. See the discussion of Nili Shupak, *Where Can Wisdom Be Found? The Sage's Language in the Bible and in Ancient Egyptian Literature*, OBO 130, 225, 398 n. 46.

Closer to Israel, the figure of El in the Ugaritic texts is the preeminent, wise creator deity (for his wisdom, see KTU 1.3 V 30–31 and 1.4 IV 41–43, presented in Smith, "The Baal Cycle," 117, 128). For discussion of El's wisdom, see Manfried Dietrich and Oswald Loretz, "Die Weisheit des ugaritischen Gottes El im Kontext der altorientalischen Weisheit," *UF* 24 (1992) 31–8. El's titles, *bny bnwt*, literally "builder of the built" (that is, "Creator of creatures"), as well as *'ab 'adm*, "father of humanity," *'ab bn 'il*, "father of the divine children," and *'ab*, "father" point to El as the creator god and father of deities and humanity; for references and discussion, see Aicha Rahmouni, *Divine Epithets in the Ugaritic Alphabetic Texts* (translated by J. N. Ford; Handbook of Oriental Studies I/volume 93; Leiden/Boston: Brill, 2008) 8–10, 11–13, 22–24, 98–101. Note that his consort Athirat is called the "establisher of the gods" (*qnyt 'ilm*); see Rahmouni, *Divine Epithets*, 275–77. The only creation account in Ugaritic (actually, an excerpt) presents El fathering gods (KTU 1.23). For a convenient presentation of this text, see Theodore J. Lewis, "The Birth of the Gracious Gods," in *UNP*, 205–14. For a detailed study, see Mark S. Smith, *The Sacrificial Rituals and Myths of the Goodly Gods, KTU/CAT 1.23: Royal Constructions of Opposition, Intersection, Integration and Domination*, SBLRBS 51. For another divine wisdom model, see the following note.

21. In the Ugaritic texts, the craftsman god Kothar wa-Hasis (whose name means "wise crafts-man") pours metals for his manufacture of furniture (KTU 1.4 I), and he is also the builder of Baal's house (KTU 1.4 V–VII); see Smith, "The Baal Cycle," 121, 131–36. In his combination of roles and character, Kothar is the most proximate Ugaritic counterpart to the biblical God in his role as the divine craftsman (see the following note). For this Ugaritic god, see Dennis Pardee, "Koshar," in *DDD*, 490; and the older work of Mark S. Smith, "Kothar wa-Hasis, the Ugaritic Craftsman God" (PhD dissertation, Yale University, 1985). Kothar, however, does not create the world; this role apparently belonged to El (see the preceding note).

The roles of builder and creator are attributed to the figure of Egyptian Ptah in some texts. See Jacobus van Dijk, "Ptah," in *The Oxford Encyclopedia of Ancient Egypt* (edited by Donald B. Redford; three volumes; Oxford/New York: Oxford University Press, 2001) 3.74–76, with relevant studies. For examples, see *ANET* 5; *COS* 1.18–23.

Within Mesopotamian tradition, creation by wisdom is attributed jointly to Anu, Enlil, and Ea, for example in an Akkadian prayer (see Clifford, *Creation Accounts*, 61). Ea, like Ugaritic El, also combines wisdom and creative capacities. On the similarity between El and Ea, see Manfred Dietrich and Oswald Loretz, "Das ugaritische Gottesattribut *ḥrš*: 'Weiser, handwerklich Tüchtiger': Eine Studie über die Götter El, Ea/Enki, *Ktr-w-ḫss* und Hyn," *UF* 31 (1999) 165–73; Jonas C. Greenfield, *'Al Kanfei Yonah: Collected Studies of Jonas C. Greenfield on Semitic Philology* (edited by Shalom Paul, Michael E. Stone, and Avital Pinnick; two volumes; Leiden/Boston: Brill; Jerusalem: Magnes, 2001) 2.895; and Tsumura, *Creation and Destruction*, 130–40. It is to be noted that both El and Ea create figures for particular situations. El's creation of Shataqat made to expel illness from Kirta (KTU 1.16 V) compares with Ea's creation of Saltu, a double of Ishtar, in order to do with battle with her and to curb her ferocity. For the former text, see Greenstein, "Kirta," in *UNP*, 38; for the latter, see Benjamin R. Foster, "Ea and Saltu," in *Ancient Near Eastern Studies in Memory of J. J. Finkelstein* (edited by Maria de Jong Ellis; Hamden, Conn.: Academy of Arts and Sciences, 1977) 79–84; for discussion, see Harris, "Inanna-Ishtar as Paradox and Coincidence of Opposites," *HR* 30/3, 266–67. For this form of ad hoc creation, see also Enki's manufacture of two professional mourners made to help Inanna out of the underworld in "Inanna's Descent to the Underworld" (see Thorkild Jacobsen, *The Harps That Once...: Sumerian Poetry in Translation*, [New Haven: Yale U. Press, 1997], 218).

22. The word *raqia'* in Gen. 1:6–7, often translated "firmament," stands in parallelism with "the heavens" in Psalm 19:1 (MT 2). In Psalm 150:1, the same word is parallel to "his holy place" and in apposition to "his strong place." From these comparisons, the firmament is located in the heavens, and it is the site of divine enthronement in the heavens. The root appears in a verbal form in Job 37:18: "Can you, like him [God], *spread out* the skies, hard as a molten mirror?" (so NRSV; see Isaiah 44:24 for the same root in another creation allusion). The translation of the verb translated "to spread out" in this context is rendered to "stretch out" in NJPS. The *D*-stem of the verb is taken to refer to beating or hammering out metal plates (Exod. 39:3, Num. 17:4, Isaiah 40:19; see *BDB* 956). The context of Job 37:18 likewise suggests the activity of metal work, perhaps with the specific sense of the word as "molten," translated as "cast metal" in NJPS. This root (°*ysq*) denotes pouring

casting liquid metal in casts. The verb applies to the pouring of molten metals for the materials of the tabernacle conducted by the craftsman Bezalel (Exod. 25:12 and 37:3) and for furniture made by Kothar in the Baal Cycle; see the preceding note). See *BDB* 955–56; *HALOT* 1291–92.

23. For this passage, see the recent study of Alan Lenzi, *Secrecy and the Gods: Secret Knowledge in Ancient Mesopotamia and Biblical Israel,* SAAS 19, 339–62.

24. Compare the role of personified Magic in the process of creation, in the *Egyptian Coffin Spell* 261 (*COS* 1.17): "I am the one whom the Sole Lord made/before two things had evolved in this world,/ when he sent his sole eye, when he was one,/ when something came from his mouth, when his million of ka was in protection of associates,/when he spoke with the one who evolved with him, than whom he is mightier,/when he took Annunciation in his mouth." See also *Coffin Spell* 648. For discussion of these two texts, see Robert Kriech Ritner, *The Mechanisms of Ancient Egyptian Magical Practice,* SAOC 54, 17–20, 23, 25.

25. Adele Berlin, "The Wisdom of Creation in Psalm 104," in *Seeking Out the Wisdom of the Ancients: Essays Offered to Honor Michael V. Fox on the Occasion of His Sixty-Fifth Birthday* (edited by Ronald L. Troxel, Kelvin G. Friebel, and Dennis R. Magary; Winona Lake, Ind.: Eisenbrauns, 2005) 83.

26. For the image as applied to human enemies, see Isaiah 33:3.

27. NRV takes the verbs as simple past (perhaps on the theory that these are short preterite past prefix forms), while NJPS takes them as simple future. The verbs might be taken as durative past in keeping with the usage of verse 16.

28. For the variety of relationships of these sorts of terms to temples and their deities, see Mark S. Smith, "Like Deities, Like Temples (Like People)," in *Temple and Worship in Biblical Israel* (edited by John Day; *Library of Hebrew Bible/Old Testament Studies,* formerly JSOTSup 422; London/New York: T & T Clark, 2005) 3–27. See further below.

29. I am using "presence" in this discussion as a shorthand term for these various expressions that are related to the temple and the presence of God in it. I would note that the Hebrew word for "presence" (*panim*) is rare at best in biblical creation accounts. See below for the discussion of Psalm 104:29; compare the notion of *panim* informing the universe in Psalm 139:7, in combination with "breath, life-force" (*ruah*). For the sanctuary background of *panim,* see Num. 6:24–26, Psalm 42:2; and compare Exod. 23:17. For a comprehensive discussion of the word and its temple background, see Friedhelm Hartenstein, *Das Angesicht JHWHs,* FAT I:55; see also Othmar Keel and Christoph Uehlinger, *Gods, Goddesses, and Images of God,* 366; and Mark S. Smith, "'Seeing God' in the Psalms: The Background to the Beatific Vision in the Hebrew Scriptures," *CBQ* 50 (1988) 171–83.

30. To be clear, divine appearance as such (theophany) does not constitute the rubric that I have in mind for divine presence, since many of the terms for divine presence involve some mark of the divine apart from physical appearance made by God. At the same time, sometimes these terms (such as name) are associated with theophany, for example in Psalm 29 (vss. 2, 9). For this subject, see George W. Savran, *Encountering the Divine: Theophany in Biblical Narrative* JSOTSup 420.

31. Compare Psalm 48:11: "like your name, O God, praise of you goes to the ends of the earth." For Psalm 8, see the lengthy discussion below.

32. See Klaus Koch, "Wort und Einheit des Schöpfergottes in Memphis und Jerusalem," ZTK 62, 251–93, esp. 273–80, republished in Koch, *Studien zur alttestamentlichen und altorientalischen Religionsgeschichte: Zum 60. Geburtstag von Klaus Koch* (edited by Eckart Otto; Göttingen: Vandenhoeck & Ruprecht, 1988) 61–105, esp. 83–90; and Clifford, *Creation Accounts,* 110–12, 143–44. For the importance of divine speech in creation, we may also compare Psalm 19. In this psalm, the universe proclaims the divine word (vv. 1–6) corresponding to divine teaching and precepts (vss. 7–10), which is worthy of human praise and contemplation (vss. 11–14). We will discuss Psalm 19 as well as creation by divine speech further in ch. 2. Note also the representation of the divine word in Isaiah 55:11.

33. In Psalm 66:4 the earth offers temple worship, bowing down to God and singing hymns to God. Compare the images in Psalm 36:6–9.

34. See Hartenstein, *Das Angesicht,* 181.

35. On divine "light" in the Hebrew Bible, see Hartenstein, *Das Angesicht,* 177–204; and Mark S. Smith, "The Near Eastern Background of Solar Language for Yahweh," *JBL* 109 (1990) 29–39.

For a broader consideration of light, see Mikkel Bille and Tim Flohr Sørensen, "An Anthropology of Luminosity: The Agency of Light," *Journal of Material Culture* 12/3 (2007) 263–84. I will return to this article in ch. 2 to discuss its general insights into light, which will contribute to our understanding of Genesis 1.

36. See Hartenstein, *Das Angeischt*, 177–209.

37. For "name," see Oskar Grethner, *Name und Wort Gottes im Alten Testament*, BZAW 34; S. Dean McBride, "The Deuteronomic Name Theology" (Ph.D. diss., Harvard University, 1969); Tryggve N. D. Mettinger, *The Dethronement of Sabaoth: Studies in the Shem and Kabod Theologies* (Lund: C. W. K. Gleerup, 1982) 38–79, 124–32; Herbert B. Huffmon, "Name," *DDD*, 610–12; and Sandra L. Richter, *The Deuteronomistic History and Name Theology*, BZAW 318. For the West Semitic evidence for the name (KTU 1.16 VI 56; KAI 14:8; personal names of the type consisting of the phrase, "name of" such and such a deity) as well as an attempt to provide an account for this anthropomorphic presentation of the name, see Smith, *Origins*, 74–76. Name is a mark of human or divine identity in the world. Compare Gen. 32:28–30, where the episode concerning knowledge of names follows a request for blessing.

38. See Grethner, *Name*. For God's word, see Psalms 33:5; compare Psalm 147:15 and 18; and Isaiah 55:11. See ch. 3 for further discussion.

39. In the West Semitic world, holiness was a characteristic adhering to shrines (as "holy places," e.g., Exod. 28:43) marked by the appearance of divinity (theophany), as well as to their cultic realia (Exod. 28:36; Zechariah 14:20; compare the censer and lyre included in Ugaritic deity lists; see Pardee, *Ritual and Cult* [Intro., n. 9], 15–16). By definition, divinity is observable in some sense in these places. They are marked and demarcated for holiness, and divinity is perceived to partake fully of holiness. In turn, the presence of divinity imparts holiness to those places. From a cultic perspective holiness of deities is a matter of liturgical experience and expression: deities are known in holy places, and both are considered holy. By extension, deities' sanctuaries and their dwellings on mountains partake of holiness. So Baal's mountain, Mount Sapan, is called "holy" (KTU 1.3 III 30; 1.16 I 7) as well as "divine" (KTU 1.3 III 29). So, too, Yahweh's dwelling-place is called the "holy mountain" (*har qodesh*; Psalm 48:2) and "the holy dwelling-place of the Most High" (*qedosh mishkene 'elyon*; Psalm 46:5).

Divine holiness, as experienced and expressed in cult, is associated with shaking, whether of places of theophany (KTU 1.4 VII; Psalm 114) or people who experience it (KTU 1.4 VII; Isaiah 6:4). The "holy voice" of the deity, whether belonging to Yahweh or Baal, signals a theophany, which may wreak destruction (Psalm 29) or revelation (as in Num. 7:89), and it may induce flight and fear on the part of the god's enemies (KTU 1.4 VII 29). Similarly, sanctuaries can be regarded as awe-inspiring like the deities who own and inhabit them.

It has been common for students of ancient religion to understand this experience of the holy in terms of awe and fear. In the modern Western discussion of religion, this idea is customarily traced to the theologian Rudolf Otto, who characterized this confrontation with the divine as *mysterium tremendum et fascinosum*. The great Sumerologist Thorkild Jacobsen, for example, followed Otto in stressing the "wholly other" character of the numinous (Thorkild Jacobsen, *Treasures of Darkness: A History of Mesopotamian Religion*, [New Haven: Yale, 1976], 3). By the same token, such a view requires balance. Because such experience is mediated by human experience and language, it is not by definition entirely "Wholly Other." It may be recognizable in natural effects of the rainstorm or dream experience at night. In these experiences, the "other" partakes of the here and now.

40. As noted above, divine light is a common motif of biblical texts, especially the Psalms. See ch. 2 for further examples and discussion. In this connection we may note the pairing of divine light (°*nr*) with glory (°*kbd*) in a Ugaritic list of deities (KTU 1.123.16). In line 21 of the same text, *kbd* is followed by *d 'il*, and may mean "*kbd* of the god. . .". See *DUL* 426–27; they reasonably view *kbd w nr* as a binomial, and they translate the generic form of the noun *kbd* as "splendor, glory." By contrast, see Pardee, *Ritual and Cult*, 151–52, which leaves *kbd* untranslated. For *kabod*, see the following note.

41. Among the expressions denoting the divine presence, one may also note the term "glory, effulgence" (*kabod*), or more precisely, "gravitas," which fits with the root meaning of the word, "to be heavy" (compare *kabod* used of a human person in Gen. 49:6). This term may be less a separate term for divine presence than a word that describes that presence; compare "the *kabod* of his name" in

Psalm 29:2. *Kabod* perhaps captures the palpable sense of that presence as marked by these terms for presence. Still, the distinction is perhaps not to be drawn too finely. For *kabod,* see Mettinger, *Dethronement,* 80–115 and 116–23.

42. A somewhat different case is "life-force, breath, wind" (*ruah*), which is a physical attribute that God has and gives to human beings (Psalm 104:29–30; Ecclesiastes 11:5), and which returns to God when they die (Ecclesiastes 12:7: compare 3:21; Psalm 146:4); see ch. 2 for further discussion of *ruah.* Compare Hittite "soul, spirit, mind, will" (*ishtanza*), shared by divinity and humanity: "Is the soul of a human and of the gods any different?" (CTH 264, col. I, paragraph 2, line 21, written with the Sumerogram ZI; quoted by Ada Taggar-Cohen, *Hittite Priesthood* (Heidelberg: Universitätsverlag Winter, 2006) 74, 95; see also p. 41; see also Smith, *God in Translation,* 74.

Divine *ruah* is used with a variety of other images for divine creation (for example, with word in Psalms 33:6 [MT 5] and 147:18). Though it denotes a sense of divine presence, it is not particular to temple settings. It is a term of divine infusion into prophets (e.g., Micah 3:8) and other figures (see Exod. 31:3; Judg. 14:6, 19; 1 Samuel 10:10). Its usage in the creation account of Psalm 104 has been traced to Egyptian material, specifically to the Hymns to the Aten from Amarna (see the discussion of Psalm 104, in sec. 2 below).

43. Ben Sira 33:8 views the creation of Genesis 1 as a matter of divine wisdom. In this presentation, this later wisdom text of the second model offers a wisdom interpretation of an earlier example of the third model. The view of Ben Sira is echoed in 2 Enoch 28:1 and in the great medieval mystical commentary, *Sefer ha-Zohar* (p. 3b, according to the Mantuan edition of 1558–60). For the former, see Francis I. Andersen, "2 (Slavonic Apocalypse of) Enoch," *OTP* 1.146; for the latter, see Daniel C. Matt, *The Zohar: Volume One* (Stanford, Calif.: Stanford University, 2004) 17. For another convenient translation, see *The Zohar* (trans. by Harry Sperling and Maurice Simon, with an Introduction by J. Abelson; vol. 1; London/Bournemouth: Soncino, 1949) 13.

44. Beyond this importance given to the word is the matter of the degree to which the production of the Bible itself represented a form of textual devotion. Compare the suggestion by Stephen A. Geller that "biblical religion is an essentially literary faith." See Geller, *Sacred Enigmas: Literary Religion in the Hebrew Bible* (London/New York: Routledge, 1996) 168. For this notion, see further Geller's discussion on 170–71.

45. Another wisdom mark may be the use of °*sih* in verse 34 as "discourse." Compare the word in Ben Sira Hebrew ms. A 31:11 (Hebrew ms. A), 32:17 (ms. B), 35:4 and 44:4 (in B and Masada mss.). The wisdom background of this psalm would explain the parting wish of verse 35, which may presume the wisdom dichotomy between the wicked and the righteous (compare Psalm 1:6). For this psalm, see sec. 2 below.

46. This is also true of texts that do not specifically discuss creation. In Psalm 29 and Isaiah 35 the appearance of God as a warrior is characterized with language of holiness (see Psalm 29:2; Isaiah 35:8). Or, a biblical passage that is grounded in the wisdom model can draw on the idea of God's nearness in a sanctuary (Psalm 73).

47. It is plausible to correlate these three models with other deities: Marduk (and to some extent Baal) exemplifies the first model; Kothar fits the second; and perhaps the seated El in his role of giving blessing and decrees is expressive of the third model. To be sure, these correlations involve some simplification and typecasting. For example, both Kothar and El are wise.

This comparison may draw our attention to the massively patriarchal conception of creation in our biblical sources, despite the fact that in older traditions, as found in the Ugaritic texts (compare Gen. 49:26 for the imagery of the pair), it is El and Asherah who produce the divine children and who bear various epithets as creators of the world and its creatures. The blessing goddess is known in Ugaritic iconography (see p. 261 n. 88 and pp. 261–62 n. 92). Keel & Uehlinger (*Gods,* 239–40, 314, 391, 401) have noted the reduction of Asherah to her symbol and her subsequent demise. This goddess with creative capacities has been lost from biblical models of creation, except in the incorporation of her character in the figure of Wisdom personified, as noted below.

48. Ronald S. Hendel, "Prophets, Priests, and the Efficacy of Ritual," in *Pomegranates and Golden Bells: Studies in Biblical, Jewish, and Near Eastern Ritual, Law and Literature in Honor of Jacob Milgrom* (edited by David P. Wright, David N. Freedman, and Avi Hurvitz; Winona Lake, Ind.: Eisenbrauns, 1995) 193.

49. "Sea" in verse 13 is a primordial figure and one of God's adversaries. Sea appears along with the monsters, identified as the Tanninim, serpentine dragon or dragons, and Leviathan in verse 14. Sea and the dragon are mentioned together in Job 7:12, as are Leviathan and the serpent in Isaiah 27:1. See p. 21 for the discussion of Sea in Psalm 89:26. As noted above, these monstrous enemies appear in the major Ugaritic story about the warrior god Baal (often called "The Baal Cycle"). In this story, Sea is the cosmic waters and a major enemy of Baal. He belongs to an older generation of divine forces in the universe. A passage in this story (KTU 1.5 I 1–4 and 27–31) also mentions Leviathan and the *Tnn*, like Isaiah 27:1 (for the Ugaritic passage, see Smith, "The Baal Cycle," 141–42).

Sea seems to belong to an older generation, while the other figures associated with Sea may belong to the next generation of watery enemies (for this characterization, I thank Andrés Piquer Otero). The Tanninim here in Psalm 74:13 are said to be on the waters, and as such they are distinguished from Sea. It is also said to be in the Sea (Isaiah 27:1; compare KTU 1.6 VI 51, in Smith, "The Baal Cycle," 164; compare also Gen. 1:21). Perhaps they were considered Sea's offspring as well. Perhaps represented as second-generation figures relative to Sea, they may be regarded as manifestations or alternate forms of Sea.

50. The versions vary between "our," "my,"and no pronoun at all.

51. The usual translations for *porarta* render "divide" or "split." Septuagint reads *ekrataiōsas,* translated "you strengthened" by Albert Pietersma in *A New English Translation of the Septuagint* (edited by Albert Pietersma and Benjamin Wright; New York/Oxford: Oxford University, 2007) 584; perhaps it could be rendered also "you ruled, subdued." There is little philological evidence for any of these renderings, and so the clause calls for another proposal. The word *porarta* is parallel with *shibbarta,* "you smashed" both morphologically and sonantly. With this immediate context of *porarta* in mind, a semantically sound cognate would be Akkadian *parāru* in the D-stem meaning, "to break up, shatter, to rupture, disperse," etc. (*CAD P*:161). See, for example, *Enuma Elish* IV 106 where the root is used of Tiamat's forces in defeat: "her forces were scattered (*up-tar-ri-ra*), her hosts were dispersed" (*CAD P*:163, #3b); for comparison of *Enuma Elish* and the Bible's creation traditions, see further below. It may be noted also that Akkadian *naparruru* is applied to enemy forces (*CAD P*:164, #4b; *AHw* 830). The root is attested in other languages as well: Arabic *farfara,* "cut," post-biblical Hebrew *pirper,* "crush, crumble, pulverize," and Ugaritic *prr,* "to break" (a vow) (in KTU 1.15 III 30; see *DUL* 681). For these words, as well as further South Semitic cognates, see Wolf Leslau, *Comparative Dictionary of Geʿez (Classical Ethiopic)* (Wiesbaden: Harrassowitz, 1987) 165. The root has also been proposed for Deir Alla, combination I, line 8 (*DNWSI* 944), but other readings have been suggested; see Jo Ann Hackett, *The Balaam Text from Deir ʿAllā* (Harvard Semitic Monographs, volume 31; Chicago, Calif.: Scholars, 1980) 48.

Leslau suggests that °*prr,* "to cut" and the like "should perhaps not be separated" from °*prr,* "to flee." See Leslau, *Ethiopic and South Arabic Contributions to the Hebrew Lexicon* (Berkeley/Los Angeles: University of California, 1958) 43, with citation of various South Semitic languages. The word in this meaning is attested also in Ugaritic in KTU 1.19 III 14 and 28 (see Parker, "Aqhat," in *UNP,* 74–75) and in Arabic *farra,* "to flee, fly." This would find contextual support in the Bible, with a different root, °*nws,* used for the fleeing waters in Psalm 104:7, another creation context, and also in Psalm 114:3 and 5. This meaning for *porarta* in Psalm 74:13 has been proposed by Greenfield, *ʿAl Kanfei Yonah,* 833–39; and *DCH* 784; cf. *HALOT* 3.975. These sources do not discuss *Enuma Elish* IV 106, nor do they address the parallelism of *porarta* with *shibbarta* in Psalm 74:13.

52. MT reads literally, "for a people, for wild beasts." Retaining the MT, Mitchell Dahood translates, "desert tribes," with the following commentary: "The defeat of Sea will be so complete that the ocean will become a desert. With this description the psalmist foreshadows the thought of vs. 15b." Dahood, *Psalms II: 51–100,* AB 17, 206. MT ʿ*am* might be defended in part for the analogy that it builds with verse 18 with its use of ʿ*am.* Despite efforts to defend the MT, most commentators consider it to be faulty.

Most tentatively I am reading *leʿamal siyye yam,* "for the labor of sea beasts," which at least involves words all known in biblical Hebrew and more or less suits the context. The idea would be that sea-beasts receive Leviathan as food for their toil, perhaps anticipating the inverse sentiment of verse 19b: "do not give your dove to the wild beast."

This reading is not much better, though hardly any worse, than what is the most popular emendation to "the sharks in the sea" (*le'amlese yam*), first proposed by Immanuel Löw, "Zur biblischen Fauna und Flora: Ein nachträglicher Beitrag zur Festnummer für I. Löw," *MGWJ* 68, 160–61. This suggestion has since entered the dictionaries of *HALOT* 845 (going back to *KB* 715) and *DCH* 6.483 and 892 (with bibliography). It has been noted and largely accepted by many commentators; for example, see Hans-Joachim Kraus, *Psalms 60–150: A Commentary* (tr. by Hilton C. Oswald; Minneapolis: Augsburg, 1989) 96; Klaus Seybold, *Die Psalmen*, HAT I/15, 286; and Frank-Lothar Hossfeld and Erich Zenger, *Psalms 2: A Commentary on Psalms 51–100* (edited by Klaus Baltzer; translated by Linda M. Maloney; Minneapolis: Fortress, 2005) 241, note m. James Barr criticized Löw's proposal for two reasons: the proposed Hebrew word for "shark" (based on °*mls*, "to be slippery, smooth") has little or no basis in ancient Hebrew, whether biblical or postbiblical; and the proposed Arabic cognate, which does refer to fish that slips out of one's hand, is not likely to be the name for a type of fish. See James Barr, *Comparative Philology and the Text of the Old Testament: With Additions and Corrections* (Winona Lake, Ind.: Eisenbrauns, 1987) 236–37.

53. Psalm 8:3 (MT 4) also use the verb, "set in place" (hiphil, or causative stem of °*kwn*) for the moon and the stars. Akkadian texts use the same verb for stars in the sense "to be stationary" and "to make stationary," for example "(the planet) Venus becomes stationary in the morning" (*mulDIL. BAT ina šēreti ikūn*) as noted by Susan Ackerman, *Under Every Green Tree: Popular Religion in Sixth-Century Judah*, HSM 46, 12. For other examples of the Mesopotamian usage in astronomical texts, see David Brown, *Mesopotamian Planetary Astronomy-Astrology* (Cuneiform Monographs, vol. 18; Groningen: Styx, 2000) 69, 86, 154 n. 367 and 194.

54. Some commentators take the first noun as a reference to the moon (see Seybold, *Die Psalmen*, 286). Dahood (*Psalms II*, 207) translates "moon," and comments that it may apply to either the sun or the moon. If it refers to the moon, the usage would be exceptional in putting the moon before the sun. The two direct objects have been taken instead as a hendiadys, "the orb of the sun" (NJPS).

55. This choice of summer (*qayis*) and winter (*horep*) might be attributed to the sonant connection that *horep* in verse 17b makes with *yeherep* in verse 10a and *herep* in verse 18a. In this manner, the hymn of verse 12–17 is connected sonantly to the lament that precedes and follows. The verb *yesartam* seems unusual for time (contrast Gen. 1:14–19).

56. The victory over the cosmic enemies (and its possible ties to creation) has been seen also in the iconography of the Ta'anach stand. Ziony Zevit proposes to relate this theme in these biblical texts to the scene on the stand's side panel between the second and third registers. In this panel, a male figure appears to be choking a snake. See Zevit, *The Religions of Ancient Israel: A Synthesis of Parallelactic Approaches* (London/New York: Continuum, 2001) 324. I wish to thank Elizabeth Bloch-Smith for drawing this information to my attention.

57. See Barbara Nevling Porter, *Images, Power, and Politics: Figurative Aspects of Esarhaddon's Babylonian Policy* (Philadelphia: American Philosophical Society, 1993).

58. For this letter, see Jean-Marie Durand, "Le mythologème du combat entre le dieu de l'orage et la mer en Mésopotamie," *MARI* 7, 41–61; and Pierre Bordreuil and Dennis Pardee, "Le combat de *Ba'lu* avec *Yammu* d'après les textes ougaritiques," *MARI* 7, 63–70. For text, translation and notes, see also Martti Nissinen, *Prophets and Prophecy in the Ancient Near East* SBLWAW 12, 22. The evidence is summarized by Daniel Schwemer, "The Storm-Gods of the Ancient Near East: Summary, Synthesis, Recent Studies," *Journal of Ancient Near Eastern Religions* 8/1 (2008) 24–27. See ch. 2 p. 69 for further discussion.

59. For the Amarna letters, readers can find a convenient translation by William L. Moran, *The Amarna Letters* (Baltimore/London: Johns Hopkins, 1992).

60. Some Egyptian texts, such as the poetical stele of Tutmoses III, dress up the king in the storm imagery of the god Baal. See E. Gaál, "Tuthmosis III as Storm-God?" *Studia Aegyptiaca* 3 (1977) 29–38. See also *ANET* 249.

61. Cross, *Canaanite Myth*, 258 n. 177. The Baal Stela in the Louvre (*ANEP* #490) depicts the Ugaritic king literally hanging from Baal, which expresses his direct dependence on the god.

62. Cf. the self-comparison of Shalmaneser III with Hadad in *ANET* 277. See David Damrosch, *The Narrative Covenant: Transformations of Genre in the Growth of Biblical Literature* (San Francisco: Harper & Row, 1987) 55, 61, 70.

63. To convey this idea, I would like to draw on metaphysical language used in the Middle Ages to convey the notion of how various beings in the world were connected to God. In metaphysical (or ontological) terms, creatures as "beings" are linked to or "participate in" the "Being" that is God. Their "being" comes from the "Being." The world of ancient Israel and the ancient Near East did not use the language of being in their manner. Instead of the language of "being," ancient creation texts often communicate this "ontological" relationship in terms of power.

64. For further discussion of this comparison of language and imagery for Baal and Yahweh, see John Day, *Yahweh and the Gods and Goddesses of Canaan,* JSOTSup 265, 91–127; and Mark S. Smith, *The Early History of God: Yahweh and the Other Deities in Ancient Israel,* (Grand Rapids: Eerdmans, 2002) 65–101.

65. In view of the Ugaritic evidence, one may wonder if *neharot* represents a plural of majesty or the like or implies a reapplication of the mythic language to the maximal borders of the Wadi el-Arish to the Euphrates.

66. Gösta W. Ahlström, *Psalm 89: Eine liturgie aus dem Ritual des leidenden Königs* (Lund: Gleerup, 1959, 108–11; Edouard Lipinski, *Le poème royal du Psaume LXXXIX 1.5.20–38,* CahRB 6, 53; J. B. Dumortier, "Un rituel d'intronisation: Le Ps. LXXXIX 2–38," *VT* 22, 188 and n. 1; Cross, *Canaanite Myth,* 258 n. 177, 261–62; Mosca, "Ugarit and Daniel 7," 496–517, here 509, 512; and "Once Again the Heavenly Witness of Ps 89:38," *JBL* 105 (1986) 33. Mosca ("Once Again," 33) points to other examples of "mythico-religious terms" in Psalm 89: the king is "the 'first-born' (*bekor,* v. 28) of 'my father'" ('*abi,* v. 27), and serves as the "Most High" ('*elyon,* v. 28) with respect to earthly kings. Cf. Moshe Weinfeld, "Zion and Jerusalem as Religious and Political Capital: Ideology and Utopia," in *The Poet and the Historian: Essays in Literary and Historical Biblical Criticism* (edited by Richard E. Friedman; Harvard Semitic Studies, volume 26; Chico, Calif., 1983) 97–98.

67. Charles F. Whitley, "Textual and Exegetical Observations on Ps 45:4–7," *ZAW* 98, 277–82.

68. The order of Earth and Heaven varies between the two passages. The Baal text is KTU 1.5 II 2–3. For English transliterations of the text and translation, see Smith, "The Baal Cycle," 143. The other text is KTU 1.23.61–62; for 1.23, see Lewis, "Birth," 213. Below in this chapter, I discuss the allusion to these deities in Psalm 8:1–2 (MT 2–3).

69. The massive mouth of Death is also described elsewhere in the Baal Cycle. KTU 1.5 I 6–8 = 33–35; see Smith, "The Baal Cycle," 141, 143. Outside of the Bible, it is to be noted that Leviathan in later Aramaic texts is presented as a demonic power that afflicts people. See Cyrus H. Gordon, "Leviathan: Symbol of Evil," in *Biblical Motifs: Origins and Transformations* (ed. Alexander Altmann; Cambridge: Harvard University Press, 1966) 1–9.

70. KTU 1.23.63–64; see Lewis, "Birth," 213. See the image also in Zechariah 12:6.

71. Some recent studies of this passage in relation to biblical tradition and the Ugaritic texts claim that the author of this verse actually knew a version of the Ugaritic myth of Baal and Death. More specifically, Isaiah 27:1 is understood to be a quotation from some version of this text. See W. G. Lambert, "Leviathan in Ancient Art," in *Shlomo: Studies in Epigraphy, Iconography, History and Archaeology in Honor of Shlomo Moussaieff* (edited by Robert Deutsch; Tel Aviv: Archaeological Center Publication) 147–54, here 154. Lambert is followed by William D. Barker, "Isaiah 24–27: Studies in a Cosmic Polemic" (Ph.D. dissertation, University of Cambridge, 2006) 8–9, 133, 149. See also John Day, *God's Conflict with the Dragon and the Sea: Echoes of a Canaanite Myth in the Old Testament* (Cambridge: Cambridge University Press, 2000) 141–51, 185–88. I wish to thank Bill Barker for providing me with a copy of his thesis.

72. For a fine survey of creation, especially in wisdom literature, see Raymond C. van Leeuwen, "Cosmos, Temple, House: Building and Wisdom in Mesopotamia and Israel," in *Wisdom Literature in Mesopotamia and Israel,* SBLSymS 36, 67–90, with comments on Genesis 1 offered on 75–76.

73. For the idiom of construction in this passage, compare Proverbs 24:3: "a house is built in wisdom, and in understanding it is established."

74. On secret knowledge as it pertains to this passage, see Lenzi, *Secrecy,* 232–33.

75. For creation in the divine speeches in Job 38–40, see further the reflections of Kathleen M. O'Connor, "Wild, Raging Creativity: Job in the Whirlwind," in *Earth, Wind, and Fire: Biblical Perspectives on Creation* (Carol J. Dempsey, O.P., and Mary Magaret Pazdan, O.P., eds.; Collegeville, Minn.: Liturgical Press, 2004) 48–56.

76. Given the emphasis on wisdom in Psalm 104:24, it might be surmised that the psalm was influenced by wisdom tradition. Still, evocation of wisdom themes with respect to creation does not necessarily require a wisdom background as such, because a general wisdom theme may have entered into the liturgical tradition by the time of Psalm 104 (see also Psalm 136:5). Despite this reservation, a comparison with Job 12:7–10 would point in the direction of wisdom influence on Psalm 104. In favor of this view, see the discussion of R. N. Whybray, *The Intellectual Tradition of the Old Testament*, BZAW 135, 96–97. Whybray compares Proverbs 3:19, as well as Jeremiah 10:12 = 51:15 in its combination of might and wisdom as the divine attributes in creation (this passage arguably reflects a combination of liturgical and wisdom perspectives within a prophetic context).

77. For this psalm and its similarities with Genesis 1, see (by date) Peter C. Craigie, "The Comparison of Hebrew Poetry: Psalm 104 in the Light of Egyptian and Ugaritic Poetry," *Semeia* 4 (1974) 10–21; Pierre Auffret, *Hymnes d'Egypte et d'Israël: Études de structure littéraire*, OBO 34; Meir Weiss, *The Bible From Within: The Method of Total Interpretation* (Jerusalem: Magnes, 1984) 85–87; Day, *God's Conflict*, 28–34; Thomas Krüger, "'Kosmos-theologie' zwischen Mythos und Erfahrung. Ps 104 im Horizont altoreiientalischer und alttestamentlicher Schöpfungs' konzepte," *BN* 68, 49–78; Matthias Köckert, "Literargeschichtliche und religionsgeschichtliche Beobachtungen zu Psalm 104," in *Schriftauslegung in der Schrift*, BZAW 300, 259–80; and Berlin, "The Wisdom of Creation," 71–83.

For the combination of Egyptian and West Semitic components, see in particular Paul E. Dion, "YHWH as Storm-god and Sun-god: The Double Legacy of Egypt and Canaan as Reflected in Psalm 104," *ZAW* 103, 43–71. The putative Egyptian elements include the psalm's extended presentation of *ruah*, which was probably mediated through Levantine centers under Egyptian hegemony during the Late Bronze and Early Iron Ages. For discussions, see Keel & Uehlinger, *Gods*, 137; and Smith, *God in Translation*, 69–76. For a rather different Egyptian comparison with Psalm 104, see Annette Krüger, "Der Weg, die Grösse zu erkennen. (pIns. 30,18)," in *Was ist der Mensch, dass du seiner gedenkst? (Psalm 8,5): Aspekte einer theologischen Anthropologie. Festschrift für Bernd Janowski zum 65. Geburtstag* (edited by Michaela Bauks, Kathrin Liess and Peter Riede; Neukirchen-Vluyn: Neukirchener Verlag, 2008) 271–80.

78. This expression means that the speaker calls on himself to bless God. It is not a general excla-mation (such as "bless my soul"), but a form of self-address. Speaking to one's soul or self (*nepesh*) is not uncommon in the Bible. This usage is well attested in hymns like Psalm 104, and we see it also in laments, for example, in Psalm 42:6, 13 and 43:5. In this verse the speaker asks his *nepesh* why it is so sad, and then commands it to keep hope in God. Perhaps compare also the benighted man who "speaks in his heart" (Psalm 14:1 = 53:1) and the rebellious son whose insides instruct him in the Ugaritic story of Kirta (KTU 1.16 VI 26; see Greenstein, "Kirta." Passages such as these raise the question of how the ancients understood the parts and the whole of the human person. For this larger question, see Robert A. Di Vito, "Old Testament Anthropology and the Construction of Personal Identity," *CBQ* 61 (1999) 217–38.

In turn, this question of the constitution of the human person affects how the ancients under-stood the personhood of deities (what we might call "divine anthropology"). Note the comments of Beate Pongratz-Leisten, "When the Gods are Speaking: Toward Defining the Interface between Polytheism and Monotheism," in *Propheten in Mari, Assyrien und Israel* FRLANT 201, 162–68; and Barbara Porter, "The Anxiety of Multiplicity: Concepts of Divinity as One and Many in Ancient Assyria," in *One God or Many? Concepts of Divinity in the Ancient World* (edited by Barbara Nevling Porter; Transactions of the Casco Bay Assyriological Institute, Volume 1; np, 2000) 248. For a discussion of this question with respect to Egyptian deities, see in the same volume the essay by John Baines, "Egyptian Deities in Context: Multiplicity, Unity, and the Problem of Change," 27–29, 31–35. I have tried to address this question in a preliminary way as it applies to Israel's chief deity; see *God in Translation*, 144–46.

79. Compare Hosea 4:19 and Zechariah 5:9 for images of the wind (*ruah*) with wings. Note also this usage in the wings of the wind in the story of Adapa; see *COS* 1.449. For another example, see Mari letter ARM vol. 26, #200; for convenient access, see Wolfgang Heimpel, *Letters to the King of Mari: A New Translation with Historical Introduction, Notes, and Commentary* (Mesopotamian

Civilizations series, volume 12; Winona Lake, Ind.: Eisenbrauns, 2003) 255. For further discussion of Psalm 104:3–4, see below p. pp. 54–55.

80. The subject in MT ("fiery flame") is singular, but the predicate is plural. As a result, the subject might be regarded as a collective governing a plural predicate. Some scholars prefer to take the adjective (more precisely, a participle) as a substantive and thus as a second noun, thereby providing two nouns as the subject to agree in number with the predicate. In this case, the particle "and" would be reconstructed between the noun and participle. See Patrick D. Miller, "Fire in the Mythology of Canaan and Israel," *CBQ* 27 (1965) 258. For the comparison with "fire" (*phos*) and "flame" (*pur*) in Philo of Byblos, *PE* 1.10.9, see Harold W. Attridge and Robert A. Oden, Jr., *Philo of Byblos. The Phoenician History: Introduction, Critical Text, Translation, Notes,* CBQMS 9, 40–41, and 81 n. 53. For a critical assessment, see Albert I. Baumgarten, *The Phoenician History of Philo of Byblos: A Commentary,* EPRO 89, 152–53

81. See the same imagery in Isaiah 17:13. For the motif, compare Eusebius' *Preparatio evangelica* 1.10.4, presented conveniently by Attridge & Oden, Jr., *Philo,* 38–39. In this regard, note the discussion of verse 4 above.

82. The waters are apparently the subject; see Berlin, "The Wisdom of Creation," 78 n. 20.

83. The construction, *meqom zeh,* is unusual. As pointed, *meqom* stands in construct to the demonstrative pronoun. See *GKC* 138g, but the alleged analogies are not precisely comparable. Joüon para. 129q and 145c regards *zeh* as an old relative particle (and note the usage in Ugaritic); para. 129q cites Ecclesiastes 1:7: *'el-meqom she-* , while para. 145c cites other cases of the particle used in this manner. For this use of *zeh,* see also verse 26b below.

84. There is no relative pronoun; rather, the relative clause is asyndetic (so also in verse 15c here). For the notion in verse 15a, see Judg. 9:13.

85. For this meaning of biblical Hebrew °*smh* with parallels, see Greenfield, *'Al Kanfei Yonah,* 679–89.

86. Literally, "the earth is full of your acquisition." The word *qinyanka* refers to "your property," or "your acquisition" (*HALOT* 1114, which takes the usage here specifically as "your possession, meaning wealth"). Cf. Proverbs 4:7: "in every acquisition of yours, acquire understanding." Note also BH *miqneh,* "purchase." Many translations, following some mss., read °*qinyaneka* in Psalm 104:25c as plural, meaning "your creatures" (see NJPS, NRSV, NAB). This is the "easier reading" and perhaps suspect for this reason.

87. Compare the use of *zeh* in verse 8 and 26.

88. Note the same use of *zeh* in verse 8. For the syntax of this clause, see Weiss, *Bible from Within,* 78–93 (also cited by Berlin, "The Wisdom of Creation," 82).

89. The language here is quite reminiscent of Gen. 1:1–2.

90. For this sense of °*sih,* see *HALOT* 1321, especially in Ben Sira Hebrew ms. A 31:11 (Hebrew ms. A), 32:17 (ms. B), 35:4 and 44:4 (in B and Masada ms.).

91. For this point, see especially B. Jacobsen, *Teaching the Traditional Liturgy: Experimental Edition* (New York: The Melton Research Center/The Jewish Theological Seminary of America, 1971) 150–9.

92. Keel & Uehlinger, *Gods,* 261.

93. For the possibilities, see Berlin, "The Wisdom of Creation," 81–82.

94. See Bernard W. Anderson with Steven Bishop, *Out of the Depths: The Psalms Speak for Us Today* (3rd ed., rev. and exp.; Louisville, Ky: Westminster John Knox, 2000) 139; and John Day, "How Many Pre-exilic Psalms are There?" in *In Search of Pre-exilic Israel: Proceedings of the Oxford Old Testament Seminar,* JSOTSup 406, 238. Based largely on these parallels, Day has argued that Genesis 1 is dependent on Psalm 104. See Day, *God's Conflict,* 51–52, 55 (brought to my attention by Ron Hendel, personal communication). To these parallels between Psalm 104 and Genesis 1, Day also appeals to the use of *lemo'adim* in Psalm 104:19 and Gen. 1:14 and the form *hayto* in Psalm 104:11, 20 and Gen. 1:24, "and apart from the latter passage attested only in poetry in the Old Testament." See the following note.

95. The psalm's mention of human work in verse 23 sounds like Genesis 2:15 rather than anything in Genesis 1. Accordingly, one may suspect that the author of Psalm 104 drew on Genesis 1 and 2.

Given its form as a hymn plus a prayer of its final verse, it would fit a temple setting. For some remarks on the development and historical background to Psalm 104, see Smith, *God in Translation*, 69–76. It is possible that Psalm 104 was used and transmitted in the Jerusalem Temple, which could explain how the author of Genesis 1 might have known it. See also p. 214 n. 2.

96. For recent discussions of these two texts, see Ute Neumann-Gorsolke, *Herrschen in den Grenzen der Schöpfung: ein Beitrag zur alttestamentlichen Anthropologie am Beispiel von Psalm 8, Genesis 1 und verwandten Texten*, WMANT 101; and Jan Christian Geertz, "Herrschen in den Grenzen der Schöpfung: ein Beitrag zur alttestamentlichen Anthropologie am Beispiel von Psalm 8, Genesis 1, und verwandten Texten," ZAW 118/2, 310–11. For Herrmann Spieckermann, the two texts show an affinity, with Psalm 8 reflecting Temple theology, specifically "tempeltheologische Anthropologie." See Spieckermann, *Heilsgegenwart: Eine Theologie der Psalmen* (Göttingen: Vandenhoeck & Ruprecht, 1989) 227–39, esp. 235. As the discussion below and in chs. 2 and 3 suggests, Spieckermann's fitting characterization applies to both texts. Note also Walter Harrelson, "Psalm 8 on the Power and Mystery of Speech," in *Tehillah le-Moshe: Biblical and Judaic Studies in Honor of Moshe Greenberg* (edited by Mordechai Cogan, Barry L. Eichler and Jeffrey H. Tigay; Winona Lake, Ind.: Eisenbrauns, 1997) 69–72. Harrelson puts a particular emphasis on the role of divine speech in both texts.

97. Note the later Stoic-Cynic idea that the true temple is the universe (Cicero, *Nature of the Gods*, 3.26; Philo, *Special Laws* 1.66–97). Compare Wisdom of Solomon 18:24, which says that the whole world was depicted on the robe of Aaron. See NRSV note (*HarperCollins Study Edition*, p. 1375) to this passage.

98. For this psalm, see the comprehensive study of Helmut Schnieringer, *Psalm 8. Text—Gestalt—Bedeutung* (Ägypten und Altes Testament, vol. 59; Wiesbaden: Harrassowitz, 2004); and the review by Bernd Janowski in OLZ 103, 211–13.

99. For verse 2, MT reads: "who gives your splendor over the heavens." The last part of the line is clear; cf. Psalm 148:13: "His splendor is over earth and heaven." Much disputed are the opening two words, read by MT as *'asher tenah*, "who gives/giving"; cf. LXX: *eperthe*, "(your magnificence) is exalted." NJPS translates "You who have covered the heavens with your splendour!" This translation appears to be informed by the similar imagery in Habakkuk 3:3. For MT *tenah* as an infinitive, see Moshe Buttenwieser, *The Psalms Chronologically Treated with a New Translation* (first published in 1938; New York: KTAV, 1969) 180. An infinitive construct following relative *'asher* as well the opening of the hymn's body with a relative clause with *'asher* seems odd, and poetically the addition of the relative clause is awkward. Given the parallel in verse 10, the clause would seem not to go with the verse 2a.

To address these difficulties, scholars have proposed various first person prefix forms derived from various roots, including °*tny*, "to reiterate," °*shyr*, "to sing," and °*shrt*, "to serve." Mitchell J. Dahood reads °*'asharetannah*, "I will praise." See Dahood, *Psalms I: 1–50*, AB 16, 49. Helmer Ringgren faults the proposed meaning as otherwise attested for °*shrt*. See Ringgren, "Some Observations on the Text of the Psalms," *Maarav* 5–6, 307–8. Ringgren instead suggests °*'ashira-nna*, "I will sing." The difficulty with this proposal is that it does not account for the medial *-t-*.

On the one hand, the versions' general agreement on °*ntn* as the verb cannot be ignored. On the other hand, the first person singular prefix form is supported by some of the versions. As a speculative proposal, I have suggested that MT *'asher tenah* may preserve two variants, *'ashirah* and *'ettenah* which passed in conflated form into MT and the other versions. See Mark S. Smith, "Psalm 8:2b-3: New Proposals for Old Problems," CBQ 59, 637–41; and Schnieringer, *Psalm 8*, 27–43. This interpretation here would accord better with the length of the following lines.

100. The parallelism between the nouns, *'oz* and *sorereka*, is difficult to fathom since the apparent meanings of these words, "strength" and "your enemies," offer little semantic similarity. It may be asked whether these are precisely the meanings involved in Psalm 8:2 (MT 3). It is possible that *'oz* may mean not "strength" as such. Instead, it may characterize the created world as a "strong place," a suitable description in view of the description of creation in these terms in Psalm 104:5 and 8. These verses use the verb, "to found" (°*ysd*), for acts of creation, as in Psalm 8:2. Psalm 8 refers to eliminating the divine enemies, which may allude to the battle between God and the cosmic enemies at the time of creation. Given this sense of the passage, the noun *sorereka* may not stand in parallelism

with *'oz* in the meaning of "your enemies." Rather, it may be related to BH *sur,* "rock," as a place of divine strength. To explain the consonantal spelling, MT *sorereka* might be viewed instead as a plural of abstraction, °*surereka*, "Your strength," understood in this context more precisely as "Your stronghold" (similar to Ugaritic *srrt spn*). For further argument and etymological support, see Smith, "Psalm 8:2b-3," 637–41. The proposal is speculative, but if it is this case, *'oz* and °*surereka* in Psalm 8:2 would be semantically parallel. In this reading, the parallel terms of Psalm 8:2 would describe the ancient, divine victory over cosmic enemies.

101. For °*kwn*, "to establish," see above n. 53; and ch. 3, sec. 3.

102. The logical flow between verses 3 and 4 (MT 4 and 5) is implicit as it stands. *GKC* 159dd suggests implicit "I exclaim," following verse 3 and prior to the question posed in verse 4. The poem is presented as the expression of an individual who uses exclamations as in verses 1 and 9; ellipsis of this sort or an implied main verb suggested by *GKC* would not be exceptional for direct discourse (for an example, see Psalm 2:2–3). In the following vv. 4–6, "her" and "him" alternate to signal the inclusion of both genders in the antecedent "the human." To be sure, Hebrew here uses the masculine pronominal element in these verses.

103. Here the *'elohim* refer to deities in the most general sense (as in Psalms 82:1b, 86:8). They are the *'elim,* "gods" (Exod. 15:11; Job 41:17), or *bene 'elim,* literally "divine sons" or "sons of God (El)," in Psalms 29:1 and 89:7 (cf. 89:6, 8). The word "god" (*'elohim*) is not reserved only for main or "high" deities such as God, but for divinities of varying statuses, including "angels" who are literally "messenger" gods, the lowest rank in the divine hierarchy. As the word is applied occasionally to the dead (1 Samuel 28:3) and rarely for the king (Psalm 45:7), it seems to refer to beings with superhuman characteristics or perhaps anyone who passes human boundaries such as death. See further ch. 2, p. 48.

104. For *soneh,* "sheep," compare *sona'akem* in Num. 32:34. The noun appears to be a biform of *so'n* (*BDB* 856), "sheep," or more precisely the smaller animals of the flocks, namely sheep and goats.

105. For this division, see Charles Augustus Briggs and Emilie Grace Briggs, *A Critical and Exegetical Commentary on the Book of Psalms, vol. I,* (ICC New York: Charles Scribner's Sons, 1906) 61, 62.

106. For the old cosmic conflict in this allusion, see Dahood, *Psalms I,* 49; and Helmer Ringgren, "Observations," 307–08. See also Smith, "Psalm 8:2b-3," 637–41. The verbs of verses 2–3 (MT 3–4) suggest a cosmic conflict at the time of creation of the universe. The root °*ysd,* "to found, establish" is commonly used for the divine creation of the world (e.g., Psalm 104:5, 8). The relation of creation to the enigmatic "mouth of babes (*'olelim*) and suckers (*yoneqim*)" is difficult. Helmer Ringgren proposes that here, as in Psalm 73:9, there is an allusion to the traditional myth as known also from the Ugaritic text, "The Rituals and Myths of the Goodly Gods" (KTU 1.23), also sometimes called the "Birth of the Beautiful Gods." Called "suckers" (*ynqm*) like the enigmatic figures of Psalm 8:2, the children of the god El in 1.23 devour all the beasts of the known world and are remanded to the desert for seven or eight years until they are allowed into the sown region. The putative parallel with Psalm 8:2 involves three features: (i) the divine "suckers"; (ii) their appetite that threatens all animals; and (iii) the possible cosmogonic setting of this myth. Perhaps a related mythic version underlies these texts, and the beasts in verses 7–8 (MT 8–9) might be interpreted with this in mind: instead of the troublesome cosmic forces devouring all the animals of the world (as in KTU 1.23), they are given instead to humanity as their ruler (Psalm 8). For the Ugaritic text, see Lewis, "Birth," 205–14; and my book, *Sacrificial Rituals.*

107. Later texts that draw on Psalm 8 likewise pass over the description of cosmic enemies. See for example Psalm 144:3 and Job 7:17. At the same time, Psalm 144 retains some of the older language of cosmic conflict, albeit in rather conventional terms (e.g., the cosmic waters of verse 7, which serve as description for foreigners). See Spieckermann, *Heilsgegenwart,* 237.

108. See George Coats, "Self-Abasement and Insult Formulas," *JBL* 89 (1970) 14–26, esp. 24–26; and Jeffrey Tigay, "What Is Man That You Have Been Mindful of Him? (On Psalm 8:4–5)," in *Love & Death in the Ancient Near East: Essays in Honor of Marvin H. Pope* (edited by John H. Marks and Robert M. Good; Guilford, Conn.: Four Quarters, 1987) 169–71. For verse 5, see the comparable formula in Psalm 144:3 and the famous satire on this saying in Job 7:17–18; cf. Hebrews 2:6. The verbs °*yd',* "to know," and °*hshb,* "to think of, conceive," in the parallel in Psalm 144:3 are mental activities suggesting the general sense of the verbs °*zkr,* "to remember" (in the sense of "to call to mind") and °*pqd* as "to be mindful." Job 7:17 follows suit in using °*shyt lb 'l,* "to set

(one's) heart on," but note the ironic reversal of °*pqd* in the Joban version: "you make him watch the cattle."

109. For this question and the anthropology reflected in the answer, see Bernd Janowski, *Konfliktgespräche mit Gott: Eine Anthropologie der Psalmen* (Neukirchen-Vluyn: Neukirchener Verlag, 2003) 11–12; and *Die Welt als Schöpfung: Beiträge zur Theologie des Alten Testaments 4* (Neukirchen-Vluyn: Neukirchener Verlag, 2008) 175–78.

110. J. P. Oberholzer, "What is Man. . .?" in *De fructu oris sui: Essays in Honour of Adrianus van Selms* (edited by Ian H. Eybers et al.; Leiden: Brill, 1971) 147.

111. This way of praising God through praise of a visible phenomenon is found also in the Jerusalem psalms (for example, Psalms 46, 48, and 87), where praise of the divine king and his divine city are inextricably linked. Like Zion in the Songs of Jerusalem, humanity here mediates the understanding of the divine-human relationship.

112. See also Schnieringer, *Psalm 8*, 182. For other proposals, see Schnieringer, *Psalm 8*, 106–20.

113. Luis Alonso Schökel, *A Manual of Hebrew Poetics, SubBi* 11, 198.

114. Jon D. Levenson, *Creation and the Persistence of Evil*, (Princeton: Princeton University, 1994) 88.

115. For studies of the divine name, see above n. 37.

116. For the temple sensibility of *kabod*, see also note 41.

117. For a consideration of the visual elements in this scene, see Keel & Uehlinger, *Gods*, 273 and 401. Based on their studies of eighth century seals, they consider the seraphim to be comparable to the four-winged Egyptian *uraeus* imagined as the black-necked cobra. They also note the absence of the cherubim iconography from the description in Isaiah 6 (p. 310 n. 21).

118. Compare Psalm 108:5 (MT 6).

119. For the temple background to Genesis 1, see Moshe Weinfeld, "Sabbath, Temple and the Enthronement of the Lord—The Problem of the Sitz im Leben of Genesis 1:1—2:3," in *Mélanges bibliques et orientaux en l'honneur de M. Henri Cazelles*, AOAT 212, 501–12; Levenson, *Creation*, 78–87; Bernd Janowski, "Tempel und Schöpfung: Schöpfungstheologische Aspekte der priesterschriftlichen Heiligtumskonzeption," *Jahrbuch für Biblische Theologie* 5 (1990) 37–69, reprinted in Janowski, *Gottes Gegenwart in Israel: Beiträge zur Theologie des Alten Testaments* (Neukirchen-Vluyn: Neukirchener Verlag, 1993) 214–46.

120. Briggs & Briggs, *Psalms I*, 61; Hans Joachim Kraus, *Psalms 1–59: A Continental Commentary* (translated by Hilton C. Oswald; Minneapolis: Fortress, 1993) 180, 185. See also Levenson, *Creation*, 113–14; and Schnieringer, *Psalm 8*, 435–70.

121. Kraus, *Psalms 1–59*, 180, 185; Levenson, *Creation*, 113–14. For the verb in Genesis 1, see further Bernd Janowski, *Die rettende Gerechtigkeit: Beiträge zur Theologie des Alten Testaments 2* (Neukirchen-Vluyn: Neukirchener Verlag, 1999) 33–48.

122. See Mettinger, *King and Messiah*, 269–71.

123. Discussed by Levenson, *Creation*, 114

124. Levenson, *Creation*, 113; and Josef Shreiner, "Her Herr hilft Menschen und Tieren (Ps 36,7)," in *Gefährten und Feinde des Menschen: Das Tier in der Lebenswelt des alten Israel* (edited by Bernd Janowski, Ute Neumann-Gorsolke and Uwe Glessmer; Neukirchen-Vluyn: Neukirchener Verlag, 1993) 228–29. See also Richard Whitekettle, "Taming the Shrew, Shrike, and Shrimp: The Form and Function of Zoological Classification in Psalm 8," *JBL* 125, 749–65.

125. On this basis of these similarities, one might think that Psalm 8 derived from a priestly background like Genesis 1. It is possible that Psalm 8 is the priestly poetic counterpart to the prose narrative of Genesis 1.

126. See ch. 4 for the possible implications for reading Genesis 1.

127. John J. Collins, "The Zeal of Phinehas: The Bible and the Legitimation of Violence," *JBL* 122 (2003) 3–21. See also the essays in *Sanctified Aggression: Legacies of Biblical and Post-Biblical Vocabularies of Violence* (edited by Jonneke Bekkenkamp and Yvonne Sherwood; London/New York: T & T Clark International, 2003).

128. In this vein, note the following cosmic characterization of one of Don Quixote's battles: "The keen-edged swords of the two valiant and enraged combatants, thus raised aloft, seemed to be threatening the very heavens, earth, and watery abysses, such was the determination displayed

by both men." Cited from the edition: Miguel de Cervantes Saavedra, *The Ingenious Hidalgo Don Quixote* (translated by John Rutherford; with an introduction by Roberto González Echevarría; New York: Penguin Books, 2003) 76–77.

129. Exegetes sometimes try to reconcile the language of dominion and subjugation of Genesis 1 with an ecological sensitivity. For example, see Haroldo Alomía, "Sujeción del Planeta en Genesis 1:26–28 y su mensaje ecológico vinculado con el mensaje de la Iglesia Adventista del Séptimo Día," *Theo* 17, 42–92. However, the language of rule and dominion in Gen. 1:26 and 28 is not to be soft-pedaled. See Hermann-Josef Stipp, "Dominium terrae: Die Herrschaft der Menschen über die Tiere in Gen 1,26.28," in *Gott Sprach Mensch: Schüler-festschrift für Walter Gross zum 60. Geburstag* (Arbeiten zu Text und Sprache im Alten Testament, vol. 68; St. Ottilien: EOS, 2001) 113–48. For the issues, see in general Norman C. Habel and Peter Trudinger, eds., *Exploring Ecological Hermeneutics* (Atlanta: SBL, 2008).

130. For the issue of what is now criticized as "speciesism," see Joan Dunager, *Speciesism* (Derwood, Md.: Ryce Publishing, 2004) especially 11–12, 57.

131. In the discussion of the third model earlier in this chapter, I discussed holiness, light, name, and word as various ways in which humanity and divinity are related or connected. In Psalm 104, it is "breath/sprit" (*ruah*) that links the human and the divine. To my mind, both *ruah* and eternity (*'olam*) are the comparable notions of Ecclesiastes' wisdom search. For a discussion of "eternity" in this verse, see Charles F. Whitley, *Koheleth: His Language and Thought*, BZAW 148, 31–33; Diethelm Michel, *Untersuchungen zur Eidenart des Buches Qohelet*, BZAW 183, 61–64. Proposals to emend Ecclesiastes 3:11 may be resisted, especially given the lack of versional evidence, and given that time is the topic at hand. This divine act means that humanity in its finitude cannot ever fully fathom infinity, as stressed by the verse; still this divine act perhaps oriented humanity toward God who is eternal. The other possibility that commentators (such as Whitley) accept requires no emendation, namely that the word is to be derived from °*'lm*, "darkness" (cf. Ugaritic °*ǵlm*). Still one may doubt that God has put "darkness into their heart." The further effort to take the word in the sense of "to be hidden" is marred somewhat by the awkwardness of reading required: "God has put the hidden/hiddenness (?) in their heart." Wordplay may be involved.

132. So the reflections on the state of sub-Saharan Africa in light of Genesis 1 by Moiseraele Prince Dibeela, "A Setswana Perspective on Genesis 1:1–10," in *The Bible in Africa: Transactions, Trajectories and Trends* (edited by Gerald O. West and Musa W. Dube; Leiden/Boston/Köln: Brill 2000) 384–99.

133. Compare various psalms of pilgrimage such as Psalms 42–43 and 84. See Mark S. Smith, "Setting and Rhetoric in Psalm 23," *JSOT* 41, 61–66.

Chapter 2: The First Day

1. For a sixth century context for Genesis 1, see Cross, *Canaanite Myth* (ch. 1, n. 16) 324.

2. Three considerations often used to date Genesis 1 involve (1) later allusions to Genesis 1; (2) references to the Sabbath; and (3) dating according to grammar.

Allusions to Genesis 1

Allusions to Genesis 1 have been detected in Jeremiah, Ezekiel, and Second Isaiah, all composed in whole or in part in the sixth century. For claims of allusions to Genesis 1–3 in Jeremiah and Ezekiel, see Richard Elliott Friedman, "Torah (Pentateuch)," *ABD VI*, 617. For Second Isaiah responding directly to Genesis 1, see Moshe Weinfeld, "The Creator God in Genesis 1 and the Prophecies of Deutero-Isaiah," *Tarbiz* 37 (1968) 120–26 (Heb.); Michael Fishbane, *Biblical Interpretation in Ancient Israel* (Oxford: Clarendon, 1985) 322–26, especially p. 325–26; and Benjamin D. Sommer, *A Prophet Reads Scripture: Allusion in Isaiah 40–66* (Stanford, Calif.: Stanford University Press, 1998) 142–43 and 216 n. 87. This view of Second Isaiah's dependence on Genesis 1 is criticized by Levenson, *Creation* (ch. 1, n. 114), 124–26. Levenson supposes that an allusion to Genesis 1 would reference the seven days of creation. This position rests on an argument from silence.

Another biblical passage sometimes cited as an allusion is Zechariah 12:1: "Oracle of Yahweh, who stretches out the heavens and establishes the earth and fashions the life-breath of humanity within it."

According to some commentators, this verse alludes to both Genesis 1 and 2. The mention of heavens and earth is thought to echo Genesis 1 (in particular, verse 1) and the reference to human creation with divine breath here is believed to reflect Gen. 2:7. If this reading of Zechariah 12 is correct, it would suggest that Genesis 1 was written and connected with Genesis 2 by the time when Zechariah 12 was written. This chapter has been dated to the mid-fifth century. So see Carol L. Meyers and Eric M. Meyers, *Zechariah 9–14: A New Translation with Introduction and Commentary*, AB 25C, 27. So it would appear that Genesis 1 was known by this time, at least in the circles that produced Zechariah 12. It might have taken some time for Genesis 1–2 to circulate and become known to the tradition that produced Zechariah 12. So Genesis 1–2 would be earlier than the fifth century.

The verbs that Zechariah 12:1 uses for creating the heavens and earth differ from the ones in Genesis 1, which raises some suspicion about this proposal. To make the claim of an allusion more convincing, a more complex model allowing for dependence and accounting for the choice of verbs is required. It might be suggested that Zechariah 12:1 uses these traditional verbs of creating (as known elsewhere) because they appear in other contexts in Zechariah. Zechariah 1:16 uses °*nth*, and 4:9 and 8:9 attest to °*ysd*. In these verses, the verbs concern the (re-)building of the temple, which is analogous to building language used in creation accounts and vice versa. For °*ysd* building language in a creation account, see for example, Psalm 104:5 and Job 38:4; for the earthly sanctuary characterized as "built" (°*bny*) like the heavens and like the earth that God "established" (°*ysd*), see Psalm 78:69; see further p. 179. I wish to thank Carol Meyers for communicating with me about this issue.

It may be noted that a reading of Genesis 1–2 has been seen also in Ben Sira 24:3; see Gerald T. Sheppard, *Wisdom as a Hermeneutical Construct: A Study in the Sapientializing of the Old Testament*, BZAW 151, 21–26, 103. Seeing this allusion rests on a rather complex argumentation. Another possible candidate of a biblical text drawing on Genesis 1–2 is Psalm 104, which uses the language of *ruah* and °*br'* in verse 30 as known from Gen. 1:2, and the image of humanity at its work in verse 23, as seen in Gen. 2:15. See p. 209–10, nn. 94 and 95. Finally, the combination of cosmic and human creation in Isaiah 42:5 might also seem to suggest the combination of Genesis 1–2.

The Date of Sabbath Texts

A sixth-century date also fits the allusion to the Sabbath with God's rest in Gen. 2:2–3. We find extensive references to the Sabbath in the sixth century priestly work of Ezekiel (20:12–24; 22:8, 26; 44:24; and 46:1–5). In this period, the Sabbath came to take on an "exalted status." This phrase as well as the point being made here comes from Brooks Schramm, *The Opponents of Third Isaiah: Reconstructing the Cultic History of the Restoration*, JSOTSup 193, 118. This status is reflected in Isaiah 56:1–8 and 66:23 and Jeremiah 17:19–27 (see also Nehemiah 13:15–22). The priestly promotion and dissemination of the Sabbath represented by these texts work well with a sixth century milieu for Genesis 1. Note also the personal name Shabbetay, in Ezra 10:15, Nehemiah 8:7 and 11:16 (BDB 992).

Biblical Hebrew Grammar

A sixth century context also works with the grammar of Genesis 1. According to scholars who study Hebrew grammar, Genesis 1 appears to contain what has been called "Standard Biblical Hebrew." This style of Hebrew dates to the period of the monarchy (ca. 1000–586 BCE), and it may have continued through the end of the sixth century. For extensive discussion, see the appendix, pp. 173–74. Indeed, biblical writers might wish to imitate the earlier style of their tradition. Cf. Adele Berlin's discussion of imitation of preexilic "historical books" by postexilic writers in order to connect the experience of postexilic communities and thereby provide continuity of identity between the two; see Berlin, "The Book of Esther and Ancient Story-Telling," *JBL* 120 (2001) 7.

3. Baruch Halpern dates P to the late seventh century at around 610, based largely on the allusions to Genesis 1 in Jeremiah. See Halpern, "The Assyrian Astronomy of Genesis 1 and the Birth of Milesian Philosophy," *ErIsr* 27, 74°-83°. "Pre-exilic times" is suggested as the date of Genesis 1 by Bill T. Arnold, *Genesis* (The New Cambridge Bible Commentary; Cambridge/New York: Cambridge University Press, 2009) 29.

4. See the remarks of Ratzinger *In the Beginning* (ch. 1, n. 2), 20.

5. Gershom Hepner takes the rationale of Genesis 1 to be the creation of the land of Israel after the Babylonian exile. See Hepner, "Israelites Should Conquer Israel: The Hidden Polemic of the First Creation Narrative," *RB* 113, 161–80. William Brown (*The Seven Pillars of Creation: The Bible, Science, and the Ecology of Wonder*, in preparation, cited with permission) has likewise suggested that Genesis 1 is programmatic for communal restoration following the Exile. Alice L. Laffey puts the chapter in the exilic or post-exilic context. See Laffey, "The Priestly Creation Narrative: Goodness and Interdependence," in *Earth, Wind, and Fire* (ch. 1, n. 75), 24–34, esp. 27.

6. For a listing of priestly language in Genesis 1, see Julius Wellhausen, *Prolegomena to the History of the Old Testament* (Gloucester, Mass.: Peter Smith, 1973; originally publ. 1878) 386–90; and Hermann Gunkel, *Genesis* (translated by Mark E. Biddle; Macon, Ga.: Mercer University, 1997; originally publ. 1901) 117 (with references to earlier literature).

7. Among major commentators, see Wellhausen, *Prolegomena*, 297–98, 386–90; Gunkel, *Genesis*, 117–22; Martin Noth, *A History of Pentateuchal Traditions* (translated with an Introduction by Bernhard W. Anderson; Englewood Cliffs, N.J.: Prentice-Hall, 1972; repr., Atlanta: Scholars Press, 1981; originally publ. 1948) 10–11, 12, 235, 241, 251; Gerhard von Rad, *Genesis: A Commentary*, OTL, 45 and 61–65; Cross, *Canaanite Myth*, 301, 306; Erhard Blum, *Studien zur Komposition des Pentateuch*, BZAW 189, 285, 289–91, 306–7; and David M. Carr, *Reading the Fractures of Genesis: Historical and Literary Approaches* (Louisville, Ky.: Westminster John Knox, 1996) 62–68.

Among recent commentators, Israel Knohl attributes Gen. 1:1—2:4a entirely to P. See Knohl, *The Sanctuary of Silence: The Priestly Torah and the Holiness School* (Minneapolis: Fortress Press, 1995) 104 and 125 n. 4; and *The Divine Symphony: The Bible's Many Voices* (Philadelphia: JPS, 2003) 120–21 and 164–65 n. 16. Edwin Firmage and Yairah Amit assign Genesis 1 to the later priestly hand that Knohl and others call "the Holiness redaction" (H). See Firmage, "Genesis 1 and the Priestly Agenda," *JSOT* 82, 97–114; and Amit, "Creation and the Calendar of Holiness," in *Tehilla le-Moshe: Biblical Studies in Honor of Moshe Greenberg* (edited by Mordechai Cogan, Barry L. Eichler, and Jeffrey H. Tigay; Winona Lake, Ind.: Eisenbrauns, 1997) 13–29 (Heb., with an English summary on 315–16). Like Firmage and Amit, Jacob Milgrom sees H material in Gen. 2:2–3, but he does not see it otherwise in Genesis 1. See Jacob Milgrom, *Leviticus 17–22*, AB 3A, 1344. The notion that Isaiah 40:28 alludes to Gen. 2:2 would preclude Milgrom's view. For this view, see Weinfeld, "The Creator God," 126; and Sommer, *A Prophet Reads Scripture*, 144. However, this view is debatable. See Knohl, *Symphony*, 163 n. 16 for the rejection of Amit's argument (and by implication, probably Milgrom's as well). Knohl claims that if Gen. 1:1—2:3 belonged to H and not P, then a prohibition against work might have been expected as in Exod. 31:14–15 and 35:2–3. See further the comments of William P. Brown, *The Ethos of the Cosmos: The Genesis of Moral Imagination in the Bible* (Grand Rapids: Eerdmans, 1998) 120 n. 228.

Because of this controversy, my consideration of Genesis 1 will prescind from treating it primarily in source-critical terms as the unit heading the larger priestly source or stratum in Genesis 1–11 and beyond, as is often done; see, for example among recent commentators, Michaela Bauks, "Genesis 1 als Programmschrift der Priesterschrift (P^g)," in *Studies in the Book of Genesis*, BETL 145, 333–46. For further discussion, see the appendix as well as ch. 4.

8. These three works are mentioned at various points in the discussion below in this chapter. For the moment, we may make some initial remarks.

For *Enuma Elish*, its overall presentation has been related to Genesis 1. For a recent discussion, see Kenton Sparks, "*Enūma Elish* and Priestly Mimesis: Elite Emulation in Nascent Judaism," *JBL* 126 (2007) 625–48. For the international context of Genesis 1 vis-à-vis Mesopotamia and the Aegean, see Halpern, "Assyrian Astronomy," 74°-83°.

In the case of the Egyptian Memphite Creation text, this text involves creation by word that is particularly suggestive for Genesis 1. See Donald B. Redford, *Egypt, Canaan, and Israel in Ancient Times* (Princeton, N. J.: Princeton University Press, 1992) 396. For the connection with Genesis 1, see Koch, "Wort und Einheit" (ch. 1, n. 32), 251–93, republished in Koch, *Studien zur alttestamentlichen*, 61–105; and Levenson, *Creation*, 107.

For Philo of Byblos, it is this text's description of the cosmos just prior to creation that arguably relates to Genesis 1; so Robert du Mesnil du Buisson, *Études sur les dieux phéniciens hérités par l'empire romain* (Études preliminaires aux religions orientales dans l'empire romain, vol. 14;

Leiden: Brill, 1970) 39–42; and Richard J. Clifford, "Phoenician Religion," *BASOR* 279, 58; see also the comparison made by Cross, *From Epic to Canon* (ch. 1, n. 6), 82–83. The comparison specifically involves Gen. 1:2 and Philo of Byblos, in Eusebius' *Praep. ev.* 1.10.1, 7, presented conveniently by Attridge & Oden, *Philo*, (ch. 1, n. 80), 36–37, 40–41, respectively. As noted below, the reference to Baau (*PE* 1.10.7) has often been compared with Hebrew *bohu* in Gen. 1:2. Philo also includes light in the creation account (*PE* 1.10.9). For these details, see the discussion below. Some scholars have considered the possibility that the influence here operated in the opposite direction; in this vein, note the comments of du Mesnil du Buisson (*Études*, 41–42) that the goddess Baau is an interpretation of Hebrew *bohu*. In this case, the evidence of Philo would provide a sense of how Genesis 1, or at least some of the ideas in it, was received in Phoenician culture. However, it is not clear that the influence runs in this direction or that it is direct.

9. Redford, *Egypt, Canaan*, 400.

10. An outstanding issue is whether this influence would have been mediated via Phoenicia or not. Clifford insightfully notes that possible Egyptian influence of the sort represented by the Memphite Creation may have been mediated to ancient Israel via a Phoenician contact, such as Philo of Byblos (see *Creation Accounts* [Intro., n. 2], 114,). Yet since divine speech is what seems to proximate the divine speaking in Genesis 1, what would make this putative line of influence via Phoenician tradition more persuasive would be a reference either to "word" (*logos*) or to divine speaking in the creation account of Philo of Byblos; there is none, however. At the same time, the place of Ptah as in the Memphite Creation text was arguably known in Phoenician cosmogony tradition, as attested in Damascius; see Attridge & Oden, *Philo*, 102–3. This source reflects this knowledge in expressing the idea of Chousor as "the first opener." This has long been recognized as a pun on the West Semitic root °*pth* inspired by the identification of Chousor and Ptah; see Attridge & Oden, *Philo*, 104 n. 6. The identification arguably goes back to the Late Bronze Age and may not reflect the seventh-sixth century period of influence.

The path of this influence is complex. Already in the Late Bronze Age material from Ugarit, one of the homes of Kothar wa-Hasis, the craftsman god, is said to be Memphis, that is Hikuptah, literally "the house of the soul (*ka*) of Ptah" (KTU/CAT 1.3 VI 15–16; cf. 1. 17 V 20–21; see Smith, "The Baal Cycle," and Parker, "Aqhat" (ch. 1, n. 51), 59 and 119. This identification between the two gods had been noted by many older commentators: G. Hoffman, "Aramäische Inschriften aus Nêrab bei Aleppo. Neue und alte Götter," *ZA* 11, 254; William Foxwell Albright, *Archaeology and the Religion of Israel* (Baltimore: The Johns Hopkins University, 1942) 82, and *Yahweh and the Gods of Canaan* (Garden City, N. Y.: Doubleday, 1968; repr., Winona Lake, Ind.: Eisenbrauns, nd) 137, 225; Theodor H. Gaster, *Thespis: Ritual, Myth, and Drama in the Ancient Near East* (New York: Henry Schuman, 1950) 156; H. L. Ginsberg, "Two Religious Borrowings in Ugaritic Literature," *Or* 8, 317–27; Keith Vine, "The Establishment of Baal at Ugarit" (Ph.D. dissertation, University of Michigan, 1965) 44–45; Michael David Coogan, *Stories from Ancient Canaan* (Philadelphia: Westminster, 1978) 118; and Redford, *Egypt, Canaan*, 40. The identification of Kothar with Ptah was based also on some similarity of divine functions: like Kothar, Ptah was associated with arts and crafts. This sort of identification was presumably inspired by the social situation in Memphis: a famous cult site of Ptah, Memphis was also a site of West Semitic trade and religious devotion, including a temple to Baal; see Redford, *Egypt, Canaan*, 228. Still, it remains unclear what weight, if any, is to be put on this information for delineating a line of influence from Egypt to Phoenicia to Genesis 1.

11. See Moshe Greenberg, *Ezekiel 21–37: A New Translation with Introduction and Commentary*, AB 22A, 395–96. For the putative Phoenician backdrop to Ezekiel 28, see Corinne Bonnet, *Melqart: Cultes et mythes de l'Héraclès tyrien en Méditerranée* (Studia Phoenicia VIII; Leuven: Peeters/Presses universitatieres de Namur, 1988) 42–46. For a general consideration, see Paolo Xella, "La Bible," in *La civilization phénicienne et punique: Manuel de recherche* (edited by Véronique Krings; HO, Nahe und mittlere Osten ser. I, vol. 20; Leiden: Brill, 1995) 63–72, esp. 72.

12. See Robert R. Wilson, "The Community of the Second Isaiah," in *Reading and Preaching the Book of Isaiah* (edited by Christopher R. Seitz; Philadelphia: Fortress Press, 1988) 53–70; and Stephen L. Cook, *Conversations with Scripture: 2 Isaiah* (Anglican Association of Biblical Scholars Study Series; Harrisburg, Penn.: Morehouse, 2008) 6–8, 27–32, 45–48, 86–93, 116–19.

Cook ties the thought of Second Isaiah to the priestly tradition as reflected in the P source as opposed to the Holiness priestly tradition represented in the Holiness Code (Leviticus 17–26) and the holiness redaction of the Pentateuch, as understood by Knohl, *Sanctuary*. Unlike Wilson, Cook (6, 15–16, etc.) works with the presupposition that Isaiah 40–66 forms a single work, a view that has some adherents but is not the consensus view of scholarship at present. Note the case that Brooks Schramm makes for the disciples of the author of Isaiah 40–55 (represented by Isaiah 56–66) as allies of the Zadokite priests. See Schramm, *Opponents*, 111; for further discussion of this question, see Lena-Sofia Tiemeyer, *Priestly Rites and Prophetic Rage*, FAT 2:19, 12–13. For a very different reading of Second Isaiah, see Diana Lipton, "Bezalel in Babylon? Anti-Priestly Polemics in Isaiah 40–55," *The Journal of the Ancient Near Eastern Society* 31 (2008) 63–84. Most of Lipton's evidence is very indirect, and some of what she reads as antipriestly polemic might be understood as part of an inner-priestly discussion.

13. For the cross-cultural dimension of Second Isaiah's thought, see Peter Machinist, "Mesopotamian Imperialism and Israelite Religion: A Case Study from Second Isaiah," in *Symbiosis, Symbolism, and the Power of the Past: Canaan, Ancient Israel, and Their Neighbors—From the Late Bronze Age through Roman Palaestina* (edited by William G. Dever and Seymour Gitin; the AIAR Anniversary Volume; Winona Lake, Ind.: Eisenbrauns, 2003) 237–64.

14. I have further considered the speculative scenario that the authors of Genesis 1 and Ezekiel were perhaps priestly "alphabet scribes," like the later Judean, Gadalama, who worked in the satrapy of Babylon in the fifth century; he is also called "chancellor" (*bel temi*). See Matthew W. Stolper, "The Governor of Babylon and Across-the-River in 486 B.C.," *JNES* 48, 284–305; and Ran Zadok, *The Earlier Diaspora: Israelites and Judeans in Pre-Hellenistic Mesopotamia* (Publications of the Diaspora Research Institute, Book 151; Tel Aviv: The Diaspora Research Institute, Tel Aviv University, 2002) 35. Thanks to discoveries of a number of cuneiform tablets since the late 1980s, we know that Judeans were settled in various locations in Babylonia, including a place called "Judah-town" (*al-Yahudu*) as well as "town of the Judeans." For discussion, see Zadok, *The Earlier Diaspora*, 33–35, 61–63; and Laurie E. Pearce, "New Evidence for Judeans in Babylonia," in *Judah and Judeans in the Persian Period* (edited by Oded Lipschits and Manfred Oeming; Winona Lake, Ind.: Eisenbrauns, 2006) 399–411, esp. 400–405 (with further bibliography). This reconstruction would fit with the book of Ezekiel (or at least the prophet), which suggests a context in Babylon (see Ezek. 1:1 and 3:15); for discussion of the setting in connection with Psalm 137, see John Ahn, "Psalm 137: Complex Communal Laments," *JBL* 127 (2008) 267–89, esp. 276–78, 281–82. Such a setting cannot be determined for Genesis 1 (compare the "windows" in Gen. 7:11, also priestly, which have been thought to reflect Mesopotamian irrigation sluice-gates; see Moshe Weinfeld, "Gen. 7:11, 8:1–2 against the Background of Ancient Near Eastern Tradition," *WO* 9, 242–44). Also suggestive of the Judean-in-exile context for Ezekiel is M. A. Dundamayev's comparison of "the elders of Judah" in Ezekiel 8:1 with "an assembly of Egyptian elders" that functioned in Babylon. See Dundamayev, "Neo-Babylonian and Achaemenid State Administration," in *Judah and Judeans in the Persian Period* (edited by Oded Lipschits and Manfred Oeming; Winona Lake, Ind.: Eisenbrauns, 2006) 374.

Generally for this sort of scribal role for the "literateur" of Genesis 1 or Ezekiel, we may also discuss the role of "interpreter scribe" (*spr pshr'*) known from the later book of Enoch; to mention only a couple references, see 4Q530, conveniently presented in Donald W. Parry and Emanuel Tov, *The Dead Sea Scrolls Reader: Part 3. Parabiblical Texts* (Leiden/Boston: Brill, 2004) 484; or Geza Vermes, *The Complete Dead Sea Scrolls in English* (fourth edition; New York/London: Penguin Books, 1998) 516–17. For discussion, see further Smith, *God in Translation* (ch. 1, n. 4), 219–20 n. 96 and 223 n. 107, which also compares Nehemiah 8:8.

15. Important groups in Israel at the time were the "sons of Aaron" (Aaronids if P) and the "sons of Zadok" (Zadokites if H); but in either case, the "sons of Levi" (Levites) were not, because they are priests of lesser rank by the sixth century. For a summary, see Mark S. Smith, "The Priestly Lines and the Production of Exodus," which appeared in my book, *Pilgrimage Pattern in Exodus*, with contributions by Elizabeth M. Bloch-Smith, JSOTSup 239, 257–61.

16. I use the term broadly to refer to the nature of the relationship.

17. Jeremiah has been viewed as an accumulation of material beginning in the sixth century. The general idea of the work as a "rolling corpus" (with some passages going back to the prophet) as advocated by William McKane has won considerable support. See McKane, *Jeremiah: Volume I. I-XXV* (ICC; Edinburgh/New York: T & T Clark, 1986) l-lxxxiii. The evidence of duplicates in Jeremiah has contributed to the issue of Jeremiah's development; see Geoffrey H. Parke-Taylor, *The Formation of the Book of Jeremiah: Doublets and Recurring Phrases*, SBLMS 51, esp. 296–306.

A primary matter of discussion is the degree to which the poetry of Jeremiah 2–25 (what Mowinckel labeled "Jeremiah A") is to be read as the prophet's words or as later compositions about the prophet. The fact that the major commentaries are so strongly split over the issue suggests that the evidence in either direction is not particularly clear. Note the sober assessment of McKane, *Jeremiah I*, lxxxviii-xcii. See also the intelligent discussion of Robert R. Wilson, "Poetry and Prose in the Book of Jeremiah," in *Ki Baruch Hu: Ancient Near Eastern, Biblical, and Judaic Studies in Honor of Baruch A. Levine* (edited by Robert Chazan, William W. Hallo, and Lawrence H. Schiffman; Winona Lake, Ind.: Eisenbrauns, 1999) 413–27.

This issue also affects later poetic sections of the book. See the discussions of Christoph Levin, *Die Verheissung des neuen Bundes in ihrem theologiegeschichtlen Zusammenhang ausgelegt*, FRLANT 137, 147–96; and Konrad Schmid, *Buchgestalten des Jeremiasbuches: Untersuchingen zur Redaktions- und Rezeptionsgeschichte von Jer 30–33 im Kontext des Buches*, WMANT 72.

A good deal of the prose material especially in Jeremiah 26–45 has been understood in the context of the early postexilic situation and later. For two approaches, see Hermann Josef Stipp, *Jeremia im Parteienstreit: Studien zur Textentwicklung von Jer 26, 36–43, und 45 als Beitrag zur Geschichte, seines Buch und jüdaischer Pateien im 6. Jahrhundert* (Athenäums Monografien: Theologie, vol. 82: Bonner Biblische Beiträge; Frankfurt: Anton Hain, 1992); and Carolyn J. Sharp, *Prophecy and Ideology in Jeremiah: Struggles for Authority in the Deutero-Jeremianic Prose* (London: T & T Clark, 2003).

18. A good deal of Ezekiel 1–32 has been placed in the sixth century, whether from the time of the prophet or later in the sixth century. Ezekiel 33–39 and 40–48 consist of restoration documents. Ezekiel is particularly marked with a historical arrangement from 593 to 573, which reflects a scribal effort at organizing the book. To explain the composition of Ezekiel, it has become quite common since the commentary of Walther Zimmerli to appeal to the notion of a priestly school or tradition that has received traditions about the prophet and has composed a good deal of the book using these traditions, with later tradition continuing to produce ongoing interpretation through the Persian period. The survey of Brevard S. Childs is helpful on this discussion. See Childs, *Introduction to the Old Testament as Sacred Scripture* (Philadelphia: Fortress, 1979) 355–72. In the meantime, other issues have come to the fore. See Ralph W. Klein, "Ezekiel at the Dawn of the Twenty-First Century," in *The Book of Ezekiel: Theological and Anthropological Approaches*, SBLSymS 9, 1–11. As a result, the issue of the dating of texts in Ezekiel 1–32 has somewhat receded.

19. For the traditional view of Second Isaiah as an exilic author, see Wilson, "Community," 53–70; Peter Machinist, "Mesopotamian Imperialism," 237–64; and Cook, *Conversations*, 6–8, 27–32, 45–48, 86–93, 116–19.

Several critics (for example, R. Kratz, J. van Oorschot, U. Berges, J. Werlitz, A. Labahn) put the beginnings of Second Isaiah in the generation that returned from Babylon in the sixth century and also see Second Isaiah going through several editions down into the fifth century. For a discussion, see Charles Conroy, "Reflections on Some Recent Studies of Second Isaiah, in *Palabra, Prodigio, Poesía: In Memoriam P. Luis Alonso Schökel, S. J.*, AnBib 151, 160. Second Isaiah has been put in the second half of the fifth century by Klaus Baltzer, *Deutero-Isaiah* (Hermeneia; Minneapolis: Fortress, 2001) 30.

Mark F. Rooker has attempted, on linguistic grounds, to put Isaiah 40–66 before the exile. See Rooker, "Dating Isaiah 40–66: What Does the Linguistic Evidence Say?" *WTJ* 58, 303–22. For critique, see Richard M. Wright, "Further Evidence for North Israelite Contributions to Late Biblical Hebrew," *Biblical Hebrew: Studies in Chronology and Typology*, JSOTSup 369, 132 n. 6.

20. See pp. 13, 14, 18, 46–47, 48, 49, 57, 58, and 122 . For a survey of Second Isaiah on this topic, see Clifford, *Creation Accounts*, 163–76.

21. Compare Ralph Klein's survey of these biblical works as responses to the exile. See Klein, *Israel in Exile: A Theological Interpretation,* OBT. Where Klein argues for these works as responses to exile, I would see exile or the sixth century more broadly as the context for precipitating a larger discussion in which these biblical works are responding, either to one another or at least to positions represented by these works.

22. For a sixth century date for Job, see Cross, *Canaanite Myth,* 343–45, esp. 344 n. 1; and J. Gerald Janzen, *Job* (Interpretation; Atlanta: John Knox, 1985) 8–10. See the critical discussions of Marvin H. Pope, *Job,* AB 15, 3rd ed., xxxv-xl; and Johannes C. de Moor, "Ugarit and the Origins of Job," in *Ugarit and the Bible: Proceedings of the International Symposium on Ugarit and the Bible, Manchester, September 1992,* UBL 11, 225–57. Pope notes the lack of any reference to the exile in the book of Job; he himself leaves the question of date open although he also suggests the seventh century as the best guess for the date of the dialogue.

A date in the early sixth century prior to the Exile might still be entertained. In this case, one might view Job as slightly earlier than Second Isaiah, a view that is consistent with the argument of Robert H. Pfeiffer, "The Priority of Job over Isaiah 40–55," *JBL* 46, 202–6. However, the opposite direction in their literary relationship has been argued. See Edward L. Greenstein, "Features of Language in the Poetry of Job," in *Das Buch Hiob und seine Interpretation: Beiträge zum Hiob-Symposium auf dem Monte Verità vom 14.-19. August 2005* (edited by Thomas Krüger, Manfred Oeming, Konrad Schmidt, and Christoph Uehlinger; ATANT 88, 95. For further comments on the literary relationship between Job and Second Isaiah by Greenstein, see his earlier essay, "A Forensic Understanding of the Speech from the Whirlwind," in *Texts, Temples, and Traditions: A Tribute to Menachem Haran* (edited by Michael V. Fox et al.; Winona Lake, Ind.: Eisenbrauns, 1996) 254. C. Leong Seow (personal communication) has argued for a date of 520–450 based on datable information in the text of Job; see his forthcoming commentary. While he finds it impossible to be further precise, he prefers a late sixth-century date. To be sure, a date later in the Persian period remains feasible as well.

Several commentators opt for a later date; see, for example, the 3rd-2nd centuries, as favored by Markus Witte, *Vom Leiden zur Lehre: Der dritte Redegang (Hiob 21–27) und die Redaktionsgeschichte des Hiobbuches,* BZAW 230, 220. For others favoring a Hellenistic date, see J. Lévêque, "La datation du livre de Job," in *Congress Volume Vienna 1980,* VTSup 32, 209 n. 13. The lack of Greek loanwords in Job does not militate in favor of such a late date. Even as a work of the sixth century, Job could of course speak to the setting that Witte proposes in the Hellenistic period. For the linguistic situation of Job, see also Greenstein, "Features of Language," 81–96; and "The Poetic Use of Akkadian in the Book of Job," in *Language Studies XI-XII: Avi Hurvitz Festschrift* (edited by Steven E. Fassberg and Aharon Maman; Jerusalem: The Hebrew University of Jerusalem, 2008) 51–68.

23. For example, in chs. 26 and 38–39, which will be discussed below. For a survey of creation in Job, see Clifford, *Creation Accounts,* 185–97.

24. It has been argued that Job knows Genesis 1–3. See T. N. D. Mettinger, "The God of Job: Avenger, Tyrant, or Victor?" in *The Voice from the Whirlwind: Interpreting the Book of Job* (edited by L. G. Perdue and W. C. Gilpin; Nashville: Abingdon: 1992) 39–49; for reservations, see James W. Watts, "The Unreliable Narrator of Job," in *The Whirlwind: Essays on Job, Hermeneutics and Theology in Memory of Jane Morse,* JSOTSup 336, 177.

25. It has also become quite common to date the so-called "Yahwist" or "J" source to the sixth century as well. See, for example, John Van Seters, *The Life of Moses: The Yahwist as Historian in Exodus-Numbers* (Louisville: Westminster John Knox, 1994); compare Christoph Levin, *Der Jahwist,* FRLANT 157; and his more recent article, "The Yahwist: The Earliest Editor in the Pentateuch," *JBL* 126, 209–30. Viewing J as a great assembler of what has been regarded as other sources, Van Seters places this source in the exilic period. For Levin, the redaction of the Jahwist is designed to address the Jewish Diaspora of the Persian period. A more radical dating would put the Pentateuch in the Hellenistic period; for an example, see Russell E. Gmirkin, *Berossus and Genesis, Manetho and Exodus: Hellenistic Histories and the Date of the Pentateuch* (Library of Hebrew Bible/Old Testament Studies, 433; Copenhagen International Series, 15; New York/London: T & T Clark, 2006). According to Gmirkin (89–139), the author of Genesis 1–11 borrowed from Berossus.

What these discussions rarely distinguish is how various Pentateuchal figures such as Abraham may have been produced earlier and how he then may have been read in a later period. To my mind, an eighth century date fits much of this material.

On the other hand, one might well situate some of the so-called "Yahwist material," such as Genesis 1–11, in the sixth century as another voice in the conversation that I am describing. Some features may suggest this period. For example, references to Ur of the Chaldees in Gen. 11:28, 31, 15:7 (cf. Neh. 9:7) may be anachronisms of the seventh-sixth centuries when Chaldeans became rulers of Babylon dominating southern Mesopotamia. This view has accepted by Moshe Weinfeld, *The Promise of the Land: The Inheritance of the Land of Canaan by the Israelites* (The Taubman Lectures in Jewish Studies 3; Berkeley/Los Angeles/Oxford: University of California Press, 1993) 4 n. 5; compare Kenneth Kitchen, *On the Reliability of the Old Testament* (Grand Rapids, Mich./Cambridge, U.K.: Eerdmans, 2003) 316, who rejects the effort of Cyrus H. Gordon and Gary A. Rendsburg (*The Bible and the Ancient Near East* [fourth edition; New York/London: W. W. Norton, 1997] 113 n. 10) to avoid the apparent anachronism by proposing an identification of the biblical Ur with Urfa in northern Mesopotamia, established as a commercial colony of the famous Ur of Sumer. The redactional situation with Genesis 1–11 is particularly complex. For a recent redaction study, see Michael Witte, *Die biblische Urgeschichte: Redaktions- und theologiegeschichtliche Beobachtungen zu Genesis 1,1–11, 26*, BZAW 265.

There remains the issue as to whether we can properly speak of such a single "Yahwist" source, in view of the wide variation of this material as it appears in the primordial history of Genesis 1–11, the patriarchal cycles of Genesis 12–36, or the Joseph material of Genesis 37–50. Many scholars are no longer inclined to the view of a single source; see the essays in Thomas B. Dozemann and Konrad Schmid, eds., *A Farewell to the Yahwist? The Composition of the Pentateuch in Recent European Interpretation*, SBLSymS 34. Even many of those who maintain the Yahwist as a source acknowledge the problem, in particular with the great variation in the Joseph cycle compared to other so-called "Yahwist" material in Genesis; see Noth, *Pentateuchal Traditions*, 208–13; Cross, *From Epic to Canon*, 36 n. 38.

26. I have already noted above (note 2) the scholars who propose allusions to Jeremiah, Ezekiel and Second-Isaiah in Genesis 1. For Second Isaiah as a response to Jeremiah and Ezekiel, see J. D. W. Watts, *Isaiah 1–33* and *Isaiah 34–66*, WBC 24 & 25, 1.xxxiii; and Sommer, *A Prophet Reads Scripture*. Sommer likewise sees Second Isaiah referring directly to Genesis 1 (see the chart on allusions on 320–21; is it of any consequence that the allusions posited are confined to Isaiah 44–46?). For Jeremiah in relationship to priestly writing in the Pentateuch, see Eckart Otto, "Scribal Scholarship in the Formation of Torah and Prophets: A Postexilic Scribal Debate between Scholarship and Literary Prophecy—The Example of the Book of Jeremiah and Its Relationship to the Pentateuch," in *The Pentateuch as Torah: New Models for Understanding Its Promulgation and Acceptance* (edited by Gary N. Knoppers and Bernard M. Levinson; Winona Lake, Ind.: Eisenbrauns, 2008) 171–84.

While it is not entirely clear that these major biblical works allude directly to one another in their final form, it may be that they respond to one another in various points in their textual development (as Otto's essay would suggest). For this reason, I would prefer to think in terms of a larger dialogue or debate (Otto's term), taking place among these writers or at least the traditions to which they belong. I would see their works as exemplars of different traditions that did interact and dialogue over these matters over the course of the sixth century and later.

27. So Arnold, *Genesis*, 36. The point has been made to me also by Tryggve N. D. Mettinger in a personal communication. See the more explicit expression in Jer. 51:48: "heaven and earth and all that is in them". Compare Ps. 135:6: "All that Yahweh desires he does in the heaven and in the earth, in the seas and in all deeps." Note also Yahweh's title in Gen. 24:3, "the God of the heaven and the God of the earth."

28. On the King James Version (named for its royal patron, James VI), see Adam Nicolson, *God's Secretaries: The Making of the King James Bible* (New York: HarperCollins, 2003). See also the interesting account of David Daniell, *The Bible in English: Its History and Influence* (New Haven/London: Yale University, 2003) 427–50.

29. For an accessible edition, see *Pentateuch with Targum Onkelos, Haptaroth, and Rashi's Commentary: Genesis*, translated into English and annotated by Morris Rosenbaum and Abraham Maurice Silbermann in collaboration with A. Blashki and L. Joseph (New York: Hebrew Publishing Company, 1934) 2. Rashi's discussion involves a rather detailed analysis.

30. For a convenient edition, see *Rabbi Abraham ibn Ezra's Commentary on the Creation*, translated and annotated by Michael Linetsky (Northvale, N.J./Jerusalem: Jason Aronson, 1998) 1. See also Leo Prijs, *Abraham ibn Esra's Kommentar zu Genesis Kapitel 1: Einleitung, Edition, und Superkommentar* (Wiesbaden: Franz Steiner Verlag GMBH, 1973) 1–7.

31. The form of *bere'shit* is what in Hebrew grammar is called a "construct" or in English a "possessive"; in other words, the preposition "of" comes after the translation of the base word, and its object follows. See further in the following note.

32. Technically, the word means "in beginning of." In this sentence structure, the noun, "beginning" followed by "of," connects to a noun or phrase after it. In Hebrew, when you have a noun standing in this "of" relationship (called a "construct" in Hebrew grammar) to a second noun that has a definite article (or some other mark of definiteness), then it makes the first noun definite, too; in these cases, the translation of the first noun should reflect this definiteness by having "the" before the noun, and only when a definite noun or clause follows it can *re'shit* (without a definite article) be translated "the beginning." Rashi compared Proverbs 8:22, where the word "beginning" similarly stands in an "of" relationship to what follows: "the beginning of his way" (*re'shit darko*; contrast *qesot derakayw*, "the ends of his ways," in Job 26:14)

The ancient Greek translator likewise omitted the definite article even though the prepositional phrase was taken as modifying the verb and not as bound to the clause that follows. See John William Wevers, *Genesis* (Septuaginta; Göttingen: Vandenhoeck & Ruprecht, 1974) 75; and *Notes on the Greek Text of Genesis*, SBLSCS 35, 1. For the Latin variants, see Erzabtei Beuron, *Genesis*, VL 2, 3; and Bonifatio Fischer, Iohanne Gribomont, H. F. D. Sparks, and W. Thiele, *Biblical Sacra: Iuxta Vulgatam Versionem* (2nd ed.; two vols.; Stuttgart: Württembergische Bibelanstalt, 1975) 1.4. Of course, in Greek, it is not necessary for the noun to have the definite article per se in order to be considered definite; the important point here is that the lack of the definite article in the Greek matches the lack of definite article as found in the Hebrew text.

33. See the preceding note.

34. This sense of the passage is echoed in the book of Ben Sira (16:26): "as God created his works from the beginning." Ben Sira 16:26 ms. A: *kbr' 'l m'syw mr'sh*. The Greek text, *en krisei kuriou ta erga autou ap' archēs,* has been rendered: "When the Lord created the first of his works"; see Patrick W. Skehan and Alexander A. Di Lella, O. F. M., *The Wisdom of Ben Sira: A New Translation with Notes*, AB 39, 276 and notes on 279–81, noting the comparison with Gen. 1:1. See also Sheppard, *Wisdom*, 74, 101. For Ben Sira on creation more broadly, see Friedrich V. Reiterer, *"Alle Weisheit stammt vom Herrn. . .": Gesammelte Studien zu Ben Sira* BZAW 1:375, 185–227.

35. See also the fine comment to this effect by Ronald Hendel in his notes to the NRSV in *HCSB* (Intro, n. 3), p. 5.

36. For considerations of the evidence and issues, see Manfred Weippert, "Schöpfung am Anfang oder Anfang der Schöpfung? Noch einmal zu Syntax und Semantik von Gen 1,1–3," *TZ* 60, 5–22; and Michaela Bauks, *Die Welt am Anfang: zum Verhältnis von Vorwelt und Weltenstehung in Gen 1 und in der altorientalischen Literatur,* WMANT 74, esp. 65–92. Bauks herself would allow for the possibility of the traditional translation for the initial word, along the lines of "In the beginning, as/when God created". Apart from the lack of definite article before "beginning," there is little in the Hebrew serving properly as a conjunction for "as/when." See also Michaela Bauks and Gerlinde Baumann, "Im Anfang war. . .? Gen 1,1ff und Prov 8,22–31 im Vergleich," *BN* 71, 26. Wellhausen (*Prolegomena*, 387 n. 1) commented on this approach to translating Gen. 1:1–2: "this translation is desperate." For a response to Bauks, see Oswald Loretz, "Gen 1,2 als Fragment aus einem amurritisch-kanaanäischen Schöpfungsmythos in neuer ägyptozentrischer Deutung," *UF* 33, 387–401.

37. A noun standing in an "of" relationship to a verbal clause that follows, as we have in Gen. 1:1, has been noted by scholars going back at least to Rashi, who have often compared Hosea 1:2:

"In the beginning of (when) the Lord spoke by means of Hosea, the Lord said to Hosea." See, for example, Cyrus H. Gordon, "'This Time' (Genesis 2:23)," in *"Sha'arei Talmon": Studies in the Bible, Qumran, and the Ancient Near East Presented to Shemaryahu Talmon* (edited by Michael Fishbane and Emanuel Tov with the assistance of Weston W. Fields; Winona Lake, Ind.: Eisenbrauns, 1992) 47–48. Note that the word *tehillat* in Hosea 1:2 is in the same general semantic range as *bere'shit* in Gen. 1:1. NRSV shows this understanding of Hosea 1:2 in its translation: "When the Lord first spoke through Hosea, the Lord said to Hosea." Compare the combination of *bari'shonim bithillat* in 2 Samuel 21:9 (mentioned in the discussion of Francis I. Andersen and David Noel Freedman, *Hosea*, AB 24, 153).

A. B. Davidson provides 21 examples of this construction with a following verb in the Hebrew Bible (not including cases with *'asher*): Exod. 4:13, 6:28, Lev. 14:46, Num. 3:1, Deut. 32:35, 1 Sam. 25:15, Isa. 29:1, Jer. 36:2, Hos. 1:2, Pss. 4:8, 18:1, 56:4, 10, 65:5, 81:6, 90:15, 104:8, 138:3, Prov. 8:32; Job 6:17; 2 Chr. 29:27; see also Pss. 59:17 and 102:3, which contain the same nominal clause following a temporal noun in construct. See Davidson, *Introductory Hebrew Grammar: Hebrew Syntax* (3rd ed.; Edinburgh: T & T Clark, 1989) 34–35, paragraph 25; see also *GKC* paragraph 130; cited in Andersen & Freedman, *Hosea*, 153. The cases with *'asher* following the noun in construct and preceding the finite verb (e.g., Gen. 39:20, 40:3; Lev. 13:46, Num. 9:18, 1 Kings 21:19; Jer. 22:12, Hos. 2:1) suggest that the cases without *'asher* (compare especially Ps. 104:8) are asyndetic relative clauses (cf. also Pss. 137:8, 9, 146:5, cited by Davidson). See the view of Holmstedt discussed below.

For Gen. 1:1, one might consider the possibility that the MT pointing may reflect the preservation of a double tradition, one that knows verse 1 both as a subordinate clause and as a self-standing sentence (my thanks to Bruce Zuckerman for suggesting this possibility). For a possible double-tradition of this grammatical sort, see the Qere/Ketib of Jeremiah 7:22.

38. This is the analysis of Robert D. Holmstedt, "The Restrictive Syntax of Genesis i 1," *VT* 58, 56–67. For this structure, Holmstedt compares Lev. 25:48, 1 Sam. 25:15, Isa. 29:1, Jer. 48:36, and Hos. 1:2 (as noted above). Two examples involve temporal constructions, as in Gen. 1:1: 1 Sam. 25:15, "all the days of (when) we went about"; and Hosea 1:2, "in the beginning of (when) God spoke." These two cases speak well for this analysis.

39. For example, Brown, *Seven Pillars*.

40. To name only a handful, see William Foxwell Albright, "Contributions to Biblical Archaeology and Philology," *JBL* 43 (1924) 365; Jack M. Sasson, "Time. . . to Begin," in *Sha'arei Talmon*, 187–88; Hans Rechenmacher, "Gott und das Chaos: Ein Beitrag zum Verständnis von Gen 1,1–3," *ZAW* 114, 1–20; Weippert, "Schöpfung am Anfang," 5–22. Arnold (*Genesis*, 35) is open to either v. 2 or v. 3 as the main clause on which v. 1 is dependent.

41. In the sense "to come to pass." *BDB* (p. 224) claims this meaning for the occurrences in Gen. 1:7, 9, 11, 15, 24, 30, but does not mention 1:3. *BDB* notes that the meaning "to come to pass" is used often "of fulfillment of prediction, command, expectation, etc." The verb here might be rendered, "to happen," a possibility suggested to me by Gordon Hamilton. This meaning, as Hamilton has reminded me, is given in *BDB* (p. 224). I have not used the translation, "to come to pass," or "to happen," in my translation, in order to be consistent with the translation of the same root in verse 2.

The common translation for °*yehi 'or* in verse 3, "let there be light," suffers from the fact that the word "there" is not in the Hebrew, but is a convention of English translations. It is helpful to mention this information so that readers do not get the impression that Gen. 1:3 is providing some sort of spatial information, which might be inferred from this conventional translation. It might be more accurate to translate "let it be light," or "may light be," or "let light be," the last of which I have adopted. Isaac Rabinowitz proposed: "let light come to be." See Rabinowitz, *A Witness Forever: Ancient Israel's Perception of Literature and the Resultant Hebrew Bible* (Bethesda, Md.: CDL Press, 1993) 51. The meaning of the verb °*hyh*, in its meaning, "to be," may denote creation as such, a picture that is debated below.

42. Below I offer a detailed discussion of this translation. For now, I would note the possibility that verse 3 might be understood: "'let light be (manifest),' and light was (manifest)."

43. Sasson, "Time. . . to Begin," 183–194, here 187–88.

44. For examples, see Clifford, *Creation Accounts*, 29–30, 49–50, 59, 61.

45. In ch. 4, I suggest the possibility that Gen. 2:4b (*beyom* plus infinitive construct) may have been the model for 1:1. For now, see Carr, *Reading the Fractures*, 65–66 and esp. n. 34. Close in syntax to Gen. 2:4b with *beyom* plus an infinitival form is Jeremiah 7:22. Ron Hendel (personal communication) notes that the construction as found in Gen. 1:1 becomes obsolete in Late Biblical Hebrew. Compare the later construction of *beyom she-* plus finite verb (for example, in Eccles. 12:3)

The general structure of Gen. 1:1–3 and 2:4b-7 is not limited to biblical texts. For example, lines 1–2 of the Siloam tunnel inscription seem to open with a temporal reference (*[ym] hnqbh*, following *wbym hnqbh* in lines 3–4), followed by conditions prevailing at the time (*b'wd. . . lhnq[b]*, followed by a *waw*-consecutive verbal clause (*[wn/yshm]' ql...*); to be sure, the reconstructions are open to dispute (see KAI 189 for the reconstruction of the opening, *[z't] hnqbh*). A somewhat similar structure also follows in the same inscription from line 3 (*wbym...*) to line 5 (*. . . bm'tym*). See K. Lawson Younger, "The Siloam Tunnel Inscription: an Integrated Reading," *UF* 26 (1994) 543–56. For another treatment, see F. W. Dobbs-Allsopp, J. J. M. Roberts, C. L. Seow, and R. E. Whitaker, *Hebrew Inscriptions: Texts from the Biblical Period of the Monarchy with Concordance* (New Haven/London: Yale University, 2005) 500–506. For further evidence, see Shmuel Aḥituv, *Echoes from the Past: Hebrew and Cognate Inscriptions from the Biblical Period* (translated by Anson F. Rainey; Jerusalem: Carta, 2008) 336–38.

46. Philo, *Creation*, 27. For the translation, see David Runia, *Philo of Alexandria on the Creation of the Cosmos according to Moses* (Philo of Alexandria Commentary Series, volume 1; Leiden/Boston/Köln: Brill, 2001) 52. For a handy translation with the Greek text, see F. H. Colson and G. H. Whitaker, *Philo: Volume I* (Loeb Classical Library series, volume 226; Cambridge, Mass./London: Harvard University, 1929) 23.

47. Wellhausen, *Prolegomena*, 387.

48. Wilfred G. Lambert, "Mesopotamian Creation Stories," in *Imagining Creation* (edited by Markham J. Geller and Mineke Schipper; Institute of Jewish Studies, Studies in Judaica, volume 5; Leiden: Brill, 2007) 15–16. For reflections in this vein, see also the insightful remarks by Clifford, *Creation Accounts*, 7–10.

49. Contrast *qesot derakayw*, "the ends of his ways," in Job 26:14.

50. Bauks & Baumann, "Im Anfang war. . .?" 24–52.

51. For these latter expressions, compare Micah 5:2: "whose origin is from of old, from ancient days."

52. Compare NJPS: "the time anything existed." For *ro'sh* for the beginning of a period of time, see also Lamentations 2:19: "at the beginning of the (night) watches."

53. The use of this word is echoed in later Second Temple literature. See the later echoes, for example, in Ben Sira 16:26: "When the Lord created his works from the beginning" (NRSV); and 24:3: "before the ages, in the beginning" (NRSV); compare Ben Sira 15:14: "It was he who created humankind in the beginning" (NRSV). I wonder whether the word has a further connotation that what is made at the beginning by God also represents what is the "sum" worth understanding in creation; for this use of *ro'sh*, see Psalm 119:160: "the *ro'sh* of your words is truth." (NJPS translates "essence," while NRSV has "sum;" perhaps compare Psalm 139:17). This, however, is speculative on my part.

54. The use of the word as marking the beginning of a time-period (and not necessarily the beginning of time as such) may be gathered also from the Ugaritic noun *r'išyt*, which has been compared with °*re'shit* in Gen. 1:1. The Ugaritic word occurs in an expression, *mtk mlkm r'išyt*, in KTU 1.119.25, which has been translated in different ways: "a royal (?) libation offering of the best [quality]/[that is] first." Perhaps under the influence of Gen. 1:1 and Proverbs 8:22, the word in this context is translated as "primordial" in *DUL* 726. Other translations of *mtk mlkm r'išyt* in KTU 1.119.25 are possible, arguably more likely. The word *r'išyt* here has been understood as "best" or "superlative"; see Pardee, *Ritual and Cult* (Intro., n. 9), 53. It has been compared with the month name "first of the wine" (*r'iš yn*) in 1.41.1, 4.182.32 and 4.387.21 (for these, see *DUL* 725).

Compare *bym pr'* in an administrative context (KTU 4.279.1), which might be rendered "on the first day" or "on the day of the first (fruit)"; see *DUL* 679. (It is perhaps to be viewed like the *qorban re'shit*, "first" or "best offering," in Leviticus 2:12; cf. *re'shit*, "best," in Deuteronomy 33:21.) Both KTU 1.41 and 1.119.25 concern "the first" as well as wine in the context of a royal setting at the start of the year. So *mtk mlkm r'išyt* might be understood in the sense of "royal (?) libation of the first (of the year in the fall)." If correct, the word would not mean "primordial," and so any connection with Gen. 1:1 would not be direct. Instead, the comparison at best would only be broader in nature: both Ugaritic *r'išyt* and °*re'shit* in Gen. 1:1 arguably refer to the beginning of a time-period.

55. Isaiah 41:4, 44:6, and 48:12. Compare the remarkable statement in Isaiah 43:10: "Before me no god was formed, and after me there shall not be (any)."

56. For this issue as it pertains to Gen. 1:14, see p. 96.

57. For *'ehad* for "(day) one" and *yom 'ehad* for "day one," see note 259 below.

58. That is, the qal or G-stem, *BDB* 135; cf. piel or D-stem used for people, in the meaning, "to cut." See the following note.

59. For example, Num. 16:30, Ps. 51:12; Isa. 40:26; 43:1, 7, 15; 45:7, 8, 18; 54:16 [2 times]; and Ps. 148:5. For a fuller listing, see *DCH II,* 258. See also the noun *beri'ah* discussed on p. 263; it occurs mostly in Second Temple literature, but also in Num 16:30. Note further the discussion of W. Randall Garr, "God's Creation ברא in the Priestly Source," *HTR* 97, 83–90.

For this root, Aramaic dialects and Arabic show the meaning, "to create" (see *HALOT* 153). The root's meaning in other Semitic languages may suggest another nuance:

Sabaean °*br'*, "to build," *mbr'*, "building" or "stonework," in A. F. L. Beeston, M. A. Ghul, W. W. Müler, and J. Ryckmans, *Sabaic Dictionary (English-French-Arabic)/Dictionnaire Sabéen (anglais-français-arabe)* [Louvain-la-Neuve: Éditions Peeters; Beyrouth: Librairie du Liban, 1982] 30; and Joan Copeland Biella, *Dictionary of Old South Arabic: Sabaean Dialect*, HSS 25, 54); Qatabanian °*br'*, "to build, construct," *br'n*, "construction," in Stephen D. Ricks, *Lexicon of Inscriptional Qatabanian* (Studia Pohl, vol. 14; Rome: Pontificio Istituto Biblico, 1989) 32–33); Soqotri *bére*, "mettre un monde, enfanter," in Wolf Leslau, *Lexique Soqotri (subarabique moderne)* (Paris: Librairie C. Klincksieck, 1938) 95; *HALOT* 153; Punic *br'*, perhaps "engraver??" or "diviner?"; and "to be created (said of the world)" (N-stem), in *DNWSI* 1.196. Hebrew (post-biblical), "to hollow out, perforate" (G-stem); and "to bore, perforate" (C-stem), in Marcus Jastrow, *A Dictionary of the Targumim, The Talmud Babli and Yerushalmi, and the Midrashic Literature* (New York: The Judaica Press, 1971) 192.

For these cognates, see *HALOT* 153; and Karl-Heinz Bernhardt, "*bārā',*" in *TDOT II,* 245. Based on these cognates, Bernhardt suggests the meaning, "to build." One might be inclined to posit "building" or some other sort of craftsmanship as the older meaning of the root. Bernhardt posits as "the original meaning 'to separate, divide.'" This is held also by Claus Westermann, *Genesis 1–11: A Commentary* (translated by J. J. Scullion; Minneapolis: Augsburg, 1984) 34–35. Both Bernhardt and Westermann base their view on E. Dantinne, "Création et Séparation," *Le Muséon* 74 (1961) 441–51.

The hypothetical semantic development of the root from "to separate, divide" to "create" is an old view going back at least to Gesenius' 1883 dictionary. It might be supported by appeal to °*br'*, "cut down, clear," applied to "forest" (*hayya'ar*) in Joshua 17:15, 18 and to "timber" (*ha'es*) in Haggai 1:8 (*HALOT* 154). For further consideration, see Ellen van Wolde, "Why Does the Verb *Bara'* in Genesis 1 Not Mean 'to Create'," paper presented at the SBL on November 22, 2008. This will appear in her book, *Reframing Biblical Studies: When Language and Text Meet Culture, Cognition, and Context* (Winona Lake, Ind.: Eisenbrauns, in preparation). For this information about her book, I am grateful to Professor van Wolde.

60. The verbs also appear in the creation allusion in Isaiah 45:6–7. See Werner H. Schmidt, *Die Schöpfungsgeschichte der Priestschrift: Zur Überlieferungsgeschichte der Priesterschrift* (3rd ed.); WMANT 17, 164–67.

61. For God as creator with this traditional verb of creation outside of Genesis 1, see Gen. 3:1; Pss. 95:5; 100:3; 119:73; Prov. 8:26; Job 9:9; 31:15; Neh. 9:6; see also the description of God as "his maker" in Isa. 17:7, Prov. 14:31; 17:15. This usage of the verb for the Israelite deity is reflected in Hebrew personal names: Asael (brother of Joab and Abishai, in 2 Sam. 3:27, 30; 2 Samuel 18 (nine

times); 23:24; also a Levitical name in 2 Chr. 17:8; 31:13; cf. Ezra 10:15); Asayah (servant of Josiah in 2 Kings 22:12, 14; a Simeonite in 1 Chr. 4:36; and a Levitical name in 1 Chr. 6:15, 9:5, and 15:6, 11); and Yaasiel (a hero of David according to 1 Chr. 11:47; and a leader in the tribe of Benjamin in 1 Chr. 27:21). See also the discussion of a proper name in the Kuntillet ʿAjrud inscriptions in Dobbs-Allsopp, et al., *Hebrew Inscriptions*, 291 and 615; cf. 339 (Lachish 22:7) and 551 and 552 (two unprovenienced inscriptions). By contrast, the traditional verb for divine creation, °*qnh*, "to acquire, establish" is not used in this account. For this verb in creation, see Gen. 14:19, 22 (cf. Deut. 32:6), and in the name of Elkunirsha (*ANET* 519). For this usage, see Patrick D. Miller, "El, Creator of Earth," *BASOR* 239, 43–46; and C. Leong Seow, *Myth, Drama, and the Politics of David's Dance*, HSM 44, 19–22. Seow notes in this connection the name of Elqanah, the name of the father of Samuel, in 1 Samuel 1–2; see further *BDB* 46.

62. Edward L. Greenstein translates *ʾelohim* here as "the Powers." See Greenstein, "Presenting Genesis 1: Constructively and Deconstructively," *Proof* 21/2, 1–22. This translation reflects the meaning thought to lie behind the middle weak root posited for the base of *ʾelohim*; evidence against this view has been noted by Marvin H. Pope, *El in the Ugaritic Texts*, VTSup 2, 16–19; and Pardee, *Les textes rituels* (Intro., n. 9), 1.36 n. 109. Pardee notes that the cognate in Akkadian *ilu* has a short vowel, which theoretically should not be expected of a middle weak root; yet this is what is seen with some Biblical Hebrew forms, such as *ger* from middle weak °*gwr* and *met* from middle weak °*mwt*. On this comparison, however, caution is in order, as the form of *ʾel* may not be middle weak and it has been categorized among non-verbal forms such as *ben*, "son," and *shem*, "name"; so Joüon, 1.240, para. 88Bb. Pardee also notes the reduction of the middle vowel in proper names such as ʾEliab, which would not be expected as a middle-weak root.

In any case, the verbs predicated of *ʾelohim* are singular, as commonly noted in the grammars (e.g., Christo H. J. van der Merwe, Jackie A. Naudé and Jan H. Kroeze, *A Biblical Hebrew Reference Grammar* [Biblical Languages: Hebrew 3; Sheffield: Sheffield Academic Press, 1999] 182 and 250). For the form and its significance, see the detailed discussion of Joel S. Burnett, *A Reassessment of Biblical Elohim*, SBLDS 183, 79–152. The subject *ʾelohim* would appear to be a collective. Frank Moore Cross notes cases of plural verbs or adjectives with *ʾelohim* in Gen. 20:13, 31:53 and 2 Sam. 7:23 (with plural verbs); and Deut. 5:23 and Josh. 24:19 (with plural adjectives). He compares the following expression with the plural verb: *kh ʾmrw ʾlhn lgr*, "Thus spoke the godhead to Gera'"; see Cross, *Leaves from Epigrapher's Notebook: Collected Papers in Hebrew and West Semitic Palaeography and Epigraphy*, HSS 51, 63; and *From Epic to Canon*, 50 n. 73. Compare the translation, "Thus said (the) gods to Gera'," as suggested by Pierre Bordreuil and Dennis Pardee, "Le papyrus du marzeaḥ," *Sem* 38, 49–68 + pls. 7–10, esp. 52–54 (in particular 54 n. 17) for discussion of the line. It remains a question as to whether this text should be admitted as evidence, since the issue of the text's authenticity is taken up by both Bordreuil and Pardee as well as Cross. The issue is discussed by Christopher Rollston, "Northwest Semitic Cursive Scripts of Iron II," in *An Eye for Form: Essays in Honor of Frank Moore Cross* (edited by Wally Aufrecht and Jo Ann Hackett; Winona Lake, Ind.: Eisenbrauns, forthcoming). Rollston notes that Cross dated the papyrus to the mid- or late-seventh century B.C.E., and he provided a brief paleographic discussion. However, Rollston is not convinced that this inscription is ancient. See also Aḥituv, *Echoes from the Past*, 428–29.

63. For the biblical material, see the fine survey of Tsumura, *Creation and Destruction* (ch. 1, n. 13), 58–76. The order heavens-earth is also attested in other creation allusions in the biblical corpus. Jer. 10:12 = 51:15 contains a creation allusion, with earth preceding heaven. Similarly, while the divine splendor covers heaven and earth in Hab. 3:3, in Ps. 148:13 it is over earth and heaven.

Note also the contrast between the traditional divine title, "maker of heaven and earth," for example in Gen. 14:19, 22, and in Pss. 115:15; 121:2; 124:8; 134:3; and 146:6, as opposed to "maker of earth," evidently underlying the divine name of Elkunirsha (*ANET* 519); for these titles, Patrick D. Miller, "El, Creator of Earth," 43–46; W. Herrmann, "Wann wurde Jahwe zum Schöpfer der Welt?" *UF* 23, 165–80, esp. 167, 173–174; Keel & Uehlinger, *Gods* (ch. 1, n. 29) 311, 345; and Wolfgang Röllig, "El-Creator-of-the-Earth," *DDD*, 280–81; see also the older work by M. Fantar, *Le dieu de la mer chez les pheniciens et les puniques* (Studi semitici 48; Rome: Consiglio nazionale delle recherche, 1977) 97–103.

The same contrast is present in Ugaritic poetry: heaven precedes earth in KTU 1.3 II 39 = 1.3 IV 43, presented in Smith, "The Baal Cycle" (ch. 1, n. 19), 109, 114. In contrast, the Ugaritic story of Kirta (KTU 1.16 III 2) uses "earth and heaven" (for the text and translation of this passage, see Greenstein, "Kirta," (ch. 1, n. 21), 35–36), and in 1.23.62 and its parallel image in 1.5 II 2 earth precedes heavens (Smith, "The Baal Cycle," 143, and Lewis, "Birth" [ch. 1, n. 20], 213).

It is to be noted further that the divine name, "Heaven-and-Earth," appears in *PRU* IV 137 (RS 18.06 + 17.365), line 6', "Earth-and-Heaven" is also attested, appearing in Ugaritic god-lists, KTU 1.47.12 = 1.118.11, and in the ritual text, 1.148.5, 24 (cf. the Akkadian form of the same list in 20.024.11), and in KTU 1.148.24 = RS 92.2004.2 (see also the reconstruction in 1.74.2–3); for these texts, see the convenient presentation in Pardee, *Ritual and Cult*, 11–19. In view of these god-lists as well as the divine name Elkunirsha, it would seem that the order, "earth and heaven," might have been particularly at home in the Levant. In view of the Ugaritic references, Pardee (*Ritual and Cult*, 23 n. 2) sees the order in these texts as a reflection of Ugaritic "theology." It is to be noted that Mesopotamian creation traditions contain both orders, as emphasized by Wilfred Lambert, "Old Testament Mythology in its ancient Near Eastern Context," in *Congress Volume: Jerusalem 1986*, VTSup 40, 138.

64. The reversal of creation of earth and heaven in Jer. 4:23 as a sign of destruction also presupposes the traditional order of heaven and earth.

65. For some examples, see Foster, *Muses*, 494–95.

66. *PRU* IV 137 (RS 18.06 + 17.365), line 6'.

67. KTU 1.47.12 = 1.118.11, and in the ritual text, 1.148.5, 24; cf. the Akkadian form of the same list in 20.024.11.

68. KTU 1.148.24 = RS 92.2004.2; see also the reconstruction in 1.74.2–3. For the Ugaritic texts, see the convenient presentation in Pardee, *Ritual and Cult*, 11–19.

69. See Pardee, *Ritual and Cult*, 186–87 n. 19 for the notion that these pairings express "cosmological origins." For creation involving cosmic pairs, see further Cross, *From Epic to Canon*, 73–83.

70. The word is often rendered "waters," but NJPS renders it in the singular (perhaps as a collective), "water." Technically, the dual form is a "pseudo-form," the result of the mimation of the plural form added to the third weak base of the noun. For the noun as a plural, see Joüon 1.272, para. 90f; 274, para. 91f; 319, para. 98e, #11; and 2.500, para. 136b; and *IBHS* 118, para. 7.3d; see also Joshua Fox, *Semitic Noun Patterns*, HSS 52, 73. In Hebrew, *mayim* is treated as a plural, serving as the subject of a plural verb (e.g., Exod. 15:8; Num. 20:11; Deut. 2:6) and governing plural adjectives (e.g., Exod. 15:10; Num. 20:11, 24:7); for a parade example, see Jer. 18:14. The form in Gen. 1:2 may be regarded as a collective, which works well with the singular forms for the cosmic realities in this verse. Verse 6 also suggests a collection of water above and a collection of water below.

71. In an earlier version of this work, this word was instead spelled "university," perhaps an interpretation worthy of further consideration.

72. This idea was commonly accepted among commentators into the twentieth century. Note the emphasis given to this idea by Elias Bickerman in a letter that he wrote to Moshe Greenberg on July 5, 1980, cited by Greenberg, *Studies in the Bible and Jewish Thought* (JPS Scholar of Distinction Series; Philadelphia/Jerusalem: Jewish Publication Society, 1995) 242–43 n. 10. Bickerman listed *creatio ex nihilo* as one of the singular hallmarks of "the Mosaic faith." Most commentators now do not accept this view, given the interpretation of Gen. 1:1–2 as noted above. For example, see the comments of Levenson, *Creation*, 47, 49, and 121; Bauks, *Die Welt am Anfang*, 3–4, 23–31, and 63; see also her article, "Big Bang or creation *ex nihilo*?" *ETR* 71 (1996/4), 481–93. For a discussion of Bauks' view, see Loretz, "Gen 1,2 als Fragment," 399–401.

73. For a recent study with bibliography, see Norbert Clemens Baumgart, "'JHWH. . . erschafft Unheil': Jes 45,7 in seinem unmittelbaren Kontext," *BZ* 49, 202–36; and Tina Nilsen, "The Creation of Darkness and Evil (Isa. 45:6c-7)," *RB* 115, 5–25. As Baumgart shows, the notion of God as creator of all these realities here relates to the presentation of the deity in Isa. 44:24 as the one who makes all (see also Jer. 51:19). For God as the creator of destructive power in Second Isaiah, see Isa. 54:16: "I have also created the ravager to destroy" (NRSV).

74. For translation, see Orval S. Wintermute, "Jubilees," *OTP*, 1.55.

75. Wintermute, "Jubilees," 1.55 n. i. See James C. VanderKam, "Genesis 1 in Jubilees 2," *Dead Sea Discoveries* 1 (1994) 300–321, reprinted in VanderKam, *From Revelation to Canon: Studies in the Hebrew Bible and Second Temple Literature* (Supplements to the Journal for the Study of Judaism, vol. 62; Leiden/Boston/Köln: Brill, 2000) 500–521; and J. T. A. G. M. van Ruiten, *Primaeval History Interpreted: The Rewriting of Genesis 1–11 in the Book of Jubilees* (Supplements to the Journal for the Study of Judaism, vol. 66; Leiden: Boston: Brill, 2000) 23–26. As these studies indicate, Jubilees involves a number of alterations to Genesis 1. Van Ruiten compares the interpretation in Jubilees with the Qumran "Hymn to the Creator" (see below), which he notes includes important differences as well. The latter retains the language of separation in Genesis 1, and the verb to "prepare" (for creation) in the two texts does not include light in the Hymn.

76. See Loretz, "Gen 1,2 als Fragment," 398, 400 n. 58, who also notes Rom. 4:17 and Heb. 11:3 (also brought to my attention by Tryggve Mettinger). See also 2 Enoch 24:2 in Francis I. Andersen, "2 Enoch" (ch. 1, n. 43), 1.142–43, as noted by Alexander Altman, "A Note on the Rabbinic Doctrine of Creation," in his essays, *Studies in Religious Philosophy and Mysticism* (Ithaca, N.Y.: Cornell University Press, 1969) 129 (reference courtesy of Elliot Wolfson).

77. For this passage and *creatio ex nihilo* in rabbinic sources, see Altman, "A Note," 128–39. This passage, as well as Rom. 4:17 and Heb. 11:3, also reflects the idea of *creatio ex nihilo*. For a distinction between these texts and the idea of *creatio ex nihilo* in sources of the second century CE and later, see Gerhard May, *Creatio Ex Nihilo: The Doctrine of 'Creation out of Nothing' in Early Christian Thought* (translated by A. S. Worrall; Edinburgh: T & T Clark, 1994) especially 6–7, 27–28. May sees the classic Christian expressions of *creatio ex nihilo* in part as a response to Gnosticism. His view that *creatio ex nihilo* is later than the biblical passages mentioned depends on his distinction between the highly philosophical view of creation in later sources espousing *creatio ex nihilo* and the less philosophical expressions about creation in these biblical passages. In any case, *creatio ex nihilo* is not the view of Genesis 1.

78. The creation account of Job 26:7 might also seem to convey the idea of creation from nothing. This verse shows a poetic matching of words, with "emptiness" or "void" (*tohu*) in the first line of the verse corresponding to "without anything" (*beli-mah*, literally, "without what") in the second line. Scholars recognize that poetic lines standing in what is called "poetic parallelism" are designed to match one another, in a number of ways. See the fine book by Adele Berlin, *The Dynamics of Biblical Parallelism* (Bloomington/Indianapolis: Indiana University Press, 1985; Midland Book Edition, 1992). So in Job 26:7, *beli-mah* expresses something of the character of *tohu*; it is "without anything." So perhaps verse 2, with its idea of a void, might seem to be a statement of nothingness.

79. Richard J. Clifford, "Cosmogonies in the Ugaritic Texts and in the Bible," *Or* 53, 183–201.

80. So Arnold, *Genesis*, 29.

81. Echoing the term "Vorwelt," used by Bauks & Baumann, "Im Anfang war. . .?", 25.

82. Reference courtesy of Tryggve Mettinger. Some later writers would distinguish between the immaterial world preceded by the material world in creation, for example Philo of Alexandria discussed later in this chapter, and also Ben Sira according to Reiterer, *"Alle Weisheit stammt von Herrn. . .",* 185–227. See the later sources discussed by Altmann, *Studies in Religious Philosophy and Mysticism,* 128–39. One may doubt whether the biblical author distinguished in this manner between the waters in Gen. 1:2 and their attestation later in the Genesis 1 account.

83. For general Mesopotamian and Egyptian parallels, see Keel, *Symbolism* (ch. 1, n. 6), 30–31 and 36. Keel emphasizes the two-part nature of the world as consisting of heaven and earth. Keel also characterizes earth in Gen. 1:12 and 24 as a "mother earth figure." See Keel, *Goddesses and Trees* (ch. 1, n. 6), 52. See also Meier Malul, "Woman-Earth" (ch. 1, n. 6), 339–63.

84. I owe this formulation essentially to Richard Clifford, and it is used here with his permission. See his longer discussion of this matter in his essay, "Cosmogonies," 183–201; as well as his book, *Creation Accounts,* 7–9.

85. This point has been made eloquently by Clifford, "Cosmogonies," 183–201. Note the later reflection on the transformation in the process of creation in Wisdom of Solomon 19:19 with respect to the nature of animals on days five and six: "For land animals were transformed into water creatures, and creatures that swim moved to the land."

86. For the parallelism in this verse, see John Kselman, "The Recovery of Poetic Fragments in the Pentateuchal Priestly Source," *JBL* 97 (1978) 163, followed by Cross, *Canaanite Myth*, 167 n. 87 and 301; Nicolas Wyatt, "The Darkness of Genesis I 2," *VT* 43/4, 545, 553–54; Loretz, "Gen 1,2 als Fragment," 388–96 (with bibliography); and David Tsumura, "Vertical Grammar: The Grammar of Parallelism in Biblical Hebrew," in *Hamlet on a Hill: Semitic and Greek Studies Presented to Professor T. Muraoka on the Occasion of his Sixty-Fifth Birthday*, OLA 18, 496. For an interesting consideration of poetry in a prose context in the Mesopotamian context, see Piotr Michalowski, "Ancient Poetics," in *Mesopotamian Poetic Language: Sumerian and Akkadian* (edited by M. E. Vogelzang and H. L. J. Vanstiphout; Cuneiform Monographs, vol. 6; Proceedings of the Groningen Group for the Study of Mesopotamian Literature, vol. 2; Groningen: Styx, 1996) 148–49.

Other scholars posit a poetic substratum to Genesis 1 as a whole. Albright thought that Genesis 1 had a prior, poetic form (*Yahweh and the Gods*, 92). Cross (*Canaanite Myth*, 301, citing Kselman noted above) suggests that Genesis 1 was "based upon a poetic document probably of catechetical origin." For this approach, see also Oswald Loretz, "Wortbericht-Vorlage und Tatbericht-Interpretation im Schöpfungsbericht GN 1,1—2,4A," *UF* 7, 279–87. The most extensive exploration of poetic parallelism for this chapter is by Frank Polak, "Poetic Style and Parallelism in the Creation Account (Gen. 1:1—2:3)," in *Creation in Jewish and Christian Tradition*, JSOTSup 319, 2–31.

According to John Day, the poetic antecedent could have been Psalm 104. He deduces this from the similarity of the imagery of the *ruah* in Gen. 1:2 and God riding on the wings of the wind in Psalm 104:3, as well as the shared motifs of Leviathan and the Tanninim. See Day, *God's Conflict* (ch. 1, n. 71), 51–52, 55; Day, "Pre-exilic Psalms" (ch. 1, n. 94), 238–39. See p. 209–10 nn. 94 and 95 and p. 214 n.2. While there may be some poetic pieces in Genesis 1 (such as verses 2 and 27), its overall rhythm might not necessarily be attributed to a poetic base-text, but to the ritual sensibility of the priestly tradition. See p. 127.

87. Some interpret the verb as pluperfect ("the earth had been"). For example, see the great medieval Jewish mystical commentary, known as the Zohar (p. 16a, according to the Mantuan text), as translated by Daniel C. Matt: "was, precisely: previously"). See Matt, *Zohar* (ch. 1, n. 43), 118. For another convenient translation, see *The Zohar* (Sperling & Simon) (ch. 1, n. 43), 66. This view in the Zohar echoes *Gen. Rab.* 1:15 ("the earth was, it already was," *wh'rs hyth kbr hyth*), as pointed out to me by Elliot Wolfson. While it is true that a suffix verb formed following another suffix verb may be pluperfect, it need not be. Most translations render it in the simple past to describe the conditions obtaining at the time in the past when God began to create.

88. Translations often prefer "wind" (NRSV, NJPS). I discuss *ruah* below.

89. The alliteration of "void and vacuum" is to match the alliteration of *tohu wabohu* that it translates. For further discussion of my translation, see below. I recognize that the alliteration of the original does not otherwise work the way that my English translation does; it instead shows its own patterns of alliteration. For example, the alliteration in the third line involves *ruah* and the participle *merahepet*. I have considered capturing this alliteration with a translation, "a *wind* of God was *winding* over the face of the waters." However, the verb used in this translation departs from the sense of the original, which is "moving/gliding" (see the discussion of the verb below). By the way, the second line shows a notable inversion of the order of the vowels, underlined here, between *hoshek* and *tehom*, but this is difficult to capture in English; "*darkness. . . deep*" comes fairly close.

90. I will return to the use of "the earth" in this context in ch. 4. See below pp. 133–34.

91. See Clifford, *Creation Accounts*, 28.

92. So Philo of Byblos, *Praep. ev.* 1.10.1, in Clifford, *Creation Accounts*, 128, 142; compare Attridge & Oden, *Philo*, 36–37. The comparison has been long noted. See Sabatino Moscati, "The Wind in Biblical and Phoenician Cosmogony," *JBL* 66, 305–10; and Cross, "Olden Gods" (ch. 1, n. 6), 83. For further scholarly discussion, see Klaus Koch, "Wind und Zeit als Konstituenten den Kosmos in phönikischer Mythologie und spätalttestamentlichen Texten," in *Mesopotamia— Ugaritica—Biblica: Festschrift für Kurt Bergerhof zur Vollendung seines 70. Lebensjahres am 7. Mai 1992*, AOAT 232, 59–91, reprinted in Koch, *Der Gott Israels und die Götter des Orients: Religionsgeschichtliche Studien II. Zum 80. Geburtstag von Klaus Koch*, FRLANT 216, 86–118; and Hans-Peter Müller, "Der Welt- und Kulturensstehungsmythos von Philo Byblios und die biblische Urgeschichte," *ZAW* 112, 161–79. There is arguably a genetic relationship between the notions in

the account in Gen. 1:1–2 and the material preserved in Philo of Byblos; the direction of borrowing, if any, is unclear, given the elaborations in both sets of material. The reference to Zophasemin in 1.10.2 might seem to militate in favor of Hebrew or Aramaic influence on the material preserved of Philo of Byblos. However, the influence, if any, might have run in the opposite direction.

93. See Robert Luyster, "Wind and Water: Cosmogonic Symbols in the Old Testament," *ZAW* 93, 1–10; and P. J. Smith, "A Semotactical Approach to the Meaning of the Term *rûaḥ 'elohim* in Genesis 1:2," *JNSL* 8, 99–104.

94. See the discussion of Tsumura, *Creation and Destruction*, 74–76.

95. The same range appears in later readings and echoes of Gen. 1:2. For example, Dan. 7:2 echoes the use of *ruah* as "wind," while the book of Jubilees (4Q416, column V, lines 2–11) interprets *ruah* in Gen. 1:2 as "spirit," in other words, "angelic spirits." For the text of Jubilees, see James VanderKam and J. T. Milik, "Jubilees," in Harold Attridge et al., *Qumran Cave 4: VIII. Parabiblical Texts, Part 1*, DJD XIII, 13–14. For convenient access, see Parry and Tov, *The Dead Sea Scrolls Reader*, 48–49. These meanings as well as others for *ruah* in the Qumran literature are dealt with by Arthur Everett Sekki, *The Meaning of* Ruaḥ *at Qumran*, SBLDS 110.

96. For *ruah* for military strength, see also Judg. 3:10.

97. Compare Hosea 4:19 and Zechariah 5:9 for images of the wind (*ruah*) with its wings. Note also this usage in the wings of the wind in the story of Adapa; see *COS* 1.449; Dalley, *Myths* (Intro., n. 6), 185. For another example, see also Mari letter ARM vol. 26, #200; for convenient access, see Wolfgang Heimpel, *Letters* (ch. 1, n. 79), 255.

98. *Enuma Elish*, tablet IV, line 50 (*ANET* 66; *COS* 1.397; Dalley, *Myths*, 251). I owe the suggestion of this parallel to Jeffrey Tigay.

99. For text and translation, see Smith, "The Baal Cycle," 147.

100. Compare *ruah* for "wind" in Ecclesiastes 2:26; 4:4, 6, 16; 5:15, 7:9, 11:4; and 12:7.

101. For example, Harry Orlinsky, "The Plain Meaning of *Rûaḥ* in Gen. 1.2," *JQR* 48/2, 174–82; and Luyster, "Wind and Water:," 1–10. See also James K. Hoffmeier, "Some Thoughts on Genesis 1 & 2 and Egyptian Cosmology," *JANESCU* 15, 44. Orlinsky ("The Plain Meaning," 181) claimed that the alternative meaning of "spirit" developed under Hellenistic influence (see *pneuma* in LXX Gen. 1:2; compare *pneumatō dē*, "like wind, air," in Philo Byblos, *Praep. ev.* 1.10.1, in Attridge & Oden, *Philo*, 36–37). According to Albright, *ruah 'elohim* means "spirit of God," but substituted for an original *ruah* (without *'elohim*), meaning wind." See Albright, "Contributions," 363–93, esp. 368.

102. I wish to thank Robert Kawashima for his presentation at the Association of Jewish Studies on 23 December 2008, who reminded me of this passage.

103. Among commentators on Genesis 1, see von Rad, *Genesis*, 47. For commentators on Daniel 7, see Louis F. Hartman and Alexander A. Di Lella, *The Book of Daniel*, AB 23, 211. Compare John J. Collins, *Daniel: A Commentary on the Book of Daniel* (edited by Frank Moore Cross; Hermeneia; Minneapolis: Fortress, 1993) 294.

104. For another instance of the parallelism of "word" and "spirit," see Ps. 147:18. For discussion, see Grethner, *Name* (ch. 1, n. 37), 156. Compare the *ruah* that gives life to the earth in Isa. 32:15, and the destructive divine *ruah* and beneficial "word" together in Isa. 40:6–7. Here the *ruah*, which desiccates the grass of the field, recalls the east wind. For this passage, see Aloysius Fitzgerald, F.S.C., *The Lord of the East Wind*, CBQMS 34, 162 n. 8 and 202–3. Job 4:16 uses *ruah* for a "spirit" (NRSV), which has a form that speaks (verses 17–18).

105. Compare Job 4:9: "From the breath of Eloah they perish, from the *ruah* of his mouth they are finished."

106. Compare the divine title in Num. 27:15, *'elohe haruhot lekol basar*, literally "god of the life-breath(s) (belonging) to all flesh" (NJPS: "Source of the breath of all flesh").

107. The usage here perhaps recalls Gen. 2:7, which uses *neshamah* for the breath of life instead; compare the creation allusion of Zech. 12:1, where God is said to have "fashioned the spirit of the human."

108. This use of *ruah* in Psalm 104 has been compared with the descriptions of the divine Aten's life-giving breath in Egyptian hymns composed at the site of Amarna, the capital built by Akhenaten (Amenophis IV) specifically for his devotion to the Aten. It is possible to trace the probable path of cultural transmission from Egypt through the Amarna corpus to the Levantine coast, and from

the coast to the Judean hinterland; see my book, *God in Translation*, 69–76. From a cultural point of view, we may guess that this idea of the divine breath was adopted and adapted in various royal centers on the coast and then in Jerusalem (see Lam. 4:20 for a remarkable similarity; and Isa. 33:17 for the idea of the king's beauty, an aesthetic notion that perhaps has older resonances that may go back to the Amarna material). This use of *ruah* perhaps entered Judean religious vocabulary readily because there was already a similar usage not only for breath or the like, but also for the divine inspiration of prophets (see Num. 11:25; Isa. 42:1; 63:1; Joel 2:28–29 [MT 3:1–2]; note 2 Sam. 23:2; Zech. 7:12, and compare Rev. 22:6). The rather particular use of *ruah* in Ps. 104:29–30 for the life-giving breath of the Aten, possibly influenced by the local Levantine adaptations of this breath, grafted rather easily onto a local traditional use of *ruah* for human breath. We may note that Ugaritic, while hardly beyond the influence of Egypt, shows the mundane use of *rh*: "[His lif]e (*npsh*) went out of him like breath (*rh*)" (KTU 1.18 IV 36; Parker, "Aqhat"). The specific semantics of the word *ruah* were at home in ancient Israel, but its application to the divine breath that infuses life into human beings might owe something to this background. Needless to say, this reconstruction remains quite speculative on my part.

109. Keel & Uehlinger, *Gods*, 137.

110. For a textual parallel to the destructive breath of the god on the iconography, see Job 4:9: "From the breath (*neshamah*) of God they perish, and from the wind/breath (*ruah*) of his anger they are consumed.

111. In English, winds do not "hover" or "glide" but "move" or "blow" (cf. *holek harruah* in Eccles. 1:6 rendered by NJPS. "blows the wind"). The most suitable translation depends on understanding the subject and the verb in tandem. Perhaps "moving" or "sweeping" would best accommodate the two sides of *ruah* under discussion here. Compare Cross, *From Epic to Canon*, 83: "the divine wind. . . soared over the surface of the waters of the deep."

112. Deuteronomy 32:11; and KTU 1.18 IV 21, 31 and 32; see Parker, "Aqhat," 66, 68. See also the root applied to Anat in KTU 1.108.8 (noted in the discussion in *HALOT* 1219–1220). The verb in the Ugaritic passages is often translated as "hover," but it is unclear that birds hover as such: flying, soaring, gliding, and swooping are more proper characterizations of how birds move. For an iconographic example of a raptor with wings outspread, see the Middle Bronze Age gold piece found under the floor of the so-called "Temple of the Obelisks" at Byblos. See Maurice Dunand, *Fouilles de Byblos: Volume 2. 1933–1938* (Paris: Geuthner, 1954) 858–59, no. 16732 and 950 plate CXXXIV; and *Beyond Babylon: Art, Trade, and Diplomacy in the Second Millennium B.C.* (edited by Joan Aruz, Kim Benzel, and Jean M. Evans; New York: Metropolitan Museum of Art; New Haven/London: Yale University Press, 2008) 56, #27.

Following citation of the biblical evidence, Brown (*Seven Pillars*) suggests: "The sense in Gen. 1:2 is that of God's breath suspended over the waters, like a vulture riding the updraft of a warm current of air, gently moving back and forth or fluctuating, but poised to act (cf. Gen. 1:9; 8:1)."

Noting the root in Ugaritic, Cross (*Canaanite Myth*, 323) regards its use in Gen. 1:2 to be an "archaism." For further discussion, see also Jacques Duchesne-Guillemin, "Genèse 1,2c, Ugarit et l'Égypte," CRAI 1982, 512–25.

113. Tsumura (*Creation and Destruction*, 76) nicely notes the relationship between *ruah* in v. 2 and divine speech in v. 3, that the former "was ready to become engaged in his [God's] creative action," signaled by divine speech.

114. Referring to what he calls "the intended ambiguity" of *ruah ʾelohim*, Agustinus Gianto says that it "makes little sense to adopt one sense to the exclusion of the other." See Gianto, "Historical Linguistics and the Hebrew Bible," in *Studi sul Vicino Oriente Antico dedicati alla memoria di Luigi Cagni* (ed. by Simonetta Graziani; Istituto universitario orientale dipartimento di Studi Asiatici, Series Minor, vol. 61; Naples: Istituto universitario orientale, 2000) 1553–1571, here 1566. The term "ambiguity" may convey to some readers a "lack of clarity," which I do not think is what Gianto intends.

115. This is hardly a singular case. For an analogy, note *qol*, "voice," used seven times for divine thunder in Psalm 29 (see Ugaritic *ql* also in KTU 1.4 V 8, VII 29; Smith, "The Baal Cycle," 129, 136), and for God's voice in Gen. 3:8 and 10 as well as Isa. 6:8 (cf. Anat's "voice" in KTU 1.3 V 10; Smith, "The Baal Cycle," 116). Note also the physical, theophanic effect of the divine *qol* in Ps. 104:4; cf.

the "voice of Baal" in the meteorological context of KTU 1.19 I 46; Parker, "Aqhat," 69. The word is used also for animals (Ps. 104:12; KTU 1.14 III 17 and IV 8–10; Greenstein, "Kirta," 16 and 20; and Deir 'Alla, combination I, line 8, in Hackett, *The Balaam Text* [ch. 1, n. 51], 25, 133, given as line 10 in *DNWSI* 1011).

Another case involves the root °*g'r*. Used for God's speech anthropomorphically, it refers to divine rebuke (see Zech. 3:2; cf. KTU 1.2 IV 28, in Smith, "The Baal Cycle," 104; and 1.114.14, in Theodore J. Lewis, "El's Divine Feast," in *UNP*, 195; see also *DUL* 290). Applied against natural phenomena or destruction of enemies (Ps. 9:6), it refers to divine physical blasts. The word in Ps. 104:7 and Job 26:11 seems to be physical in nature in view of their surrounding context, yet *BDB* 172 lists these references under the meaning, "rebuke." The word may operate on both levels. For other theophanic passages with °*g'r*, see also Fitzgerald, *The Lord of the East Wind*, 27, 30, 37, 68, 162. Fitzgerald translates °*g'r* by either "roar" or "rebukes/roars at." Compare also the use of the root for horses blowing or roaring in the Ugaritic hippiatric texts (KTU 1.72.27 and 1.82.5; *DUL* 291).

116. The language here is quite reminiscent of Gen. 1:1–2.

117. This suggestion seems to suffer from the fact that the human persons are infused with divine *neshamah* not in Genesis 1, but in Gen. 2:7 (see *nishmat-ruah* in Gen. 7:22; cf. Isa. 42:5 for the parallelism of *neshamah* and *ruah*). Yet, if the author of Genesis 1 knows Genesis 2 (as suggested in ch. 3 herein), then perhaps this sense of *ruah* lurks behind the account of Genesis 1. The usage of *ruah* in Gen. 6:3 was perhaps also known to the author of Genesis 1.

118. Not only the work of creation, but perhaps even God's rest may be tied to the divine *ruah*. Compare the thematic connection between *ruah* and rest in Isa. 63:14: "The *ruah* of Yahweh gave them rest."

119. For discussion of this pair, see Westermann, *Genesis 1–11*, 102; David Toshio Tsumura, *The Earth and the Waters in Genesis 1 & 2*, JSOTSup 83, 30–31, 32–36, 42–43, 156, and *Creation and Destruction*, 28–35; and Rechenmacher, "Gott und das Chaos," 1–20.

120. Note also the echo in the War Scroll, 1QM 17:4.

121. This issue is discussed above in note 2. For this passage, see also Michael Fishbane, "Jeremiah IV 23–26 and Job III 3–13: A Recovered Use of the Creation Pattern," *VT* 21, 151–67.

122. See *DCH II*, 97. Note also the older survey of Armin Schwarzenbach, *Die geographische Terminologie im Hebräischen des Alten Testamentes* (Leiden: Brill, 1954) 105–7; and the detailed discussion of David Toshio Tsumura, *Creation and Destruction*, 9–35. Tsumura understands the phrase to mean "desolate and empty." My conclusion about the meaning of the phrase is proximate to his.

123. Scholars compare Arabic *bahâ*, "vacuum"; see Zorrell, 97; and *bahiya*, "to be empty," so *BDB* 96. For *tohu*, scholars note Arabic cognates such as *tahâ*, so Zorrell, 889: "via erravit mente, turbatus fuit." *HALOT* 1689 cites Arabic *tîh*, "wilderness"; see Hans Wehr, *A Dictionary of Modern Written Arabic* (edited by J. Milton Cowan; 4th ed.; Wiesbaden: Otto Harrassowitz, 1979) 121. Similarly, Albright long ago cited Arabic *tih*, "desert," and *bahw*, "vast plain." See Albright, "Contributions," 365–66 (Albright also characterized *tohu* as a "blend" of *tehom* and *bohu*). For *tohu*, *BDB* 1062 comments: "primary meaning difficult to seize."

For proposals for Egyptian cognates, see Manfred Görg, "*tohu wabohu*—ein Deutung-Vorschlag," *ZAW* 92, 431–34; and "Zur Ikonographie des Chaos," *BN* 14, 18. See further Hoffmeier, "Some Thoughts," 39–49, here 43–44. See also *HALOT* 4.1689.

BH *bohu* has long been compared with *Baau* in the cosmology of Philo of Byblos (in Eusebius *PE* 1.10.7), presented conveniently in Attridge & Oden, *Philo*, 40–41; for example see Wilhelm Gesenius, *Hebräisches und Aramäisches Handwörterbuch* (edited by Frants Buhl; seventeenth edition; Berlin/Göttingen/Heidelberg: Springer-Verlag, 1959) 85; *HALOT* 1.111; Koch, "Wind und Zeit," 68, repr. in Koch, *Der Gott Israels*, 94; Attridge & Oden, *Philo*, 80 (with discussion of alternatives); and Cross, *From Epic to Canon*, 82–83. Attridge and Oden suggest that the interpretation of Baau in this cosmology as "night" works in favor of the comparison. See further Baumgarten, *Phoenician History* (ch. 1, n. 80), 132, 146.

124. *HALOT* 1689. This entry compares Ugaritic *thw* (see below) as well as the disputed interpretation of *tu-a-bi [-u(?)]* in the *Ugaritica* V polyglot (p. 243, line 23). For a sympathetic attitude

toward the reading, see Tsumura, *Creation and Destruction*, 16–22; for a very critical assessment, see John Huehnergard, *Ugaritic Vocabulary in Syllabic Transcription: Revised Edition*, HSS 32, 84 (for the entry, see #184.2 on 38–39). Despite his favorable disposition toward the reading, Tsumura also discusses the difficulties with it.

125. Compare the description of God's punishment in Ps. 107:40: "he pours contempt on leaders and he makes them wander in a wasteland (*tohu*) with no path." This verse is closely paralleled by Job 12:24. See also in this vein Job 6:18.

126. As noted by many commentators, such as Tsumura, *Creation and Destruction*, 10–12.

127. KTU 1.5 I 14–16 = 1.133.2–4. For the texts, see Smith, "The Baal Cycle," 142, 177. For the contrast of sea and wilderness in these Ugaritic parallels, compare the apparent contrast of sea and st[eppe] in Ahiqar; see James M. Lindenberger, *The Aramaic Proverbs of Ahiqar*, JHNES 1983, 209, saying #110.

It has been argued that *btwm* in KTU 4.320.13 means "in the steppe"; so see Josef Tropper, *Ugaritische Grammatik*, AOAT 273, 192, para. 33.312.31b. If correct, *tw* in this case would be a shortened form of *thw*. However, *btwm* in this context may mean "houses."

128. This "presentist" sense of *tohu* is insightfully captured in the reflections of Dibeela, "Perspective" (ch. 1, n. 132), 388–89, 398.

129. Sasson, "Time. . . to Begin," 188.

130. Note the pattern of vowels, /o/ and /u/, in both nouns; this is what scholars call a °*qutl* formation for nouns with the letter *heh* as the third consonant of the word. See J. Barth, *Die Nominalbildung in den semitischen Sprachen* (Leipzig: J. C. Hinrichs'sche Buchhandlung, 1894) 38, para. 25b.

131. Compare French "pêle-mêle," mentioned by du Mesnil du Buisson (*Études*, 41 n. 4), for *tohu wabohu*. I wish to thank Bruce Zuckerman for making a number of fine suggestions (personal communications) about the translation of *tohu wabohu* that would capture the alliteration and the quality of the watery world: "masses and messes," "vastness and masses" (quite good!), "a mish and a mash," or "a vast mish mash." His point, which is quite right, is that the world is full and not empty as my translation might suggest. My point is that is it is empty of the life that is to be created; moreover, my translation stays closer to the meaning and usage of these words in Hebrew.

132. The verse echoes three primordial pairs denoting cosmological origins: "Heavens" and "Deep," then "blessings of Breasts and Womb" and "blessings of your father, warrior Most High," a pair of images going back to the blessing goddess and god (perhaps Asherah and El?); and "Mountains" and "Hills" ("blessings of everlasting mountains" and "the outlying (?) eternal hills").

Like the first pair, the third is cosmological; compare Ugaritic "Mountains" paired with "Deep" (see Pardee, *Ritual and Cult*, 14–15 in slot 19 and 18–19, slot 29). These are primordial mountains in biblical creation accounts (compare Prov. 8:25; Ps. 104:6, 8). In some accounts, the mountains serve as pillars for the foundation of the world (Prov. 8:25; cf. Zaphon in Job 26:7). In others, these mountains serve to contain the waters (Ps. 104:8). Hebrew *ta'awat* in Gen. 49:25 for the mountains is understood as "boundary" (NJPS: "utmost bounds"; see also textual note to NRSV), and so perhaps the word suggests the sort of primordial mountains lying at the edge of the earth (compare "the two hills at the edge of the earth," in KTU 1.4 VII 4; Smith, "The Baal Cycle," 138).

For El and Asherah and their blessings, see pp. 261 n. 88, 261–62 n. 92. It is possible to read "warrior Most High" differently. See Raymond de Hoop, *Genesis 49 in its Literary and Historical Context*, OtSt 39, 24 (on 216, 231, he reads the third pair and the syntax of the last clause differently than what I am proposing here). Contrast Christian Frevel, *Aschera und der Ausschließlichkeitsanspruch YHWHs* (Athenäums Monografien: Theologie series, vol. 94/1: BBB; Frankfurt: Anton Hain, 1995) 163: "Brüste und Mutterschoß sind hier auf die generative Fruchtbarkeit bezogen und haben keine Beziehung zu Aschera." What Frevel does not discuss are the other cosmological pairs in this context. These are more specific than in the sorts of blessings in Gen. 27:28 and 39, which are not as cosmological by comparison.

133. For the former text, see Pardee, *Ritual and Cult*, 174. For the latter text, see A. Caquot and A. S. Dalix, "Un Texte Mythico-magique (n. 53)," in *Études Ougaritiques I: Travaux 1985–1995* (edited by M. Yon and D. Arnaud; Paris: Editions Recherche sur les Civilisations, 2001) 393–405. Note also the feminine noun *thtm*, "deep," and the dual form *thmtm*, "double-deeps," part of the description of

the home of the god, El. The singular form is used with cosmic significance also in the message of Baal to Anat (in KTU 1.3 III 25 and 1.3 IV17; see Smith, *UNP*, 110 and 112–13, respectively).

134. For KTU 1.100.1, see Pardee, *Ritual and Cult*, 174. Note also RS 92.2016.9.

135. In view of the pairs, it is perhaps notable that the composer does not use "sea" (*yam*), in view of its common attestation as a term for the cosmic waters or sea. For "mighty waters," see Herbert Gordon May, "Some Cosmic Connotations of *Mayim Rabbim*, 'Many Waters'," *JBL* 74, 9–21.

136. The expression also appears in the creation context in Proverbs 8:27.

137. Note also Gen. 1:29: "over the face of all the earth." For the expression, compare Zech. 5:3.

138. Levenson, *Creation*, 47–50.

139. Levenson is hardly alone. Compare also the characterization of the primordial monsters of the sea as "primordial evil" by Bilha Nitzan, "Evil and Its Symbols in the Qumran Scrolls," in *The Problem of Evil and its Symbols in Jewish and Christian Tradition*, JSOTSup 366, 83. It may be indicative of the lack of evil in Genesis 1 that a single sentence out of this entire volume is devoted to Genesis 1.

140. To be clear, I am not claiming that Levenson says this about the waters as they appear in Genesis 1. I have yet to find an exact characterization about this question in his book, but the discussion on p. 122, calls the waters in Genesis 1 "neutralized," "demythologized," and "depersonalized." If they are "depersonalized," they have no will and do not offer any "opposition" (as also noted by Levenson here); they are likely then not "evil."

141. Levenson, *Creation*, 127.

142. Greenstein, "Presenting Genesis 1," 1–22.

143. Compare Isa. 27:1, 51:9; Ezek. 29:3, 32:2; Pss. 44:20, 148:7; and Job 7:12. See the discussion of the biblical and Ugaritic evidence by Gordon, "Leviathan" (ch. 1, n. 69), 1–9. Gordon also notes Leviathan the *tnyn'* in later Aramaic magical bowls. The Aramaic proverbs of Ahiqar (line 106) include a reference to *tnyn* (*DNWSI* 1223): "The k[ing]'s tongue is gentle, but it breaks a dragon's ribs." Lindenberger (*The Aramaic Proverbs of Ahiqar*, 91) connects this usage to "kindred mythological traditions."

Like Yamm and Leviathan, *tnn* is one of the cosmic enemies attested also in the Ugaritic texts, for example in KTU 1.3 III 38b-40. This name appears to be vocalized in the *Ugaritica* V polyglot (# 137:8') as *tu-un-na-nu*. Unfortunately, the Sumerian, Akkadian and Hurrian equivalents are not preserved on the tablet, though #135:15', which is probably a parallel, reads *MUŠ* = *ṣi-i-ru*, "snake" in the Sumerian and Akkadian column. See Huehnergard, *Ugaritic Vocabulary*, 34, 72, 379. The name is also found in an uncertain context in KTU 1.82.1, where it is preceded before a break by *]mḫṣbʿl[*. This strongly suggests that the line is describing a conflict between Baal and Tunnanu. The name almost certainly appears too in KTU 1.83.8, where the text reads *ṯʿan*. The context of the passage, with references to Yamm/Nahar (lines 4, 6, 11–12) and the appearance of the root *šbm*, which also occurs with *tnn* in KTU 1.3 III 40, seems to assure that the *'a* in *ṯʿan* is a mistake for *n* (simply missing a third horizontal wedge). Another Ugaritic reference to Tunnanu, alongside *'arš*, is found at the very end of the Baal Cycle, in KTU 1.6 VI 51. For a recent discussion of Tunnanu in these Ugaritic passages, see Mark S. Smith and Wayne T. Pitard, *The Ugaritic Baal Cycle: Volume 2. Introduction with Text, Translation and Commentary of KTU 1.3–1.4*, VTSup 114, 248–49, 253–55, 259. See also Wayne T. Pitard, "Just How Many Monsters Did Anat Fight (*KTU* 1.3 III 38–47)?" in *Ugarit at Seventy-Five* (edited by K. Lawson Younger Jr.; Winona Lake, Ind.: Eisenbrauns, 2007) 75–88. Unlike Pitard, I consider the cosmic enemies in the sea, such as Ugaritic Tunnanu and the biblical *tanninim* of Gen. 1:21, as related but separate figures relative to Sea personified. Sea seems to belong to an older generation, while the other figures associated with Sea may belong to the next generation of watery enemies dwelling in it (for this characterization, I thank Andrés Piquer Otero).

144. See Gordon, "Leviathan," 1.

145. Levenson, *Creation*, 122. Compare Brown, *Ethos*, 42: "The waters are drained of all potential hostility before creation even commences."

146. Hendel, personal communication.

147. Compare the *tannin* generated by Moses in another priestly passage of Exod. 7:8–12. Here, the *tannin* (plural *tanninim*) is produced from a staff both by Moses and Aaron and by the Egyptian

magicians. With the staff of Moses and Aaron swallowing up that of the Egyptian magicians, the power of Yahweh is demonstrated. The two sets of *tannin* play a role in the competition, and the description of them is fairly neutral. There is no sense in the narrative that these are symbolic of opposition to God as such. See Brevard S. Childs, *The Book of Exodus,* OTL, 151–53. According to Childs, the idea of the staff turning into *tannim* comes from God in the story (verse 9). In context, it is hardly inimical to God; on the contrary. The power at stake in this episode involves the manipulators of the staffs, not what the staffs turn into. The *tanninim* are subservient to this theme.

Ezekiel 29:3 constitutes another priestly passage with a stronger presentation of the *tannin* imagery. Here it stands for the king of Egypt and his opposition to God, and it is presented as an enemy. In this passage, the traditional symbolism of the *tannin* is used more fully as the enemy, and this is an enemy to be defeated by God (see vv. 4–6). In contrast, the symbolism of the *tannin* in Exod. 7:8–12 may be implicitly recognized, especially if viewed in light of Ezek. 29:3–6, but with the relatively neutral and flat presentation of Exod. 7:8–12, the traditionally potent symbolism is eviscerated and neutralized. For a different approach, see Ziony Zevit, "The Priestly Redaction and the Interpretation of the Plague Narrative in Exodus," *JQR* 66, 194–205. The neutralization apparent in Exod. 7:8–12 is even clearer in Gen. 1:21. (My thanks go to Aaron Tugenhaft for our discussion of this issue.)

148. Mary Douglas, *Natural Symbols: Explorations in Cosmology* (New York: Pantheon Books, 1970). For further reflections on water as a powerful cultural symbol, see Veronica Strang, "Common Senses: Water Sensory Experience and the Generation of Meaning," *Journal of Material Culture* 10/1 (2005) 92–120. Note her comment in connection with water in Genesis 1 as well as Psalm 104: "Water's diversity is, in some respects, a key to its meanings" (p. 98). Cf. Strang's comments on p. 105 regarding biblical descriptions of water.

149. Biblical scholars commonly use the words "chaotic" or "chaos" to characterize the waters or Sea or the cosmic enemies such as Leviathan. For example, among scholars who have worked on creation in Genesis 1, see Day, *Yahweh and the Gods and Goddesses* (ch. 1, n. 64), 102; and Levenson, *Creation,* 14–25. Note also Johann Cook, "The Exegesis of Greek Genesis," in *VI Congress of the International Organization for Septuagint and Cognate Studies: Jerusalem 1986* SBLSCS 23, 106; and Phyllis Trible, *God and the Rhetoric of Sexuality,* OBT, 12.

Recently, some scholars have criticized the use of this term. Following her lengthy study of divine conflict in the Hebrew Bible, Rebecca S. Watson concludes "that the language of 'chaos' has been inappropriately applied to the material considered here, and that there is therefore a strong case for abandoning it in respect of the Old Testament." Watson, *Chaos Uncreated: A Reassessment of the Theme of "Chaos" in the Hebrew Bible,* BZAW 341, 369. For another strong critique of using "chaos" for the situation in Gen. 1:2, see Tsumura, *Creation and Destruction,* 9–35, 75, 196. Arguably, chaos is a meaning that doesn't quite fit the situation in Gen. 1:1–2. In Greek the word *chaos* refers to the first state of the universe, but it also has the following senses: space and the expanse of air; the nether abyss, infinite darkness, or darkness generally; and any vast gulf or chasm. See LSJ, 1976. See the survey of Watson, *Chaos Uncreated,* 13–19. Accordingly, we might follow suit and avoid the translation, "chaos." (I wish to thank Bruce Zuckerman for our conversations about the unsuitability of "chaos" for pre-Hellenistic Near Eastern texts.)

It is to be noted also that the ancient Greek translations for this verse do not use *chaos.* See Wevers, *Genesis,* 75. The LXX reading, *aoratos kai akataskeuastos,* "invisible and unformed," is thought to have been influenced by *aoraton eidos ti kai amorphon,* "invisible and formless being," in Plato, *Tim.* 51A; see J. C. M. van Widen, O. F. M., "Some Observations on the Patristic Interpretation of Genesis 1:1," *Vigilae christianae* 17/2 (1963) 105–21, here 105 n. 3. At the same trime, *chaos* does occur in the account of Philo of Byblos (*PE* 1.10.1); see Attridge & Oden, *Philo,* 36–37 and 75 n. 24; Baumgarten, *The Phoenician History,* 106–8. Both of these secondary works discuss the possible comparison with Gen. 1:2.

150. In this respect, the waters and darkness seem to embody what is captured by the book title, *Sacred Chaos: Reflections on God's Shadow and the Dark,* by Françoise O'Kane, (Toronto: Inner City Books, 1994). Reference courtesy of Stephen Cook.

151. This is opposite to the view of Job. For reflections on Job in this vein that serve as a counterpart to my discussion of Genesis 1 here, see Corrine L. Patton (Carvalho), "The Beauty of the

Beast: Leviathan and Behemoth in Light of Catholic Theology," in *The Whirlwind: Essays on Job, Hermeneutics, and Theology in Memory of Jane Morse*, JSOTSup 336, 142–67. See in the same volume the remarks on Job and Genesis 1 made by Ellen F. Davis, "Job and Jacob: The Integrity of Faith," 115–16.

152. See Gordon, "Leviathan," 1.

153. As noted by Gordon, "Leviathan," 1.

154. For example, see Hermann Spieckermann, "Is God's Creation Good?" 79–94, esp. 79 and 81, and Jean-Luis Ska, "Genesis 2–3: Some Fundamental Questions," 21, both in *Beyond Eden: The Biblical Story of Paradise and Its Reception History*, FAT 2/34. Contrast the view taken by Greenstein, "Presenting Genesis 1," 1–22. In his deconstruction of Genesis 1's presentation of a good creation created by a good God, Greenstein suggests that "good" in Genesis 1 is only "good" as it appears to God, not morally good. He also compares Gen. 6:2, which does not suggest moral good: "the divine beings saw how good the daughters of men were." Here "good" refers to their appearance ("beautiful" in NJPS) to the divine beings. (Ron Hendel [personal communication] suggests that Gen. 6:2 represents an intertextual *reversal* of Gen. 1:4.) Despite Greenstein's interesting comparison, it is reasonable to think that references to God's seeing creation as good in Genesis 1 do mean that they are good (cf. Jer. 24:3, where the prophet sees the good figs are "very good," *tobot me'od*).

Greenstein's reading not only questions the explicit mentions of "good" in Genesis 1, but also imputes evil to waters, darkness, and *tanninim* even though these are not called evil. It may be asked why one should impute evil to these components of reality in Genesis 1 but not impute good when the text says so explicitly (for "good" in Genesis 1, see further below). Greenstein's citations of Job perhaps suggest that his reading of Genesis 1 is strongly influenced by Job. However, the sensibility about God and evil in Job arguably does not fit Genesis 1. For contrasts between the two texts, see the reflections of Knohl, *Symphony*, 120–21. As noted at the outset of this chapter, Genesis 1 may be read as a *response to* the ideas found in other texts such as Job.

155. See also Brown, *Ethos*, 120–21.

156. See Trible, *God and the Rhetoric of Sexuality*, 13. Compare the reflections of Dibeela, "Perspective," 396–98.

157. "Weal and woe" is a common translation for these terms in Isaiah 45:7; see for example NRSV and NJPS. Compare Job's question to his wife (Job 2:10): "Shall we accept good from God and not accept evil?" See also 1 Kings 22:18, which uses *tob* and *ra'* for a good outcome and a bad outcome.

158. It may be that the word *tob* is not used even more often for good people (for example in the book of Proverbs), because it holds the additional sense of benefit.

159. For the integral relationship of ethics and ritual in priestly thinking, see the insightful essay by Ronald S. Hendel, "Prophets" (ch. 1, n. 48) 185–198, esp. 194.

160. Compare the discussion of S. David Sperling, "Pants, Persians, and the Priestly Source," in *Ki Baruch Hu*, 384–85. Sperling sees "a Hebrew adaptation of the Iranian notion that creation is all good" (p. 385). This broad comparison is difficult to confirm or refute.

161. Compare the *tanninim* created in verse 21, discussed below in sec. 4. As divine creations, they are "good" (verse 21).

162. For comments in this vein, see also Ratzinger, *In the Beginning*, 13–14.

163. Culler, *Literary Theory: A Very Short Introduction* (Oxford/New York: Oxford University, 1997) 82. To be clear, Culler here is explicating narrative theory (or narratology), not his own view as such.

164. Naming is not an uncommon motif in Mesopotamian creation accounts. For example, see very opening of *Enuma Elish*: "When skies above were not yet named,/Nor earth below pronounced by name" (see Clifford, *Creation Accounts*, 88).

165. Creation by word in Genesis 1 has been emphasized by Klaus Koch, "Wort und Einheit," 251–93, republished in Koch, *Studien zur alttestamentlichen*, 61–105; Levenson, *Creation*, 107; and Michael Fishbane, *Biblical Myth and Rabbinic Mythmaking* (Oxford: Oxford University, 2003) 34–35, 101.

166. Perhaps as opposed to speech directed to other divine parties such as angels. One can understand why such an idea might seem possible, given Ps. 103:20: "Bless the Lord, O His angels,

mighty strong ones who do his word"; and Ps. 148:5: "For He commanded [*siwwah*] and they were created" (see also Ps. 33:6–9).

The exception in Genesis 1 is the first person plural pronouns in Gen. 1:26 ("in our image, according to our likeness"). Scholars have generally taken this usage as reflecting divine beings (cf. "the intelligent and holy beings whom he had already created," R. V. Foster, "The Word *Elohim* in Genesis I," *The Old Testament Student* 6/8 [1887] 241–43, here 242). This "polytheistic echo," as Gunkel (*Genesis*, 121) called it, is reflected elsewhere by the older first person plural language used by the head god of the divine council. Compare Isa. 6:8, 40:3 and 8 (in contrast with the singular in 1 Kings 22:19–22). In addition to these passages, Cross (*Canaanite Myth*, 186–88, esp. 187 n. 176) notes first person plural forms in Gen. 3:22 and 11:7 as well as KTU 1.4 IV 43–44, which is paralleled in KTU 1.3 V 32–33. See also Ronald Hendel, in notes to NRSV to Gen. 1:26–28 of *HCSB*, p. 6; and Savran, *Encountering* (ch. 1, n. 30), 166; cf. Lyle Eslinger, "The Enigmatic Plurals like 'one of us' (Genesis I 26, iii 22, and xi, 7) in "Hyperchronic Perspective," *VT* 56, 171–84. Note also, the second person plural used by Ea in the divine council in the Hurrian myth called "the Song of Hedammu": "[Ea], King of Wisdom, spoke among the gods. [The god Ea] began to say: 'Why are you [*plural*] destroying [mankind]?. . . If you [*plural*] destroy mankind, they will no longer [worship] the gods", quoted (including the italics) from Harry A. Hoffner, Jr., *Hittite Myths* SBLWAW 2, 49. See also the Old Hittite myth called "The Disappearance of the Sun God," in Hoffner, *Hittite Myths*, 27. This model of the heavenly divine council with discourse in the plural person has reflexes in biblical cases of the human assembly (see Num. 13:30; Jdg. 1:1; 1 Kgs. 22:15).

Had the composer of Genesis 1 wished to convey the idea of God speaking to other members of the divine assembly in Gen. 1:4 and all the other verses lacking the first person plural marker, it would have been possible to do so in accordance with the first person plural in v. 26. Instead, it would seem that v. 26 is the departure from the other divine speech-acts, which comports with proposals that the first person plural use in v. 26 is vestigial, deriving from the older divine council background (see 1 Kgs. 22:19–22; Isaiah 6; Job 1–2); it seems in this context to present God as a royal figure. For discussion, see in addition to the references above, the important study of W. Randall Garr, *In His Own Image and Likeness: Humanity, Divinity, and Monotheism* (Culture and History of the Ancient Near East, vol. 15; Leiden/Boston: Brill, 2003) 85–92, 152–69.

167. See Klaus Koch, "Wort und Einheit," 251–93, republished in Koch, *Studien zur alttestamentlichen,* 61–105; Frederick L. Moriarty, S. J., "Word as Power in the Ancient Near East," in *Light Unto My Path: Old Testament Studies in Honor of Jacob M. Myers* (edited by Howard N. Bream, Ralph D. Klein, and Carey A. Moore; Philadelphia: Temple University, 1974) 345–62; and Clifford, *Creation Accounts*, 110–12, 144.

For Egyptian evidence for creation by divine word, see in addition to Koch's study, the valuable presentation by James P. Allen, *Genesis in Egypt: The Philosophy of Ancient Egyptian Creation Accounts* (Yale Egyptological Studies, vol. 2; New Haven, Conn.: Yale Egyptological Seminar, 1988) 15, 24, 28, 31–32, 43–47. Note also Hoffmeier, "Some Thoughts," 39–49, here 45; Susanne Bickel, *La cosmogonie égyptienne: Avant le Nouvel Empire,* OBO 134, 100–11; and Shupak, *Wisdom* (ch. 1, n. 20), 225. It has been common to compare Genesis 1 with the Memphite theology; for handy access, see *ANET* 5 ("all the divine order [literally, every word of the god] really came into being through what the heart thought and the tongue commanded"); see also Allen, *Genesis in Egypt,* 43–47, 59–61; Clifford, *Creation Accounts,* 110–12, 114; and Keel and Schroer, *Schöpfung,* 170–76 (the latter reference courtesy of Christoph Uehlinger). Noting creation by word already in the Pyramid texts, Bickel disputes the common conception that this mode of creation in Egyptian texts is particular to the Memphite theology; she calls it "certainement erronée" (p. 101). Note also *ANET* 5 n. 12; and Hoffmeier, "Some Thoughts," 45.

Creation by magic in Egyptian texts (see Coffin Spell 261, in *COS* 1.17–18) appears to be related to the category of creation by speech. Note its emphasis on the divine mouth in creating:

> I am the one whom the Sole Lord made
> before two things had evolved in this world,
> when he sent his sole eye, when he was one,
> when something came from his mouth, when his million of ka was in protection
> of associates,

when he spoke with the one who evolved with him, than whom he is mightier, when he took Annunciation in his mouth (COS 1.17).

See also Coffin Spell 648. For discussion of these two texts, see Ritner, *Mechanisms* (ch. 1, n. 24) 17–20, 23, 25.

168. This verse uses "word," but it may be misleading to characterize the other texts using verbs of speech as "word." Unlike Ps. 36:5 (compare Ps. 147:18), neither Psalm 19 nor Genesis 1 uses "word," but verbs of speech; accordingly, one should not boil down all the usage of divine speech to some sort of essentialist sounding "word" or "Word." Such a usage might also conjure up the Greco-Roman concept of *logos*, literally "word" but also the principle of reason built into the universe by which it was made; this notion would be foreign to this material. For *logos*, see LSJ, 1058, #7. The divine speech of Genesis 1 would be interpreted in this manner in the Greco-Roman period (for example, John 1:1: "In the beginning was the word"; cf. 4 Ezra 6:38, in Bruce Metzger, "The Fourth Book of Ezra," *OTP*, 536). It would be an anachronism to interpret the Hebrew Bible references to either divine speech or divine word in these terms. The English word that more closely captures what is going on in Psalm 19 is "speech" (see vv. 3 and 4; cf. "their words," *millehem*, in v. 5), which derives from the verb "to speak," the main verb of speaking in Genesis 1. For this point about Genesis 1, see also below.

169. Compare the parallelism of *ruah* and mouth in Isa. 34:16.

170. See Grethner, *Name*, 137–38.

171. Compare Isa. 55:10–11, with its idea that the divine word goes forth from God and returns to God only when it has accomplished what God has sent it to do.

172. Useful literature includes Alan Cooper, "Creation, Philosophy, and Spirituality: Aspects of Jewish Interpretation of Psalm 19," in *Pursuing the Text: Studies in Honor of Ben Zion Wacholder on the Occasion of his Seventieth Birthday*, JSOTSup 184, 15–33; K. A. Deurloo, "Psalm 19: Riddle and Parable," in *Goldene Äpfel in silbernen Schalen: Collected Communications to the XIIIth Congress of the International Organization for the Study of the Old Testament*, BEATAJ 20, 93–100; Fishbane, *Biblical Text and Texture: A Literary Reading of Selected Texts* (Oxford: Oneworld, 1979) 84–90; Rolf Knierim, "On the Theology of Psalm 19," in *Ernten was man sät. Festschrift für Klaus Koch zu seinem 65. Geburtstag* (Neukirchen-Vluyn: Neukirchener Verlag, 1991) 439–50; Herb J. Levine, *Sing Unto God a New Song: A Contemporary Reading of the Psalms* (Indiana Studies in Biblical Literature; Bloomington/Indianapolis: Indiana University, 1995) 11–21, 83–85; Nahum Sarna, "Psalm XIX and the Near Eastern Sun-god Literature," in *Fourth World Congress of Jewish Studies; Papers I* (Jerusalem: World Union of Jewish Studies, 1967) 171–75; idem, *Songs of the Heart*, 70–96; J. Glen Taylor, *Yahweh and the Sun: Biblical and Archaeological Evidence for Sun Worship in Ancient Israel*, JSOTSup 111, 220–25.

173. From the parallelism, °*qaw* is some sort of sound. BDB (876) proposes "music." NJPS p. 1126 n. b compares Arabic *qawwah*, "to shout." Dahood arrives at this solution on the basis of context; see Dahood, *Psalms I*, 122.

174. This language of nature, which humans do not hear, is a traditional motif also in ancient Near Eastern literature. The speech of the heavens and earth in the Ugaritic Baal Cycle is a notable case (KTU 1.3 III 22–25, presented in Smith, "The Baal Cycle," 110). Relevant to the theme is a Sumerian cosmological account (sometimes referred to as the "Barton Cylinder"). In this text, the raging of the storm is represented as the speech of heaven and earth to one another (Clifford, *Creation Accounts*, 25): "Heaven (An) spoke with Earth (Ki), Earth (Ki) spoke with Heaven (An)." This image is presented in the context of the beginning of a creation account.

175. Grethner, *Name*, 136: "das Wort. . . das Prinzip der Schöpfung."

176. Clifford, *Creation Accounts*, 144.

177. This point is made also by Ron Hendel in a personal communication. As he notes, "the priests (from whom the P source came) often discharged their duties by effective speech-acts, declaring a thing holy or profane, clean or unclean (Lev. 10:10)." To be sure, priests are not the only authorities to make pronouncements. Kings give pronouncements as well, and so the comparison with royal decrees is hardly inapt. See David Carr, *The Erotic Word: Sexuality, Spirituality, and the Bible* (New York: Oxford University Press, 2003) 24. The application of the royal idea of kings

delivering decrees is given explicit formulation in a Sumerian text sometimes called "The Duties and Powers of the Gods," an inscription on a statue of Kurigalzu. In this text, the Igigi gods are said to be "the kings who pronounce the word, who are gods of true decrees" (*ANET* 458). In Genesis 1, the blessings among its acts of speech suggest a priestly model and not simply a royal one. It may be that an older royal model (possibly underlying an earlier version of this text) has been taken over in Genesis 1 and recast in priestly terms by its priestly composer.

178. Many of the passages are prophetic critiques of the priesthood to maintain their proper teaching role. For interesting comments on such prophetic critiques of the priesthood from a socio-logical perspective, see the article by Hendel, "Prophets," 185–198, esp. 194.

179. Following Yehezkel Kaufmann, Menahem Haran, and Moshe Greenberg, Israel Knohl has argued that the priests conducted sacrifices in silence. See Kaufmann, *The Religion of Israel: From Its Beginnings to the Babylonian Exile* (Chicago: University of Chicago Press, 1960) 303–5, 309–10; and Knohl, *Sanctuary.* See also Knohl, "Between Voice and Silence: The Relationship between Prayer and Temple Cult," *JBL* 115, 17–30. Knohl himself notes some exceptions (Lev. 16:21; Num. 5:19–22) as pointed by Michael Fishbane. Knohl's discussion works with a grid running from pagan to nonpagan and from monotheistic to polytheistic without much consideration of specific corpora outside of the Bible. It may be that what he regards as priestly silence was not simply a matter of the temple sacrifice, but reflects the genres of biblical sources detailing sacrifices. Ugaritic ritual texts often lack elements of speech (there are some interesting exceptions). If scholars discovered only those ritual texts in Ugaritic without any speech (which is the majority of Ugaritic ritual texts), then one might have arrived at the similar conclusion for Ugaritic temple ritual. In any case, this issue does not matter for the discussion here, as it does not involve priestly sacrifice, but priestly acts of teaching and blessing. See further the comments of Brown, *Ethos,* 76 n. 110.

180. This is not to say that other motifs in other accounts are not absent from Genesis 1. It also omits the motif of sport/laughter; see Prov. 8:30; Ps. 104:26 and Job 40:29. My point here is the importance of the conflict motif's omission for understanding the shift represented by Genesis 1.

181. In a major challenge to this view, Tsumura (*Creation and Destruction*, 36–57) rightly notes the lack of extrabiblical West Semitic evidence for creation following conflict (*Chaoskampf*). I also agree with Tsumura that the Ugaritic material and a good deal of the Bible lack references to creation following divine conflict. Still, there are problems with Tsumura's position. Tsumura notes a problem with passages describing divine conflict without any mention of creation (for exam-ple, Psalm 18; Habakkuk 3). While this critique applies to these texts, a number of other biblical poems work against his position. For example, Ps. 74:12–17 does reflect creation following battle against the cosmic enemies named in vv. 13–14. It seems that Tsumura's discussion of this pas-sage (192–93, 194) simply ignores the text's discussion of creation in the wake of divine conflict. Similarly, Job 26:7–13 mentions both creation and the cosmic enemies whom God defeated (see also Job 38:4–11). For discussion, see Terry Fenton, "Nexus and Significance: Is Greater Precision Possible?" in *Ugarit and the Bible: Proceedings of the International Symposium on Ugarit and the Bible, Manchester, September 1992,* UBL 11, 78–80. In the case of these biblical passages, Tsumura's position is less persuasive. The same difficulty affects the otherwise valuable study of Watson, *Chaos Uncreated*; for example, the denial of the link between creation and conflict in Ps. 74:12–17 (157–59) seems forced. Note also H. W. F. Saggs, *The Encounter with the Divine in Mesopotamia and Israel* (London: Athlone Press, 1978) 54–60. On passages such as Ps. 74:12–17 and Job 26:7–13, Tsumura and Watson have, to my mind, overstated their objections. In their defense, their critique is otherwise helpful.

182. For a recent, detailed discussion of this passage, see Jeremy M. Hutton, "Isaiah 51:9–11 and the Rhetorical Appropriation and Subversion of Hostile Theologies," *JBL* 126, 271–303. Hutton's interpretation requires the speculative reconstruction of a hymn to the goddess Anat that was known to the author of Isa. 51:9–11. No such hymn is known in this period or from any period. Hutton's reconstructed first millennium hymn is based largely on the Late Bronze Age story of the god Baal from Ugarit (KTU 1.3 III 38–IV 3). For the text and translation of the Ugaritic passage, see Smith, "The Baal Cycle," 111–12. Despite the lack of evidence, Hutton's article contains several fine observations. It may be that the emphasis on God's arm in Isaiah 51:9–11 represents a sort of

metaphor to emphasize divine power; this would be especially fitting for a text that may have been responding to perceptions of a lack of divine power in the sixth century.

183. Greenfield, 'Al Kanfei Yonah (ch. 1, n. 21) 114.

184. In the Bible, Sea appears with personified monsters, including the dragons Leviathan and Twisting Serpent. See Ps. 74:13–14; Isa. 27:1. As the cosmic ocean, Sea belongs to an older generation of divine forces in the universe, and these other figures associated with Sea may belong to the next generation of watery enemies that dwell in the sea (see Gen. 1:21–22; Isa. 27:1; KTU 1.6 VI 51; see Greenfield, 'Al Kanfei Yonah, 833–839; Mark S. Smith, The Ugaritic Baal Cycle: Volume 1. Introduction with Text, Translation, and Commentary of KTU 1.1–1.2, VTSup 55, 164); and they might be Sea's offspring (see KTU 1.6 V 1–4; see Smith, "The Ugaritic Baal Cycle," 160). Compare Tiamat and her army of monstrous creatures in Enuma Elish, tablet II, lines 10–30 (ANET 63; COS 1.393).

185. So Wilfred G. Lambert, "A New Look at the Babylonian Background of Genesis," JTS 16, 298. See also the discussions of Clifford, Creation Accounts, 141; Sparks, "Priestly Mimesis," 625–48, esp. 630–31; and Arnold, Genesis, 31–32. Note also the study of Lenzi, Secrecy (ch. 1, n. 23), 358. Lenzi compares Mesopotamian Tiamat in Enuma Elish with tehom in Prov. 8:27–28, and argues for a direct literary dependence of the latter on the former. In this connection, Lenzi (349–50) further notes the usage of tehom in Genesis 1. In this connection, it is also worth noting Edward Greenstein's proposal that the author of the Joban poetry knows Enuma Elish; see Greenstein, "Poetic Use," 51–68 (Heb., with English summary on IX-X).

As Ugaritic thm and thmt show, this basic cosmological term was known in the West Semitic milieu. As a result, a view of direct borrowing of Genesis 1 from Enuma Elish while possible is not required by the available evidence. Note the comment of Jack M. Sasson about tehom: "(it) has become an interpretive bête noire ever since cuneiform documents introduced the Tiamat of Babylonian myths, so much so that it is now practically impossible to locate a biblical commentary which does no devote many pages to Enuma Elish and its influence on the Genesis creation account. I doubt, however, that Israel was much interested in the theologies of other nations, if only because its own theologians did not have ready access to Pritchard's hefty ANET from which to mount their polemics. Linguistically, tehom could be related to Tiamat only indirectly, through a link that is missing from the evidence at hand. Tehom as an adversary for God makes fullest sense only in creations where the combat metaphor is dominant. While this particular metaphor appears frequently in Scripture, it is not featured in Genesis where there are metaphors of rearrangement and of craftsmanship. Therefore, we should recognize that here, as elsewhere, tehom is a poetic term for bodies of water." See Sasson, "Time. . . to Begin," 183–194, here 188–89.

Given the evidence noted above (in particular Ugaritic thm and its cosmological usage, cited above on pp. 232–33 n. 133), ancient Israelites would not have needed Pritchard's volume to know about the cosmic tehom. One might demur from Sasson's comment about a link missing between Mesopotamian Tiamat and biblical tehom, in light of the Mari evidence noted above for tamtum as an Akkadian rendering of the West Semitic cosmic Sea (for references, see note 188). See also the detailed discussion of Tsumura (Creation and Destruction, 36–57), which is no less dismissive of the connection between biblical tehom and Akkadian Tiamat/tâmtum. While the evidence is not as strong as one might like, Tsumura minimizes the cosmological significance of Ugaritic thmt, and it is not clear that the connection between the cosmic thmt and biblical tehom can be ruled out as conclusively as he would suggest. Despite these criticisms, Tsumura has noted some important difficulties in the standard position.

186. In the form, thm. See pp. 232–33 n. 133.

187. The form appears as thmt in KTU 1.1 III 14 (reconstructed)//1.3 III 25//1.3 IV 17 (UNP, 91, 110, 113, respectively), as well as the fragmentary 1.17 VI 12 (UNP, 60). Note also the admittedly obscure KTU 1.92.5, translated by J. C. Greenfield, "the abyss was roiled." See Greenfield, 'Al Kanfei Yonah, 882 n. 36. For another translation, see Wyatt, Religious Texts from Ugarit (Intro., n. 8), 371. Wyatt relates this occurrence to Gen. 1:7.

188. The evidence is summarized by Schwemer, "Storm-Gods" (ch. 1, n. 58), 24–27. For the Mari evidence in particular, see Durand, "Le mythologème" (ch. 1, n. 58) 41–61; and Bordreuil &

Pardee, "Le combat" (ch. 1, n. 58) 63–70. For text, translation and notes, see also Nissinen, *Prophets* (ch. 1, n. 58) 22. Note also Jack M. Sasson, "The Posting of Letters with Divine Messages," in *Florilegium marianum II: Recueil d'études à la mémoire de Maurice Birot, Mémoires de N.A.B.U.* 3 (edited by Dominique Charpin and Jean-Marie Durand; Paris: Sepoa, 1994) 299–316, esp. 310–14; see also Sasson, "Mari Historiography and the Yahdun-Lim Disc Inscription," in *Lingering Over Words: Studies in the Ancient Near Eastern Literature in Honor of William L. Moran,* HSS 37, 444 n. 12; and Smith, *Early History* (ch. 1, n. 64), 56–57.

This Mari text fits with the theory of Thorkild Jacobsen that the description of the conflict between Marduk and Tiamat in *Enuma Elish* was borrowed from West Semitic prototypes (this hardly precludes local Mesopotamian influence as well as various aspects of the description in *Enuma Elish*, as Assyriologists have long noted). Jacobsen had in mind the conflict of Baal and Yamm (Sea) in the Ugaritic Baal Cycle; the Mari text provides a sort of "missing link" in-between. See Jacobsen, "The Battle between Marduk and Tiamat," *JAOS* 88, 104–8. See the discussion and further defense of this view in Mark S. Smith, *The Ugaritic Baal Cycle*, 108–14.

189. For Mesopotamian traditions of cosmic battle, see Theodore J. Lewis, "*CT* 13.33–34 and Ezekiel 32: Lion-Dragons Myths," *JAOS* 116/1 (1996) 28–47, and the literature cited therein; and Schwemer, "Storm-Gods," 26–27, with reference to other literature. Schwemer addresses Hittite evidence on 25–26. In this context, Schwemer disputes the evidence from Ebla.

190. See Day, *God's Conflict*, 51–52, 55; and *Yahweh and the Gods and Goddesses,* 101. For further discussion, see above in ch. 1, p. 18; and the appendix, p. 183.

191. These passages show a shared tradition between Ugaritic and biblical texts. See Day, *God's Conflict*, 141–188. It is to be mentioned that the Baal Cycle is not a creation text as such, however. The point here is the antiquity of the tradition of conflict involving Sea and Tanninim.

In perhaps what is the most extreme claim for textual proximity between the Ugaritic and biblical texts detailing divine conflict, some scholars suggest that Isa. 27:1 is a quotation from the Baal Cycle, specifically of KTU 1.5 I 1–3. So Lambert, "Leviathan" (ch. 1, n. 71), paper read to the University of Cambridge Faculty of Divinity and Faculty of Oriental Studies Senior Old Testament Seminar, Oct. 29, 2003, as reported and followed by Barker, "Isaiah 24–27" (ch. 1, n. 71), 133. There is a great difficulty with this argument for a quotation as such: the Isaiah passage mentions a sword as the instrument of divine attack, but this is absent from the so-called Ugaritic quotation; and the Ugaritic does not mention *tnn*, but it is mentioned in Isaiah 27:1. So it is unclear how one passage is a quote of the other (what sort of quote would this be?). Instead, considering both the similarities as well as the differences, it would appear instead that the two texts belong to a shared tradition of material.

192. Levenson, *Creation,* 82, 84, 88.

193. See Levenson, *Creation*, 86–87. For another description of this sort, see Psalm 24.

194. Compare Philo, *Creation,* 55. See Runia, *Philo of Alexandria,* 60, 204. Runia traces Philo's view to Plato, *Timaeus,* 37c7.

195. Joy does appear in Psalm 19; see below. It is also an old theme in ancient Near Eastern accounts. See "Enki and the World Order" (Clifford, *Creation Accounts,* 35). Note also Atum's joy in the Heliopolis cosmogony in *ANET* 3.

196. Contrast Ps. 19:9, where divine precepts make the heart rejoice; note also Ps. 119:14, 111.

197. Compare the divine word of Isaiah 40:8, itself located within a series of divine voices announcing salvation of the divine glory (see verse 5). For comparison of the divine word in Gen. 1:3 and Isa. 40:1–11, see Manfred Görg, "Revision von Schöpfung und Geschichte: Auf dem Wege zu einer Strukturbestimmung von Jes 40,1–8 (11)," in *Ich bewirke das Heil und schaffe das Unheil (Jesaja 45,7): Studien zur Botschaft der Propheten* (edited by Friedrich Diedrich and Bernd Willmes; FS Lothar Ruppert; Würzburg: Echter Verlag, 1988) 135–56, esp. 151–54; and Antje Labahn, *Wort Gottes und Schuld: Untersuchungen zu Motiven deuteronomistischer Theologie im Deuterojesajabuch mit einem Ausblick auf das Verhältnis von Jes 40–55 zum Deuteronomismus,* BWA(N)T 143, 101 n. 36.

198. The issues in this section were broached by me earlier in my article, "Light in Genesis 1:3—Created or Uncreated: A Question of Priestly Mysticism?" in *Birkat Shalom: Studies in the*

Bible, Ancient Near Eastern Literature, and Postbiblical Judaism presented to Shalom M. Paul on the Occasion of His Seventieth Birthday (edited by Chaim Cohen et al.; Winona Lake, Ind.: Eisenbrauns, 2008) 125–34. There are some modifications in my presentation here and in the final section of this chapter.

199. The approach taken to this question here was inspired originally by the discussion of James Kugel, *Traditions on the Bible: A Guide to the Bible as It Was at the Start of the Common Era* (Cambridge, Mass./London: Harvard, 1998) 47–48.

200. For example, see Albright, "Contributions," 363–93, here 368; Herbert Gordon May, "The Creation of Light in Genesis 1 3–5," *JBL* 58, 203–11; Ephraim A. Speiser, *Genesis: Introduction, Translation and Notes,* AB 1, 10; von Rad, *Genesis,* 49; Claus Westermann, *Creation* (translated by J. J. Scullion; Philadelphia: Fortress, 1974) 13–14, and his commentary, *Genesis 1–11,* 112; Levenson, *Creation,* 55; William P. Brown, *Structure, Role, and Ideology in the Hebrew and Greek Texts of Genesis 1:1—2:3,* SBLDS 132, 217; Ronald A. Simkins, *Creator and Creation: Nature in the Worldview of Ancient Israel* (Peabody, MA: Hendrickson, 1994) 197; and Jacob Milgrom, "The Alleged 'Hidden Light,'" in *The Idea of Biblical Interpretation: Essays in Honor of James L. Kugel* (edited by Hindy Najman and Julie H. Newman; Supplements to the Journal for the Study of Judaism, vol. 83; Leiden/Boston: Brill, 2004) 41–44, here 41.

Umberto Cassuto suggested that the light of this verse was an "immaterial phenomenon," but he does not expand on this observation; see Cassuto, *A Commentary on the Book of Genesis: Part I. From Adam to Noah, Genesis I—VI 8* (trans. by Israel Abraham; Jerusalem: Magnes, 1978) 16, 26.

The discussion is quite careful in Odil H. Steck, *Der Schöpfungsbericht der Priesterschrift: Studien zur literarkritischen und überlieferungsgeschichtlichen Problematik von Genesis 1,1—2,4a,* FRLANT 115, 95–100. He addresses the creative acts in days two through six, but not in day one. Steck's discussion on p. 237 touches on the question of creation in verse 3. He does not characterize the light as created as such.

201. For translation, see Wintermute, "Jubilees," 1.55.

202. Wintermute, "Jubilees," 1.55 n. i; and van Ruiten, *Primaeval History,* 23–26. Van Ruiten compares this interpretation in Jubilees with the Qumran "Hymn to the Creator" (see below), which as he notes also includes important differences. The latter retains the language of separation in Genesis 1. See James C. VanderKam, "Genesis 1," 300–321, reprinted in VanderKam, *From Revelation to Canon,* 500–521.

203. As noted above, also related to the context of Gen. 1:1–3 is Gen. 2:4b-7. Since scholars (including myself) see Gen. 1:1–3 as similar structurally to Gen. 2:4b-7, then the events in the two passages may be similar. Gen. 2:7 involves creation of the human person, and so it would seem that Gen. 1:3 involves creation of light.

204. Weinfeld, "The Creator God" (ch. 2, n. 2), 120–26; Fishbane, *Biblical Interpretation* (ch. 2, n. 2), 322–26, especially p. 325; and Sommer, *A Prophet Reads Scripture,* 142–43. Fishbane (p. 326) does use the term, "polemical challenge" in the context of this textual relationship, but he puts the stress on interpretational dimension of the response. He comments that Second Isaiah "exegetically reappropriated Gen. 1:1—2:4a and transposed it into a new theological key." Clifford, (*Creation Accounts,* 167–68) positively comments on Fishbane's approach. For cautionary remarks, see de Moor, "Ugarit and the Origins of Job," 227–28.

205. The following texts are cited by Kugel, *Traditions on the Bible,* 47–48. For some of these texts, see also Gregory E. Sterling, "'Day One': Platonizing Traditions of Gen. 1:1–5 in John and Jewish Authors," *SPhilo* 17, 118–40. Milgrom ("The Alleged 'Hidden Light,'" 41) also observes the idea of the hidden, divine light in Jewish sources, such as bT. Hagigah 12a and compares *Gen. Rab.* 3:6, 11:2.

206. Metzger, "The Fourth Book of Ezra," 520.

207. Metzger, "The Fourth Book of Ezra," 536. The brackets (| |) in the translation are the editor's suggestion that the word was added secondarily at some point in antiquity.

208. See Andersen, "2 Enoch," 1.94–97.

209. Andersen, "2 Enoch," 1.144.

210. For example, the Psalms scroll from Cave 11 at Qumran contains a poem known as the "Hymn to the Creator" (11QPs[a], column 16, lines 9–12):

> Great and holy is Yahweh,
> Holy of the holy ones (i.e., the holiest one)
> for generation upon (literally, and) generation (i.e., forever).
> Before Him *glory* goes,
> And after Him, the roar of many waters.
> Mercy and truth surround his *Presence* (literally, face).
> {Truth and} justice and right are the establishment of his throne.
> Separating (*mabdil*) light from *deep darkness*,
> He established dawn by the knowledge of his heart.
> Then the angels saw all of His works and rejoiced,
> For He showed them what they had not known.

See James A. Sanders, *The Psalms Scroll of Qumrân Cave 11: 11QPs[a]*, DJD IV, 89–90; Patrick W. Skehan, "A Liturgical Complex in 11QPs[a]," *CBQ* 35, 195–205; and "Jubilees and the Qumran Psalter," *CBQ* 37, 343–47; and Moshe Weinfeld, "The Angelic Song over the Luminaries in the Qumran Texts," in *Time to Prepare the Way in the Wilderness: Papers in the Qumran Scrolls, STDJ* 16, 131–57. The hymn recalls God's presence in the form of divine procession, which leads into the first act of creation. This initial act of creation involves no creation of light as such, but its separation from "deep darkness" (*'plh*), and not simply "darkness" (*hshk*) found in the biblical account (Gen. 1:4). The poem echoes Gen. 1:4 in using the root "to divide, separate" (*bdl) for separating light from darkness. Preceding the poem's reference to light is God processing in divine glory, described further in terms of the divine presence, literally "face" (on divine "face," *panim*, see ch. 1). The picture of God just before the separation of light from darkness would seem to suggest that the light in this poem is not a creation of God, but uncreated light of the divine presence.

211. Philo (*Creation*, 31) expresses his view of the light in philosophical terms: "That invisible and intelligible light has come into being as image of the divine Logos which communicated its genesis." For this translation and discussion, see Runia, *Philo of Alexandria*, 53 and 168. For a handy translation with the Greek original, see Colson & Whitaker, *Philo: Volume I*, 25. This invisible light preceded the pronouncement of the divine word that made it perceptible as an image of itself. For Philo, the light (*phos*) is in the image (*eikon*) of the word (*logos*). The word, "image," *eikon*, is important for Philo. The word is Philo's term for the relationship between divine word and divine light. Later Philo characterizes the light as the "original intellectual light" that belongs to the "order of the incorporeal world." See Philo, *Creation*, 55. For translation, see Runia, *Philo of Alexandria*, 60; and Colson & Whitaker, *Philo: Volume I*, 43. In this view, this light was not created, as it belongs to the eternal world of day one and not to the sense-perceptible world of days two through six.

212. NRSV. For the light in Genesis 1 and John 1 (as well as *Gen. Rab.* 3:4), see Sterling, "Day One," 118–40; and John Painter, "Rereading Genesis in the Prologue of John," *Neotestamentica et Philonica* (Leiden/Boston: Brill, 2003) 179–201. See also the brief comments in Calum M. Carmichael, *The Story of Creation: Its Origin and Its Interpretation in Philo and the Fourth Gospel* (Ithaca, N.Y.: Cornell University, 1996) 46–47; Elaine H. Pagels, "Exegesis of Genesis 1 in the Gospels of Thomas and John," *JBL* 118, 477–96; and Gregory E. Sterling, "The Place of Philo of Alexandria in the Study of Christian Origins," in *Philo und das Neue Testament. Wechselseitige Wahrnehmungen: I. Internationales Symposium zum Corpus Judaeo-Hellenisticum 1.-4. Mai 2003, Eisenach/Jena*, WUNT 172, 50–51. Note also Gary A. Anderson, "The Interpretation of Genesis 1:1 in the Targums," *CBQ* 52, 21–29.

213. For the notion of the *logos* in Philo and John 1, see Thomas H. Tobin, "The Prologue of John and Hellenistic Wisdom Speculation," *CBQ* 52, 252–69; note also John J. Collins, "Jewish Monotheism and Christian Theology," in *Aspects of Monotheism: How God is One* (edited by Hershel Shanks and Jack Meinhardt; Washington, D. C.: Biblical Archaeology Society, 1997) 92; and Adela Yarbro Collins and John J. Collins, *King and Messiah as Son of God: Divine, Human, and Angelic Messianic Figures in Biblical and Related Literature* (Grand Rapids, Mich.: Eerdmans, 2008) 176–77. For two wide-ranging discussions of the Jewish background of the *logos* in John 1,

see Daniel Boyarin, *Border Lines: The Partition of Judaeo-Christianity* (Philadelphia: University of Pennsylvania Press, 2004) 113–16, 128–47, 296 n. 6; and Eliot R. Wolfson, "Inscribed in the Book of the Living: *Gospel of Truth* and Jewish Christology," *Journal for the Study of Judaism* 38 (2007) 234–71. Note Jesus as the word of God also in Revelation 19:13; see Collins & Collins, *King and Messiah*, 198–201, 211.

214. LSJ 1058, #7.

215. Milgrom ("The Alleged 'Hidden Light,'" 41) cites the idea of the hidden, divine light in Jewish sources, such as bT. Hagigah 12a and he compares *Gen. Rab.* 3:6, 11:2. For further discussion of rabbinic sources for this idea, see Altmann, *Studies*, 128–39. Milgrom (44) rejects the idea and calls the rabbinic notion of the light reserved in God's treasury for the righteous "a beautiful but fanciful midrash." For some of these texts, see also Sterling, "'Day One,'" 118–40.

216. The Zohar is noted in this regard by Milgrom ("The Alleged 'Hidden Light,'" 41). See below for discussion. Medieval Jewish commentators also viewed the light as uncreated, for example Abraham Ibn Ezra in his commentaries on Genesis 1. See *Rabbi Abraham ibn Ezra's Commentary on the Creation*, 13–25, esp. 17 n. 91. For discussion, see Shlomo Sela, "La creacíon del mundo supralinear según Abraham Ibn Ezra: un estudio comparativo de sus dos comparatives a Genesis 1,14," *Sef* 63, 148–81. I wish to thank Mario Gómez for the information about Ibn Ezra.

217. Page 15a, according to the Mantuan text. The translation comes from Matt, *Zohar*, 107. For another convenient translation, see *The Zohar* (Sperling & Simon), 61.

218. Page 16b; Matt, *Zohar*, 123.

219. As pointed out to me by Elliot Wolfson.

220. Compare Judg. 6:39–40: "'Let the fleece be (*yehi*) dry,' and God did so (*wayya'as*) that night."

221. See the remarks of Karl Eberlein, *Gott der Schöpfer—Israels Gott: eine exegetisch-hermeneutische Studie zur theologischen Funktion alttestamentlicher Schöpfungsaussagen*, 2nd. ed., BEATAJ 5, 298–99; and Wilfried Warning, "Terminologische Verknüpfungen in der Urgeschichte," *ZAW* 114/2, 262–69, esp. 266–67.

The closest parallel to the verbs in Gen. 1:3 comes from another priestly narrative quoting a verbal wish on the part of the deity, followed by the recording of the fact that it did take place. In Exod. 7:8–10, Yahweh expresses the wish that the staff become a serpent and the narrative then relates that it so happened, without further action taken by the deity. The pertinent verbal correspondences to Gen. 1:3 in Exod. 7:8–10 are "and Yahweh said. . .' let it (the staff) become a serpent,' . . . and so it became a serpent" (*wayyo'mer yhwh. . . yehi letannin. . . wayhi letannin*). The staff, like the light in Gen. 1:3, already existed. Despite some imprecision in the analogy between the two passages, it might be argued that in both cases, the deity is presented as effecting a transformation by using a prior existing element, light in the case of Gen. 1:3 and the staff in the case of Exod. 7:8–10. From this line of interpretation, this analogy may be read to suggest that light is a preexisting element, given a new purpose in the perceptible universe. As a possible argument against using Exod. 7:8–10 as an analogy to Gen. 1:3, it may be noted that the preexisting element of the staff is turned into a snake, while in the case of Gen. 1:3 there is no second term for light, nor is there anything pre-existent turned into (*l-*) light. In addition, in order to turn the rod into a snake, other actions are commanded and followed by Moses. I wish to thank Baruch Schwartz for directing my attention to some of these differences.

222. Von Rad, *Genesis*, 45, cited by Brown, *Structure, Role, and Ideology*, 249–50.

223. Brown, *Structure, Role, and Ideology*, 249.

224. The connection is implicit at best; note the comment of Westermann (*Genesis 1–11*, 174) about how the light of verse 3 relates to the sun, moon and stars: "P does not answer the question of how these are related to each other." An implicit connection between the day and night with the stars and sun is suggested in Ps. 74:16: "Yours is the day, yours also the night; you established the luminary of the sun." For this psalm, see the discussion in ch. 1 on 12–13, 17–18.

225. There is another aspect of Genesis 1 that points to the light as not created. In the other two verses (verses 9 and 11) where God speaks and an act of creation follows without any verb of making, the act of creation is based on some aspect of reality already present in the universe. In these two instances, both acts take place on day three. In verse 9, "God said, 'Let the water below

the heavens be gathered to one place so that dry land may appear.' And it was so." In this verse the waters already exist. Compare the gathering of the waters by Enki in the Sumerian composition, "Bird and Fish" (Clifford, *Creation Accounts*, 39), where the creation of dry land proceeds not from an act of divine making, but from the waters being collected. In verse 11, "God said: 'Let the earth sprout vegetation' and so it was." Again creation involves a component of reality already in existence, in this case the earth, and there is no divine act of manufacture. Since these two cases of creation involve only a divine act of speech, their narration stands the closest to what we see with the light on day one. They would suggest that just as the waters and the earth are in existence before day three, so also the light exists prior to creation on day one. Viewed from this perspective, the light in the immediate context of Genesis 1 appears not to be created.

226. The connection appears already in Benno Jacob, *Das Buch Genesis: Übersetzt und erklärt* (Berlin: Schocken Verlag, 1934); repr. as *Das erste Buch der Tora: Genesis* (Stuttgart: Calwer, 2000) 67. See also Martin Buber, "Der Mensch von heute und die Jüdische Bibel," in *Die Schrift und ihre Verdeutschung* (edited by Martin Buber and Franz Rosenzweig; Berlin: Schocken, 1936) 13–45, here 40–45; and Franz Rosenzweig, "Das Formgeheimnis der biblischen Erzählungen," in *Die Schrift und ihre Verdeutschung*, 239–61, here 254. Note also Martin Buber, *Die Schrift und ihre Verdeutschung* (Berlin: Schocken, 1961) 39–40.

227. This relationship between Genesis 1 and Exodus 39–40 has been addressed by several scholars: Joseph Blenkinsopp. "The Structure of P," *CBQ* 38, 275–92, here 280; and *Prophecy and Canon: A Contribution to the Study of Jewish Origins* (Notre Dame, Ind.: University of Notre Dame Press, 1977) 54–79, here 60–69; Peter J. Kearney, "Creation and Liturgy: The P Redaction of Ex 25–40," *ZAW* 89, 375–87; Moshe Weinfeld, "Sabbath" (ch. 1, n. 119), 501–12; Levenson, *Creation*, 78–87; Blum, *Studien*, 306; Janowski, "Tempel" (ch. 1, n. 119), 37–69; and *idem*, "Der Tempel als Kosmos: Zur kosmologischen Bedeutung des Tempels in der Umwelt Israels," in *Egypt—Temple of the Whole World/Ägypten—Tempel der gesamten Welt: Studies in honour of Jan Assmann* (edited by Sibylle Meyer; Leiden/Boston: Brill, 2003) 163–186; Brown, *Ethos*, 77–78, 82–89; Hanna Liss, "The Imagining Sanctuary: The Priestly Code as an Example of Fictional Literature in the Hebrew Bible," in *Judah and the Judeans in the Persian Period* (edited by Oded Lipschits and Manfred Oeming; Winona Lake, Ind.: Eisenbrauns, 2006) 675–76; and van Leeuwen, "Cosmos" (ch. 1, n. 72), 67–90, esp. 75–76. These scholars characterize the relationship as one of likeness between descriptions of building temples and creating the world.

Kearney further suggests that seven divine instructions in Exodus 25–31 correspond to the seven days of creation in Genesis 1. For criticism of this proposal, see Levenson, *Creation*, 83.

Note also the comments of Milgrom ("The Alleged 'Hidden Light,'" 42), which compare the light of Genesis 1 with "the lampstand of tabernacle" in Exod. 35:14, 28, 39:27 and Num. 4:9, 16, and with the "oil of the luminary" in Exod. 25:6, 27:20, 35:8 and Lev. 25:2. Note also Thomas Römer, "Le Pentateuch toujours en question. Bilan et perspectives après un quart de siècle de débat," in *Congress Volume: Basel 2001*, VTSup 92, 351–52, esp. n. 27.

In connection with the comparison of Genesis 1 and Exodus 39–40, we may note a late Akkadian creation account that ends with the gods moving into their temple-dwelling on earth; see Foster, *Muses*, 494.

228. These parallels are laid out by a number of these scholars, including Levenson, *Creation*, 85–86; Blum, *Studien*, 306–7; and Liss, "The Imagining Sanctuary," 676.

229. If the comparison really works, then one should explain why *'or* is used in Gen. 1:3 instead of *kabod*. Three reasons may be suggested. First, in the immediate context, *'or* resonates well with, and anticipates, *me'orot* in Gen. 1:14. Second, *'or* is used theophanically elsewhere (as in Ps. 104:1b-2, discussed further below); so perhaps the use of "light" follows this usage. Third, *'or* connects to a theme central to the program of the priestly writer (to be discussed below).

230. Milgrom ("The Alleged 'Hidden Light,'" 43) compares Ps. 104:2 (like many commentators), and adds 2 Sam. 23:4, Eccles. 12:2, and Isa. 30:26. For Ps. 104, see ch. 1, pp. 23–24.

231. See pp. 26–27.

232. Note the verb "to stretch out," also a reference to creation in Isa. 42:5 and 44:24 as well as Job 9:8 and 26:7. See Norman Habel, "'He Who Stretches out the Heavens'," *CBQ* 34, 417–30.

233. This idea appears in Job 37:18: "Can you make a firmament like Him (God) for the heavens, strong as a mirror of cast metal?" The association with metal is suggested by Phoenician *mrq'*

(KAI 38:1) made of gold, perhaps a bowl or plate; see *DNSWI* 696; and Charles R. Krahmalkov, *Phoenician-Punic Dictionary*, OLA 90, 313. For speculations about such an idea of a cosmic dome in Mesopotamian cosmology, see the critical remarks by Wilfred Lambert, "The Pair Lahmu—Lahamu in Cosmology," *Or* 54, 202. Compare the discussion of the Esharra in *Enuma Elish* IV 143–146, as understood by Alisdair Livingstone, *Mystical and Mythological Explanatory Works of Assyrian and Babylonian Scholars* (Oxford: Clarendon, 1986) 80–81. Note that the lower heaven is made of jasper with stars on it, according to VAT 8917, obverse, line 33; see Livingstone, *Mystical and Mythological*, 82–83, 86.

234. Some occasionally question the comparison. For example, the great giant of German biblical scholarship of the twentieth century, Gerhard von Rad, dismissed the comparison of this psalm with Gen. 1:3. He expressed his objections in these terms: "In contrast to a few freer poetic declarations (Ps. 104.2), here [in Gen. 1:3] the creatureliness even of light is emphasized. It is not somehow an overflow of the essence of deity but rather an object, even though preferential, of God's creation." Von Rad, *Genesis*, 49. The parallel has been noted by other scholars, though without a discussion of the implications that the comparison may hold for interpreting the light in Gen. 1:3; see Levenson, *Creation*, 55; and Milgrom, "The Alleged 'Hidden Light,'" 43. In von Rad's view, Ps. 104:1b-2 is not to be associated with the light in Gen. 1:3, despite the fact that both involve light relating to God at the beginning of creation. To be sure, there are differences between the two texts, as we saw in ch. 1, but there is no reason to disconnect their use of the same word for light. Psalm 104, with its long description of divine creation, represents the light at the beginning of creation as God's own light. In view of the overall similarities between Psalm 104 and Genesis 1, it seems reasonable to conclude that the light of Gen. 1:3 is in fact the divine light which is not created on day one.

235. Yair Zakovitch, *Mashmia' shalom mevasser tob: shiv'ah pirqe hazon lišlom yerushalayim* (Jerusalem/Haifa: University of Haifa, 2004) 39–40 (reference courtesy of Gary Anderson); compare the older study of May, "The Creation of Light," 211. The classic idea of *Urzeit* being reflected in descriptions of *Endzeit* goes back to the late nineteenth century work by the great German scholar Hermann Gunkel. He noted the relationship between several motifs in accounts of creation and in descriptions of the future in apocalyptic literature. The book has appeared recently in English as *Creation and Chaos in the Primeval Era and the Eschaton. A Religio-Historical Study of Genesis 1 and Revelation 12* (trans. and with a preface by K. William Whitney, Jr.; foreword by Peter Machinist; Grand Rapids: Eerdmans, 2006). Compare the following comments of Culler (*Literary Theory*, 84) about narrative: "A mere sequence does not make a story. There must be an end relating to the beginning—according to some theorists, an end that indicates that what has happened to the desire that led to the events in the first place."

236. See also Isa. 24:23 and note Rev. 21:23 and 22:5.

237. So Meyers & Meyers, *Zechariah 9–14*, 433. See their discussion more broadly on 432–34.

238. For the connections between Genesis 1 and Ezekiel 1, see Ben Zion Wacholder, "Creation in Ezekiel's *merkabah*: Ezekiel 1 and Genesis 1," in *Of Scribes and Sages: Early Jewish Interpretation and Transmission of Scripture. Volume 1: Ancient Versions and Traditions* (edited by Craig A. Evans; Studies in Scripture in Early Judaism and Christianity, vol. 9; Library of Second Temple Studies, vol. 50; London/New York: T & T Clark, 2004) 14–32, here 18–22. Noting the connections, Wacholder draws few conclusions except that Ezekiel 1 adumbrates what is presented in Genesis 1. The reference to the throne (Ezek. 1:26) locates this scene inside the heavenly temple where God is enthroned. God is on the divine throne "above the firmament" (Ezek. 1:25–26), "above the earth" (1:21; compare Ps. 150:1 and Job 22:12). Ezekiel 1:27 mentions God's fiery appearance, in other words divine theophanic light, not the sun or the moon, but God's own light. It is the divine light of the future that is to transform the world as known to Israel. As such, this light is at once like and unlike any light perceptible to human beings. (I want to thank Stephen Cook for this point.) In short, Ezekiel 1 presents a mysterious description of God brilliant in light and enthroned in the heavenly temple. With these descriptions from Ezekiel as well as well Isa. 60:19 and Zech. 14:6–7, we need to be aware that this is no ordinary light. We might even say that this is an otherworldly or mystical light. It is a divine, noncreated light.

Ezekiel's presentation echoes older theophanic traditions that represent the divine cherub chariot surrounded by brilliant light (as in Ps. 18:10–12 [MT 11–13] = 2 Sam. 22:11–13). Compare also the light of the divine theophany in Hab. 3:4. For the idea of the heavenly temple on the top of God's mountain on earth, see the description in Exod. 24:9–11. One may compare the pavement of sapphire of Exod. 24:10 with the gleam of sapphire in the account of Ezek. 1:26. Both may belong to the construction of the heavenly temple. The precious stone in these passages for the heavenly palace appears in the Songs of the Sabbath Sacrifice (ShirShabb) from Qumran and in the Book of Revelation (21:11; note also 4:6, 15:2); see Mark S. Smith, "Biblical and Canaanite Notes to the Songs of the Sabbath Sacrifice from Qumran," *RevQ* 12, 585–88.

Genesis 1 mentions some of the features in Ezekiel 1, including God and the light, the cosmic waters and the firmament. At the same time, Genesis 1 does not provide much description of them. Ezekiel 1 shows that the priestly tradition was aware of this idea of God enthroned above the firmament, but Genesis 1 makes no mention of these details. Yet as a member of the priestly tradition, its author probably knew of these matters. Perhaps then the writer implicitly understood the mention of light in v. 3 as proceeding from this heavenly temple to the perceptible universe that is only darkness in creation in v. 2. I will return below to the question of why the author of Genesis 1 did not make the picture of the light more explicit. However, for the moment we may observe that the light and the cosmic waters mentioned in Ezekiel's description inform Genesis 1 as well.

239. Ezekiel 43:2 describes the procession of divine glory, with its light: "There, the glory (*kabod*) of the God of Israel was coming from the direction of the east, And his voice was like the sound of the mighty waters, And the earth was lit up (°'*wr*) from his glory." This verse describes the prophetic vision of the divine "glory" (or "effulgence") that lights up the world. According to Ezek. 43:4–5, this "glory" will enter the Jerusalem temple. In this description, this passage connects the divine "effulgence" (*kabod*) with the temple. Behind Ezekiel's presentation lies the traditional association of divine light and presence in the temple. A particularly good example of this is Psalm 36, which describes experience of God in the temple. In this context, verse 10 declares: "In your light we see light." Psalm 27 provides another case. Verse 1 calls God "my light," and vv. 4–7 describe the speaker's desire to be in God's temple. The psalmists were generally familiar with the idea that God was manifest in divine glory and light in the temple. Beyond the Psalms, divine light is a generally recognized feature of God (see Job 25:3; compare Dan. 2:22: "light dwells with him"). Ezekiel 43 plays off this notion in its description.

240. Clifford, *Creation Accounts*, 28.

241. Chapter 1 also describes this text in connection with the tradition of creation in texts such as Ps. 74:12–17; see 12–13, 17–18. In ch. 5, I return to the larger literary significance of the comparison; see 148, 157–58.

242. Speiser, *Genesis*, 10. Speiser adopted this list of correspondences from Alexander Heidel, *The Babylonian Genesis: The Story of Creation* (second edition; Chicago/London: The University of Chicago Press, 1951) 129. See also Clifford, *Creation Accounts*, 140.

243. The Akkadian reads as follows:

```
101   marī UTU marī UTU
102   marī šamši šamši ša ilī
103   labiš melammi ešret ilī šaqîš etpur
104   pulḫātu ḫaššāsina elīšu kamra
```

For the fourth line, see *CAD* K:113 *sub kamāru 1c*. Cf. Jean Bottéro and Samuel Noah Kramer, *Lorsque les dieux faisaient l'homme. Mythologie mésopotamienne* (Paris: Gallimard, 1989) 609. I wish to thank Avigdor Hurowitz for availing me of his notes to these passages.

244. Translation from Benjamin Foster, "Epic of Creation (1.111)," in *COS* 1.392; cf. *ANET* 62.

245. The presentation of the god resumes (tablet IV, lines 57–58), shortly before he engages Tiamat in battle: "He was garbed in a ghastly armored garment./On his head he was covered with terrifying auras." The Akkadian reads:

```
57   naḫlapta āpluḫti pulḫati ḫalipma
58   melammī rašubbāti aper rāšuššu
```

The translation comes from Foster, "Epic of Creation (1.111)," *COS* 1.397. Foster's translation captures something of the alliteration of the original, on which see Speiser, *ANET* 66 n. 67. See also Bottéro & Kramer, *Lorsque les dieux faisaient l'homme*, 627.

This passage, too, describe Marduk's appearance, both passages use the words, "aura" (*melammu*) and "fear" (*puluḫtu*). The classic treatment of these theophanic terms is A. Leo Oppenheim, "Akkadian *pul(u)ḫ(t)u* and *melammu*," *JAOS* 63, 31–34. The two passages also share the verb, "to provide with a headdress" (*apāru*); *CAD A/2*:166. For the root and its forms in these two passages, see *AHw* 57; *CAD A/2*:166. The G-stem form is used also for the *melammu* of Adad-nirari II (cited in *CAD A/2*:167a).

246. Compare the same root in Isa. 59:17 and 63:1, and in Ps. 93:1. I thank Jeffrey Tigay for suggesting these parallels.

247. Although Mesopotamia provides very rich resources for creation stories outside the Bible, it is hardly the only culture outside of Israel to contain creation stories. Closer to ancient Israel, the site of Ugarit produced an important excerpt of creation. The text is presented in a handy edition by Lewis, "Birth," 205–14; see also Smith, *Sacrificial Rituals*.

This text contains an account of how the major god, El, fathered children at the dawn of time. These children included the deities, Dawn and Dusk. The relevant section involves lines 49–54, which describes El's sexual relations, the children's births, and their birth-announcement:

> He bends down, kisses their lips,
> See how sweet their lips are,
> Sweet as pomegranates.
> As he kisses, there's conception,
> As he embraces, there's passion.
> The two cr[ouch and] give birth
> to Dawn and Dusk.
> Word to El was brought:
> "El's [two wi]ves have given birth."
> "What have they born?"
> "A new-born pair, Dawn and Dusk."
> "Make an offering to Lady Sun,
> And to the stationary stars."

This passage presents the beginning and end of the day as two deities. In the Ugaritic texts, this pair is one of three sets of day-markers represented as deities. In addition to Dawn and Dusk, the sun and the moon as well as the morning and evening stars (Athtart and Athar) are divinities marking day and night. Evidently they are also all children of the god El. In the context of the quote above, Dawn and Dusk may be the last of these astral deities born to El, since the Sun and stars are presumed to be there at the time of the birth-announcement. As a divine child, Dawn is construed as divine in nature. It is understood as the divine light within the context of this creation excerpt. A further detail in this account pertinent to our discussion is the understanding of the sun and moon. As divinities, their light is likewise divine. This text seems to show then the older West Semitic tradition of divine lights inherited by ancient Israel as expressed in the biblical texts discussed above.

248. Before concluding, we may note that in Ugaritic, light is represented as a divinity. One Ugaritic list of gods and goddesses pairs divine "light" (*nr*) with divine "glory" or "effulgence" (*kbd*) KTU 1.123.16. In line 21 of the same text, *kbd* is followed by *d 'il*, and may mean "*kbd* of the god"; see Pardee, *Ritual and Cult*, 151–52, which leaves *kbd* untranslated; see also Pardee, *Les textes rituels*, 1.694, 702. See also *DUL* 426–27.

This light was known as divine outside the Bible in both Mesopotamian and Ugaritic sources. Cf. light as one of the children in the divine genealogy in *The Phoenician History* of Philo of Byblos, as preserved in Eusebius' *Praep. Ev.* 1.10.9. See Attridge & Oden, *Philo*, 40–41.

249. Earlier we noted von Rad's objections to the comparison of Gen. 1:3 with Ps. 104:2–3. In order to fully entertain the question, I mention what I could imagine would be further objections. One might point to differences between the presentations of divine light in other biblical passages and the light of Gen. 1:3. For example, the light is presented explicitly in Psalm 104 metaphorically as the god's theophanic garment. Gen. 1:3 does not present the light in this manner. Instead, it is placed within the structure of creative acts. Another argument that might be marshaled in favor of the light as created is that Gen. 1:3 does not present it in terms of the conventional priestly terms of

"glory" (*kabod*), as in Exodus 39–40 and Ezek. 43, which moves perceptibly in the form of a theophany. However, the light ('*or*) of day one in Gen. 1:3 corresponds to the "lights" (*me'orot*) of day four, and it is not designed to be a moving light in the manner of a theophany. For these reasons, these sorts of objections do not seem compelling.

250. Bille & Sørensen, "Luminosity" (ch. 1, n. 35) 263–84.

251. Bille & Sørensen, "Luminosity," 280. Their italics.

252. Bille & Sørensen, "Luminosity," 263.

253. So the Greek and Latin versions in closely following the Hebrew; see Wevers, *Genesis*, 75; and *Notes on the Greek Text of Genesis*, 2. For the Latin variants, see Beuron, *Genesis*, 7–8; and Fischer et al., *Biblical Sacra: Iuxta Vulgatam Versionem*, 1.4. For details see J. N. Ford, "Ninety-nine by the Evil Eye and One from Natural Causes": KTU2 1.96 in its Near Eastern Context, *Ugarit Forschungen* 30 (1998) 202, 218–22, esp. 221–22 n. 69.

This approach for verse 4 is defended grammatically by Pardee (*Ritual and Cult*, 165 n. 16), who says that the word "that" here "introduces a nominal object clause of the verb of perception; it has no particular emphatic function." Here Pardee is evidently responding to a traditional view of the so-called "asseverative *kaph*." See Robert Gordis, "The Asseverative Kaph in Ugaritic and Hebrew," *JAOS* 63, 176–78, 181. For sophisticated treatments of the Hebrew particle *ki*, see A. Aejmelaeus, "Function and Interpretation of כ in Biblical Hebrew," *JBL* 105, 193–209; Barry Bandstra, "The Syntax of the Particle KY in Biblical Hebrew and Ugaritic" (Ph.D. dissertation, Yale University, 1982); W. T. Claassen, "Speaker-Oriented Functions of *ki* in Biblical Hebrew," *JNSL* 11, 29–46; and Tamar Zewi, "Subordinate Nominal Clauses Involving Prolepsis in Biblical Hebrew," *JSS* 41, 1–20. The same construction appears in Gen. 49:15, also introduced by a verb of visual perception: "And he saw security that it was good, and the earth that it was lovely." This case in Gen. 49:15 stands closer to the Ugaritic example that Pardee (*Ritual and Cult*, 165 n. 16) compares with Gen. 1:4, namely KTU 1.96.2: "she/it saw her/its brother that he was good, her/its brother that he was lovely."

254. Compare the theme of separation of heaven and earth in Mesopotamian creation accounts. For examples, see the introduction to "Gilgamesh, Enkidu and the Underworld" (discussed in Clifford, *Creation Accounts*, 23), "Praise of the Pickax" (Clifford, *Creation Accounts*, 30), and KAR 4 (Clifford, *Creation Accounts*, 49). In these cases, separation applies to heaven and earth. By comparison, Genesis 1 applies this notion widely to various aspects of creation.

255. For the context of this verse, see James L. Crenshaw, "W^edōrēk 'al-bâmotê 'âreṣ," *CBQ* 34, 39–53. Amos 5:8 uses a similar formulation, that God "turns deep darkness into morning." Compare Job 12:22: God "brings deep darkness to light."

256. The combination °*qr' l*- appears for naming the stars in Ps. 147:4; compare also the verb-preposition combination in Gen. 2:19–20 (the possible implications of this comparison are explored in ch. 4). Does the verb "he called" (*qara*') bear any further nuance? In context it does not seem to do so; still I am reminded of the verb's cosmic usage in Ps. 42:8: "Deep to Deep calls (*tehom 'el tehom qore'*)."

257. For the sequence of morning and evening, see also Isa. 21:12; note also morning and evening in parallelism, for example in Gen. 49:27.

258. This point has been emphasized by many commentators. For example, see Robert V. McCabe, "A Defense of Literal Days in the Creation Week," *Detroit Baptist Seminary Journal* 5 (2000) 97–123; David M. Fouts, "Selected Lexical and Grammatical Studies in Genesis I," *AUSS* 42, 79–90; and Walter M. Booth, "¿Son los días de Génesis 1 literales o no literals?" *Theo* 19, 2–41.

259. See also Aramaic *bywm ḥd* in Cowley 15:28, translated "on a certain day" (*DNWSI* 1.33) or "on one day" (Bezalel Porten et al., *The Elephantine Papyri in English: Three Millennia of Cross-Cultural Continuity and Change* [Leiden/New York/Köln: Brill, 1996] 182).

Contrast *yom 'ehad* in Gen. 27:45, 33:13, Lev. 22:28, 1 Kings 20:29, Isa. 9:13, 10:17, 47:9, 66:8, Zech. 3:9, Esther 3:13, 8:12 in the sense of "a single day" (see also Jon. 3:4 and 2 Chron. 28:6) and in 1 Sam. 2:34 for "the same day" (NJPS). First Samuel 27:1 uses the expression in an indefinite manner, "some day" (NJPS), and it means "one day" in the sense of "single" ("and one day [became like two days]") in Ben Sira B manuscript 46:4 as completed by the versions (LXX: *kai mia hēmera egenēthē pros duo*). Note also Zech. 14:7 for "a continuous day"; this case strikes me as a possible echo of the usage in Gen. 1:5 (see sec. 5 below for discussion). Note the expression in Neh. 5:18 for "each day"; cf. the Vulgate *quotidie* in Neh. 5:15, as noted in BHS and regarded as exegetical in the edition of David Marcus, *Biblia Hebraica quinta editione: Ezra and Nehemiah* (Stuttgart: Deutsche Bibelgesellschaft, 2006) 54.

All told, the expression *yom 'ehad* is hardly uncommon in the Hebrew Bible (23 times including Ben Sira B 46:4). See *DCH I*, 180, 182–83.

260. The biblical parallels indicates that *yom 'ehad* in Gen. 1:5 means "day one" as the first day in the sequence and not simply "a day." Contrast Peter Weimar, "Struktur und Komposition der priesterschriftlichen Schöpfungserzählung (Gen 1,1—2,4a)," in *Ex Mesopotamia et Syria Lux: Festschrift für Manfried Dietrich zu seinem 65. Geburtstag*, AOAT 281, 816, republished in Peter Weimar, *Studien zur Priesterschrift*, FAT I.56, 191–234, esp. 127; and Andrew E. Steinmann, "אחד as an Ordinal Number and the Meaning of Genesis 1:5," *JETS* 45, 577–84.

261. In contrast to the phrase, "on the first day" (*bayyom hari'shon*), in Lev. 23:7, 35, 39, 40 and Num. 28:18.

262. The text in question is KTU 1.115.14, conveniently presented by Pardee, *Ritual and Cult*, 66–67; see also Pardee, *Les textes rituels*, 1.643–44, 650–51. The *editio princeps* was published by Charles Virolleaud in *Ugaritica V* (Mission de Ras Shamra, vol. XVI; Paris: Imprimerie Nationale/ Geuthner, 1968) 586–88.

263. Pardee, *Ritual and Cult*, 107 n. 84. See also Pardee, *Les textes rituels*, 1.650–51. Baruch A. Levine, in contrast, stresses that Ugaritic *ym 'ahd* here does mean "the first day." See Levine, *In the Presence of the Lord*, SJLA 5, 11 n. 23. Compare "day six" for "sixth day" in CAT 1.78.1.

264. For further discussion, see the older study of Loren Fisher, "An Ugaritic Ritual and Genesis I, 1–5," in *Ugaritica VI*, 197–205. Fisher proposes a broader parallel between Gen. 1:1–5 and this ritual: Gen. 1:1–2 and lines 1–3 as "circumstance"; Gen. 1:3–5a and lines 4–13 as "action"; and Gen. 1:5b and line 14 as "time clause." The force of the parallel structure depends in part in seeing the initial word in the ritual, *'id*, as meaning "when" and not "at that time" (so Pardee) or the like. In the first translation, Fisher is followed by Levine, *In the Presence of the Lord*, 10; see also *DUL* 16. At the same time, even if *'id* means "at that time" or the like, the opening line does involve a term of temporal "circumstance" like Gen. 1:1.

265. That this is a particularly ritual usage in the Ugaritic texts is suggested by the fact that it never occurs in the literary texts, which for "first day" simply use the word for "a day" (*ym*). This usage occurs, for example, in the seven-day counting formula for the construction of Baal's palace in the Baal Cycle in KTU 1.4 VI 24. See Smith, "The Baal Cycle," 133. Compare *bym pr'* in an administrative context (KTU 4.279.1), which might be rendered "on the first day" or "on the day of the first (fruit)"; see *DUL* 679. For the counting of the other ritual days from the second through the seventh, Genesis 1 otherwise use ordinals, like Ugaritic and biblical rituals (see Num. 29:17, 20, 23, 26, 29, 32; see also Deut. 16:8).

266. Fisher, "An Ugaritic Ritual," 200. Fisher speaks of a "ritual tradition." Levine (*In the Presence of the Lord*, 11 n. 23) instead emphasizes the calendrical formula involved in both; this conclusion fits with a number of the other biblical attestations of *yom 'ehad* noted above. Without positing a liturgical background as Fisher does (note here Levine's criticisms), it is possible that a liturgical tradition with its calendrical reckoning has informed the literary production of Gen. 1:1–5.

267. On the "ritual style" of the priestly author, see Liss, "The Imagining Sanctuary," 674–76.

268. As suggested by Israel Knohl; see Knohl, *Sanctuary*, 18, 104, 125 n. 4, 137. This is Knohl's "Holiness Redaction." Note also Firmage, "Genesis 1," 97–114. See also Carr, *Reading the Fractures*, 62–68, 122, 316–17.

269. Compare Prov. 6:23: "a commandment is a lamp, and teaching (*torah*) is a light." See also light as an image for the moral situation of humans in relation to Yahweh in Isa. 50:10: "Who among you reveres Yahweh and heeds the voice of his servant? Whoever walks in darkness and has no light, let him trust in the name of Yahweh and depend upon his god."

270. See also Mic. 7:8: "Though I dwell in darkness, Yahweh is a light for me." Compare also Mic. 7:9; Job 12:25, 29:3, 33:28, 30.

271. In Isa. 42:6 and 49:6, Israel is called by God to serve as "a light to the nations," by bringing knowledge and salvation of God. For an older discussion of these verses, see Mark S. Smith, "*Běrît 'ām/běrît 'ôlām*: A New Proposal for the Crux of Isaiah 42:6," *JBL* 100, 241–43.

272. Psalm 19:2–7 discusses the divine glory spoken about by the heavens, then vv. 8–11 praise the teaching of the Lord, which in the words of v. 9 "illuminates the eyes." The glory of God known to the heavens parallels the divine teaching known to humans (compare "in your light we see light," in Ps. 36:10).

273. For this reference, I am indebted to Geza Vermes, "The Torah is a Light," *VT* 8, 436–38.

274. For the idea of secret knowledge in Israelite priestly literature, see Chaim Cohen, "Was the P Document Secret?" *JANESCU* 1/2, 39–44. See also Yaakov Ellman, "Authoritative Oral Tradition in Neo-Assyrian Scribal Circles," *JANESCU* 7, 19–32. For secret knowledge in Mesopotamia, see Karel van der Toorn, *Scribal Culture and the Making of the Hebrew Bible* (Cambridge, Mass./ London: Harvard University, 2007) 65–66, 104, 219–21; for both Mesopotamia and Israel, see Lenzi, *Secrecy*; for priestly material in the Hebrew Bible, see in particular 277–97, esp. 288–89. Against Cohen, Lenzi stresses the ultimately public purpose of this literature and notes the lack of data for the idea of secret knowledge for the priestly material. I agree. However, the lack of data does not preclude Cohen's basic claim that there may well have been a prior and contemporary private background for some priestly literature. A lack of data is precisely what might be expected for secret or private material. Moreover, such secret priestly material is well in keeping with the comparative evidence from Mesopotamia marshaled by Lenzi. The further development of public priestly material in the Hebrew Bible may represent an inner-Israelite development, not entirely a major cultural feature of ancient Israel.

275. See the study of this verse by Michael Segal, "The Responsibilities and Rewards of Joshua the High Priest according to Zechariah 3:7," *JBL* 126, 717–34. Segal's interpretation of the verb *tadin* in light of Akkadian *dunnunu*, "to strengthen, to increase, to reinforce," is persuasive.

For the end of the verse, Segal does not adopt the usual sort of translation. Literally I would render: "then I will give you access among *those standing there*" (NJPS: "and I will permit you to move about among *these attendants*"; cf. NRSV: "then I will give you the right of access among those *who are standing here*"). Segal instead proposes: "then I will grant you (people) who walk among *these pillars.*" A revocalization for the final noun to "pillars" is required, which seems less convincing.

276. Judges 3:19, 1 Sam. 20:25; compare Gen. 18:8; Exod. 18:13, 14; and Dan. 7:16.

277. For discussion of the divine council in 1 Kings 22:19, KTU 1.2 I and other biblical and West Semitic texts, see Smith, *The Ugaritic Baal Cycle*, 295. For a convenient presentation of the text and translation of 1.2 I, see Smith, "The Baal Cycle," 98–101.

278. Compare the notion of royal ascent, discussed by Bernard Lang, *The Hebrew God: Portrait of an Ancient Deity* (New Haven/London: Yale University Press, 2002) 20. If Lang is correct, this royal background is suggestive for the situation with the priesthood.

279. For the lamps and the lampstand, see Carol L. Meyers, *The Tabernacle Menorah* (American School of Oriental Studies Dissertation Series, vol. 2; Missoula, Mont.: Scholars Press, 1976) 18, 26, 32–33, 166–68. For the Tabernacle's lamp, see also William H. C. Propp, *Exodus 19–40*, AB 2A, 398–401, 509–12. For a common household lamp, compare Jer. 25:10: "the light of the lamp" (for the parallelism of "light" and "lamp," see Prov. 13:9). In the context of discussing the Tabernacle lamp, Propp (p. 512) mentions the light of Gen. 1:3, and his heading for the section (p. 509) is likewise fitting for the light in Genesis 1: "The Light Shineth in the Darkness: The Lampstand." It would seem reasonable to suppose that the priestly writer made the connection between the Temple lamp and God's light on day one. It would be quite speculative to suggest that the seven-branched structure of the lampstand with three pairs of lamps on either side in Exod. 25:32 and 37:18 (see 37:21 for the three pairs of branches) corresponds to the structure of Genesis 1 with its three pairs of days plus its seventh day (specifically days one to three corresponding to days four through six), and that this parallel influenced the priestly writer's arrangement of days in Genesis 1. See also p. 253 n. 19.

280. It has been thought that Egyptian religious influence may underlie this practice. See Keel & Uehlinger, *Gods*, 353. Solar practice hardly requires an Egyptian background; at the same time, it is not precluded.

281. This is what some scholars have dubbed "solarized Yahwism." This solarized Yahwism would fit into the larger picture of Israelite religion. For discussion, see Smith, "Solar Language" (ch. 1, n. 35), 29–39. Such solarized devotion also would fit into the monarchic worldview. According to the royal ritual language of Ps. 110:3, the king on his coronation is to "go forth toward the dawn"; for this understanding, see William P. Brown, "A Royal Performance: Critical Notes on Psalm 110:3a-b," *JBL* 117, 93–96.

282. Malachi 4:2 [MT 3:20] may represent a metaphorical response that gets away from the sort of solar devotion suggested by Ezek. 8:16: "But for you who revere my name the sun of righteousness shall rise, with healing in its wings" (NRSV). The sun is still part of the imagery, but the imagery may involve no formal devotion.

283. Compare the view of Ibn Ezra that Genesis 1 was written for laypeople, not about supernal matters, but about sublunar realities. In his view laypeople could not grasp matters pertaining to the supernal realm. For this information I thank Mariano Gómez Ariano.

284. For discussion of the pertinent texts from the Dead Sea Scrolls, see Philip Alexander, *The Mystical Texts* (Companion to the Dead Sea Scrolls; London: T & T Clark International, 2005). Note also the briefer discussion in Smith, "Biblical and Canaanite Notes" 585–88. For the broader context, see Elliot R. Wolfson, "Seven Mysteries of Knowledge: Qumran Esotericism Recovered," in *The Idea of Biblical Interpretation: Essays in Honor of James L. Kugel* (edited by Hindy Najman and Julie H. Newman; Leiden/Boston: Brill, 2004) 177–213; and Peter Schäfer, *The Origins of Jewish Mysticism* (Tübingen: Mohr Siebeck, 2009). I recognize the difficulty with the terms "mystical" and "mysticism." For a helpful discussion, see Schäfer, *The Origins of Jewish Mysticism*, 1–26.

285. For secret knowledge in Mesopotamia in general, see the extensive survey of material in Lenzi, *Secrecy*, 67–219. Simo Parpola has made strong claims for mysticism in Neo-Assyrian royal sources in his essay, "The Assyrian Tree of Life: Tracing the Origins of Jewish Monotheism and Greek Philosophy," *JNES* 52, 161–208, and his book, *Assyrian Prophecies* SAA IX, xv–xliv. Parpola compares the structures of neo-Assyrian state theology with forms of Jewish Kabbalistic speculation. Parpola's work in this area has been strongly criticized by Jerrold Cooper, "Assyrian Prophecies, the Assyrian Tree, and the Mesopotamian Origins of Jewish Monotheism, Greek Philosophy, Christian Theology, Gnosticism, and Much More," *JAOS* 120, 430–43. Compare the responses by Barbara Nevling Porter in *BO* 61, 685–90; and Ithamar Gruenwald, "'How Much Qabbalah in Ancient Assyria?'—Methodological Reflections on the Study of a Cross-Cultural Phenomenon," in *Assyria 1995: Proceedings of the 10th Anniversary Symposium of the Neo-Assyrian Text Corpus Project. Helsinki, September 7–11, 1995* (edited by Simo Parpola and Robert M. Whiting; Helsinki: The Neo-Assyrian Text Corpus Project, 1997) 115–27. Despite criticisms, Parpola's work challenges the field to give thought to Assyrian religious expression and its possible heuristic value for exploring other systems of ancient thought.

286. See Altmann's discussion, especially of Bereshit Rab. 3:4 (with variants), in *Studies*, 129–30.

Chapter 3: The First Week

1. The specifically priestly elements from Genesis 1 strongly feature in days one, six, and seven, and the nonpriestly material concentrates in days two through five. This corresponds somewhat also with the use of the verb, "to make" (°*'sh*), as opposed to the verb, "to create" (°*br'*). Day five in fact uses both verbs. The summaries at the end of the story include both verbs (see 2:2–3 as well as 2:4a). Apart from the use of the seven-day structure and the emphasis on divine speech throughout, the priestly features of this account strongly cluster on days one and seven. On °*br'*, see ch. 2, especially pp. 48 and 224 n. 59.

2. It should be noted that two manuscripts of Genesis (4QGenesis[b] and 4QGenesis[g]) in the Dead Sea Scrolls as well as the medieval Masoretic texts mark the end of each day of creation with an open section. See Emanuel Tov, *Scribal Practices and Approaches Reflected in the Texts Found in the Judean Desert*, STDJ 54, 157.

3. The relevant texts are: KTU 1.4 VI 24–31 (*UNP*, 133–34); 1.14 V 3–8 (*UNP*, 20); 1.17 I 5–16 (*UNP*, 51–52); 1.22 I 21–26 (*UNP*, 204); see also 1.16 V 9–23 (*UNP*, 37–38). These passages generally show no concern for clarifying the exact time when the action takes place on the seventh day.

The exception is 1.14 III 3–4 and 14–15, which explicitly name the time of day on the seventh. These two exceptions also show that sometime during the seventh day is intended by reference to the seventh day, a point that applies to Gen. 2:1–3 (see further below).

KTU 1.4 VI 24–33, which describes the final phase of the building of Baal's palace over the course of seven days, was compared with Genesis 1 by Loren R. Fisher, "Creation at Ugarit and in the Old Testament," *VT* 15, 313–24. Fisher maintained that because of the resemblances, the building of Baal's palace is to be regarded as a "cosmogony" or a creation account. However, the palace construction is not a creation account. Rather, it is the description of creation in Genesis 1 that looks somewhat like temple building as we see it in the account of Baal's house.

Older research on this motif includes the studies of Samuel Loewenstamm, "The Seven-Day Unit in Ugaritic Epic Literature," *IEJ* 15, 122–33, reprinted in his volume of studies entitled *Comparative Studies in Biblical and Ancient Oriental Literatures,* AOAT 204, 192–209; and David N. Freedman, "Counting Formulae in the Akkadian Epics," *JANESCU* 3/2, 65–81. See also the comments of David P. Wright, *Ritual in Narrative: The Dynamics of Feasting, Mourning, and Retaliation Rites in the Ugaritic Tale of Aqhat* (Winona Lake, Ind.: Eisenbrauns, 2001) 39 n. 77. As the Akkadian instances show, seven is attested not only in West Semitic literature, but also in Mesopotamia literature. For seven in a series of figures in a Sumerian context, see "Dumuzu's Dream," in Jacobsen, *Harps* (ch. 1, n. 21), 45. For general examples of seven in Sumerian literature, see Jacobsen, *Harps,* 174 (the seven leading gods who formulate divine decisions), and 243 (the seven-headed serpent in Lugal-e; see the same sort of seven-headed figure on a plaque of unknown provenience, *ANEP* #671, and on a seal from Tell Asmar, in *ANEP* #691). The Descent of Inanna is replete with the use of seven. See Jacobsen, *Harps,* 207 and 211 (for the seven powers of office, also in Enheduanna's hymn to Inanna, in *COS* 1.519), 212–13 (for the seven gates of the underworld palace of Ereshkigal), 215 (for the seven judges) and 225 (for the seven churns). Insofar as the seven powers of office reflect Inanna's status, and her passage through the seven gates of the underworld undo her, these two sets of seven may be regarded as one of the text's salient literary structures.

4. The number forty is used at the next higher scale of numbers, namely tens. Hence Moses is on the mountain for forty days (Exod. 34:28), echoed in Jesus' forty days in the wilderness (Mark 1:13).

5. For the following references with discussion, see Marvin H. Pope, "Seven, Seventh, Seventy," *IDB* 4, 294–95; and Coogan, *Stories* (ch. 2, n. 10), 17–18. For a broader consideration of the number seven from the perspective of the working memory of humans, see G. A. Miller, "The Magical Number Seven, Plus or Minus Two: Some Limits on Our Capacity for Processing Information," *Psychological Review,* 63 (1956) 81–97,

6. For journeys, forty is also used for the next higher scale. Elijah journeys in the wilderness for forty days (1 Kings 19:8). The unit is also used for years, in the Israelites' forty years in the wilderness (Deut. 1:3; Ps. 95:10; Amos 2:10, 5:25).

7. For text and translation, see Parker, "Aqhat" (ch. 1, n. 51), 52.

8. Similarly, only on the seventh day of the Kotharat's ritual in Aqhat did Danil's wife conceive (KTU 1.17 II 39). For text and translation, see Parker, "Aqhat," 57.

9. For the ritual dimensions of this chapter, see Daniel E. Fleming, "The Seven-Day Siege of Jericho in Holy War," in *Ki Baruch Hu* (ch. 2, n. 17), 211–28. This study nicely makes observations about the ritual use of the number seven in battle contexts.

10. Note also units of seven "periods," for example the period of time that Nebuchadnezzar is driven from society to live like a beast (Dan. 4:20, 22, 29). Compare the "seven cycles" that the Goodly Gods are to sojourn in the "desert" (perhaps better, "outback") in the Ugaritic narrative of "The Goodly Gods" (KTU 1.23.66–68); see Theodore J. Lewis, "CAT 1.23," in *UNP*, 214.

11. Note also the counting by seven weeks in Lev. 23:15; see also the reference to the seventh month in 23:24, 27.

12. Organization of the ritual calendar "in sevens" is quite pronounced in Num. 28–29, especially compared with the rituals at Ugarit.

13. See also Num. 23:8 and Deut. 16:8 for "the seventh day." The "seventh day" also marks the end of the wedding feast in Judg. 14:12, 15, 17–18 (LXX and Syriac have "fourth" for verse 15). The same usage of the ordinal for "the seventh" (without the word "day") occurs in Ugaritic

ritual texts, for example, in KTU 1.119.22; see Pardee, *Ritual and Cult* (Intro., n. 9), 51. See also Weimar, "Struktur und Komposition" (ch. 2, n. 260), 816–17, 819, repr. in Weimar, *Studien zur Priesterschrift* (ch. 2, n. 260), 191–234.

14. KTU 1.41//1.87, lines 47–48; see Pardee, *Ritual and Cult*, 61, 65; and *Les textes rituels* (Intro., n. 9), 1.149, 151, 199–208. Compare also KTU 1.112.10; see Pardee, *Ritual and Cult*, 37; and *Les textes rituels*, 1.630, 632, 633, 638–39.

15. Pardee, *Ritual and Cult*, 106 n. 74.

16. For comments in this direction, see Noth, *Pentateuchal Traditions* (ch. 2, n. 7), 11 n. 21; von Rad, *Genesis* (ch. 2, n. 7), 62; and Westermann, *Genesis 1–11* (ch. 2, n. 59), 90.

17. The basic arrangement has been traced back to Johann Gottfried von Herder. See J. Richard Middleton, *The Liberating Image: The* Imago Dei *in Genesis 1* (Grand Rapids, Mich.: Brazos Press, 2005) 74. It has since been followed by many scholars. See Gunkel, *Genesis* (ch. 2, n. 6), 120; Bernard W. Anderson, "A Stylistic Study of the Priestly Creation Story," in *Canon and Authority* (George W. Coats and Burke Long, eds.; Philadelphia: Fortress, 1977) 148; Joseph Blenkinsopp, *Treasures Old and New: Essays in the Theology of the Pentateuch* (Grand Rapids, Mich./Cambridge, U. K.: Eerdmans, 2004) 48; Clifford, *Creation Accounts* (Intro., n. 2), 142; Tsumura, *Creation and Destruction* (ch. 1, n. 13), 34. See also (with modifications) Jacob Milgrom, *Leviticus 17–22* (ch. 2, n. 7), 1344. For a detailed discussion, see Beauchamp, *Création et séparation* (ch. 1, n. 1), 41–44. See also Brown, *Ethos* (ch. 2, n. 7), 37–39. Brown suggests that *tohu*, "formless," is covered by the creation of days one through three, while *bohu*, "empty," is overcome in creation on days four through six; in this schema, day seven stands apart for the Sabbath.

Compare Weimar, "Struktur und Komposition," 803–43, esp. 836 (repr. in Weimar, *Studien zur Priesterschrift*, 191–234, esp. 127:

First Day	Time
Second Day	Schöpfungswelt ("world creation")
Third Day	Schöpfungswelt
Fourth Day	Time
Fifth Day	Lebewesen ("living things")
Sixth Day	Lebewesen
Seven Day	Time

18. The repetition is discussed by many scholars. See Westermann, *Genesis 1–11*, 84–88; and Loretz, "Wortbericht-Vorlage," (ch. 2, n. 86), 279–87.

19. In ch. 2 (see pp. 84, 93), we noted the possible relationship between the light of day one and the lamps of the sacred spaces of the Tabernacle and the Temple. It would be quite speculative to suggest that the seven-branched structure of the lamp stand with three lamps on either side in Exod. 25:32 corresponds to the structure of Genesis 1 with days one to three corresponding to days four through six and that this parallel influenced the priestly writer's arrangement of days in Genesis 1. See further p. 250 n. 279.

20. The scope of blessing on these days is discussed by Frank Crüsemann, "Der erste Segen: Gen 1,26—2,3: Übersetzung und exegetische Skizze," *BK* 58, 108–18.

21. Sasson, "Time. . . to Begin," (ch. 2, n. 40), 183–194, here 186.

22. Brown, *Ethos*, 52. For more "sevens" in Genesis 1, see Levenson, *Creation* (ch. 1, n. 114) 66–68.

23. For these approaches, see the appendix on 165–67.

24. To take only a few examples, see the Sumerian texts known as "Gilgamesh, Enkidu, and the Underworld," in the prologue (lines 8–9, in Clifford, *Creation Accounts*, 23); "Praise of the Pickaxe" (lines 4–5, in Clifford, *Creation Accounts*, 31); and KAR 4, (lines 1–2, in Clifford, *Creation Accounts*, 49).

25. For discussion, see Wilfred G. Lambert, "Mesopotamian Creation Stories," in *Imagining Creation* (ch. 2, n. 48), 18–19. See also Keel, *Symbolism* (ch. 1, n. 6), 30–31, 36. Keel emphasizes the two-part nature of the world as consisting of heaven and earth. Keel also characterizes earth in Gen. 1:2 and 24 as a "mother earth figure." See Keel, *Goddesses and Trees* (ch. 1, n. 6), 52. Note also Malul, "Woman-Earth" (ch. 1, n. 6), 339–63.

26. For further discussion of the usage in Genesis 1, see Beauchamp, *Création et séparation*, 235–39.

27. Echoing this notion is the divine title in 1QM (War Scroll) 10:12: "the one who creates earth and the boundaries of its divisions" (*hbwr' 'rs whwqy mplgyh*). For a convenient edition of the text with translation, see *The Dead Sea Scrolls. Hebrew, Aramaic, and Greek Texts with English Translations: Volume 2. Damascus Document, War Scroll, and Related Documents* (James Charlesworth, ed.; The Princeton Theological Seminary Dead Sea Scrolls Project; Tübingen: J. C. B. Mohr (Paul Siebeck); Louisville: Westminster John Knox, 1995) 116–17. For a recent grammatical discussion of this expression, see Søren Holst, *Verbs and War Scroll: Studies in the Hebrew Verbal System and the Qumran War Scroll* (Studia Semitica Upsaliensia, vol. 25; Uppsala: Uppsala Universitet, 2008) 115.

28. Below we will discuss the fundamental place of the Sabbath in Genesis 1's blueprint for human time, as recognized by commentators; see Philippe Guillaume, "Genesis 1 as a Charter of a Revolutionary Calendar," *Theological Review* 24/2 (2003) 141–48; and Klaas Smelik, "The Creation of the Sabbath (Gen 1:1—2:3)," in *Unless Some One Guide Me. . . : Festschrift for Karel A. Deurloo* (Masstricht: Shaker, 2000) 9–11.

29. See pp. 201–2 n. 22.
See also the parallelism of "the heavens" and "firmament" in Ps. 19:1 [MT 2]; compare Dan. 12:3.

30. For the periphrastic form *wiyhi mabdil* in v. 6, see Jonas C. Greenfield, *'Al Kanfei Yonah* (ch. 1, n. 21) 66. Greenfield considers this case and the one in 2 Sam. 3:17 as "early examples," in comparison with the vast number of examples in postexilic books. Note also Takamitsu Muraoka, "The Participle in Qumran Hebrew with Special Reference to its Periphrastic Use," in *Sirach, Scrolls, and Sages: Proceedings of a Second International Symposium on the Hebrew of the Dead Sea Scrolls, Ben Sira, and the Mishnah, held at Leiden University, 15–17 December 1997*, STJD 33, 199; and Martin Ehrensvärd, "Linguistic Dating of Biblical Texts," in *Biblical Hebrew*, (ch. 2, n. 20), 171.

31. The association of the root in these priestly contexts is a commonplace of biblical scholarship, e.g., Brown, *Ethos*, 104–106; Edward L. Greenstein, *Essays on Biblical Method and Translation*, BJS 92, 50.
The view further classifying the animals according to realms is often associated with the anthropologist Mary Douglas. Her work in this area has received considerable attention and it has been quite influential in biblical studies, though not without some criticism and modifications. See Jacob Milgrom, *Leviticus 1–16*, AB 3, 719–30; Walter Houston, *Purity and Monotheism: Clean and Unclean Animals in Biblical Law*, JSOTSup 140, 96–111; and Firmage, "Genesis 1" (ch. 2, n. 7), 104–11. While there may be divergences between the understanding of animals and their environments in Genesis 1 versus Leviticus 11 and elsewhere (as Houston notes), it seems nonetheless that Genesis 1 shows an interest in this relationship. For a recent appreciation of the work of Mary Douglas, see Ronald Hendel and Saul M. Olyan, "Beyond Purity and Danger: Mary Douglas and the Hebrew Bible," which heads a series of five articles devoted to her work in the *Journal of Hebrew Studies* 8, art. 7 (available online at: http://www.arts.ualberta.ca/JHS/Articles/article_84.pdf—89.pdf).

32. For an iconographic study of the animals in Genesis 1, see Othmar Keel and Thomas Staubli, *Les animaux de 6ème jour: les animaux dans le Bible et dans l'Orient ancien* (Zurich: Editions universitaires Fribourg Suisse, Musée de zoologie Lausanne, 2003).

33. See the interesting discussion of Second Temple literature by David Bryan, *Cosmos, Chaos, and the Kosher Mentality*, JSPSup 12.

34. The comparison has often been made. Among recent authors, see Richard Whitekettle, "Where the Wild Things Are: Primary Level Taxa in Israelite Zoological Thought," *JSOT* 93 17–37; and Hannah Liss, "Ritual Purity and the Construction of Identity," in *The Books of Leviticus and Numbers*, BETL CCXV, 337–38, 348. Whitekettle comments on the differences among the many schemas of animals embedded within the two texts. Whitekettle sees a three-fold schema in Genesis 1:20–25, 28 (19, 34) but a four-fold schema in Genesis 1:26 MT (24, 34).

The priestly tradition embodied by Genesis 1 and Leviticus 11 drew in part on Israel's older tradition for words designating the various animals of the universe. For animal taxonomy in biblical sources, including Genesis 1, see Whitekettle, "Where the Wild Things Are," 17–37; and "Rats are Like Snakes, and Hares are Like Goats: A Study in Israelite Land Animal Taxonomy," *Bib* 82, 345–62. The matter of the animals in Genesis 1 is touched upon by a number of essays in *Gefährten und Feinde* (ch. 1, n. 124); see in particular, Marie Louise Henry, "Das Tiere im religiösen Bewusstsein des alttestammentlichen Menschen," 33–36; Albert de Pury, "Gemeinschaft und Differenz: Aspeket der Mensch-Tier-Beziehung im alten Israel," 138–46; and Josef Schreiner, "Der Herr hilft Menschen und Tieren (Ps 36,7)," 228–29. Genesis 1 shows some of the older, poetic terms for the division of the various animals in the world. In this connection, we may note Umberto Cassuto's argument that some phrasings reflected an older epic version as opposed to a more recent composition. He suggested, for example, that the first term in the formulation of "beast of the earth" in Gen. 1:24, *hayto 'eres*, reflected an older poetic usage (for example, in Pss. 50:10, 104:11, 20), compared with a later form of the same expression in Genesis 1:25, 30, namely *hayyat ha'ares* (see Jer. 28:14; Hos. 4:3; cf. 13:8). See Cassuto, *Genesis: Part I*, 10–11. For discussion of the construction in Gen. 1:24, see Aḥituv, *Echoes from the Past* (ch. 2, n. 45), 254. For other cases of the same construction with *hayto*, he notes Pss 50:10, 104:11, 20. Following older commentators, Aḥituv regards it as a genitive construction. In view of the disagreement of gender between the masculine suffix and the following feminine noun (cf. *'eres* treated as masculine in Ezek. 21:24), the construction does not seem to involve a "prospective" suffix on the word standing in construct to a noun in a genitive relationship (for this construction in biblical Hebrew, see *GKC* 128d and 131r and perhaps add Jer. 3:11, and perhaps in the Gezer Calendar; so see Patrick Skehan, as cited by Frank Moore Cross, Jr. and David Noel Freedman, *Early Hebrew Orthography: A Study of the Epigraphic Evidence*, AOS 36, 47 n. 11).

Genesis 1 ends with a summary of the animals with the divine command to humanity: "rule the fish of the sea, the birds of the sky, and all the living things that creep on the earth" (1:28). These expressions are part of Israel's poetic tradition not only in creation references (Pss. 104:12, 14, 25; cf. 146:6; Hab. 1:14), but also in the poetic tradition more broadly (see, for example, Pss. 50:10–11, 148:10; Job 5:23, 12:7–8, 35:11; Jer. 7:33, 9:9, 12:4, 15:3, 16:4, 19:7, 34:20; Ezek. 29:5, 31:6; Hos. 4:3, 7:12, 13:8; Zeph. 1:3; cf. Joel 1:20, 2:22). The priestly tradition inherited these terms as well as the poetic division of the world into heaven, earth, and sea (compare Ps. 146:6). They also developed other terms (such as the verb, "to swarm") to describe some of these animals.

The stock formulations for animals in the Bible are known from older West Semitic poetic tradition. A variation on the biblical formulary for creatures is used in an Ugaritic excerpt of the creation-story, in 1.23.61–63: "birds of the sky, and fish from the sea." For a handy edition of the text (KTU 1.23), see Lewis, "Birth" (ch. 1, n. 20), 205–14, esp. 213. For a detailed study of this text, also with text and translation, see my book, *Sacrificial Rituals* (ch. 1, n. 20).

35. Other aspects of priestly thinking also draw on the idea of proper separation, for example, Israel's separation from other nations (see Lev. 20:26). I wish to thank Robert Kawashima for his presentation at the Association of Jewish Studies on December 23, 2008, which drew my attention to this passage.

36. See the general situation as put by Jacob Milgrom: "The entire sacrificial system, though its operation is solely the job of the priests, should be revealed—and taught—to all Israelites." See Milgrom, *Leviticus 1–16*, 143. At a minimum, Israelites knew something of the dietary traditions by participating in the pilgrimage festivals held at sanctuaries. See Houston, *Purity and Monotheism*, 51–52, 212–17, 221–25. That the dietary laws were part of the priestly regimen in the Temple fits the content of Leviticus 11 and is suggested by its following Leviticus 10. See Baruch Levine, *The JPS Torah Commentary: Leviticus* (Philadelphia/New York/Jerusalem: Jewish Publication Society, 1989) 220. Ezek. 4:14 may reflect the general expectations for priests. It is evident from Lev. 11:1 and Deut. 14:4–21 that the idea of maintaining distinctions between clean and unclean animals laws was taught to laypeople; see Levine, *Leviticus*, 224. Milgrom (*Leviticus 1–16*, 698–704) has argued that the dietary laws in Deuteronomy 14:4–21 are based on Leviticus 11; cf. Levine, *Leviticus*, 64–65. The priestly background of the dietary laws is put succinctly by Lawrence H. Schiffman: "these laws represent the ancient heritage of the priesthood"; Schiffman, *Reclaiming the Dead Sea*

Scrolls: Their True Meaning for Judaism and Christianity, ABRL 336. Note the discussion in the Second Temple context also by Aharon Oppenheimer, "Haverim," in *Encyclopedia of the Dead Sea Scrolls* (edited by Lawrence H. Schiffman and James C. VanderKam; two volumes; Oxford/New York: Oxford University Press, 2000) 1.333–34.

37. It is hardly surprising to see this sort of explanatory or etiological function of a creation story for dietary norms. Note the explicit taboo against eating pork in Egyptian spells (Coffin Text 157 and its later appearance in Book of the Dead 112), which explains the prohibition by reference to an etiological myth about Re and Horus. For translations of the text, see *ANET* 10; and *COS* 1.30–31.

38. For God as the one who makes pure (*tahor*), see Jer. 33:8. For God's eyes as *tahor*, see Hab. 1:13. Compare Job 14:4: "Who can make a clean thing (*tahor*) out of an unclean thing (*tame'*)? No one." Reverence of Yahweh is labeled as *tehorah* in Ps. 19:10.

39. See pp. 101–02; see also 208–9.

40. Zechariah 4:10 explicitly understands the lamp in the temple as a symbol of God's watchfulness.

41. For these oppositions, see especially Saul M. Olyan, *Rites and Rank: Hierarchy in Biblical Representation* (Princeton: Princeton University, 2000) 15–62, with reference to earlier literature.

42. There is some evidence, such as KTU 1.108.26–27, suggesting that "days and years" not only simply stands for the annual cycle in Genesis 1:14, but also for the length of time for which the sun and moon are to stand as signs. See Greenfield, *'Al Kanfei Yonah,* 717–18. For discussion of the biblical and inscriptional evidence for the pairing of days and years in royal blessings, see Michael L. Barré, "An Analysis of the Royal Blessing in the Karatepe Inscription," *Maarav* 3/2 (1982) 177–95, esp. 184–86 and 192–93; and Ahituv, *Echoes from the Past,* 365–66. It is to be noted that some of these royal blessings include both pairs, days and years as well as sun and moon, as we see in Genesis 1:14.

43. Cf. the same root "to rule" in Job 41:33 [MT 25], toward the very end of a discussion of Leviathan: "there is no one on earth ruling him."

44. For a translation with a transliteration of this text in English letters, see Edward L. Greenstein, "Kirta," (ch. 1, n. 21), 32. The technical citation is: KTU 1.16 I 36–38. The second title, *nyr rbt,* is to be translated literally, "the light, the great one," according to Aicha Rahmouni, *Divine Epithets* (ch. 1, n. 20), 244–45. Rahmouni points out that the *nyr* is masculine and *rbt* is feminine; therefore *rbt* does not modify *nyr* as such, but represents a substantized adjective in apposition to *nyr.*

Many commentators take *nyr rbt* in this passage as a title of the moon, for example, as Greenstein renders the title on p. 32 and discusses on p. 46 n. 121. Opposed to this view is Dennis Pardee ("The Kirta Epic," in *COS* 1.340 n. 73), who compares the same title for the sun in KTU 1.161.18–19; and also Rahmouni, *Divine Epithets,* 242–43. It might be argued that the same title may be used for the sun in one context but for the moon in another; if so, the variation would be due to which astral body a given text emphasizes. Compare the title of the moon, *nyr šmm,* "light of the heavens," in KTU 1.24.16, and 31; for discussion, see Rahmouni, *Divine Epithets,* 244–45. For the sun, compare the title *nrt 'il(m),* "light of El/the gods," attested thirteen times in the Ugaritic corpus; see Rahmouni, *Divine Epithets,* 252–53. The second word in this title is ambiguous, with the final -*m* possibly enclitic; the attestation without the -*m* in RS 92.2016 would seem to militate in this direction. It is to be observed that Shapshu conducts her role as divine communicator on El's behalf (see 1.6 III 22—IV 24 and 1.6 VI 22–29), which would also seem to work well with *nrt 'ilm* as "light of El." Still, caution is warranted.

45. For a translation with a transliteration of this text in English letters, see Smith, "The Baal Cycle" (ch. 1, n. 19), 116, 139, 151, 156. The technical citations are: KTU 1.3 V 17, 1.4 VIII 21, 1.6 I 8–9, 11, 1.6 II 24. See Rahmouni, *Divine Epithets,* 252–53.

46. See Rahmouni, *Divine Epithets,* 242–45, 252–53 for discussion of the Ugaritic evidence and 242 for the comparison with Gen. 1:16.

47. This is explicit in the interpretation of Letter of Jeremiah (EpJer) 6:60.

48. For a handy translation with a transliteration of the Ugaritic text, see Lewis, "Birth," 205–14; and my book, *Sacrificial Rituals.*

49. For discussion of El and his astral family consisting of these figures, see my book, *Origins* (ch. 1, n. 14), 61–66. The biblical references to the figures of El and his astral family are also discussed in this context.

50. For example, see Sarna, "Psalm XIX" (ch. 2, n. 172), 171–75; Milgrom, "The Alleged 'Hidden Light'" (ch. 2, n. 200), 42; and Ahituv, *Echoes from the Past,* 446. See also Ratzinger *In the Beginning* (ch. 1, n. 2), 47–48. The theory is also considered by Richard S. Hess, *Israelite Religions: An Archaeological and Biblical Survey* (Grand Rapids, Mich.: Baker; Nottingham, England: Apollos, 2007) 171–72. Hendel (personal communication) likewise sees a desacralization of the astral bodies.

The idea of polemical purposes is at best implicit in the text, which hardly makes it impossible. This view arguably flies in the face of texts such as Ps. 148:3, which personifies the sun, moon, and the stars in a positive manner. Genesis 1 and Psalm 148 would presumably have functioned in the post-exilic Jerusalem community led by the priesthood. It seems questionable whether a priestly leadership that authorized a putative polemic against the sun, moon, and the stars in one text would also sanction such a positive anthropomorphizing of the same astral bodies in another text. Cultic devotion to the sun, moon, and stars as such is not at stake in either text (compare Job 31:26–28 for religious devotion associated with the moon, discussed in the preceding note).

The appreciation for astral imagery may be a hallmark by the sixth century date of Genesis 1. Earlier, Amos 5:26 refers to a Mesopotamian deity explicitly designated as "your astral deity." A dramatic increase in astral symbols in iconography in the Iron IIC period has been noted by Keel & Uehlinger, *Gods* (ch. 1, n. 29), 317–18. The later polemics against "the sun, moon, and the stars" in texts such as 2 Kings 23:5 (cf. 21:3; and Zeph. 1:9) may correlate with this increase. At the same time, it remains unclear that Genesis 1 is to be read as polemic. For further discussion, see my treatments in Smith, *Origins,* 38; and "When the Heavens Darkened: Yahweh, El, and the Divine Astral Family in Iron Age II Judah," in *Symbiosis, Symbolism, and the Power of the Past: Canaan, Ancient Israel, and Their Neighbors from the Late Bronze Age through Roman Palaestina* (edited by William G. Dever and Seymour Gitin; the AIAR Anniversary Volume; Winona Lake, Ind.: Eisenbrauns, 2003) 265–77.

51. Compare God's covenant with "the stones of the field" and "the beast(s) of the field" as God's allies in Job 5:23.

52. Foster, *Muses,* 495.

53. ^mul^*DIL.BAT ina šēreti ikūn,* as noted by Ackerman, *Green Tree* (ch. 1, n. 53), 12. For other examples of the Mesopotamian usage in astronomical texts, see Brown, *Mesopotamian Planetary* (ch. 1, n. 53) 69, 86, 154 n. 367, 194.

54. Instead, the miraculous response of nature to God's salvation of Israel itself will be the divine "sign that shall not be cut off." That this idea marks the very last verse of Second Isaiah (Isa. 55:13) may point to the importance of this idea of "signs" in this work. Isa. 44:7, a decidedly a difficult verse, may be claiming that "signs" (?) (*'tywt*) are to be part of the Lord's divine power in predicting the future.

55. Compare the less astronomically specific formulation about Israel's God: "He delivers and saves, and performs signs and wonders in heaven and on earth" (Dan. 6:28).

56. This sense of the word as "omen" has been read in a divinatory text, KTU 1.103.1 (*DUL* 121). However, the line has been read differently; see Pardee, *Ritual and Cult,* 136. In any case, this text does not involve a specifically astronomical context. The word *'atm* in KTU 1.3 III 28 has been translated "sign" in reference to Baal's lightening as a "sign" in the world, but it also may be translated as the imperative "come" as a command to the address, Baal's sister, Anat (see Smith, "The Baal Cycle," 110).

57. EpJer 6:67 uses the language of signs deliberately echoing Gen. 1:14. Compare also EpJer 6:60.

58. A. Leo Oppenheim, "A Babylonian Diviner's Manual," *JNES* 33, 197–220, esp. 204, lines 38ff. See also Keel & Uehlinger, *Gods,* 318–19; W. van Binsbergen and F. Wiggermann, "Magic in History. A Theoretical Perspective, and Its Application to Ancient Mesopotamia," in *Mesopotamian Magic: Textual, Historical, and Interpretative Perspectives* (edited by Tzvi Abusch and Karel van der Toorn; Ancient Magic and Divination series, vol. I; Groningen: Styx, 1999) 33. For further discussion

of the manual, see Clemency Williams, "Signs from the Sky, Signs from the Earth: The Diviner's Manual Revisited," in *Under One Sky: Astronomy and Mathematics in the Ancient Near East,* AOAT 297, 473–85. Compare the moon providing omens in one of the prologues to the "Great Astrological Treatise," which is discussed by Clifford, *Creation Accounts,* 67–68.

59. See the contributions of Baruch Halpern on this score in his essays, "Assyrian Astronomy" (ch. 2, n. 3), 74*-83*; and "Late Israelite Astronomies and the Early Greeks," in *Symbiosis, Symbolism,* 323–52. Compare the view of J. Severino Croatto that Gen. 1:14–19 represents an act of resistance to Babylonian-Persian hegemony and their lunar-based calendar. See Croatto, "Reading the Pentateuch as a Counter-Text: A New Interpretation of Genesis 1:14–19," in *Congress Volume: Leiden 2004,* VTSup 109, 383–400.

60. See also *mo'ed* in Lam. 1:4, 2:6, 7, 22.

61. It is to be noted that the command to desist from work on the Sabbath applies also to the festivals in the priestly calendars of Leviticus 23 (vv. 8, 21, 24, 28, 30–32) and Numbers 28–29 (28:18, 25; 29:7, 12, 35).

62. The sun in Ezek. 8:16 might seem to be the object of worship by priests in the Temple. Some scholars have viewed this passage as suggesting that these priests are not worshipping the sun as such, but that they are worshipping Yahweh via the sun. Ezekiel 8 may be an inner-priestly polemic aimed against veneration of Yahweh as the divine light. The priestly side favored by the author of Ezekiel 8 might be reflected in the imagery of light in the priestly blessing. The issues surrounding solar imagery of the Bible are discussed by Bernd Janowski, "JHWH und der Sonnengott: Aspekte der Solarisierung JHWHs in vorexilischer Zeit," in *Pluralismus und Identität* (edited by J. Mehlhausen; Gütersloh: Gütersloher, 1995) 214–241, repr. in *Die rettende Gerechtigkeit* (ch. 1, n. 121), 192–219; and Frank Zeeb, "Jahwe und der Sonnengott," in *Ex Mesopotamia et Syria Lux: Festschrift für Manfred Dietrich zu seinem 65. Geburtstag* AOAT 281, 899–917. While Zeeb does not address the situation in Ezekiel, he does raise the question of the priestly blessing (see the next section) as showing a priestly response on the issue of light imagery for God. See also Smith, "Solar Language" (ch. 1, n. 35) 29–39.

Job 31:26–28 comments on some sort of religious devotion associated with the moon: "If I saw light while it was shining, with a full moon on the move, and it enticed my heart in secret, and I kissed my hand with my mouth, that too would be a criminal offense, for I would have denied God above." This does not seem to be a cultic act so much as a matter of personal practice and belief. Note also the popular belief in the potential threats posed by the sun and moon, as named in Ps. 121:6 and conveyed by Ps. 91:6.

63. Compare the description of wisdom in Wisd. of Sol. 7:29 that "she is more beautiful than the sun" (NRSV). See also Philo's *Biblical Antiquities* 12.1–3, where the light on the face of Moses exceeds the brightness of the sun and the moon. For an association of the moon with a deity in the divine scheme of things, compare "the moon of Thoth," in *ANET* 8.

64. For a lengthy review of the image and likeness in this passage, see Middleton, *The Liberating Image.*

65. For this sort of plural usage, compare Gen. 3:22, 11:7, and Isa. 6:8. As the context of the third passage would suggest, the usage in Gen. 1:26 appears to many scholars to be vestigial of the setting of the divine council, where the head god addresses the council as a whole in the first person plural forms. For full discussion, see Garr, *In His Own Image* (ch. 2, n. 166), 202–12. Garr sees an implicit polemic behind the use of the plural followed by the singular.

66. For the poetic structure and its significance, see Trible, *God and the Rhetoric of Sexuality* (ch. 2, n. 149), 12–23.

67. See ch. 4 for discussion, and in particular note pp. 276–77 n. 106.

68. For example, see Westermann, *Genesis 1–11,* 152–54. For further discussion of Mesopotamian material, see Peter Machinist, "Kingship and Divinity in Imperial Assyria, in *Text, Artifact, and Image: Revealing Ancient Israelite Religion,* BJS 346; Providence, R. I.: Brown University, 2006) 152–88; and Bernard F. Batto, "The Divine Sovereign: The Image of God in the Priestly Creation Account," *David and Zion: Biblical Studies in Honor of J. J. M. Roberts* (edited by Bernard F. Batto and Kathryn L. Roberts; Winona Lake, Ind.: Eisenbrauns, 2004) 143–86. For the Egyptian evidence, see Klaus Koch, *Imago Dei: Die Wurde des Menschen im biblischen Text* (Göttingen: Vandenhoeck

und Ruprecht, 2000). The Mesopotamian and Egyptian material and more proximate sources have been surveyed by J. Richard Middleton, *The Liberating Image*. As the discussion here indicates, I tend toward reading Genesis 1 more "locally," within the context of West Semitic and biblical sources, without disputing the potential value of the broader evidence. Many commentators overlook the language of *demut* in the priestly work of Ezekiel; see below.

Middleton offers a distinctive reading of the royal idea behind the image and likeness language. Like most commentators, he accepts the royal model of the image language of Genesis 1. His claim about the meaning of the image, that "the sort of power or rule that humans are to exercise is generous, loving power" (295), is difficult to derive from Genesis 1; it sounds quite modern. See also his comment (294): "Genesis 1 depicts what is precisely a loving, parental exercise of power on God's part." A similar difficulty may be perceived in Walter Brueggemann's *Genesis* (Interpretation; Atlanta: John Knox, 1982, 32) cited by Middleton (296).

69. See the original edition of A. Abou Assaf, Pierre Bordreuil, and Alan R. Millard, *La statue de Tel Fekherye et son inscription bilingue assyro-araméenne* (Etudes assyriologiques; Cahiers 10; Paris: Editions Recherche sur les civilisations, 1982) 23–25 (consistently rendering both terms as "statue"). See Greenfield, *'Al Kanfei Yonah,* 219 (with Aaron Schaeffer) and 252; and W. Randall Garr, "'Image' and 'Likeness' in the Inscription from Tell Fakhariyeh," *IEJ* 50, 227–34. For Akkadian *ṣalmu* and its relevance to Gen. 1:26–27, see also the remarks of M. Stol, *Birth in Babylonia and in the Bible: Its Mediterranean Setting* (Cuneiform Monographs 14; Groningen: Styx, 2000) 147–51.

70. For this word elsewhere in Aramaic of this period, see Dirk Schwiderski, *Die alt- und reicharamäischen Inschriften/The Old and Imperial Aramaic Inscriptions. Band I: Konkordanz* (Fontes et Subsidia ad Bibliam pertinentes, Band 4; Berlin/New York: de Gruyter, 2008) 211.

71. Garr, "'Image' and 'Likeness,'" 231–32.

72. See the reflections of Bernd Janowski, "Die lebendige Statue Gottes: zur Anthropologie der priesterlichen Urgeschichte," in *Gott und Mensch im Dialog. Volume I* (Berlin/New York: de Gruyter, 2004) 183–214. Walter Gross would see a more direct connection with the notion of statuary, since he takes *selem* in Gen. 1:26–27 to mean, "statue." See Gross, "Gen 1,26–27; 9,6: Statue oder Ebenbild Gottes? Aufgabe und Würde des Menschen nach dem hebräischen und griechischen Wortlaut," *Jahrbüch für Biblische Theologie* 15 (2000) 11–38.

73. Note Westermann's criticism of viewing Gen. 1:26–28 in terms of the royal background given the priestly context of Genesis 1. See Westermann, *Genesis 1–11*, 153. As I hope is clear from my comments here and elsewhere, the priestly composer of Genesis 1 draws on language with monarchic roots and puts it to use in expressing a priestly vision of reality.

74. This connection between Ezekiel 1 and Genesis 1 on *demut* has been noted by various commentators, for example, John F. Kutsko, "Ezekiel's Anthropology and Its Ethical Implications," in *The Book of Ezekiel: Theological and Anthropological Approaches* (Margaret D. Odell and John T. Strong, eds.; Symposium Series, vol. 9; Atlanta: Society of Biblical Literature, 2000) 119, 125–27; Wacholder, "Creation in Ezekiel's *merkabah* (ch. 2, n. 238), 30; and Peter Schäfer, *The Origin of Jewish Mysticism* (Tübingen: Mohr Siebeck, 2009) 44. For the following interpretation of Gen. 1:26–28 and Ezek. 1:26, see Mark S. Smith, "God Male and Female in the Old Testament: Yahweh and his *'Asherah,*" *TS* 48, 333–40; and Smith, *Early History* (ch. 1, n. 64), 102.

75. For a discussion of this anthropomorphism, see Keel & Uehlinger, *Gods*, 305 and 407. Note also Bryan, *Cosmos*, 42–44. Bryan's discussion includes reflexes in Second Temple literature.

76. For this word as applied to the figure of God, compare Isa. 40:18: "To whom can you liken (*°dmh*) God, what form (*demut*) would you compare to him?" See also 40:25 and 46:5. Weinfeld, followed by Fishbane and Sommer, see in these passages polemic against Genesis 1:26. For Weinfeld and Sommer, it involves polemic, while for Fishbane, it is a matter of maintaining "it in a newly understood way." See Weinfeld, "The Creator God" (ch. 2, n. 2), 124–25; Fishbane, *Biblical Interpretation* (ch. 2, n. 2), 325–26; Sommer, *A Prophet Reads Scripture* (ch. 2, n. 2), 143–44, 216 n. 87. For cautionary remarks about this sort of argumentation, see de Moor, "Ugarit and the Origin of Job" (ch. 2, n. 22), 227–28.

77. For a proposal about the iconography behind this description, see Keel & Uehlinger, *Gods*, 296, 345, and 402.

78. Contrast the juxtaposition of praise of Yahweh as Creator with passages satirizing the images of other deities. This presentation in Second Isaiah (especially ch. 44) suggests the idea that while the human person is the sign of the living God, the lifeless idols of the nations are indicators that their deities are equally without reality. See Smith, *Origins*, 191–92.

79. See Bernd Janowski, "Herrschaft über die Tiere: Gen 1,26–28 und die Semantik von רדה," in *Biblische Theologie und gesellschaftlicher Wandel: Für Norbert Lohfink SJ* (edited by Georg Braulik OSB, Walter Gross, and Sean McEvenue; Freiburg/Basel/Vienna: Herder, 1993) 183–98, reprinted in *Die rettende Gerechtigkeit*, 33–48; and Keel and Schroer, *Schöpfung*, 176. See also Simkins, *Creator and Creation* (ch. 2, n. 200), 201, 205–6. Simkins would play down the possible violent connotations of these two verbs in Gen. 1:26, 28. Simkins (253) suggests that the priestly source sees humanity as both part of creation and holding mastery over it.

80. There is an immense literature on the image and likeness, especially emphasizing the usage's royal background in Assyrian and Egyptian sources (e.g., Merikare in *ANET* 417). See Hans Wildeberger, "Das Abbild Gottes," *TZ* 21, 245–49, 481–501; Kraus, *Psalms 1–59*, 180, 185; Tryggve N. D. Mettinger, "Abbild oder Urbild? *Imago Dei* in traditionsgeschichtlicher Sicht," *ZAW* 86, 403–24, esp. 412–15 (with a good deal of older bibliography); Hoffmeier, "Some Thoughts," (ch. 2, n. 101), 46–48; Levenson, *Creation*, 113–14; Clifford, *Creation Accounts*, 142–44; Janowski, "Herrschaft über die Tiere," 183–98, repr. in *Die rettende Gerechtigkeit*, 33–48; Andreas Schüle, "Made in the 'image of God': The concept of divine images in Gen 1–3," *ZAW* 117, 1–20; and Keel and Schroer, *Schöpfung*, 177–81. This matter is raised also in ch. 1, sec. 3, in the comparison of Genesis 1 and Psalm 8. See pp. 27–30 above.

81. The tent of meeting in Josh. 18:1 is particularly suggestive of the priestly background for at least this verse. See Richard D. Nelson, *Joshua: A Commentary*, OTL, 9. For a discussion of the relationship between the uses of this verb in Gen. 1:28 and Josh. 18:1, see A. Graeme Auld, *Joshua Retold: Synoptic Perspectives*, OTS, 65–68 (with discussion of earlier literature on this point). I am indebted to Bill Brown for our conversation about °*kbsh* in Joshua 18 as a possible key to understanding the use of the same root in Gen. 1:27.

82. The translation here largely follows NJPS.

83. As noted by commentators. See the essays of Ed Noort, "Bis nur Grenze des Landes? Num 27,12–23 und das Ende der Priesterschrift," 119, and Jean-Louis Ska, "La récit sacerdotal: Une histoire sans fin?" 632–33, both in *The Books of Leviticus and Numbers*, BETL CCXV.

84. See Trible, *God and the Rhetoric of Sexuality*, 17. Citing Phyllis Bird, Simkins (*Creator and Creation*, 200) states against the poetic structure of 1:27 that "'male and female' describes how humans are *not* in the image of God" (Simkins' italics).

85. Liss ("Ritual Purity," 350) connects the command to be fruitful and multiply in this verse to the priestly discussions of *shikbat zara'/zera'* in Lev. 15:16–18, 32, and 19:20. The connection would be conceptual, not terminological. For another discussion of Lev. 15:18 (without connection to Genesis 1), see Richard Whitekettle, "Leviticus 15.18 Reconsidered: Chiasm, Spatial Structure, and the Body," *JSOT* 49, 31–45. The connection that Whitekettle sees between Genesis 1 and Leviticus 15 involves a homology between the cosmos of Genesis 1 and the conditions for the production of human life in Lev. 15:19–24. See Whitekettle, "Levitical Thought and the Female Reproductive Cycle: Wombs, Wellsprings, and the Primeval World," *VT* 46, 376–91, esp. 385–89.

86. So Simkins, *Creator and Creation*, 201–2. However, note the discussion of Saul M. Olyan, "'And with a Male You Shall Not Lie the Lying Down of a Woman': On the Meaning and Significance of Leviticus 18:22 and 20:13," *Journal of the History of Sexuality* 5 (1994) 179–206; repr. in *Que(e)rying Religion: A Critical Anthology* (G. D. Comstock and S. E. Henking, eds.; New York: Continuum, 1997) 398–414, 513–24. Olyan notes that the Leviticus laws lack any such citation of the P creation story, which may suggest otherwise.

According to Olyan, the prohibition in Leviticus does not simply outlaw such relations. Instead, it is forbidding a male to assume what is considered culturally to be the female role of reception by male penetration. For a critique of this understanding, see Jerome T. Walsh, "Leviticus 18:22 and 20:13: Who is Doing What to Whom?" *JBL* 120, 201–19.

87. Might the command, "be fruitful and multiply" (*peru urbu*) in v. 28 also echo the verb °*br'*, "to create," in the preceding verse?

88. Compare the god El blessing king Kirta and his wife upon their marriage in KTU 1.15 II 18–26; see Greenstein, "Kirta," 25. The Ugaritic texts attribute the role to the god, but the iconography also shows female figures offering the gesture of blessing. For Late Bronze examples of iconography of divine blessing (seated deity with an upraised hand) by male and female figures, see Keel & Uehlinger, *Gods*, 86; and Izak Cornelius, *The Many Faces of the Goddess: The Iconography of the Syro-Palestinian Goddesses Anat, Astrate, Qedeshet, and Asherah c. 1500–1000 BCE*, OBO 204, 115, plates 3.9, 3.10, and figs. 14–18, 22. It is in light of this iconographic situation that "the blessings of breast and womb" in Gen. 49:25 may be viewed. This may be an allusion to a goddess; for discussion, see Smith, *Early History*, 48–52. See also favorably Raymond de Hoop, *Genesis 49* (ch. 2, n. 132), 24 (on 216, 231 he reads the third pair and the syntax of the last clause differently than what I am proposing here). Contrast Frevel, *Aschera* (ch. 2, n. 132), 163: "Brüste und Mutterschoß sind hier auf die generative Fruchtbarkeit bezogen und haben keine Beziehung zu Aschera." What Frevel does not discuss are the other cosmological pairs in this context. These are more specific than in the sorts of blessings that we find, for example in Genesis 27:28, 39, which are not nearly as cosmological by comparison.

For the Iron Age, anthropomorphic representation of blessing is displaced by icons of blessing, according to Keel & Uehlinger (*Gods*, 147–49). In the famous Kuntillet Ajrud inscriptions (see note 92), blessing is offered in the name of "Yahweh and his asherah"; this is not Yahweh and Asherah, but Yahweh and something that is his; the symbol has become the symbol of his blessing according to Keel and Uehlinger. Criticism of the asherah as an icon of Yahweh's blessing may have been motivated as a protection against worship of the goddess (or against goddesses more broadly). As one result of the religious differences, Asherah is channeled into the female figure of Wisdom personified, who is said to have a tree offering well-being: "She is a tree to those who lay hold of her, those who hold her fast are called happy" (Proverbs 3:18). This sort of comparison is hardly uncommon; see Michael David Coogan, "The Goddess Wisdom—'Where Can She Be Found?' Literary Reflexes of Literary Religion," in *Ki Baruch Hu*, 203–9, esp. 204, 206. It generally goes unnoted that the word for "happy" in Prov. 3:18 arguably plays on the word *'asherah* (see Smith, *Early History*, 134 n. 102, following a personal communication from Anthony Ceresko).

89. For the language of blessing, see J. K. Aitken, *The Semantics of Blessing and Cursing in Ancient Hebrew* (Ancient Near Eastern Studies Supplement Series, vol. 23; Leuven: Peeters, 2008). For the religious backdrop of blessing, see Martin Leuenberger, *Segen und Segenstheologien im alten Israel: Untersuchungen zu ihren religions—und theologiegeschichtlichen Konstellationen und Transformationen*, ATANT 90. For inscriptional evidence, see Timothy G. Crawford, *Blessing and Curse in Syro-Palestinian Inscriptions of the Iron Age* (American University Studies, Series VII: Theology and Religion, vol. 120; New York: Peter Lang, 1992).

90. For the syntax of verse 22c, see Elisha Qimron, "A New Approach to the Use of Forms of the Imperfect without Personal Endings," in *Sirach, Scrolls and Sages: Proceedings of a Second International Symposium on the Hebrew of the Dead Sea Scrolls, Ben Sira and the Mishnah, held at Leiden University, 15–17 December 1997*, STJD 33, 179–81. Qimron notes the exceptional character of the syntax of this clause, with its subject preceding the jussive form. In this context, he also notes 1 Sam. 17:37 and 2 Sam. 14:17.

91. In his discussion of Genesis 1, Hermann Gunkel comments: "Blessing is the priest's function." See Gunkel, *Genesis*, 119. See also Westermann, *Genesis 1–11*, 140: "A typical and rather late use of the word [to bless] which is characteristic of P is the cultic use, e.g., Lev 9:22f., and especially Num 6:22–24." For blessing in the priestly worldview, see Hendel, "Prophets" (ch. 1, n. 48), 185–198, esp. 191–93.

92. See the priestly blessing in Numbers 6 as preserved in an inscription from Ketef Hinnom. See Gabriel Barkay, Andrew G. Vaughan, Marilyn J. Lundberg, and Bruce Zuckerman, "The Amulets from Ketef Hinnom: A New Edition and Evaluation," *BASOR* 334, 41–71. Note also Keel & Uehlinger, *Gods*, 363–66; and Zeeb, "Jahwe und der Sonnengott," 910–12.

The blessings in the Kuntillet 'Ajrud inscriptions arguably fit priestly blessing. In particular, the blessing written on Pithos A echoes the priestly blessing of Num. 6:22–24: "I bless you to (*l-*) Yahweh Teiman and to his asherah/Asherah; may he bless you and may he guard you, and may he be with my lord." The parallel is noted by scholars, such as Keel & Uehlinger, *Gods*, 226 n. 75;

and Zevit, *Religions* (ch. 1, n. 56), 396–97. Keel & Uehlinger (*Gods*, 239–40; cf. 314) regard the Asherah in these inscriptions as "the medium or entity through which" Yahweh's blessing happens and not as a goddess: "only one divine power, namely Yahweh, is considered the active agent." This approach casts doubt on the notion that these inscriptions witness to a goddess who is Yahweh's consort, though the representation in these inscriptions could go back to such a notion earlier (see Smith, *Early*, 108–47).

Zevit (*Religions*, 368) has suggested that a mantic was involved in the blessing of the Khirbet el-Qom inscription (see Keel & Uehlinger, *Gods*, 361–62). It might be argued that priestly blessing to people was an important task of the priesthood. At the same time, it is to be recognized that in a number of biblical passages, blessings are offered on behalf of persons by nonspecialists including family members, as in Judg. 17:2, Ruth 3:10, 1 Sam. 15:13, 23:21, and 2 Sam. 2:5 (references courtesy of Stephen Russell).

93. See Otto Mulder, *Simon the High Priest: An Exegetical Study of the Significance of Simon the High Priest as Climax to the Praise of the Fathers in Ben Sira's Concept of the History of Israel* (Leiden/Boston: Brill, 2003).

94. It is in the context of a visit to the temple, God's "holy place," in Psalm 24 that the pilgrim receives a divine blessing: "he shall bear a blessing from the Lord" (v. 5). Similarly, Ps. 118:26 locates blessing in the house of the Lord: "May the one who enters be blessed in the name of the Lord; we bless you from the House of the Lord." Divine blessing in Jerusalem is a stock motif in the Psalms (for example, in the "Songs of Ascents," in Pss. 128:5; 129:5–8; 133:3; 134:3).

95. The following discussion is hardly a comprehensive treatment of the Sabbath in ancient Israel. For recent surveys of the Sabbath in the Hebrew Bible, see Baruch A. Levine, "Scripture's Account: The Sabbath," in *Torah Revealed, Torah Fulfilled: Scriptural Laws in Formative Judaism and Earliest Christianity*, by Jacob Neusner, Bruce D. Chilton, and Baruch A. Levine (New York/London: T & T Clark, 2008) 77–88; and Alexandra Grund, "Gerdenken und Bewahren: Studien zu Zeitkonzept und Erinnerungskultur Israel am Beispiel des alttestamentlichen Sabbats" (Habitilationschrift, Eberhardkarls Universität Tübingen, 2008) 206–333 (this work is to be published in FAT). Note also further secondary literature cited below.

96. One might compare and contrast Job's cursing of the day of his birth (Job 3:1). The cursing of this time opens a lament in Job 3 over his condition in life. In other words, Job's cursing of his first time, the day of his birth, is a rhetorical act aimed at heightening the expression of his present condition. In its own way, God's ancient blessing of the Sabbath likewise is a rhetorical act that heightens the meaning of Sabbath rest in the present.

97. See also the later Isa. 66:23, which may be informed by the use in 1:13; note also the parallelism of new moon and full moon in Ps. 81:4, and compare the story of the new moon feast in 1 Samuel 20. For the new moon in this passage as the interlunium, see Karel van der Toorn, *Family Religion in Babylonia, Syria, and Israel: Continuity and Change in the Forms of Religious Life* (Studies in the History and Culture of the Ancient Near East, volume VII; Leiden/New York/Köln: Brill, 1996) 212–13; Jan A. Wagenaar, "In the Sixth Month: the Day of the New Moon of Hiyaru," *Ugarit-Forschungen* 34 (2002) 913–19, and *Origin and Transformation of the Ancient Israelite Festival Calendar* (Beihefte zur Zeitschrift für Altorientalische und Biblische Rechtsgeschichte, vol. 6; Wiesbaden: Harrassowitz, 2005) 145 n. 107. This is consistent with Michael Fishbane's view, who sees in the new moon and Sabbath not two days within the month, but two lunar phases. See Fishbane, *Biblical Interpretation,* 149–51. The biblical evidence may suggest an older practice of celebrating the Sabbath as a seven-day unit within the monthly calendar, parallel to the interlunium.

A number of scholars have compared the Sabbath with Akkadian *shapattu*, for example in Atraḥasīs I 206, 221: "On the days of the new moon, the seventh and the fifteenth (*shapattu*)" (*COS* 1.451; *CAD* Sh/1:450). See the critical discussions of William W. Hallo, "New Moons and Sabbaths," *HUCA* 48, 1–18; and William W. Hallo, *Origins: The Ancient Near Eastern Background of Some Modern Western Institutions* (Leiden/New York/Köln: Brill, 1996) 127–35; Mayer Gruber, "The Source of the Biblical Sabbath," *JANESCU* (1969) 14–21; and Levine, "Scripture's Account," 77. Note also *COS* 1.451 n. 5, also citing *Enuma Elish,* tablet V, lines 14–18 (*COS* 1.399 and n. 10); and *HCSB* (Intro., n. 3), p. 118, note to Exod. 20:8. Hallo also considers proposals that the Sabbath and the week more broadly developed under Babylonian influence. For presentations of evidence with critical discussion, Hallo cites the work of Ellen Robbins on offerings made weekly in Neo-Babylonian sources; see her article, "Tabular Sacrificial Records and the Cultic Calendar of Neo-Babylonian Uruk," *JCS* 48, 61–87.

As these discussions show, the origins of the Sabbath are not entirely clear. As my colleague Daniel Fleming reminds me, the Sabbath is unusual for the ancient Near East, unprecedented both for calendar and for the idea that everyone would stop their regimens and festivals on a regular basis, and so frequently (though perhaps early on, it was not so frequent). The Sabbath became part of the priestly purview as it involved sacrifices. Whatever the earlier situation, the combination of Sabbath and new moon survives in priestly tradition (see Num. 28:9–15); in priestly tradition the celebration of the new moon is overshadowed generally by the concern for Sabbath observance.

98. For an older discussion of this theme, see G. Robinson, "The Idea of Rest in the Old Testament and the Search for the Basic Character of Sabbath," *ZAW* 92, 32–42.

99. Unlike the verses cited here from Exodus and Leviticus, Gen. 2:2–3 does not address Israel in particular. Rather, its description applies to humanity as a whole. While there is no doubt that Gen. 2:2–3 anticipates the commandment of Sabbath rest to Israel in Exodus and Leviticus, it does not restrict the Sabbath to Israel. In short, Gen. 2:2–3 offers a claim about God's modeling rest for humanity in general.

100. The theme of "rest" is discussed shortly below.

101. For further discussion, see Gary A. Rendsburg, "Alliteration in the Exodus Narrative," in *Birkat Shalom* (ch. 2, n. 198), 93.

102. This is indicated by the use of the same verb in other contexts, for example, in Lam. 5:15: "the joy of our heart has ceased" (and not "rested").

103. For a convenient presentation of the text (in Hebrew transliteration) with translation, see James M. Lindenberger, *Ancient Aramaic and Hebrew Letters*, SBLWAW 4, 96–98. For discussions, see Shemaryahu Talmon, "The New Hebrew Letter from the Seventh Century B.C. in Historical Perspective," *BASOR* 176, 32; John C. L. Gibson, *Textbook of Syrian Semitic Inscriptions: Volume 1. Hebrew and Moabite Inscriptions* (Oxford: Clarendon Press, 1971) 28–29; Dennis Pardee, "The Judicial Plea from Meṣad Ḥashavyahu (Yavneh-Yam): A New Philological Study," *Maarav* 1/1 (1978) 36–37, 44; Anson Rainey, "Syntax and Rhetorical Analysis in the Hashavyahu Ostracon," *JANESCU* 27, 75–79; and Dobbs-Allsopp, et al., *Hebrew Inscriptions* (ch. 2, n. 45), 358–59, 362. Talmon compares Exod. 21:19 and Ruth 2:7; Gibson also notes Ruth 2:7, which describes Ruth either stopping or resting (for the latter, see NRSV, NJPS, NAB) after working. According to NJPS, the meaning of the Hebrew here is uncertain. As Pardee and Dobbs-Allsopp et al. observe, it is also possible that *shbt* in this inscription means the "the Sabbath day" itself or "sabbath" "in the nontechnical sense of a holiday or simply a time of rest" (p. 362). They further note that if the Sabbath day itself were meant, then the word might have also had a definite article on it as in Neh. 13:19. Compare Cross, *Epigrapher's Notebook,* (ch. 2, n. 62), 123 n. 47; Rainey, "Syntax," 78; and Levine, "Scripture's Account," 85.

104. See also Exod. 23:12. The verb occurs only in the niphal; see Exod. 23:12; 2 Sam. 16:14. Since it occurs only three times, while the corresponding noun occurs hundreds of times, it would seem that the Hebrew verb derived from the noun. For the idea of the verb, perhaps compare Ps. 19:7 [MT 8]: "The teaching (*torat*) of the Lord is perfect, renewing life (*meshibat nepesh*)" (NJPS); and Ps. 23:3: "he restores (*yeshobeb*, literally 'causes to turn') my life (*nepesh*)." For an analogous semantic development, compare the verb °*rwh* that derives from the noun *ruah*, as in 1 Sam. 16:23 and Job 32:30, "to be relief" (*BDB* 926). This sort of verb derived from an old noun of the human person is seen also with °*lbb*, from *leb, lebab*, "heart"), in the *N*-stem, "to get a heart (or mind) in Job 11:12, and in the *D*-stem, "to entice" in Song of Sol. 4:9 (cf. *BDB* 525).

105. Compare the command in the Psalms, "bless the lord, O my soul (*napshi*)." For an example with discussion, see Psalm 104, on p. 208 n. 78. Technically speaking, "soul" is not the correct translation for *nepesh*.

106. Divine rest occurs in other ancient Near Eastern literatures, in particular with the root °*nwḥ*. The motif of divine rest occurs in *Enuma Elish* I 50 and 75, IV 135 and VII 128 (cited in *CAD N/1*:147; see Foster, *Muses*, 441, 461, 483). For divine rest in Ugaritic, note the rest of El in KTU 1.6

III 18–19 (see Smith, "The Baal Cycle," 158). In this context El expresses contentment or ease at the wellbeing of the cosmos, with the return of Baal to life. In Ugaritic, the royal throne—whether divine or human—is said to be "the resting-place, the seat of rule" (see KTU 1.3 IV 2–3; 1.16 VI 22–23; 1.22 II 17–18; the expression may be taken as a hendiadys; see Cross, *Canaanite Myth*, [ch. 1, n. 16], 94 n. 14); note also Brown, *Ethos*, 50.

In KTU 1.17 II 12–14, rest for Danil signals the achievement of the proper social order, namely in the form of a son (Parker, "Aqhat," 56). One Ugaritic letter KTU 2.11.10–14a likewise adds to the usual formula to convey a general sense of wellbeing by using the same word, °*nwḥ*: "here with me [us—there are two senders] all is very well, and I am indeed at rest" (*hnny 'mny kll m'id šlm w 'ap 'ank nḫt*). There is also the Phoenician phrase, "that the Danuneans may dwell in rest" (*lšbtnm dnnym bnḥt lbnm*), in other words in peace and security from enemies (KAI 26 I 17–18). The motif of dwelling in rest or peace informs the Akkadian expression, "to let dwell in security," *šubat nēḫti šūšubu* (*CAD* N/2:150–51). For these texts, see Jonas C. Greenfield, "Notes on the Asitawadda (Karatepe) Inscription," *ErIsr* 14, 74–75 (Heb.).

Akkadian texts commonly express the idea of the heart or innards at rest; see *CAD* N/1:146a. Note the wish expressed to the king in the Mari letters that his heart be at rest (see for example M.14546, in Maurice Birot, *Correspondance des gouverneurs de Qaṭṭunân*, ARMT XXVII, 208); compare its opposite, namely the heart not at rest (for example, A.2172, in Jean-Robert Kupper, *Lettres royales du temps de Zimri-Lim*, ARMT XXVIII, 64).

With respect to biblical "rest," Levenson (*Creation*, 107) relates this theme to the Temple; several of the biblical texts that he cites pertain equally to the king or Jerusalem as a whole. Still, he may be correct in stressing the connection between Temple and the theme of rest.

The expression *nw/yḥ npš* later appears in Jewish inscriptions to commemorate the deceased. See, for example, #109, line 3 (an epitaph from an ossuary from Nazareth) and #A.12, line 3 (a synagogue inscription from Beth Gubrin), in Joseph A. Fitzmyer and Daniel J. Harrington, *A Manual of Palestinian Aramaic Texts*, BibOr 34, 176–77, 258–39, respectively; cf. A.50.1 and A. 52.1, in Fitzmyer & Harrington, *Manual*, 270–73. Note also a fifth or sixth century Hebrew note layered within a Latin epitaph from Venosa: "resting place of Faustina, may (her) soul rest, peace"; see Pieter W. van der Horst, *Ancient Jewish Epitaphs: An Introductory Survey of a Millennium of Jewish Funerary Epigraphy (300 BCE-700 CE)*, CBET 2, 147.

107. See above pp. 31–32. For the semantic use, compare the same root in Ps. 89:45: "You have ended." Note also the root in Neo-Punic, in the G-stem, meaning, "to come to an end," in Mactar B I 1–2; and in the D-stem, meaning, "to remove, destroy," in CIS I 5510. For references, see *DNWSI* 1107; and Krahmalkov, *Phoenician-Punic Dictionary* (ch. 2, n. 233), 455.

108. At one point in David's rule (°*yshb*), God is said in 2 Sam. 7:1 to have given him rest from all his enemies (for the causative or Hiphil stem A of °*nwḥ* in this idiom, see BDB 628, #1b (2)). Jonas C. Greenfield noted the same collocation of words (°*yshb* and °*nwḥ*) in Lam. 1:3, Ps. 132:14 and Isa. 12:15. See Greenfield, "Notes," 74–77.

109. Compare Zech. 6:8: those who went to the land of the north are said to give rest to the divine spirit.

110. For example, in *Enuma Elish*, tablet VI, line 8; see *ANET* 68; *COS* 1.400; Foster, *Muses*, 469. Note also the account in Atra-ḫasīs, in *COS* 1.451. For discussion of the gods' work in Atra-asīs, see William L. Moran, *The Most Magic Word*, CBQMS 35, 48. The comparison between these Mesopotamian works and Genesis 1 on the matter of divine rest is noted by Levenson, *Creation*, 106–107.

111. Ezekiel 20:12, 16, 21, 24; 22:26; 23:38. Note also references to the Sabbath in Jer. 17:22–24, 27. Both prophets are attributed priestly lineages (see Jer. 1:1; Ezek. 1:3). Note also Isa. 56:2–6, 58:13; see Leszek Ruuskowski, "Der Sabbat bei Tritojesaja," in *Prophetie und Psalmen: Festschrift für Klaus Seybold zum 65. Geburstag*, AOAT 280, 61–74. For discussion of the Sabbath in biblical sources, see further Heather McKay, *Sabbath and Synagogue: The Question of Ancient Worship in Ancient Judaism* (Religions in the Greco-Roman World Series, vol. 122; Leiden/New York/Köln: Brill, 1994) 15–42. See also the Aramaic expressions *shbh*, "Sabbath," and *ywm shbh* "day of Sabbath," in texts from Elephantine in southern Egypt ca. 475 (Lindenberger, *Ancient Aramaic and Hebrew Letters*, 40, 46, 49). See also the recent discussions of Levine, "Scripture's Account," 85; and Bob Becking,

"Sabbath at Elephantine: A Short Episode in the Construction of Jewish Identity," in Empsychoi Logoi—*Religious Innovations in Antiquity: Studies in Honour of Pieter Willem van der Horst* (Alberdina Houtman, Albert de Jong, and Magda Misset-Van de Weg, eds.; Ancient Judaism and Early Christianity, vol. 73; Leiden: Brill, 2008) 177–189.

112. Compare the words of Levenson (*Creation*, 106): "the prominence of rest on the seventh day in the creation story of Genesis 1:1—2:3 reflects a much more widespread theology in which creation is a paradigm of God's gracious and perdurable will to save the defenseless."

113. Here we may consider two scholarly proposals. One is offered by Wevers, *Notes* (ch. 2, n. 32), 20. To resolve the problem in the Masoretic text, Wevers suggests that the Hebrew verbs in 2:2a may be taken in the pluperfect and so no emendation would be necessary. While this solution suits the second verb ("the work that he had made"), it does not work as well with the *waw*-consecutive form at the outset of the verse; this form suggests sequence of action in the same time frame as the preceding verb. In view of 2:1, which states that the creation was completed before reference to the seventh day in 2:2, there may be a tension between the two verses, which could reflect some complexity of the text's compositional history.

Another route is to reread the word for "finishing" in Gen. 2:2, which is usually understood to mean that on the seventh day God "finished (*waykal*) the work." Anson Rainey has proposed a rather elegant solution for this verb. He notes that the similar looking verb °*kwl*, "to measure," is used in the description of God's creation in Isa. 40:18. In light of this usage, Rainey suggests that while the first verb in Gen. 2:1 means to be finished, Gen. 2:2 really means that God "measured the work." See Rainey, "Syntax," 75–79, here 77–78 (my thanks go to Anson Rainey for drawing my attention to this article). See also his piece, "Grammar and Syntax of Epigraphic Hebrew" (review essay of Sandra Gogel, *Grammar of Epigraphic Hebrew*), *JQR* 90, 419–27, here 424–27 (I wish to thank David Goldenberg for bringing this discussion by Rainey to my attention and for lending me a copy of it). For the idea, Rainey also compares *Enuma Elish*, tablet IV, lines 141–143. Rainey also observes that the verb °*kwl* is known in precisely this meaning in Hebrew inscriptions. For the meaning, "to measure," see the Gezer Calendar, line 6: "A month of harvesting (wheat) and measuring (grain)," as rendered in Dobbs-Allsopp et al., *Hebrew Inscriptions*, 157, with discussion on 162. For the usage in Meṣad Ḥashavyahu (Yavneh Yam), lines 5, 6, 8, see Dobbs-Allsopp et al., *Hebrew Inscriptions*, 358–61. For further bibliography and discussion, see *DNWSI* 1.507–8. For the form in the causative stem (hiphil), in the sense "to hold," see 1 Kings 7:26–38, 8:64, Ezek. 23:32, and 2 Chron. 4:5, 7:7, as cited in *HALOT* 2.464; for this general meaning, compare Akkadian *kullu* (*CAD* K:508). See further Alexander Rofé, "A Neglected Meaning of the Verb כול and the Text of 1QS VI:11–13," in *Sha'arei Talmon* (ch. 2, n. 37), 315–21, esp. 318. The word also fits the spelling of the verb in Gen. 2:2 particularly well. For this form, compare *wykl* in Meṣad Ḥashavyahu line 5 (Dobbs-Allsopp et al., *Hebrew Inscriptions*, 358). Rainey suggests that measuring is the activity of God on day seven and that work belongs to days one through six. Rainey may be right, but there are problems. Elsewhere the combination of this Hebrew verb (*waykal*) with "blessing" (°*brk*) does not suggests measuring. For example, 1 Chron. 16:2 presents David in the manner of a priest: "And David finished (*waykal*) offering the *'olah*-offerings and the 'well being' offerings and he blessed (*waybarek*) the people in the name of Yahweh." No measuring is involved here.

Furthermore, Rainey's proposal may introduce a new problem: is "measuring" work or not? It indeed seems to be part of the construction work in Isa. 40:12 (the creation account of Job 38:5 also describes measuring before the construction work of sinking of bases and setting of the cornerstone in verse 6). In one inscription that Rainey compares, the act of measuring is listed between the activities of harvesting and storing, and all three of these activities are said to take place "before stopping (*shbt*)." We noted this passage above, where the word for "stopping" here comes from the same word as the Sabbath. Some commentators, including Rainey himself, take this word in the Meṣad Ḥashavyahu inscription to refer to the Sabbath. So it looks as if measuring is part of the activity that happens before ceasing or before the Sabbath, and here measuring seems to be part of the labor. So the text as proposed by Rainey might still pose a problem. It still looks as if God is completing or measuring the work on the seventh day and this might have been seen as labor by the priestly tradition in the Bible (as reflected in Exod. 31:15–17) and later commentators.

I wish to thank Anson Rainey for our e-mail conversation about this matter and for his permission to cite his comments from it. From Rainey's perspective, it matters little whether measuring involves work or not, since God does not bless the day until after measuring the work of creation. Given the emphasis on work in the priestly tradition elsewhere (for example, in Exod. 31:15–17), it might be thought that work would seem to matter to a priestly author.

114. For the text-critical issues in this verse, see Wevers, *Notes*, 20. Some scholars believe that the evidence of these versions of Gen. 2:2 is secondary because it does away with the difficulty; they prefer the "more difficult" reading of the Hebrew Masoretic text precisely it does not get rid of the problem.

115. See pp. 251–52 n. 3.

116. For further discussion, see Avigdor Hurowitz, "When Did God Finish Creation," *BRev* 3/4, 12–14. I wish to thank Avigdor Hurowitz and Gary Rendsburg for a discussion of the problem via e-mail on May 8–9, 2000.

117. See pp. 75–76.

118. Compare a modern "priestly" view of "God-centered and sacramental view of the universe" with its notion that "The whole universe is God's dwelling." See "Catholic Social Teaching and Environmental Ethics," in *Renewing the Face of the Earth* (Washington, D. C.: United States Conference of Catholic Bishops, 1994). Note also its comment: "Earth, a very small, uniquely blessed corner of that universe, gifted with unique natural blessing, is humanity's home, and humans are never so much at home as when God dwells with them."

119. Compare the theological reflections of Iain Provan, "Holistic Ministry: Genesis 1:1—2:3," *Crux* 37/2 (2001) 22–30.

120. See Ratzinger, *'In the Beginning,'* 15.

121. With its use of the speech, Genesis 1 responds to the role of the divine word announced in Isa. 40:8, itself located within a series of divine voices announcing salvation of the divine glory (see v. 5). For comparison of the divine word in Gen. 1:3 and Isa. 40:1–11, see Manfred Görg, "Revision von Schöpfung" (ch. 2, n. 197), 135–56, esp. 151–54; and Labahn, *Wort Gottes und Schuld*, 101 n. 36.

122. So the reflections on the state of sub-Saharan Africa in light of Genesis 1 by Dibeela, "Perspective" (ch. 1, n. 132), 384–99.

123. Compare the generation of mythic narrative in response to colonial domination in the study of Eric Hirsch, "Landscape, Myth and Time," *Journal of Material Culture* 11/1–2 (2006) 151–65. For the presentation of time in Genesis 1 (see further below), note in particular the reflections in this essay on the role of time in mythic narrative in contrast to the time reckoned by outside forces of foreign government and missionaries.

124. For reflections on the priestly construction of memory in the book of Numbers, see Adriane B. Leveen, *Memory and Tradition in the Book of Numbers* (Cambridge/New York: Cambridge University Press, 2008).

125. For an example of the biblical critique of priestly power, see Jer. 5:31. For a sociological approach to the prophets and their criticism of the priesthood, see Hendel, "Prophets," 185–198; see also Lena-Sofia Tiemeyer, *Priestly Rites* (ch. 2, n. 12).

126. Ratzinger recognizes that the revelation of Israel arises from within ancient Israel. See Joseph Cardinal Ratzinger, *Truth and Tolerance: Christian Belief and World Religions* (trans. by Henry Taylor; San Francisco: Ignatius Press, 2004) 198–99. (For bringing this book to my attention, I wish to thank my family's old friend, the late lamented Avery Cardinal Dulles.) At the same time, one might resist the stress placed on the universal versus the particular with respect to revelation of and in ancient Israel (see *Truth and Tolerance*, 199). This may strike one as a Christianizing of the Old Testament, which itself never lessens the particularity of Israel's election even as it offers expression of universal salvation.

127. Ratzinger (*Truth and Tolerance*, 147, 196) rightly recognizes some measure of continuity with ancient Near Eastern traditions. The range of biblical texts with deep roots in ancient Near Eastern tradition has been emphasized for many decades; a full detailing of the cases lies beyond the scope of this discussion, but for starters one may consult Kenton L. Sparks, *Ancient Texts for the Study of the Hebrew Bible: A Guide to the Background Literature* (Peabody, Mass.: Hendrickson

Publishers, 2005). Thus, further wrestling with this issue is needed on the part of biblical theologians and theologians more generally, including the Magisterium. Difference is emphasized often at the expense of continuity. Balance, or better dialectical analysis, is needed.

128. Ratzinger, *Truth and Tolerance*, 145.

129. I am not claiming a singular achievement of Israel over and against the ancient Near East. In its way, *Enūma Elish* combines a description of reality with a number of prescriptive elements for humanity. Just as Genesis 1 describes divine rest as an implicit model for humans, so too *Enūma Elish* declares divine rest for the gods in Marduk's temple, the Esagila (see tablet VI:54; Foster, *Muses*, 470; *COS* 1.401), with the implicit notion that the gods are to be properly served there. In addition, *Enūma Elish* may make reference humanity's service in tablet V:139 (see Foster, *Muses*, 468, n. 2; *COS* 1.400; see also VI:5–9 and 34, Foster, *Muses*,469, 470, and *COS* 1.400, 401; and VII 113, Foster, *Muses*, 473 and *COS* 1.402). Humanity is not only to relieve the gods of their burdens, but also to tell of Marduk's ways and make offerings (VII:108–109, Foster, *Muses*, 473 and *COS* 1.402). The text closes with instructions to various human groups (VII:145–162, in Foster, *Muses*, 484–85, and *COS* 1.402).

As noted in the appendix, it has been argued that Genesis 1 represents a response to *Enūma Elish*. See Sparks, "Priestly Mimesis" (ch. 2, n. 8), 625–48. If so, *Enūma Elish* would be its model for the linkage of ontology and ethics. The history of ancient Near Eastern texts (including biblical texts) linking descriptions of reality (ontology) with prescriptions for human action (ethics) remains a desideratum for research.

130. Many authors have commented in this vein. See, for example, Bauks, "Genesis 1" (ch. 2, n. 7), 333–45. For further discussion, see ch. 4 and the appendix.

Chapter 4: The First Creation Story

1. Carr, *Reading the Fractures* (ch. 2, n. 7).

2. Carr, *Reading the Fractures*, 67–68, 316–19. See also Tryggve N. D. Mettinger, *The Eden Narrative: A Literary and Religio-historical Study of Genesis 2–3* (Winona Lake, Ind.: Eisenbrauns, 2007) 134.

It has also been argued that the second creation story presupposes the priestly creation account. See Eckart Otto, "Paradierzählung Genesis 2–3: Eine nachpriesterschriftliche Lehrerzählung in ihrem Religionsgeschichtlichen Kontext," in „*Jedes Ding hat seine Zeit": Studien zur israelitischen und altorientalischen Weisheit*, BZAW 241, 167–92, followed by Ska, "Genesis 2–3" (ch. 2, n. 154), 1–27. Ska works with a theory that the Yahwist is postexilic (16). Ska suggests that Genesis 2–3 represents the postexilic response of "the people of the land" to the Jerusalemite priesthood that produced Genesis 1. The production of the two accounts together in the present text of Genesis 1–3 represents "a sort of 'historical compromise'" for Ska (23). Ska (16) cites John Van Seters and Christoph Levin as putting the Yahwist in the postexilic period, but these authors generally date this work to the exilic period. Levin favors a dating in the early Diaspora (post-587 BCE): Levin, *Der Jahwist* (ch. 2, n. 25), 433–34, and "The Yahwist" (ch. 2, n. 25), 230. An exilic dating is proposed by Van Seters, *Prologue to History: The Yahwist as Historian in Genesis* (Louisville, Ky.: Westminster/John Knox, 1992) 332; and *The Life of Moses* (ch. 2, n. 25), 468. To be sure, other scholars dispute a Yahwist source altogether. See the debate in the volume of essays edited by Dozemann & Schmidt, *A Farewell to the Yahwist?* (ch. 2, n. 25). See the German forerunner to this volume, *Abschied vom Jahwisten: Die Komposition des Hexateuch in der jüngsten Diskussion*, BZAW 315; and the response to that volume by Christoph Levin, "Abschied vom Jahwisten?" *TRu* 69/3, 329–44.

While I am assuming with most critical scholarship the priority of the second account, Ska's opposite view deserves serious consideration. Whether Genesis 1 presupposes Genesis 2 or vice-versa and whatever their precise dates and backgrounds, Ska seems correct to my mind in suggesting a dialogue about the nature of creation between the traditions represented by Genesis 1 and 2–3.

3. I take this term from S. Dean McBride, "Divine Protocol: Genesis 1:1—2:3 as Prologue to the Pentateuch," in *God Who Creates: Essays in Honor of W. Sibley Towner* (edited by William P. Brown and S. Dean McBride Jr.; Grand Rapids, Mich./Cambridge, U.K.: Eerdmans, 2000) 3–41.

For a treatment of Genesis 1 that also addresses its scope within the Pentateuch, see also Brown, *Ethos* (ch. 2, n. 7), 35–132.

4. Traditional source criticism, as we will note in the appendix, paid little attention to these facets of writing, but these can work with its theory.

5. For further studies of various aspects of orality and literacy, readers may consult the appendix.

6. Carr, *Writing on the Tablet of the Heart: Origins of Scripture and Literature* (Oxford/New York: Oxford University Press, 2005).

7. Memorization has moved to the center stage of other fields, for example in Catherine Hezser's work, *Jewish Literacy in Roman Palestine* (Texts and Studies in Ancient Judaism, vol. 81; Tübingen: Mohr Siebeck, 1998) 99–100, 427–29. For medieval Europe, see the two books by Mary Carruthers, *The Book of Memory: A Study of Memory in Medieval Culture* (Cambridge Studies in Medieval Literature, vol. 10; Cambridge/New York: Cambridge University, 1990); and *The Craft of Thought: Meditation, Rhetoric, and the Making of Images, 400–1200* (Cambridge Studies in Medieval Literature, vol. 14; Cambridge/New York: Cambridge University, 1998).

8. Somewhat neglected in biblical studies until recently is the broader subject of collective memory. For recent studies, see Marc Brettler, "Memory in Ancient Israel," in *Memory and History in Christianity and Judaism* (edited by Michael Signer; Notre Dame, Ind.: University of Notre Dame, 2001) 1–17; Daniel Fleming, "Mari and the Possibilities of Biblical Memory," *Revue Assyriologique* 92 (1998) 41–78; Ronald S. Hendel, "The Exodus in Biblical Memory," *JBL* 120 (2001): 601–22; and his book, *Remembering Abraham: Culture, Memory, and History in the Hebrew Bible* (Oxford/New York: Oxford University, 2005); and Mark S. Smith, *The Memoirs of God: History, Memory, and the Experience of God in Ancient Israel* (Minneapolis: Fortress Press, 2004); "Remembering God: Collective Memory in Israelite Religion," *CBQ* 64 (2002) 631–51; and Leveen, *Memory and Tradition* (ch. 3, n. 124). Brettler, Hendel, and I have been influenced by Yosef Hayim Yerushalmi, *Zakhor: Jewish History and Jewish Memory* (Seattle/London: University of Washington, 1982; rev. ed., 1989).

9. Van der Toorn, *Scribal Culture* (ch. 2, n. 274).

10. This matter comes up in the Epilogue below.

11. Readings and discussion are based on Dennis Pardee, in Dennis Pardee et al., *Handbook of Ancient Hebrew Letters: A Study Edition,* SBLSBS 15, 84–89. I have not included partial brackets in Pardee's reconstruction. See also Johannes Renz, *Handbuch der althebräischen Inschriften: Teil I. Text und Kommentar* (Darmstadt: Wissenschaftliche Buchgesellschaft, 1995) 412–19; and Sandra Goegel, *A Grammar of Epigraphic Hebrew,* SBLRBS, 23, 416–18. I wish to thank David Marcus for questions that required me to clarify some of my thinking about the Lachish letters and their relevance for the discussion below.

12. Cf. the reading *shlhth 'l* in Renz, *Handbuch der althebräischen Epigraphik, Band I,* 417. This difference does not affect the discussion below.

13. Renz as well as Goegel takes this clause as a declarative sentence, while Pardee regards it as a question.

14. Recent commentators agree on the meaning, "to recite" for this form; for example, Pardee, Goegel, and Renz ("kann ich nacher bis ins Detail wiederholen" in *Handbuch der althebräischen Inschriften,* 418). The outstanding issue is the root of the form, whether it is to be derived from °*ntn,* "to give" (Renz, *Handbuch der Althebräischen Epigraphik: Teil 2. Zusammenfassende Erörterungen, Paläographie und Glossar* [Darmstadt: Wissenschaftliche Buchgesellschaft, 1995] 227; Goegel, *A Grammar,* 356) or °*thny* or °*thnn* "to recite" (for the latter, see *DCH* V, 116, #3b).

The best candidate seems to be the root °*thny* (Judg. 5:11, 11:40); for further discussion of this root, see Baruch Halpern, "Dialect Distribution in Canaan and the Deir Alla Inscriptions," in *"Working with No Data": Semitic and Egyptian Studies Presented to Thomas O. Lambdin* (edited by David M. Golomb, with the assistance of Susan T. Hollis; Winona Lake, Ind.: Eisenbrauns, 1987) 124; and Avigdor Hurowitz, "The Seventh Pillar—Reconsidering the Literary Structure and Unity of Proverbs 31," *ZAW* 113, 215 n. 10. The verb is well attested in Ugaritic in the meanings "to repeat, reiterate" particularly in the literary texts; see *DUL* 924–25; it evidently means "to pronounce" in KTU 1.79.3: "he has pronounced (a complaint)." See Pardee, *Ritual and Cult* (Intro., n. 9), 119.

For the meaning "to repeat," William W. Hallo (personal communication) suggests comparing the use of Akkadian *sunnû* in its meaning "to repeat" a text. Referring to the master and his pupil learning the fifty names of Marduk, *Enūma Elish* VII 147 admonishes *li-šá-an-ni-ma abu māri lišāḫiz*, "let the father repeat (the poem) and make his son learn (it) by heart" (*CAD Š/1*:401). The writing of the word of Marduk is encouraged in line 158. The *CAD* entry also contains uses of the word that involve repetition of an oral text.

The use of °*ntn* in this meaning is questionable. The closest meanings given by the *DCH V*, 801 # 3 are "to give out, sound out, utter voice, send," but these are hardly the same as "to recite" (a text). Appeal to Psalm 8:3 for °*ntn* in the meaning to "recite" is dubious; see Smith, "Psalm 8:2b-3" (ch. 1, n. 99), 637–41.

The proposal °*thnn* seems to assume a "polel" form, which is better understood as the alternative piel of °*thny*; it is possible, however, that the second *nun* is part of the ending of the suffix (°*-enhu*). However this question is to be resolved, it does not affect the discussion that follows.

15. Not the suffix *-h* (for which there are no biblical examples with this word), but the adverbial *-h*, as noted by Theophilus J. Meek ("The Hebrew Accusative of Time and Place," *JAOS* 60, 231): "demonstrative or emphatic, parallel to the emphatic *-ma* ending in the Akkadian indefinite pronoun *mimma*, 'anything.'"

16. Pardee, in Pardee et al., *Handbook*, 92.

17. Or, *beth* of essence?

18. Performative perfect.

19. Following NJPS, assuming the *hl* particle (instead of the interrogative *heh* plus the negative). See Michael L. Brown, "'Is it Not?' or 'Indeed!': *HL* in Northwest Semitic," *Maarav* 4/2 (1987) 201–19.

20. Evidently a reference to the thirty sets of sayings thought to follow. For discussion of these "thirty" relating to the precepts of Amenemope, long recognized as the basis for the material following in Proverbs 22–24, see Richard J. Clifford, *Proverbs: A Commentary*, OTL, 199–206. For an ingenious proposal to see the name of Amenemope behind the MT consonants in the words, *hwd'tyk hywm 'ap 'ath*, in Prov. 22:19b, see Gary Rendsburg, "Hebrew Philological Notes (II)," *HS* 42, 187–195, here 192–95. The words are commonly taken to mean, "I have informed you today, indeed you" or the like.

21. Compare the heart as a "site of text," for prayer in Ps. 19:15 and for incorrect speech in Eccles. 5:1 and Ps. 14:1 = 53:1 [MT 2].

22. Clifford, *Proverbs*, 206.

23. See note 14 above.

24. See Susan Niditch, *Oral World and Written Word: Ancient Israelite Literature* (Louisville, Ky.: Westminster John Knox, 1996). Note also Michael David Coogan, "Literacy and the Formation of Biblical Literature," in *Realia Dei: Essays in Archaeology and Biblical Interpretation in Honor of Edward F. Campbell, Jr. at His Retirement* (edited by P. H. Williams, Jr. and T. Hiebert; Scholars Press Homage Series, vol. 23; Atlanta: Scholars, 1999) 47–61; James Crenshaw, *Education in Ancient Israel: Across the Deadening Silence*, ABRL; and Menachem Haran, "On the Diffusion of Literacy and Schools in Ancient Israel," in *Congress Volume: Jerusalem 1986*, VTSup 40, 81–95.

25. The complexity of these interrelated features has been underscored for prophecy in the book edited by Ehud Ben-Zvi and Michael H. Floyd, *Writings and Speech in Israelite and Ancient Near Eastern Prophecy*, SBLSymS 10. The crucial chapter Jeremiah 36 has been studied in this vein by Aaron Schart, "Combining Prophetic Oracles in Mari Letters and Jeremiah 36," *JANESCU* 23, 75–93. For a redactional examination of Jeremiah 36, see also Hermann Josef Stipp, *Jeremia im Parteienstreit* (ch. 2, n. 17), 73–129.

26. For comments on Second Isaiah as a written composition, see Smith, *Early History* (ch. 1, n. 64), 153–54. For reading, writing and interpretation in Second Isaiah, see Sommer, *A Prophet Reads Scripture* (ch. 2, n. 2).

27. Harold Louis Ginsberg, "A Strand in the Cord of Hebraic Psalmody," *ErIsr* 9, 45–50.

28. See my comments on this matter in my article, "Biblical Narrative between Ugaritic and Akkadian Literature: Part II," *Revue Biblique* 114 (2007) 189–207.

29. Smith, *The Memoirs of God*, 107–10, 151–52.

30. For rather different treatments of these passages, see Jon D. Levenson, *The Death and Resurrection of the Beloved Son: The Transformation of Child Sacrifice in Judaism and Christianity* (New Haven/London: Yale University Press, 1993); and John Van Seters, "From Child Sacrifice to Paschal Lamb: A Remarkable Transformation in Israelite Religion," *Old Testament Essays* 16/2 (2003) 453–63.

Luis Alberto Ruiz Cabreo recently analyzed the Phoenician evidence for the *mlk*-sacrifice in "El Sacrificio Molk entre los feninicio-punicis: Cuestiones demografias y ecologicas" (Tesis, Departamento de Historia Antigua, Universidad Complutense de Madrid, 2007; reference courtesy of the author). This work accepts the view of Otto Eissfeldt, Paul G. Mosca, and others that *mlk* is not the name of a deity in the Phoenician material and that offerings of children were indeed involved. For Eissfeldt, see his monograph, *Molk als Opferbegriff im Punichen und Hebräischen und das Ende des Gottes Moloch* (Beitrage Religionsgeschichte des Alterums, vol. 3; Halle: Max Niemeyer, 1935). Eissfeldt's work has been translated into Spanish as *El Molk concepto Sacrificio Punico y Hebreo y final del Dios Moloch*, edited by Carlos C. Wagner and Luis Ruiz Cabreo (Madrid: Centre de Estudios Fenicios y Punicos, 2002), published together with articles on the subject by Enrico Acquario, Maria Giulia Amadasi, Antonia Ciasca, and Edward Lipiński. For Mosca, see "Child Sacrifice in Canaanite and Israelite Religion: A Study in *Mulk* and *mlk*" (Ph.D. dissertation, Harvard University, 1975). For the view that archaeological research has confirmed that sacrifice of children was involved and not simply burial of deceased children, see Lawrence E. Stager and Samuel Wolff, "Child Sacrifice at Carthage: Religious Rite or Population Control? Archaeological Evidence Provides Basis for a New Analysis," *BAR* 10/1, 30–51.

31. A discussion can be found in Scott Walker Hahn and John Seitze Bergsma, "What Laws Were 'Not Good'? A Canonical Approach to the Theological Problem of Ezekiel 20:25–26," *JBL* 123, 201–18. Compare the remarks of Moshe Greenberg, *Ezekiel 1–20*, AB 22, 368–70. Without providing reasons or evidence, Greenberg regards the practice, much less such an interpretation of it in this regard, as "intrinsically improbable."

32. So see the discussion of Jeffrey H. Tigay, *The JPS Commentary: Deuteronomy* (Philadelphia: The Jewish Publication Society, 1996) 162–63. Child sacrifice appears to be understood also in Mic. 6:7; see also Num. 3:12–13, 8:17–18. Parenthetically, it is to be noted that in proposing Levites as a substitute for first-born Israelites, the passages from Numbers shows that the commandment was taken to apply to first-born humans.

33. So Tigay, *Deuteronomy*, 162–63.

34. Note the post-exilic account of such study and interpretation in Neh. 8:13–15.

35. Regarding Ezekiel's alteration of tradition, see the reflections of Moshe Greenberg, "Notes on the Influence of Tradition on Ezekiel," *The Journal of the Ancient Near Eastern Society* 22 (1993) 37 n. 11.

36. Compare the parallel expression found in an Akkadian pseudonymous letter attributed to Samsuiluna and thought to date to the reign of Nebuchadnezzar II. It concerns the holy places and critiques their priestly staffs for their dishonesty, sacrilege, and other offenses, including the following statement: "They establish for their gods matters that the gods did not command." See Foster, *Muses*, 288. For the publication of this text, see F. H. N. Al-Rawi and A. R. George, "Tablets from the Sippar Library III. Two Royal Counterfeits," *Iraq* 56 (1994) 135–48, particularly 138–39. According to Al-Rawi and George, "'Things that the gods commanded' are presumably the correct ritual procedures of the temple, which in Babylonia were considered matters of divine revelation dating from time immemorial" (139).

37. Yet note also Hosea 8:12: "I wrote for him a multitude of my teachings, like something foreign have they been reckoned."

38. I use the term "scriptures" for the beginning of the process of scriptural collection and transmission at this point in Israel's religious-scribal history. Its later and full accomplishment as a religiously recognized reality is signaled by the explicit use of the term in the Hellenistic and Roman periods, as indicated by the following references:

> "the law, the prophets, and the later authors"; and "the law, the prophets, and the rest
>   of the books of our ancestors": Ben Sira prologue;
> "Torah, prophets, and Psalms," *tō nomō. . . tois prophētēs. . . psalmois* (Luke 24:44);

"in the writings," *basseparim* (Dan. 9:2);
"the holy works," *ta biblia ta hagia* (1 Macc. 12:9);
"holy writings," *graphais hagiais* (Rom. 1:2);
"writings," *tōn graphōn* (Rom. 15:4);
"writings," *graphas* (1 Cor. 15:3, 4);
"For what does the writing say?" *ti gar hē graphē legei* (Rom. 4:3; = Gen. 15:6); cf.
    Rom. 9:17; 10:11; 11:2; Gal. 3:8, 22; 4:30;
"the writing," *tēn graphēn*, John 20:9;
"(it says) in the writing," *en graphē*, 1 Pet. 2:6;
"there is no prophecy of scripture," *graphēs*, 2 Pet. 1:20;
"scripture (is inspired by God)," *graphē*, and "the holy writings," *hiera grammata* in
    2 Tim. 3:15–16;
"the holy writings," *hai hierai graphai*: Josephus, *C. Ap.*, 2.4, para. 45 (see also "our
    biblia" in 1.38–40);
Philo, *Abr.*, 61; *Congr.*, 34, 90.

For discussions of these terms, see *The Canon Debate* (Lee Martin McDonald and James A. Sanders, eds.; Peabody, Mass.: Hendrickson Publishers, 2002) 128–145; Jonathan G. Campbell, "4QMMT(d) and the Tripartite Canon," *JJS* 51, 181–190; Timothy H. Lim, "The Alleged Reference to the Tripartite Division of the Hebrew Bible," *RevQ* 20, 23–37; Eugene Ulrich, "The Non-attestation of a Tripartite Canon in 4QMMT," *CBQ* 65, 202–214. (A number of these references come courtesy of Moshe Bernstein.) For an optimistic view of a relatively early tripartite canon (especially compared to the discussions of Ulrich), see Stephen Dempster, "From Many Texts to One: The Formation of the Hebrew Bible," in *The World of the Aramaeans I: Studies in Language and Literature in Honour of Paul-Eugène Dion*, JSOTSup 324, 19–56. I do not use the term "Bible," since this term is a postbiblical anachronism.

39. Compare J. R. Lundbom, "Baruch," in *ABD* 1:617: "as far back as the Old Babylonian period. . . scribes were known to cluster in families."

40. I have discussed this passage in my book, *God in Translation* (ch. 1, n. 4), 219–20.

41. On the Holiness Code of Leviticus 17–26 in recent discussion, see in particular Baruch Schwartz, *The Holiness Legislation: Studies in the Priestly Code* (Jerusalem: Magnes, 1999) (Heb.). Recent discussion on the Holiness redaction and its relationship to other priestly corpora has been studied by Israel Knohl, *Sanctuary* (ch. 2, n. 7); and Jacob Milgrom, *Leviticus 1–16* (ch. 3, n. 31), 13–42. For a constructive response to Knohl, see Olyan, *Rites and Rank* (ch. 3, n. 41); and his study, "Exodus 31:12–17: The Sabbath According to H or the Sabbath According to P and H?" *JBL* 124, 201–9. See also Alan Cooper and Bernard Goldstein ("Exodus and Maṣṣôt in History and Tradition," in *Maarav* 8/2 [1992] = *Let Your Colleagues Praise You: Studies in Memory of Stanley Gevirtz* [edited by Robert Ratner et al.; two vols.; Rolling Hill Estates, Calif.: Western Academic Press, 1992], 2.15–37, esp. 25 n. 35), who also regard H as a redaction postdating P. On the relationship between the Holiness Code and P, see further H.-W. Jüngeling, "Das Buch in der Forschung seit Karl Eligers Kommentar aus dem 1966," in *Levitikus als Buch*, BBB 119, 1–45. A discussion of various positions has been laid out by Jeffrey R. Stackert, *Rewriting the Torah: Literary Revision and the Holiness Legislation*, FAT I:52.

42. For detailed discussion of these chapters, readers are encouraged to consult the commentaries by Levine, *Leviticus* (ch. 3, n. 36); and Jacob Milgrom, *Leviticus 1–16*, 13–42. Note also Milgrom's comments in his introduction and notes to Leviticus in NRSV (*HCSB*, [Intro., n. 3]).

43. On the "ritual style" of the priestly author, see Hanna Liss, "The Imagining Sanctuary" (ch. 2, n. 227), 674–76.

44. I owe these observations to Chaim Cohen, "The Genre of Priestly Instructions in the Torah and the Isolation of a New Torah Source—PI" (unpublished paper, cited with permission). Cohen is head of the Department of Hebrew Language at Ben-Gurion University in Beersheba.

45. Carr, *Reading the Fractures*. Cf. Gary A. Rendsburg, *The Redaction of Genesis* (Winona Lake, Ind.: Eisenbrauns, 1996). Despite the use of the word "redaction" in its title, the book does not address what is generally regarded as redaction or redactional activity in the book of Genesis. Rendsburg's work is largely engaged in identifying large-scale literary patterning in Genesis, and for

this agenda, he offers several fine literary observations. The sort of patterning that he discerns in the book may well be part of the redactional activity underlying its formation. Cf. Jack M. Sasson, "The 'Tower of Babel' as a Clue to the Redactional Structuring of the Primeval History [Gen. 1—11:9]" in *The Bible World: Essays in Honor of Cyrus H. Gordon* (edited by Gary Rendsburg et al.; New York: KTAV, 1980) 211–219; and "Love's Roots: On the Redaction of Genesis 30:14–24," in *Love and Death in the Ancient Near East: Essays in Honor of Marvin H. Pope* (edited by John H. Marks and Robert M. Good; Guilford, Conn.: Four Quarters, 1987) 205–209.

46. Blum, *Studien* (ch. 2, n. 7). See further Witte, *Die biblische Urgeschichte* (ch. 2, n. 25).

47. See Cross, *Canaanite Myth* (ch. 1, n. 16), 305, 324–25, where he argued against narrative continuity in the priestly source. See also Childs, *Introduction* (ch. 2, n. 18), 147. Other scholars, such as Joseph Blenkinsopp, *The Pentateuch: An Introduction to the First Five Books of the Bible,* ABRL, 78, 119, essentially return to Martin Noth's view of narrative continuity of the priestly source (see Noth, *Pentateuchal Traditions* [ch. 2, n. 7], 8–9). See also Klaus Koch, "P—kein Redaktor! Erinnerung an zwei Eckdaten der Quellenescheidung," *VT* 37, 446–67; and John A. Emerton, "The Priestly Writer in Genesis," *JTS* 39, 381–400, cited by Blenkinsopp, *The Pentateuch*, 132 n. 19. Note also Graham I. Davies, "Reflections on the Theses of Erhard Blum," in *Texts, Temples, and Traditions* (ch. 2, n. 22), 79–80.

48. This model (or something similar) may apply in the case of Genesis 1. Exodus 31:17 resembles Gen. 2:2–3. It looks like a textual repetition or echo of Gen. 2:2–3 in summary form. At the same time, the departure in Exod. 31:17, with its use of *wayyinnapash,* "and was refreshed" (NJPS), arguably looks like a variant, perhaps an oral one. Note also the slight variation in Exod. 20:11 in its echo of Gen. 2:2–3. Exodus 20:11 and 31:17 look like presentations of material attested in narrative form in Gen. 2:2–3. One might prefer a synchronic reading of Genesis and Exodus and view the Exodus passages as reflections of Gen. 2:2–3, but such an approach does not explain the appearance of *wayyinnapash* in Exod. 31:17. This departure suggests that these three passages may reflect the process of drafting of what became Gen. 2:2–3 (and Gen. 1:1—2:3 by implication). See Yair Hoffman, "The First Creation Story: Canonical and Diachronic Aspects," in *Creation in Jewish and Christian Tradition,* JSOTSup 319, 32–53. For discussion of the context of Exod. 31:17, see Saul M. Olyan, "Exodus 31:12–17," 201–9.

49. See Childs, *Introduction*, 147.

50. See Marc Vervenne, "Genesis 1,1—2,4: The Compositional Texture of the Priestly Overture to the Pentateuch," in *Studies in the Book of Genesis,* BETL 145, 35–79, esp. 55–64, which critically evaluates arguments in favor of the priority of Genesis 2–3 relative to Genesis 1. In this connection, it may be noted that Hoffman ("The First Creation Story," 32–53) also believes that Genesis 1 was a very late addition. See further below.

51. Pardee, *Ritual and Cult*, 3.

52. Pardee, *Ritual and Cult*, 2.

53. Pardee, *Ritual and Cult*, 2. Particularly interesting in this regard are what Pardee calls the "check marks" on deity-lists (see 13), used to check off offerings as they were given to deities.

54. Pardee, *Ritual and Cult*, 3.

55. Again I owe this observation to Chaim Cohen, "The Genre of Priestly Instructions."

56. Many rituals listing what animals are to be offered to which god or goddesses use a preposition, "for such and such a deity, such and such an animal (as an offering)," but sometimes the rituals do not use a preposition in a manner that recalls administrative lists, "deity-name: a given animal." Both styles are used in KTU 1.109 (see Pardee, *Ritual and Cult*, 29–31).

57. In addition to the commentaries, see the older study of Baruch Levine, *In the Presence of the Lord* (ch. 2, n. 263); and the summary of Pardee, *Ritual and Cult*, 233–41. Ugaritic rituals alternate between the largely dominant third-person prefix forms and second-person prefix forms (they also contain some imperatives addressed to the officiating priest); the same basic verbal usage appears in Leviticus 2. Both corpora also display the converted suffix form in the second person (for example, see Leviticus 2:5–6 and KTU 1.39.20, in Pardee, *Ritual and Cult*, 68). They also vary in the parties addressed. Lev. 1:2—6:7, 7:11–36 are addressed to lay people as opposed to Lev. 6:8—7:10, which is addressed to priests. The Ugaritic ritual texts are addressed to priests

and perhaps sometimes to the king. They also mention various figures who are neither, for example, women in 1.115.8, "the woman/women may eat (of the sacrificial meal)," and participants in general in 1.115.10, "all may eat of it"; see Pardee, *Ritual and Cult*, 66. Leviticus 1–7 provides far greater detail about the manner of handling the sacrifices compared with the Ugaritic ritual texts. For other differences of content (including some differences and similarities in the names of the offerings), consult Pardee, *Ritual and Cult*, 233–41. The similarities suggest a broadly shared West Semitic ritual tradition, while the differences suggest local variation as well as individuation from this older tradition.

58. Cohen, "The Genre of Priestly Instructions."

59. For example, the structuring note of Exod. 31:18, discussed in Mark S. Smith, *The Pilgrimage Pattern in Exodus*, with contributions by Elizabeth M. Bloch-Smith, JSOTSup 239, 161, 169, 187, 190, 197, 244, 246–47, 259–60.

60. For a broad discussion of the oral, literary tradition of early Israel (largely influenced by the work of Frank M. Cross), see Robert S. Kawashima, *Biblical Narrative and the Death of Rhapsode* (Indiana Studies in Biblical Literature; Bloomington/Indianapolis: Indiana University Press, 2004). See also the important essay of Edward L. Greenstein, "The Formation of the Biblical Narrative Corpus," *Association of Jewish Studies Review* 15 (1990) 151–78. Note also the qualifications expressed by Michael H. Floyd, "Oral Tradition as a Problematic Factor in the Historical Interpretation of Poems in the Law and the Prophets" (Ph.D. dissertation, Claremont Graduate School, 1980). For the Ugaritic backdrop to this storytelling tradition, see Simon B. Parker, *The Pre-Biblical Narrative Tradition*, SBLRBS 24. For reflections on this subject, with discussion of various proposals, see my two essays, "Biblical Narrative between Ugaritic and Akkadian Literature: Part I: Ugarit and the Hebrew Bible: Consideration of Recent Comparative Research," *RB* 114/1, 5–29; and "Biblical Narrative: Part II," 189–207.

61. It has become quite common to place the so-called "Yahwist" or "J" source in the sixth century as well. See, for example, Van Seters, *The Life of Moses;* compare Christoph Levin, *Der Jahwist;* and his more recent article, "The Yahwist," 126, 209–30. Viewing J as a great assembler of what has been regarded as other sources, Van Seters places J in the exilic period. For Levin, the redaction of the Jahwist is designed to address the Jewish Diaspora of the Persian period. Other scholars hold out for an earlier date. For a consideration of the date of the so-called "Yahwist" as ninth-seventh century, see John A. Emerton, "The Date of the Yahwist," in *In Search of Pre-Exilic Israel: Proceedings of the Oxford Old Testament Seminar,* JSOTSup 406, 107–29. Many scholars are no longer inclined to the view of a single source; see the essays in Dozemann & Schmid, eds., *A Farewell to the Yahwist?* (ch. 2, n. 25). See further the discussion of Levin, "Abschied vom Jahwisten?" 329–44.

The Elohist is arguably even more problematic. For the so-called "Elohist source" as seventh century, see Robert K. Gnuse, "Redefining the Elohist?" *JBL* 119, 201–20. For a recent defense of the Elohist, see Joel Baden, *J, E, and the Redaction of the Pentateuch,* FAT (2009). For the purposes of this discussion, the precise nature or dates of these so-called sources is unimportant. The discussion below assumes only that Genesis 1:1—2:3 postdates 2:4b-25.

62. For broader discussions of priestly narrative, see Cross, *Canaanite Myth*, 293–325; and Sean McEvenue, *The Narrative Style of the Priestly Writer,* AnBib 50.

63. See Cross, *Canaanite Myth*, 293–325. Note also Childs, *Introduction*, 147, where he observes that the priestly blocks of material in Genesis have their own integrity, even they do not constitute a source running the length of the book. He has notes that the book reflects different redactional levels within the priestly material itself, and he cites 2:4 and 5:1 in this connection.

64. Note the explorations in this vein by Sparks, "Priestly Mimesis" (ch. 2, n. 8), 625–48.

65. So Levenson, *Creation* (ch. 1, n. 114), 76.

66. Compare the studies of Marc Vervenne, "Genesis 1,1—2,4," 35–79; and Weimar, "Struktur und Komposition," 803–43.

67. See the important essay of Polak, "Poetic Style" (ch. 2, n. 86), 2–31.

68. For scholars who hold to a priestly source (see the appendix), Genesis 1 would have originated as the prologue to that source; it became the prologue for the Pentateuch when the priestly or holiness compiler (or redactor) combined the priestly source with the other narrative material of

the other sources. For recent reflections on the larger placement of Genesis 1, see Otto, "Scribal Scholarship" (ch. 1, n. 26), 171–75. In any case, I have already expressed my doubts about a continuous priestly source parallel to the other so-called sources, but this issue little affects the discussion here.

69. Gerhard von Rad, *Deuteronomy: A Commentary,* OTL, 48, 55; Georg Braulik, "Literarkritik und archäologisches Stratigraphie: Zu S. Mittmanns Analyse von Deuteronomium 1,1–40," *Bib* 59, 351–83; and "Literarkritik und die Einrahmung von Gemälden: Zur literarkritischen und redaktionsgeschichtlichen Analyse von Dtn 4,1—6,3 und 29,2—30.20 durch D. Knapp," *RB* 96, 266–86; A. D. H. Mayes, "Deuteronomy 4 and the Literary Criticism of Deuteronomy," *JBL* 100 23–51; and Sven Petry, *Die Entgrenzung Jhwhs: Monolatrie, Bilderverbot und Monotheismus im Deuteronomium, in Deuterojesaja und im Ezechielbuch,* FAT II:27, 70–100.

70. This view is based largely on the near repetition of Josh. 24:28–31 by Judg. 2:6–10. See the discussion of Marc Z. Brettler, *The Book of Judges* (Old Testament Readings; London/New York: Routledge, 2002) 94–102. That this view has received broad acceptance is reflected in its mention by *HCSB,* 350, note to 2:6–10. Judg. 1:1—2:5 arguably represents two sets of introductory material to Judges.

71. The only known exemplar of the Middle Babylonian Version of the introduction was discovered in 1994 at the site of ancient Ugarit. See Daniel Arnaud, *Corpus des texts de bibliothèque de Ras Shamra-Ougarit (1936–2000) en sumérien, babylonien, et assyrien* (Sabadell: Editorial AUSA, 2007) 130–34 for transliteration and translation, and 252–54 for transcription. For the Standard Babylonian Version, see Andrew R. George, *The Babylonian Gilgamesh Epic: Introduction, Critical Edition and Cuneiform Texts* (two vols.; Oxford/New York: Oxford University Press, 2003) 1.29–33; and van der Toorn, *Scribal Culture,* 126–28. To be sure, there are significant differences between the Middle Babylonian and Standard Babylonian versions. I wish to thank my student Elizabeth Knott for sharing her work comparing the Middle Babylonian and the Standard Babylonian Versions. As she reminds me, the Standard Babylonian Version is a hypothetical reconstruction of a supposed standard text reconstructed from many, but not identical, fragments.

72. Von Rad, *Genesis* (ch. 2, n. 7), 45, cited by Brown, *Structure, Role, and Ideology* (ch. 2, n. 200), 249–50.

73. Brown, *Structure, Role, and Ideology,* 249.

74. The Ugaritic example of KTU 1.86 has been compared with the *pesharim.* See Pardee, *Ritual and Cult,* 144. Note also the discussion of *Ezra and Ishum* as commentary (on p. 150).

75. For presentation of KTU 1.86 = RS 18.041, see Pardee, *Ritual and Cult,* 144–48. Lines 2 and 7 attest to *rgm,* "word" in this usage (the last letter in line 2 is somewhat damaged).

76. For an interesting case for an interpretative clause somewhat along these lines (using *hi'*), see Jer. 45:4 in comparison with 1:10, 18:7, 24:6, 31:28, and 38:40. For this sort of interpretational marking with a pronominal deictic particle relative to the *pesher* form, see Fishbane, *Biblical Interpretation* (ch. 2, n. 2), 454–55; and for the wider context of this usage of the pronoun as a deictic marker, see 44–46. For discussion of the motif in Jeremiah, note Carolyn J. Sharp, "The Call of Jeremiah and Diaspora Politics," *JBL* 119, 426–27.

77. Carr, *Reading the Fractures,* 74–75, 317. See also Cross, *Canaanite Myth,* 301–5; Sven Tengström, *Die Toledotformel und die literarische Structur der priestlichen Erweiterungsschicht im Pentateuch,* ConBOT 17; and the 1974 essay by Peter Weimar, "Die Toledotformel in der priesterschriftlichen Geschichtsdarstellung," conveniently accessible in his collection of essays, entitled *Studien zur Priesterschrift,* FAT I:56, 151–84. See also the valuable review of Terje Stordalen, "Genesis 2,4: Restudying a *locus classicus,*" *Zeitschrift für die alttestamentliche Wissenschaft* 104 (1992) 163–77; Marc Vervenne, "Genesis 1,1—2,4," 35–79; and Hendel, *Remembering Abraham,* 105. These studies presuppose that P knows J rather than the other way around; for Genesis 2–3 as an elaboration of Genesis 1, see Craig Y. S. Ho, "The Supplementary Combination of the Two Creation Stories in Genesis 1–3," in *Stimulation from Leiden: Collected Communications to the XVIIIth Congress of the International Organization for the Study of the Old Testament, Leiden 2004,* BEATAJ 54, 13–21. Such an approach may be maintained as a matter of synchronic reading and arguably reflects diachronically the goals and strategy of the priestly author/editor that placed these chapters together.

78. The view is discussed by many scholars; see for example, Stordalen, "Genesis 2,4," 163–77; and Christoph Levin, "Die Redaktion R^{JP} in der Urgeschichte," in *Auf dem Weg zur Endgestalt von Genesis bis II Regum: Festschrift Hanns-Christoph Schmitt zum 65. Geburstag* (Martin Beck and Ulrike Schorn, eds.; Berlin/New York: de Gruyter, 2006) 15–34, esp. 24–27. See also the discussion in the appendix.

79. See for example, Cross, *Canaanite Myth*, 301–5; Tengström, *Die Toledotformel;* the 1974 essay by Weimar, "Die Toledotformel," 151–84; and Carr, *Reading the Fractures*, 74–75. See also the valuable review of Terje Stordalen, "Genesis 2,4," 163–77.

80. Childs, *Introduction*, 145–46.

81. Many scholars take Gen. 2:4a as a priestly redactional addition made secondarily to the priestly composition of Gen. 1:1—2.3. Vervenne ("Genesis 1,1—2,4," 69) has questioned this assumption that Gen. 2:4a derives from a different hand than Gen. 1:1—2:3, rightly in my opinion. As a related matter, it is sometimes thought that the priestly editor of 2:4a also added "God" (*'elohim*) to the name of Yahweh throughout Gen. 2:4b through the end of Genesis 3. Von Rad, *Genesis*, 75; Speiser (ch. 2, n. 200), *Genesis*, 15–16; S. McBride, "Divine Protocol," 8 n. 10. The result of this editorial commentary is to state that Yahweh is God (compare "Yahweh—he is God," *yhwh hu' ha'elohim*, in 1 Kings 18:39). In effect, this editorial addition specifies what *'elohim* in Genesis 2–3 means (cf. Sarna, *Genesis*, 5). If this observation is correct, then the editorial commentary involved an editor importing an element from his own textual tradition or material into a preexisting text that he transmitted and modified.

82. Compare the remarks of Levin, "Die Redaktion R^{JP}," 24–27.

83. For the purposes of the discussion here, it does not matter whether the author of Gen. 1:1—2:3 is also the priestly redactor responsible for 2:4a. The comments that follow stand either way.

84. For example, Carr, *Reading the Fractures,* 62–68. See also Vervenne, "Genesis 1,1—2,4," 69–70.

85. Speiser, *Genesis*, 18.

86. Westermann, *Genesis 1–11* (ch. 2, n. 59), 197.

87. Schmidt, *Die Schöpfungsgeschichte* (ch. 2, n. 60), 196.

88. Sarna, *Genesis*, 16.

89. Carr, *Reading the Fractures*, 66 n. 34.

90. For these orders in other texts, see ch. 2.

91. Sarna, *Genesis*, 16–17. Contrast Vervenne ("Genesis 1,1—2,4," 69) on the literary function of Gen. 2:4.

92. As support, one might invoke "Seidel's law," that a word pair in an older text may occur in a later one in reverse order. See Moshe Seidel, "Parallels between the Book of Isaiah and the Book of Psalms," *Sinai* 38 (1955–56) 149–72, 229–42, 272–80, 333–55, esp. 150 (Heb.). Sommer (*A Prophet Reads Scripture*, 219 n. 11) comments on Seidel's law: "The value of this observation is limited, however, since coincidentally shared terms could very well appear in different order in two texts. Indeed, even stock parallel terms in Hebrew and Ugaritic sometimes appear with one term first and other times with the other first. . . . Further, the inversion that Seidel notes does not help us recognize which text is the source and which the borrower." With respect to Gen. 2:4, however, little looks coincidental, and there is a general consensus concerning the relative sequence of source and borrower. With respect to the Ugaritic examples, thematic reversal appears to be involved in some instances, which would suggest that other literary conventions govern them, and they therefore should not be invoked as counterevidence to Seidel's law. For example, in the reversal of *'urbt ḥln* in KTU 1.4 V 61–62, 64–65, VI 5–6, 8–9 and in 1.4 VII 17–19, 25–27, commentators have suggested that the inversion marks the reversal of Baal's decision to install a window in his new palace. For a convenient presentation of the text and translation of these Ugaritic passages, see Smith, "The Baal Cycle," 132–33, 136. I thank Alan Cooper for reminding me of the possible pertinence of Seidel's law for the discussion of Gen. 2:4.

93. To my mind, these problems are not sufficiently addressed by Stordalen, "Genesis 2,4," 163–77. His translation of the verse seems somewhat forced.

94. Schökel, *Hebrew Poetics* (ch. 1, n. 113), 189.

95. See the discussion in ch. 2.

96. Bauks & Baumann, "Im Anfang war. . .?" (ch. 2, n. 36), 24–52. See ch. 2 for discussion.

97. This root is used not uncommonly in creation references. Besides Genesis 1 and Prov. 8:22, see also Prov. 8:23, Job 15:7, 40:19.

98. See ch. 3. See further p. 244 n. 227, with citations of other scholars who accept the comparison of language of temple building and creation.

99. Schmidt, *Die Schöpfungsgeschichte*, 164–67.

100. For an extended discussion, see David Toshio Tsumura, *Creation and Destruction* (ch. 1, n. 13) 9–140, esp. 9–35, 77–85, 127–30, 196.

101. One might even speculate that the noun, "darkness" (*hoshek*) in 1:2 aurally echoes the verb, "and it would water" (*wehishqah*) in 2:6; this, though, may be going too far. It is likewise tempting, though speculative, to see Gen. 3:8, with its use of both *ruah* and *'elohim*, as another possible source text informing the composition of Gen. 1:2.

102. See p. 57 and p. 232 n. 125.

103. For some discussion of the two in tandem, see Tsumura, *The Earth and the Waters* (ch. 2, n. 119), 165.

104. Two more suggestions are appropriate; although they are rather speculative, they are in keeping with the idea of Genesis 1 playing off Genesis 2, and perhaps Genesis 3 as well. First, the refrain of Genesis 1 (vv. 4, 10, 12, 18, 21, 25; cf. 1:31), "and God *saw* that it was *good*" (*wayyar' 'elohim ki tob*), was perhaps inspired in part by the phrasing in Genesis 2:9, "pleasing in *appearance*, and *good* for food" (*nehmad lemar'eh wetob lema'akal*). Both phrases use the word, "good" (*tob*) and both contain a form of the word "to see" (the verb *wayyar'* in one case and the noun form *mar'eh* in the other). We may note that Gen. 2:9 is echoed later in 3:6 in a formulation that stands closer to the refrain verses of Genesis 1: "and the woman *saw* that the tree was *good* (*wattere' ha'ishsha ki tob ha'es*). Second, perhaps the human acts of naming (*qr' l-*) in Gen. 2:19, 20, 23 (cf. Gen. 3:9, 20) inspired the use of divine naming (*qr' l*) in Gen. 1:5, 8, 10, since divine naming does not seem to be a particularly priestly feature. In the case of Genesis 3, "calling" in verse 20 precedes "making" in verse 21, a collocation of acts that marks Gen. 1:7–8.

105. See, in addition to the commentaries, Phyllis Bird, "Gen 1:27b in the Context of the Priestly Account of Creation," *HTR* 74, 138–44; Janowski, "Herrschaft über die Tiere" (ch. 3, n. 79), 183–98; and Edwin Firmage, "Genesis 1" (ch. 2, n. 7), 97–114. Note the discussion above on pp. 99, 101–02. See also the literature cited in the next note.

106. For this presentation of human creation by God, compare Job 10:8–12 and 33:6 (see also 4:19, 27:3, 30:19 for various aspects of this idea); note also Isa. 29:16, 45:8–9, 64:7–8; Jer. 18:3–6; Wisd. of Sol. 15:7–8; Rom. 9:21. Genesis 2:7 is echoed in Ben Sira 17:1. Compare how Ben Sira 33:13 uses this image of God the potter following the allusion to Gen. 2:7 in Ben Sira 33:10. For discussion, see Edward L. Greenstein, "God's Golem: The Creation of the Human in Genesis 2," in *Creation in Jewish and Christian Tradition*, JSOTSup 319, 219–39; and Mettinger, *The Eden Narrative*, 29.

Creation of the human person from the dirt of the ground is attested in ancient Near Eastern literature as well. For example, the account of human creation in *Atra-ḫasis* includes clay from the ground; see Old Babylonian *Atra-ḫasis*, tablet I, lines 203, 210–234; see W. G. Lambert and A. R. Millard, *Atra-ḫasis: The Babylonian Story of the Flood* (Oxford: At the Clarendon, 1969; reprint edition, Winona Lake, Ind.: Eisenbrauns, 1999) 56–59; and Stol, *Birth* (ch. 3, n. 69), 112–14. Similarly, the goddess "pinched off its clay" for the creation of the human king; see Foster, *Muses*, 496. This is also the method of creation used by El to make the female figure "expeller" (cf. the human male attributed this job in KTU 2.82.5), who cures King Kirta of his illness in KTU 1.16 V 28–30: "He fills his hands [with soil], With good soil fills his [fingers]. He pinches off some clay." For this translation as well as an English transcription of the Ugaritic letters, see Greenstein, "Kirta" (ch. 1, n. 21), 38. For the Egyptian god Khnum creating human beings like a potter, see Bickel, *La cosmogonie égyptienne* (ch. 2, n. 167), 202–4; for an iconographic example, note *ANEP* #569. For basic presentations of the manufacture of pottery from clay in ancient Israel, see Robert H. Johnston, "The Biblical Potter," *BA* 37/4, 86–106, repr. in *BARead IV*, 213–26; and Philip J. King and Lawrence E. Stager, *Life in Biblical Israel* (Library of Ancient Israel; Louisville/London: Westminster John Knox, 2001) 133–46. Compare Gloria Anne London, "Past and Present: The Village Potters of Cyprus," *BA* 52, 219–29; and Gloria Anne London, F. Egoumenidou, and V. Karageorghis, *Traditional Pottery in Cyprus* (Mainz am Rhein: Philipp von Zaubern, 1990). See also the promotional Web page for Gloria London's 2000 video *Women Potters of Cyprus* at http://home.earthlink.net/~galondon/Kornos/index.html.

The element mixed with the dirt or clay of the earth varies in these accounts. In some instances, it is a component that links human life with divinity in some manner, for example, divine *neshamah*, "breath" in the case of Gen. 2:7 (see also Isa. 57:16), while it is *ruah*, "breath" in Isa. 42:5; in *Atra-ḥasīs* it is the flesh and blood of the slain god that contains his "spirit," as *eṭemmu* is translated by Lambert and Millard, and also by Foster, *Muses*, 236. The word elsewhere often means "ghost," and so this "spirit" is in some sense the ghost of this slain god incorporated into the human person. It is to be noted that several levels of wordplay inform this account. For discussion, see Lambert & Millard, *Atra-ḥasīs*, 153; Foster, *Muses*, 236 n. 1; compare and Tzvi Abusch, "Ghost and God: Some Observations on a Babylonian Understanding of Human Nature," in *Self, Soul and Body in Religious Experience*, SHR 78, 363–83. The element of the god's blood occurs not only in *Atra-ḥasīs*, but also in *Enūma Elish*, tablet VI, lines 32–33 (Foster, *Muses*, 470) and in the bilingual "Creation of Humankind" (in Foster, *Muses*, 491–93), which describes human creation from the blood of the "Alla-gods."

For a rather imaginative discussion of biblical and ancient Near Eastern accounts of the creation of humanity, see Irit Ziffer, "The First Adam, Androgyny, and the 'Ain Ghazal Two-Headed Busts in Context," *IEJ* 57, 129–52, esp. 140–43.

107. For a recent discussion of biblical anthropomorphism, see Esther J. Hamori, "*When Gods Were Men*": *The Embodied God in Biblical and Near Eastern Literature*, BZAW 384; for her comments on Genesis 1–2, see 32.

108. Compare Eccles. 12:7: "And the dust returns to the ground as it was, and the life breath returns to God who bestowed it" (compare also Isa. 38:16). Note also *ruah* fashioned in the human person as mentioned in the creation allusion in Zech. 12:1.

109. Trible, *God and the Rhetoric of Sexuality*, 20–21. The italics are Trible's. For a response to some of Trible's ideas about this passage, see Robert S. Kawashima, "A Revisionist Reading Revised: On the Creation of Adam and Then Eve," *VT* 5, 46–57.

110. See earlier pp. 99–100.

111. See the detailed comments of Carr, *Reading the Fractures*, 63–64.

112. With its reference to creation of heaven and earth followed by the fashioning of human *ruah* by God, Zech. 12:1 shows that the general approach of Genesis 1 ("heavens and earth") need not overwhelm the idea of human creation as put forth in Gen. 2:7. See Meyers & Meyers, *Zechariah 9–14* (ch. 2, n. 2), 311.

113. The priestly writer is also thought to offer here an implicit polemic against polytheism, that human beings are the living images pointing to a living God, while statues of others' deities are lifeless images of lifeless deities. For these points, especially as they involve Second Isaiah, see Smith, *Origins* (ch. 1, n. 14), 179–93, esp. 181–82. While certainly there is no room for other deities in the priestly understanding of reality, it is unclear that a deliberate polemic is in evidence.

114. Wellhausen, *Prolegomena* (ch. 2, n. 6), 307: "We cannot regard it as fortuitous that in this point Gen. i asserts the opposite of Gen. ii. iii.; the words spoken with such emphasis, and repeated i. 27, v. 1, ix. 6, sound exactly like a protest against the view underlying Gen. ii-iii.".

115. *Atra-ḥasīs*, in *COS* 1.451. See also *Enūma Elish*, tablet VI, line 8; see *ANET* 68; *COS* 1.400; Foster, *Muses*, 469; and the discussion of Levenson, *Creation*, 106–7.

116. Aquinas, *Commentary on the Metaphysics*, para. 301–305. See also Aquinas, *De Trinitate*; and his *Commentary on Romans* 1:20. These references came courtesy of my teacher of metaphysics, Professor John Whipple of The Catholic University of America. He is, of course, not responsible for my simplification of Aquinas' point here.

117. In the book of Deuteronomy, God becomes the unseen, disembodied Speaker of the heavenly word. For discussion, see Smith, *Early History*, 205–6.

118. I have discussed these ideas in the context of Israel's larger narrative traditions in Genesis through Kings in an article, entitled, "Biblical Narrative: Part II," 189–207.

119. Arguably the priestly tradition did so in tandem or dialogue with Deuteronomy and other works influenced by this book (what scholars have called "deuteronomic" and "deuteronomistic" viewpoints). See Smith, "Biblical Narrative: Part II," 205–7.

Chapter 5: Is Genesis 1 a Creation Myth?

1. For the religious views of the sources of the biblical flood story as well as their resultant redaction together, see P. J. Harland, *The Value of Human Life: A Study of the Story of the Flood (Genesis 6–9)* VTSup LXIV.

2. For handy reference, see Dalley, *Myths* (Intro., n. 6). For a survey of ancient Near Eastern traditions about the flood, see Brian B. Schmidt, "Flood Narratives of Ancient Western Asia," *CANE IV*, 2337–51. Atra-ḫasīs is discussed further below. Regarding the combination of Inanna's divine roles, note the comment of Rivkah Harris: "The composer of the so-called standard version of the Gilgamesh Epic incorporated the original separate flood story into his version, surely aware of the contradictory depictions of the goddess." See Harris, "Inanna-Ishtar" (ch. 1, n. 21), 261–78, here 264.

3. This is a fairly typical approach to myth. Among more general treatments, see Robert A. Segal, *Myth: A Very Short Introduction* (Oxford: Oxford University Press, 2004) 4–5, 84–85; and G. S. Kirk, *The Nature of Greek Myths* (London: Penguin Books, 1990) 23, 28–29. Among biblical scholars, see Robert A. Oden, *The Bible Without Theology: The Theological Tradition and Alternatives to It* (San Francisco: Harper & Row, 1987) 56; and Mettinger, *The Eden Narrative* (ch. 4, n. 2), 68–69.

4. Here note the comments of George W. Coats: "If ancient Near Eastern myths lie behind this unit, it is nonetheless clear that the unit is no longer myth. The generic character of parallel mythology is not reproduced in the narrative itself." See Coats, *Genesis with an Introduction to Narrative Literature*, FOTL I, 47. Coats concludes that Genesis 1 is to be classified as a "report."

5. For example, note the following comment of Fritz Graf, "Myth," in *Religions of the Ancient World. A Guide* (Sarah Iles Johnston, ed.; Cambridge/London: Harvard University, 2004) 53: "In monotheistic Israel, every intervention of God in the visible world—from the creation to the ongoing protection of God's people—is understood as history: where God reveals the past, there is no place for myth."

6. LSJ 1151.

7. For an explicit expression of this contrast, Nagy cites Pindar, *Olympian*, 1.27–29. See Nagy, "Can Myth Be Saved?" in *Myth: A New Symposium* (edited by G. Schrempp and W. Hansen; Bloomington/Indianapolis: Indiana University, 2002) 240–48, esp. 241. Nagy attributes the change in the meaning of myth to the breakdown of the symbiosis between myth and ritual in the archaic and classical periods of ancient Greece. Prior to this breakdown, myth was at home, according to Nagy, in contexts of ritual performance.

8. Andrew Von Hendy, *The Modern Construction of Myth* (Bloomington/Indianapolis: Indiana University, 2002).

9. Von Hendy, *The Modern Construction*, 3.

10. See Jonathan Z. Smith, "Religion, Religions, Religious," in *Critical Terms for Religious Studies* (edited by Mark C. Taylor; Chicago/London: University of Chicago, 1998) 269–84.

11. Von Hendy, *Modern Construction*, xviii.

12. See also the critique by Kirk, *The Nature of Greek Myths*, 13–91. Note also the critique about the more recent tendency to privilege the political in myths by C. Sourvinou-Inwood, "Reconstructing Change: Ideology and the Eleusinian Mysteries," in *Inventing Ancient Culture: Historicism, Periodization, and the Ancient World* (edited by Mark Golden and Peter Toohey; London/New York: Routledge, 1997) 143; see also Elizabeth A. Clark, *History, Theory, Text: Historians and the Linguistic Turn* (Cambridge/London: Harvard University, 2004) 175–76.

13. Dalley, *Myths*, 259. See also J. J. Glassner, "The Use of Knowledge in Ancient Mesopotamia," in *CANE* 3, 1815.

14. Dalley, *Myths*, 257; note also the discussion of the flood stories on pg. 7 of Dalley.

15. Lambert & Millard, *Atra-ḫasīs* (ch. 4, n. 106) 163; Dalley, *Myths*, 34, 38 n. 42.

16. Let me add a qualification to this point: we should not dismiss the potential contributions of these approaches out of hand. They all have important perspectives to contribute to our understanding of the texts that we tend to regard as myths.

For example, a book formative in my education was Eric Neumann's captivating work, *The Origins and History of Consciousness* (the foreword to the book was penned by Carl G. Jung). See

Neumann, *The Origins and History of Consciousness*, with a foreword by Carl G. Jung (translated by R. F. C. Hull; New York: Pantheon Books, 1954). This book offered a systematic presentation of Jung's thought as it applied to myth, to show how myths from across the globe captured different points in human psychological development. This is a contribution, and it is one that is perhaps being extended by those who attempt to include potential insights from neural science. See, for example, the essays in *The New Unconscious* (R. R. Hassin, J. S. Uleman, and J. A. Bargh, eds.; Oxford Series in Social Cognition and Social Neuroscience; Oxford/New York: Oxford University, 2005). One wonders what interesting sort of theorizing of myth may develop out of these sorts of studies.

Perhaps each person has what Nick Wyatt calls "the mythic mind"; see Wyatt, *The Mythic Mind: Essays on Cosmology and Religion in Ugaritic and Old Testament Literature* (London/Oakville, Conn.: Equinox, 2005). Still the differences among myths are at least as interesting as those that are shared. Note the critique of Dundes, "Madness in Method Plus a Plea for Projective Inversion in Myth," in *Myth and Method* (Laurie L. Patton and Wendy Doniger, eds.; Charlottesville/London: University Press of Virginia, 1996) 150–151, for the variety of myths in the world, which arguably undermines the notion of universal archetypes. One might be inclined to reformulate the contribution coming from such quarters, namely that different cultures generate myths that draw on their different cultural perceptions of human development. For a productive use of such theory, see Neal Walls, *Desire, Discord, and Death: Approaches to Ancient Near Eastern Myth* (Boston: American Schools of Oriental Research, 2001).

17. Segal, *Myth*, 2, Segal's italics. This point is generally borne out by Segal's short survey of nineteenth and twentieth century theories of myth and by the probing survey of this territory from the eighteenth century on produced by Von Hendy, *The Modern Construction*. Von Hendy places a particular emphasis on the importance of German Romanticism on later modern theorizing about myth, as he believes this point has been overlooked in several quarters.

18. Von Hendy (*The Modern Construction*, xiii) puts this point in his introduction to his fine book: "I was surprised in the course of this project, however, to discover how overwhelmingly the true century of myth is the twentieth."

19. On this point, I take Segal's *Myth* as representative of modern theorizing. Symptomatic of this classical bias in Segal's book is his otherwise engaging use of the Adonis myth to test various theories of myth; neither Segal nor the authors whom he discusses ever mention the foreign setting of the story in Cyprus.

Some modern theorists, such as Erich Neumann and Joseph Campbell, have trodden into ancient Near Eastern texts, but their efforts tend to conform these texts or their interpretation to the notion that they have derived on the basis of other material and hardly reflect a substantive engagement with them.

20. Graf, "Myth," 54.

21. Nagy, "Can Myth Be Saved?" 240–48.

22. Jacobsen, *Harps* (ch. 1, n. 21), xiii.

23. Dalley, *Myths*, xvii.

24. Michael Fishbane, *Biblical Myth* (ch. 2, n. 165), 11 n. 46.

25. Kirk, "On Defining Myths," in *Sacred Narrative. Readings in the Theory of Myth* (Alan Dundes, ed.; Berkeley/Los Angeles/London: University of California, 1984) 60.

26. See Kirk, *The Nature of Greek Myths*, 23.

27. Kirk, *The Nature of Greek Myths*, 63–64.

28. Leach, "Anthropological Approaches to the Study of the Bible during the Twentieth Century," in *Humanizing America's Iconic Book*, SBLCP 1980, 74.

29. Dundes, "Madness in Method," 148.

30. Segal, *Myth*, 5: "The story can take place in the past. . ., or in the present or the future."

31. Niditch, *Oral World* (ch. 4, n. 24).

32. Kirk, *The Nature of Greek Myths*, 14.

33. Dundes, "Madness in Method," 147–159.

34. Segal, *Myth*, 1.

35. *UNP*.

36. This is so even if at the end of the day one might jettison the category of myth altogether or at least avoid the idea of myth as a particular genre. For the latter, see Fishbane, *Biblical Myth*, 11 n. 46.

37. The square brackets here are a convention scholars use to mark a letter that is not represented on the tablet where it may be damaged. The letter was probably there in ancient times, but today it cannot be seen.

38. These may all reflect the name or title of the tablet series to which they belong. In addition to this designation that the Baal Cycle is "about Baal," it also refers to the text as *mspr*, "an account, recitation" (KTU 1.4 V 42), as does the story of Aqhat (1.19 IV 62). For discussion of *mspr* in this meaning, see Mark S. Smith and Wayne T. Pitard, *The Ugaritic Baal Cycle Volume 2: Introduction with Text, Translation and Commentary of KTU 1.3-1.4* (Vetus Testamentum Supplement series, volume 114; Leiden: Brill, 2009) 574–76.

39. Dalley, *Myths*, 274.

40. This is perhaps a bit ironic in view of Enlil's role in the text.

41. See van der Toorn, *Scribal Culture* (ch. 2, n. 274), 13.

42. Lambert & Millard, *Atra-ḫasīs*, 7; Dalley, *Myths*, 274.

43. Lambert & Millard, *Atra-ḫasīs*, 7, 104–5 (in the end of the Old Babylonian version, C = British Museum). See also Dalley, *Myths*, 38 n. 46.

44. Lambert & Millard, *Atra-ḫasīs*, 165.

45. This written representation of the narrative as a song serves as a claim for divine authorship. This may be the earliest case of a claim of divine pseudonymous authorship; Atra-ḫasīs is "Pseudo-Nintu." Insofar as later readers regard the biblical Pentateuch as ultimately authored by God, it may be considered as "Pseudo-God." The text itself represents some of the laws and not the narratives as actually written by God. See Exod. 24:12, 31:18, 32:16, 34:1; and Deut. 5:22; compare Exod. 24:4, 34:27 (Moses writing).

46. On Atra-ḫasīs and its musical sensibility, see the insightful essay by Anne Draffkorn Kilmer, "Fugal Features of Atra-ḫasīs The Birth Theme," in *Mesopotamian Poetic Language:* (ch. 2, n. 6), 127–39.

47. Dalley, *Myths*, 38 n. 46.

48. Lambert & Millard, *Atra-ḫasīs*, 7; Dalley, *Myths*, 38 n. 46. Dalley says that the opening lines to Ishum and Erra, and she says that the opening lines are modeled on the opening of Anzu; see Dalley, *Myths*, 313 n. 1.

49. Van der Toorn, *Scribal Culture*, 41–42. Van der Toorn attributes this unusual presentation to the text's purpose as prophecy, specifically regarding the "man of Akkad" who will defeat the Suteans (tablet IV, lines 131–136; tablet V, lines 25–38). Functioning as prophecy (or pseudo-prophecy), the text, so van der Toorn suggests, "needed the name of the prophet."

50. For this point, see Hoffner, *Hittite Myths* (ch. 2, n. 166), 38. For a convenient translation of the "songs," see Hoffner, *Hittite Myths*, 40–60.

51. For a convenient presentation of the text and translation of this Ugaritic text, see David Marcus, "The Betrothal of Yarikh and Nikkal-Ib," *UNP*, 215–18.

52. Note also the opening of RIH 98/02, lines 1–2, with the first-person invocation preceded by a third person address for Athtart. See Dennis Pardee, "A New Ugaritic Song to ʿAṭtartu (RIH 98/02)," in *Ugarit at Seventy-Five* (edited by K. Lawson Younger Jr.; Winona Lake, Ind.: Eisenbrauns, 2007) 27–39, esp. 30–31.

53. Jacobsen, *Harps*, xiii.

54. This point has been emphasized recently by Fishbane, *Biblical Myth*, 37–44, 50–52.

55. Lambert & Millard (*Atra-ḫasīs*, 8) mention the conclusion as suggestive of the impression that the poem was intended for public recitation. See also Dalley, *Myths*, xv, xvi, and especially 38 n. 46. Note also Jacobsen, *Harps*, xiii.

56. See van der Toorn, *Scribal Culture*, 12.

57. As noted by Dalley, *Myths*, xvi.

58. For this text, see Smith, *Sacrificial Rituals* (ch. 1, n. 20). For a convenient presentation of the text and translation of this Ugaritic text, see Lewis, "Birth" (ch. 1, n. 20), 205–14.

59. Richard E. Averbeck, "Myth, Ritual, and Order in 'Enki and the World,'" *JAOS* 123, 757–71. I wish to thank Professor Averbeck for bringing this example to my attention.

60. *COS* 1.152.

61. Dalley, *Myths*, 154.

62. *COS* 1.32, 33.

63. For a convenient presentation of the text and translation of these Ugaritic passages, see Lewis, "El's Divine Feast" (ch. 2, n. 115), 193–96, esp. 196.

64. Dalley, *Myths*, 315 n. 52.

65. Dalley, *Myths*, 90, 130 n. 81; Benjamin R. Foster, trans. and ed., *The Epic of Gilgamesh* (New York/London: Norton, 2001) xxi, and *Muses*, 24.

66. Jonathan Z. Smith, "Good News is No News: Aretalogy and Gospel," in *Christianity, Judaism, and Other Greco-Roman Cults: Studies for Morton Smith at Sixty*, SJLA 1:12, 37–38.

67. So Foster, *From Distant Days: Myths, Tales, and Poetry of Ancient Mesopotamia* (Bethesda, Md.: CDL, 1995) 7, 10.

68. See Dalley, *Myths*, 230, 240, 277.

69. See Ibid., 261.

70. See Jacobsen, *Harps*, 240.

71. Jacobsen, "The Battle" (ch. 2, n. 188), 104–108. This proposal has gained in plausibility since the publication of an apparent "missing link" at the ancient site of Mari located on the great bend of the Euphrates. See Durand, "Le mythologème" (ch. 1, n. 58) 41–61; and Bordreuil & Pardee, "Le combat" (ch. 1, n. 58), 63–70. For text, translation and notes, see Nissinen, *Prophets* (ch. 1, n. 58) 22. For further discussion, see Sasson, "The Posting of Letters" in (ch. 2, n. 188) 299–316, esp. 310–14; see also Sasson, "Mari Historiography" (ch. 2, n. 188), 444 n. 12; and Smith, *Early History* (ch. 1, n. 64), 56–57. By the way, this Mari text goes a considerable way toward confirming the theory of Thorkild Jacobsen that the description of the conflict between Marduk and Tiamat in *Enūma Elish* was borrowed from West Semitic prototypes (this hardly precludes local Mesopotamian influence as well as various aspects of the description in *Enūma Elish*, as Assyriologists have long noted). Jacobsen had in mind the conflict of Baal and Yamm (Sea) in the Ugaritic Baal Cycle, but the Mari text provides a sort of "missing link" in between. See Jacobsen, "The Battle," 104–8. See the discussion and further defense of this view in my book, *The Ugaritic Baal Cycle* (ch. 2, n. 188) 108–14.

72. Foster, *From Distant Days*, 9.

73. See Jacobsen, *Treasures* (ch. 1, n. 39), 227–28. See also the observations made by Peter Machinist in his study, "Order and Disorder: Some Mesopotamian Reflections," in *Genesis and Regeneration* (Shaul Shaked, ed.; Jerusalem: Israel Academy of Sciences and Humanities, 2005) 31–61.

74. Jonathan Z. Smith, "No News is Good News: The Gospel as Enigma," in *Secrecy in Religions* (edited by Kees W. Bolle; Studies in the History of Religions, volume XLIX; Leiden: Brill, 1987) 78–79.

75. *COS* 1.149.

76. *COS* 1.35.

77. By contrast, ritual perhaps migrates and translates less; in this respect, law seems closer. For discussion, see my essay, "Biblical Narrative: Part II," (ch. 2, n. 28) 189–207.

78. For the text and translation of this passage, see Mark S. Smith, "The Baal Cycle," (ch. 1, n. 19), 109–110.

79. The mythic dimensions of Genesis 2 are discussed in a recent study by Mettinger, *The Eden Narrative*. See also the earlier studies of Manfred Görg, "Mensch und Tempel" (ch. 1, n. 8), 191–215; Terje Stordalen, *Echoes of Eden* (ch. 1, n. 8); and Howard N. Wallace, *The Eden Narrative*, HSM 32.

80. See above ch. 2, p. 63 and in particular the remarks of Jonathan Culler cited there.

81. See the theory of myth as *aetia*, in modern times associated with the name of Andrew Lang; for a convenient discussion, see Kirk, *The Nature of Greek Myths*, 53, 59. More recently, Glassner ("The Use of Knowledge," 1815) has emphasized the importance of explanation for Mesopotamian myth.

82. Compare the notion of myth as narrative that is "the temporalizing of essence" by the literary critic, Kenneth Burke (1897–1993), in his book, *The Rhetoric of Religion: Studies in Logology* (Berkeley/Los Angeles: University of California Press, 1970) 201; cited and commented on by Segal, *Myth*, 85. Note also the idea of the anthropologist Paul Radin (1883–1959): "Myths deal with metaphysical topics of all kinds, such as the ultimate conceptions of reality" cited from Segal, *Myth*, 37. In other words, myths map reality in the form of narrative sequence.

83. I have discussed this idea for Genesis 1:1–3 in ch. 2; see 63–64.

84. See the discussion of Oden, *The Bible without Theology*, 40–91, esp. 93; and Fishbane, *Biblical Myth*, 1–92, with comments on Genesis 1 on 34–35.

85. I have discussed this contrast between the relative rarity of myths in the Bible and its many mythic images in an article, "Myth and Myth-making in Ugaritic and Israelite Literatures," in *Ugarit and the Bible: Proceedings of the International Symposium on Ugarit and the Bible, Manchester, September 1992*, UBL 11, 293–341. To this degree I am in agreement with Fishbane's emphasis on the mythic in the Bible. See Fishbane, *Biblical Myth*, 1–52. Fishbane's discussion does not address sufficiently this difference between what might be regarded as biblical myths and biblical mythic images. In this regard, ancient Israel perhaps stands closer to the situation in ancient Greece. Here it may be helpful to recall Kirk's observation that I quoted earlier: "The vital fact is that myths in Greek literature exist for the most part only in brief allusions. . . . The myths were so well known that formal exposition was unnecessary, and in the high classical period, at least, it was felt to be provincial. This changed in the Hellenistic world after the conquests of the Alexander the Great." See Kirk, *The Nature of Greek Myths*, 14. In longer biblical narrative, there are little more than allusions to myth, yet the Bible contains many mythic images. Biblical narrative may be a product of a scribal culture accustomed to mythic images yet concerned with matters other than myth, as in pre-Alexandrian Greek literature. Or, one might simply wonder if the sample of the Bible is simply too small. Perhaps in the matter of myth, there may be something simply incidental involved. In the end this may be one of the major differences that we scholars need to think about more. There is an abundance of mythic material in the ancient Near East; in comparison, prior to the Hellenistic period, Israel barely has a whole Bible.

86. Sometimes with additional critique of them; see Moran, *The Most Magic Word* (ch. 3, n. 110), 45; or perhaps, with admiration.

87. Bernard F. Batto, *Slaying the Dragon: Mythmaking in the Biblical Tradition* (Louisville, Ky.: Westminster John Knox, 1992).

88. McBride, "Divine Protocol," 3–41.

89. See Cross, *Canaanite Myth* (ch. 1, n. 16), 301–5; Tengström, *Die Toledotformel* (ch. 4, n. 77); and the 1974 essay by Peter Weimar, "Die Toledotformel" (ch. 4, n. 77), 151–84.

90. For a convenient translation of the Sumerian King List, see A. Leo Oppenheim's in *ANET* 265–66. The older critical edition of this text is Thorkild Jacobsen, *The Sumerian King List*, AS 11. For a good discussion of the text, see Piotr Michalowski, "History as Charter: Some Observations on the Sumerian King List," *JAOS* 103, 237–248. The discussion of Brian B. Schmidt locates the Sumerian King List within the wider context of Mesopotamian flood traditions: "Flood Narratives," 2337–51, esp. 2340–41. Note also William W. Hallo, *Origins* (ch. 3, n. 97), 7–15. Hallo's concerns are largely comparative (see below).

91. As noted by commentators such as Gunkel, *Genesis* (ch. 2, n. 6), 103.

92. For theogonies, see the summary discussion of Cross, *From Epic to Canon* (ch. 1, n. 6), 73–83. See also the discussions in chs. 1 and 2.

93. Perhaps the scope in question should be Genesis through Deuteronomy. For a fine consideration of the latter, see McBride, "Divine Protocol," 3–41.

94. According to Hallo (*Origins*, 10–13), some of the names in Gen. 4:17, in particular Lamech, reflect a number of the figures also known in the Sumerian King List.

95. This number is given by Herman L. J. Vanstiphout, "The Old Babylonian Literary Canon: Structure, Function and Intention," in *Cultural Repertoires: Structure, Function, and Dynamics* (edited by Gillis J. Dorleijn and Herman L. J. Vanstiphout; Groningen Studies in Cultural Change, volume 3; Leuven/Paris/Dudley, Mass.: Peeters, 2003) 12 n. 55.

96. Before proceeding to a final consideration of our question as to whether or not Genesis 1 is a myth, I would like to briefly consider two general differences between ancient Near Eastern myths

and the Bible, one involving an external, formal difference and the second a matter of content. The first is prose versus poetry, and the second is space as represented in ancient Near Eastern myths versus biblical narrative. One textual feature of the longer biblical narratives is their construction primarily in prose, in contrast to the long, poetic versions of myths as generally known in the ancient Near East. As Dennis Pardee remarks, Ugaritic prose is "an extremely rare feature of texts of a mythological nature." See Pardee, *Ritual and Cult* (Intro., n. 9), 171. With little narrative poetry beyond isolated, single chapters, the longer biblical narrative agglomerations are not constructed primarily as poetry, but as prose. What is one to make of this difference? Are there any leads that might be helpful here? It is true that Gilgamesh tablet XII is thought by commentators to be prose, which was added by an editor to bring the Akkadian closer to the known Sumerian version. See George, *The Babylonian Gilgamesh Epic* (ch. 4, n. 71), 489, 450. More specifically, the Sumerian text, "Gilgamesh, Enkidu, and the Netherworld" was translated into Akkadian as Gilgamesh tablet XII, lines 129f. So Foster, *Epic of Gilgamesh*, 129. Perhaps one key then to the biblical situation is not simply an aversion on the part of Israel's textual elites to depicting the divine. The use of prose itself may be important here.

It has been thought that the prosaic character of most biblical narrative might be at least in part a matter of scribal production overtaking the oral settings that generated Israel's older stories. So Kawashima, *Biblical Narrative* (ch. 4, n. 60). It is not clear that this is generally the case. I say this because Kawashima's book does not examine or demonstrate the cultural and historical conditions that would support his reconstruction. Instead, he presupposes that this reconstruction was the situation involved and then reads various biblical passages in light of this reconstruction. For example, he assumes the view of Frank M. Cross that ancient Israel enjoyed a longstanding epic tradition until "the death of the rhapsode" (as he expresses the point in his subtitle) and the passing of this oral tradition. The question of epic, and in particular Cross's arguments for it, however, have been highly contested. Dissent from this view from within the tradition of William Foxwell Albright comes from Delbert R. Hillers and Marsh McCall, Jr., "Homeric Dictated Texts: A Reexamination of Some Near Eastern Evidence," *Harvard Studies in Classical Philology* 80 (1976) 19–23 (reference courtesy of Seth Sanders). See also Simon B. Parker, *Stories in Scripture and Inscriptions: Comparative Studies on Narratives in Northwest Semitic Inscriptions and the Hebrew Bible* (New York: Oxford University, 1997) 7. Note also the older comments of Shemaryahu Talmon, "Did There Exist a Biblical National Epic?" in *Proceedings of the Seventh World Congress of Jewish Studies: Studies in the Bible and the Ancient Near East* (Jerusalem: World Union of Jewish Studies, 1981) 57. In his discussion of Judges 5, Volkmar Fritz emphatically denies epic in ancient Israel. See Fritz, "The Complex of Traditions in Judges 4 and 5 and the Religion of Pre-state Israel," in *"I Will Speak the Riddles of Ancient Times": Archaeological and Historical Studies in Honor of Amihai Mazar on the Occasion of His Sixtieth Birthday* (edited by Aren M. Maier and Pierre de Miroschedji; vol. 2; Winona Lake, Ind.: Eisenbrauns, 2006) 695: "There was no development of epic verse, as occurred, for example, in ancient Greece." I have noted some reservations about Cross's use of the term. See Smith, "Biblical Narrative: Part I," (ch. 4, n. 60), 5–29. What Cross regards at the vestiges and indicators of Israel's epic, I view as something of an "anti-epic" that rejects or displaces Israelite's Canaanite heritage. Despite its use of Cross's notion of epic, Kawashima's book is quite sophisticated and offers a number of important observations.

When we do see poetic passages in our long narrative texts in the Bible, they display a rather different effect than our ancient Near Eastern myths. In the case of the great poems of Judges 5 and Exodus 15, it seems that they function in context to link the older world of the events being described. These poems are written in an older Hebrew relative to their contexts composed in prose, which are linguistically closer to the world of the human audience of the narrative. As a result, the older poetic pieces evoke that distant past of the purported events, and they are linked to—and interpreted for—the world of the audience's present via the prose accounts. And yet the presence of both poetry and prose also marks their difference in time and context for their scribal composers: these poetic events are ancient for them. So poetry in the longer narratives of the Bible may have a very different function than the long poetic myths of the ancient Near East.

97. Compare the discussion of biblical theology in the appendix on 161–62, 181.

98. See the appendix on 175, 177–81.

99. Contrast the theological approaches of Alomía, "Sujeción" (ch. 1, n. 129), 42–92; and Norman Habel, "Playing God or Playing Earth? An Ecological Reading of Genesis 1:26–28," in *"And God Saw That It Was Good": Essays on Creation and God in Honor of Terence E. Fretheim* (edited by Frederick J. Gaiser and Mark A. Throntveit; Word & World Supplement, vol. 5; St. Paul, Minn.: Word & World, Luther Seminary, 2006) 33–41. See also Keel and Schroer, *Schöpfung*, 26–29, 237.

100. There are, to be sure, further complexities beyond these considerations. See Claus Westermann, *Genesis 1–11*, 175.

101. For this issue, see the discussion in ch. 2.

102. I am not claiming or speaking to the matter of intertextual relations among texts in other ancient Near Eastern traditions. It may be the development of such intertextual relations within scribal traditions or canons that underlies Israel's developments of its Bible. I would also place a certain importance in the replacement of a royal-priestly scribal situation in the pre-exilic context by a priestly scribal situation in the post-exilic context, but these large developments lie beyond the scope of this discussion. See van der Toorn, *Scribal Culture*.

Appendix: Modern Scholarly Approaches

1. For an accessible synthesis drawing heavily on archaeological research, see King & Stager, *Life in Biblical Israel* (ch. 4, n. 106).

2. The research of Othmar Keel and his former student and colleague Christoph Uehlinger, as well as other scholars associated with the so-called Fribourg School of Iconographic Studies, have made major contributions to the study of iconography in ancient Israel and its neighbors. For example, see Keel & Uehlinger, *Gods,* (ch. 1, n. 29). For iconography pertinent to divine creation, see Keel & Schroer, *Schöpfung*. Note also Othmar Keel, *Goddesses and Trees* (ch. 1, n. 6). See also his more general book, *Symbolism*.

3. For surveys and critical discussions, see Henning Graf Reventlow, *Problems of Biblical Theology in the Twentieth Century* (Philadelphia: Fortress, 1986); Bernd Janowski, "Biblische Theologie heute: Formale und materiale Aspekte," in *Biblical Interpretation: History, Context, and Reality,* SBLSymS 26, 17–32; *idem*, "Kanonhermeneutik: eine problemgeschichtliche Skizze," *BThZ* 22, 161–80. For an important Jewish biblical scholar engaged with the issues of this approach, see Jon D. Levenson, *The Bible, the Old Testament, and Historical Criticism: Jews and Christians in Biblical Studies* (Louisville, Ky.: Westminster John Knox, 1993). For a significant Catholic, see John J. Collins, *Encounters with Biblical Theology* (Minneapolis: Fortress, 2005). For a work of biblical theology that pays considerable attention to the ancient context, see Erhard S. Gerstenberger, *Theologies in the Old Testament* (translated by John Bowden; Minneapolis: Fortress, 2002). Compare Walter Brueggemann, *Theology of the Old Testament: Testimony, Dispute, Advocacy* (Minneapolis: Fortress, 1997). Note also the series, Overtures to Biblical Theology (OBT), published by Fortress Press. For a classic theological treatment of Genesis 1, see Dietrich Bonhoeffer, *Creation and Fall, A Theological Interpretation of Genesis 1–3* (translated by Douglas Stephen Bax; Minneapolis: Fortress, 1997).

4. For the "canonical approach" (as opposed to the "canonical criticism" of James Sanders), see Childs, *Introduction* (ch. 2, n. 18); *The New Testament as Canon* (Philadelphia: Fortress, 1985); *Old Testament Theology in a Canonical Context* (Philadelphia: Fortress, 1986); *The Struggle to Understand Isaiah as Christian Scripture* (Grand Rapids, Mich.: Eerdmans, 2004). Note also Mark G. Brett, *Biblical Criticism in Crisis? The Impact of the Canonical Approach on Old Testament Studies* (Cambridge/New York: Cambridge University, 1991); and Paul R. Noble, *The Canonical Approach: A Critical Reconstruction of the Hermeneutics of Brevard S. Childs* (Biblical Interpretation, volume 16; Leiden/New York: Brill, 1995). Childs' best-known student in this approach is Christopher R. Seitz. See his books *Word without End: The Old Testament as Abiding Theological Witness* (Grand Rapids, Mich.: Eerdmans, 1998) and *Figured Out: Typology and Providence in Christian Scripture* (Louisville, Ky.: Westminster John Knox, 2001). See as well the entry in this discussion by Seitz's student, William Ross Blackburn, "The Missionary Heart of Exodus" (Ph.D. dissertation, Saint Andrews University, 2005). Note also the appreciative examination of Childs' approach by

Joseph W. Groves, *Actualization and Interpretation in the Old Testament,* SBLDS 86. For critiques of Childs' opponents and an uncritical appreciation of his vision of the "canonical approach," see Daniel R. Driver, "Brevard Childs: The Logic of Scripture's Textual Authority in the Mystery of Christ" (Ph.D. dissertation, Saint Mary's College, University of Saint Andrews, 2008).

One of the most difficult issues for historical critics involved the question of the "final form" of the Hebrew Bible. See James A. Loader, "The Finality of the Old Testament 'Final Text,'" *OTE* 15, 739–53. See also the comments of Carr, *Reading the Fractures* (ch. 2, n. 7), 317. Objections to the "canonical" approach include its effort to ground its legitimacy on a disputed notion of the "final form" of the biblical text, which itself contains historical and theological presuppositions that often go unexamined. The text-critical basis for the "final form" is also a subject of considerable debate. Some scholars view it as a mirage with little or no basis. For a sympathetic appreciation, see Rolf Rendtorff, *The Problem of the Process of Transmission in the Pentateuch* (trans. by John J. Scullion), JSOTSup 89, 18, 24, 30; "'Covenant' as a Structuring Concept in Genesis and Exodus," *JBL* 108 (1989) 385–93, esp. 386; and *The Canonical Hebrew Bible: A Theology of the Old Testament* (trans. by David E. Orton; Leiden: Deo, 2005).

For interesting reflections on Genesis 1 with related concerns, see Hoffman, "The First Creation Story" (ch. 4, n. 48), 32–53; and John Sailhammer, "Genesis 1–11 and the Canon," *BBR* 10/1, 89–106. Canon criticism or the canonical approach may be viewed as a combination of biblical theology and redaction and literary criticism, using the "final form" of the text as the fulcrum point for interpretation. See the discussion further below.

5. This area is associated particularly with the name of Michael Fishbane, in particular his book, *Biblical Interpretation* (ch. 2, n. 2). See the important survey of innerbiblical exegesis by Bernard M. Levinson, *Legal Revision and Religious Renewal in Ancient Israel* (Cambridge/New York: Cambridge University Press, 2008) 95–181.

6. For an accessible collection of postbiblical interpretations of biblical texts, see James Kugel, *Traditions on the Bible* (ch. 2, n. 199). The Ancient Christian Commentary on Scripture (ACCS), a new series published by InterVarsity Press, collates interpretations from Christian writers through the eighth century on books of the Bible by chapter and verse. For Genesis 1, see Andrew Louth, ed., *Genesis 1–11,* ACCS(OT) I.

7. It might seem logical to move immediately to the more detailed survey of the older approaches at this point before mentioning newer approaches. However, our sense of the older approaches has been influenced by the impact of approaches that have developed in the meantime. Whether or not scholars think it looks logical to go in this order, we view past approaches in light of where we are; so it is logical to mention the newer approaches that influence our present context as interpreters. In her capacity as one of the nonspecialists who reviewed this appendix for me, my daughter, Shula Smith, suggested that it is helpful for her as a reader to have all the approaches, both old and new, put on the table before going into more detail about the older approaches. I wish to thank her for her editorial advice.

8. Steven L. McKenzie and Stephen R. Haynes, eds., *To Each Its Own Meaning: An Introduction to Biblical Criticisms and Their Application* (revised and expanded; Louisville, Ky.: Westminster/John Knox, 1999); Gale A. Yee, ed., *Judges and Method: New Approaches in Biblical Studies* (2nd ed.; Minneapolis: Fortress, 2007). See also *The People's Bible: New Revised Standard Version, with the Apocrypha* (Minneapolis: Fortress, 2008).

9. Zevit, *Religions* (ch. 1, n. 56) 1–79.

10. Many of the approaches are allied more with historical or literary studies. As we continue this discussion, I would also mention that "history" and "literature" are terms alien to the world of the Bible, so we need to be mindful of the gap between the horizons of the ancient world and our own reflected in the terms that we use. See Jacques Berlinerblau, "The Bible as Literature?" *HS* 45, 9–26. Berlinerblau criticizes the assumption of harmony within texts as well as the presupposition of individual biblical authors, especially as literary virtuosos. The problem has been noted among scholars of Mesopotamia as well. Note the comment of Piotr Michalowski: "Here is the rub. No matter how hard we try, it is extremely difficult for modern scholars to abandon the notion of 'literature' and high art." See Michalowski, "The Libraries of Babel: Text, Authority, and Tradition

in Ancient Mesopotamia," in *Cultural Repertoires* (ch. 5, n. 95), 125. The upshot of this critique, whether by Berlinerblau or by Michalowski, is that the term "literature" may not always apply properly to ancient texts. At the same time, what is considered worthy of literary critical attention has expanded vastly in the past two decades; everything textual now attracts the attention of literary critics (see the discussion below).

The relationship between literature and history in biblical studies has attracted considerable attention. For some reflections in recent years, see two essays by Edward L. Greenstein, "The State of Biblical Studies," and "Theory and Argument in Biblical Criticism," in his volume, *Essays on Biblical Method*, (ch. 3, n. 31), 3–27, 53–68, respectively; Marc Zvi Brettler, *The Creation of History in Ancient Israel* (London/New York: Routledge, 1995) 8–19; Erhard Blum, "Historiography or Poetry? The Nature of the Hebrew Bible Prose Tradition," in *Memory in the Bible and Antiquity: The Fifth Durham-Tübingen Research Symposium (Durham, September 2004)* (Stephen C. Barton, Loren T. Stuckenbruck, and Benjamin G. Wold, eds.; Tübingen: Mohr Siebeck, 2007) 25–45; and Peter Machinist, "Let a Hundred Flowers Bloom: Some Reflections on Reading and Studying the Hebrew Bible," in *The Hebrew Bible: New Insights and Scholarship* (Frederick E. Greenspahn, ed.; New York/London: New York University, 2008) 209–18. Compare Stephen A. Geller's proposal for understanding the relationship between "Literature, History, and Religion," in his volume, *Sacred Enigmas* (ch. 1, n. 44), 168–94.

11. John Barton, *Reading the Old Testament: Method in Biblical Study* (Philadelphia: Westminster Press, 1984); Collins, *The Bible after Babel: Historical Criticism in a Post-modern Age* (Grand Rapids, Mich.: Eerdmans, 2005). See also the thoughtful, critical review of Collins' book by Steven Weitzman, "Rebuilding the Tower of Babel," *Jewish Quarterly Review* 98/1(2008) 103–12.

12. John Sandys-Wunsch, *What Have They Done to the Bible? A History of Modern Biblical Interpretation* (Collegeville, Minn.: Liturgical Press, 2005).

13. Another bibliography along these lines is being created at: http://sites.google.com/site/biblicalstudiesresources/Home/biblical-studies-resources/hebrew-bible/bibliography-of-old-testament-studies.

14. See the introductions to this area of anthropological and sociological research: Robert R. Wilson, *Sociological Approaches to the Old Testament* (Philadelphia: Fortress, 1984); and *Community, Identity, and Ideology: Social Science Approaches to the Hebrew Bible* (Charles E. Carter and Carol L. Meyers, eds.; Winona Lake, Ind.: Eisenbrauns, 1996); and *The Social World of the Hebrew Bible: Twenty-Five Years of Social Sciences in the Academy, Semeia* 87. Social science work made a major impact in biblical studies beginning in mid-1970s. For an example, see the republication of studies mostly from this period in Bernard Lang, ed., *Anthropological Approaches to the Old Testament*, IRT 8. For a book-length application in the area of prophecy, see Robert R. Wilson, *Prophecy and Society in Ancient Israel* (Philadelphia: Fortress, 1980). Note the reflections by Jacques Berlinerblau, "The Delicate Flower of Biblical Sociology," in *Tracking the Tribes of Yahweh: On the Trail of a Classic* (edited by R. Boer; Sheffield: Sheffield Academic Press, 2002) 59–76. To be sure, sociological interest in the Hebrew Bible is hardly novel. See already the classic study of Max Weber, *Ancient Judaism* (New York: Free Press Paper, 1967).

Classic work on the priestly worldview, which pertains to Genesis 1, was done by the recently deceased anthropologist, Mary Douglas. Her work in this area has received considerable attention and it has been quite influential in biblical studies, though not without some criticism. See Houston, *Purity and Monotheism* (ch. 3, n. 31), 96–111. It is endorsed with modifications by Firmage, "Genesis 1" (ch. 2, n. 7), 104–11. While there may be divergences between the understanding of animals and their environments in Genesis 1 versus Leviticus 11 and elsewhere (as Houston notes), it seems nonetheless that Genesis 1 shows an interest in this relationship. For a recent appreciation of the work of Mary Douglas for the priestly writings of the Bible, see Hendel & Olyan, "Beyond Purity" (ch. 3, n. 31). For an instructive piece about the priestly worldview pertinent to Genesis 1 that takes its cue from Douglas' work, see Ronald S. Hendel, "Prophets" (ch. 1, n. 48), 185–98.

15. See esp. Carr, *Writing on the Tablet of the Heart* (ch. 4, n. 6); and van der Toorn, *Scribal Culture* (ch. 2, n. 274). These studies provide discussion of prior works in this vein. See ch. 4 above for discussion of these works. Michael Fishbane has nicely noted the related role that interpretation plays in scribal practice. See Fishbane, *Biblical Interpretation* (ch. 2, n. 2).

16. For a nice representation of New Historicism studies, see the essays in *The New Historicism* (H. Aram Veeser, ed.; New York/London: Routledge, 1989). For New Historicism and biblical studies, see Gina Henz-Piazza, *The New Historicism* (Minneapolis: Fortress, 2002).

17. The quote comes from a characterization of New Historicism by Culler, *Literary Theory* (ch. 2, n. 163), 130.

18. This language is a modification of Culler, *Literary Theory*, 130.

19. See comments above.

20. For a survey of the study of collective memory in the French Annales tradition since World War I and its application to ancient Israel, see Smith, *The Memoirs of God* (ch. 4, n. 8). The best-known figure of the Annales tradition was Ferdnand Braudel. The Annales work on collective memory began with Maurice Halbwachs.

21. Since the late 1990s, this topic has been pursued in biblical studies by Ronald Hendel, Marc Brettler of Brandeis University, my New York University colleague Dan Fleming, and myself. See Brettler, "Memory in Ancient Israel" (ch. 4, n. 8), 1–17; Fleming, "Mari and the Possibilities" (ch. 4, n. 8) 41–78; Hendel, "The Exodus in Biblical Memory" (ch. 4, n. 8), 601–22; and his book, *Remembering Abraham* (ch. 4, n. 8); Smith, *The Memoirs of God*, and "Remembering God" (ch. 4, n. 8), 631–51. See also the collection of essays, entitled *Memory in the Bible*. Brettler, Hendel, and I have been influenced by Yerushalmi, *Zakhor* (ch. 4, n. 8). Hendel and I were influenced also by the work on collective memory undertaken by the Annales School in France. For a recent entry into this area especially as it bears on priestly tradition, see Leveen, *Memory and Tradition* (ch. 3, n. 124).

22. See the essays in *Psychology and the Bible: A New Way to Read the Scriptures (Psychology, Religion, and Spirituality)* (J. Harold Ellens and Wayne G. Rollins, eds.; four volumes; New York: Prager, 2004). See also Wayne G. Rollins, *Soul and Psyche: The Bible in Psychological Perspective* (Minneapolis: Fortress, 1999). For an application to ancient Near Eastern myth, see the sophisticated study of Walls, *Desire, Discord, and Death* (ch. 5, n. 16). Recent work on trauma theory has advanced the understanding of biblical expressions of societal loss. See Amy Kalmanofsky, *Terror All Around: The Rhetoric of Horror in the Book of Jeremiah* (New York/London: T & T Clark, 2008); and Kathleen O'Connor, "The Book of Jeremiah: Reconstructing Community After Disaster," in *Character Ethics of the Old Testament: Moral Dimensions of the Scriptures* (M. Daniel Carroll Rodas and Jacqueline Lapsley, eds.; Westminster John Knox, 2007) 81–92. Genesis 1 might be read in light of this approach. An essay involving Genesis 1 that combines psychoanalysis and historical analysis is Roland Boer, "The Fantasy of Genesis 1–3," *BibInt* 14/4, 309–31.

23. Feminist commentary on Genesis 1 may be traced to the two-volume work, *The Woman's Bible*, authored by a team of women headed by Elizabeth Cady Stanton in 1895 and 1898, and reprinted as *The Woman's Bible: A Classic Feminist Perspective* (Mineola, N.Y.: Dover Publications, 2002; see 14–19 for comments on Genesis 1 by Elizabeth Cady Stanton, Ellen Battelle Dietrick, and Lillie Devereux Blake.

An important pioneering work in feminist study of the Bible was authored by Trible, *God and the Rhetoric of Sexuality* (ch. 2, n. 149); see 12–23 for her discussion of Genesis 1 and in particular on 1:26–28, representing "gender balance." Since Trible, these sorts of reflections on Genesis 1 have become common. See the comments of Susan Niditch, "Genesis," in *Women's Bible Commentary: Expanded Edition* (edited by Carol A. Newsom and Sharon H. Ringe; Louisville, Ky.: Westminster John Knox, 1998) 16; and Tamara Cohn Eskenazi, "Genesis," in *The Torah: A Women's Commentary* (ed. Tamara Cohn Eskenazi; New York: URJ Press and Women of Reform Judaism, 2008) 8. Note also the essays in *Earth, Wind, and Fire* (ch. 1, n. 75). See as well L. Juliana Claasens, "And the Moon Spoke Up: Genesis 1 and Feminist Theology," *RevExp* 103, 325–42; and Jerome I. Gellman, "Gender and Sexuality in the Garden of Eden," *Theology and Sexuality* 12/3 (2006) 319–35. For a response to feminist readings of Genesis creation stories, see Joseph Abraham, *Eve: Accused or Acquitted? An Analysis of Feminist Readings of the Creation Narrative Texts in Genesis 1–3* (Cumbria: Paternoster Press, 2002).

A superb biblical scholar whose work combined a feminist perspective and concern with an excellent knowledge of extrabiblical texts was the late lamented Tikva Simone Frymer-Kensky. See in particular her two books *Reading the Women of the Bible: A New Interpretation of Their Stories*

(New York: Shocken Books, 2002) and *In the Wake* (ch. 1, n. 6). Susan Ackerman has written a fine study of several women in the Bible: *Warrior, Dancer, Seductress, Queen: Women in Judges and Biblical Israel*, ABRL 17. She is currently at work on a book called *Women and the Religion of Ancient Israel* (Anchor Yale Bible Reference Library; New Haven: Yale University). See also the various volumes published in the series *A Feminist Companion to the Bible*, ed. by Athalya Brenner and published by Sheffield Academic Press. Note as well the reference work *Women in Scripture: A Dictionary of Named and Unnamed Women in the Bible, the Apocryphal/Deuterocanonical Books, and the New Testament* (Carol L. Meyers, gen. ed.; Toni Craven and Ross S. Kraemer, assoc. eds.; Boston: Houghton Mifflin, 2000).

24. See *Take Back the Word: A Queer Reading of the Bible* (edited by Robert E. Goss and Mona West; Cleveland: Pilgrim Press, 2000); and Stephen D. Moore, *God's Beauty Parlor, and Other Queer Spaces in and around the Bible* (Stanford: Stanford University, 2001). Compare the work of Susan Ackermann, *When Heroes Love: The Ambiguity of Eros in the Stories of Gilgamesh and David* (Gender, Theory, and Religion Series, vol. 2; New York: Columbia University Press, 2005).

25. Culler, *Literary Theory*, 128.

26. Culler, *Literary Theory*, 126.

27. See with earlier literature on the subject, Hanne Løland, *Silent or Salient Gender: The Interpretation of Gendered God-Language in the Hebrew Bible Exemplified in Isaiah 42, 46, and 49*, FAT 2:32, 3–90.

28. Carol L. Meyers wrote a groundbreaking archaeological study informed by feminist studies, entitled *Discovering Eve: Ancient Israelite Women in Context* (New York: Oxford University, 1988). See also her book, *Households and Holiness: The Religious Culture of Israelite Women* (Minneapolis: Fortress, 2005).

29. See the critical assessment of Jacques Berlinerblau, "Max Weber's Useful Ambiguities and the Problem of Defining 'Popular Religion,'" *JAAR* 69, 605–626.

30. See Cain Hope Felder, *Race, Racism, and the Biblical Narratives* (Minneapolis, Minn.: Fortress, 2002); and Vincent L. Wimbush, *The Bible and African Americans: A Brief History* (Minneapolis, Minn.: Fortress, 2002). For issues of class, see Norman Gottwald, "Social Class as an Analytic and Hermeneutical Category in Biblical Studies," *JBL* 112 (1993) 3–22.

31. As with all these fields, the literature is vast. For starters, see Mark G. Brett, *Ethnicity and the Bible* (Biblical Interpretation, vol. 19; Leiden/New York: Brill, 1996). For ethnicity theory and early Israel, see Elizabeth M. Bloch-Smith, "Israelite Ethnicity in Iron Age I: Archaeology Preserves What Is Remembered and What Is Forgotten in Israel's History," *JBL* 122, 401–25.

32. See Fernando F. Segovia, *Decolonizing Biblical Studies: A View from the Margins* (Maryknoll, N.Y.: Orbis Books, 2002); and Miguel A. De La Tore, *Reading the Bible from the Margins* (Maryknoll, NY: Orbis Books, 2002). See also the series of volumes edited by R. S. Sugirtharajah entitled The Bible and Postcolonialism. The sixth volume in the series is *Postcolonial Biblical Criticism: Interdisciplinary Perspectives*, edited by Stephen Moore and Fernando F. Segovia (London: T & T Clark, 2005).

For an annotated bibliography for postcolonial studies in general and for biblical studies in particular, see Stephen D. Moore, *Empire and Apocalypse: Postcolonialism and the New Testament* (Bible in the Modern World, vol. 12; Sheffield: Sheffield Phoenix Press, 2006) 124–51. For a general introduction, see Robert J. C. Young, *Postcolonialism: An Historical Introduction* (Oxford: Blackwell, 2001). I wish to thank Gale Yee for these two references.

For work involving Genesis 1, see Hironori Minamino, "Genesis 1 as Critique of Japanese Culture," *Direction* 34/2 (2005) 159–69; Ann Nasimiyu-Wasike, "Genesis 1–2 and Some Elements of Diversion from the Original Meaning of the Creation of Man and Woman," in *Interpreting the Old Testament in Africa* (New York/Washington: Lang, 2001) 175–80; and Dibeela, "Perspective" (ch. 1, n. 132), 384–99. The last of these essays has influenced my thinking in chs. 2 and 3. Note also the older work of Modupe Oduyoye, *The Sons of the Gods and the Daughters of Men: An Afro-Asiatic Interpretation of Genesis 1–11* (New York: Maryknoll; Ibbadan: Daystar Press, 1984).

33. For the issues, see in general Habel & Trudinger, *Exploring* (ch. 1, n. 129). See also the ecologically sensitive edition of *The Green Bible: New Revised Standard Version* (New York: HarperCollins, 2008).

34. For a handy discussion, see Culler, *Literary Theory*. See also Terry Eagleton, *Literary Theory: An Introduction* (2nd ed.; Minneapolis: University of Minnesota, 1996); and *Critical Terms for Literary Study* (Frank Lentricchia and Thomas McLaughlin, eds. [2nd ed.]; Chicago/London: University of Chicago, 1995). For literary theory and biblical studies, see *The Book and the Text: The Bible and Literary Theory* (Regina Schwartz, ed.; Oxford: Blackwell, 1990).

35. Culler, *Literary Theory*, 83.

36. French structuralism is often associated with the name of Roland Barthes (1915–1980) and his work on what he called semiology, the science of textual signs. His work contributed to the major shift from seeking meaning in what authors think (or seem to think) toward what texts say and do; this turn Barthes called "the death of the author." See Jonathan Culler, *Barthes: A Very Short Introduction* (Oxford/New York: Oxford University, 2002) 69, 71. For his "science of signs" and its binary oppositions, Barthes was influenced by the French linguist, Ferdinand de Saussure (see Culler, *Barthes*, 57–60). The complete writings of Barthes have been published as a three-volume set by Seuil, which has been translated into English. For bibliography, see Culler, *Barthes*, 136–40. As Culler's sketch of Barthes indicates, his thought was considerably more complex than what the classic structuralist project involved (see further below). The structuralist intellectual project deeply influenced other French luminaries, such as the anthropology of Claude Lévi-Strauss, the history and "archaeology" of systems of thought of Michel Foucault, and the post-Freudian psychoanalysis of Jacques Lacan.

The structuralist effort, often aimed at trying to disentangle codes of a work without assigning meaning to them, seems problematic. How does one understand codes such that one can disentangle them without treading on the issue of meaning? In the end, it is to be noted that structuralism and its binary codes work well with texts where such binary oppositions constitute their surface structure. In the case of biblical texts, many priestly texts are founded on basic binary oppositions. For an exposition of such priestly oppositions, see in particular the masterful study of Olyan, *Rites and Rank* (ch. 3, n. 41); for his comments on modern theory of binary oppositions, see 123 n. 1. This issue plays a role in my discussion in sec. 3 below.

37. For postmodernism, see J. Lyotard, *The Postmodern Condition: A Report on Knowledge* (Theory and History of Literature, vol. 10; Manchester: Manchester University, 1984); and H. Bertens, *The Idea of the Postmodern* (London/New York: Routledge, 1995). For postmodern in biblical studies, see for example, *The Postmodern Bible*, by the Bible & Culture Collective (George Aichele et al.; New Haven: Yale University, 1995). See also A. K. M. Adam, *Postmodern Interpretations of the Bible: A Reader* (St. Louis: Chalice Press, 2001). For an example dealing with the primeval history, see George Aichele, "Sitcom Mythology," in *Screening Scripture* (Harrisburg, Penn.: Trinity Press International, 2002) 100–19. For reflections on postmodernism and the study of the Bible, see Craig G. Bartholomew, *Reading Ecclesiastes: Old Testament Exegesis and Hermeneutical Theory*, AnBib 139, 173–203; and George Aichele, Peter Miscall, and Richard Walsh, "An Elephant in the Room: Historical-Critical and Postmodern Interpretations of the Bible," *Journal of Biblical Literature* 128 (2009) 383–404. Steven Weitzman wisely reminds biblical scholars that postmodern approaches are not readily accommodated to modern (traditional) biblical study, nor should they be. See Weitzman, "Rebuilding the Tower of Babel," *Jewish Quarterly Review* 98/1 (2008) 103–12.

38. Again I draw on Culler, *Literary Theory*, 126. Deconstruction is often associated with the name of Jacques Derrida. Derrida is treated in Jonathan Culler's book, *On Deconstruction: Theory and Criticism after Structuralism* (Ithaca, N.Y.: Cornell University, 1982). For Derrida, see Geoffrey Bennington, *Jacques Derrida* (Chicago: University of Chicago, 1993). Among Derrida's works, one of his best known is *Of Grammatology* (Baltimore: The Johns Hopkins University, 1976). For Derrida's impact in biblical studies, see the essays in *Derrida's Bible: Reading a Page of Scripture with a Little Help from Derrida*, edited and with an introduction by Yvonne Sherwood (New York: Palgrave Macmillan, 2004). For a deconstructionist reading of Genesis 1, see Edward L. Greenstein, "Presenting Genesis 1" (ch. 2, n. 62), 1–22.

39. Here I draw on Culler, *Literary Theory*, 126.

40. Cited in Culler, *Literary Theory*, 126. To be fair, Barthes himself moved away from the structuralist project, in particular in his work entitled *S/Z*. Here Barthes explored not only the manifestation of the underlying system in works of literature; he also explored what Culler (*Barthes*, 74)

calls such a system's "unmasterable evasiveness, and the way it outplays the codes on which it seems to be based." In this respect, Culler notes, Barthes has moved into a deconstructionist mode. Over the course of his life, Barthes was a protean figure (compare Culler, *Barthes*, 123 for his discussion of this characterization).

41. www.epress.monash.edu/bc/about.html.

42. This point has been emphasized by Jacques Berlinerblau, *The Secular Bible: Why Nonbelievers Must Take Religion Seriously* (Cambridge: Cambridge University Press, 2005). See also his essay, "'Poor Bird, Not Knowing Which Way to Fly': Biblical Scholarship's Marginality, Secular Humanism, and the Laudable Occident," *BibInt* 10, 267–304. At the same time that he recognizes this point, Berlinerblau condemns religious readings of the Bible that gave rise to this critical sensibility against fundamentalism. He would advocate the abolition of biblical scholarship as it is presently constituted in the United States (for example, in the SBL). To my mind, Berlinerblau can't have it both ways.

He also paints biblical scholarship too broadly as theological. It is more than evident that biblical scholarship, especially in the hands of its best practitioners, is not simply a theological enterprise. Furthermore, Berlinerblau's views represent his own subjectivity favoring the secularism that he personally embraces. It is never clear why his own subjective view is intellectually superior to those he criticizes. The implicit claim is that it is somehow less biased, but is this really true?

43. We may compare this situation with what see at the Catholic Biblical Association national meetings. These continue to privilege historical criticism even as they have been adding a variety of more recent approaches. It will be interesting to see how this situation develops over the next decade. This difference with the SBL is perhaps reflected in their journals. The *CBQ* continues to be weighted to historical criticism and its associated interpretive practices, with newer approaches making their impact increasingly felt. In contrast, the SBL has sponsored two major journals, perhaps marking recognition of an intellectual divide. The older *JBL* has been oriented toward historical criticism, though with some exceptions and with some healthy hybrids working between the old and the new. The newer journal, *Semeia*, has actively sought to work with more recent approaches, sometimes drawing on older historical criticism. The founding of *Semeia* was largely to provide a balance to the older journal of the Society.

44. Quoted by Culler, *Barthes*, 107, 109 (the italics are Barthes'), where he also provides the French text.

45. See this critique of the modern study of the Bible by Hector Avalos, *The End of Biblical Studies* (Amherst, N.Y.: Prometheus Books, 2007). For Avalos, biblical studies largely constitutes a theological tool and not a respectable academic discipline. Cf. the more balanced and helpful discussion of Aichele, Miscall, and Walsh, "An Elephant in the Room", 383–404.

46. This is beautifully illustrated in the case of Roland Barthes. His theory of literary pleasure in *Le Plaisir du texte* dovetailed with his concern with his own pleasure, with what he also called his hedonism (see Culler, *Barthes*, 76–86). Culler (*Barthes*, 12) relates this part of Barthes' theorizing to his personal history, to the "nagging poverty of a middle-class family in reduced circumstances." Barthes himself would refer to the factor of his own "childhood configuration" (quoted by Culler, *Barthes*, 77). In his later work, Barthes turned to the biographical in his literary criticism of a number of writers (see Culler, *Barthes*, 104). This turn is ironic according to Culler, as it was a literary criticism informed by a biography, a practice that had been shunned by literary critics since New Criticism. As Culler observes, this turn came from the very critic who had proclaimed "the death of the author" (Culler, *Barthes*, 69, 71, 104). Reading Barthes in this manner, the deceased author of his earlier criticism is resurrected in his later criticism.

This turn was perhaps ironic for another reason. Barthes' emphasis on pleasure and the body was seen as a return to the old western dichotomy of mind and body, the very sort of opposition that his earlier work challenged. Culler (*Barthes*, 104) also sees the discredited dichotomy of nature and culture coming back into Barthes' work). In the end, though, to be pleased by a text and to be moved by it in some way really is fundamental to reading, and Barthes was quite daring in emphasizing pleasure and the body in his literary criticism and in seeking a critical basis for doing so.

47. For a survey of the ancient textual witnesses to Genesis 1, see Julio Trebolle Barrera, "La tradición textual griega y Latina. Texto e interpretación: unidad y pluralidad," *ILUSup* 7 (2002) 35–62.

48. For Genesis 1 in the Samaritan Pentateuch, see Luis-Fernando Girón Blanc, "La version samaritana del Pentateuco," *ILUSup* 7 (2002) 75–82.

49. A particularly important source for the Septuagint of Genesis 1 is Wevers, *Notes* (ch. 2, n. 32), 1–23.

50. Brown, *Structure, Role, and Ideology* (ch. 2, n. 200).

51. Contrast Martin Rösel, *Überlieferung als Vollendung der Auslegung: Studien zur Genesis-Septuaginta*, BZAW 223. According to Rösel, the Greek translator deliberately adjusted a Hebrew text virtually identical with the MT. This reference came courtesy of the essay by Jennifer Dines (see her discussion cited below in note 55). Rösel also sees significant Platonic influence on the LXX. See the response by William P. Brown, "Reassessing the Text-Critical Value of Septuagint Genesis 1: A Response to Martin Rösel," *BIOSCS* 32, 35–39. Note the fairly critical discussion of the text-critical work on Genesis by Brown, Hendel, and Rösel by Johann Cook, "The Septuagint of Genesis: Text and/or Interpretation," in A. Wénin, ed., *Studies in the Book of Genesis: Literature, Redaction and History*, BETL 155, 315–29. Among the few positive conclusions that he draws, Cook suggests that the differences over the water in LXX versus MT are interpretational.

52. Brown, *Structure, Role, and Ideology*, 192. As a comparison of Brown's translations for LXX (24) and MT (60) show, the differences seem rather minimal for the broad distinction that Brown sees.

53. Hendel, *The Text of Genesis 1–11: Textual Studies and Critical Edition* (New York/Oxford: Oxford, 1998). The model works with text reconstructed from many variants issuing in an "eclectic text." At present, Hendel is one of the editors of the new series of text-critical works devoted to the text criticism of all of the books of the Bible. In contrast, the text-critical enterprise favored in Israel, especially at the Hebrew University, uses the attested text of the MT as its basic text, and notes the other versions where they diverge from it (e.g., Moshe Goshen-Gottstein, Shemaryahu Talmon, Emanuel Tov). See the discussion in Melvin K. H. Peters, "A New Critical Edition of the Book of Genesis," *HS* 40, 251–57.

54. Here Hendel's view is informed by Sean McEvenue's study of the priestly style. See Hendel, *The Text of Genesis 1–11*, 21, 156, citing McEvenue, *The Narrative Style* (ch. 4, n. 62).

55. Jennifer Dines, "Creation under Control: Power Language in Genesis 1:1—2:3," in *Studies in the Greek Bible: Essays in Honor of Francis T. Gignac, S.J.*, CBQMS 44, 3–16. See also Cook, "The Exegesis of Greek Genesis" (ch. 2, n. 149), 101–13.

56. For an engaging introduction, see Richard Elliott Friedman, *Who Wrote the Bible?* (rev. ed.; San Francisco: HarperSan Francisco, 1997).

57. For a critical assessment of the assumption of RJE, see Baden, *J, E, and the Redaction of the Pentateuch* (ch. 4, n. 61).

58. J has been dated to the exile by John Van Seters, *Prologue to History* (ch. 4, n. 2), 332, and *The Life of Moses* (ch. 2, n. 25). See the early Diaspora setting proposed by Levin, *Der Jahwist* (ch. 2, n. 25), 433–34; and his article, "The Yahwist" (ch. 2, n. 25), 230.

Other scholars dispute a Yahwist source altogether. See the debate in the essays in Dozemann & Schmid, *A Farewell to the Yahwist?* (ch. 2, n. 25). See the German forerunner to this volume, *Abschied vom Jahwisten* (ch. 4, n. 2); and the response to that volume by Levin, "Abschied vom Jahwisten?" (ch. 4, n. 2) 329–44.

59. The so-called "Elohist source" is arguably more problematic. For the "Elohist" as seventh century, see Gnuse, "Redefining the Elohist?" (ch. 4, n. 61), 201–20. For a recent defense of the Elohist, see Baden, *J, E, and the Redaction of the Pentateuch*.

60. For a recent statement, see Bauks, "Genesis 1" (ch. 2, n. 7), 333–45. See further studies cited below. For some dissent, see Nahum Sarna, *Genesis: The JPS Commentary* (Philadelphia/New York/Jerusalem: The Jewish Publication Society, 1989) 16.

61. Cassuto, *Genesis: Part I* (ch. 2, n. 200), 96–97.

62. Knohl, *Sanctuary* (ch. 2, n. 7). Chapter 1 of Knohl's study was published originally as "The Priestly Torah Versus the Holiness School: Sabbath and the Festivals," *HUCA* 58, 65–117. See also Milgrom, *Leviticus 1–16* (ch. 3, n. 31), 13–42. Note also Milgrom's comments in his introduction to Leviticus in NRSV (*HCSB*, [Intro., n. 3]), 151.

Cooper & Goldstein ("Exodus and *Maṣṣôt*" [ch. 4, n. 41] = *Let Your Colleagues Praise You* [ch. 4, n. 41], 2.15–37, esp. 25 n. 35) also regard H as a redaction postdating P. Compare the opposite view of Cross (*Canaanite Myth* [ch. 1, n. 16], 297 n. 18, 319). His approach is characteristic of older critics, that P reworked H in Leviticus 26. On the relationship between the Holiness Code and P, see further Jüngeling, "Das Buch" (ch. 4, n. 41), 1–45.

63. Knohl attributes Genesis 1:1—2:4a entirely to P. See Knohl, *Sanctuary*, 104 and 125 n. 4. Building on Knohl's work, Firmage and Amit assign Genesis 1 to H. See Firmage, "Genesis 1," (ch. 2, n. 7), 97–114; and Amit, "Creation" (ch. 2, n. 7), 13–29, 315–16. Jacob Milgrom initially argued for H in Genesis 2:2–3. See Milgrom, *Leviticus 17–22* (ch. 2, n. 7), 1344. Milgrom has since argued for Genesis 1:1—2:3 as entirely H. See Milgrom, "H$_R$ in Leviticus and Elsewhere in the Torah," in *The Book of Leviticus: Composition and Reception*, VTSup 93, 33–40. The notion that Isa. 40:28 alludes to Gen. 2:2 would preclude Milgrom's view. For this view, see Moshe Weinfeld, "The Creator God" (ch. 2, n. 2), 126; and Sommer, *A Prophet Reads Scripture* (ch. 2, n. 2), 144. However, this view is debatable.

See Knohl, *Symphony* (ch. 2, n. 7), 163 n. 16 for the rejection of Amit's argument (and by implication, probably Milgrom's as well). Knohl claims that if Gen. 1:1—2:3 belonged to H and not P, then a prohibition against work might have been expected as in Exod. 31:14–15, 35:2–3. See further the comments of Brown, *Ethos*, (ch. 2, n. 7), 120 n. 228.

64. For a survey, see Thomas Römer, "Le Pentateuch" (ch. 2, n. 227), 343–74, esp. 346–54. For Genesis 1, see 351–52.

65. See further Carr, *Reading the Fractures*, 120–40.

66. For example, blocks of P material set side by side with non-P material (as in Gen. 1:1—2:4a and 2:4b-24, or Exod. 6:2 and following appended to Exodus 3–5), as opposed to P material filched into non-P material "paragraph by paragraph" (as in Genesis 6–9 or Exodus 14).

67. Chaim Cohen, "The Genre of Priestly Instructions" (ch. 4, n. 44).

68. For example, the structuring note of Exod. 31:18, discussed in Smith, *The Pilgrimage Pattern*, (ch. 4, n. 59), 161, 169, 187, 190, 197, 244, 246–47, 259–60.

69. For Kaufmann's dating of P, see his monumental *Toledot ha-emunah hay-Yisra'elit miy-yeme qedem 'ad sof bayit sheni* (vol. 1; Tel Aviv: Mosad Bialik-Dvir, 1937) 113–42. For an English version of this section, see Kaufmann, *The Religion of Israel* (ch. 2, n. 179), 175–200.

Several major scholars have followed Kaufmann's preexilic dating. These include Menachem Haran, Moshe Weinfeld, Jacob Milgrom, and Israel Knohl. See the essays of Haran and Weinfeld in *Proceedings of Eighth World Congress of Jewish Studies, Jerusalem, August 16–21, 1981: Panel Sessions. Bible Studies and Hebrew Language* (Jerusalem: World Union of Jewish Studies, 1983) and Weinfeld, *The Place of the Law in the Religion of Ancient Israel*, VTSup 100. For Milgrom, see *Numbers: The JPS Commentary* (Philadelphia/New York/Jerusalem: The Jewish Publication Society, 1990) xxxii-xxxv; *Leviticus 1–16* (ch. 3, n. 31), 3–12. See Knohl's two works, *Sanctuary* and *Symphony*. Many American scholars have followed this line: Friedman, *Who Wrote the Bible?* and his article, "Torah" (ch. 2, n. 2), 605–22.

For Kaufmann's views about the antiquity of the priestly source, see Thomas M. Krapf, *Yehezkel Kaufmann: ein Lebens- und Erkenntnisweg Theologie der Hebräischen Bibel* (Berlin: Institut Kirche und Judentum, 1990). For the intellectual roots of Kaufmann's views, see Benjamin Uffenheimer, "Some Reflections on Modern Jewish Biblical Research," in *Creative Biblical Exegesis: Christian and Jewish Hermeneutics through the Centuries*, JSOTSup 59, 161–74. See also Moshe Greenberg, "Kaufmann on the Bible: An Appreciation," *Judaism: A Quarterly Journal of Jewish Life and Thought* 13/1 (1964), reprinted in Greenberg, *Studies* (ch. 2, n. 72), 175–88.

70. Contrast Albright and Cross who may be understood as simply opting between two alternatives clearly outlined by their German contemporaries. Like Albright, Cross accepted the general outlines of source criticism as well as a sixth century date for P. However, influenced by the views of Mowinckel and Volz, Albright viewed E as a recension of J, thereby dissenting from Noth's positing of J and E as fully independent narrative sources. See Albright, *Yahweh and the Gods* (ch. 2, n. 10), 29. In contrast, Cross closely aligned his analysis with Noth's, even working heavily with his notion of the *Grundlage* and the Israelite epic attested in it. Indeed, it cannot be overstated that in this pillar of his analysis, he is deeply indebted to Noth. See Cross, *Canaanite Myth*, 79–90. For interesting discussions of Cross's overall approach, see Charles Conroy, "Hebrew Epic: Historical Notes and Critical Reflections," *Biblica* 61 (1980) 1–30; Simon B. Parker, "Some Methodological Principles

in Ugaritic Philology," *Maarav* 2/1 (1979) 7–41. Note also Mark S. Smith, "Biblical Narrative: Part I," 5–29.

71. On the European front, it has been common to fault Kaufmann and company for not distinguishing between older material and later composition and redaction. See Erhard Blum, *Studien* (ch. 2, n. 7), 221. Blum could accept the idea of some earlier priestly material, but the fulcrum point in his general approach is the exilic or postexilic period. See somewhat similarly Blenkinsopp, *The Pentateuch* (ch. 4, n. 47), 238. The force of this approach lies in looking at the collection of the priestly tradition rather than an analysis of linguistic evidence. This approach favoring the later collection as the basis for analysis seems part and parcel of the larger consideration of the Pentateuch as a whole as a book of authorization for the postexilic Jewish community headed up by a priestly leadership. See Rolf Rendtorff, "Chronicles and the Priestly Torah" in *Texts, Temples, and Traditions* (ch. 2, n. 22), 259–266; Blum, *Studien*, 346–56; Frank Crüsemann, *The Torah: Theology and Social History of Old Testament Law* (translated by Allan W. Mahnke; Minneapolis: Fortress, 1996) 260–61; Rainer Albertz, *A History of Israelite Religion in the Old Testament Period* (trans. by John Bowden; vol. 2; Louisville, Ky.: Westminster John Knox, 1994) 138–39. It may be said that in Europe a postexilic dating for priestly material is fairly standard.

In the United States, this approach also enjoys considerable support, for example in the work of Blenkinsopp, *The Pentateuch*, 120, 156, 171, 238; Carr, *Reading the Fractures*, 325–33; Jon L. Berquist, *Judaism in Persia's Shadow: A Social and Historical Approach* (Minneapolis: Fortress, 1995) 138–39; and James W. Watts, *Reading Law: The Rhetorical Shaping of the Pentateuch* (Biblical Seminar, vol. 59; Sheffield: Sheffield Academic Press, 1999) 137–44. See also the essays edited by Watts in *Persia and Torah: The Theory of Imperial Authorization of the Pentateuch*, SBLSymS 17. This approach on the whole tends to pass over linguistic evidence with little or no discussion. This may be reminiscent of the suspicions about linguistic evidence expressed by Rendtorff (see *The Problem*, 117–19, 141–42, 170). An exception in this regard has been Baruch A. Levine who, following Ephraim A. Speiser, has argued for some Persian period material in the priestly corpus. He argued that *mishhah*, "measure," in Lev. 7:35 (written as *moshah* in Num. 18:8), as well as *degel* (see Num. 1:52, as well as several instances in chs. 2 and 10), can be shown to derive from Aramaic borrowings best situated in the Persian period. Levine argues further that terms of land holdings in priestly material (such as *'ahuzza*) fit better in the Persian period than in the Iron II. See Levine's contribution to *Proceedings of Eighth World Congress*; also Levine, *Leviticus* (ch. 3, n. 36), xxix-xxx; and *Numbers 1–20*, AB 4, 103–9. Levine's argument also includes the question of when the institutions and practices described in priestly literature would best fit with historical circumstances. He concludes against the Kaufman tradition that these would suit the postexilic context. Levine's arguments were challenged by Hurvitz (see the *Proceedings* volume cited in this note) and have not been accepted within the Hebrew University circle (discussed in note 69). Compare also the Persian period dating of S. David Sperling, "Pants" (ch. 2, n. 160), 373–85. Yair Hoffman regards Genesis to be a very late addition. See Hoffman, "The First Creation Story," 32–53. Following the general thinking found in many European studies, Gershom Hepner takes the rationale of Genesis 1 to be the creation of the land of Israel after the Babylonian exile. See Hepner, "Israelites Should Conquer" (ch. 3, n. 5), 161–80.

72. For a succinct statement of his view, see Raphael Kutscher, *A History of the Hebrew Language* (Raphael Kutscher, ed.; Jerusalem: Magnes; Leiden: Brill, 1982) 81–84.

73. Hurvitz's basic bibliography in English for this approach includes: "Linguistic Criteria for Dating Problematic Biblical Texts," *Hebrew Abstracts* 14 (1973) 74–79; "The Relevance of Biblical Hebrew Linguistics for the Historical Study of Ancient Israel," in *Proceedings of the Twelfth World Congress of Jewish Studies. Division A: The Bible and Its World* (Jerusalem: World Union of Jewish Studies, 1999) 21°-33°; and "Can Biblical Texts be Dated Linguistically? Chronological Perspectives in the Historical Study of Biblical Hebrew," in *Congress Volume: Oslo 1998*, VTSup 80, 143–60.

74. See Hurvitz, *A Linguistic Study of the Relationship Between the Priestly Source and the Book of Ezekiel: A New Approach to an Old Problem*, CahRB 20; "The Evidence of Language in Dating the Priestly Code—A Linguistic Study in Technical Idioms and Terminology," *RB* 81, 24–56; "Dating the Priestly Source in Light of the Historical Study of Biblical Hebrew a Century after Wellhausen," *ZAW* 100, suppl. vol., 88–100; and "Once Again: The Linguistic Profile of the

Priestly Material in the Pentateuch and its Historical Agenda. A Response to J. Blenkinsopp," *ZAW* 112, 180. His approach to this question is followed and refined in two studies by Mark F. Rooker, *Biblical Hebrew in Transition: The Language of the Book of Ezekiel*, JSOTSup 90; and "Ezekiel and the Typology of Biblical Hebrew," *HAR* 12, 133–55. Cf. Jackie A. Naudé, "The Language of the Book of Ezekiel. Biblical Hebrew in Transition?" *OTE* 13, 46–71.

75. For a partial list, see Young, *Biblical Hebrew*, (ch. 2, n. 20) 3.

76. Hurvitz's method has been the subject of two recent treatments. The first is edited by Ziony Zevit, "Symposium: Can Biblical Texts Be Dated Linguistically?" *HS* 46, 321–76. The second is edited by Young, *Biblical Hebrew*. Part I of this volume is dedicated to essays by Hurvitz and his defenders, while Part II gives voice to his critics. The counterargument boils down to three issues: (a) the exile does not serve as an adequately indicated break-point between stages of Hebrew, as there is a "linguistic" drift in the use of preexilic Hebrew through and after the exile (Davies, Ehrensvärd, Talshir, with his own variation); (b) the distinction between Standard Biblical Hebrew (SBH) and Late Biblical Hebrew (LBH) does not reflect the reality in the great variation of dialects, style, etc., of Biblical Hebrew (Naudé, Young); (c) Chronicles may not have used Samuel-Kings as a source (Rezetsko).

Concerning the first argument, it may or may not be possible in individual cases to examine whether the phenomenon of drift is manifest. Two basic facts deserve mention. One or two features do not a whole composition make, and therefore isolating a single feature or two to make a case for a whole work as properly imitative would be insufficient. Furthermore, the analogy between Dead Sea Scrolls (DSS) imitation of biblical style is imprecise as it is used to address the argument for drift. Indeed, the imitation of old biblical style in DSS may not aspire to the same sort of biblical imitation that LBH composition may aspire of SBH. In the case of the second argument, it could be well be true that the SBH and LBH distinction does not encompass all the variety of Hebrew in these periods. Indeed, many of Hurvitz's supporters have been looking at other aspects of Hebrew for quite some time. For example, for decades Rendsburg has placed a great deal of emphasis on northern Hebrew (or Israelian Hebrew) as opposed to southern Hebrew (or Judean Hebrew) within SBH. Others have noted the additional complication of direct discourse versus narrative underlying the differences that he sees as a matter of north versus south. For an excellent study, see William Schniedewind and Daniel Sivan, "The Elijah-Elisha Narratives: A Test Case for the Northern Dialect of Hebrew," *JQR* 87, 303–37. Polak has beautifully explored aspects of style in tandem with linguistic features to help address the diachronic divide between earlier and later Hebrew (cf. the response by Young on 296, which does not address the value of linguistic evidence *in tandem* with style). In view of these studies, under some circumstances a distinction between SBH and LBH may well be manifest within the wider variety of Hebrew attested. (From a linguistic point of view, the third argument is actually irrelevant.)

A few observations on the part of Hurvitz's sympathizers in the volume deserve mention. Loanwords may help in discerning periods (Eskhult), but there are limits here. For example, postexilic works do not all have Persian loans (as noted by Young, 284–85). Aramaisms in particular can be tracked and distinguished in the SBH and LBH corpora (Hurvitz, Rendsburg). Some LBH features go back to the preexilic regional variation from SBH. Differing styles may indeed cut across the SBH-LBH divide, but these too may be tracked for diachronic development (Polak). It bears mentioning that Polak's study is particularly impressive for its consideration of sociolinguistic interface.

On the whole, the critics of the SBH-LBH distinction improve our appreciation for the complexities of the Hebrew, yet in any given case, the SBH-LBH distinction is not invalidated, even if it does not account for all data. This is revealed in the fact that the more critical discussions of Hurvitz's method hardly attack his cases head-on and falsify them. Some cases are mentioned with a critical tone (314), but there is no discussion of the evidence with any actual falsification. At the same time, in given instances some linguistic drift is to be expected through the exile and wherever possible ascertained (e.g., the discussion about Second Isaiah summarized in Wright's contribution, 132–33, esp. n. 6; cf. his circular argument about *'olamim* as an LBH feature in Second Isaiah versus 134–35 on 1 Sam. 8:12–13, where he argues that this same feature is preexilic northern Hebrew).

After this manuscript was completed, a crucially important new work appeared by Ian Young and Robert Rezetko, with the assistance of Martin Ehrensvärd, *Linguistic Dating* (ch. 3, n. 30). This two-volume work offers a very substantial alternative to the diachronic approach, preferring instead to see "Early Biblical Hebrew" and "Late Biblical Hebrew" as two styles (or ranges) of style. These volumes add many arguments to the critics of Hurvitz's approach. At the same time, there are notable difficulties with the alternative paradigm emphasizing style to the near exclusion of diachronic considerations. One may wonder whether a range of styles (perhaps with some sort of diglossia) was operative within various diachronic levels (perhaps early, transitional and late).

77. The linguistic evidence has been dismissed or virtually ignored in the European context, which has continued the older tendency to situate the priestly material in general in the Persian period. See Blum, *Studien*, 221–360; Erhard Gerstenberger, *Leviticus: A Commentary* OTL, 6–14; cf. Jean Louis Ska, *Introduction to Reading the Pentateuch* (translated by Pascale Dominique; Winona Lake, Ind.: Eisenbrauns, 2006) 188–207.

78. Hurvitz's approach fits the conclusions of Israel Knohl and Jacob Milgrom, who generally follow several Israeli scholars in seeing P as monarchic, perhaps as early as the eighth century (for references, see n. 63). Baruch Halpern dates P to the late seventh century, rather precisely to around 610. See Halpern, "The Assyrian Astronomy" (ch. 2, n. 3), 74°-83°.

79. Such resistance begins with the domination of the Assyrian empire in the eighth century and remained a feature of Israelite intellectual life through the Roman period. I explore this theme in my book, *God in Translation* (ch. 1, n. 4), 151–52, 160–63.

80. For example, see May, "The Creation of Light" (ch. 2, n. 200), 203–11.

81. Gunkel, *Genesis* (ch. 2, n. 6), 120–22, 132.

82. Noth, *Pentateuchal Traditions* (ch. 2, n. 7), 10–11.

83. Noth, *Pentateuchal Traditions*, 11 n. 20. Noth's italics.

84. See the comments of Brown, *Structure, Role, and Ideology*, 192–95. Among other difficulties, Brown does not think that days 2 and 5 line up tightly.

85. See, for example, Fisher, "An Ugaritic Ritual" in (ch. 2, n. 264), 197–205; and Sasson, "Time. . . to Begin," (ch. 2, n. 40), 183–194, here 191. Fisher sees the influence of "the Priestly Code" limited to "the removal of the seventh-day time clause and the addition in II, 2b-3." Without disallowing such a possibility, priestly influence can be seen more broadly in the account, for example, in the use of the verb °*lehabdil*, "to separate," throughout the account as well as the mention of festivals (*mo'adim*) in 1:14; see the discussion in chs. 2 and 3 for details. These additional feature cast doubt on the model proposed by Fisher.

See also the view of Jacob Milgrom that Genesis 2:2–3 derived from a "Holiness" editor; see Milgrom, *Leviticus 17–22*, 1344. Israel Knohl claims that if Genesis 1:1—2:3 belonged to H and not P, then a prohibition against work might have been expected as in Exod. 31:14–15 and 35:2–3. See Knohl, *Symphony*, 163 n. 16.

For this approach to Genesis 2:1–3 as seen by both Fisher and Milgrom, compare Claus Westermann, *Genesis 1–11* (ch. 2, n. 59), 167–73.

For substantial redactional studies, see Schmidt, *Die Schöpfungsgeschichte*; Steck, *Der Schöpfungsbericht* (ch. 2, n. 200); Loretz, "Wortbericht-Vorlage" (ch. 2, n. 86), 279–87; Janowski, "Tempel" (ch. 1, n. 119), 37–69, reprinted in Janowski, *Gottes Gegenwart* (ch. 1, n. 119), 214–46, esp. 232–37; and Weimar, "Struktur und Komposition" (ch. 2, n. 260), 805–43, rep. in Weimar, *Studien zur Priesterschrift* (ch. 2, n. 260), 91–134.

86. Cassuto, *Genesis: Part I*, 10–11.

87. These are discussed by Richard Whitekettle, "Where the Wild Things Are" (ch. 3, n. 31), 17–37. Whitekettle sees a three-fold schema in Gen. 1:20–25, 28 (19, 34) but a four-fold schema in Gen. 1:26 MT (24, 34).

88. For a listing of priestly language in Genesis 1, see Wellhausen, *Prolegomena* (ch. 2, n. 6), 386–90; and Gunkel, *Genesis*, 117 (with references to earlier literature).

89. See Polak, "Poetic Style" (ch. 2, n. 86), 2–31.

90. See ch. 1 for comparisons of these psalms with Genesis 1.

91. Alonso Schökel describes the idea of secondary unity in the following terms: "A later writer could take already completed pieces and bring them together skillfully to form a new and complex unity." Schökel, *Hebrew Poetics* (ch. 1, n. 113), 189.

92. To test this matter, it would be helpful to consider what the text and translation would look like without any redactional elaborations. See Loretz, "Wortbericht-Vorlage," 279–87.

93. John Day has argued that Genesis 1 is dependent on Psalm 104. See Day, *God's Conflict* (ch. 1, n. 71), 51–52, 55; and Day, "Pre-exilic" (ch. 1, n. 94), 238–39. For further discussion, see pp. 23–27, 54–55. Whether or not direct dependence is involved, the similarities witness to an overall shared schema of creation known in Hebrew poetry.

94. As an analogy, we may point to the royal-priestly setting of the literary work of the Ugaritic Baal Cycle. The scribal colophon at the end of the six-tablet work (KTU 1.6 VI 54–58) provides the name of the scribe who produced the text and that he was a student under the chief of the priests who was also an official of the king. For the text, translation, and commentary for the colophon, see Smith & Pitard, *The Ugaritic Baal Cycle: Volume 2* (ch. 2, n. 143), 725–30 as well as the discussions on xxxvii and 14. For a comparison of this colophon with the scribal situation in ancient Israel, see van der Toorn, *Scribal Culture*, 82–89, esp. 85–86.

95. For example, Cross, *Canaanite Myth*, 301–5; Sven Tengström, *Die Toledotformel* (ch. 4, n. 77); the 1974 essay by Weimar, "Die Toledotformel" (ch. 4, n. 77), 151–84; and Carr, *Reading the Fractures*, 74–75. See also the valuable review of Terje Stordalen, "Genesis 2,4," (ch. 4, n. 77), 163–77.

96. Childs, *Introduction*, 149–50. A great deal has been written about Childs' canonical approach, much of it negative. For a recent survey of responses to Childs, with an effort to read Childs on his own terms, see Daniel R. Driver, "Brevard Childs." See n. 4.

97. Childs, *Introduction*, 150. Childs characterizes the relationship in this manner: "the structure of the literature guides the reader to recognize in the shift of idiom a literary device by which further to illuminate the relationship between creation (ch. 1) and offspring (ch. 2)."

98. For examples in his work, see Childs, *Old Testament Theology*, 30–34, 188–95.

99. For intertextuality (or "figuration") in Childs' work, see Childs, "Critique of Recent Intertextual Canonical Interpretation," *ZAW* 115/2, 173–84, esp. 177, cited in Driver, "Brevard Childs," 58. In this same piece, Childs distinguishes intertextuality as a subset of allegory for Christian tradition as opposed to intertextuality within Jewish Midrash. See further Driver, "Brevard Childs," 99–105.

100. Ratzinger, *In the Beginning* (ch. 1, n. 2).

101. Jacob, *Das Buch Genesis,* (ch. 2, n. 226); repr. as *Das erste Buch der Tora: Genesis* (Stuttgart: Calwer, 2000) 67; Buber, "Der Mensch" (ch. 2, n. 226), 13–45, here 40–45; Rosenzweig, "Das Formgeheimnis" (ch. 2, n. 226), 239–61, here 254; see also Buber, *Die Schrift* (ch. 2, n. 226), 39–40.

102. These parallels are laid out by Levenson, *Creation* (ch. 1, n. 114), 85–86.

103. Cooper believes that the priestly writer had a written copy of RJE in front of him. See Alan Cooper and Bernard Goldstein, "The Festivals of Israel and Judah and the Literary History of the Pentateuch," *JAOS* 110, 19–31, and "Exodus and *Maṣṣôt*," = *Let Your Colleagues Praise You,* 2.15–37.

104. Levenson, *Creation*, 82, 84, 88.

105. The translation of the latter comes from Jacobsen, *Harps* (ch. 1, n. 21) 419. For discussion of these two texts, see Avigdor Hurowitz, *I Have Built You an Exalted House: Temple Building in the Bible in Light of Mesopotamian and Northwest Semitic Writings*, JSOTSup 115; JSOT/ASOR Monograph Series, vol. 5, 332–35. Horowitz notes several Mesopotamian examples of temple building rendered in cosmic terms.

106. In alphabetical order: Blenkinsopp, "The Structure of P" (ch. 2, n. 227), 275–92, esp. 276–78; Brown, *Ethos*, 77–78, 82–89; Fishbane, *Text and Texture* (ch. 2, n. 172), 12; Fisher, "Creation at Ugarit" (ch. 3, n. 3), 313–24; Janowski, "Tempel," 37–69; *idem*, "Der Tempel als Kosmos" (ch. 2, n. 227), 163–186; Kearney, "Creation and Liturgy" (ch. 2, n. 227), 375–81; Levenson, *Creation*, 78–99; Liss, "The Imagining Sanctuary" (ch. 2, n. 227), 675–76; McBride, "Divine Protocol" (ch. 4, n. 3), 11–15; van Leeuwen, "Cosmos" (ch. 1, n. 72), 67–90, especially 75–76; Weinfeld, "Sabbath," (ch. 1,

n. 119), 503. In this connection, we may note a late Akkadian creation account that ends with the gods moving into their temple-dwelling on earth; see Foster, *Muses*, 494.

107. For references, see Smith, *God in Translation*, 219–220.

108. See Driver, "Brevard Childs," 184–86 for Childs on these issues.

109. Smith, *The Memoirs of God*, (ch. 4, n. 8), 107–10, 151–52.

110. Carr, *Reading the Fractures*. Cf. Rendsburg, *The Redaction of Genesis* (ch. 4, n. 45). Despite the use of the word redaction in its title, the book does not address what is generally regarded as redaction or redactional activity in the book of Genesis. Rendsburg's work is largely engaged in identifying large-scale literary patterning in Genesis, and for this agenda, he offers several fine literary observations. The sort of patterning that he discerns in the book may well be part of the redactional activity underlying its formation. Cf. Sasson, "The 'Tower of Babel'" (ch. 4, n. 45), 211–219; and "Love's Roots" (ch. 4, n. 45), 205–209.

111. Blum, *Studien*, 293–312.

112. See Cross, *Canaanite Myth*, 305, 324–25, where he argued against narrative continuity in the priestly source. See also Childs, *Introduction*, 147. Many others, such as Blenkinsopp (*The Pentateuch*, 78, 119), essentially return to Martin Noth's view of narrative continuity of the priestly source. See Emerton, "The Priestly Writer in Genesis," (ch. 4, n. 47), 381–400, cited by Blenkinsopp, *The Pentateuch*, 132 n. 19. Note also Graham I. Davies, "Reflections" (ch. 4, n. 47), 79–80.

113. See Jeffrey H. Tigay's influential contributions in *Empirical Models for Biblical Criticism* (Jeffrey H. Tigay, ed.; Philadelphia: University of Pennsylvania, 1985).

114. This is a vast area of research. Single-author works that address the matter of deities in Israel include: the worthwhile collection of essays of Manfred Weippert, collected as *Jahwe und die anderen Götter*, FAT 18; the fine summary by Day, *Yahweh* (ch. 1, n. 64); the popular historical overview produced by André Lemaire, *Naissance du monothéisme: Point de vue d'un historian* (Paris: Bayard, 2003), translated as *The Birth of Monotheism: The Rise and Disappearance of Yahwism* (Washington, D. C.: Biblical Archaeology Society, 2007); and my books, *Early History of God:* (ch. 1, n. 64); and *Origins* (ch. 1, n. 14). A streamlined discussion of these matters appears in my work, *The Memoirs of God*, esp. ch. 3. See also the study of Herbert Niehr, *Der höchste Gott: Alttestamentlicher JHWH-Glaube im kontext syrisch-kanaanäischer Religion des 1. Jahrtausends v. Chr.*, BZAW 190; and the monograph-length article by Meindert Dijkstra, entitled "El, Yhwh, and their Asherah: On Continuity and Discontinuity in Canaanite and Ancient Israelite Religion," in *Ugarit: Ein ostmediterranes Kulturzentrum im Alten Orient. Ergebnisse und Perspektiven des Forschung*, ALASP 7, 43–73. In addition, important collections of essays include: *Ein Gotte allein? JHWH-Verehrung und biblischer Monotheismus im Kontext der israelitischen und altorientalischen Religionsgeschichte*, OBO 139; Bob Becking, et al., *Only One God? Monotheism in Ancient Israel and the Veneration of the Goddess Asherah* (The Biblical Seminar, vol. 77; London/New York: Sheffield Academic Press, 2001); *The Crisis of Israelite Religion: Transformation of Religious Tradition in Exilic and Post-Exilic Times* (Bob Becking and Marjo C. A. Korpel, eds.; Leiden/Boston/Köln: Leiden, 1999); *Polytheismus und Monotheismus in den Religionen des Vorderen Orients*, AOAT 298; *Der eine Gott und die Götter: Polytheismus und Monotheismus im antiken Israel* (Manfred Oeming and Konrad Schmidt, eds.; Zürich: Theologischer Verlag, 2003); *Yahwism After the Exile: Perspectives on Israelite Religion after the Exile* (Rainer Albertz and Bob Becking, eds.; Studies in Theology and Religion (STAR), vol. 5; Assen: Royal Van Gorcum, 2003).

115. Schmidt, *Die Schöpfungsgeschichte*; Levenson, *Creation*, 66–77; Clifford, *Creation Accounts* (Intro., n. 2), 137–44. See also Smith, *The Pilgrimage Pattern*, 110–17.

116. Ephraim A. Speiser, "The Creation Epic," in *ANET*, 60–72. See also his treatment of Genesis 1 in his commentary, *Genesis* (ch. 2, n. 200).

117. Clifford, "Cosmogonies," (ch. 2, n. 79), 183–201, here 185.

118. Sasson, "Time. . . to Begin," 190. For another example, see Sverre Aalen in *TDOT* 1, 151.

119. These have been collected in a handy edition by Richard J. Clifford in his book, *Creation Accounts*. For a fine collection of Mesopotamian creation texts in French, see Bottéro & Kramer, *Lorsque les dieux faisaient l'homme* (ch. 2, n. 243). For Egyptian creation texts, see James P. Allen, *Genesis in Egypt* (ch. 2, n. 167).

120. The text has been called by different names: "Dawn and Dusk," "The Birth of the Beautiful Gods," or "The Birth of the Gracious Gods." I have discussed the question of the text's title in my book, *Sacrificial Rituals* (ch. 1, n. 20). For a handy translation with a transliteration of the Ugaritic signs into English letters, see Lewis, "Birth," 205–14. This text might be further classified under the subgenre of creation accounts known as "theogonies," namely accounts of the creation of the gods and goddesses. To be clear, the Baal Cycle is not a creation account. Sometimes it has been labeled a cosmogony, in large measure because of its account of building the palace of the god Baal, but this is not a creation account nor would I call it a cosmogony, since it does not narrate the creation of deities or the world as such. For this view, see Loren Fisher, "Creation at Ugarit," 313–24; compare Clifford, "Cosmogonies," 183–201.

121. See Klaus Koch, "Wind und Zeit" (ch. 2, n. 92), 59–91; reprinted in Koch, *Der Gott Israels* (ch. 2, n. 92), 86–118; and Müller, "Der Welt- und Kulturensstehungsmythos" (ch. 2, n. 92), 161–79.

122. See, for example, Loretz, "Gen 1,2 als Fragment" (ch. 2, n. 36), 387–401.

123. For example, see James Atwell, "An Egyptian Source for Genesis 1," *JTS* 51, 441–77; Manfred Görg, "Genesis und Trinität: Religionsgeschichtliche Implikationen des Glaubens an den dreieinigen Gott," in *Ägypten und der östliche Mittelmeerraum im 1. Jahrtausend v. Chr: Akten des interdisziplinären Symposions am Institut für Ägyptologie der Universität München 25.-27.10.1996* (Manfred Görg and Günther Hölbl, eds.; Aegypten und Altes Testament, vol. 44; Wiesbaden: Harrassowitz, 2000) 47–68; and John Strange, "Genesis 1 og aegyptisk skabelsesteologi [Genesis 1 and Egyptian creation-theology]," *DTT* 70, 3–10.

124. See, for example, Hoffmeier, "Some Thoughts" (ch. 2, n. 101), 39–49; and Redford, *Egypt, Canaan,* (ch. 2, n. 8), 396–400. Redford (p. 400) entertains the possibility of borrowing ca. 725–525, but he also suggests that "it may turn out to be a mere sideshow in a far more widespread and complex pattern of cultural exchange." Note also the brief remark of Jan Assmann, *Of God and Gods: Egypt, Israel, and the Rise of Monotheism* (Madison, Wis.: University of Wisconsin, 2008) 18.

125. See Hans-Peter Müller, "Eine grieschische Parallele zu Motiven von Genesis I-II," *VT* 47, 478–86.

126. See the sophisticated study by Sparks, "Priestly Mimesis" (ch. 2, n. 8), 625–48. Note also the more popular essay by Victor Hurowitz, "The Genesis of Genesis: Is the Creation Story Babylonian?" *BRev* 21/1, 37–48, 52–53.

127. Sasson, "Time. . . to Begin," 191.

128. Sasson, "Time. . . to Begin," 189 n. 17.

129. Halpern, "Assyrian Astronomy," 74°-83°.

130. See among recent authors Shalom Paul, *Divrei Shalom: Collected Essays of Shalom M. Paul on the Bible and the Ancient Near East 1967–2005* (Culture and History of the Ancient Near East, vol. 23; Leiden/Boston: Brill, 2005) 348 n. 42; Jacob Milgrom, "H$_R$ in Leviticus," 34–35; Jean-Luis Ska, "Genesis 2–3" (ch. 2, n. 154), 22, and Spieckermann, "Is God's Creation Good?" (ch. 2, n. 154), 81. For a broader argument for Genesis 1–11 as a response to Mesopotamian cultural ideals, see Middleton, *The Liberating Image* (ch. 3, n. 17), 201–28, 235. Middleton grants this background is speculative on his part; indeed, the presuppositions required for this view exceed the level of assumption required for a source-division of Genesis 1, which he rejects. Middleton also fails to recognize the specific priestly language of Genesis 1. Middleton's book is highly commendable, especially for its broad scope, but it does tend to reject some views for their speculative quality, even as it engages in speculation of its own.

131. Sparks, "Priestly Mimesis," 625–48.

132. See Sparks, "Priestly Mimesis," 625–48, esp. 626.

133. For excesses of the comparative approach to Genesis 1, see Cyrus H. Gordon, "Gnostic Light on Genesis 1 and 2 via Maśśa'," in *Eblaitica: Essays on the Ebla Archives and Eblaite Language* Vol. 4 (Cyrus H. Gordon and Gary A. Rendsburg, eds.; Winona Lake, Ind.: Eisenbrauns, 2002) 197–98.

134. Cassuto, "The Israel Epic," *Knesset* 8 (1943) 121–42 (Hebrew), published in English in *Biblical and Oriental Studies* (trans. by Israel Abraham; vol. 2; Jerusalem: Magnes, 1975) 69–109.

135. For this view of Genesis 1, see my discussion in *The Pilgrimage Pattern*, 110–17.

136. A classic work on the subject is Klaus Koch, *The Growth of the Biblical Tradition: The Form-Critical Method* (trans. from the German 2nd ed. by S. M. Cupitt; New York: Charles Scribner's Sons, 1969).

137. To be sure, there were many efforts at interpreting the Bible as literature well before the 1970s. For example, a classic work in this vein is Erich Auerbach's 1946 book, *Mimesis: The Representation of Reality in Western Literature* (trans. by Willard R. Trask; Princeton: Princeton University Press, 1953) esp. 3–23, which compares the styles of biblical narrative and Homer. The lack of literary study of the Bible was noted by James Muilenberg ("Form Criticism and Beyond," *JBL* 88 [1969] 1–18), well before Robert Alter's initial forays into this area, by his own account, in the mid-1970s. See Alter, *The Art of Biblical Narrative* (New York: Basic Books, 1981) xi. See also the references below.

138. See Hermann Gunkel, "The Influence of Babylonian Mythology Upon the Biblical Creation Story," trans. and abridged from his *Schöpfung und Chaos in Urzeit und Endzeit* (Göttingen: Vandenhoeck & Ruprecht, 1895), in *Creation in the Old Testament* (Bernard W. Anderson, ed.; Philadelphia: Fortress Press, 1984) 25–52. See also Gunkel, *Creation and Chaos* (ch. 2, n. 235).

139. For theogonies, see the summary discussion of Cross, *From Epic to Canon* (ch. 1, n. 6), 73–83. For cosmogonies, see Clifford, *Creation Accounts*, esp. 2–10, 200–201.

140. See chs. 1 and 2 for discussion.

141. For examples, see Clifford, *Creation Accounts*, 29–30, 49–50, 59, 61. See ch. 2 for discussion.

142. For various views, see Coats, *Genesis* (ch. 5, n. 4), 47.

143. For prominent work in this vein, see Robert Alter, *The Art of Biblical Narrative*. For literary theory and the Bible, see also *The Literary Guide to the Bible* (Robert Alter and Frank Kermode, ed.; Cambridge, Mass.: The Belknap Press of Harvard University Press, 1987). A response to this work appears in a volume produced out of evangelical circles: *A Complete Literary Guide to the Bible* (Leland Ryken and Tremper Longman III, eds.; Grand Rapids, Mich.: Zondervan, 1995); see the comments on 10. See also *The Book and the Text*. For a handy, accessible treatment of literary theory in the twentieth century, see Culler, *Literary Theory.*

144. The most prominent scholar associated with rhetorical criticism may be the feminist Bible scholar Phyllis Trible. For her work on Genesis 1, see her book, *God and the Rhetoric of Sexuality,* 12–23 for her discussion of Genesis 1 and in particular on 1:26–28, representing "gender balance."

145. See the programmatic essay for rhetorical criticism by James Muilenberg, "Form Criticism and Beyond," 1–18.

146. For example, see Frederick E. Coggin, *The First Story of Genesis as Literature* (Cambridge [Cambridgeshire]: W. Heffer, 1932).

147. See the literary studies of Greenstein, "Presenting Genesis 1," 1–22; and E. J. van Wolde, "The Text as Eloquent Guide: Rhetorical, Linguistic and Literary Features in Genesis 1," in *Literary Structure and Rhetorical Strategies in the Hebrew Bible* (L. J. de Regt, J. de Waard, and J. Fokkelman, eds.; Assen: van Gorcum; Winona Lake, Ind.: Eisenbrauns, 1996) 134–51. For an analysis informed by structuralism, see Pierre Auffret, "L'ouvrage qu'il avait fait: Étude structurelle de Gn 1 à 2:4a," *SJOT* 14, 28–55. See further below.

148. Walter Eichrodt, "In the Beginning: A Contribution to the First Word of the Bible," in *Creation in the Old Testament*, 65.

149. Sasson, "Time. . . to Begin," 189.

150. In chs. 2 and 4, I have suggested that the style is informed by the priestly tradition's ritual sensibility. See Hanna Liss, "The Imagining Sanctuary," 674–76.

151. Older research on this motif includes the studies of Samuel Loewenstamm, "The Seven-Day Unit" (ch. 3, n. 3), 122–33, repr. in *Comparative Studies in Biblical and Ancient Oriental Literatures* (ch. 3, n. 3), 192–209; and Freedman, "Counting Formulae" (ch. 3, n. 3), 65–81. The Ugaritic passages with this motif are: KTU 1.14 III 2–5, 10–16 (cf. IV 31–48); V 3–8, VI 24–33; 1.17 I 5–16; II 32–40; 1.22 I 21–26. KTU 1.4 VI 24–33, as a description of the creation of Baal's palace, was compared with Genesis 1 by Fisher, "Creation at Ugarit," 313–24. Despite Fisher's character-ization of the construction of Baal's house (heavenly palace/earthly temple) as a creation-story or cosmogony, his comparison of temple and creation holds. See further n. 106, with citations of other scholars who likewise accept the comparison of language of temple building and creation.

152. For example, Sasson ("Time. . . to Begin," 186) notes that °*qr' l*- occurs only in days 1–3 and that °*brk* occurs only in days 5 and 6, suggesting day 4 is pivotal between the other two sets.

153. Cassuto, *Genesis: Part I*, 16–17; Sarna, *Genesis*, 4; Anderson, "A Stylistic Study" (ch. 3, n. 17), 148; Fishbane, *Text and Texture*, 10; Clifford, *Creation Accounts*, 142–43; and Milgrom, "The Alleged 'Hidden Light,'" 41–44, here 43. See also the review in Brown, *Structure, Role, and Ideology*, 192–95.

154. Carr, *Reading the Fractures*, 20. Drawing on Jeffrey Tigay's work on the history of the different editions of Gilgamesh, Carr offers a useful summary of the processes of transmission of ancient Near Eastern texts. I have also noted above recent comparative work on scribalism: Carr, *Writing on the Tablet of the Heart;* and van der Toorn, *Scribal Culture*.

155. Niditch, *Oral World;* Person, Jr., "The Ancient Israelite Scribe as Performer," *JBL* 117 (1998) 601–9.

156. Coogan, "Literacy," (ch. 4, n. 24), 47–61; Crenshaw, *Education* (ch. 4, n. 24); Haran, "On the Diffusion of Literacy" (ch. 4, n. 24), 81–95.

157. See above note 32. I have been particularly struck by the reflections by Dibeela, "Perspective," 384–99.

158. Culler, *Literary Theory*, 120.

159. Frank Moore Cross, "The History of Israelite Religion: A Secular or Theological Subject?" *BAR* 31/3, 42.

160. See my book, *God in Translation*, 32–34.

161. This sense of the problem came up when I was researching a book on the history of the biblical field, which takes a look at the moving currents of modern scholarship over the better part of a century: *Untold Stories: The Bible and Ugaritic Studies in the Twentieth Century* (Peabody, Mass.: Hendrickson Publishers, 2001). From this work, it seemed that the lives of scholars are marked not simply by major periods (birth, youth, university years, early career, middle and old age, and death). Their lives also involve changes in the course of months, sometimes even just weeks and days. They are not simply like the long ages; life also involves tiny, nearly imperceptible changes that affect and sometimes alter human existence and affect people's identity and reality.

To convey the impact of such microchanges, I would suggest an analogy with two views of evolution. On the one hand, Charles Darwin's perspective on the long ages of natural selection and evolution was influenced by ideas of geological ages that he found in Charles Lyell's three-volume work, *Principles of Geology* published in 1830–1833. On the other hand, late twentieth century scholarship on evolution has examined small, very short-term changes, even week-by-week; for this sort of work, see Jonathan Weiner, *The Beak of the Finch* (New York: Random House, 1994). The lives of scholars, and people generally, may look like a series of major periods, and both modern biographies and people's memory often structure human life this way. At the same time, human lives also involve many small changes, month-by-month or even day-by-day, that are experienced blended together and may seem like the undifferentiated matter of long phases of life. For the most part, they often go unnoted or even unnoticed, yet they may be core to the development of human intellects. The changes in human intellects are largely beyond their capacity to track them.

162. This issue has been discussed recently by Russell T. McCutcheon, "'It's a Lie. There's No Truth in It! It's a Sin!' On the Limits of Humanistic Study of Religion and the Costs of Saving Others from Themselves," *JAAR* 74/3, 720–50, with a response by Paul B. Courtright, "The Self-Serving Humility of Disciplining Liberal Humanist Scholars: A Response to Russell McCutcheon," 751–54; and McCutcheon, "A Response to Courtright," 755–56.

I have become concerned about the responsibility of academics, as we come to grips with the fact that scholarship of religion can have serious effects on communities beyond academia. I offer some comments in this vein in *God in Translation*, 328–39. Scholars of the Bible are, to use an image of Roland Barthes, its modern "echo chambers" (quoted in Culler, *Barthes*, 88); and in our writings and classes, we potentially give voice to what the Bible reverberates within us. For that we are responsible.

Index

Subjects and Terms

Aaron, 103,126
Aaronids, 124
Abihu, 124
Abraham, 103,114
Aleppo, 69
Anat, 152
Anu, 77, 96, 97
Anzu, 145, 147, 150
Apocalyptic, 48, 144, 153, 154
Apsu, 18
Assur (empire), 19
Assur (god), 19
Astronomy, 80, 97, 151, 154, 194. *See also* signs
Athtar, 94
Athtart, 94

Baal, 20, 21, 22, 54, 58, 88, 94, 146, 152
    titles, 20
Babylon, x, 18, 19, 42, 43, 94, 142
Biblical Theology, 161, 181, 190
"beginning" (*re'shit*), xvii, xxiv–7, 44, 46–48, 132
Bel, 77
Big Bang, 34
Blessing, divine, x, 3, 16, 64, 66, 90, 102, 104, 109, 110

bohu. See "void and vacuum"

calendar, 80. *See also* priestly calendar
Canonical approach, 157, 162, 175, 177–79, 188
chiasm, 29
    definition of, 29
child sacrifice, 122–23
collective memory, 118, 163, 164, 169. *See also* priestly memory
commentary, narrative as implicit, 2, 4, 118, 128–36, 150, 155
Comparative Study, 138, 161, 182–85, 186, 188
cosmological pairs, 49, 53, 59, 91, 155, 186
cosmogony, 12, 183, 184, 186, 187
    definition of, 186
    Phoenician, 42, 184
    Mesopotamian, 183
creatio ex nihilo, 49, 50
creation
    and divine holiness, 15, 16, 137
    and divine kingship, 12, 13, 137
    and divine light, 15, 16
    and divine name, 15
    and divine word/speech, 15, 16, 67

301

Index

Biblical References

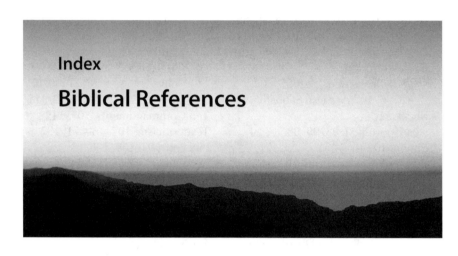

Index

Extrabiblical References